INTRODUCTION TO DIRECT INSTRUCTION

NANCY E. MARCHAND-MARTELLA

Eastern Washington University

TIMOTHY A. SLOCUM

Utah State University

RONALD C. MARTELLA

Eastern Washington University

PEARSON

Boston   New York   San Francisco
Mexico City   Montreal   Toronto   London   Madrid   Munich   Paris
Hong Kong   Singapore   Tokyo   Cape Town   Sydney

Executive Editor: *Virginia Lanigan*
Editorial Assistant: *Robert Champagne*
Executive Marketing Manager: *Amy Cronin-Jordan*
Production Editor: *Paul Mihailidis*
Manufacturing Buyer: *Andrew Turso*
Cover Administrator: *Kristina Mose-Libon*
Electronic Composition: *Galley Graphics*
Editorial-Production Services: *Chestnut Hill Enterprises, Inc.*

Copyright © 2004 Pearson Education, Inc.

For related titles and support materials, visit our online catalog at www.ablongman.com

Library of Congress Cataloging-in-Publication Data

Marchand-Martella, Nancy E.
    Introduction to direct instruction / Nancy E. Marchand-Martella,
  Timothy A. Slocum, Ronald C. Martella.
       p. cm.
  Includes bibliographical references and index.
    ISBN 0-205-37761-0
  1. Effective teaching—United States.   2. Direct instruction—United
  States.   3. Academic achievement—United States.   I. Slocum, Timothy A.
  II. Martella, Ronald C.   III. Title.
    LB 1025.3.M33715 2004
    371.39—dc22

                                                    2003015332

Printed in the United States of America
10 9 8 7 6 5 4 3 2 1   07 06 05 04 03

Dedication

Our dedication of *Introduction to Direct Instruction* is twofold. First, we wish to dedicate this text to Siegfried Engelmann. Engelmann and colleagues developed the Direct Instruction model over thirty years ago, and since that time have continually improved, elaborated, and extended the model. Over the years, Engelmann has submitted his work to close empirical scrutiny through years of field-testing, evaluation, and impartial scientific investigation. Throughout, Engelmann has remained committed to the idea that student learning is our measure of success. For his tireless energy and dedication to improving the lives of children, we say thank you.

Second, we wish to dedicate this text to the countless teachers, administrators, parents, trainers, professors, and others who use Direct Instruction because it works. They have changed the lives of our children, opening doors for them that were otherwise closed, setting them on paths to success rather than failure. To their conviction for doing what is right for children and their dedication to the profession called *education,* we say thank you.

CONTENTS

About the Editors   xv

Preface   xvii

Foreword by Siegfried Engelmann   xix

Contributing Authors   xxvii

PART ONE   The Need for and Aspects of Direct Instruction   1

CHAPTER ONE

The Importance of Effective Instruction   1

OBJECTIVES   1

THE NEED FOR QUALITY EDUCATION   2

A LITANY OF DISADVANTAGE   3

CONCERN OVER EDUCATIONAL OUTCOMES   4

STUDENTS WHO PERFORM POORLY   5

Minority and Disadvantaged Students   5
Learning Disabilities   6
Unexpected Groups   6
High School and Beyond   7

THE DEVELOPMENT OF SERIOUS ACADEMIC PROBLEMS   7

Matthew Effects   8
Reading Participation   8
Vocabulary Development   8
Increasing Problems   9

PREVENTING ACADEMIC FAILURE   10

IMPORTANCE OF INSTRUCTION   10

THE LACK OF IMPACT OF RESEARCH ON PRACTICE   11

    Obstacles to Research-Driven Teaching   12

    Need for Communication   13

    Linking Professional Practices and Research   13

HOW OTHER PROFESSIONS CONNECT RESEARCH TO PRACTICE   13

    Medicine   13

    Clinical Psychology   14

HOW EDUCATION ADDRESSES THE RESEARCH ISSUE   15

RESEARCH ON EFFECTIVE INSTRUCTION   16

    Characteristics of Effective Instruction   16

    Principles of Effective Instruction   17

    Support for the Power of Effective Instruction   18

HISTORY OF DIRECT INSTRUCTION   19

    Increased Interest in Direct Instruction   21

    Continued Research and Program Development   21

REFERENCES   22

CHAPTER TWO

The Components of Direct Instruction   28

    OBJECTIVES   28

    MAIN COMPONENTS OF DIRECT INSTRUCTION   29

        Program Design   29

        Organization of Instruction   40

        Teacher–Student Interactions   43

    DIRECT INSTRUCTION AND EFFECTIVE TEACHING   52

    STUDENTS FOR WHOM DIRECT INSTRUCTION IS APPROPRIATE   53

        Students with Diverse Learning Needs   53

        Students with Diverse Language Backgrounds   55

        Children with Various "Learning Styles"   56

        Students of Different Ages   56

    RESEARCH ON DIRECT INSTRUCTION   57

        Project Follow Through   57

Independent Reviews of Research on Direct Instruction   61

Long-Term Follow-Up Research   62

REFERENCES   63

PART TWO   Direct Instruction Programs   66

CHAPTER THREE
Language   66

OBJECTIVES   66

IMPORTANCE OF ORAL LANGUAGE   67

Oral Language and Beginning Reading Achievement   67

Oral Language and Reading Comprehension   68

Oral Language Skills and Social Interaction   68

Long-Term Effects of Poorly Developed Oral Language   69

IMPORTANCE OF ORAL LANGUAGE INSTRUCTION   70

OVERVIEW OF DIRECT INSTRUCTION LANGUAGE PROGRAMS   71

Language for Learning   71

Language for Thinking   72

Commonalities between *Language for Learning* and *Language for Thinking*   72

Language for Writing   73

CONTENT ANALYSIS AND FORMAT FEATURES   74

Language for Learning   74

Language for Thinking   84

TEACHING TECHNIQUES   90

Signals   90

Error Corrections   92

ASSESSMENT AND TROUBLESHOOTING   92

Assessment Systems   93

Troubleshooting   93

EXTENSIONS AND ADAPTATIONS   94

Extensions of *Language for Learning*   94

Adaptations to *Language for Learning* and *Language for Thinking*   94

RESEARCH ON DIRECT INSTRUCTION LANGUAGE PROGRAMS   95

REFERENCES   97

CHAPTER FOUR
Reading   100

OBJECTIVES   100

IMPORTANCE OF READING   101

CRITICAL COMPONENTS OF READING PROGRAMS   102

    Phonemic Awareness   103

    Phonics   103

    Fluency   104

    Vocabulary   104

    Text Comprehension   105

OVERVIEW OF DIRECT INSTRUCTION READING PROGRAMS   106

    Critical Features   106

    Lesson Events   106

    Program Descriptions   107

CONTENT ANALYSIS AND FORMAT FEATURES   110

    Reading Mastery   110

    Horizons   119

    Corrective Reading   124

OTHER DIRECT INSTRUCTION READING PROGRAMS   129

TEACHING TECHNIQUES   129

    Signals   130

    Error Corrections   130

ASSESSMENT AND TROUBLESHOOTING   132

    Assessment   132

    Troubleshooting   133

EXTENSIONS AND ADAPTATIONS   133

    Phonics   134

    Fluency   134

    Vocabulary   134

    Comprehension   135

RESEARCH ON DIRECT INSTRUCTION READING PROGRAMS   135

Reading Mastery   136

Horizons   136

Corrective Reading   137

REFERENCES   137

CHAPTER FIVE

Writing   140

OBJECTIVES   140

IMPORTANCE OF WRITING   141

IMPORTANCE OF WRITING INSTRUCTION   143

SIX DESIGN PRINCIPLES OF EFFECTIVE INSTRUCTION   144

Big Ideas   144

Conspicuous Strategies   145

Mediated Scaffolding   145

Strategic Integration   145

Primed Background Knowledge   146

Judicious Review   146

OVERVIEW OF DIRECT INSTRUCTION WRITING PROGRAMS   147

Cursive Writing   147

Basic Writing Skills   150

Expressive Writing   150

Reasoning and Writing   151

CONTENT ANALYSIS AND FORMAT FEATURES   154

Big Ideas   154

Conspicuous Strategies   159

Mediated Scaffolding   160

Strategic Integration   161

Primed Background Knowledge   163

Judicious Review   165

TEACHING TECHNIQUES   165

Signals   166

Error Corrections   166

ASSESSMENT AND TROUBLESHOOTING   167

Placement Tests   167

Mastery Tests   168

Continuous Assessment for Troubleshooting   169

EXTENSIONS AND ADAPTATIONS   170

Extensions   170

Adaptations   173

RESEARCH ON DIRECT INSTRUCTION WRITING PROGRAMS   174

REFERENCES   175

CHAPTER SIX
Spelling   178

OBJECTIVES   178

IMPORTANCE OF SPELLING   179

IMPORTANCE OF SPELLING INSTRUCTION   180

INSTRUCTIONAL APPROACHES TO SPELLING   181

Phonemic Approach   181

Whole-Word Approach   182

Morphemic Approach   182

OVERVIEW OF DIRECT INSTRUCTION SPELLING PROGRAMS   183

Spelling Mastery   183

Spelling Through Morphographs   184

CONTENT ANALYSIS AND FORMAT FEATURES   184

Phonemic Approach   184

Whole-Word Approach   188

Morphemic Approach   188

TEACHING TECHNIQUES   193

Signals   194

Error Corrections   196

ASSESSMENT AND TROUBLESHOOTING   197

Curriculum-Based Assessment   197

Troubleshooting   199

EXTENSIONS AND ADAPTATIONS   200

Extensions: Writing   200

Extensions: Practice Activities   201

Adaptations: Acceleration or Deceleration   201

Adaptations: Equalizing   202

RESEARCH ON DIRECT INSTRUCTION SPELLING PROGRAMS   203

REFERENCES   204

CHAPTER SEVEN
Mathematics   206

OBJECTIVES   206

IMPORTANCE OF MATHEMATICS   207

IMPORTANCE OF MATHEMATICS INSTRUCTION   208
   Goals   209
   History   210
   Implicit versus Explicit Instruction   210
   Basic Skills versus Conceptual Understanding   211

DESIGN FEATURES OF EFFECTIVE MATHEMATICS PROGRAMS   212
   Integrated Strand Curriculum   212
   Big Ideas and Strategies   214

OVERVIEW OF DIRECT INSTRUCTION MATHEMATICS PROGRAMS   215
   DISTAR Arithmetic   215
   Corrective Mathematics   215
   Connecting Math Concepts   216

CONTENT ANALYSIS AND FORMAT FEATURES   216
   DISTAR Arithmetic   216
   Corrective Mathematics   219
   Connecting Math Concepts   219

TEACHING TECHNIQUES   235
   Signals   235
   Error Corrections   236

ASSESSMENT AND TROUBLESHOOTING   237
   Placement   237
   Mastery   238

EXTENSIONS AND ADAPTATIONS   239
   Math Facts and Fluency   239
   Word Problems   240
   Videodisc   241

RESEARCH ON DIRECT INSTRUCTION MATHEMATICS PROGRAMS   241

REFERENCES   243

CHAPTER EIGHT

Content Areas   246

OBJECTIVES   246

IMPORTANCE OF CONTENT AREAS   248

IMPORTANCE OF CONTENT AREA INSTRUCTION   249

Teacher Preparation   249

Concept-Based Instruction   250

PRINCIPLES OF CURRICULAR DESIGN   251

Big Ideas   251

Strategic Integration   251

Conspicuous Strategies   251

Scaffolding   252

Primed Background Knowledge   252

Judicious Review   252

OVERVIEW OF DIRECT INSTRUCTION CONTENT AREA PROGRAMS   252

History/Social Studies   253

Science   254

CONTENT ANALYSIS AND FORMAT FEATURES   254

Big Ideas from History   254

Big Ideas from Science   258

Strategic Integration in History   259

Strategic Integration in Science   259

Conspicuous Strategies in History   259

Conspicuous Strategies in Science   261

Scaffolding in History   261

Scaffolding in Science   262

Primed Background Knowledge in History   264

Primed Background Knowledge in Science   265

Judicious Review in History   265

Judicious Review in Science   266

ANOTHER DIRECT INSTRUCTION CONTENT AREA PROGRAM   266

TEACHING TECHNIQUES   266

Unison Responding and Signals   267

Error Corrections   267

ASSESSMENT AND TROUBLESHOOTING   268

History   268

Science   269

EXTENSIONS AND ADAPTATIONS   270

Big Ideas and Writing   273

Strategic Integration and Writing   273

Conspicuous Strategies and Writing   274

Scaffolding and Writing   274

Primed Background Knowledge and Writing   274

Judicious Review and Writing   275

RESEARCH ON DIRECT INSTRUCTION CONTENT AREA PROGRAMS   275

History   275

Science Videodisc Programs   276

REFERENCES   276

PART THREE   Additional Issues in Direct Instruction Implementations   280

CHAPTER NINE

Applying Direct Instruction Principles to New Content   280

OBJECTIVES   280

OVERVIEW OF DESIGNING EFFECTIVE INSTRUCTION   281

PLANNING UNITS AND GENERAL STRATEGIES   283

Identifying Objectives   283

Analyzing the Content and Identifying Big Ideas   283

Sequencing Content   286

LESSON PLANNING AND DELIVERY   286

Activity Planning   289

Formats   290

Designing and Delivering Lesson Plans   293

EVALUATION   299

Student Performance   299

Instructional Interactions with Students   299

Structure of Lesson   299

SUPPORTING RESEARCH   300

REFERENCES   301

CHAPTER TEN

Aspects of Schoolwide Implementations   304

OBJECTIVES   304

ELEMENTS AND LEARNING ENVIRONMENTS OF EFFECTIVE SCHOOLS   305

Criterion Content Covered   306

Academic Learning Time   307

Minimizing Time Needed to Learn   308

DIRECT INSTRUCTION IN AN EFFECTIVE SCHOOL FRAMEWORK   309

CRITICAL ISSUES AND GUIDELINES FOR IMPLEMENTING DIRECT INSTRUCTION PROGRAMS   310

Scope and Sequence of Implementation   310

Organizing the Student Learning Environment   313

Monitoring Mission Progress   317

Staff Development   319

COACHING AS A MEANS OF STAFF DEVELOPMENT   320

Common Types of Coaching Interventions   321

Direct Instruction Coaching Format   322

TUTORING AS A MEANS OF INCREASING SUPPORT FOR STUDENTS   324

Advantages of Tutoring   325

Tutoring Models   325

Implementing and Evaluating a Tutoring Program   326

Research on Tutoring Using Direct Instruction   328

EFFECTIVE SUPERVISION OF PRESERVICE TEACHERS   329

Research on the Direct Instruction Supervision System   331

REFERENCES   332

APPENDIX   Direct Instruction Programs   335

Name Index   357

Subject Index   365

ABOUT THE EDITORS

Dr. Nancy E. Marchand-Martella is a professor of Special Education in the Department of Counseling, Educational, and Developmental Psychology at Eastern Washington University. She has worked for over eighteen years with students with and without disabilities in public and private school settings. Dr. Marchand-Martella teaches courses in effective instructional practices and assessment. She is co-editor of the *Journal of Direct Instruction* and is a board member of the National Association for Direct Instruction. She serves on the Reading First review panel for the State of Washington. Dr. Marchand-Martella has written or cowritten over ninety journal articles, book chapters, and manuals and has conducted over 130 professional research presentations and workshops. The content of her most recent publications and presentations has focused on the use of research-validated instructional practices, with a focus on Direct Instruction programs.

Dr. Timothy A. Slocum is an Associate Professor in the Department of Special Education and Rehabilitation at Utah State University, and directs the special education doctoral program at the University. Dr. Slocum teaches teacher-preparation courses in special education teaching methods and assessment, and graduate research courses in statistics and research methods. Dr. Slocum is co-editor of the *Journal of Direct Instruction* and is a member of the Board of Directors of the Association for Direct Instruction. Dr. Slocum's recent research has been focused on reading instruction and effective teacher-preparation practices. Dr. Slocum is also co-director of a private school that uses Direct Instruction with a wide range of students with and without disabilities.

Dr. Ronald C. Martella is a professor of Special Education in the Department of Counseling, Educational, and Developmental Psychology at Eastern Washington University. He has worked for over eighteen years with students with and without disabilities in public and private school settings, and currently serves on four editorial boards of refereed journals. Dr. Martella has written or cowritten over ninety books, book chapters, journal articles, and manuals. Additionally, he has conducted over 100 professional research presentations. The content of his most recent publications and presentations has focused on individualized behavior-management procedures including the use of functional academic/behavioral assessments.

Part One provides an overview and discusses the importance of Direct Instruction. In Chapter 1, Hempenstall sets the stage for the text by describing why we need quality education and how so many of our children fail to experience success and, instead, participate in a cycle of failure. Hempenstall describes the importance of using research to guide our practices and the obstacles to using research to drive education. Finally, Hempenstall defines effective instruction (**d**irect **i**nstruction) and **D**irect **I**nstruction and chronicles the history of the Direct Instruction model and its founder, Siegfried Engelmann. In Chapter 2, Watkins and Slocum describe the three main components of Direct Instruction: program design, organization of instruction, and teacher–student interactions. Watkins and Slocum note the results of Project Follow-Through, independent reviews of Direct Instruction research, and long-term follow-up investigations.

Part Two provides an overview and analysis of Direct Instruction academic programs. In particular, these chapters describe the importance of each academic area and instruction in the area, critical elements of focus, an overview of programs with corresponding content analyses and format features, teaching techniques specific to the programs, assessment and trouble-shooting aspects, extensions and adaptations, and a summary of the research supporting these programs. In Chapter 3, Waldron-Soler and Osborn describe the language programs. Stein and Kinder discuss the various reading programs in Chapter 4. In Chapter 5, Fredrick and Steventon provide a discussion of writing programs. Simonsen and Dixon discuss spelling programs in Chapter 6. Snider and Crawford discuss various math programs in Chapter 7. Finally, in Chapter 8, Harniss, Hollenbeck, and Dickson describe content area programs in history/social studies and science.

Part Three focuses on additional issues in Direct Instruction implementation. In Chapter 9, Lignugaris/Kraft describes how Direct Instruction principles can be applied to new content. A lesson plan format is provided to guide teachers in providing effective instruction to students when Direct Instruction programs are not available. Marchand-Martella, Blakely, and Schaefer discuss aspects of schoolwide implementations in Chapter 10. These aspects include critical issues and guidelines for implementing Direct Instruction programs, coaching as a means of staff development, tutoring to increase support for students, and effective supervision of preservice teachers.

Additional Chapters

Two additional chapters on Direct Instruction published in the Summer Issue, Volume 4(2), of the *Journal of Direct Instruction* (*JODI*) can be obtained by calling the Association for Direct Instruction (ADI) at (800) 995-2464, by faxing ADI at (541) 683-7543, or by accessing ADI's website at www.adihome.org. These chapters include what was to be Chapter 11: Evaluation of Direct Instruction Implementations by Timothy Slocum, Utah State University and Chapter 12: Managing Classroom Behavior by Ronald C. Martella,

Eastern Washington University, and J. Ron Nelson, University of Nebraska-Lincoln. Due to space limitations, both chapters were cut and subsequently published in *JODI*. In the chapter on evaluating Direct Instruction implementations, Slocum notes how Direct Instruction implementations should be evaluated. Slocum describes issues of assessment, evaluation, and validity, as well as formative and summative evaluation. Evaluation designs are also illustrated. In the chapter on managing classroom behavior, Martella and Nelson overview how to manage classroom behavior using primary prevention, secondary, and tertiary techniques. Martella and Nelson focus on the connection of Direct Instruction programs and their elements to classroom management. We encourage readers to purchase this issue of *JODI* for further information on aspects of Direct Instruction implementations.

Acknowledgments

Several individuals were involved in completing this text. We would like to thank everyone at Allyn and Bacon for their continued support of this project, especially Virginia Lanigan, without whom this project would not have come to fruition. To the contributing authors who painstakingly wrote chapters in their areas of expertise, we extend our sincere thanks. We also wish to thank those individuals who helped with the production of this text including Karen Sorrentino, Anne Desjardins, Don Stenhoff, Amy Griffin, and Bryan Wickman. Finally, we wish to thank the following reviewer who provided invaluable feedback and suggestions to help us produce a better book: Kathleen Beaudoin, University of Washington, Tacoma.

FOREWORD

SIEGFRIED ENGELMANN

All details of Direct Instruction are referenced to teaching effectively. Most of the details evolved from our failure to teach something well or to achieve the effect that we had intended. Our assumption from the beginning was that children would learn if we taught them effectively. When all children did not learn or didn't learn in a timely manner, the conclusion was not that they lacked readiness or were incapable of learning, but that our procedure was ineffective and should be modified to communicate more effectively with the children. Fortunately, our initial work, starting in the 1960s, was directed at accelerating the performance of preschool-age, low-performing children who had older siblings in classes for individuals with mild mental retardation. These children were relatively hard to teach and manage, which meant that, when we succeeded in teaching skills or operations, we knew that the techniques were solid and would work with the full range of students who lacked these skills or operations.

The overall strategy that evolved was to let these children's performance show where they could begin an instructional sequence—a point at which we could start a small-step staircase of skills that didn't attempt to teach everything in one "lesson," or even in a few days, but that built progressively, a little bit during each lesson. The idea was that, if children were able to learn only so much new information at a time, we would teach only that much. But if we designed the sequence properly, any child who could stand firmly on the first step of the staircase—performing perfectly on the basic skills—could learn enough to reach the next step and the next and, ultimately, reach the goal of the sequence.

The result would be that we would be able teach children anything. The trick was simply to start them where they would be successful and to design a sequence that would not overwhelm them by trying to teach too much new material during any lesson. For instance, if children could not follow directions that told them to touch the top of their paper, we taught them the difference between top and not top. If they could not say the sentence, "I touched the top of my paper," we taught the sentence. If they had trouble with large classes of sentences, we taught them. Basically, we simply tried to teach them all of the things they would have to know to learn the next thing we planned to teach them.

In addition to being sequential and characterized by small steps, the instructional sequences had to be scrupulously efficient. Children at-risk are significantly behind middle-class children both in what they know and in their strategies about how to learn and retain information being taught to them. If these children are to catch up, the task facing teachers is a paradox: to achieve more learning for these children during each period than the middle-class child in a traditional program learns during the same amount of time. The paradox is that, if these children have learned at a slower-than-average rate during their entire life, and if they are relatively naïve about learning from "instructional presentations," how is it possible to accelerate their performance so they are able to catch up to children who know more and learn faster?

The most obvious implication is that, if we use the same programs and techniques traditionally employed with middle-class children, the children at-risk would continue to learn at a rate slower than that of middle-class children. So, in addition to having small steps that allow all children to learn everything we teach, the program would have to be designed so that it packed more total learning into each lesson than a traditional program did.

Because there is no magic in instruction, the advantage had to come about through design of the program and the various techniques the program used. If children produced unison responses, where possible, teachers would receive feedback about the children's learning at a far faster rate than individual turns could generate. If the materials were designed so that teachers did not engage in long explanations, simply short ones, and the children produced a very high rate of responses per minute—possibly ten to twenty—it would be possible to pack more practice into a period. If the program were designed so that it communicated very directly and clearly to the students, the number of misinterpretations would be reduced and learning would occur faster. If the program had no "fluff"—material that was not analytically necessary for the immediate learning objective—a great savings in time would be possible.

Eliminating the fluff requires a careful analysis of what children are to learn and how the introduction can be sequenced so that it involves a minimum of baggage. For instance, if the traditional program requires children to learn all their letters before actual reading is introduced, a great savings could occur if the reading commenced after these children learn possibly only eight or nine letters. A further savings could be realized by completely eliminating the requirement of learning letter names before reading instruction commences. These children do not need letter names, but letter sounds, to attack words. If they learn the letter names first, they must later learn the sounds, then learn to read. The letter–name teaching could be eliminated because it is not necessary.

Children entering kindergarten would first learn some language skills and become familiar with following directions and with learning from teachers. Then reading instruction would start. After fewer than thirty lessons into the sequence, children would be reading their first words.

The sequence must be not only small-stepped, efficient, and capable of generating responses at a high rate, but must be complete, which means that, if there is a skill component children need for a task like initial word reading, the program must provide it. For instance, if we expect beginning readers to "sound out" a word by saying the "sounds" of the letters in sequence and then identifying the word, we have to make sure that they have the skills they need. Again, we were able to identify some of these skills by observing the mistakes they made. Some children we worked with could not identify the word if they sounded it out in the traditional way—with pauses between each sound—for instance, in saying the sounds for the word *mat*, "mmm, aaa, t." By teaching these children to sound out without pauses, they would actually be saying the word slowly ("mmmaaat"); this made it a lot easier for them to identify the word.

But even with this modification, some children could not identify the word. Even when teachers tried to correct by modeling the sounding-out procedure, the children would either produce no response or would say the last part of the word.

"James, watch me touch the letters and say the sounds: mmmaaat.
"What word?" "*At.*"
"James, it's *mat.*"

The correction didn't work because the children lacked the skill. The simplest form of the task they failed was a verbal task that involved no written word. "Listen, mmmaaat. Say it fast." Unfortunately, that example is too hard for some children. The solution is to introduce easier examples and work up to the harder ones. Again, the children's responses showed us when we had reached the appropriate starting point, which was verbal words presented in two parts with a pause between them. "Listen: *ham burger.* Say it fast." With this starting point in place, the children practiced saying it fast with simple words, starting on the first day of reading instruction (many days before they would read their first word). These examples were followed by progressively harder words until the children practiced three-sound words and two-sound words (the hardest for them). "Listen: *nnnōōō.* Say it fast." When they completed this sequence, children had the phonemic skill they needed to approach written words. The only difference was who said the sounds. To decode, the children, not the teacher, said them. Furthermore, the children had the skills necessary for teachers to correct them, so the children figured out the word. "Listen: *mmmaaat.* Say it fast. . . . Now do it by touching and saying the sounds. Sound it out. . . . Say it fast. . . . You read the word *mat.* Good for you."

Our beginning reading program (*DISTAR Reading,* now titled *Reading Mastery*) was the first to introduce these phonemic-awareness exercises, but phonemic awareness was not an end in itself or something that had only an amorphous relationship to what we were teaching. It was a small-step progression that taught a skill that a fair percentage of children hadn't learned and that was a necessary preskill to learning and understanding basic reading procedures.

For some tasks, children need to have knowledge of letter names. So letter names were taught in the sequence, but not before children started reading, only when they needed the information about letter names. In the same way, children learned math facts, but not before they had learned the logic of math operations like addition.

The same analytical approach used in reading applies to all content and skills the children are expected to learn in school. The approach frequently results in procedures that are different not only from traditional approaches but from standards and what is typically measured by achievement tests. For instance, the tradition calls for the introduction of fractions proceeding from the "concrete singular" to the "more complex." The traditional sequence first introduces three fractions, and the children work on these extensively:

$$\frac{1}{2}, \frac{1}{3}, \text{ and } \frac{1}{4}.$$

The expectation is that they are basic examples and, from them, the children learn a fundamental understanding of simple fractions. Later teaching expands the scope. The analysis is poor and is easily contradicted by the behavior of children who go through the sequence. Children learn "misrules" about fractions because the sequence generates these misrules. In other words, it is possible for children to go through the sequence, perform perfectly on every verbal task and worksheet task the sequence presents, and come away with serious misunderstanding of what fractions are. The most common misunderstanding is that all fractions have only one part that is colored or referred to. Another is that you don't have to attend to the top number of the fraction, only the bottom number. (To find the picture on the worksheet that shows

$$\frac{1}{4},$$

just look for the group that has four parts.) The most dangerous misunderstanding is that a fraction is always less than one group.

To avoid all these misunderstandings, the Direct Instruction sequence starts by teaching children how to analyze any fraction. The bottom number tells the number of parts in each group. The top number shows the number of parts that are "used" (colored or referred to). This analysis applies to

$$\frac{11}{7}$$

as well as it applies to

$$\frac{5}{5} \text{ or } \frac{1}{4}.$$

It requires very little time to teach and apply, and it sets the stage for everything children are to learn about fractions. "Improper" fractions are simply those that have a larger number on top than on the bottom. Fractions that equal whole numbers follow logically. (If you can count by the bottom number to reach the top number, the fraction equals a whole number.) For fractions that equal *one,* if there are four parts in each group and you wanted to color one group, how many parts would you color? So the fraction for one group is

$$\frac{4}{4}.$$

For larger fractions, the number of times you count tells the number of wholes.

The analysis even implies why it is impossible to "divide by zero." The fraction

$$\frac{7}{0}$$

tells you to count by zero until you end up with seven. It can't be done. Zero times any other number yields zero, not 7. On the other hand,

$$\frac{0}{7}$$

is easily demonstrated as a legitimate fraction—strange but legitimate. According to the analysis there are seven parts in each group but none of the parts is colored or used.

A further extension of the analysis relates fractions to division (rather than introducing labels like *numerator* and *denominator* that give the impression that fractions are something strange and unique). Fractions are division problems that are written in a column rather than a row. The problem

$$7\overline{)28}$$

is the same as the fraction

$$\frac{28}{7}$$

The Direct Instruction mathematics programs show this relationship by requiring students to treat the problems in the same way. They read the standard division problem as 28 divided by 7. Then they read the fraction as the same division problem: 28 divided by 7. These conventions promote knowledge of relationships that many students never develop going through traditional programs and virtually none develop going through programs in which they make up math algorithms.

In the end, the process that we tried to follow in developing effective instruction was to identify *all* the variables that we could manipulate within the school setting to create savings in time and make the instruction more effective. We scripted what teachers said because teachers we worked with learned faster and performed better when we did this. In a full-school implementation, we required all teachers to be part of the same plan, so that we would know exactly where the various children were performing now and would be performing at the end of the year. We needed this information to coordinate efforts from classroom to classroom, from grade to grade.

We developed recommended schedules for daily periods of instruction because we observed that, unless the instruction was scheduled this way, teachers were not able to teach enough or spent too much time on a particular subject. We grouped children homogeneously for instruction so that all children were on the same step of the instructional sequence. With heterogeneous groups, some of the children were far below where they would have to be to master everything taught in the lesson. (They would have to learn much more during the period than children who were placed on the appropriate stair.) Other children already know the material being presented and do not benefit from whatever instruction teachers provide.

We introduced behavior-management techniques and practices because without these, teachers would often not issue a ratio of praise-to-corrective comments that promote confident, positive learners. Finally, we developed detailed procedures for training teachers and for monitoring and collecting the data that helped us identify current problems. The purpose of identifying problems is not to blame teachers but to provide timely solutions to the problems so children are able to proceed at a good rate through the program.

With all these pieces in place, and with academic work in reading, language, and math beginning in kindergarten, we are able to accelerate the performance of children who were behind. At-risk schools are able to perform far above their current achievement levels.

Figure 1 shows the fifth-grade reading performance of eleven schools in Baltimore where Direct Instruction programs were implemented. All but one at least doubled its 1998 reading level. Some were implemented better than others. City Springs was the best-implemented school (it solved more of the problems and effectively controlled more of

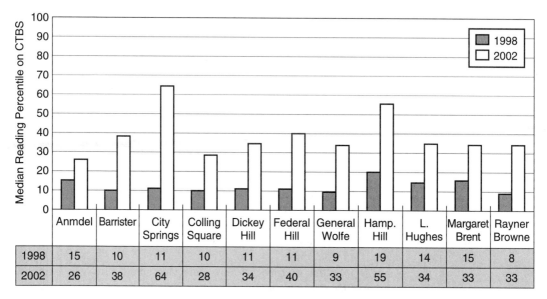

FIGURE 1   Comprehensive Test of Basic Skills (CTBS) Median Percentile Reading Scores in fifth grade in eleven Direct Instruction Schools in Baltimore, Maryland for the years 1998 and 2002.

the variables), and went from an overall 1997 placement (math and reading) of 115th of 117 schools in the district to being sixth in 2002. Note that all of these schools have more than 25 percent turnover of students each year. So the average fifth-grader has been in the program less than three years. Children who have gone through the entire K–5 sequence score about 30 percent higher than the 2002 values shown in Figure 1. The data show that it can be done, but it requires a great deal of work and coordination.

During the 1960s, we worked not only with preschoolers but with a variety of school-age children who were not performing well in academic work. Some were students who failed to learn to read well or to perform well in math. To develop appropriate instruction for them, we followed a variation of the same strategy we used with children in the preschool and elementary grades. We assumed that, if the teaching was appropriate, they would learn. We recognized that most of them were victims of very bad instruction. In reading, for instance, they had been taught to guess at words, to use sentence contexts, pictures, or hints provided by teachers to figure out words. They didn't learn that, for an overwhelming number of words, a particular arrangement of letters signaled a particular pronunciation. Most of these students had gone through various, magical approaches, such as those based on the idea that students simply weren't motivated and that, if they really wanted to read, they would. In fact, these students couldn't read accurately if their lives depended on it. They came away from their attempts to read high-interest material even more frustrated because they were very confused about what reading actually involved. Their confusion was revealed by the discrepancy between their performance at reading words in lists and reading the same words in sentences. Many of them could accurately read words like *the, a, what,* and *that* in lists but would make frequent mistakes when they tried to read these words in passages. For them, reading words in passages involved a formula far more complex than the word-reading strategy for words in lists.

Because these students had to relearn habits and notions they had about reading, the program had to be designed to provide them with both the information about what they needed to do and the amount of practice they needed to establish new habits. The approach was logical, not magical.

The corrective reading sequences that we have designed do not try to avoid the students' reading problems but rather confront them directly. The beginning parts of the sequence were designed so that, if students used any of their ineffective strategies, they would make mistakes and thereby receive immediate feedback about exactly where their current strategies must be changed. One technique we used was to design the text so it was not predictable. Instead of saying something like,

> Tim and Jim said, "Let's go to the store." So Tim and Jim went to the store,
>> the text would say,
> Tim and Jim said, "Let's go to the store." So the boys rode their bikes there.

Any guessing would probably result in a mistake. We also designed the material so there were no pictures (eliminating the possibility of predicting the text on the basis of pictures). We even created some stories so that the students read lists of words that were not actually in lists. For instance, one of the characters was a dog named Chee. When she got excited, she would say things that made no sense. The words she would say were those the students tended to confuse most frequently. For instance,

> Chee was very mad. She said, "Of what for to go that who."

Some students who could read these words accurately in a list would find this task very difficult, but it served to show them that reading is grounded in identifying the same words that the program presented in daily lists.

The common thread for all subjects and all students—from the preschooler learning to follow basic directions to the high school-age students learning chemistry—is that instruction is logical and that learners respond in lawful ways. They learn to hate reading if they can't figure out how to do it. They like reading if they succeed.

Furthermore, their performance history gives them a good idea of what to expect. Children who have learned everything teachers have set out to teach them are understandably confident that they will be able to learn the next thing teachers present. In contrast, those children who have a history of failing to learn what teachers try to teach have a pretty good idea that they will fail the next thing teachers present. So if we want children to feel good about themselves, we give them evidence that shows them they have a reason for being confident. We don't try to seduce them through slogans and songs that say how smart they are. We respond to their successes as if they are important and thereby show them how smart they are. We don't give them noncontingent praise or ignore the problems they have in learning. We view children as lawful beings who have the capacity to learn if we identify the appropriate starting point and provide them with a sufficient amount of practice.

Both the starting point and the amount of practice are determined not by applying formulas that have nothing to do with performance, but by letting the children show you, through actual behavior, what they don't know and how much practice they require to learn it. The most important rule for anyone who wants to become a superior teacher—one who is able to teach virtually any learner with an IQ of 70 or more—is to reference everything that is taught to the performance of the learner. This rule holds not only for everything in the Direct Instruction sequences but everything else teachers do whether you are teaching learners the rules about how to store the volleyballs and use them during recess, a unit on Sweden, or quadratic equations, find a starting point that permits the learners to perform at least 70 percent correctly on the tasks you present. Then proceed a step at a time, with each step referenced to whether the learners achieve mastery.

Remember, the learner is not segment to learn one way during structured lessons and learn another way in response to the unit on Sweden. It's the same learner, with the same repertoire, habits, and motivation. Sometimes, teachers fail to learn this truth. Instead of using the same positive management techniques they use during the Direct Instruction lessons, they nag and scold children at other times, and basically fail to apply what they have learned through their Direct Instruction training about teaching to mastery.

Not only can it be done, it's worth the work because the superior teacher is able to change the learner's life more than doctors, social workers, or any other professional. A superior teacher in a superior school can create options for the learner that nobody else is able to create, such as the option of going to college and becoming a journalist, an engineer, or a teacher.

CONTRIBUTING AUTHORS

Molly Blakely, Ed.D.
Educational Resources, Inc.

Donald Crawford, Ph.D.
Otter Creek Institute

Shirley Dickson, Ph.D.
Education Commission of the States

Robert Dixon, M.A.
Classical Learning Systems

Laura D. Fredrick, Ph.D.
Georgia State University

Mark Harniss, Ph.D.
University of Washington

Keith Hollenbeck, Ph.D.
University of Oregon

Kerry Hempenstall, Ph.D.
RMIT University

Diane Kinder, Ph.D.
University of Washington–Tacoma

Benjamin Lignugaris/Kraft, Ph.D.
Utah State University

Nancy Marchand-Martella, Ph.D.
Eastern Washington University

Jean Osborn, M.Ed.
Educational Consultant

Ed Schaefer, M.Ed.
Educational Resources, Inc.

Flint L. Simonsen, Ph.D.
Eastern Washington University

Timothy A. Slocum, Ph.D.
Utah State University

Vicki E. Snider, Ph.D.
University of Wisconsin–Eau Claire

Marcy Stein, Ph.D.
University of Washington–Tacoma

Candace Steventon, Ed.S.
Georgia State University

Kathleen M. Waldron-Soler, Ph.D.
Eastern Washington University

Cathy L. Watkins, Ph.D.
California State University–Stanislaus

CHAPTER ONE

THE IMPORTANCE OF EFFECTIVE INSTRUCTION

KERRY HEMPENSTALL
Royal Melbourne Institute of Technology University

OBJECTIVES

After studying this chapter you should be able to:

1. describe the economic, social, and political benefits for society of ensuring all students' competence in basic skills;

2. describe the areas of disadvantage for those individuals who do not develop competence in basic skills;

3. compare the basic skill development of students in the United States relative to comparable countries and relative to the past;

4. describe the process of decline typically endured by students who make slow initial progress in basic skills;

5. describe the relationship between student achievement and teacher behavior;

6. explain why empirical research had such little impact on teaching practice in the past;

7. compare the experiences of various professions in the shift toward research-based practice;

8. summarize the research on effective instruction;

9. describe the history of Direct Instruction.

A universal and high-quality education is acknowledged by the community as among the most highly valued of its priorities. When education is successful, citizens have the opportunity to reach their potential and nations are able to thrive, making the best use of their human resources in an increasingly competitive world.

In gauging the success of educational policies in achieving this goal, state and national student assessments have become the accepted measure. The current view is that the results, particularly in the core skills such as reading and math, are unacceptably poor. This finding is deeply troubling, especially when we consider the increasing amount of money assigned to education each year. One explanation for this outcome is that education has never forged strong links to research and has failed to acknowledge and promote methods of teaching that are demonstrably effective. There is ample evidence that most student failure is a predictable and preventable phenomenon, and even the step-by-step process of student decline is well understood.

There has long been ample evidence that some teaching behaviors are more conducive to student success than others. However, until recently these effective practices have had little impact in the classroom. It is now recognized that events in the classroom represent the most powerful opportunity to influence student progress available to the education system, and we are beginning to see interest in training teachers in effective instructional methods. These methods are viewed as helpful to student learning but have particular importance in the national efforts to overcome failure among disadvantaged groups.

An important model consistent with these effective instructional practices is known as Direct Instruction. Direct Instruction includes design principles and teaching behaviors incorporated into a set of instructional programs typically published by Science Research Associates and associated with Siegfried Engelmann and the University of Oregon. Direct Instruction has a relatively long history, though one that has not been well accepted by the educational community. This model has many notable features that are consistent with the research on effective instruction (described later). Each of these features can be readily observed in the range of programs available for a variety of curricular areas.

An increasing number of schools are adopting Direct Instruction programs. For example, when Thaddeus Lott became principal of Wesley Elementary in Houston, a school in an area of extreme disadvantage, only 18 percent of third graders were at or above grade level in reading comprehension on the Iowa Test of Basic Skills. Within five years that proportion had increased to 85 percent. In 1996, 100 percent of the third graders passed the Texas Assessment of Academic Skills (TAAS) in reading (Palmaffy, 1998). Further, in poverty-ridden City Springs Elementary School in Baltimore, literacy levels have improved from among the district's lowest to fifth highest after implementing Direct Instruction programs (Viadero, 2002b). In some of the most disadvantaged schools in Houston, Direct Instruction reading with students in kindergarten, first grade, and second grade, under the auspices of the Rodeo Institute for Teacher Excellence, have produced consistent and accelerated growth throughout the program duration (Viadero, 2002b).

In this chapter the importance of basic skills in our society and how individuals are disadvantaged without these skills are described. How research can inform educational practice as well as why empirical research has had little impact on teaching practice in the past is discussed. The history of the Direct Instruction model and its major contributors is provided.

THE NEED FOR QUALITY EDUCATION

It is more apparent than ever before that our society requires an educated population (American Federation of Teachers, 1998). Governments recognize that, unless the nation's workforce is skilled, the economy will always be under threat because of intense global competition. Parents are aware that their children's economic and social futures depend on their capacity to respond productively to a rapidly changing workplace.

We live in a complex world in which no country can afford to be insular. Our nation's policies have an impact at a global level in addition to their domestic impact. Citizens' awareness of national and international issues is crucial to the development of a nation's policies; only an educated population can provide the needed support and guidance for their political leaders in a democratic society.

Flesch (1955) exemplified the broad societal concern when expressing his dismay at the methods of teaching reading that were popular at the time. He argued that an alleged decline in reading standards among the children of the working class represented a threat to democracy, and he hinted at conspiracies to disempower sections of the community by deliberately using methods of teaching that were ineffective. "The American dream is, essentially, equal opportunity through free education for all. This dream is beginning to vanish in a country where public schools are falling down on the job" (Flesch, p. 132). This concern about educational outcomes, and particularly illiteracy, has remained in the public eye and is even more evident today (Rochester, 2002).

It is tempting to blame the rapid increase in technology as a major factor in altering the employment mix between those entailing mostly physical abilities and those requiring predominantly intellectual qualities. Yet, as long ago as 1984, Kirsch and Guthrie indicated that the demands of the workplace for literacy skills were obviously increasing, and that jobs without a strong literacy requirement were becoming rare.

A LITANY OF DISADVANTAGE

The completion of high school was originally the province of the middle class, it being seen as unnecessary for individuals who would inevitably spend their working life in an unskilled occupation. It was the increased desire of those in poorly paid, and often unsafe, employment that their children have the opportunity for a better life that led to the strong community interest in education. Stedman and Kaestle (1987) show why our society has such deep concerns about education when they describe the day-to-day disadvantages caused by serious deficits in functional literacy.

> Among the lowest fifth in functional literacy skills are many who are unable to read product labels and have to depend upon brand name logos for selection of items in a grocery store. Many are unable to determine whether they are getting the correct change. Many cannot read recipes very well and cannot read the directions on frozen food packages (p. 34).

Further difficulties for these adults include reading traffic signs, street names and maps, transport schedules, children's homework, school reports, medical information, and emergency phone numbers.

The report of the National Institute for Literacy (1998) pointed to a strong association between illiteracy, unemployment, poverty, and crime. It is generally acknowledged that the availability of employment for those with underdeveloped basic skills has declined markedly in the last twenty years. This trend is evident in the U.S. Department of Labor (2003) finding that the majority of the 20 occupations in most rapid decline are of the unskilled type, while all seven of the education and training categories expected to demonstrate above average growth in employment opportunities require postsecondary vocational or academic work.

A high proportion of individuals with inadequate academic achievement are unemployed. About 80 percent of adults with at least a university degree are employed compared with 65 percent of high school graduates, and only 43 percent of those who did not complete high school (Snyder & Hoffman, 2002).

The Condition of Education (U.S. Department of Education, 2002a) report noted that health and welfare are strongly related to education levels. Problems in the understanding and practice of good nutrition and mental health, access to health services, and the appropriate use of medical services are all characteristic of those with poor literacy. Further, the less educated are involved in more workplace accidents. Lyon (2001a) reported that about 50 percent of those with a history of substance abuse have reading problems. Forty-three percent of those individuals at the lowest literacy skill level live in poverty (National Institute for Literacy, 1998).

Among the prison population, 70 percent demonstrate literacy at the two lowest levels of reading proficiency (National Institute for Literacy, 1998). Lyon (2001a) made the chilling observation that in some states the accommodation needs of their prisons ten years into the future can be reliably predicted by the current fourth-grade rates of reading failure.

CONCERN OVER EDUCATIONAL OUTCOMES

It was not only a concern for democracy that elevated education-for-all to the status of a national priority. The issues have concerned the community's perception of the absolute level of success, and whether the level is improving or declining. In *A Nation at Risk* (National Commission on Excellence in Education, 1983) it was argued that the literacy demands of an increasingly sophisticated society were exceeding supply.

> Each generation of Americans has outstripped its parents in education, in literacy, and in economic attainment. For the first time in the history of our country, the educational skills of one generation will not surpass, will not equal, will not even approach, those of their parents (Copperman, 1978, cited in National Commission on Excellence in Education, 1983, paragraph 17).

Only 36 percent of Americans in 1999 expressed either *a great deal* or *quite a lot* of confidence in the public schools. In 1988, the proportion was 49 percent, and in 1973 it was 58 percent (Public Agenda, 2002).

Concerns about public education are not new; however, their focus in recent times has shifted. Issues that have arisen over the last ten to twenty years include apparent national and state test score declines, unflattering international achievement comparisons, the failure of funding increases to produce discernible results, excessive high school dropout rates, and a perception that schooling and work are insufficiently closely aligned (Levin, 1998).

It is not simply a public impression that there are serious problems in the education system's capacity to meet expectations. Numerous surveys and reports have reached similar conclusions. The U.S. Department of Education reported in 1999 that across the nation 40 percent of fourth graders failed to demonstrate even partial mastery of the literacy levels required for school success, and among high-poverty schools that figure rose to 70 percent. Only one of ten students in high-poverty schools read at the *proficient* level on the National Assessment of Educational Progress (U.S. Department of Education, 1999). Similar results were presented in the *Nation's Report Card: Fourth-Grade Reading 2000* (U.S. Department of Education, 2001a) in the finding that only 32 percent of students could be considered proficient.

Recently, in a report to the Office of Educational Research and Improvement, Snow et al. (1998) noted that U.S. students are falling behind students in comparable countries because their underdeveloped basic skills limit their attainment in the challenging subject-specific demands of the high school curriculum.

STUDENTS WHO PERFORM POORLY

Many groups of students have been identified as performing poorly in school. These groups include minority and disadvantaged students, students with learning disabilities, and even those from advantaged backgrounds.

Minority and Disadvantaged Students

According to the Office of Educational Research and Improvement (2001) almost 40 percent of students nationally read below a *basic* level; that is, they struggled to comprehend even the simplest of texts. These figures are even more alarming for some groups of individuals: 63 percent of African American fourth graders, 60 percent of children in poverty, and 47 percent of children in urban schools read below a *basic* level. In New York State in 2001, only 30 percent of students passed the eighth-grade English test (Hartocollis, 2002), and nearly 65 percent of students were unable to compute at grade level (Campanile, 2002).

Another major concern with educational attainment is the gap between the affluent and the middle class, compared with those less advantaged—those students from minority and low income groups. Social objectives of equality cannot be achieved while there are glaring gaps in the attainments of different segments of society. A generally accepted social value is that such groups should be assigned sufficient assistance to enable their full participation in the economic and social riches of the nation. This goal has resisted attainment over a long period, though in recent times there has been a concerted multilevel attack on inequality at the preschool and elementary levels. Such initiatives have been partly driven and informed by the failure to make much headway with the teaching models most prevalent during the 1990s.

In fact, the achievement levels of minority and disadvantaged students declined during the 1990s in comparison with those of other students (Haycock, 2001; Office of Educational Research & Improvement, 2001). The reading performance of the nation's fourth graders may appear to have remained relatively stable across the last decade. However, while the 2000 national average reading scale score was similar to that of 1992, the reading of higher performing students improved and that of the low performing students declined, thereby increasing the gulf between them (Office of Educational Research & Improvement, 2001). Adding to the early disadvantage suffered by minority and low-income children is the finding that they are far more likely to be saddled with lower-quality teachers (Wayne, 2002).

Learning Disabilities

Apart from the debate about whether a learning disability category really exists or whether it serves a useful function (U.S. Department of Education, 2001b), there is consensus that such a category can account for the failure of no more than about 5 percent of the population (U.S. Department of Education, 1995). In fact, there is concern that the expanding learning disability category may serve to mask the major issue in educational failure. "Learning disabilities have become a sociological sponge to wipe up the spills of general education. It's where children go who weren't taught well" (Lyon, cited in Colvin & Helfand, 1999, p. 1). According to the Commission on Excellence in Special Education (2002) about 50 percent of those in special education programs are identified as having a specific learning disability, a category that has tripled in numbers diagnosed since 1976. Of those students, 80 percent are so classified because they haven't been effectively taught how to read. Further, few children placed in special education programs make adequate progress or close the gap on their peers in literacy and school attainment.

The Commission on Excellence in Special Education (2002) further reported that students with disabilities fail to complete high school at twice the rate of their nondisabled peers, and enrollment rates in higher education remain 50 percent lower than enrollment among the general population.

Unexpected Groups

It appears that students who are educationally disadvantaged include those we might anticipate: those in poverty, minority race groups, those with disabilities, and English-language learners. Yet, the figures suggest that a portion of struggling students do not arise from those groups but appear rather unexpectedly.

When the head of the reading programs at the federal government's National Institute of Child Health and Human Development, G. Reid Lyon (1998), testified to the Senate Committee, he pointed out that half of the children reading below the *basic* level in California were from the homes of parents who were college graduates.

> In fact, the children of college-educated parents in California scored lowest with respect to their national cohort. These data underscore the fact that reading failure is a serious problem and cannot simply be attributed to poverty, immigration, or the learning of English as a second language (p. 3).

Based on this finding, it seems that reading difficulties are seen across the board, not just with groups who are typically found to be educationally disadvantaged.

Similarly, for mathematics, the TIMSS study observed that even bright students were lagging in comparison with those in other countries. Interestingly, the countries that did very well in math and science had "a common, coherent, rigorous curriculum" (Schmidt, Houang, & Cogan, 2002, p. 16).

> In mathematics a score at the 75th percentile in the U.S. was below the 25th percentile in Singapore. The problems we must address affect not only our average students, but even those who are above average. . . . What we can see in the Third International Mathematics and Science Study is that schooling makes a difference. Specifically, we can see that the curriculum itself—what is taught—makes a huge difference (Schmidt et al., 2002, pp. 2–3).

High School and Beyond

Lyon (2001a) observed that, of those who receive special assistance because of early reading problems, only 2 percent will complete a four-year college program. Further, more than three-fourths of the approximately 15 percent of children who fail to complete high school ascribe major significance to the difficulties experienced in learning to read. The extent of their basic skill deficit is evident in the U.S. Department of Education (1999) finding that 60 percent of the unemployed lack the basic skills required to be trained successfully for high-tech positions.

The basic skills of many high school graduates fall below community expectations. Most employers and college professors say that high school graduates generally display *poor* or *only fair* basic skills such as written expression, spelling, and math (Johnson & Duffett, 2002). The American Management Association Survey on Workplace Testing (American Management Association, 2001) found that about one-third of assessed applicants lacked the basic skills necessary to perform the jobs they sought, and 85 percent of the companies did not hire such applicants.

Even at the college level, problems in the basic skills of entrants were of concern as noted in the Condition of Education report (U.S. Department of Education, 2002a). Numerous universities have found it necessary to institute programs for teaching basic skills, including, literacy to newly enrolled students.

It seems that skill performance for disadvantaged students as well as advantaged ones is a concern across multiple academic areas such as reading and mathematics. Additionally, basic skills for high school and beyond are of concern; these skill deficits may lead to even more serious academic problems.

THE DEVELOPMENT OF SERIOUS ACADEMIC PROBLEMS

Problems in basic educational skills commence early in an individual's life, have snowballing negative effects, and their consequences are felt over a lifetime and in numerous domains of an individual's life (Binder, 1996; Lewis & Paik, 2001). Hart and Risley (1995) noted major differences in the amount and quality of conversation between parents and young children from professional, working-class, and welfare families (described in detail in Chapter 3). Lyon (2001b) pointed out that early vocabulary deficits are more likely among disadvantaged children whose parents may be unable to provide them with the early language and literacy experiences that provide many other students with a flying start.

The area of literacy development, and, in particular, initial progress in reading, represents the fulcrum on which students' educational progress balances. Several studies (e.g., Becker, 1977; Farkas & Beron, 2001) have noted that students entering school with underdeveloped vocabularies are very likely to fail in their basic skill development, yet they also found the effects could be countered by intensive early school-based assistance. There is ample evidence (America Reads, 2001; Ceci, 1991) that students who do not make good initial progress in learning to read find it increasingly difficult ever to master the process.

Matthew Effects

Stanovich (1986, 1988a, 1988b, 1993) outlined a model in which problems with early phonological skills lead to a downward spiral whereby all other school skills and even higher cognitive skills are eventually affected by slow reading development. Stanovich (1986) described this process as the Matthew Effects: "For unto everyone that hath shall be given, and he shall have abundance; but from him that hath not shall be taken away even that which he hath" (Matthew, XXV: 29, Revised Standard Version). Commencing at the initial stages of reading, children with strong skills gain new skills with ease, and those with weak skills struggle to learn subsequent skills, thereby falling further behind. Children with a clear understanding of the sound structure of spoken words (phonological awareness) are well placed to make sense of our alphabetic system and learn the sounds for letters. Their rapid development of letter–sound correspondences allows the development of independent reading, high levels of practice, and the subsequent fluency that is critical for comprehension and enjoyment of reading.

In contrast, initial difficulties with prereading skills can undermine students' capacity to learn the code of written English. This deficit can inhibit the learning of word meanings, reading comprehension, spelling, written expression, and even the motivation to engage in subsequent language-based learning (Moats, 1996). In their study, Chapman, Tunmer, and Prochnow (2000) reported a negative self-concept among struggling readers arising within the first two years of their schooling.

Reading Participation

These cycles of failure can be exacerbated because struggling students do not participate in reading as much as their peers. Allington (1984), in a study of first-grade students, noted vastly different reading-exposure ratios. In his study, the number of words read per week ranged from 16 in the less skilled group to 1933 in the upper group. Exacerbating this problem of differential exposure is the finding that struggling readers are often presented with reading materials that are too difficult for them (Stanovich, 1986). Slow, halting error-prone reading of difficult material, unsurprisingly, reduces comprehension and leads to avoidance of reading activities and further disadvantage.

Vocabulary Development

There is evidence that vocabulary development from about third grade is largely a function of volume of reading (Nagy, 1998; National Reading Panel, 2000; Stanovich, 1988b). Nagy and Anderson (1984) estimate that struggling readers may read around 100,000 words per year in school, whereas, for keen upper-elementary students the figure may be closer to 10,000,000, that is, a hundred-fold difference. For out-of-school reading, Fielding, Wilson, and Anderson (1986) suggested a similar ratio, indicating that fifth-grade children at the 10th percentile of reading ability read about 50,000 words per year out of school, while those at the 90th percentile read about 4,500,000 words per year.

Increasing Problems

Contrary to the hope that initial slow progress is merely a maturational lag to be redressed by a developmental spurt at some later date, even relatively minor delays typically tend to become increasingly major over time (Stanovich, 1993). Juel (1988) reported that poor readers in first grade had an 88 percent chance of remaining so in fourth grade. Jorm, Share, Maclean, and Matthews (1984) followed a group of students with poor prereading skills. In kindergarten, children with poor prereading skills were matched with other children who had similar verbal IQs. By first grade, the group with stronger prereading skills was four months more advanced, and by second grade, nine months more advanced than the group who had lower skills in kindergarten.

Lyon (1998) provides a sobering reminder of the importance of identifying and intervening early in students' educational careers.

> However, we have also learned that if we delay intervention until nine-years-of-age, (the time that most children with reading difficulties receive services), approximately 75% of the children will continue to have difficulties learning to read throughout high school. To be clear, while older children and adults can be taught to read, the time and expense of doing so is enormous (p. 9).

Thus, the idea that differences in early reading development can be taken lightly, as children will catch up later, appears to be a very dangerous myth. This sobering picture is even more serious because early reading problems are not restricted to reading. Empirical research increasingly supports the notion that that even intellectual development can be markedly influenced by literacy attainment (Ceci, 1991; Fletcher, Francis, Rourke, Shaywitz, & Shaywitz, 1993; Stanovich, 1993). Further support from a longitudinal study in New Zealand is provided by Share, McGee, and Silva (1989) and Share and Silva (1987). They matched groups of students with and without reading disabilities on their vocabulary scores attained at age three. At age eleven, marked differences were noted in vocabulary, listening comprehension, and general language skills in favor of the nondisabled group. They demonstrated that the changes in IQ between ages seven and thirteen were predicted by changes in reading over that period. Growth in reading ability between the ages of seven and thirteen accounted for a significant proportion of the IQ-score variability even after controlling for IQ and reading ability at age seven.

Hoskyn and Swanson (2000) reviewed a large body of scientific research and found additional support for this perspective, noting the development of generalized cognitive deficits in older children with a history of significant reading problems. This apparent cognitive decline is thought to be a result of a lower rate of vocabulary development compared to that of students who are capable and regular readers.

The implications of these findings are both disturbing and instructive. That there is increasing agreement about a specific cause of most inadequate reading progress is encouraging. Early intervention has the potential to preclude failure with its attendant personal and social cost. That an initially small and specific deficit rapidly broadens into generalized language, intellectual, and motivational deficits is worrisome for those attempting to alleviate the reading problems of students in mid-elementary school and beyond. In these cases, the consequences of reading failure may remain even if the cause of the reading problem has been successfully addressed.

PREVENTING ACADEMIC FAILURE

Many researchers (Adams, 1990; Ball, 1993; Ball & Blachman, 1991; Blachman, 1994; Bradley & Bryant, 1983; Byrne & Fielding-Barnsley, 1989; Catts, 1991; Cunningham, 1990; Felton, 1993; Foorman, Francis, Novy, & Liberman, 1991; Hatcher, Hulme, & Ellis, 1994; Juel, 1993; Simmons, 1992; Stanovich, 1986, 1988a, 1992, 1993; Torgesen, Wagner, & Rashotte, 1994) have noted the cost-beneficial effects of early intervention. Although early intervention has long been regarded as logical, even programs as intensive as Head Start for disadvantaged children have not achieved the outcome success that was sought. The reasons may relate to the varying quality of educational programs offered and to the difficulty in overcoming very early language disadvantage. More recent efforts may overcome some of the deficits of former initiatives as they are informed by up-to-date research.

The *Condition of Education* report (U.S. Department of Education, 2002a) noted the research finding that childhood education programs, when well designed, can help compensate children for a language disadvantage in early childhood (Engelmann, 1999; Hart & Risley, 1995). This initiative involves increasing the educational elements in preschool programs where these activities have formerly been considered an inappropriate forum for such activities. Such early intervention initiatives are crucial if the community expectations are to be met. Without such large-scale programs, the trajectory for students with early disadvantage is sadly predictable.

The value of empirical research since the beginning of Head Start has been in the narrowing of the focus of the early intervention for reading—from a broad range of "readiness" activities to specific emphases on (1) phonemic awareness as a screening tool and a possible intervention focus, and (2) the critical role of systematic, explicit phonics in initial reading instruction (National Reading Panel, 2000). Further, the evidence indicates the value of effective systematic instruction as a means of enhancing the learning of basic skills for all students, not only for those who are disadvantaged.

IMPORTANCE OF INSTRUCTION

There is strong evidence that the quality of teaching makes a great difference in educational outcomes. This research is exemplified in the Sanders and Rivers (1996) finding that students who were in classes with effective teachers for three years in a row achieved 50 percent more learning than those in classes with poor teachers over the same period.

A year-long study in Boston noted that the best 30 percent of teachers evoked in their students six times the learning growth as did the lowest 30 percent of teachers (Boston Public Schools, 1998). Similar research in Tennessee and Texas highlighted the cumulative nature of these effects and their presence regardless of student background or attainment levels (Sanders & Rivers, 1996).

In Texas, for example, concerted action in assisting teachers to identify and respond effectively to students at-risk has been based on this expectation. Thaddeus Lott, a successful Texas principal, expressed it this way: "A child's self-esteem and success at learning are determined by his having an opportunity to be taught at the rate and level that he is capable of being taught" (Just for the Kids, 2000, p. 18). Based on his analysis of empirical findings available since the 1970s, Jencks has altered his earlier view that other issues were overwhelmingly powerful in determining educational attainment (e.g., Jencks et al., 1972) and now argues for the preeminent role of education in significantly reducing inequality in student achievement (Jencks & Phillips, 1998).

The major school influence on student achievement is clearly classroom practice (DeCourcey Hinds, 2002). Despite the evidence for this link, a great deal of policy continues to be devoted to issues outside of the classroom and school (Lyon & Fletcher, 2001; Wenglinsky, 2000). Of course, there are also other important elements in building successful schools (see Chapter 10 for further details). The Report of the Education Trust (1999) described the characteristics of schools that were successful in the difficult job of improving the achievement of disadvantaged children. In successful schools, increased time was devoted to reading and math. A recognition that many teachers have had little training in effective teaching practice required that funds be made available to enable carefully focused professional development. In order for school and district accountability, comprehensive monitoring of student progress and consequences for inadequate teaching were incorporated. The provision of additional school and home-based student support helps ensure that students at-risk do not remain unassisted. These elements of effective school reform have their most powerful effect in ensuring effective practices are employed in the classroom.

THE LACK OF IMPACT OF RESEARCH ON PRACTICE

Education has frequently adopted new ideas, but it has done so without the wide-scale assessment and scientific research that is necessary to distinguish effective from ineffective reforms (and to promote the former while eliminating the latter). This absence of the scientific perspective has precluded systematic improvement in the education system, and it has impeded growth in the teaching profession for a long time (Carnine, 1995a; Hempenstall, 1996; Marshall, 1993; Stone, 1996). Maggs and White (1982) wrote despairingly, "Few professionals are more steeped in mythology and less open to empirical findings than are teachers" (p. 131).

Carnine (1991) described educational decision makers as lacking a scientific framework and inclined to accept proposals based on good intentions and unsupported opinions. Carnine (1995a) also points to teachers' lack of training and direction in seeking out and evaluating research. For example, he estimates that fewer than 1 in 200 teachers are experienced users of the ERIC educational database.

From a different perspective, Meyer (1991, cited in Gable & Warren, 1993) blames the research community for being too remote from classrooms. She argued that teachers would not become interested in research until its credibility was improved. Research is often difficult to understand, and the careful scientific language and cautious claims may not have the same impact as the wondrous claims of ideologues and faddists unconstrained by scientific ethics.

Obstacles to Research-Driven Teaching

Fister and Kemp (1993) considered several obstacles to research-driven teaching, important among them being the absence of an accountability link between decision makers and student achievement. Such a link was unlikely until recently, when regular mandated state or national test program results became associated with funding. They also apportion some responsibility to the research community for failing to appreciate the necessity of connecting research with teachers' concerns in an adequate manner. The specific criticisms included a failure to take responsibility for communicating findings clearly and with the end-users in mind. Researchers have often validated practices over too brief a time frame, and in too limited a range of settings to excite general program adoption across settings. Without considering the organizational ramifications (such as staff and personnel costs) adequately, the viability of even the very best interventions cannot be guaranteed. The methods of introduction and staff training in innovative practices can have a marked bearing on their adoption and continuation.

Fister and Kemp (1993) also argued that researchers often failed to meet their own criterion by not incorporating research-validated staff training procedures and organizational analysis in their strategies for promoting program adoption. Their final criticism involved the rarity of the establishment of model sites exemplifying excellent practice. When prospective adoptees are able to see the reality rather than the rhetoric of a program, they are more likely to take the often uncomfortable steps toward adoption. In addition, it is possible to discuss with on-site teachers the realities of being involved in the innovation.

Woodward (1993) pointed out that there is often a culture gulf between researchers and teachers. Researchers may view teachers as unnecessarily conservative and resistant to change, whereas teachers may consider researchers unrealistic in their expectations and lacking in understanding of the school system and culture. Teachers may also respond defensively to calls for change because of the implied criticism of their past practices and the perceived devaluation of the professionalism of teachers. Leach (1987) argued strongly that collaboration between change agents and teachers is a necessary element in the acceptance of novel practice. In his view, teachers need to be invited to make a contribution that extends beyond solely the implementation of the ideas of others. There are some positive signs that such a culture may be in the early stages of development. Viadero (2002a) reports on a number of initiatives in which teachers have become reflective of their own work, employing both quantitative and qualitative tools. She also notes that the American Educational Research Association has a subdivision devoted to the practice.

Need for Communication

There are three groups with whom researchers need to be able to communicate if their innovations are to be adopted. At the classroom level, teachers are the focal point of such innovations and their competent and enthusiastic participation is required if success is to be achieved. At the school administration level, principals are being given increasing discretion as to how funds are to be disbursed; therefore, time spent in discussing educational priorities and cost-effective means of achieving them may be time well-spent, bearing in mind Gersten and Guskey's (1985) comment on the importance of strong instructional leadership. At the broader system level, decision makers presumably require different information and assurances about the viability of change of practice.

The Coalition for Evidence-Based Policy (2002) report to the U.S. Department of Education blamed the "disconnect between practice and evidence" (p. 3) for the lack of progress over the past thirty years in raising student achievement in K–12 math, reading, and science. This report also noted the importance of both small- and large-scale studies being of strong design to enable confident recommendations to ensue.

Perhaps because of the frustration over the problems experienced in ensuring effective practices are employed across the nation, we are beginning to see a top-down approach, in which research-based educational practices are either mandated, as in Great Britain (Department for Education and Employment, 1998), or a prerequisite for funding as in the 2001 *No Child Left Behind Act* (U.S. Department of Education, 2002b). Whether this approach will be successful in changing teachers' practices remains to be seen. In any case, there remains a desperate need to address teachers' and parents' concerns regarding classroom practice in a cooperative and constructive manner.

Linking Professional Practices and Research

Over the past twenty to thirty years there has developed a consensus among empirical researchers about a number of issues crucial to education, and a great deal of attention is now directed at means by which these findings can find fruition in the classroom (Gersten, Chard, & Baker, 2000). Carnine (2000) noted that education has appeared impervious to research on effective practices. He examined differences between education and other professions, such as medicine, that are strongly wedded to research as a powerful contributor to practice.

HOW OTHER PROFESSIONS CONNECT RESEARCH TO PRACTICE

Medicine

The term *evidence-based medicine* was popularized during the 1990s. The intention was to enable practitioners to gain access to knowledge of the effectiveness and risks of different interventions before choosing whether or not to implement them, using as a guide reliable estimates of benefit and harm. Even before that time, the U.S. Food and Drug Administration played an important role in approving procedures related to medications and medical devices.

The intent of evidence-based medicine is to make available to practitioners the complex information from a large number of individual studies. Practitioners do not have the time and expertise in research methods and statistics to enable them to draw appropriate conclusions about risks and benefits of every procedure.

Despite the current imperfections, there is strong support within the medical profession for this direction because it offers a cooperative system that will be in a constant cycle of improvement, thereby providing better health outcomes for their patients.

Clinical Psychology

In an initiative parallel to that of the medical profession, the American Psychological Association (APA) (Chambless & Ollendick, 2001) introduced the term *empirically supported treatments* (ESTs) to clinical psychology as a means of focusing attention on the issue of effective psychotherapy. Through examination of research evidence, the Division 12 (Clinical Psychology) Task Force on Psychological Interventions arrived at three classes of interventions that could be applied to any treatment for any particular psychological problem. The criteria for a treatment to be considered *well established* were (1) efficacy through two controlled clinical outcomes studies or a large series of controlled single-case design studies, (2) the availability of treatment manuals to enhance treatment fidelity and reliability, and (3) the provision of clearly specified client characteristics. A second level involved criteria for *probably efficacious* treatments, criteria requiring fewer studies, and/or a lesser standard of rigor. The third category comprised *experimental* treatments, those without sufficient evidence to achieve status in the other two categories.

Initially included as *well-established* treatments were twenty-two treatments for twenty-one different syndromes and seven *probably efficacious* treatments for seven disorders. With a couple of exceptions, all the *well-established* treatments were behavioral or cognitive-behavioral. The exceptions were family education programs for schizophrenia and interpersonal therapy for bulimia and for depression. Similarly, all but one *probably efficacious* treatment were behavioral, the exception being brief psychodynamic therapy.

The EST emphasis on empiricism also has obvious implications for other fields, such as education, in which decisions about the choice of approach have not previously been based on any mutually agreed-on criteria. There are interesting similarities between the response of some psychotherapists to the EST initiative and that of some educators to the "reliable replicable research" criterion for federal funding in literacy programs in the United States.

Objections to Empirically Supported Treatments.   Some of the objections raised have been that ESTs should be ignored because this effort has been the work of a powerful lobby of biased individuals within the APA. Critics view qualitative rather than quantitative research as the appropriate approach to place research into psychotherapy. To be considered a *well-established* treatment requires a treatment manual, and their use (it has been argued) leads to poor quality psychotherapy by diminishing personal judgment. Another perspective rejects ESTs because every client has different needs, and the use of single treatments based on problem analysis cannot meet their needs. Some have asserted that there is no discernible difference in efficacy among the various forms of psychotherapy, thus ESTs are not relevant.

Finally, some consider EST research as irrelevant to clinical practice as it originates in controlled clinical settings and does not translate well to the real world. The degree to which documented treatments can be implemented in settings outside of those from which they originated are now being assessed in large-scale effectiveness studies under the auspices of the National Institute of Mental Health (NIMH). The APA's approach to empirically supported treatments provides a model that may be adapted to the needs of education.

HOW EDUCATION ADDRESSES THE RESEARCH ISSUE

The first obvious sign that education was taking a similar path was in the United States in 1998 when the Reading Excellence Act (The 1999 Omnibus Appropriations Bill, 1998) was introduced because of the unacceptably low reading achievement of students in public schools. It acknowledged that part of the responsibility for the perilous state rested with methods of reading instruction, and that policies had been insensitive to developments in the understanding of the reading process. The Act, and its successors, attempted to bridge the gulf between research and classroom practice by mandating that only programs in reading that had been shown to be effective according to strict research criteria would receive federal funding. This reversed a trend in which the criterion for adoption of a model was that it met preconceived notions of "rightness" rather than that it was demonstrably effective for students, a situation in which process was more highly regarded than was student outcome.

Federal funding is now only available for programs with demonstrated effectiveness evidenced by reliable replicable research.

> Reliable replicable research means objective, valid, scientific studies that: (a) include rigorously defined samples of subjects that are sufficiently large and representative to support the general conclusions drawn; (b) rely on measurements that meet established standards of reliability and validity; (c) test competing theories, where multiple theories exist; (d) are subjected to peer review before their results are published; and (e) discover effective strategies for improving reading skills (The 1999 Omnibus Appropriations Bill, 1998, p. 960).

In recent times, Congress and President George W. Bush have offered unequivocal support for an emphasis on what works in U.S. classrooms. The 1965 Elementary and Secondary Education Act (ESEA) was reauthorized in 2001 and makes clear its concern that scientifically-based research underpins instructional practices; the No Child Left Behind Act of 2001 (U.S. Department of Education, 2002b) is equally explicit that educators' classroom activities must be demonstrably effective in teaching children. Slavin (2002) considers that these initiatives will reduce the pendulum swings that have characterized education thus far and could produce revolutionary consequences in redressing achievement differences among the population.

The National Research Council's Center for Education (Towne, 2002) suggests that educators attend to research that (1) poses significant questions that can be investigated empirically; (2) links research to theory; (3) uses methods that permit direct investigation of the question; (4) provides a coherent chain of rigorous reasoning; (5) replicates and generalizes; and (6) ensures transparency and scholarly debate. The Council's message is clearly to improve the quality of educational research and reaffirm the link between scientific research and educational practice. Ultimately, the outcomes of sound research should inform educational policy decisions, just as a similar set of principles have been espoused for the medical profession. Shavelson and Towne (2002) noted that fields such as medicine, technology, transportation, and agriculture that have embraced research as the prime determinant of practice have displayed unprecedented development over the last century.

RESEARCH ON EFFECTIVE INSTRUCTION

Fortunately, a large body of research has produced findings that enable judgments about specific educational practices and their effectiveness with students. Much of this research involves observation of what teachers actually do in their classrooms to promote learning. Student attainment is assessed, and teacher strategies that occur in the classrooms with the highest student performance are noted. Across a large number of successful classrooms, patterns emerge and particular teacher behaviors are consistently present. Those elements of instruction are then considered to be effective.

Rosenshine (1979a) described a set of instructional variables relating teacher behavior and classroom organization to high levels of academic performance for elementary school students. Rosenshine called these effective teaching procedures *direct instruction*. However, because this term is easily confused with *Direct Instruction* (with capitalized first letters), we will refer to these procedures as *effective instruction*. Recall that Direct Instruction includes effective instruction design principles and teaching behaviors incorporated into a set of published instructional programs. Effective instruction, on the other hand, involves effective teacher behaviors but *not* a specified published curriculum.

In summarizing the findings of research into those teacher variables displaying a positive relationship with student learning, Rosenshine and Berliner (1978) described effective instruction as:

> a set of teaching behaviors focussed on academic matters where goals are clear to students; time allocated for instruction is sufficient and continuous; content coverage is extensive; student performance is monitored; questions are at a low cognitive level and produce many correct responses; and feedback to students is immediate and academically oriented. In direct [effective] instruction, the teacher controls the instructional goals, chooses material appropriate for the students' ability level, and paces the instructional episode (p. 7).

Characteristics of Effective Instruction

High levels of student achievement are related to a number of variables such as the amount of content covered and mastered. Hence, the pacing of a lesson is considered an important instructional emphasis because optimizing coverage enhances student learning.

Additionally, a strong academic focus was found to be characteristic of teachers using effective instruction. Nonacademic activities, though perhaps enjoyable or directed at other educational goals, were consistently negatively correlated with achievement. That is, classrooms that had more time devoted to nonacademic activities tended to produce lower achievement. In Rosenshine's (1979b) review of studies, it was clear that an academic focus rather than an affective emphasis also produced classrooms with a warm atmosphere and high student self-esteem among students. Less structured programs and teachers with an affective focus had students with lower self-esteem. This finding may well be counterintuitive, as some teachers consider activities that stimulate self-esteem as a prerequisite for student motivation and progress. It follows from this finding that establishing competence is more helpful to student self-esteem than are approaches directly concerned with esteem elevation.

Teachers who were strong leaders and did not base their teaching around student choice of activities produced higher achievement. Solomon and Kendall (1976, cited in Rosenshine, 1979b) indicated that permissiveness, spontaneity, and lack of classroom control were "negatively related, not only to achievement gain, but also to positive growth in creativity, inquiry, writing ability, and self-esteem for the students in those classrooms" (p. 18).

The instructional procedure called demonstration-practice-feedback had strong support from this research. This deceptively simple strategy combines three elements of teaching directly related to achievement. It comprises a sequence in which a short demonstration of the skill or academic material is followed by guided practice, during which feedback is provided to the student (and further demonstration offered if necessary). The second phase usually involves response to teacher questions about the material previously presented. The third phase is that of independent practice, a feature especially important in assisting retention of knowledge and skill sequences.

Principles of Effective Instruction

Ellis, Worthington, and Larkin (1994) summarized effective instruction as classroom behaviors emanating from a set of ten principles:

Principle 1: Students learn more when they are engaged actively during an instructional task.

Principle 2: High and moderate success rates are correlated positively with student learning outcomes, and low success rates are correlated negatively with student learning outcomes.

Principle 3: Increased opportunity to learn content is correlated positively with increased student achievement. Therefore, the more content covered, the greater the potential for student learning.

Principle 4: Students achieve more in classes in which they spend much of their time being directly taught or supervised by their teacher.

Principle 5: Students can become independent, self-regulated learners through instruction that is deliberately and carefully scaffolded.

Principle 6: The critical forms of knowledge associated with strategic learning are (1) declarative knowledge, (2) procedural knowledge, and (3) conditional knowledge. Each of these must be addressed if students are to become independent, self-regulated learners.

Principle 7: Learning is increased when teaching is presented in a manner that assists students in organizing, storing, and retrieving knowledge.

Principle 8: Students can become more independent, self-regulated learners through strategic instruction.

Principle 9: Students can become independent, self-regulated learners through instruction that is explicit.

Principle 10: By teaching sameness both within and across subjects, teachers promote the ability of students to access potentially relevant knowledge in novel problem-solving situations.

Support for the Power of Effective Instruction

More recent support for the power of effective instruction (i.e., specific teacher behaviors) to enhance the learning of students arose from the systematic review of scientific research of Swanson, Carson, and Sachse-Lee (1996) that examined seventy-eight group-intervention studies published between 1967 and 1993 on students with learning disabilities. This review found that interventions employing these effective instruction strategies produced large positive results. Swanson and Sachse-Lee (2000) also reviewed single-subject-design intervention research, and noted that the most important element producing large positive effects arose from studies that included the effective instructional components of drill-repetition-practice-review, lesson segmentation, small interactive groups, and the use of strategy cues. In addition to this list of crucial features, a review by Swanson, Hoskyn, and Sachse-Lee (1999) had previously noted the importance of designing instructional sequences that evoked a high proportion of correct responses.

Vaughn, Gersten, and Chard (2000) also reviewed the effective instruction research literature from a general education perspective and found that the same techniques also enhance the learning of typically achieving students. This finding should not be surprising because the characteristics described above merely represent systematic, thoughtful, and considerate communication between teachers and students. These practices are not only logically consistent with good teaching but have also been shown to make measurable and educationally significant improvements in students' learning.

For those students at-risk of the Matthew Effects because they struggle at any point in their educational development, these effective instructional procedures become critically important. As we noted earlier, without a strong and effective intervention, minor problems can grow into severe problems in the academic domain, in broader cognitive areas, and in attitudes toward schooling.

We can provide effective instruction in necessary language, math, and reading skills. However, unless students at-risk learn at a more rapid rate than their affluent peers, they will remain behind. Therefore, curricular and programmatic formats employed must be efficient, implying high degrees of structure and large amounts of practice with corrective feedback. By so doing, progress is achieved in a fraction of the time than would occur through incidental interactions (Engelmann, 1999).

To enable Direct Instruction programs to alter the educational trajectory of these students, Engelmann focused attention on the tasks that students need to master rather than on the qualities of the learners. He made use of the principles for presenting curricula described above, but added to this a focus on the logical analysis of the curriculum itself, to enable unambiguous teaching and accelerated learning. These principles are described in detail in Chapter 2.

HISTORY OF DIRECT INSTRUCTION

The person most responsible for the development of the Direct Instruction model is Siegfried ("Zig") E. Engelmann, born in Chicago in 1931. He completed a philosophy major at the University of Illinois, before working as an investment counsellor for five years. He then commenced a brief career in advertising in which the campaigns designed to be attractive to children aroused his interest in how children learn. Engelmann's subsequent enduring passion for instruction was further piqued through his experiences in teaching his fraternal-twin sons, Owen and Kurt.

The Direct Instruction model in Project Follow Through had its beginnings in the early 1960s through the work of Carl Bereiter and Siegfried Engelmann at a preschool associated with the University of Illinois. Carl Bereiter was engaged in research on accelerating intellectual development in young children. When he happened to see a film of Engelmann teaching math in 1963, he was sufficiently impressed to offer the unqualified Zig a position on his team. The group also included Jean Osborn, who has played a long and important role in the history of Direct Instruction programs. Engelmann accepted the position but immediately sought to have their research formalized into that of a functional preschool rather than continuing with a series of experimental projects.

The group was particularly interested in what impact the early and systematic teaching of academic skills to children from economically deprived circumstances could achieve. The underlying belief was that cognitive growth could be stimulated by careful instruction, and progress could be achieved at an accelerated rate compared to that achieved by relying on everyday environmental events and genetic propensity as the spurs toward learning.

Together, Bereiter and Engelmann (1966) published *Teaching Disadvantaged Children in the Preschool*. The book created considerable controversy in a field dominated by Piagetian concepts of developmental levels as the determinant of the timing of exposure to educational experiences. The notion of withholding instruction until students reached appropriate levels of readiness was not one that Bereiter and Engelmann endorsed. To them, disadvantaged children could not afford the luxury of such educational extravagance. In fact, Engelmann's first formal report to Bereiter of his activities related to a project entitled, "Accelerating intellectual development in young children." When asked what he was doing, Engelmann replied, "I'm teaching formal operations to children who flunk concrete operations. Is that accelerated enough for you?" Bereiter acknowledged that indeed it was.

To many in the field at the time, the Engelmann/Bereiter ideas and practices were simplistic and likely to be harmful to children's development. How little has changed in the last thirty-five years! In their preschool, four- and five-year-old disadvantaged children were provided with intensive, carefully sequenced, teacher-directed verbal instruction for two hours per day in small groups. Despite the rancor that surrounded their ideas and program, their systematic approach to the design of instruction and attention to detail produced remarkable success with these youngsters.

Because of the success at the Bereiter-Engelmann Preschool, a Carnegie Foundation grant became available. However, Carl Bereiter had elected to take a position at the Ontario Institute of Studies, and Engelmann did not have the academic qualifications to direct the preschool program. He enlisted as codirector Wes Becker (who was also at the University of Illinois), a well-respected authority in behavior analysis and its application to classroom management. However, Wes was more than an educational researcher. His careful explanation of the principles of teacher attention, classroom rules, and reinforcement contingencies, while never having received the attention they deserved in general education classrooms, do have an important role in all of the Direct Instruction programs. He produced more than one hundred papers, four textbooks on educational psychology, a valuable book for parents, *Parents Are Teachers* (Becker, 1971), and was coauthor of several levels of the *Corrective Reading* series. Wes was also a major figure in the data analysis associated with Project Follow Through.

Accompanying Wes Becker was one of his former undergraduate students, Doug Carnine. It was shortly after these events in 1967 that Engelmann and Becker were invited by the Office of Education to develop a program appropriate for children from kindergarten to grade three. Thus, the Direct Instruction model was selected to participate in the Project Follow Through study.

The University of Illinois was not prepared to offer Engelmann a staff position and there were also other difficulties with the sponsorship, so the group contacted thirteen universities known for an expressed concern for disadvantaged children, offering to bring with the group their $1.5 million per annum grant. Presaging the negative attitudes toward Direct Instruction in academic and education circles (which were to remain a feature), only two universities responded, one of which voted unanimously to oppose the acceptance of the group behind the Direct Instruction model.

So it was that in 1970, partly through the intercession of Barbara Bateman at the University of Oregon, the group with the grant headed for Eugene, Oregon. Enlisting Wes Becker and Doug Carnine was a most felicitous occurrence, as they brought with them skills and interest in behavior analysis, subsequently one of the important components of the teaching programs that began to be published from 1968 under the acronym, DISTAR (Direct Instruction System for Teaching Arithmetic and Reading, later also known as Direct Instruction System for Teaching and Remediation, reflecting a wider curriculum interest).

In 1984, Western Michigan University celebrated Engelmann's contributions with an honorary doctorate. In 1994, the American Psychological Association presented Engelmann with the Fred Keller Award of Excellence. He is currently a professor of special education at the College of Education at the University of Oregon.

Doug Carnine was a college senior when he coauthored DISTAR Arithmetic I, and he continued to collaborate with Engelmann in subsequent revisions of this program. He also acted as a field supervisor and teacher trainer, developing the Direct Instruction teacher-training program at the University of Oregon. When Wes Becker moved in 1978 from his position as Director of the Direct Instruction Follow Through model, Carnine took over the post.

Doug Carnine is currently Professor of Education at the University of Oregon and is Director of the National Center to Improve the Tools of Educators (NCITE), a body devoted to promoting community understanding of the importance of research-based educational strategies. Doug has produced many research papers and essays and has made innumerable conference presentations. He has coauthored several books on Direct Instruction. In 2002, Doug was among ten individuals nominated by President George W. Bush to serve on the National Institute for Literacy Advisory Board.

There have been many other significant figures in the development of Direct Instruction programs. These individuals include, but are not limited to, Jerry Silbert, Bob Dixon, Gary Johnson, and Susan Hanner.

Increased Interest in Direct Instruction

Interest in Direct Instruction has become more widespread during the last fifteen years. An issue of *Education and Treatment of Children* (Becker, 1988) was devoted to Direct Instruction. The National Reading Conference in the United States has regular sessions on the pedagogical impact and appropriateness of Direct Instruction (Kameenui & Shannon, 1988). The *Journal of Learning Disabilities* (1991) devoted two issues to "sameness analysis," an instructional design principle central to Direct Instruction (Engelmann & Carnine, 1982). Another special issue, this time of *School Psychology Review,* was edited by Carnine (1994), and provided a similar focus on curricular design features.

Writers of texts on teaching (Becker, 1986), special education (Cole & Chan, 1990; Gable & Warren, 1993; Greaves & McLaughlin, 1993; Lloyd, Kameenui, & Chard, 1997; Scruggs & Wong, 1990; Wolery, Ault & Doyle, 1992), and educational psychology (Joyce, Weil & Showers, 1992; Kameenui & Simmons, 1990; Tuckman, 1991) have included Direct Instruction as an effective approach for a range of educational challenges. From one of the most respected writers and researchers on the problems of *learning disability* (a term coined by Kirk and Bateman in 1962) comes the highest praise: "The documented success of Siegfried Engelmann and his colleagues' direct instruction reading programs with thousands of hard-to-teach and high risk children is unsurpassed in the annals of reading history" (Bateman, 1991, p. 11).

In the United States, the shift toward reliable, replicable research as a basis for educational decision making has led to a strong interest in Direct Instruction from states, districts, and schools. Numerous reports (see Chapter 2) have included the model among those with strong empirical support.

Continued Research and Program Development

Direct Instruction research and program development has also been maintained. The first programs focused on beginning reading and math and were published by Science Research Associates in 1968. There are now more than sixty programs, some being sequential programs designed for all students; others are remedial programs directed at specific skill areas. Together these curricula constitute a comprehensive school reform model known as the Direct Instruction model, one that has been implemented in more than 150 schools in the United States alone. Apart from whole-school implementations, Direct Instruction materials have also been used in scores of other schools.

Chapters 3–8 highlight the use of Direct Instruction programs across academic skill areas. However, the model no longer has a sole emphasis on basic skills programs such as reading or mathematics but has broadened its area of application to include higher order skills, for example, literary analysis, logic, chemistry, critical reading, geometry, and social studies (Carnine, 1991; Casazza, 1993; Darch, 1993; Grossen & Carnine, 1990; Kinder & Carnine 1991). Use has been made of technology through computer-assisted instruction, low-cost networking, and videodisc courseware (Kinder & Carnine, 1991); researchers have tested the model in non-English-speaking countries, for example, third-world countries (Grossen & Kelly, 1992) and Japan (Nakano, Kageyama, & Kinoshita, 1993). It has also shown promise in teaching a most challenging group of students—school-aged children with TBI, traumatic brain injury (Glang, Singer, Cooley, & Tish, 1992).

REFERENCES

Adams, M. J. (1990). *Beginning to read: Thinking and learning about print.* Cambridge, MA: MIT Press.

Allington, R. L. (1984). Content coverage and contextual reading in reading groups. *Journal of Reading Behavior, 16,* 85–96.

American Federation of Teachers. (1998). *Building a profession: Strengthening teacher preparation and induction.* K–16 Teacher Education Task Force. Retrieved December 19, 2002, from http://www.aft.org/higher_ed/downloadable/k16report.pdf

American Management Association. (2001). *AMA Survey on workplace testing: Basic skills, job skills, psychological measurement—Summary of key findings.* New York: American Management Association.

America Reads. (2001). *Starting out right: A guide to promoting children's reading success.* Retrieved December 12, 2002, from http://www.ed.gov/inits/americareads/educators_early.html

Ball, E. W. (1993). Phonological awareness. What's important and to whom? *Reading and Writing: An Interdisciplinary Journal, 5,* 141–159.

Ball, E. W., & Blachman, B. A. (1991). Does phoneme awareness training in kindergarten make a difference in early word recognition and developmental spelling. *Reading Research Quarterly, 25,* 49–66.

Bateman, B. (1991). Teaching word recognition to slow learning children. *Reading, Writing and Learning Disabilities, 7,* 1–16.

Becker, W. C. (1971). *Parents are teachers.* Champaign, IL: Research Press.

Becker, W. C. (1977). Teaching reading and language to the disadvantaged: What we have learned from field research. *Harvard Educational Review, 47,* 518–543.

Becker, W. C. (1986). *Applied psychology for teachers: A behavioral-cognitive approach.* Columbus, OH: SRA.

Becker, W. C. (1988). Direct Instruction (Special Issue). *Education and Treatment of Children, 11*(4).

Bereiter, C., & Engelmann, S. (1966). *Teaching disadvantaged children in the preschool.* Englewood Cliffs, NJ: Prentice-Hall.

Binder, C. (1996). Behavioral fluency: Evolution of a new paradigm. *The Behavior Analyst, 19,* 163–197.

Blachman, B. A. (1994). What we have learned from longitudinal studies of phonological processing and reading, and some unanswered questions: A response to Torgesen, Wagner, & Rashotte. *Journal of Learning Disabilities, 27,* 287–291.

Boston Public Schools. (1998, March 9). *High school restructuring.* Boston: Author.

Bradley, L., & Bryant, P. (1983). Categorizing sounds and learning to read—A causal connection. *Nature, 301,* 419–421.

Byrne, B., & Fielding-Barnsley, R. (1989). Phonemic awareness and letter knowledge in the child's acquisition of the alphabetic principle. *Journal of Educational Psychology, 81,* 313–321.

Campanile, C. (2002, July 11). Two-thirds flunk math. *New York Post.* Retrieved December 12, 2002, from http://www.nypost.com/news/regionalnews/52299. htm

Carnine, D. (1991). Curricular interventions for teaching higher order thinking to all students: Introduction to the special series. *Journal of Learning Disabilities, 24,* 261–269.

Carnine, D. (1994). Introduction to the mini-series: Educational tools for diverse learners. *School Psychology Review, 32,* 341–350.

Carnine, D. (1995a). The professional context for collaboration and collaborative research. *Remedial and Special Education, 16*(6), 368–371.

Carnine, D. (1995b). Trustworthiness, useability, and accessibility of educational research. *Journal of Behavioral Education, 5,* 251–258.

Carnine, D. (2000). *Why education experts resist effective practices (and what it would take to make education more like medicine).* Washington, DC: Thomas B. Fordham Foundation.

Casazza, M. E. (1993). Using a model of direct instruction to teach summary writing in a college reading class. *Journal of Reading, 37,* 202–208.

Catts, H. W. (1991). Early identification of reading disabilities. *Topics in Language Disorders, 12*(1), 1–16.

Ceci, S. (1991). How much does schooling influence general intelligence and its cognitive components? A reassessment of the evidence. *Developmental Psychology, 27,* 703–722.

Chambless, D. L., & Ollendick, T. H. (2001). Empirically supported psychological interventions: Controversies and evidence. *Annual Review of Psychology, 52,* 685–716.

Chapman, J. W., Tunmer, W. E., & Prochnow, J. E. (2000). Early reading-related skills and performance, reading self-concept, and the development of academic self-concept: A longitudinal study. *Journal of Educational Psychology, 92* (4), 703–708.

Coalition for Evidence-Based Policy. (2002). *Bringing evidence driven progress to education: A recommended strategy for the U.S. Department of Education.* Council for Excellence in Government's Coalition for Evidence-Based Policy. Retrieved December 12, 2002, from http://www.excelgov.org/displayContent.asp?Keyword=prppcEvidence

Cole, P., & Chan, L. (1990). *Methods and strategies for special education.* Sydney: Prentice-Hall.

Colvin, R. C., & Helfand, D. (1999, Dec 12). Special education a failure on many fronts. *LA Times.* Retrieved December 12, 2002, from http://www.latimes.com/news/state/reports/specialeduc/lat_special991212.htm

Commission on Excellence in Special Education. (2002). *A new era: Revitalizing special education for children and their families.* Retrieved December 12, 2002, from http://www.ed.gov/inits/commissionsboards/whspecialeducation/

Cunningham, A. (1990). Explicit vs. implicit instruction in phonemic awareness. *Journal of Experimental Child Psychology, 50,* 429–444.

Darch, C. (1993). Direct Instruction: A research-based approach for designing instructional programs. In R. C. Greaves & P. J. McLaughlin (Eds.), *Recent advances in special education and rehabilitation* (pp. 88–106). Boston: Andover Medical.

De Courcey Hinds, M. (2002). *Teaching as a clinical profession: A new challenge for education.* New York: Carnegie Corporation of New York. Retrieved December 12, 2002, from www.carnegie.org/pdf/teachered.pdf

Department for Education and Employment. (1998). *The national literacy strategy: Framework for teaching.* London: Crown.

Ellis, E. S., Worthington, L. A., & Larkin, M. J. (1994*). Executive summary of the research synthesis on effective teaching principles and the design of quality tools for educators.* Technical Report No. 6 produced for the National Center to Improve the Tools of Educators, University of Oregon. Retrieved December 12, 2002, from http://idea.uoregon.edu/~ncite/documents/techrep/tech06.html

Engelmann, S. (1999). The benefits of direct instruction: Affirmative action for at-risk students. *Educational Leadership, 57* (77), 79.

Engelmann, S., & Carnine, D. (1982). *Theory of instruction: Principles and applications.* New York: Irvington.

Farkas, G., & Beron, K. (2001, March). *Family linguistic culture and social reproduction: Verbal skill from parent to child in the preschool and school years.* Presentation at the session on Consequences of Child Poverty and Deprivation, at the Annual Meetings of the Population Association of America, Washington, DC, March 31. Retrieved December 12, 2002, from http://www.pop.psu.edu/general/pubs/working_papers/psu-pri/wp0105.pdf

Felton, R. H. (1993). Effects of instruction on the decoding skills of children with phonological processing problems. *Journal of Learning Disabilities, 26,* 583–589.

Fielding, L., Wilson, P., & Anderson, R. (1986). A new focus on free reading: The role of trade books in reading instruction. In R. Raphael and R. Reynolds (Eds.), *Contexts in literacy* (pp. 149–160). New York: Longman.

Fister, S., & Kemp, K. (1993). Translating research: Classroom application of validated instructional strategies. In R. C. Greaves & P. J. McLaughlin (Eds.), *Recent advances in special education and rehabilitation* (pp. 107–126). Boston: Andover Medical.

Flesch, R. (1955). *Why Johnny can't read.* New York: Harper & Row.

Fletcher, J. M., Francis, D. J., Rourke, B. P., Shaywitz, S. E., & Shaywitz, B. A. (1993). Classification of learning disabilities: Relation to other childhood disorders. In G. R. Lyon, D. B. Gray, J F. Kavanagh, & N. A. Krasnegor (Eds.), *Better understanding of learning disabilities: New views from research and their implications for education and public policies* (pp. 153–170). Baltimore: Brooks.

Foorman, B., Francis, D., Novy, D., & Liberman, D. (1991). How letter–sound instruction mediates progress in first grade reading and spelling. *Journal of Educational Psychology, 83,* 456–469.

Gable, R. A., & Warren, S. F. (1993). The enduring value of instructional research. In R. Gable & S. Warren (Eds.), *Advances in mental retardation and developmental disabilities: Strategies for teaching students with mild to severe mental retardation* (pp. 1–7). Philadelphia: Jessica Kingsley.

Gersten, R., Chard, D., & Baker, S. (2000). Factors enhancing sustained use of research-based instructional practices. *Journal of Learning Disabilities, 33,* 445–457.

Gersten, R., & Guskey, T. (1985, Fall). Transforming teacher reluctance into a commitment to innovation. *Direct Instruction News,* 11–12.

Glang, A., Singer, G., Cooley, E., & Tish, N. (1992). Tailoring direct instruction techniques for use with elementary students with brain injury. *Journal of Head Trauma Rehabilitation, 7,* 93–108.

Greaves R. C., & McLaughlin, P. J. (Eds.). (1993). *Recent advances in special education and rehabilitation.* Boston: Andover Medical.

Grossen, B., & Carnine, D. (1990). Diagramming a logic strategy: Effects on difficult problem types and transfer. *Learning Disability Quarterly, 13,* 168–182.

Grossen, B., & Kelly, B. F. (1992). The effectiveness of Direct Instruction in a third-world context. *International Review of Education, 38*(1), 81–85.

Hart, B., & Risley, T. R. (1995). *Meaningful differences in the everyday experiences of young American children.* Baltimore: Brookes.

Hartocollis, A. (2002, July 11). Reading scores drop sharply in 8th Grade. *New York Times.* Retrieved December 12, 2002, from http://www.nytimes.com/ 2002/07/11/education/11SCOR.html?pagewanted =print&position=top

Hatcher, P., Hulme, C., & Ellis, A. (1994). Ameliorating reading failure by integrating the teaching of reading and phonological skills: The phonological linkage hypothesis. *Child Development, 65,* 41–57.

Haycock, K. (2001, March). Helping all students achieve: Closing the achievement gap. *Educational Leadership 58*(6). Retrieved December 12, 2002, from http://www.ascd.org/readingroom/edlead/ 0103/ haycock.html

Hempenstall, K. (1996). The gulf between educational research and policy: The example of Direct Instruction and Whole Language. *Behaviour Change, 13,* 33–46.

Hoskyn, M., & Swanson, H. L. (2000). Cognitive processing of low achievers and children with reading disabilities: A selective meta-analytic review of the published literature. *School Psychology Review, 29,* 102–119.

Jencks, C. S., & Phillips, M. (1998). America's next achievement test. *The American Prospect, 9*(40). Retrieved December 12, 2002, from http://www. prospect.org/print/V9/40/jencks-c.html

Jencks, C. S., Smith, M., Acland, H., Bane, M. J., Cohen, D., Ginits, H., Heyns, B., & Michelson, S. (1972). *Inequality: A reassessment of the effect of family and schooling in America.* New York: Basic Books.

Johnson, J., & Duffett, A. (2002). Reality check, 2002. *Public Agenda.* Retrieved December 12, 2002, from http://www.publicagenda.org/specials/teachers/ teachers.htm

Jorm, A., Share, D., McLean, R., & Matthews, R. (1984). Phonological recoding and learning to read: A longitudinal study. *Applied Psycholinguistics, 5,* 201–207.

Joyce, B., Weil, M., & Showers, B. (1992). *Models of teaching* (4th ed.). Boston, MA: Allyn & Bacon.

Juel, C. (1988). Learning to read and write: A longitudinal study of 54 children from first through fourth grades. *Journal of Educational Psychology, 80,* 437–447.

Juel, C. (1993). The spelling-sound code in reading. In S. Yussen & M. Smith (Eds.), *Reading across the life span* (pp. 95–109). New York: Springer-Verlag.

Just for the Kids. (2000). *Promising practices study of high-performing schools.* National Center for Educational Accountability. Retrieved December 12, 2002, from http://www.just4kids.org/US/pdf/PP_O Summary.pdf

Kameenui, E. J., & Shannon, P. (1988). Point/counterpoint: Direct instruction reconsidered. In J. E. Readence & R. S. Baldwin (Eds.), *Thirty-seventh Yearbook of the National Reading Conference* (pp. 36–41). Chicago: National Reading Conference.

Kameenui, E. J., & Simmons, D. C. (1990). *Designing instructional strategies: The prevention of academic learning problems.* Columbus, OH: Merrill.

Kinder, D., & Carnine, D. (1991). Direct Instruction: What it is and what it is becoming. *Journal of Behavioral Education, 1,* 193–213.

Kirsch, I., & Guthrie, J. (1984). Adult reading practices for work & leisure. *Adult Education Quarterly, 34,* 213–232.

Leach, D. J. (1987). Increasing the use and maintenance of behaviour-based practices in schools: An example of a general problem for applied psychologists? *Australian Psychologist, 22,* 323–332.

Levin, B. (1998). Criticizing the schools: Then and now. *Education Policy Analysis Archives, 6*(16). Retrieved December 12, 2002, from http://epaa.asu.edu/epaa/v6n16.html

Lloyd, J., Kameenui, E. J., & Chard, D. (Eds.). (1997). *Issues in educating students with disabilities.* Mahwah, NJ: Erlbaum.

Lewis, L., & Paik, S. (2001). *Add it up: Using research to improve education for low-income and minority students.* Washington, DC: Poverty & Race Research Action Council. Retrieved December 12, 2002, from http://www.prrac.org/additup.pdf

Lyon, G. R. (1998). *Overview of reading and literacy initiatives. Statement to Committee on Labor and Human Resources.* Retrieved December 12, 2002, from http://www.nichd.nih.gov/publications/pubs/jeffords.htm

Lyon, G. R. (2001a). *Measuring success: Using assessments and accountability to raise student achievement.* Subcommittee on Education Reform Committee on Education and the Workforce, U.S. House of Representatives.Washington, DC. Retrieved December 12, 2002, from http://www.nrrf.org/lyon_statement3-01.htm

Lyon, G. R. (2001b, July 30). Summary comments White House Early Childhood Cognitive Development Summit. *EducationNews.org.* Retrieved December 12, 2002, from http://www.educationnews.org/white_house_early_childhood_cogn.htm

Lyon, G. R., & Fletcher, J. M. (2001, Summer). Early warning system: How to prevent reading disabilities. *Education Matters, 1* (2), 22–29. Retrieved December 12, 2002, from http://www.educationnext.org/20012/22.html

Maggs, A., & White, R. (1982). The educational psychologist: Facing a new era. *Psychology in the Schools, 19,* 129–134.

Marshall, J. (1993). Why Johnny can't teach. *Reason, 25*(7), 102–106.

Moats, L. C. (1996). Implementing effective instruction for students with LD: A challenge for the future. In S. C. Cramer & W. Ellis (Eds.), *Learning disabilities: Lifelong issues* (pp. 87–93). Baltimore, MD: Brookes.

Nagy, W. E. (1998). *Increasing students' reading vocabularies.* Presentation at the Commissioner's Reading Day Conference, Austin, Texas.

Nagy, W. E., & Anderson, R. C. (1984). How many words are there in printed English? *Reading Research Quarterly, 19,* 304–330.

Nakano, Y., Kageyama, M., & Kinoshita, S. (1993). Using Direct Instruction to improve teacher performance, academic achievement, and classroom behavior in a Japanese public junior high school. *Education and Treatment of Children, 16,* 326–343.

National Commission on Excellence in Education. (1983). *A nation at risk: The imperative for educational reform.* Washington, DC: U.S. Government Printing Office. Retrieved December 12, 2002, from http://www.ed.gov/pubs/NatAtRisk/risk.html

National Institute for Literacy. (1998). *Facts sheets.* Washington, DC: National Institute for Literacy. Retrieved December 12, 2002, from http://www.nifl.gov/nifl/facts/reference.html

National Reading Panel. (2000). *Teaching children to read: An evidence-based assessment of the scientific research literature on reading and its implications for reading instruction.* Washington, DC: U.S. Department of Health and Human Services.

Office of Educational Research and Improvement. (2001). *The Nation's Report Card: Fourth-Grade Reading 2000.* Washington, DC: U.S. Dept. of Education. Retrieved December 12, 2002, from http://nces.ed. gov/nationsreportcard/pubs/main2000/2001499.asp)

Ohio Literacy Network. (2002). Key facts about adult under-education. Retrieved December 12, 2002, from http://www.ohioliteracynetwork.org/fact.html

Palmaffy, T. (1998). *No excuses: Houston educator Thaddeus Lott puts failing schools to shame.* Washington, DC: Heritage Foundation. [On-line.] Available: http://www.noexcuses.org/articles/shame.html

Public Agenda. (2002). *Understanding the issues: Quick takes.* Retrieved December 12, 2002, from http://www.publicagenda.org/issues/angles.cfm?issue_type=education

Report of the Education Trust. (1999). *Dispelling the myth: High poverty schools exceeding expectations.* Washington, DC: Education Trust. Retrieved December 12, 2002, from http://www.edtrust.org/main/documents/dispell.pdf

Rochester, J. M. (2002). *Class warfare: Besieged schools, bewildered parents, betrayed kids and the attack on excellence.* San Francisco, CA: Encounter Books.

Rosenshine, B. V. (1979a). Content, time and direct instruction. In P. L. Peterson & H. J. Walberg (Eds.), *Research on teaching: Concepts, findings and implications* (pp. 28–56). Berkeley, CA: McCutchan.

Rosenshine, B. V. (1979b). *Direct instruction for skill mastery.* Paper presented to the School of Education, University of Milwaukee, Wisconsin.

Rosenshine, B. V., & Berliner, D. C. (1978). Academic engaged time. *British Journal of Teacher Education, 4,* 3–16.

Sanders, W., & Rivers, J. (1996). *Cumulative and residual effects of teachers on future student academic achievement.* Knoxville, TN: University of Tennessee Value-Added Research and Assessment Center.

Schmidt, W., Houang, R., & Cogan, L. (2002, Summer). A coherent curriculum: The case of mathematics. *American Educator.* Retrieved December 12, 2002, from http://www.aft.org/american_educator/summer2002/curriculum.pdf

Scruggs, T., & Wong, B. (Eds.). (1990). *Intervention research in learning disabilities.* New York: Springer-Verlag.

Share, D. L., McGee, R., & Silva, P. (1989). IQ and reading progress: A test of the capacity notion of IQ. *Journal of the American Academy of Child and Adolescent Psychiatry, 28,* 97–100.

Share, D. L., & Silva, P. A. (1987). Language deficits and specific reading retardation: Cause or effect? *British Journal of Disorders of Communication, 22,* 219–226.

Shavelson, R. J., & Towne, L. (Eds.). (2002). *Scientific research in education.* Washington, DC: National Academy Press.

Simmons, D. C. (1992). Perspectives on dyslexia: Commentary on educational concerns. *Journal of Learning Disabilities, 25,* 66–70.

Slavin, R. E. (2002). Evidence-based education policies: Transforming educational practice and research. *Educational Researcher, 31*(7), 15–21.

Snow, C. E., Burns, S., & Griffin, P. (Eds.). (1998). *Preventing reading difficulties in young children. Report of the National Research Council.* Retrieved December 12, 2002, from http://www.nap.edu/readingroom/books/reading/

Snyder, T. D., & Hoffman, C. M. (2002). *Digest of Education Statistics, 2001.* Washington, DC: U.S. Department of Education, NCES.

Stanovich, K. E. (1986). Matthew effects in reading: Some consequences of individual differences in the acquisition of literacy. *Reading Research Quarterly, 21,* 360–406.

Stanovich, K. E. (1988a). Explaining the differences between the dyslexic and the garden-variety poor reader: The phonological-core variable-difference model. *Journal of Learning Disabilities, 21,* 590–612.

Stanovich, K. E. (1988b). The right and wrong places to look for the cognitive locus of reading disability. *Annals of Dyslexia, 38,* 154–157.

Stanovich, K. E. (1992). Speculation on the causes and consequences of individual differences in early reading acquisition. In P. Gough, L. Ehri, & R. Treiman, *Reading acquisition* (pp. 307–342). Mahwah, NJ: Erlbaum.

Stanovich, K. E. (1993). Does reading make you smarter? Literacy and the development of verbal intelligence. *Advances in Child Development and Behavior, 24,* 133–180.

Stedman, L., & Kaestle, C. (1987). Literacy and reading performance in the United States, from 1880 to the present. *Reading Research Quarterly, 23*(1), 8–46.

Stone, J. E. (1996, April 23). Developmentalism: An obscure but pervasive restriction on educational improvement. *Education Policy Analysis Archives* [On-line.] 4, 1950 lines. Available: http://seamon-key.ed.asu.edu/epaa

Swanson, H. L., Carson, C., & Sachse-Lee, C. M. (1996). A selective synthesis of intervention research for students with learning disabilities. *School Psychology Review, 25,* 370–391.

Swanson, H. L., Hoskyn, M., & Sachse-Lee, C. M. (1999). *Interventions for students with learning disabilities: A meta-analysis of treatment outcomes.* New York: Guilford.

Swanson, H. L., & Sachse-Lee, C. M. (2000). A meta-analysis of single-subject-design intervention research for students with LD. *Journal of Learning Disabilities, 33,* 114–136.

The 1999 Omnibus Appropriations Bill. (1998). *The Reading Excellence Act,* pp. 956–1007. Retrieved December 12, 2002, from http://www.house.gov/eeo

Torgesen, J. K., Wagner, R. J., & Rashotte, C. A. (1994). Longitudinal studies of phonological processing and reading. *Journal of Learning Disabilities, 27,* 276–286.

Towne, L. (2002, February 6). *The principles of scientifically based research.* Speech presented at the U.S. Department of Education, Washington, DC. Retrieved December 12, 2002, from www.ed.gov/nclb/research/

Tuckman, B. W. (1991). *Educational psychology: From theory to application.* New York: Harcourt Brace Jovanovich.

U.S. Department of Education. (1995). *Seventeenth annual report to Congress on the implementation of the Individuals with Disabilities Education Act.* Washington, DC: U.S. Government Printing Office.

U.S. Department of Education. (1999). P. L. Donahue, K. E. Voelkl, J. R. Campbell, & J. Mazzeo (Eds.). *The 1998 NAEP Reading Report Card for the Nation,* NCES 1999-459. Washington, DC: Author.

U.S. Department of Education. (2001a). *The Nation's Report Card: Fourth-Grade Reading 2000,* NCES 2001-499, by P. L. Donahue, R. J. Finnegan, A. D. Lutkus, N. L. Allen, and J. R. Campbell. Washington, DC: U.S. Government Printing Office.

U.S. Department of Education. (2001b). OSEP by D. Fuchs, L. S. Fuchs, P. G. Mathes, Mark W. Lipsey, & P. H. Roberts. *Is "learning disabilities" just a fancy term for low achievement?: A meta-analysis of reading differences between low achievers with and without the label.* The Learning Disabilities Summit: Building a Foundation for the Future. Washington, DC: U.S. Government Printing Office.

U.S. Department of Education. (2002a). *The Condition of Education 2002,* NCES 2000-602. Washington, DC: U.S. Government Printing Office.

U.S. Department of Education. (2002b). *No Child Left Behind Act, 2001.* Retrieved December 12, 2002, from http://www.ed.gov/offices/OESE/esea/

U.S. Department of Labor (2003). *Occupational Outlook Handbook.* Bureau of Labor Statistics, Bulletin 2540. Retrieved January 4, 2003 from http://www.bls.gov/oco/print/oco2003.htm

Vaughn, S., Gersten, R., & Chard, D. J. (2000). The underlying message in LD intervention research: Findings from research syntheses. *Exceptional Children, 67,* 99–112.

Viadero, D. (2002a). Research: Holding up a mirror. *Editorial Projects in Education, 21*(40), 32–35.

Viadero, D. (2002b). Studies cite learning gains in Direct Instruction schools. *Editorial Projects in Education, 21*(31), 15.

Wayne, A. (2002, June 13). Teacher inequality: New evidence on disparities in teachers' academic skills. *Education Policy Analysis Archives, 10*(30). Retrieved June 20, 2002 from http://epaa.asu.edu/epaa/v10n30/

Wenglinsky, H. (2000). *How teaching matters.* Princeton, NJ: Milken Foundation and Educational Testing Service. Retrieved December 12, 2002, from www.ets.org/research/pic/teamat.pdf

Wolery, M., Ault, M. J., & Doyle, P. M. (1992). *Teaching students with moderate to severe disabilities.* New York: Longman.

Woodward, J. (1993). The technology of technology-based instruction: Comments on the research, development, and dissemination approach to innovation. *Education & Treatment of Children, 16,* 345–360.

CHAPTER TWO

THE COMPONENTS OF DIRECT INSTRUCTION

CATHY L. WATKINS
California State University–Stanislaus

TIMOTHY A. SLOCUM
Utah State University

OBJECTIVES

After studying this chapter you should be able to:

1. identify the three major elements of Direct Instruction;
2. explain what it means to teach a general case;
3. describe each of the five juxtaposition principles and explain how they contribute to clear communication;
4. explain the shifts that occur in formats over time;
5. explain what tracks are and how track design differs from more traditional instruction;
6. explain the guidelines for sequencing tasks;
7. describe effective teacher–student interaction techniques;
8. summarize the results of Project Follow Through.

The purpose of Direct Instruction is to teach subject matter efficiently so that all the students learn all the material in the minimum amount of time. Every strategy, tactic, and specific technique employed in Direct Instruction is designed to serve this purpose. Accomplishing this goal requires keen attention to all aspects of teaching. It would be much easier if we could focus on one or two "key issues" and produce measurably superior instruction, but this is not the case. Producing highly effective teaching requires that we attend to a wide variety of details concerning the design, organization, and delivery of instruction. If any one element of instruction is not done well, high-quality instruction in other areas may not compensate for it. For example, superior instructional delivery cannot make up for poorly designed instructional materials. Likewise, well-designed programs cannot compensate for poor organization.

Three main components enable Direct Instruction to accomplish the goal of teaching all children effectively and efficiently: (1) program design that identifies concepts, rules, strategies, and "big ideas" to be taught and clear communication through carefully constructed instructional programs to teach these; (2) organization of instruction, including scheduling, grouping and ongoing progress monitoring to assure that each student receives appropriate and sufficient instruction; and (3) student–teacher interaction techniques that assure that each student is actively engaged with instruction and masters the objectives of each lesson.

Direct Instruction has been the focus of a vast amount of research and has been shown to be highly effective for a wide range of content and with diverse learners, from those identified as gifted to students who require special education services. Studies have shown excellent outcomes in basic skills, complex cognitive tasks, and affective areas such as students' self-concepts and confidence. This chapter will describe the three main components of Direct Instruction and briefly review the research base on the effectiveness of Direct Instruction.

MAIN COMPONENTS OF DIRECT INSTRUCTION

In this section, we describe the three main components of Direct Instruction: the program design, organization of instruction, and student–teacher interactions that make Direct Instruction effective.

Program Design

Program design includes five main elements. First, program design begins by carefully analyzing the content matter and identifying central organizing ideas and generalizable strategies that enable students to learn more in less time. Second, clear communication is designed to minimize ambiguity for students. Third, instructional formats are designed to structure the dialogue between teachers and students. Fourth, skills are sequenced to maximize student success and minimize points of confusion. Fifth, instructional topics and objectives are organized into tracks that allow for systematic skill development across the length of a program and support cumulative review and application. Together, these elements result in instructional programs that are highly effective for a wide range of learners.

Content Analysis.   The goal of Direct Instruction is to teach generalized skills; thus, the first step in developing a Direct Instruction program is analysis of the content and identification of concepts, rules, strategies, and "big ideas" (i.e., those concepts that provide strategies that students can use to further develop their expertise in subject matter) to be taught. The content area, such as reading or earth science, is carefully analyzed to find key big ideas that can be taught to students to enable them to exhibit generalized performance to the widest possible range of examples and situations. Identification of these generalizations is the foundation of Direct Instruction.

Becker (1971) illustrated the power and efficiency of strategy-based instruction with an example from the area of basic reading. A nonstrategic or rote teaching approach would teach students to recognize whole words. In this rote approach, each word would be taught as a separate entity with no system for teaching generalizable strategies for decoding new words. In the rote approach, after the teacher has taught ten words, students should be able to read (at best) ten useful words. In contrast, a strategic approach would be to teach ten letter–sound relations and the skill of sounding out words. When students have learned these ten sounds and the sounding-out skill, they can read 720 words made up of three sounds (e.g., *cat*), 4,320 words of four sounds (e.g., *cram*), and 21,600 words of five sounds (e.g., *scram*) for a total of over 25,000 words. Not all of these words would be real words, some would be pseudowords (e.g., *blums*), but the example illustrates the power of strategic instruction. (This strategy and other reading strategies are described in more detail in Chapter 4.) The efficiency that results from teaching generalizable big ideas is the goal of the content analysis that underlies Direct Instruction. This example also illustrates that even in difficult content areas that are fraught with exceptions, such as reading in English, powerful generalizations are possible.

Spelling is often taught by rote memorization of whole words resulting in little or no generalization. However, wide generalizations are possible. Teaching the skill of detecting individual sounds in a spoken word and matching sounds to written letters is a very efficient beginning point. In addition, if students learn to spell the parts of words called *morphographs* (prefixes, base words, and suffixes) and rules for combining them, they can correctly spell many new words that they have never encountered. Table 2.1 shows seven morphographs and some of the words that can be correctly spelled by using rules to combine them. The

TABLE 2.1   Seven Morphographs and Some of the Words Derived from Them

PREFIXES	BASES	SUFFIXES
re	cover	ed
dis	pute	able
un		

WORDS FORMED

recover, recoverable, recovered, unrecoverable, unrecovered, repute, reputable, reputed, disreputable, disrepute, coverable, covered, uncover, uncoverable, uncovered, discover, discoverable, discovered, undiscoverable, undiscovered, dispute, disputable, disputed, undisputable, undisputed, etc.

Direct Instruction program, *Spelling Mastery,* teaches 750 morphographs that can be combined to form over 12,000 words. (This program is described in detail in Chapter 6.)

These examples from reading and spelling illustrate the goal and importance of content analysis to Direct Instruction. Direct Instruction is about teaching strategies that enable students to go beyond the particular items that are taught and to apply their learning to new items or situations.

A common and persistent misunderstanding is that Direct Instruction teaches students to memorize simple responses to specific stimuli, commonly referred to as *rote learning.* In reality, Direct Instruction programs enable students to learn more in less time for the very reason that they are *not* learning isolated, unrelated bits of information by rote, but are learning strategies that can be broadly applied across numerous examples, problems, and situations.

This mistaken notion that Direct Instruction is a rote learning approach not only reflects a fundamental misunderstanding of the approach but also fails to recognize that so-called higher-order thinking depends on the mastery of more basic skills and involves the integration of concepts, rules, and strategies. Virtually all Direct Instruction programs concern higher-order thinking skills: classifying, learning rules, making inferences, testing generalizations, analyzing arguments, and solving problems. Carnine and Kameenui (1992) have described how the principles of design have been applied to teach sophisticated problem-solving skills to a variety of learners and across various domains. As the American Federation of Teachers (1998a) noted, although the early mastery of basic skills is a key element, Direct Instruction programs also address students' general comprehension and analytic skills.

Clear Communication.   Identification of generalizable strategies that students can use to solve a wide variety of problems is the foundation of Direct Instruction. The first step of building on this foundation is designing a sequence of instruction that communicates these strategies and enables students to display generalized skills to the full range of appropriate situations. Becker, Engelmann, and Thomas (1975) and Engelmann and Becker (1978) called this "general case programming" because the goal is to teach the general case rather than to teach a set of discrete specific cases. General case programming is the design of instruction that clearly communicates one and only one meaning and enables students to exhibit generalized responding.

General case programming is based on principles for the logical design of clear communication sequences (Engelmann & Carnine, 1982). It enables Direct Instruction program developers to design effective and efficient "learner friendly" instruction. In order to teach a general case, it is necessary to show students a set of items that includes examples and nonexamples arranged so that similarities and differences are readily apparent. Irrelevant aspects of the teaching must be held constant to minimize confusion and relevant aspects must be carefully manipulated to demonstrate important differences. Engelmann and Carnine (1982) developed five principles for sequencing and ordering examples to communicate clearly:

1. *The wording principle.* To make the sequence as clear as possible, we should use the same wording on all items (or wording that is as similar as possible). This wording helps focus students' attention on the details of the examples by reducing distraction or confusion that may be caused by variations in teacher language. Figure 2.1 shows a pair of items that

Following the wording principle		Not following the wording principle	
$\dfrac{3}{2}$	$\dfrac{2}{3}$	$\dfrac{3}{2}$	$\dfrac{2}{3}$
The larger number is on top.	The smaller number is on top.	The larger number is on top.	In this ratio statement, the denominator is greater than the numerator.

FIGURE 2.1   The Wording Principle

follow the wording principle; teachers use nearly the same wording for the two items. The figure also shows a pair of items that does not follow the wording principle; teachers add potential confusion by excessive variation in their wording.

   2. *The setup principle.* Examples and nonexamples selected for the initial teaching of a concept should share the greatest possible number of *irrelevant* features. In Figure 2.2 the pair of items on the right does not follow the setup principle. The two items differ in several ways, so there are many possible interpretations. Naïve students might think that the label *on* means 'rectangle' or 'things with corners'. It might mean 'gray'. It might mean 'horizontal'. Or, it could mean 'on'. Any of these interpretations is possible, and there is no way of determining which interpretation students will make. From a Direct Instruction perspective, this ambiguity is considered poor communication.

   The pair on the left of Figure 2.2 follows the setup principle. The items are exactly alike except in the critical aspect of being (or not being) *on*. The other interpretations (rectangle, having corners, gray, horizontal) are eliminated because these features are shared by both the positive and negative example. This pair of positive and negative examples differs in a single feature, so only one interpretation is possible. In later lessons, additional examples would be used to further expand the range of the concept. For example, by changing the setup (that is, by using different materials) in subsequent lessons, we would demonstrate that the concept *on* holds for all objects and surfaces.

   3. *The difference principle.* In order to illustrate the limits or boundaries of a concept, we should show examples and nonexamples that are similar to one another except in the critical

Following the setup principle		Not following the setup principle	
This is on.	This is not on.	This is on.	This is not on.

FIGURE 2.2   The Setup Principle

Following the difference principle		Not following the difference principle	
This line is horizontal	This line is not horizontal	This line is horizontal	This line is not horizontal

FIGURE 2.3   The Difference Principle

feature and indicate that they are different. The difference principle is most effective when the items are *juxtaposed*—that is, they are shown next to each other or consecutively in a series—making the similarities and differences most obvious. In Figure 2.3, the juxtaposed items on the left side follow the difference principle. The nonexample (not horizontal) is highly similar; it is just different enough to change a positive example of the concept (horizontal) into a negative example of the concept (not horizontal). In the pair that does not follow the difference principle, the item that is *not horizontal* is quite different. Failing to follow the difference principle leaves students with limited information about the point at which an example is no longer horizontal. Students might assume that an object must be quite tilted in order to be *not horizontal.*

   4. *The sameness principle.* To show the range of variation of the concept, we should juxtapose examples of the concept that differ from one another as much as possible yet still illustrate the concept and indicate that they are the same. This sequence is intended to foster generalization to unfamiliar concept examples that fall within the demonstrated range. In Figure 2.4, the set of examples on the left demonstrates the sameness principle by presenting a sequence of examples that are greatly different from one another, but are treated the same; that is, they are all called *dog.* The set of examples on the right does not show the possible range of variation. Presenting students with a set of examples that are very similar to one another may suggest to them that the label *dog* only applies to examples that are very similar to those shown. Thus, students may not show generalized responding to the full range of possible examples.

Following the sameness principle		Not following the sameness principle	
	Example shown		Example shown
"This is a dog"	Chihuahua	"This is a dog"	Cocker spaniel
"This is a dog"	Irish Wolfhound	"This is a dog"	Beagle
"This is a dog"	Cocker Spaniel	"This is a dog"	Fox Terrier

FIGURE 2.4   The Sameness Principle

Following the testing principle		Not following the testing principle	
$\frac{2}{4}$	Is this an improper fraction?	$\frac{4}{3}$	Is this an improper fraction?
$\frac{3}{5}$	Is this an improper fraction?	$\frac{3}{5}$	Is this an improper fraction?
$\frac{8}{5}$	Is this an improper fraction?	$\frac{8}{5}$	Is this an improper fraction?
$\frac{48}{32}$	Is this an improper fraction?	$\frac{15}{32}$	Is this an improper fraction?
$\frac{18}{12}$	Is this an improper fraction?	$\frac{18}{12}$	Is this an improper fraction?
$\frac{6}{7}$	Is this an improper fraction?	$\frac{6}{7}$	Is this an improper fraction?
$\frac{9}{3}$	Is this an improper fraction?	$\frac{9}{3}$	Is this an improper fraction?
		Note the alternating order: yes, no, yes, no, yes, no, yes	

FIGURE 2.5   The Testing Principle

5. *The testing principle.* To test for acquisition, we should juxtapose new, untaught examples and nonexamples in random order. The left side of Figure 2.5 shows an unpredictable order that provides a good test of students' understanding of the concept of *improper fraction.* The right side of the figure shows an alternating order. This order could be predictable; it is possible for students to get all answers correct simply by responding *yes* or *no* in accordance with the pattern. Therefore, it is not a good test because teachers could receive inaccurate information about students' understanding.

Instructional Formats.   After the concepts, rules, and strategies have been identified and sequences for clear communication of the general case have been outlined, then instructional *formats* are constructed. A format specifies the way that teachers will present each example, explanations that they will give, questions that they will ask, and corrections that they will use. Formats are carefully designed to be clear and concise, to help students focus on the important aspects of items, to provide appropriate support for students' developing skills, and, above all, to communicate clearly with students. The consistency of wording helps students focus on the content to be learned rather than on irrelevancies such as how teachers are asking for a response. This consistency is also very helpful to teachers as it allows them to use very effective, well-designed, and precise language to communicate clearly with all students.

For example, suppose that a group of students is learning the strategy for reading words that end with the pattern of a vowel followed by a consonant, followed by the letter "e" (VCe words) such as *rate, note,* and *slope.* The main difficulty of reading these words is to say the long sound for the medial (middle) vowel. In order to know when to say the long sound for the vowel, students must distinguish these words from words that end with the pattern of a vowel followed by a consonant (VC words) such as *rat, not,* and *slop.* The reading program could use a format like the one shown in Figure 2.6 (format 1). This format would be used with many examples of words that end with a VCe pattern (e.g., *rate, slope*) and a VC pattern (*rat, slop*).

Formats change as students become more proficient. Initially, formats include a great deal of structure and support for students' use of skills. Format 1 in Figure 2.6, for example, gives students strong support in use of the VCe rule. This support is important to ensure a high level of success when strategies are initially introduced. However, formats must gradually be modified so that the students learn to apply the skills independently. If teachers continued to use this format indefinitely, some students would come to depend on the sequence of questions to apply the rule and would falter when they encounter new examples of VCe words in story reading.

The support that is so important during initial instruction must be gradually reduced until students are using the skill independently, with no teacher assistance. The process of fading the format from highly supportive to highly independent is shown in the series of five formats in Figure 2.6. In the early stages of instruction of a particular strategy, teaching is

---

Format 1
1. Teacher: Remember, when there is an 'e' on the end, this letter (point to it) says its name.
2. Teacher: Is there an 'e' on the end? Students: yes
3. Teacher: Will this letter (point) say its name. Students: yes
4. Teacher: What is its name? (or what sound will it make?) Students: ā
5. Teacher: So what is the word? Students: *rate.*
Repeat Steps 2 through 4 for each of the following words: *name, not, vote, rat, him, fine*

Format 2
1. Teacher: Is there an 'e' on the end? Students: yes
2. Teacher: What sound will this letter make? Students: ā
3. Teacher: So what is the word? Students: *rate.*
Repeat Steps 1 through 3 for each of the following words: *name, not, vote, rat, him, fine*

Format 3
1. Teacher: What sound will this letter make: Students: ā
2. Teacher: So what is the word? Students: rate.
Repeat Steps 1 and 2 for each of the following words: *name, not, vote, rat, him, fine*

Format 4
1. Teacher: What is the word? Students: rate.
Repeat Step 1 for each of the following words: *name, not, meat, first, boy, turn*

Format 5
Students encounter VCe words in story reading with no additional assistance.

FIGURE 2.6   A Series of Formats for Teaching Students to Read Words That End VCe

highly teacher directed. However, by the completion of the instructional program the students' performance is independent, widely generalized, and applied in various contexts and situations. Becker and Carnine (1980) described six "shifts" that should occur in any well-designed teaching program to facilitate this transition.

Shift from overtized to covertized problem-solving strategies. Initially, formats assist students by leading them through the steps of a strategy out loud (overtly). Later, formats gradually shift to allow students to complete the strategy "in their head" (covertly).

Shift from simplified contexts to complex contexts. Formats for introducing each skill use a simplified context so students can focus on the critical new learning. Later, formats include increasing complexity. By the end of instruction on a skill, students should be applying it in a natural and complex context.

Shift from prompted to unprompted formats. In the early stages of instruction, formats include prompts to help focus students' attention on important aspects of the item and to increase their success. These prompts are later systematically removed as students gain a skill. By the end of the instruction, students apply the skill without any prompts.

Shift from massed practice to distributed practice. Initially, students learn a new skill best when they have many practice opportunities in a short period of time. In later learning, retention is enhanced by practice opportunities conducted over a long period of time. Thus, formats begin with massed practice and progress to distributed practice.

Shift from immediate feedback to delayed feedback. Early in an instructional sequence, teachers provide immediate feedback to encourage students and to provide them with immediate information about the accuracy of their responses. As students become more capable and confident, feedback is increasingly delayed to create a more natural situation.

Shift from an emphasis on the teacher's role as a source of information to an emphasis on the learner's role as a source of information. Initially, teachers model new skills and provide very explicit instruction in concepts, then later they fade out as the students themselves become the source of information on how to solve a problem.

Taken together, these six shifts in instruction constitute a coherent system for providing sufficient support to ensure initial success with learning and applying complex strategies and skills, then maintaining a high level of success as students systematically move to independent, generalized, real-world application of strategies and skills.

Sequencing of Skills.   The sequence in which skills are taught in an instructional program is another important contributor to its success. Learning can be made more or less difficult for students depending on the order in which skills are taught. The key principle is that students should be well prepared for each step of the program to maintain a high rate of success. That is, instructional programs should set students up for success. Direct Instruction uses four main guidelines for deciding the order, or sequence, of skills.

First, prerequisite skills for a strategy should be taught before the strategy itself. Students learn strategies most easily when they have already mastered the components or prerequisites of that strategy. For example, students will learn column addition most easily if they have already mastered basic math facts.

Second, instances consistent with a strategy should be taught before exceptions to that strategy. Students learn a strategy best when they do not have to deal with exceptions. Once students have mastered the basic strategy, they should be introduced to exceptions. For example, when the VCe rule is first introduced, students apply the rule to many examples (e.g., *note*) and nonexamples (e.g., *not*). Only when they are proficient with these kinds of words will they be introduced to exception words (e.g., *done*).

Third, easy skills should be taught before more difficult ones. Students are more likely to experience success if they begin with tasks that are easier to accomplish. For example, some sounds are easier to produce than others. Easy sounds (such as /a/, /m/, and /s/) are taught before more difficult sounds (such as /t/, /d/, /p/) are introduced. (Note: When a letter is enclosed in slashes [e.g., /a/] it refers to the *sound* of the letter. Thus, /a/ refers to the first sound in *at*.)

Finally, strategies and information that are likely to be confused should be separated in the sequence. The more similar things are, the more likely it is that students will confuse them; therefore, items that are most confusable should *not* be introduced together. For example, the symbols *b* and *d* look very similar, and they make sounds that are very similar. Therefore, students are likely to confuse these two letters. In the Direct Instruction beginning reading program, *Reading Mastery Classic Level 1,* the sound /d/ is introduced in Lesson 27, while introduction of /b/ is delayed until Lesson 121. Thus, ninety-four lessons separate the introduction of these two very similar sound–symbol correspondences.

Track Organization.   Traditional programs are typically organized in units where skills and strategies are introduced, practiced, and tested within a limited period of time. For example, a math program may have a unit on adding fractions with different denominators. In this unit, there may be a great deal of work on finding common denominators and adding the numerators. But after this, when students go on to the next unit (perhaps on multiplying fractions), practice on adding with different denominators often ends suddenly. Information in one unit is seldom incorporated into subsequent units. This lack of incorporated information results in predictable errors when students (1) forget to watch for different denominators when adding fractions, (2) forget how to find common denominators, and (3) confuse the multiplication procedure with addition procedure. In contrast, *tracks* rather than units, provide the organizational framework for all Direct Instruction programs. Tracks are sequences of activities that teach a skill across multiple lessons. Each lesson contains activities from several tracks. This way, Direct Instruction can extend teaching and practice of a skill across many lessons and weave prerequisite skill tracks into the tracks that integrate these skills into more complex strategies.

Figure 2.7 shows the scope and sequence chart for *Connecting Math Concepts Level C*. The horizontal rows show skill development tracks and the vertical lines show lessons. For example, lesson 1 includes activities from the tracks on Addition and Subtraction Number Families, Addition Facts, Place Value, and Column Addition. Lesson 30 includes Addition and Subtraction Number Families but does not include Addition Facts. The Addition Facts

Level C
Scope and Sequence

Connecting Math Concepts, Level C places a strong emphasis on higher-order thinking. Students learn a variety of mapping techniques for relating problem solving to real-life situations. With word problems, measurement, money, time, and various projects, students graphically represent information before they attempt to calculate an answer. The

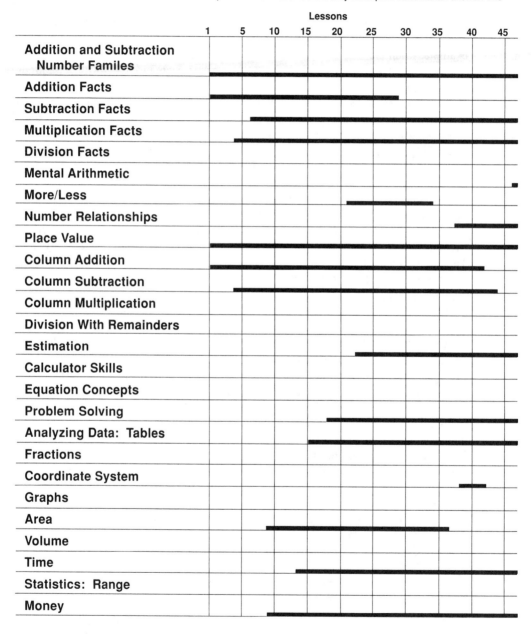

FIGURE 2.7   Scope and Sequence Chart from *Connecting Math Concepts Level C.* Reprinted with permission of the McGraw-Hill Companies, Inc.

detailed instruction leads both teachers and students to develop positive feelings about problem solving.

In addition, instruction covers place value, geometry, estimation, and calculator use.

Concepts and computational skills are also taught for regrouping, multiplication, division, and fractions. The Scope and Sequence Chart shows where each track or major topic begins and where it ends.

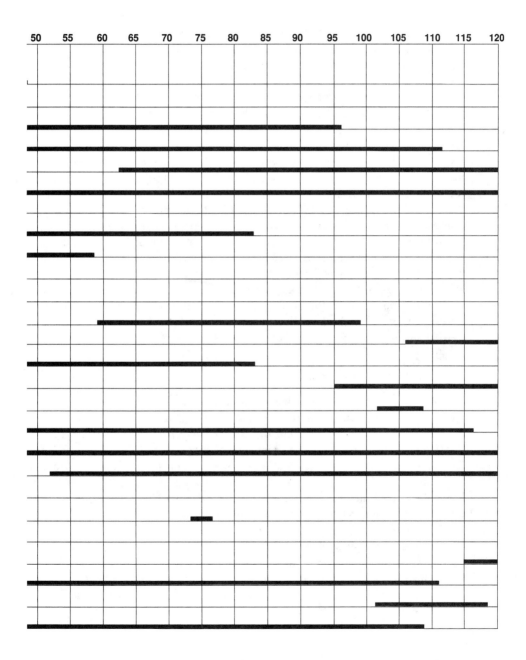

track has been completed at this point and is folded into the tracks on Column Addition, Estimation, and applications such as Analyzing Data: Tables. As shown in this scope and sequence chart, no Direct Instruction lesson is devoted to a single topic. Instead, each lesson consists of activities that develop skills from several instructional tracks, so each lesson provides instruction and practice on multiple concepts, rules, and strategies. In essence then, each lesson is composed of a collection of mini-lessons on a variety of objectives.

There are numerous advantages to designing programs in tracks. First, student attention is better maintained because they do not work on a single skill for an extended period. Instead, lessons are made up of relatively short exercises that call on a variety of skills. Difficult tasks are interspersed among easier ones. Newly introduced skills are mixed with well-practiced ones. Each lesson includes a variety of skills, formats, and difficulty levels. This variety can be seen in the scope and sequence chart by scanning down a line and noting how many different tracks are touched in a single lesson. Second, skills can be introduced and developed gradually over a number of lessons. Each lesson can include a very small step in the development of the skill because skills may be developed across many lessons. Note, for example, that the track on Analyzing Data: Tables extends across 105 lessons. This track development provides the time necessary to elaborate the strategies gradually. Third, practice can be massed within a lesson to promote learning and distributed across lessons to promote retention. Students receive a sufficient number of examples in each exercise so that they can master each step in the sequence. In addition, practice is distributed over a substantial period of time. Organizing programs in tracks also makes it possible to integrate information. In Direct Instruction programs, no skill is ever introduced and then dropped. However, some tracks are discontinued as the skills in that track are incorporated into other tracks. For example, when the track on Addition Facts ends, other tracks such as Column Addition provide ongoing practice in these facts.

Organization of Instruction

In addition to program design whereby the characteristics are embodied in the written program, we turn to the second major component of Direct Instruction: how the teacher organizes instruction. There are four key elements to organizing instruction. First, Direct Instruction teachers organize students into groups to best meet the needs of each individual. Second, Direct Instruction teachers allocate sufficient time for teaching and assure that the time is used well. Third, Direct Instruction teachers implement precise and careful plans for instruction though the use of a scripted presentation. Fourth, Direct Instruction teachers engage in continuous assessment of student performance.

Instructional Grouping.   Every teacher faces choices about how to group students for instruction. Teachers may teach to the entire class or may arrange the class into smaller instructional groups. If teachers use smaller groups they must decide how many groups to create and which students should be in each group. The principle that guides grouping in Direct Instruction is that each student should receive instruction that is appropriate to his or her individual needs. That is, students should be placed at a level where they have the necessary prerequisite skills and have not yet mastered the objectives. The skills that are to be taught are close to those students have already learned but somewhat beyond their current competence. Psychologists refer to this as the student's "zone of proximal development" (Vygotsky, 1997). To enable all students to participate in instruction that is well suited to their individual needs, Direct Instruction teachers organize their class into groups of students who have similar zones of proximal development. This type of grouping enables teachers to present instruction to the *group,* to interact with the *group,* and to address the needs of all the *individuals* in that group.

Of course, each student has individual strengths and needs. Therefore, students who are in the same group for reading may not be in the same group for math; their placement in each subject depends on their needs in each subject. In constructing groups, we are less concerned with students' general achievement or broad cognitive skills than we are with their mastery of the specific skills that are prerequisite to a given lesson and the particular skills that are taught in that lesson. Each Direct Instruction program has a placement test (or other placement guidelines) that guides teachers in forming appropriate groups. The placement tests are designed specifically to identify students' performance on the key skills that are important for them to be successful in the program. The results of these tests indicate the program level and lesson that is an appropriate starting place for students. However, no test is perfect. Therefore, when teachers form groups based on placement test scores, they should anticipate making adjustments when they see how students respond to the first several lessons. Students who make no errors and appear to be bored should be moved to more advanced groups and students who make many errors should be moved to less advanced groups.

Even if students are placed into ideal groups at the beginning of the year, we expect students to progress at different rates. Some students who were appropriately placed into less advanced groups learn quickly and show that they would now be better served in a more advanced group. Conversely, other students may struggle to learn the material at the rate of other members of their group. Direct Instruction grouping should be *flexible* to accommodate students' changing needs.

This flexible skill grouping based on students' instructional needs is very different from the practice of "tracking" in which students are assigned to rigid, inflexible groups based on general characteristics such as "intelligence." Tracking is *absolutely incompatible* with Direct Instruction because it does not allow for adjustment according to students' changing needs.

Instructional Time.   An important factor in determining how much students learn is the amount of time students are directly engaged with the material. Of course, this makes logical sense to most people, but anyone who needs to be convinced can refer to a large amount of research that demonstrates this simple fact (e.g., Rosenshine & Berliner, 1978). Thus, Direct Instruction teachers must allocate sufficient time in their schedule for teaching the most important academic areas. Of course, it is not sufficient to allocate or schedule time for instruction; this allocated time must also be used efficiently. Direct Instruction teachers will organize smooth transitions, have materials at hand, and develop efficient routines to maximize the time that is actually available for instruction. Teachers must ensure that students are actually *engaged* in instruction during the designated time. However, it is even more important that students are engaged in tasks they can perform with high levels of success. The time that students are engaged and have high success rates is called *academic* *learning time* and is one of the strongest predictors of student achievement. In other words, we must allocate sufficient time, then make sure that we use that time efficiently and make certain that students are involved in learning activities that they can perform successfully.

Scripted Presentation.   When we attempt to create performances of great complexity and we want consistently successful outcomes, we generally plan very carefully. For example, critical parts of space missions such as liftoff, difficult operations in space, and reentry are scripted in detail and practiced extensively. In the theater, sophisticated drama with complex characters and multiple levels of meaning are scripted in advance and practiced thoroughly. Casual planning and dependence on extensive improvisation are simply not successful ways of producing these complex results. Similarly, from a Direct Instruction perspective, teaching important and complicated skills such as reading, math, and language arts requires careful planning and precise implementation. Therefore, Direct Instruction programs employ detailed scripts with carefully developed explanations, examples, and wording.

Scripts are tools designed to accomplish two goals: (1) to assure that students access instruction that is extremely well designed from the analysis of the content to the specific wording of explanations, and (2) to relieve teachers of the responsibility for designing, field-testing, and refining instruction in every subject that they teach. One of the main premises that leads to the use of scripts is that students deserve precisely planned instruction. Some might argue that the level of thought about the content of instruction, the details of clear communication, and the careful sequencing of tasks that are embodied in Direct Instruction scripts are not really important and that instruction that is largely improvised is sufficient. It is certainly true that some students will master some of the objectives with instruction that is casually planned and loosely organized. But it is also true that many students will fail to master many objectives with casually planned instruction. Students who, for whatever reason, are most at risk of learning difficulties are disadvantaged by instruction that is not carefully planned and well implemented. Flaws in instruction are reflected in students who have poor skills. Even those students who are capable of learning from weak instruction can learn more if instruction is well planned. If we aspire to reach all the students and teach all the objectives, we must plan instruction very carefully. Careful and detailed planning of instruction is important to the degree that we value excellent educational outcomes.

As we might guess, planning lessons is extremely time-consuming. Even for a team of expert instructional designers, developing a new math or language arts program is a daunting task. For an individual teacher who has several hours of planning time each day after school and must prepare lessons for several subject areas, it is simply impossible to produce instructional plans that meet these high standards. Scripts can provide carefully developed, field-tested, and detailed plans for teachers. However, as with any plan, there are limits to what scripts can accomplish.

Armed with these Direct Instruction scripts, the teacher's role becomes similar to an actor's. Actors have a critical role in delivering planned performances. They are the ones who breathe life into the words that are written on the page. Without their skill and art in conveying the script, there is no drama. However, depending on the actors' inspiration to perform is far different from asking them to go on stage and spontaneously create drama. Like actors, Direct Instruction teachers are performers who put life into scripts. They relate to the students through the words on the scripts. These teachers are the source of warmth, excitement, and life in the presentation. They make the expected adjustments for individual differences among students. Teachers are the only ones who can motivate students with praise and other feedback on their work. Teachers are also the only ones who can adjust the pace to the needs of the group, allowing more time for tasks that are difficult for a particular group and moving more quickly through tasks that are easier. Teachers must also play the critical roles of problem solver and decision maker, identifying problems with student learning and adjusting the instruction accordingly. These jobs are extremely demanding but are made much easier if teachers are given excellent tools including a well-designed scripted curriculum. Relieved of the instructional design role, teachers can focus on the critical job of delivering instruction, adjusting it to the unique needs of individual students, and solving unexpected problems.

Continuous Assessment.   It is important to monitor students' progress toward program objectives continuously. All Direct Instruction programs include various types of ongoing in-program assessments. These assessments provide teachers with feedback on the effectiveness of their teaching and allow them to evaluate the adequacy of their students' skill development. Data provided by these assessments can be used to make critical instructional decisions. If progress is inadequate, teachers need to adjust instruction. They may determine that some students are inappropriately placed and regroup students accordingly. They may develop additional instruction and practice for students who have not yet mastered a particular skill.

On the other hand, students may perform above the specified criterion on these measures. Teachers may elect to skip lessons when data indicate that a group of students is capable of moving at a faster pace. Or, teachers may find that some students in a group are able to move at a faster pace and may elect to change those students' group placement. All decisions, from initial placement and grouping to acceleration of instruction, are made based on students' assessment performance, not on "hunches."

Teacher–Student Interactions

Direct Instruction defines the teacher's role more clearly and explicitly than most other forms of instruction. Scripted programs relieve teachers of the role of instructional designer. Instead, their role is to deliver instruction in a way that is effective and motivating to the particular group of students and to make the critical decisions about how the program should be adapted to the needs of the particular group. This role emphasizes (1) knowing the students as individuals and creatively motivating them through presentation of the script and by adding motivational systems that are appropriate to the particular group, and (2) knowing the students' ever-changing skills and adjusting the pacing of lessons, amount of practice, and other factors according to their needs. These roles emphasize problem solving and creativity. However, this creativity is not unstructured and undirected. It is creativity within the context of well-conceived lessons and with the clear goal of enhancing learning and motivation.

There are seven components for promoting effective teacher–student interactions: active student participation, group unison responding, signals, pacing, teaching to mastery, correction procedures, and motivation.

Active Student Participation.   Students learn best when they are actively engaged with the material. Active engagement is important for three reasons. First, and most obviously, students learn when they interact with the instructional material and receive relevant feedback. More interaction and more feedback result in more learning. A student who reads twenty words and receives feedback on each will tend to learn more than a similar student who reads only five words. Thus, actively responding to a large number of relevant items would be expected to increase learning directly.

The second reason for maximizing engagement has to do with the pragmatics of the classroom. When students are engaged, they are less likely to become distracted and to distract others. Therefore, active engagement reduces time that would otherwise be devoted to management of behavior problems. In this way, active engagement can actually increase the time available for teaching. (Martella and Nelson [in press] provide further information on behavior management issues related to the teaching of Direct Instruction.)

The third reason to maximize active engagement involves knowledge of student skill levels. When teachers have an excellent understanding of each student's current level of mastery, they can make the best decisions about instruction. Ideally, they would have very rich information on students' skills in order to make well-informed decisions. When we consider these three reasons for active engagement, it becomes clear why active engagement is one of the centerpieces of Direct Instruction.

Group Unison Responses.   There are many ways to organize active student engagement. One of the most common is to call on individual students to answer questions orally. If the items are relevant and the questions well designed, oral responses can give individual students practice, keep them attentive, and give teachers immediate information on individual student skill levels. However, individual oral responses also have several limitations. While the teacher is interacting with one student, other students may not be paying attention. Each question that is directed to a single student may constitute down time for the other students and not promote active engagement. In addition, with individual questions, the teacher receives information about only one student at a time. It is possible that the student who answered the question is the only one who understood the material. This possibility is even greater if the teacher calls on volunteers. Students who do not know the answer are the least likely to volunteer. Calling on volunteers may give the teacher a distorted picture of the group's performance. Additionally, it directs the response opportunities to students who are the most skilled and away from those who are most in need of active engagement.

In order to provide practice and to assess many students, teachers can provide numerous individual questions. However, this questioning leads to a great deal of down time for students. If there are ten students in a group, each student may waste nine-tenths of the time devoted to individual questions. In addition, if teachers repeatedly ask a small set of questions, then the first students to answer the question get a high-quality opportunity to figure out the answer. Other students who respond to a question after having heard several other students answer that same question get lower-quality opportunities because they may simply be repeating what they heard from the other students. They may not have had a chance to figure it out for themselves.

An alternative way to organize student responses is to pose a question to all the students and have them all write the answer. This technique can be very useful if written answers are appropriate and students have strong writing skills. However, many students we teach do not yet have strong and fluent writing skills, and much of the content does not lend itself to written answers. In addition, teachers must circulate around the group very quickly to assess the skills of all the students. If they do not circulate quickly and check answers as students write them, then they will not have the high-quality assessment information that is one of the goals of student engagement.

Another alternative, one that is often (though not always) employed in Direct Instruction, is to ask all the students to answer orally *in unison.* This responding is often described as *choral responding* because it is similar to a choir singing in unison. If students answer in unison, then (1) all students get high-quality practice on every item because they provide their own response and cannot echo other students, (2) all students are busy learning the material and are less likely to become distracted, and (3) teachers can assess the skills of all the students in an instant and be well informed about their skills. If teachers can orchestrate group unison responses, they can greatly increase students' opportunities to be engaged with the content and greatly increase their understanding of each student's skill level. Group unison responses are highly efficient. Suppose a teacher has a group of ten students and he can ask ten questions per minute. If he asks all individual questions, each student makes one oral response per minute. In contrast, if he asks group questions and gets unison responses, each student can make ten responses per minute.

Group unison responses have some substantial advantages; however, they should not be the only form of response. Group unison responses are useful when the answer is relatively short and when all students would be expected to provide the same answer. For example, a teacher might show students a fraction and ask, "Is this a proper fraction?" All students would respond "No." The teacher might then ask, "How do you know?" and the group would respond, "The top number is larger." In both of these instances, the use of a group unison response would be appropriate. On the other hand, if the teacher gave a request such as, "Give an example of an improper fraction," we would expect students to give a variety of answers so a group unison response would not be appropriate. For this item it would be best to call on an individual or to ask all students to write an answer.

In addition, group unison responses should be followed by individual questions. Individual turns provide information about the skill levels of different students to respond to a task when there is no support from the group. Individual turns are generally presented after the group has been brought to mastery. When teachers provide individual turns (usually signaled by teachers as "time for turns"), they provide an instruction to all students and then place an individual student's name at the end of this instruction. For example, "Read the second row of words, James" or "Say these sounds, Sally" as compared to "James, read the second row of words" or "Sally, say these sounds." In this way, all students are prepared to answer the teacher until a specific student's name is called.

Signals.   The group unison oral response is a very useful tool. However, if answers are not quite in unison, if some students answer slightly earlier or slightly later than the others, or if students drone their answers, then these group responses become much less powerful and may even be counterproductive. The problem is that if responses are not crisp and in unison, then students who answer later may simply be echoing those who answered earlier. Thus, they may not be practicing the academic task but, rather, practicing the skill of chiming in after other students. In addition, when responses are crisp and in unison, teachers can easily hear a single error in a group. However, if answers are dragged out or unsynchronized, it is much more difficult to detect errors. As a result, it is very important that teachers use some system to enable all students to answer simultaneously.

In many noneducational pursuits, people want to coordinate their actions. In an orchestra or choir, musicians watch the conductor for visual signals and listen to each other for auditory cues about when to begin. In football, a quarterback usually gives auditory signals by yelling. Coordination of our driving in traffic is mostly arranged by visual signals of traffic lights, signs, and (depending on where you are driving) other drivers' turn signals. The common element among these diverse examples is that we use various kinds of signals to coordinate groups of people.

The goal in signaling for a group unison response is to enable all students to initiate the answer at exactly the same time. In this way, teachers gain precise information about student performance that one-to-one instruction permits, while still achieving the efficiency of group instruction. Teachers hear a single response, are able to evaluate the response, and can proceed accordingly. In order for students to initiate a response at the same time, we must use some kind of signal to coordinate their answers. Direct Instruction teachers use various signals, depending on the circumstances. For example, when students are reading words from a textbook, they are not looking at the teacher. Therefore, an auditory signal such as a snap, tap, or clap is useful because it does not require students to look away from their books. On the other hand, if students are reading words that are written on a chalkboard, teachers may use a visual signal, such as pointing to the word, because they are already looking at that word. In each Direct Instruction program, the teacher's guide and teacher presentation book specifies how to signal for each task.

Figure 2.8 illustrates the parts of a basic signal. To signal a unison response during group instruction, teachers provide (1) a focus cue to gain students' attention to the task, (2) think time that varies, depending on the skills of the students, (3) a verbal cue followed by a pause (interval), and (4) a signal. To focus the students' attention, teachers may point to an item on the board or in a teacher presentation book or may direct students to point to an item in their book. In giving directions, teachers tell the students the type of response they will make. For example, they may say, "Spell each word after I say it" or "Read these words the fast way." Next, think time is provided. The length of think time depends on the difficulty of the task. If the task is relatively simple for students in the group, the think time may be very brief. For instance, after sufficient practice with letter–sound correspondence, most students would need little think time to respond to the question, "What sound does this letter make?" However, for more difficult tasks, teachers need to provide more think time. When asked to read words that follow the VCe pattern, students need sufficient time to determine if the word ends in an *e,* to think about what sound the medial vowel makes, then to sound out the word overtly with the appropriate vowel sound. This task obviously will take several seconds when the skill is being acquired. If think time is too short, students will not answer on signal or will make errors. As students become more proficient in application of a particular skill, teachers reduce this think time.

Following think time teachers provide a verbal cue such as "get ready" or "what word." This verbal cue has teacher voice inflection built in (e.g., get READY) as illustrated by the curved line under the verbal cue column in Figure 2.8; this cue is immediately followed by

Basic Signal

Focus Cue	Think Time	Verbal Cue	Interval	Signal

Focus Cue: Point to task, Ask question, Give direction

Verbal Cue: "Get ready", "What word", "What sound"

Signal: Snap, Clap, Touch, Hand drop

FIGURE 2.8   Parts of a Basic Signal (Illustrated by Tracey Hall.)

a short pause (interval). Right after this short pause, teachers provide a signal. Teachers may indicate this signal by making a gesture (such as touching the board or dropping their hand) or an audible cue (such as a clap or tap). It is critical that teachers do not "talk and move" at the same time; that is, teachers should not overlap what they say with their signal. The interval after the verbal cue and before the signal should be maintained. Students are to come in "on signal"; that is, they respond when teachers snap their fingers or tap the board.

Signals tell students when to answer and provide all students the opportunity to participate. The signal is a tool that enables all students to be actively engaged with instruction and gives teachers the opportunity to monitor student responses and adjust their instruction accordingly.

Pacing.   Active student engagement is further enhanced when teachers maintain a brisk pace in their teaching. Brisk pacing of instruction is important for several reasons. First, a rapid pace allows teachers to cover, and students to learn, more material (Brophy & Good, 1986). Second, a brisk pace holds student attention and reduces time between related information, thereby enhancing student learning. When we speak too slowly, we can actually be harder to understand, especially by distractible children. Third, well-paced instruction keeps students engaged and, in turn, reduces behavior problems. Inappropriate behavior often occurs during down time when students are not occupied with productive tasks. Engelmann and Becker (1978) reported that when teachers maintained a pace of about twelve responses per minute, students answered correctly about 80 percent of the time and were off-task only 10 percent of the time. However, when teachers asked only four questions per minute, the students' accuracy dropped to 30 percent and they were off-task about 70 percent of the time. Clearly, a brisk pace contributes to the effectiveness of instruction.

Proper pacing is a difficult teaching technique to master. The pace should be relatively quick, but must give students sufficient think time. Experienced Direct Instruction teachers become very sensitive to the demands of the task and the skills of the individual students and adjust their pace accordingly. Finding an appropriate pace is an important and subtle skill, one that is learned from experience and close observation of students' learning.

Teaching to Mastery.   The difficulty of a learning task depends on how well students are prepared for it. When students are well prepared they will find a task easy, even "natural." However, those same students would find that same task extremely difficult if they were not well prepared for it. This simple, even self-evident, logic is the basis of the Direct Instruction principle of teaching to mastery. Mastery involves performing skills at high levels. Engelmann (1999) likens mastery to a stairway: "Mastery is the guarantee that students are able to reach each stair without falling" (p. 4). Effective teachers carefully design instruction around this goal.

Direct Instruction programs are designed to prepare students for each new challenge and set the students up for success. If students have mastered the skills taught in lessons 1–80 of a Direct Instruction program, they will be well prepared for lesson 81. However, if students are weak on the tasks from the previous lessons, then lesson 81 will be more difficult. Therefore, we can make the program easiest for students and enhance their success by bringing them to mastery on every lesson. Some teachers are tempted to reduce their mastery standards for groups of students who are struggling. We often hear that a group's performance is "pretty good for the low group." The problem is that students who tend to struggle are the very students who most benefit from mastery and are most disadvantaged when lessons are made more difficult. Thus, from a Direct Instruction perspective, it is very important to assure that every group reaches mastery on every lesson; mastery is particularly crucial for students who struggle with the material.

Mastery should generally be gauged by the performance of the lowest-performing student in the group. If that student has mastered the material, we can assume that others in the group have as well. It also means that the student who is most in need of support will not be further disadvantaged on the next lesson. Engelmann (1969) advised that we "seek flattery from the lowest-performing children. When they succeed, the teacher should indeed feel that she has received the highest form of professional compliment" (p. 46).

Four criteria allow precise interpretation of how students respond during lessons as noted by Engelmann (1999):

1. Students should be at least 70 percent correct on information that is being introduced for the first time. (If they are only at 50 percent, they are at chance levels and are probably guessing.)
2. Students should be at least 90 percent correct on skills taught earlier in the program (assuming previous skill mastery).
3. At the end of a lesson, all students should be "virtually 100 percent firm on all tasks and activities" (p. 6).
4. Student error rates should be low enough to ensure that teachers have sufficient time to complete a lesson.

Teaching to mastery involves closely monitoring student performance and making appropriate adjustments.

Correction Procedures.   Effective instruction requires effective correction procedures. While Direct Instruction is designed to minimize student errors, mistakes are inevitable when students are acquiring new information. Teachers must notice every error, determine the type of error that was made, provide an appropriate correction, and arrange for additional practice on items of that type. Without effective corrections, learning is difficult or impossible.

Many different types of correction procedures are used in Direct Instruction. The particular correction procedure used depends on the teachers' diagnosis of errors. However two features characterize all corrections in Direct Instruction: (1) they are immediate, and (2) they are direct. Teachers should correct mistakes immediately when they occur. Corrections explicitly and directly provide information that enables students to answer questions correctly. In addition, during group responses, corrections are presented to the entire group. The individual student who makes an error is never singled out. All students can benefit from the additional practice provided by the correction procedure. If the errors occur in individual responses, corrections are typically directed to the student who responded.

The basic correction procedure for student response errors in Direct Instruction programs consists of reteaching and retesting students. Figure 2.9 shows the basic Direct Instruction correction procedure of model-test-retest.

Immediately after the error, teachers (1) demonstrate the correct answer (*model*), (2) ask the students to respond to the original item (*test*), (3) give several other items, then retest the item that was missed (*retest*). Each step in this correction procedure has a specific purpose. The *model* step clearly communicates what students should do. The *test* step assesses whether the model was effective and students can now respond correctly to that item. However, because the test immediately follows the teacher's model, it does not show whether students can answer correctly and independently. Thus, the *retest* step (also called "starting over") is crucial. The retest comes after several other items. If students can make the correct response after these other items, then teachers have greater confidence that

Step	Teacher says	Student says
Model Clear communication of what students should do.	This word is *eventually*	
Test Opportunity for students to perform skill correctly.	What word is this?	*eventually*
Retest Teacher intersperses several other items before retesting eventually.	What word is this? (*treatments*)	*treatments*
	What word is this? (*submarine*)	*submarine*
Gives students opportunity to perform skill independently.	What word is this? (*eventually*)	*eventually*

FIGURE 2.9   Steps in a Basic Correction Procedure

students have learned the response. In addition to these basic steps, teachers may decide to use *delayed tests* of missed items after completing the exercise or lesson. Delayed tests may be given at varying intervals throughout the day and on subsequent days to ensure that students remember important information.

In some situations, teachers may add steps to the basic correction procedure. Chapters 3–8 provide specific correction procedures for the various academic programs (presented under Teaching Techniques in the chapters). For example, if students err in applying an explicit rule, teachers can replace the model step with a *rule.* If students misread the word *note,* (saying *not*) teachers could assist students in applying the rule for reading VCe words by asking, "Is there an 'e' on the end of the word?" followed by, "So what do you say for this letter (pointing to the letter 'o')." They then proceed with the test and retest.

Students may make errors because they have trouble producing the response. For example, students may have difficulty making the sound for a particular letter, saying the sounds in a word without pausing between sounds, or reciting a list such as days of the week. In these situations, teachers should add a *lead* step after the model. They initiate the response by asking students to, "Say it with me," and respond with students on a lead step. Assume that students made a mistake when asked to say the sounds in *sat* without stopping. Figure 2.10 illustrates an appropriate correction procedure that includes a lead step. Teachers may lead (respond with the students) several times and must monitor the students' responses closely by watching and listening. Only when teachers are confident that students can produce the response without their assistance are students asked to respond independently.

The teacher's guide and teacher's presentation book for all Direct Instruction programs provide very detailed guidelines for effective correction procedures of common types of mistakes in that particular program. All of these corrections are variations on the basic correction procedure of model-test-retest.

In addition to correcting student response errors, teachers should also correct signal errors. When signal errors occur it means that students did not answer together on signal. To

Step	Teacher says	Student says
Model	My turn to say the sounds in *sat,* sssaaat.	
Lead Teacher and students say the response together. The lead may be repeated several times if necessary.	Say it with me, sssaaat	sssaaat
Test	Say the sounds in *sat* all by yourselves.	sssaaat
Delayed Test	Say the sounds in *sat.*	sssaaat

FIGURE 2.10   Correction with Lead Step

correct this error, teachers might say, "I need to hear everyone together" or "Everyone should respond right at my signal" and repeat the task (starting over).

Motivation.   In Direct Instruction, learning and motivation are seen to be closely related. Motivation begins with success, and success requires motivation. The experience of success is one of the most important bases of motivation in the classroom. Thus, motivation begins, as instruction does, by appropriate placement. Placement in excessively difficult material results in failure and reduced motivation. Placement in excessively easy material results in boredom and reduced motivation. When placement is appropriate and instruction is well designed and well delivered, students experience a high level of success. Classroom experiences that produce success are one of the foundations for motivation. Thus, to maximize student motivation, we refer to the same instructional issues we have been concerned with in maximizing student learning.

In a well-designed program, day-to-day success will result in continual learning and improvement of skills. For students, the reward of seeing their own improvement can provide powerful motivation. Learning, of course, has other natural rewards. Learning basic language skills results in communicating more effectively, opening vast possibilities. Learning to read has the great reward of access to literature as well as the social rewards of reading such as being complimented by one's parents.

Teachers play a key role in motivation. They arrange a classroom environment that results in success for all students. They recognize that success and make it more apparent to students. By frequently commenting on success and praising students for their efforts, teachers amplify the effects of the success and add a positive social element. Teacher recognition is a strong motivator for most students, but the effects of praise depend on the relationship between teachers and students as well as the way in which teachers deliver praise. When teachers have a warm and positive relationship with their students, their praise will be more powerful. Also, if they are sincere, specific, and age-appropriate in their praise, the effect will be most powerful.

Admonishments, reprimands, nagging, and other forms of attention given to undesirable behavior should be minimized. Reprimands and other forms of attention given to undesirable behavior are generally ineffective. Madsen, Becker, Thomas, Koser, and Plager (1968) compared the effects of reprimanding students for being out of their seats versus ignoring them and praising students who were in their seats and on-task. The authors concluded that, if the primary way that children get attention is by misbehaving, they actually misbehave more often. That is, teacher attention, even though intended to reduce the undesired behavior, may actually make it more frequent. Thus, one of the basic slogans of motivation for a Direct Instruction teacher is "Catch them being good."

Much of the time the immediate rewards of success, learning, and recognition from the teacher are sufficient to produce strong motivation. However, when learning is harder, more rewards may be required. Also, for a wide variety of reasons, some children are not sufficiently motivated by these simple motivational techniques. Thus, additional strategies are necessary. These additional strategies may include more focused praise. For example, if teachers know that particular students are struggling with math facts, they may be alert for situations in which those students succeed with math facts. They may also make a point of recognizing student effort and persistence in this area. Teachers can make student progress more obvious. For example, they may teach students to graph their performance on certain skills or activities such as each day's math assignment. Beating one's own best score is often a powerful motivator.

These relatively simple techniques used consistently and thoughtfully are sufficient for creating a positive, motivated, and productive classroom. However, this is not to claim that these techniques will eliminate *all* behavior management problems. When problems arise, the first question for teachers should be whether these basic motivation systems are in place. They should ask whether students are placed at an appropriate level and are experiencing success in the program and they should ask whether students are aware of their successes and are receiving sufficient recognition for their efforts. This simple analysis can unravel the reasons, and suggest solutions, for many behavior challenges. However, there will still be challenges that require even more focused analysis and intervention. Martella and Nelson (in press) describe strategies for working with a wider variety of classroom management techniques.

DIRECT INSTRUCTION AND EFFECTIVE TEACHING

The practices that have been identified by the "effective teaching" literature (described in Chapter 1 as effective instruction) are integrated into Direct Instruction. The organization of instruction in Direct Instruction includes a general academic focus with an emphasis on maximizing engaged time and instruction in small interactive groups, all characteristics of effective instruction (Rosenshine & Stevens, 1986). Direct Instruction includes organizational elements beyond those described in the effective teaching literature. These elements include grouping students with similar instructional needs and scripted presentations. Direct Instruction student–teacher interaction practices such as brisk pacing, high success rates, and explicit instruction, followed by guided practice and independent practice with emphasis on mastery of content, are all prominent recommendations from the effective teaching literature (Rosenshine & Stevens). Direct Instruction builds on these techniques by adding specific practices such as unison responding to further increase active participation by students, signals to coordinate student answers, and specific recommendations for error corrections.

The most important way that Direct Instruction extends effective teaching is in program design. Effective teaching does not deal with program design: it takes the program as a given and focuses on effective methods for delivering the content. Direct Instruction, on the other hand, is built on the foundation of instructional programs that embody efficient strategies and carefully crafted explanations. This attention to what is taught takes Direct Instruction beyond the recommendations of effective instruction. Thus, Direct Instruction is consistent with the recommendations of the effective teaching literature and goes beyond it by further specifying teaching techniques and attending to the design of programs.

Direct Instruction is often confused with the more general techniques described in the effective teaching literature. In fact, the term *direct instruction* (note the lack of capital letters) is often used to refer to any form of instruction involving direct interactions between teachers and students. Many professional educators and professional publications fail to distinguish between direct instruction, which is a set of teacher practices for organizing instruction and interacting with students, and Direct Instruction, which is an integrated system of curriculum and instruction (Schaefer, 2000).

In a recent popular educational psychology text, Slavin (2003) states that "the research on direct instruction models has had mixed conclusions. . . ." However, he also points out "Studies of Direct Instruction . . . a program built around specific teaching materials and structured methods, have found strong positive effects" (p. 239).

STUDENTS FOR WHOM DIRECT INSTRUCTION IS APPROPRIATE

Research has confirmed that Direct Instruction has been effective for students with diverse learning needs (including students in special education and general education), students with diverse language backgrounds, and students of all ages from preschool through adult.

Students with Diverse Learning Needs

Students who are receiving special education services are particularly at-risk for academic failure. If these students are to be successful, they often require careful instruction in which details are carefully planned and well implemented. Direct Instruction has been successful in accelerating the achievement of students who receive special education services.

Even students who would be predicted to have low levels of achievement benefit greatly from Direct Instruction. Gersten, Becker, Heiry, and White (1984) examined the yearly achievement test profiles of students in Direct Instruction classrooms to determine whether annual gains made by students with low IQ scores differed significantly from the gains made by students with average or superior IQ scores.

Figure 2.11 shows the yearly gains made by students in reading as measured by the Wide Range Achievement Test. As shown in this figure, students with higher IQ test scores started at higher achievement levels and ended with higher levels than their peers with lower scores. However, the pattern of growth of students with low IQ scores is remarkably similar to that of other students. The group with the lowest scores (under 70) gained nearly as much each year in reading as students with much higher scores. By the end of third grade, those students with the lowest IQ scores were performing at the seventieth percentile or a grade equivalent of 4.3.

The results are even more pronounced in math as seen in Figure 2.12. This figure shows the students' performance on the Metropolitan Achievement Test. The growth rate for *all* groups of students corresponds to one grade equivalent for each year in school.

These results provide evidence that Direct Instruction is appropriate for, and effective with, a wide variety of individuals including those with low IQ scores, those with IQ scores in the average range, and those with high IQ scores. In addition, because children in this study were taught in small homogeneous groups (having students with relatively the same skill levels), the gains of students with lower IQ scores were not made at the expense of other students nor the other way around.

Several reviews of research focusing on the use of Direct Instruction with special education populations have all converged on the finding that Direct Instruction is measurably effective with these students. White (1988) reviewed twenty-five such studies and found that

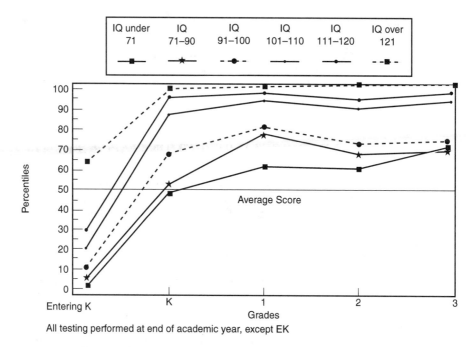

FIGURE 2.11   Results of Direct Instruction on Reading as Measured by the Wide Range Achievement Test for Students with Diverse IQ Scores. Adapted from Gersten et al. (1984).

all comparisons favored the Direct Instruction group. Forness, Kavale, Blum, and Lloyd (1997) conducted an analysis of various intervention programs for special education and determined Direct Instruction to be one of only seven interventions with strong evidence of effectiveness.

Perhaps because Direct Instruction programs have been so successful with students who have failed in other instructional programs, their use is commonly associated with children who are behind, who are failing, or who are at-risk for failure. And some have questioned their appropriateness for general education. However, Figures 2.11 and 2.12 provide direct evidence of the effectiveness of Direct Instruction for students with IQ scores in the middle range and those in the upper range.

Engelmann and Carnine (1989) found that typical second graders who had received two years of Direct Instruction scored an average 4.6 grade equivalent in reading on a standardized achievement test. The children's average scores in science and math were 4.0 and 3.4, respectively. Other researchers have arrived at similar findings. Tarver and Jung (1995) investigated the effects of a Direct Instruction math program (*Connecting Math Concepts*) and a discovery learning math program on the math achievement and attitudes of general education students in the primary grades. They found that, at the end of second grade, the children in the Direct Instruction program scored higher on measures of math computation and math concepts than children in the comparison group. In addition, children in the Direct Instruction program had significantly higher scores on a survey of attitudes about

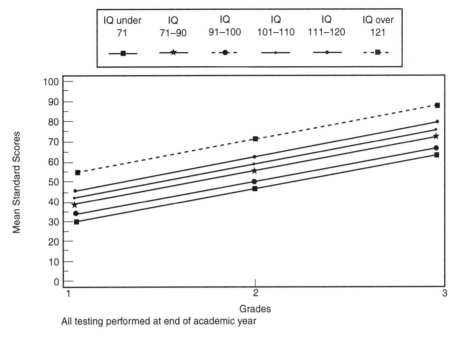

FIGURE 2.12   Results of Direct Instruction on Math as Measured by the Metropolitan Achievement Test for Students with Diverse IQ Scores. Adapted from Gersten et al. (1984).

math. Finally, Tarver and Jung reported that the Direct Instruction program was equally effective for lower- and higher-performing children who participated in the study. Other studies provide additional evidence that Direct Instruction programs accelerate the learning of high-performing students in language (Robinson & Hesse, 1981), reading (Schaefer, 1989; Sexton, 1989), and science (Vitale & Romance, 1992).

Students with Diverse Language Backgrounds

Children who have no English oral language are not ready to start in a Direct Instruction program any more than they are in any other program that delivers instruction in English. However, Direct Instruction programs are appropriate for students who have very basic English language skills (Grossen & Kelly, 1992). More generally, they are appropriate for those students who demonstrate the specific prerequisite skills necessary for success in the program based on performance on the placement test that accompanies every program. Gersten (1997) suggested that, because of the careful sequencing of prerequisite skills, controlled vocabulary, and ongoing assessment of mastery, Direct Instruction seems to provide "a workable basis for establishing a structured immersion program for limited- and non-English-speaking students" (p. 22). Gersten also suggested that the design of Direct Instruction programs "allow[s] for one of the cardinal principles of structured immersion— that new material be introduced in English but at a level understood by the children" (p. 28).

Duran (1982) showed that instructional materials developed according to Engelmann and Carnine's (1982) instructional design principles, discussed earlier in this chapter, resulted in more rapid acquisition of math concepts by Hispanic students with limited English proficiency than traditional math programs.

Gersten, Taylor, Woodward, and White (1997) described the evaluation of a fourteen-year implementation of Direct Instruction in Uvalde, Texas, whose population is 98 percent Hispanic. The authors concluded that the approach had a consistent, positive effect on the achievement of language minority students. They reported that achievement levels were at or near grade level in math, reading, and written language for more than a decade. Scores in reading comprehension and vocabulary were at the twenty-eighth to thirty-first percentiles. These scores are, according to Gersten et al., "appreciably above typical levels for low-income Hispanic students" (p. 37). Perhaps more importantly, follow-up studies conducted two and three years after students left the program indicated that the achievement effects had been maintained.

Children with Various "Learning Styles"

Many educators believe that students have different "learning styles" and that learning can be maximized by matching instruction to individual students' learning style. However, despite its common appeal and widespread acceptance, reviews of controlled research studies have consistently failed to find *any* relationship between instruction and learning styles (Snider, 1992; Stahl, 1999; Stahl & Kuhn, 1995). That is, there is no empirical evidence that matching instruction to a student's so-called learning style results in better outcomes for the student than instruction that is not "matched." The idea is simply not supported by research findings.

Attempts to prescribe specific teaching approaches based on measures of learning styles have systematically failed. However, it is clear that effective teaching does depend on a much more focused approach to adjusting instruction to the needs of individual students. Students' instructional needs are based on the skills that they currently possess. Direct Instruction places a high value on continually adjusting students' placement in programs, pace of lesson coverage, and amount of repetition on each activity based on students' performance. This approach eschews the hypothetical and elusive characteristics of learning styles and instead focuses on students' needs that are clearly seen in their performance and are directly relevant to making specific adjustments in instruction.

Students of Different Ages

When educators discuss whether a particular instructional program is appropriate to a specific child or group of children, they often use the term "developmentally appropriate." According to Church (2002), developmentally appropriate practice is an approach that involves providing children with programs that fit their age and needs. The principles of Direct Instruction are entirely consistent with this position (Kozloff & Bessellieu, 2000). Each Direct Instruction program includes extensive techniques for assessing the individual needs of children and responding to those needs.

Studies have shown Direct Instruction to be effective in teaching learners of all ages, from preschool to adult. The origins of Direct Instruction are in the Engelmann-Bereiter preschool where children demonstrated a substantial increase in language skills as well as IQ scores (Bereiter & Engelmann, 1966). Later, Weisberg (1988) reported that preschool children who received two years of Direct Instruction consistently performed above the ninety-eighth percentile on measures of reading. More recently, research has demonstrated significant improvements in language and social interactions of preschool children (Waldron-Soler et al., 2002). Chapter 3 discusses further research conducted with preschoolers.

At the other end of the age spectrum are older learners. It is not surprising that Direct Instruction is also effective in teaching older students. Effective programs are not differentially effective; they are effective for learners of all ages. Research has demonstrated that it is possible for high school students to make achievement gains of more than two years in only nine months of instruction (Campbell, 1988). (See Chapter 10 for further information on studies involving high school students in remedial reading programs.) Herr (1989) showed that even adult learners with a long history of failure and severe skill deficits can be successful when taught with Direct Instruction.

RESEARCH ON DIRECT INSTRUCTION

More than any other commercially available instructional programs, Direct Instruction is supported by research. Numerous studies provide empirical support for the specific Direct Instruction design principles and teaching practices that were discussed previously (Engelmann & Carnine, 1982; Kameenui, Simmons, Chard, & Dickson, 1997). We have already seen a number of examples of research on Direct Instruction with diverse learners. Several summaries are available providing additional research with a range of learners, in various settings, and in different content areas (e.g., Adams & Engelmann, 1996; Becker, 1978; Kameenui et al., 1997; MacIver & Kemper, 2002). In addition, current research and evaluation of Direct Instruction may be found in the *Journal of Direct Instruction*. In the following sections, we describe Project Follow Through, a large-scale research project that included Direct Instruction, independent reviews of research and evaluation literature related to Direct Instruction, and several studies of long-term outcomes from early experiences with Direct Instruction.

Project Follow Through

Project Follow Through was originally conceived as a large-scale comprehensive service program for economically disadvantaged children that would essentially extend Head Start into the primary grades. However, because the funds needed for such an ambitious undertaking were not appropriated, the United States Office of Education (now the U.S. Department of Education) decided to implement Follow Through as an educational research program. Follow Thorough provided an opportunity to compare different educational approaches in order to accumulate evidence about their effectiveness in teaching children who are economically disadvantaged. Follow Through is the largest educational experiment in history, costing close to one billion dollars, and involving nearly 100,000 children from 170 communities throughout the United States. The experimental phase of Follow Through lasted from 1968 to 1976. Follow Through continued as a service program until funding was discontinued in 1995.

Follow Through created a sort of national learning laboratory and the design, called planned variation, provided a unique opportunity to implement various instructional approaches (or models) in classrooms and then evaluate their effects (Watkins, 1997). Developers of the different approaches acted as "sponsors" of their model. The models fell into three categories: those that emphasized instruction of academic skills, those that emphasized cognitive growth, and those that stressed affective (i.e., self-esteem) development. The major models are described in Table 2.2.

The study measured three kinds of outcomes: *basic skills* (word recognition, spelling, language, and math computation), *cognitive-conceptual skills* (reading comprehension, math concepts, and problem solving) and *affective* (self-concept). Children were tested with these measures when they entered the program (in kindergarten or first grade) and at the end of each school year until they completed third grade. The evaluation data were collected and analyzed by researchers from two independent agencies. Two main analyses were conducted. One made comparisons between each model and a control group, the other made direct comparisons among the models.

In the first type of analysis, the performance of students at each Follow Through (FT) site was compared to the performance of a Non-Follow Through control group (NFT) in the same community with similar economic and social circumstances. If the difference on a given outcome favored the Follow Through group, that is, if the scores of the Follow Through group were significantly higher than the scores of the control group, the outcome was considered positive. Conversely, when the performance of the control group surpassed that of students in a particular Follow Through model, the outcome was considered negative. An index of significant outcomes (Stebbins, St. Pierre, Proper, Anderson, & Cerra , 1977) for each model is shown in Figure 2.13.

On this graph, a score of zero (represented by the vertical dividing line) would indicate that there was no difference on that measure between the Follow Through group and the control group. Bars extending to the right of the vertical line indicate positive outcomes for the Follow Through model. Bars extending to the left of the center line indicate negative outcomes for the Follow Through model (Stebbins et al., 1977).

As can be seen, the Direct Instruction model was the *only* model to demonstrate significant positive outcomes on basic skills measures, cognitive-conceptual measures, and affective measures. The majority of the other models had negative outcomes, which means that the performance of students who participated in those models was lower than that of the control group.

It is particularly important to observe that the Direct Instruction model was more effective on cognitive-conceptual measures than any other model, including those whose explicit goal was cognitive-conceptual development (Parent Education, TEEM, Cognitively-Oriented Curriculum). These findings are important because one common misunderstanding is that Direct Instruction promotes only rote learning. In fact, the children in the Direct Instruction model demonstrated higher scores on cognitive-conceptual measures (problem solving and thinking skills) than students in the control group. Without exception, the other

TABLE 2.2   Follow Through Models

MODEL	SPONSOR	DESCRIPTION
Direct Instruction	University of Oregon College of Education	The curriculum emphasis was reading, arithmetic, and language. Behavioral methods were used in conjunction with sponsor-developed teaching materials. Carefully sequenced lessons specified teacher behaviors (scripted presentation). Instruction took place in small, homogenous groups. Children's progress assessed frequently.
Behavior Analysis	University of Kansas	Primary objective was mastery of reading, writing, spelling, and math skills. A token economy was implemented and programmed instructional materials were used. 3 or 4 adults staffed classrooms. Children's progress was continuously monitored.
Parent Education	University of Florida	Curriculum objectives varied depending on the assessed needs of individual children. No particular curriculum or teaching strategies were recommended. Focus was on motivating and training parents to serve as teaching aides in the classroom and to visit the parents of children in the class and teach them how to teach their children.
Tucson Early Educational Model (TEEM)	University of Arizona	Emphasis was development of broad intellectual skills and positive attitudes toward school. Language was emphasized as the medium of skill development. Children's interests determined the curriculum.
Cognitively Oriented Curriculum	High Scope Educational Research Foundation	This developmental model was based in part on Piagetian theory. The focus was on developing children's reasoning abilities. Children scheduled their own activities. Teachers were trained to function as catalysts rather than providers of information. Science, math, and reading were emphasized.
Responsive Education	Far West Laboratory	Instruction was self-paced and self-determined. The primary objective was the development of problem-solving skills, sensory discrimination, and self-confidence. A basic assumption was that given self-esteem and an appropriate learning environment, acquisition of academic skills would follow.
Bank Street	The Bank Street College of Education	The curriculum objectives of this model included the development of positive self-image, creativity, coping skills, and the use of language to formulate and express ideas. Instructional procedures were not described.
Open Education	Education Development Center	The primary objectives were development of self-respect, imagination, and openness to change. The schedule was flexible with children initiating and terminating activities. The open classroom approach stressed a stimulating environment. The model assumed basic academic skills would be more readily acquired if they were not treated as academic exercises.
The Language Development (Bilingual Education) Approach	Southwest Educational Development Laboratory	This model stressed bilingual language development for Spanish-speaking children. Positive emphasis on the child's native language and culture was emphasized. Spanish and English were taught simultaneously; teaching procedures were not specified.

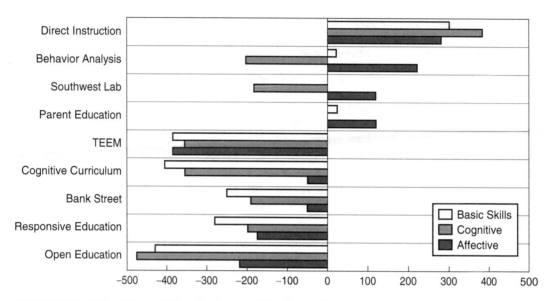

FIGURE 2.13   Follow Through Results: Index of Significant Outcomes for All Models. Adapted from Stebbins et al. (1977).

models were unable to demonstrate significant positive results on cognitive-conceptual measures.

It is also noteworthy that the Direct Instruction model produced positive results on affective (self-esteem) measures. The children in the Direct Instruction model had higher scores on this set of outcome measures than the control group. It is striking to note that those models that focused on affective development (Bank Street, Responsive Education, Open Education) had negative effects on those measures. This finding means that students who experienced these models demonstrated lower self-esteem than students in the control group. The results of the independent evaluation of Project Follow Through support the conclusion that young children who acquire the skills that enable them to be successful in school feel more positive about themselves and their school experiences.

The second type of analysis provides information about the achievement level of students in each of the models. This comparison uses results from the reading, math, spelling, and language subtests of the Metropolitan Achievement Test. Figure 2.14 shows the results of the major models in these four areas.

To fully appreciate these data, we must understand that, although the national norm is the fiftieth percentile, disadvantaged students (as a group) typically score in the twentieth percentile. Thus, the twentieth percentile can be used as a standard for measuring the benefits of receiving instruction according to the various Follow Through models (Becker, 1978). That is, if students who participated in a Follow Through model were expected to be performing at the twentieth percentile at the end of third grade without intervention, then an outcome above the twentieth percentile would be judged to be an improvement over that prediction. Conversely, if the children who participated in a particular Follow Through model

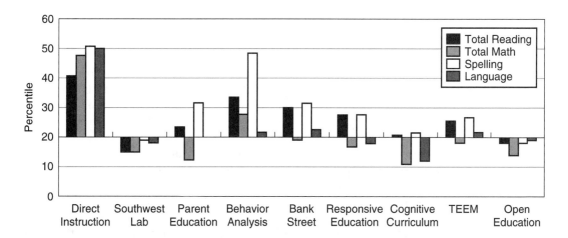

FIGURE 2.14   Comparison of Third-Grade Follow Through Children on the Metropolitan Achievement Test

scored below the twentieth percentile, we could conclude that their performance was actually worse than it would have been without participation in that Follow Though model.

We see that *only* the Direct Instruction model demonstrated substantial improvement over the twentieth percentile on all measures of academic achievement. At the end of third grade, the average of students in the Direct Instruction model was the forty-first percentile in reading and the forty-eighth percentile in math. The children in the Direct Instruction model scored, on average, at the fifty-fourth percentile in spelling and at the fiftieth percentile in language.

The purpose of the Follow Through evaluation was to study instructional methods that were intended to reduce the disparity between children who are economically disadvantaged and their peers. The Direct Instruction model was the sole model that succeeded in raising student performance to a level on a par with national norms by the end of third grade. At the end of third grade, children in the Direct Instruction model were performing at or near the national norm on each measure. These data provide clear evidence of the measurable effectiveness of Direct Instruction. The independent evaluators (Stebbins et al., 1977) summarized the results as follows: "When all Direct Instruction sites are grouped and compared with the Metropolitan Achievement Test norms, students on the average are performing at grade level in Reading, Math, and Spelling" (p. A-168). Stebbins concluded that the Direct Instruction model was generally effective in raising the achievement of Follow Through children to a level comparable with national norms.

Independent Reviews of Research on Direct Instruction

It has been argued (e.g., Allington, 2002) that, because the Follow Through evaluation was completed thirty years ago, the data are no longer relevant. However, the findings of the

Follow Through evaluation have not been contradicted by more recent research findings. In fact, recent evaluations have affirmed the findings of Project Follow Through. The American Federation of Teachers (AFT) (1998a) identified Direct Instruction as one of seven promising programs for teaching reading and language arts. The AFT report summarized the research on Direct Instruction saying, "when this program is faithfully implemented, the results are stunning" (p. 17). In a separate report the AFT (1998b) also identified Direct Instruction as one of six school reform programs. In the third report the AFT (1999) named Direct Instruction as one of five remedial reading intervention programs that are backed by strong research results.

The American Institutes of Research (AIR) was commissioned to provide an independent review of literature on twenty-four prominent schoolwide reform approaches. After an extensive review of research reports, AIR concluded that Direct Instruction was one of only three approaches that could show strong evidence of positive outcomes on student achievement (Herman et al., 1999).

In a fifth independent review, the Center for Research on the Education of Students Placed at Risk analyzed the research related to twenty-nine of the most widely implemented comprehensive school reform models. This review found that Direct Instruction was one of only three models that could be rated as having the strongest evidence of effectiveness. The review concluded that Direct Instruction had "statistically significant and positive achievement effects based on evidence from studies using comparison groups or from third-party comparison designs" (Borman, Hewes, Overman, & Brown, 2002, p. 29).

Long-Term Follow-up Research

A small, but widely publicized, research study followed up on graduates from several preschool programs when they were fifteen years old (Schweinhart, Weikert, & Larner, 1986). In this study participants were asked to provide a self-report (i.e., complete a questionnaire) about their antisocial acts. The eighteen students who had graduated from a Direct Instruction preschool program reported more antisocial acts than those who had completed other kinds of preschools. This single study has been widely cited and, in some circles, the idea that participation in Direct Instruction can have negative effects measured ten years later has been accepted as a proven fact.

Recently, however, other researchers conducted a similar study with many more participants (at least seventy-seven per group compared to only eighteen in the Schweinhart et al. study) and substantially stronger experimental methods (Mills, Cole, Jenkins, & Dale, 2002). This recent research also contacted fifteen-year-olds and used the same survey as in the earlier study. The authors found no substantial differences between graduates of a Direct Instruction program and graduates of a "child-centered" program. In fact, the very small differences that did exist actually favored the Direct Instruction program. In a careful comparison of the two studies Mills et al. concluded that the differences found in the Schweinhart study were most likely due to the fact that the Direct Instruction group in that study included a higher ratio of boys than did the other groups, and boys are known to participate in unlawful behavior at a much higher rate than girls.

REFERENCES

Adams, G. L., & Engelmann, S. (1996). *Research on Direct Instruction: 25 years beyond DISTAR.* Seattle, WA: Educational Achievement Systems.

Allington, R. (2002). *What do we know about the effects of Direct Instruction on student reading achievement?* Retrieved September 15, 2002, from http:www.educationnews.org

American Federation of Teachers. (1998a). *Seven promising schoolwide programs for raising student achievement.* Washington, DC: Author. Retrieved November 2002 from www.aft.org/edissues/downloads/seven.pdf

American Federation of Teachers. (1998b). *Six promising schoolwide reform programs.* Washington, DC: Author. Retrieved November 2002 from www.aft.org/edissues/rsa/promprog/wwschoolwidereform.htm

American Federation of Teachers. (1999). *Five promising remedial reading intervention programs.* Washington, DC: Author. Retrieved November 2002 from www.aft.org/edissues/whatworks/wwreading.htm

Becker, W. C. (1971). *An empirical basis for change in education.* Chicago: Science Research Associates.

Becker, W. C. (1978) The national evaluation of Follow Through: Behavioral-theory-based programs come out on top. *Education and Urban Society, 10*(4), 431–458.

Becker, W. C., & Carnine, D. W. (1980). Direct Instruction: An effective approach to educational intervention with disadvantaged and low performers. In B. B. Lahey & A. E. Kazdin (Eds.), *Advances in clinical child psychology* (Vol. 3, pp. 429–473). New York: Plenum.

Becker, W. C., Engelmann, S., & Thomas, D. R. (1975). *Teaching 2: Cognitive learning and instruction.* Chicago: SRA.

Bereiter, C., & Engelmann, S. (1966). *Teaching disadvantaged children in the preschool.* Englewood Cliffs, NJ: Prentice-Hall.

Borman, G. D., Hewes, G. M., Overman, L. T., & Brown, S. (2002). *Comprehensive school reform and student achievement: A meta-analysis* (Report No. 59). Baltimore, MD: Center for Research on the Education of Students Placed At Risk, Johns Hopkins University. Retrieved November 2002 from www.csos.jhu.edu

Brophy, J., & Good, T. (1986). Teacher behavior and student achievement. In M. C. Wittrock (Ed.), *Third handbook of research on teaching* (3rd ed., pp. 328–375). New York: Macmillan.

Campbell, M. L. (1988). Corrective Reading Program evaluated with secondary students in San Diego. *Direct Instruction News, 7*(4), 15–17.

Carnine, D., & Kameenui, E. (Eds.). (1992). *Higher order thinking: Designing curriculum for mainstreamed students.* Austin, TX: Pro-Ed.

Church, E. B. *Defining developmentally appropriate.* Retrieved November 18, 2002 from www.scholastic.com/smartparenting/earlylearner/childcare/pre_devappr.htm

Duran, E. (1982). Hispanic children can be taught: Or which teaching method is most effective. *Teaching and Learning Review, 2,* 4–6.

Engelmann, S. (1969). *Conceptual learning.* Sioux Falls, SD: ADAPT Press.

Engelmann, S. (1999, July). *Student-program alignment and teaching to mastery.* Paper presented at the 25th National Direct Instruction Conference, Eugene, OR.

Engelmann, S., & Becker, W. C. (1978). Systems for basic instruction: Theory and applications. In A. C. Catania and T. A. Brigham (Eds.), *Handbook of applied behavior analysis* (pp. 325–377). New York: Irvington.

Engelmann, S., & Carnine, D. W. (1989). DI outcomes with middle-class second graders. *Direct Instruction News, 8*(2), 2–5.

Engelmann S., & Carnine, D. W. (1982). *Theory of instruction: Principles and applications.* New York: Irvington.

Forness, S. R., Kavale, K. A., Blum, I. M., & Lloyd, J. W. (1997). Mega-analysis of meta-analysis: What works in special education. *Teaching Exceptional Children, 19*(6), 4–9.

Gersten, R. (1997). Structured immersion of language minority students: Results of a longitudinal evaluation. *Effective School Practices, 16*(3), 21–29.

Gersten, R., Becker, W., Heiry, T., & White, W. A. T. (1984). Entry IQ and yearly academic growth in children in Direct Instruction programs: A longitudinal study of low SES children. *Educational Evaluation and Policy Analysis, 6*(2), 109–121.

Gersten, R., Taylor, R., Woodward, J., & White, W. A. T. (1997). Structured English immersion for Hispanic students in the U.S.: Findings from the fourteen-year evaluation of the Uvalde, Texas program. *Effective School Practices, 16*(3) 30–38.

Grossen, B., & Kelly, B. (1992). Effectiveness of Direct Instruction in a third-world context. *Direct Instruction News, 9*(4), 4–11.

Herman, R., Aladjem, D., McMahon, P., Masem, E., Mulligan, I., O'Malley, A., et al. (1999). *An educators' guide to schoolwide reform.* Washington, DC: American Institutes for Research. Retrieved November 2002 from www.aasa.org/issues_and_insights/district_organization/Reform

Herr, C. (1989). Using Corrective Reading with adults. *Direct Instruction News, 8*(2), 18–21.

Kameenui, E. J., Simmons, D. C., Chard, D., & Dickson, S. (1997). Direct Instruction reading. In S. A. Stahl & D. A. Hayes (Eds.), *Instructional models in reading* (pp. 59–84). Mahwah, NJ: Erlbaum.

Kozloff, M. A., & Bessellieu, F. B. (2000). *Direct Instruction is developmentally appropriate.* Retrieved July, 9, 2002 from http://people.uncw.edu/kozolffm/didevelapp.html

MacIver, M. A., & Kemper, E. (2002). Guest editors' introduction: Research on Direct Instruction reading. *Journal of Education for Students Placed At-Risk, 7,* 107–116.

Madsen, C. H., Becker, W. C., Thomas, D. R., Koser, L., & Plager, E. (1968). An analysis of the reinforcing function of "sit down" commands. In R. K. Parker (Ed.), *Readings in educational psychology* (pp. 265–278). Boston: Allyn & Bacon.

Martella, R. C., & Nelson, J. R. (in press). Managing classroom behavior. *Journal of Direct Instruction.*

Mills, P. E., Cole, K. N., Jenkins, J. R., & Dale, P. S. (2002). Early exposure to Direct Instruction and subsequent juvenile delinquency: A prospective examination. *Exceptional Children, 69,* 85–96.

Robinson, J. W., & Hesse, K. (1981). Morphemically based spelling program's effect on spelling skills and spelling performance of seventh grade students. *Journal of Educational Research, 75,* 56–62.

Rosenshine, B. V., & Berliner, D. C. (1978). Academic engaged time. *British Journal of Teacher Education, 4,* 3–16.

Rosenshine, B., & Stevens, R. (1986). Teaching functions. In M. C. Whittrock (Ed.), *Third handbook of research on teaching* (3rd ed., pp. 376–391). New York: Macmillan.

Schaefer, E. (1989). Is DI only for low achievers? *Direct Instruction News, 8*(2), 6–9.

Schaefer, E. (2000, July). *Creating world class schools: Peak performance through Direct Instruction.* Presented at the annual conference of the Association for Direct Instruction, Eugene, OR.

Sc̶h̶w̶e̶i̶n̶h̶a̶r̶t̶, L̶.̶, W̶e̶i̶k̶a̶r̶t̶, D̶.̶, &̶ L̶a̶r̶n̶e̶r̶, M̶.̶ (1986). Consequences of three preschool curriculum models through age 15. *Early Childhood Research Quarterly,* 1̶, 15–45.

Se̶r̶w̶o̶s̶ (1̶9̶8̶9̶). Effectiveness of the DISTAR Reading I program in developing first graders' language

S̶ ... (7th ed.). Boston: Allyn & Bacon.

S̶ ... que. *Remedial and Special Education, 13,*

S̶ ... learning styles. *American Educator, 23*(3),

S̶ ... es whole language or instruction matched ... *Review, 24,* 393–404.

S̶ ... B., & Cerva, T. R. (1977). *Education as ...V-A: An evaluation of Follow Through).*

T̶ ... achievement and mathematics attitudes of ... earning mathematics curriculum or a direct ... 57.

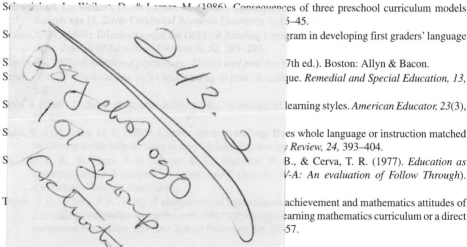

Vitale, M., & Romance, N. (1992). Using videodisc instruction in an elementary science methods course: Remediating science knowledge deficiencies and facilitating science teaching. *Journal of Research in Science Teaching, 29,* 915–928.

Vygotsky, L. S. (1997). *Educational psychology* (R. Silverman, Trans.). Boca Raton, FL: St. Lucie Press. (Original work published in 1926.)

Waldron-Soler, K. M., Martella, R. C., Marchand-Martella, N. E., Tso, M. E., Warner, D. A., & Miller, D. E. (2002). Effects of a 15-week Language for Learning implementation with children in an integrated preschool. *Journal of Direct Instruction, 2*(2), 75–86.

Watkins, C. L. (1997). *Project Follow Through: A case study of the contingencies influencing instructional practices of the educational establishment.* (Monograph). Concord, MA: Cambridge Center for Behavioral Studies.

Weisberg, P. (1988). Reading instruction for poverty level preschoolers. *Direct Instruction News, 7*(4), 25–30.

White, W. A. T. (1988). Meta-analysis of the effects of Direct Instruction in special education. *Education and Treatment of Children, 11,* 364–374.

CHAPTER THREE

LANGUAGE

KATHLEEN M. WALDRON-SOLER
Eastern Washington University

JEAN OSBORN
Educational Consultant

OBJECTIVES

After studying this chapter you should be able to:

1. describe the importance of oral language;

2. describe the importance of language instruction;

3. explain how oral language competence is related to beginning reading achievement and reading comprehension;

4. explain the impact of poorly developed oral language on social interaction skills;

5. describe the skills taught in the concept or skill groups of the *Language for Learning* and *Language for Thinking* programs;

6. describe guidelines for use of various formats included in *Language for Learning* and *Language for Thinking*;

7. describe the *Language for Learning* and *Language for Thinking* management systems;

8. describe various extensions and adaptations to the *Language for Learning* and *Language for Thinking* programs;

9. describe what the *Language for Writing* program teaches and for whom it is intended;

10. describe the research on Direct Instruction language programs.

For children to be successful in their classrooms, they must understand and use the language of learning and thinking. Teachers use oral language to present rules, directions, and demonstrations, while children are often asked to use oral language to communicate their understanding of what they are learning. Children must understand the oral language used in their teachers' directions and demonstrations as well as the written language they encounter in textbooks, workbooks, and other instructional materials.

Poorly developed oral language can have both an immediate and long-term negative impact on children. Research has repeatedly demonstrated the close relationship between oral language competence and academic achievement. Children with poorly developed oral language competence tend to have lower beginning reading achievement and lower overall academic performance. Social interactions are also closely related to oral language competence. Children with poorly developed oral language tend to have greater difficulty making friends, feel more isolated, and demonstrate a higher frequency or intensity of inappropriate behavior. Of even greater concern, the social interactions of these children often remain below average into adulthood (Aram, Ekelman, & Nation, 1984; Hall & Tomblin, 1978; King, Jones, & Lasky, 1982; Rescorla, 2002; Silva, Williams, & McGee, 1987; Weiner, 1974).

Although many children learn the language of learning and thinking through informal experiences, other children will benefit from some formal language instruction in school. The focus of this chapter is on Direct Instruction language programs that are designed to help children learn the words, concepts, and statements important to both receptive and expressive language and to written language as well. We will first discuss the importance of oral language in greater detail and then describe the concepts and skills taught in Direct Instruction language programs and how they are taught. We will also describe extensions and adaptations of the programs and ways for troubleshooting potential problems. Finally, we will present the existing research on Direct Instruction language programs.

IMPORTANCE OF ORAL LANGUAGE

Oral language competence is critical for beginning reading achievement, reading comprehension, and successful social interaction. Children with poorly developed oral language are at a disadvantage as they learn to read, and later as they are expected to comprehend text. In addition, they often interact inappropriately with other children and adults. The following sections discuss how oral language is tied to learning to read, reading comprehension, and social interactions.

Oral Language and Beginning Reading Achievement

Children with poorly developed oral language tend to have lower beginning reading achievement than children whose language development is average or above average. For example, Catts (1993) showed that children with language delays demonstrated lower reading achievement in the first and second grade than did children with average to above average oral language skills. Rescorla (2002) found that children with language delays between the ages of twenty-four and thirty-one months had lower reading skills at ages eight and nine. These findings suggest that language delay may be predictive of poor reading progress in the elementary grades.

Research on phonemic awareness provides consistent evidence that one cause of reading delay can be attributed to children's lack of skill in relating the sounds of spoken language to the letters and words of language (Baker, Kameenui, Simmons, & Stahl, 1994; Blachman, 1991). Research suggests that phonemic awareness is highly correlated to beginning reading achievement (e.g., Adams, 1990; Institute of Child Health and Human Development, 2000; Stanovich, Cunningham, & Cramer, 1984). For example, Stuart (1999) found that instruction with a phonemic-awareness language program accelerated children's acquisition of phonemic awareness and their skill in applying it to reading and writing. Children should be taught to relate the sounds of language to written words. Children who acquire phonemic awareness at least as soon as (if not before) they are formally introduced to reading and writing are at an advantage for gaining these skills.

Oral Language and Reading Comprehension

The purpose of learning to read words accurately is for children to comprehend the meanings of written words and the combinations of the words. Just as oral language serves as a foundation for learning to read the words, oral language is also important to successful reading comprehension. If children do not understand a word or group of words in oral language, then it is highly unlikely they will understand the same words in written language. Research suggests that by increasing their oral language vocabulary children will make greater gains in reading comprehension (Beck, Perfetti, & McKeown, 1982; Brett, Rothlein, & Hurley, 1996; Curtis, 1987; Recht & Leslie, 1988; Snow, Burns, & Griffin, 1998).

Beck et al. (1982) found that children who received oral vocabulary instruction prior to reading learned more word meanings and were able to process instructed words more efficiently in comprehension tasks than children who did not receive vocabulary instruction. Medo and Ryder (1993) found that both average and highly skilled children benefited from text-specific oral vocabulary instruction prior to reading expository texts. Children were able to make causal connections within the text after oral vocabulary instruction.

Oral Language Skills and Social Interaction

Oral language is not only important for learning to read and comprehend text but also greatly affects the social interactions of children. Oral language is used to accomplish social functions such as carrying on a conversation to obtain information and expressing a particular point of view. Research suggests that poorly developed oral language is related to social rejection, feelings of isolation, and inappropriate behaviors (Brinton, Fujiki, Spencer, & Robinson, 1997; Craig, 1993; Hadley & Rice, 1991).

Oral language and communication skills are related to the emergence and maintenance of social status among young children (Brinton et al., 1997; Craig, 1993; Hadley & Rice, 1991). Gertner, Rice, and Hadley (1994) asked children in a preschool classroom to nominate their most and least preferred playmates. The authors found that limited language skills are associated with lower levels of social acceptance among peers. More specifically, Gertner et al. found that general receptive language appears to be a discriminating factor that separates children who fare well in regard to social acceptance from those who do not. Children with poor communication skills were generally rated as being less popular than their linguistically typical classmates. In fact, oral language competence was found to be a better predictor of peer status than age or intelligence.

Poorly developed oral language has been associated with feelings of social isolation. Research has shown that children with specific language impairments rate themselves as feeling significantly more lonely at school than their typically developing age-matched classmates (Fujiki, Brinton, & Todd, 1996).

Inappropriate social behaviors are frequently noted in populations of children with poorly developed oral language (Aram et al., 1984; Baker & Cantwell, 1982, 1987; Silva et al., 1987; Tallal, 1988; Tallal, Townsend, Curtiss, & Wulfeck, 1991). For example, children with emotional and behavioral disorders (EBD) tend to struggle with language and reading more than any other content area (Griffith, Rogers-Adkinson, & Cusick, 1997; Hinshaw, 1992; Kaiser & Hester, 1997). In one study, approximately 54 percent of children with EBD were found to have language deficits (Benner, Nelson, & Epstein, 2002).

Long-Term Effects of Poorly Developed Oral Language

Several longitudinal studies suggest that young children with poorly developed oral language continue to experience social and academic consequences as adolescents and adults (e.g., Aram et al., 1984; Hall & Tomblin, 1978; King et al., 1982; Silva et al., 1987; Weiner, 1974). In 1971, Aram et al. (1984) administered a battery of language tasks designed to measure comprehension, formulation, and repetition of certain semantic (word meaning), syntactic (sentence structure), and phonological (sound) features as well as several nonlanguage measures to forty-seven preschool children with language disorders. Ten years later, twenty of these children were located and evaluated in four areas: (1) intelligence, (2) speech and language, (3) academic achievement, and (4) social adjustment. Overall, Aram et al. found that children who experience language disorders in the preschool years are highly likely to have long-standing language, academic, and behavioral problems. The majority of the children in the Aram et al. study scored within or below the low average range on intelligence tests. Additionally, they required special academic attention, were less socially competent, and demonstrated more behavior problems than their peers.

In a similar study, Hall and Tomblin (1978) compared the long-term effects of language disorders (difficulties with expressive and/or receptive language) compared to articulation disorders (atypical production of speech sounds). Hall and Tomblin found that over time individuals with articulation disorders performed better than individuals with language disorders. Tests of academic achievement showed a definite and persistent limitation for individuals with language disorders.

Undoubtedly, poorly developed oral language has both immediate and long-term consequences for children. Not only do children with poorly developed oral language enter school with a lower probability of learning to read at the level of their peers with typical language development, they will gain less information from text as they read. They are also at high risk for social interaction problems including social rejection, feelings of isolation, and inappropriate behaviors. Finally, these children may continue to experience the impact of poorly developed language into adolescence and adulthood.

IMPORTANCE OF ORAL LANGUAGE INSTRUCTION

Clearly, oral language impacts a child's academic and social achievement. If all children entered school with well-developed oral language, basic language instruction would be unnecessary. Although many children acquire the language of learning and instruction through informal experiences before entry into school, other children begin school with less-developed oral language. For example, children who come from homes where there is less positive adult–child contact and adults with less education tend to have lower oral language competence (Hart & Risley, 1995).

Hart and Risley (1995) followed forty-two families for two-and-one-half years to determine why children differ greatly in terms of the age when they begin to learn language and how fast they learn once they begin. The families included in the investigation represented a broad spectrum of society, including welfare, lower, middle, and upper socioeconomic status (SES) families. Hart and Risley found that neither race nor gender was a significant factor influencing a child's acquisition of language. However, the economic status of the family greatly impacted the language development of the children. Figure 3.1 shows that by the age of three children living in poverty were found to have acquired less than a third of the vocabulary of high SES families. Although children from all of the families had similar language experiences, the number of these experiences differed greatly. Hart and Risley found that in a typical hour the average child in a high SES family heard 2,153 words while a child in a low SES family heard less than a third that many, only 616 words.

For children who lack sufficient language experience, formal language instruction can give them the knowledge and vocabulary of the average child. Children with poorly developed oral language make gains in oral language and social interactions when provided language instruction (e.g., Friedman & Friedman, 1980; Gray & Ryan, 1973; Hedge, Noll,

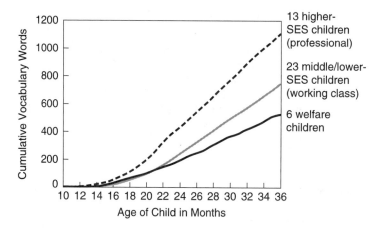

FIGURE 3.1   Average Number of Vocabulary Words Across Age for Socioeconomic Groups, from *Meaningful differences in the everyday experience of young American children,* by B. Hart & T. Risley, 1985, Baltimore, MD: Paul H. Brookes. Reprinted with permission.

& Pecora, 1979; Prelock & Panagos, 1980; Warren & Gazdag, 1990). For example, Warren and Gazdag improved language forms of three-year-old children with developmental delays during naturalistic play using a combination of two nonexplicit, immersion-based language instruction approaches, incidental teaching and mand-model techniques. Incidental teaching involves the teacher taking the opportunity to promote the best possible language use when a child wants something from the teacher. Incidental teaching procedure requires the child to initiate the interaction either verbally or nonverbally. Mand-model techniques involve the teacher initiating the interaction by "manding" a target response. For example, the teacher may ask a target probe question about an activity to which the child is attending. Other studies (e.g., Cole & Dale, 1986; Cole, Dale, & Mills, 1991; Cole, Dale, Mills, & Jenkins, 1993; Dale & Cole, 1988) used a more explicit approach using Direct Instruction language programs (i.e., *DISTAR Language II and III*) with young children with developmental disabilities and also children without developmental disabilities.

OVERVIEW OF DIRECT INSTRUCTION LANGUAGE PROGRAMS

DISTAR Language I and II have been revised, and are now titled *Language for Learning* and *Language for Thinking. DISTAR Language III* is also currently being revised and is titled *Language for Writing,* published in 2003. In addition a fourth program, *Español to English,* has been developed. The *Language for Learning* and *Language for Thinking* programs are the focus of this chapter, although *Español to English* and *Language for Writing* will also be discussed.

Language for Learning

The *Language for Learning* curriculum is the current, accelerated revision of the *DISTAR Language I* program. It is intended for five and six year olds in kindergarten and first grade who have less than adequate language knowledge and skill for their age; four-year-old children in preschool programs; primary-age children in bilingual and ESL programs; primary-age children in Title 1 and Special Education programs; and children in speech correction and language classes.

The *Language for Learning* curriculum differs from the *DISTAR Language I* program in several ways. First, *Language for Learning* is easier to use. The presentation books are larger, the type is bigger and easier to read, and the illustrations are bigger and in color. Second, the lesson events are reorganized. A lesson now begins with exercises that do not involve illustrations. Once these are complete, the teacher and children move to exercises with illustrations. The children then do workbook activities. At the end of a lesson the teacher and children engage in reading stories and poems that go with the lesson. Third, the illustrated exercises have been redesigned so that they are easier to use. The directions for teachers are now on the left and the illustrations are to the right of the presentation book. Finally, the presentation of concepts and skills is accelerated so children learn more content.

Regardless of the age or grade of the children, all children instructed with *Language for Learning* must possess several prerequisite language behaviors. First, they must be able to imitate a word or phrase spoken by an adult (e.g., they should be able to repeat "a cat" or "under the table"). Second, they must be able to answer questions such as, "What is this?" or "What are you doing?" or they must be able to learn to do so quickly. Third, they must be able to answer simple yes/no questions such as, "Are you standing?" or "Is this a chair?" Fourth, they must be able to point to and label common objects such as "a door," and complete simple actions such as "sitting." Finally, children must be able to describe pictures of objects and actions using the same words that are used to name actual objects and actions. Children that do not demonstrate these language behaviors should be taught them before beginning the program (Osborn & Becker, 1980).

Language for Thinking

Language for Thinking is intended for children who are older or have higher skill levels than children placed in *Language for Learning.* It is intended for children who have completed, or almost completed *Language for Learning,* and first and second graders who have less than adequate language knowledge and skill and are having trouble comprehending what they read. The program is also used with older children who are in bilingual and ESL programs, primary school children who are in Title I or special education programs, and older children in speech correction and language classes.

    Language for Thinking is the current revision of *DISTAR Language II.* The program extends teaching of the language of learning and instruction to more advanced concepts, and differs from *DISTAR Language II* in many ways. First, the initial ten lessons of the program are a review of some of the most important concepts from *Language for Learning.* Second, the program includes new content (e.g., making inferences, retelling accounts, reporting on pictures, determining meanings of sentences, and practicing language conventions). Other changes are similar to the changes made in *Language for Learning. Language for Thinking* is easier to use, the lessons are reorganized, and the introduction of the concepts and skills is accelerated.

Commonalties between *Language for Learning* and *Language for Thinking*

Both *Language for Learning* and *Language for Thinking* assume that language can be systematically taught by limiting the scope of the content, by organizing the content into teachable exercises, and by carefully sequencing the exercises into a daily program. Lessons are scripted. Teachers know what to do and say as well as what the children are to do and say. The lessons are comprised of exercises constructed as elements of sequences in which related sets of concepts are presented. Sequences of instruction, for example, include prepositions (e.g., *on/over*), identity statements (e.g., identify objects with two-word responses [e.g., *a cat*] and then "saying the whole thing" [e.g., *This is a cat*]), opposites (e.g., hot and cold), and *if–then* reasoning (e.g., If it is made to take you places, it is a vehicle). Each lesson includes eight to ten exercises. Children work on several instructional sequences during one lesson. Within sequences, exercises progress from those in which there is a lot of teacher demonstration to those in which the children respond to minimal teacher cues.

    Previously taught sequences are often used as a component of more advanced sequences that appear later in the programs. The use of information that has been taught in previous sequences serves two functions: (1) it permits children to learn new, more complex concepts more quickly, and (2) it provides practice and promotes generalization of basic language concepts to a broader spectrum of situations. The initial lessons in the programs involve the children spending much of their time in oral interaction with the teacher. As the children progress through the programs, they spend more time engaged in less teacher-directed activities in their workbooks.

Language for Learning and *Language for Thinking* are designed for daily instruction. Teachers present demonstrations and ask questions. The children respond orally or by performing actions and then describing their actions. Most of the time, the children respond in unison. Unison responding provides children with practice and instant, immediate feedback to teachers about what the children are learning. Correct responses are praised. Errors are corrected immediately. The children's responses dictate the rate at which teachers can proceed through the lesson. Lessons typically last for twenty to forty minutes.

Both programs maximize practice through several instructional strategies. First, responses from the children are evoked as a part of the presentation. For example, the teacher says, "Everyone, *show me* the frog that jumped," and not *"Look at* the frog that jumped." Second, unison responding increases the opportunities for children to respond. All children are asked to respond to a question or direction as opposed to calling on only one child at a time to respond. Children are given individual turns only after demonstrating that they have acquired the new information through group responses. Finally, fast pacing provides motivation and prevents boredom.

Language for Learning and *Language for Thinking* should be implemented with small, instructional groups of children. Small groups are particularly important when working with children most in need of language instruction. Teachers can hear individual responses from children more accurately and can engage the children in the practice necessary to achieve the mastery of the program's content.

Language for Writing

The revised *DISTAR Language III* program is called *Language for Writing*. The new program is for second- through fifth-grade students who have been through *Language for Learning* and *Language for Thinking*. The *Language for Writing* program can also be used with students who have not been in the first two programs if their scores on the placement test indicate they are ready for the third-level program. Students placed in the program should be reading and writing at an end of second-grade or beginning of third-grade level, and have adequate knowledge of basic spoken school English. In addition, the program can be used with older students who possess the skills just described and who pass the placement test.

Language for Writing is particularly suitable for students who will benefit from careful writing instruction. The exercises in the program focus on the concepts and skills important to clear writing: grammar (including parts of speech), sentence constructions (statements, questions, commands), mechanics (capitalization and punctuation rules), and critical thinking (including deductions, definitions, and analogies), as well as on writing itself. Every lesson includes a teacher-directed writing lesson. The writing exercises in the first half of the program center on the writing of narrative prose. As the program progresses, the writing exercises center on the writing of expository prose.

The program materials consist of a teacher-presentation book that contains the teacher-directed exercises for each of the program's lessons. Students work in workbooks and a textbook. Teachers and students work together to do exercises in the textbooks and the workbooks. Students then work independently on the review exercises that appear in their textbooks and workbooks, and on the completion of their writing assignments. In addition to a teacher's guide and answer book, the program also provides a progress monitoring system that includes the placement test and program-based assessments that are to be given at the completion of every ten lessons.

CONTENT ANALYSIS AND FORMAT FEATURES

The content of each Direct Instruction language program is broken into several skill or concept groups. Each group is then organized into several tracks, formats, and exercises. A format serves as one step in the programming of a concept or skill. It is a pattern of teaching steps repeated in a number of successive lessons, but with different examples.

For example, here is a typical format from the *Language for Learning* program that provides a pattern for a series of exercises:

IDENTITY STATEMENTS

(Point to a picture of an object in the teacher-presentation book.) This is a (name of object). What is this? (Touch.) The children respond.

Say the whole thing. (Touch). Children respond with a complete sentence.

By putting different objects into the format, or pattern, several tasks are created:

1. (Point to a fish) What is this? (Touch) *A fish.*
   Say the whole thing. (Touch) *This is a fish.*
2. (Point to a sandwich) What is this? (Touch) *A sandwich.*
   Say the whole thing. (Touch) *This is a sandwich.*
3. (Point to a ruler) What is this? (Touch) *A ruler.*
   Say the whole thing. (Touch) *This is a ruler.*

Children master a skill, such as saying complete sentences, by practicing it with many different examples. Formats also make it easier for teachers to implement the program.

The following sections provide descriptions of each skill or concept group and examples of important formats found in each of these skill or concept groups of the *Language for Learning* and *Language for Thinking* programs.

Language for Learning

The content of *Language for Learning* is organized into six groups: (1) actions, (2) descriptions of objects, (3) information and background knowledge, (4) instructional words and problem-solving concepts, (5) classification, and (6) problem-solving strategies and applications.

Each of the groups includes several tracks that extend through a number of lessons (see Table 3.1). The following section briefly describes concept and skill groups for the program and the tracks within each group.

TABLE 3.1 *Language for Learning* **Concept or Skill Groups and Tracks**

CONCEPT OR SKILL GROUP	TRACKS
Actions	Beginning Actions
	Actions-Parts of the Body
	Actions-Pictures
	Actions-Pronouns
	Tense
	Tense-Pictures
	Actions-Review
Description of Objects	Object Identification
	Identity Statements
	Common Objects
	Missing Objects
	Opposites
	Plurals
	Comparatives
Information and Background Knowledge	Names
	School Information
	Days of the Week
	Months of the Year
	Seasons
	Part/Whole
	Materials
	Common Information
	Locations
Instructional Words and Problem-Solving Concepts	Spatial and Temporal Relations
	Prepositions
	And-Actions
	Same-Different
	Some, All, None
	Actions-Or
	Before/After
	If-Then Rules
	Where, Who, When, What

CLASSIFICATION	CLASSIFICATION
Problem-Solving Strategies and Applications	Review
	Concept Applications
	Absurdities

Actions (Lessons 1–150).   Action exercises are included at the beginning of each *Language for Learning* lesson. Action exercises are intended to provide a clear demonstration of language concepts (e.g., changing from present-tense verbs to past-tense verbs) and word meanings (e.g., naming the parts of the body) that are used in everyday activities. These language concepts and word meanings are taught by asking children to perform and describe various actions. Performing and describing actions allows children to practice and review language concepts in a fun and enjoyable manner. The basic concepts and word meanings taught in the early action exercises establish a foundation for teaching more difficult language-usage conventions through actions, such as those associated with pronouns and tenses.

In the early lessons of the program, the exercises focus on specific actions such as "stand up" and "sit down." The children perform these simple actions in response to directions from the teacher (e.g., the children stand up and sit down), and label what they are doing (e.g., the children say, "standing up" and "sitting down"). They also describe people and animals performing actions in illustrations in the teacher-presentation book (e.g., the children look at a picture of a dog sitting and in response to the question, "What is the dog doing?" say, "Sitting."). The children learn the names of parts of the body in many of the beginning action exercises. The children either perform an action involving a part of the body (e.g., touching their chin) and label their action (the children say, "touching my chin") or label the action of the teacher touching a body part (e.g., the teacher touches his chin and the children say, "touching your chin" in response to "What am I doing?") In later lessons, the children learn to say the full statements that describe an action (e.g., the children say, "You are touching your chin").

As children progress through the basic actions, the children describe their actions and pictures of actions in present tense (e.g., the children say, "The pencil **is** on the table"), past tense (e.g., the children say, "The pencil **was** on the table"), and future tense (e.g., the children say, "The pencil **will be** on the table"). Review action exercises are provided throughout the lessons of the program as opportunities for the children to practice what they are learning.

Action exercises are also used in the development of concepts in the tracks of other groups. Action exercises are used as a part of the introductory instruction on prepositions, spatial and temporal relations, plurals, and/or, some/all/none, same/different, before/after, and *if–then* rules. For example, when teaching *and,* the children are asked to "Stand up **and** touch your head." Figure 3.2 represents a typical format for action exercises.

The following guidelines should be followed when teaching this type of format:

1. Keep a brisk pace by stating the directions quickly.
2. Follow each instruction with a precise hand-drop signal.
3. In Step a, after asking the question and giving the signal, wait only long enough for the children to do the action. Then immediately move on to the next instruction.
4. Emphasize the critical words in the instructions (e.g., touch your **nose**).
5. Make sure the children are responding on signal. The children should not respond to a question or instruction until the signal is given.
6. If the children do not do the actions, physically help them do the actions.
7. Make sure children are touching the correct body part.
8. In Part 3, lead the children through the statement as many times as necessary so that at Steps e and f the children can make the statement without the teacher's help.

LESSON 8—EXERCISE 1 Actions—Statements	

1. Get ready to do some actions. Watch my hand. Remember to wait for the signal.
  a. Everybody, stand up. (Signal, Wait.)
    Everbody, touch your nose. (Signal, Wait.)
    Everbody, put your hand down. (Signal.)
    Everbody, sit down. (Signal.)
    (Repeat step a until all children's responses are firm.)
  b. Everybody, stand up. (Signal, Wait.)
    What are you doing? (Signal.) *Standing up.*
  c. Everybody, touch your nose. (Signal, Wait.)
    What are you doing? (Signal.) *Touching my nose.*
    Put your hand down. (Signal.)
  d. Everybody, sit down. (Signal, Wait.)
    What are you doing? (Signal.) *Sitting down.*
2. (Repeat part 1 until all children's responses are firm.)
3. Now let's try this.
  a. Everybody, stand up. (Signal.)
    What are you doing? (Signal.) *Standing up.*
  b. Watch me. (You stand up.)
    I'll say the whole thing. I am standing up.
  c. Let's all say the whole thing. (Signal. Respond with the children.) I am standing up.
  d. Again. (Repeat the sentence with the children until they can say it with you.)
  e. Your turn. Say the whole thing. (Signal. Do not respond with the children.) *I am standing up.*
  f. Again. Say the whole thing. (Signal.)
    I am standing up.
	(Repeat until all children can say the sentence.)
	  g. Everybody, sit down.
	4. Let's go a little faster.
	  a. Everybody, stand up. (Signal.)
	    What are you doing? (Signal.) *Standing up.* •
	  b. Say the whole thing. (Signal.)
	    I am standing up.
	    (Repeat until all children can make the statement.)
	    Sit down.
	5. (Repeat part 4 until all children's responses are firm.)
	
	Individual Turns
	(Repeat part 4, calling on different children for each step.)
	
	Corrections
	EXERCISE 1
	• **Error**
	  (Children say the entire sentence.)
	Correction
	1. Stop. My turn. Listen. What are you doing? Standing up.
	2. Your turn. What are you doing? (Signal.) *Standing up.*
	3. Now say the whole thing. (Signal.) *I am standing up.*
	4. (Repeat steps 2 and 3 until all children can answer correctly.)
	5. (Repeat part 4.)

FIGURE 3.2 *Language for Learning,* **Lesson 8, Exercise 1. Reprinted with permission of the McGraw-Hill Companies.**

    9. In Part 3, the children should be doing the action as they are describing what they are doing.

    Descriptions of Objects (Lessons 1–150). The exercises in the Descriptions of Objects group are intended to teach children to respond to questions and to make statements about objects that are essential to the language of instruction. Children begin by learning to name objects that are commonly found in the classroom (e.g., a door, a chalkboard, a cupboard). Beginning exercises teach children to give the name of an object when asked, "What is it?" and to describe objects in complete sentences (e.g., the children say, "This is a cup."). In

---

EXERCISE 7   Identity Statements

1. We're going to talk about a table and a book.
   a. (Point to the table.) Everybody, what is this?
      (Touch.) *A table.*
      Yes, a table.
   b. I can say the whole thing. Listen. This is a
      table. Say the whole thing with me.
      (Touch. Respond with the children.)
      This is a table.
   c. Again. (Touch. Respond with the children.)
      This is a table.
      (Repeat until all children can make the
      statement with you.)
   d. Your turn. Say the whole thing. (Touch.
      Do not respond with the children.)
      This is a table.
   e. Again. (Touch. Do not respond with the
      children.) *This is a table.*
      (Repeat until all children can make the
      statement.)

2. Let's talk some more about these things.
   a. (Point to the book.) Everybody, what is
      this? (Touch.) *A book.*
      Yes, a book.
   b. I can say the whole thing. Listen. This is a
      book. Say the whole thing with me.
      (Touch. Respond with the children.)
      This is a book.
   c. Again. (Touch. Respond with the children.)
      This is a book.

   (Repeat until all children can make the
   statement with you.)
   d. Your turn. Say the whole thing. (Touch. Do
      not respond with the children.) *This is a
      book.*
   e. Again. (Touch. Do not respond with the
      children.) *This is a book.*
      (Repeat until all children can make the
      statement.)

FIGURE 3.3 *Language for Learning,* **Lesson 6, Exercise 7. Reprinted with permission of the McGraw-Hill Companies.**

later exercises children respond to yes/no questions (e.g., "Is this a dog?"), produce *not* statements for questions that are answered *no* (e.g., "This is not a dog"), and name common objects in the classroom and how to make statements about those objects (e.g., window, door, chalkboard). Figure 3.3 demonstrates aspects of the formats used for the Object Identification and Identity Statements tracks.

The following guidelines should be followed when teaching this type of format:

1. Point to the letter under the picture before asking the question.
2. Pause for one second before touching the letter of the picture.
3. Look at the picture when touching the letter.
4. Quickly look back at the children when they begin to respond.

5. Continue to touch the picture until the children finish responding.
6. Move rapidly from picture to picture.
7. When leading a response, as in Part 1, Step b, be sure to lead the children at the same rate you used to model the statement.
8. Lead the children through the statement until they are firm at saying each word and saying the words at an appropriate rate.
9. In Part 1, Step d, the children respond on their own. If they do not respond correctly after seven trials, move to another exercise and return to the identification exercise later.

Information and Background Knowledge (Lessons 1–150). Exercises included in the Information and Background Knowledge skill group are intended to teach children the basic information that relates to school routines (e.g., their names, the names of their teacher and school, the name of the city or county where they live, the days of the week, the months, and the seasons of the year). Children are also taught about the relationship between common objects and their parts (e.g., a table has a top and legs) and to identify the materials of which common objects are made (e.g., wood, plastic, etc.). Additionally, children learn some basic information about occupations, natural phenomena, and locations. Figure 3.4 shows a typical format for Information and Background Knowledge exercises.

The following guidelines should be followed when teaching this type of format:

1. Model saying the days of the week with a rhythm to make it sound interesting. For example, the teacher might put strong emphasis on every other word, *Sunday,* **Monday,** *Tuesday,* **Wednesday,** *Thursday,* **Friday,** *Saturday.*
2. If the children already know the days of the week, do these exercises quickly.

EXERCISE 2   Information—Days of the Week

Let's do the days of the week.
a. Everybody, how many days are there in a week? (Signal.) *Seven.*
b. My turn. I'll say the days of the week. Listen. Sunday, Monday, Tuesday, Wednesday, Thursday, Friday, Saturday. I said the days of the week.
c. Listen. Sunday, Monday, Tuesday, Wednesday, Thursday, Friday, Saturday. Say all the days of the week with me. (Signal. Respond with the children.) Sunday, Monday, Tuesday, Wednesday, Friday, Saturday.
d. Again. (Signal. Respond with the children.) Sunday, Monday, Tuesday, Wednesday, Thursday, Friday, Saturday.
e. All by yourselves. Say the days of the week. (Signal. Do not respond with children.) *Sunday, Monday, Tuesday, Wednesday, Thursday, Friday, Saturday.*
f. (Repeat step e until all children can say the days.)

Individual Turns
(Repeat step e, calling on different children.)

FIGURE 3.4 *Language for Learning,* **Lesson 41, Exercise 2. Reprinted with permission of the McGraw-Hill Companies..**

3. All children should say new days of the week by the end of the exercise in which they are introduced. Some children will need additional practice to achieve this goal. If many repetitions are necessary, have the children practice at other times of the school day.

Instructional Words and Problem-Solving Concepts (Lessons 1–150). Children learn the meanings and uses of a number of words and concepts important to following instructions, solving logical problems, and answering questions in the Instructional Words and Problem-Solving Concepts group. Initially, most of the concepts are introduced in action exercises. For example, the concept of first/next is introduced by asking children to do an action, such as clap, *first* and then do another action, such as smile, *next.* Later, concepts appear in picture exercises, in track reviews, and in applications and absurdity exercises. Additional practice of these concepts is provided through workbook activities. Figure 3.5 demonstrates a common teaching pattern used in the Instructional Words and Problem-Solving Concepts group of tracks.

The following guidelines should be followed when teaching this type of format:

1. Keep a brisk pace during the exercise by quickly saying each statement or instruction.
2. Many of these exercises require the teacher to manipulate objects or do various actions to demonstrate the concepts. Therefore, study these exercises so that they can be presented without looking at the teacher-presentation book.
3. Emphasize the concepts being taught (e.g., Is the eraser **on** the chair?).

EXERCISE 4   Prepositions—On (Demonstration)

[Note: You will need an eraser and a chair for this exercise.]

1. We're going to talk about an eraser and a chair.
   a. (Hold up an eraser.) What is this? (Signal.)
      An eraser.
      (Point to the chair.) What is this? (Signal.)
      A chair.
   b. Your turn. Tell me if I hold the eraser on the chair.
      (Hold the eraser on the seat of the chair.)
      Is the eraser on the chair? (Signal.) *Yes.*
      (Hold the eraser over the chair.) Is the eraser on the chair? (Signal.) *No.*
      (Hold the eraser next to the chair.) Is the eraser on the chair? (Signal.) *No.*
      (Hold the eraser on the seat of the chair.)
      Is the eraser on the chair? (Signal.) *Yes.*
      (Hold the eraser over the chair.) Is the eraser on the chair? (Signal.) *No.*

2. Now, we're going to say the whole thing. Watch.
   a. (Put the eraser on the chair.) Is the eraser on the chair? (Signal.) *Yes.*
      Say the whole thing with me. (Point to each object and respond with the children.) The eraser is on the chair.
   b. All by yourselves. Say the whole thing about where the eraser is. (Signal. Do not respond with the children.) *The eraser is on the chair.* Again.
3. (Repeat part 2 until all children can make the statement.)

Individual Turns
(Repeat part 2, calling on different children for each step.)

FIGURE 3.5 *Language for Learning,* **Lesson 29, Exercise 4. Reprinted with permission of the McGraw-Hill Companies.**

Classification (Lessons 51–136). The *Language for Learning* program teaches nine classification concepts (vehicles, food, containers, clothing, animals, buildings, plants, tools, and furniture). In addition to learning the labels for a number of new objects, the children are taught that some objects (e.g., pants, shirts, hats) share a particular set of features, thus making them members of a particular class of objects (e.g., clothing). The children learn the names of a number of objects that are found in each class, and statements for describing the objects and the classes to which they belong (e.g., "This piece of clothing is a shirt"). They are introduced to the concept of rules. In classification exercises, the word *rule* refers to a statement that is true of all the examples covered by the rule. For example, the rule for clothing is *if you can wear it, it is clothing.* Figure 3.6 represents the typical format used to teach children about various classes.

EXERCISE 7 Classification

1. We're going to talk about vehicles.
   (Point to a.) This is a vehicle.
   (Point to b.) This is a vehicle.
   (Point to c.) This is not a vehicle.
   (Point to d.) This is not a vehicle.
   (Point to e.) This is a vehicle.
   (Point to f.) This is not a vehicle.

2. Get ready to tell me which objects are vehicles.
   (Point to each object and ask:)
   Is this a vehicle? •
   (The children are to answer *yes* or *no.*)

3. Now let's look at some more vehicles. (Turn the page quickly.)

Corrections
EXERCISE 7
• Error
  (Children name the object.)
  Correction
  1. You're right. It is a (name of object).
     But it is also a vehicle or
     But it is not a vehicle.
  2. (Repeat parts 1 and 2.)

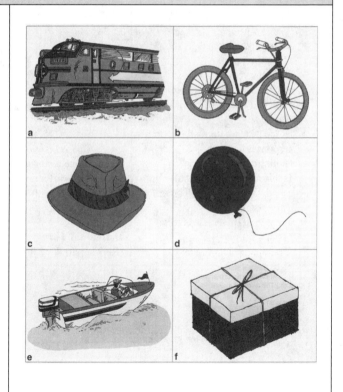

FIGURE 3.6 *Language for Learning,* Lesson 52, Exercise 7. Reprinted with permission of the McGraw-Hill Companies.

EXERCISE 7   Classification (continued)

4. Let's talk about these pictures.
   a. (Point to a.)
      Is this a vehicle? (Touch.) *Yes.*
      Say the whole thing. (Touch.)
      This is a vehicle.
   • What kind of vehicle is this?
      (Touch.) *A train.*
      Yes, this vehicle is a train.
      Say the whole thing about this
      vehicle. (Touch.) *This vehicle
      is a train.*
   • (Repeat step a until all children's
      responses are firm.)
   b. (Point to b.)
      Is this a vehicle? (Touch.) *Yes.*
      Say the whole thing. (Touch.)
      This is a vehicle.
   • What kind of vehicle is this?
      (Touch.) *A boat.*
      Yes, this vehicle is a boat.
      Say the whole thing about this
      vehicle. (Touch.) *This vehicle
      is a boat.*
   • (Repeat step b until all children's
      responses are firm.)
   c. (Point to c.)
      Is this a vehicle? (Touch.) *Yes.*
      Say the whole thing. (Touch.)
      This is a vehicle.
   ù What kind of vehicle is this?
      (Touch.) *A bike.*
      Yes, this vehicle is a bike.

      Say the whole thing about this vehicle. (Touch.)
      This vehicle is a bike.
   ù (Repeat step c until all children's responses are firm.)
5. (Call on different children to answer the question.)
   ù These are all vehicles. Which vehicle would you like
      to be on?

Individual Turns
(Repeat part 4, calling on different children for each step.)

FIGURE 3.6 (continued)

The following guidelines should be followed when teaching this type of format:

1. Emphasize the class name (e.g., **vehicle**) and the word **not** when talking about objects
   that are **not** included in the class.
2. When checking for understanding, ask questions such as *Is this a vehicle?* quickly.
3. In Part 4, emphasize the words **this vehicle** to reduce the likelihood that children will
   respond with *This is a vehicle,* instead of *This vehicle is a train.*

Problem-Solving Strategies and Applications (Lessons 38–149).   The problem-solving
strategies and applications group provides exercises that allow children to use concepts they

have been taught in other tracks of the program in new contexts. Specifically, children learn new uses and new statements for the concepts. In the problem-solving strategies and applications group a rule is a statement that is used to solve a problem. These exercises require the children to apply a rule (e.g., "The big frog will jump") to solve a problem presented in an illustration (e.g., the children look at an illustration of various sized frogs and use the description of a specific frog to predict which frog will be jumping in the next illustration). Exercises in the absurdity track expand on the concept applications track and ask children to use what they have learned to tell what is wrong with an illustration and why it is wrong. Figure 3.7 shows an example of a typical format used in the Problem-Solving Strategies and Applications group of tracks.

EXERCISE 6   Concept Application

1. You're going to figure out a problem about a goat and some flowers.
   The goat will jump over only some of these flowers. Here's the rule: The goat will jump over the flowers with leaves.
   Everybody, say the rule. (Signal.) *The goat will jump over the flowers with leaves.*
   Again. (Signal.) *The goat will jump over the flowers with leaves.*
   (Repeat until all children can say the rule.)
2. Now answer these questions.
   a. (Point to a.) Do these flowers have leaves? (Touch.) *Yes.*
      So what do you know about these flowers?
      (Touch.) *The goat will jump over these flowers.*
   b. (Point to b.) Do these flowers have leaves? (Touch.) *No.*
      So what do you know about these flowers?
      (Touch.) *The goat won't jump over these flowers.*
3. Everybody, what's the rule? (Signal.) *The goat will jump over the flowers with leaves.*

a. (Point to a.) Do these flowers have leaves? (Touch.) *Yes.*
   So what do you know about these flowers?
   (Touch.) *The goat will jump over these flowers.*
b. (Point to b.) Do these flowers have leaves? (Touch.) *No.*
   So what do you know about these flowers?
   (Touch.) *The goat will not jump over these flowers.*
4. (Call on two children.)
   • Show me the flowers that the goat will jump over. (Wait.)
     Let's see if you're right. (Turn the page quickly.)

FIGURE 3.7 *Language for Learning,* **Lesson 75, Exercise 6. Reprinted with permission of the McGraw-Hill Companies.**

EXERCISE 6   Concept Application (continued)

5. Answer these questions.
    a. (Point to a.) Do these flowers
        have leaves? (Touch.) *Yes.*
        What is the goat doing? (Touch.)
        Jumping over these flowers.
        Say the whole thing about what
        the goat is doing. (Touch.) *The
        goat is jumping over these
        flowers.*
    b. (Point to b.) Do these flowers
        have leaves? (Touch.) *No.*
        What is jumping over these
        flowers? (Touch.) *A frog.*
        Say the whole thing about what
        the frog is doing. (Touch.)
        *The frog is jumping over these
        flowers.*
    c. (Repeat part 5 until all children's
        responses are firm.)
6. (Call on different children.)
    • Does the goat look happy?
    • Does the frog look happy?
    • Would you like to jump over a
       flower?
    • Would you like to jump over a
       frog?

Individual Turns
(Repeat part 5, calling on different children for each step.)

The following guidelines should be followed when teaching this type of format:

1. The exercises are divided into parts that are indicated by numbers. Each part should
    be presented as a unit.
2. In Part 4, a child from the group should be asked to show the teacher the flowers the
    goat will jump over. If the child selects the correct bunch of flowers, quickly turn the
    page.
3. Be sure to ask the questions in Part 6. The children will use language in a freer and
    more personal manner.

Language for Thinking

Language for Thinking is also organized into six groups: (1) information and background
knowledge, (2) reasoning and critical thinking, (3) vocabulary development, (4) observing
and describing, (5) comprehension concepts, and (6) interpreting graphic displays. The first

ten lessons of *Language for Thinking* are a review of many of the concepts and skills taught in *Language for Learning.*

Each of the groups includes several tracks that extend through a number of lessons (see Table 3.2). The following section briefly describes concept and skill groups for the program and the tracks within each group.

TABLE 3.2 *Language for Thinking* **Concept or Skill Groups and Tracks**

CONCEPT OR SKILL GROUP	TRACKS
Review Lessons	
Information and Background Knowledge	Part/Whole Calendar Locations
Reasoning and Critical Thinking	Classificaiton Absurdity If/Then Only Statements Analogies Same/Different
Vocabulary Department	Opposites Synonyms Definitions Verb Tense Usage: Double Negatives Contractions Superlatives Homonyms
Observing and Describing	Actions Description Sequence Comparing Reporting on Pictures
Comprehension Concepts	Who, What, Where, When, Why, How Questioning Skills Can Do Retelling Inferences
Interpreting Graphic Displays	From/To Left/Right Map Reading

Information and Background Knowledge (Lessons 11–150). In this group of tracks, children learn the names of objects and their parts. In addition, they learn basic calendar information and the names of a number of locations important to children's general knowledge (e.g., the beach, the park).

The three tracks included in the Information and Background Knowledge group extend the instruction provided in the same group for *Language for Learning;* for example, in that program the children are taught the names of the days of the week, the months, and the seasons. In *Language for Thinking* these concepts are also taught along with instruction on the meanings of *yesterday, today, tomorrow, one week from today, today's date,* and *tomorrow's date.* Figure 3.8 provides an example of a format from this group.

The following guidelines should be followed when teaching this type of format:

1. Use a large calendar for this type of exercise.
2. Practice the script for these exercises before teaching the children. This will allow you to attend to the calendar and not the script.
3. When stating the date, say, for example, *Today is Tuesday, June 18.*
4. You may add the year if you wish.

EXERCISE 2 Calendar

1. Look at the calendar.
   a. (Present calendar. Point to month.)
      What month is it now? (Signal.)
   b. The calendar shows day of the week.
   • (Point to Sunday column.) What day of the week does the first column show? (Signal.) *Sunday.*
   • (Point to Monday column.) What day does the next column show? (Signal.) *Monday.*
   • (Point to Tuesday column.) What day does the next column show? (Signal.) *Tuesday.*
2. I'll touch columns. You tell me the day of the week for the number.
   • (Touch a number for Sunday.) What day? (Signal.) *Sunday.*
      (Touch another number for Sunday.) What day? (Signal.) *Sunday.*
   • (Touch a number for Monday.) What day? (Signal.) *Monday.*
      (Touch another number for Monday.) What day? (Signal.) *Monday.*

   • (Touch a number for Tuesday.) What day? (Signal.) *Tuesday.*
   • (Touch a number for Monday.) What day? (Signal.) *Monday.*
   • (Touch a number for Tuesday.) What day? (Signal.) *Tuesday.*
   • (Touch a number for Wednesday.) What day? (Signal.) *Wednesday.*
   • (Touch a number for Thursday.) What day? (Signal.) *Thursday.*
   • (Touch a number for Friday.) What day? (Signal.) *Friday.*
   • (Touch a number for Saturday.) What day? (Signal.) *Saturday.*
      (Repeat part 2 until firm.)
3. I'll show you the number for today.
   (Touch the number. Say date: day, month, number; e.g.: Today is Thursday, September 16th.)
   • Your turn. Say the date. (Signal.)
      (Repeat part 3 until firm.)

FIGURE 3.8 *Language for Thinking,* **Lesson 12, Exercise 2. Reprinted with permission of the McGraw-Hill Companies.**

EXERCISE 6 True/False	
1. I'm going to make statements about a box. Say **yes** if I make a statement that is right. Say **no** if I make a statement that is not right. • What are you going to say if I make a statement that is right? (Signal.) *Yes.* • What are you going to say if I make a statement that is not right? (Signal.) *No.* 2. Listen to these statements. • Listen. A box can hold things. Is that right? (Signal.) *Yes.* • Listen. A box has wheels. Is that right? (Signal.) *No.* • Listen. A box grows in the ground. Is that right? (Signal.) *No.* • Listen. A box has sides and a bottom. Is that right? (Signal.) *Yes.* • Listen. A box has wings. Is that right? (Signal.) *No.* (Repeat part 2 until firm.)	3. Listen again. This time say **true** if I make a statement that is right. Say **false** if I make a statement that is not right. • What are you going to say if I make a statement that is right? (Signal.) *True.* • What are you going to say if I make a statement that is not right? (Signal.) *False.* 4. Listen to these statements. • Listen. A box can hold things. Is that true or false? (Signal.) *True.* • Listen. A box has wheels. Is that true or false? (Signal.) *False.* • Listen. A box is a container. Is that true or false? (Signal.) *True.* • Listen. A box is a living thing. Is that true or false? (Signal.) *False.* • Listen. A box has sides and a bottom. Is that true or false? (Signal.) *True.* (Repeat part 4 until firm.)

FIGURE 3.9 *Language for Thinking,* **Lesson 17, Exercise 6. Reprinted with permission of the McGraw-Hill Companies.**

Reasoning and Critical Thinking (Lessons 11–150). Although this group of tracks is rather diverse, the exercises presented in these tracks share some common features. The exercises require the children to solve problems using information taught about the relationships between objects and events. For example, when confronted with a picture of a boat, a bike, and a plane the children are asked to make up a statement that is true only of the boat. The children are asked to determine if information provided is true only of the boat or if it is true of the boat and the bike. These exercises provide complex instructions to the children. Figure 3.9 illustrates an example of a format from this group.

The following guideline should be followed when teaching this type of format: Present the questions in Parts 2 and 4 quickly. Provide at least a one-second pause after each question and before the signal.

Vocabulary Development (Lessons 11–150). The Vocabulary Development group teaches children a number of words as well as a variety of ways to manipulate these words. The children complete the following types of activities in these tracks: (1) naming and recognizing pairs of words that are opposite, (2) naming and recognizing synonyms, (3) defining words, (4) identifying objects that are described with clues, (5) practicing transformation of statements in one tense to another tense, (6) forming contractions with pronouns and verbs, (7) "untangling" sentences with double negatives, (8) using superlatives

---

EXERCISE 4   Synonyms

1. We're going to talk about synonyms. Remember the rule: A synonym is a word that means the same thing as another word. Say that. Get ready. (Signal.) *A synonym is a word that means the same thing as another word.* (Repeat part 1 until firm.)
2. What's a word that means the same thing as another word? (Signal.) *A synonym.* Say the rule. Get ready. (Signal.) *A synonym is a word that means the same thing as another word.*
3. Let's make up statements that mean the same thing as other statements.
   a. Listen. The book is thin. Say that. (Signal.) *The book is thin.*
   b. Here's the statement that has a synonym: The book is skinny. Say that. (Signal.) *The book is skinny.*

   c. I'll say one of the statements. You say the statement that has a synonym. My turn. The book is thin. Your turn. (Signal.) *The book is skinny.* (Repeat steps a through c until firm.)
4. Here's another one.
   a. Listen. Please close the window. Say that. (Signal.) *Please close the window.*
   b. Here's a statement that has a synonym: Please shut the window. Say that. (Signal.) *Please shut the window.*
   c. I'll say one of the statements. You say the statement that has a synonym. My turn. Please close the window. Your turn. (Signal.) *Please shut the window.* (Repeat step c until firm.)

FIGURE 3.10   *Language for Thinking,* Lesson 22, Exercise 4. Reprinted with permission of the McGraw-Hill Companies.

correctly, and (9) matching up words that are homonyms. Figure 3.10 provides an example of a format for this group.

The following guidelines should be followed when teaching this type of format:

1. Help the children say the word *synonym* correctly.
2. In Part 1, the children practice saying the rule until they can all say it accurately.
3. To help children remember the rule, you can state it with a rhythm or in a song-type fashion. Emphasize the words **same thing.**
4. Check for the children's understanding by giving individual turns to say the rule.
5. If children continue to have difficulty with the rule, break the rule into two parts. Practice saying the first part, then join it with the last part so that the children state the whole rule.

Observing and Describing (Lessons 11–150).   The exercises in this group help children learn to use spoken and written language more precisely. Children are provided with the opportunity to describe what they are doing, make comparisons, observe details in pictures, and sequence events in time. In the final exercises, children are asked to listen to stories and draw conclusions from the information provided in the stories. Figure 3.11 shows an example of a format used in this group.

The following guidelines should be followed when teaching this type of format:

1. Keep a brisk pace during these formats.
2. Be sure the children are responding on signal.

EXERCISE 1 Actions	

1. It's time for some actions.
   Watch me. Tell me if I hold up all of my
   fingers or some of my fingers or none of my
   fingers.
   a. (Hold up three fingers.) Is this all of my
      fingers or some of my fingers or none of my
      fingers? (Signal.) *Some of your fingers.*
   b. (Hold up two fists.) Is this all of my fingers
      or some of my fingers or none of my fingers?
      (Signal.) *None of your fingers.*
   c. (Hold up ten fingers.) Is this all of my fingers
      or some of my fingers or none of my fingers?
      (Signal.) *All of your fingers.*
2. Now it's your turn.
   a. Everybody, hold up none of your fingers.
      Get ready. (Signal.) ✓
   • What are you holding up? (Signal.) *None
     of my fingers.*
   • Say the whole thing. Get ready. (Signal.)
     I am holding up none of my fingers.
	b. Everybody, hold up some of your fingers.
	   Get ready. (Signal.) ✓
	• What are you holding up? (Signal.) *Some
	  of my fingers.*
	• Say the whole thing. Get ready. (Signal.)
	  I am holding up some of my fingers.
	  (Repeat part 2 until firm.)
	3. Here's another action game.
	   a. (Stand up.) Everybody, I will sit down.
	      Say the whole thing about what I will do.
	      Get ready. (Signal.) *You will sit down.*
	   • Am I sitting down now? (Signal.) *No.*
	   • What am I doing now? (Signal.) *Standing up.*
	   • What will I do? (Signal.) *Sit down.*
	   b. (Sit down.) What am I doing now? (Signal.)
	      Sitting down.
	   • What was I doing before I sat down?
	     (Signal.) *Standing up.*
	   • Say the whole thing about what I was doing.
	     (Signal.) *You were standing up.*

FIGURE 3.11 *Language for Thinking,* **Lesson 25, Exercise 1. Reprinted with permission of the McGraw-Hill Companies.**

3. Make sure all children have performed the action before giving the next instruction.
4. In Part 1, emphasize the word **or.**

Comprehension Concepts (Lessons 11–150).   This diverse set of tracks prepares children for reading comprehension and the grammatical analysis of written language. In the Who, What, Where, When, Why track, children learn to identify which part of a sentence provides these pieces of information. For example, the sentence "At dinner, Tim ate slowly because there was a lot of food" provides information about who, how, why, and where eating took place. Children learn to discriminate between a question, answer, and statement in the Questioning Skills track. In the Can-Do track, children apply the concepts of what is being done, what can be done, and what cannot be done to objects and to people's actions. Exercises in the Retelling track help children learn to retell short accounts in preparation for remembering important details about the content and sequence of events in a story. In the Inferences track children are read a passage from which they learn to draw inferences. Figure 3.12 gives an example of a format used in this group.

The following guideline should be followed when teaching this type of format: Be sure the children answer the question. For example, when answering the question about where the girls were, the children should answer, *On the playground* and not *On the playground just after 11 o'clock.*

EXERCISE 5 Who, Where, When	

I'm going to say sentences that answer a lot of questions. You'll answer the questions.

a. Listen. The girls were on the playground just after 11 o'clock.
- Your turn. Say the sentence. Get ready. (Signal.) *The girls were on the playground just after 11 o'clock.* That sentence has words that tell who, words that tell where, and words that tell when.

b. Listen. The girls were on the playground just after 11 o'clock.
- Who was on the playground? (Signal.) *The girls.*
- Where were the girls? (Signal.) *On the playground.*

- When were the girls on the playground? (Signal.) *Just after 11 o'clock.*

c. Listen. The girls were on the playground just after 11 o'clock.
- Everybody, say the whole sentence. Get ready. (Signal.) *The girls were on the playground just after 11 o'clock.*
- Which words tell who? (Signal.) *The girls.*
- Which words tell where? (Signal.) *On the playground.*
- Which words tell when? (Signal.) *Just after 11 o'clock.*
  (Repeat steps b and c until firm.)

FIGURE 3.12   *Language for Thinking*, Lesson 30, Exercise 5. Reprinted with permission of the McGraw-Hill Companies.

Interpreting Graphic Displays (Lessons 43–115). The Interpreting Graphic Displays group of tracks ensures that children learn the meaning of *from, to, left, right, north, south, east, west,* and how to interpret a simple map. These concepts are learned by providing demonstrations of these concepts and practice in making statements that contain these words. In addition, children solve problems that require the use of directional concepts. Figure 3.13 shows an example of a format used in this group.

The following guidelines should be followed when teaching this type of format:

1. Be sure the children are facing the correct direction.
2. Allow enough time for each child to turn to the correct direction.
3. Repeat the exercise if children have difficulty responding correctly.
4. Be sure that children are not copying one another.

TEACHING TECHNIQUES

The following section describes two teaching techniques, signals and correction procedures, used in the *Language for Learning* and *Language for Thinking* programs.

Signals

As noted in Chapter 2, signals are used so that all children in a group respond to a question or instruction at the same time. By having children respond together teachers can maximize the practice of a skill or concept for each child. Three types of signals are used across the

---

EXERCISE 1   Map Reading

1. Everybody, stand up. ✓
   a. You're going to face north. (Pause.)
      Get ready. (Signal. The children face
      north.) What are you doing? (Signal.)
      Facing north.
      • Say the statement. Get ready. (Signal.)
        I am facing north.
   b. Everybody, you're going to face east.
      (Pause.) Get ready. (Signal. The children
      face east.) What are you doing? (Signal.)
      Facing east.
      • Say the statement. Get ready. (Signal.)
        I am facing east.
   c. Everybody, you're going to face west.
      (Pause.) Get ready. (Signal. The children
      face west.) What are you doing? (Signal.)
      Facing west.

   • Say the statement. Get ready. (Signal.)
     I am facing west.
     (Repeat steps a through c until firm.)
2. Everybody sit down. ✓
   a. (Point south.) Tell me the direction I'm
      pointing. (Pause.) Get ready. (Signal.)
      South.
      Say the statement. Get ready. (Signal.)
      You are pointing south.
   b. (Point east.) Tell me the direction I'm
      pointing. (Pause.) Get ready. (Signal.)
      East.
      Say the statement. Get ready. (Signal.)
      You are pointing east.
      (Repeat steps a and b until firm.)

FIGURE 3.13   *Language for Thinking,* Lesson 101, Exercise 1. Reprinted with permission of the McGraw-Hill Companies.

Language for Learning and *Language for Thinking* programs: the touch signal, hand-drop signal, and the auditory signal. The directions in the teacher-presentation book tell teachers which type of signal to use.

Touch Signals.   Touch signals are used in the *Language for Learning* program for exercises with pictures. The teacher points and then touches the picture and the children respond to the question or instruction. The following sequence of events constitutes a touch signal and response: (1) the teacher looks at the picture, (2) the teacher points to the picture by holding his or her finger about an inch from the page just over the picture, (3) the teacher asks the question, (4) the teacher continues to hold his or her finger in the point position for one second, (5) the teacher quickly and decisively touches the picture, (6) the children respond at the moment the teacher's finger touches the picture, (7) the teacher continues to touch the picture for the duration of the children's responses, and (8) the teacher drops his or her finger when the children finish responding.

Hand-Drop Signals.   Hand-drop signals are used in both the *Language for Learning* and *Language for Thinking* programs during exercises that do not include pictures. For example, many of the action exercises simply require the children to respond to the directions of the teacher. The following sequence of events constitutes a hand-drop signal and response: (1) the teacher holds out his or her hand at the beginning of each step of the exercise, (2) the teacher asks the question or gives the instruction, (3) the teacher pauses for one second, then quickly drops his or her hand, and (4) the children respond the moment the teacher's hand drops. Although an auditory signal is not necessary during exercises for which hand-drop signals are used, a clap or tap may be added.

Auditory Signals.   An auditory signal is used in the *Language for Thinking* program for exercises that require the children to look at a picture in their picture book or their workbook. Because their eyes must be on these pictures or on the workbook, the children must be able to *hear* when to respond. An auditory signal can be a finger-snap, clap, or tap of the pencil on a part of the book. The same timing is used for auditory signals as is used for hand-drop and touch signals. The teacher asks the question or gives the instruction, pauses, and then signals.

Error Corrections

Language for Learning and *Language for Thinking* use three correction procedures: general, specific, and statement corrections.

General Corrections.   Three general errors include: not attending, not responding, and responding before and after the signal. To determine which kind of error has occurred, the teacher observes the children closely and makes sure their eyes are on appropriate materials. To correct not attending, the teacher says, "Let's try it again" and then returns to the beginning of the exercise. To correct not responding, the teacher says, "I have to hear everybody" and then returns to the beginning of the exercise. To correct responding before or after the signal, the teacher says, "I need everybody to respond to my signal" and then returns to the beginning of the exercise.

Specific Corrections.   Correction procedures vary from exercise to exercise for specific response errors. These specific correction procedures are presented in the teacher presentation book under the initial exercises for which they apply. The teacher follows these correction procedures for specific errors made in those exercises and in other similar exercises.

Statement Corrections.   Regardless of the exercise or type of statement, the same statement correction procedure can be used for all statement errors. The teacher follows these steps: (1) she models the correct statement (e.g., "My turn. This is a chair"), (2) she leads the correct statement (e.g., "Let's say it together. This is a chair"), (3) she tests the children (e.g., "Your turn. Say the whole thing"), and (4) she retests the children by going back to an earlier part of the exercise and presenting the subsequent steps. The goal is that the children will say the statement correctly when it occurs in the context of the entire exercise.

ASSESSMENT AND TROUBLESHOOTING

The following section describes assessment systems included in the *Language for Learning* and *Language for Thinking* programs. Suggestions for troubleshooting common problems with the implementation of these programs are also provided.

Assessment Systems

Language for Learning and *Language for Thinking* include assessment systems that are designed to help teachers place children in the programs and to assist them in monitoring the achievement of children as they progress through the programs. In addition, directions for extra instruction are specified. These systems include a Placement Test (*Language for Learning*) or an Entry Test (*Language for Thinking*) and mastery tests (both programs). The *Language for Learning* Placement Test and the *Language for Thinking* Entry Test are individually administered assessments of receptive and expressive oral language. These tests should be given to each child before beginning instruction to ensure that the children are placed in the programs at an appropriate instructional level. Children's scores on the Placement Test and Entry Test will help teachers determine the appropriate beginning lesson for each child. The teacher can use this information to organize the children into instructional groups and to place each group in the program (not all groups begin at Lesson 1).

Fifteen program assessments have been designed for each program to help teachers monitor their students' progress through the programs. These assessments can be given to each child individually at ten- or twenty-lesson intervals beginning after completion of Lesson 10. These criterion-referenced assessments measure each child's achievement. Each assessment measures mastery of a specific set of concepts taught in the programs. Teachers use these assessments to help ensure children are learning concepts and skills taught in the program and to determine if reteaching of specific concepts or practice of specific skills is necessary.

Troubleshooting

Children will sometimes respond to questions or tasks in the *Language for Learning* and *Language for Thinking* programs with correct, but alternative responses or loud and draggy responses. This section describes procedures teachers should follow when these responses are observed.

Alternative Responses.   When a child responds with a correct, but alternative response (different from the response in the teacher-presentation book), the teacher acknowledges the response. The teacher then indicates that although the response is correct the group is going to use the response specified in the book (e.g., If a child refers to the point of a pencil as the tip, the teacher says, "Right. Some people call this part a **tip.** But it's also called a **point.** Let's use **point.**") The teacher does this because the children will use the specified response in the exercises of many future lessons.

Loud and Draggy Responses.   When children respond in a loud or draggy fashion, the teacher immediately stops the children and then follows this sequence of events: (1) she models a more acceptable way of responding and tells the children what she is doing (e.g., "I can say the sentence in a nice way. Listen. I am standing up"), (2) she leads the children through the response (e.g., "Let's all say that sentence the nice way"), and (3) she tests the children (e.g., "Let's hear you say the sentence the nice way, all by yourselves").

EXTENSIONS AND ADAPTATIONS

The following section describes various ways to extend and adapt the *Language for Learning* and *Language for Thinking* programs.

Extensions of *Language for Learning*

Three options are provided for the content of the *Language for Learning* program. Expanded language activities are included in the front of the teacher-presentation book for each level of the program to give children additional practice using and applying the language concepts and skills of the program. Each activity corresponds to a set of lessons in the program. Activities include songs, games, and drawing activities. These activities provide opportunities for the children to apply the concepts and skills taught in the program to new situations and contexts.

Language Activity Masters (a supplemental book of thirty activity lessons with accompanying blackline masters published by Science Research Associates) is available for use with the *Language for Learning* program. The activities reinforce the skills and concepts taught in the program. The book contains one activity for every fifth lesson. Rather than an extension of the daily lessons, these activities are intended to serve as a "treat" for good work in the daily lessons. For example, the first activity is a matching game that requires the children to match cards with pictures of objects taught in the program. Many of these activities can be used in the classroom and then sent home for extra practice of the concepts and skills with family members.

Sets of picture cards also published by Science Research Associates can also be purchased as a supplement to the program. The picture cards have been developed to give children additional opportunities to work with the concepts they are learning in *Language for Learning*. Language concepts taught in the program are illustrated with sixteen sets of picture cards. These cards have a picture on the front and the corresponding vocabulary word on the back. Several matching and sorting activities are suggested in the directions contained in the box of picture cards.

Adaptations to *Language for Learning* and *Language for Thinking*

Several adaptations of the *Language for Learning* and *Language for Thinking* programs are available.

Fast Cycle.   Some children may be able to progress through the *Language for Learning* program at an accelerated rate. For these children, the program includes a Fast Cycle option. Children who are placed at Lesson 31 or 41 in the program should be considered for the Fast Cycle, as should any group of children who are making rapid progress through the program. Beginning with Lesson 31, exercises marked with a yellow star are designated as Fast Cycle exercises. Children in the Fast Cycle are taught only the starred exercises. Although provided with less practice, children in the Fast Cycle are taught the same concepts and skills as children who complete the program at a regular rate. *Language for Thinking* does not include a fast cycle.

Children Whose First Language Is Not English. *Language for Learning* and *Language for Thinking* may be used with children for whom English is a second language, and some adaptations of the program for ESL children are recommended in the Teacher's Guide. For example, teachers are advised to use the action exercises as the initial teaching vehicle and to teach all of the action exercises in Lessons 1–10 until the children's responses are firm. The exercises in the information track can also be taught as part of the initial lessons. Once the children are firm on the action and information exercises in Lessons 1–10, return to the beginning of Lesson 1 and present one complete lesson per day.

Teachers are also advised to be particularly careful that ESL children's responses to questions and instructions are firm. Teachers should be prepared to have children repeat full statements not only during the language lesson but at other times during the school day as well.

The Direct Instruction program, *Español to English,* may be used with *Language for Learning* with children whose first language is Spanish because the program is fully integrated with *Language for Learning.* The program provides Spanish prompts and explanations when new information is presented to get Spanish-speaking students started in classrooms where English is spoken. The lessons in Spanish are gradually phased into English. The prompts and explanations in Spanish permit the children to understand what the teacher is saying and what they are expected to do or say when they respond in English.

Lessons 1–40 are self-contained within the *Español to English* presentation book. The directions in these lessons are in Spanish. Spanish directions gradually fade from lesson to lesson as the children become more familiar with English vocabulary and statements. Lessons 41–128 are bilingual lessons that use the both the *Español to English* and *Language for Learning* presentation books. *Español to English* lessons are used when new concepts and vocabulary are introduced. The children then practice these concepts and vocabulary in English in *Language for Learning,* which is used for Lessons 129–150. At this point, although the children are still learning new English vocabulary, they respond in English to the *Language for Learning* lessons.

Children with Disabilities. Depending on the nature of the disability, *Language for Learning* and *Language for Thinking* can be adapted to accommodate children with disabilities. For children with cognitive or communication delays, teachers can follow the guidelines for the use of both programs with children for whom English is a second language. For children with physical disabilities, the action exercises and workbook activities may need to be adapted. If the children are physically unable to complete the action exercises, they should observe another child doing the actions and then describe the actions as if they were completing them. Workbook activities can be completed with the physical assistance of the teacher. The responses should come from the child as much as possible.

RESEARCH ON DIRECT INSTRUCTION LANGUAGE PROGRAMS

Due to the recent publication of *Language for Learning* and *Language for Thinking,* most of the published research on Direct Instruction language programs is on *DISTAR Language I, II,* or *III.* Nine studies have investigated the *DISTAR Language* programs (Beveridge & Jerrams, 1981; Cole & Dale, 1986; Cole et al., 1991; Cole et al., 1993; Darch, Gersten, &

Taylor, 1987; Gersten & Maggs, 1982; Lloyd, Epstein, & Cullinan, 1981; Maggs & Morath, 1976; Mitchell, Evans, & Bernard, 1978). Two investigations have examined the use of *Language for Learning* (Benner et al., 2002; Waldron-Soler et al., 2002), but no published research has been conducted on *Language for Thinking*. In general, the research has shown the *DISTAR Language* programs to be as effective or more effective than other language instruction approaches.

Several studies have compared the effects of *DISTAR Language I* with other language programs/approaches (e.g., Cole & Dale, 1986; Cole et al., 1991; Cole et al., 1993; Dale & Cole, 1988). For instance, Cole and Dale (1986) compared the relative effectiveness of *DISTAR Language I* to interactive language instruction with preschool children. Cole and Dale found little difference between the effectiveness of the *DISTAR Language I* program and the interactive instruction in increasing language development in language-delayed children.

Further, a series of studies examined the relative effectiveness of Direct Instruction (DI) and Mediated Learning (ML) (Cole et al., 1991; Cole et al., 1993; Dale & Cole, 1988). Mediated Learning was defined as a program that emphasizes the development and organization of the cognitive processes such as comparison, classification, perspective changing, and sequencing of input, elaboration, and output, rather than specific academic content. In the first study, Dale and Cole (1988) investigated the effects of DI (*DISTAR Language I* was one of the DI curricula used) and ML with preschool and kindergarten children with disabilities. Overall, the children in the DI group made greater gains in language than children instructed with ML. Cole et al. (1991) conducted the second study examining the relative effectiveness of DI and ML with children ages three to seven years enrolled in a special- education program. Although no statistically significant difference in the effectiveness of the two programs were found, relatively higher-performing children gained more from the DI program, while the relatively lower-performing children gained more from the ML program. Cole et al. (1993) conducted the third study investigating the relative effectiveness of DI and ML with children who were eligible for special education. Relatively higher-performing children gained more from the DI program, and relatively lower-performing children gained more from the ML program.

Two published investigations have explored the effects of *Language for Learning*. First, Waldron-Soler et al. (2002) investigated the effects of a fifteen-week implementation of the program on the language and social interaction skills of children in an integrated preschool. Results showed that children with developmental delays instructed with *Language for Learning* had greater improvement in receptive and expressive language skills, and social interaction skills. Analyses also indicated that children instructed with the curriculum had reduced problem behaviors as measured by the SSRS compared to children in the control group. Additionally, the receptive language and social interaction skills of children without developmental delays instructed with *Language for Learning* were statistically and educationally greater than children's skills in the control group.

Second, Benner et al. (2002) investigated the effects of the curriculum on the receptive language skills of kindergarten children. Children in the experimental group were found to have scored statistically significantly higher on receptive language measures than children in the control group. The authors concluded that the observed effects were due to instruction with the *Language for Learning* curriculum.

Although these investigations suggest that *Language for Learning* is an effective instructional curriculum, further research is needed to determine if it is effective with other populations and increases other skills besides receptive language, expressive language, and social interaction skills. Additionally, research needs to be conducted on the new revision of *DISTAR Language II, Language for Thinking,* as well as *Español to English.*

REFERENCES

Adams, M. J. (1990). *Beginning to read: Thinking and learning about print.* Cambridge, MA: MIT Press.

Aram, D. M., Ekelman, B., & Nation, J. (1984). Preschoolers with language disorders: 10 years later. *Journal of Speech and Hearing Research, 27,* 232–244.

Baker, L., & Cantwell, D. (1982). Developmental, social and behavioral characteristics of speech and language disordered children. *Child Psychiatry and Human Development, 12,* 195–206.

Baker, L., & Cantwell, D. (1987). A prospective psychiatric follow-up of children with speech/language disorders. *Journal of the American Academy of Child and Adolescent Psychiatry, 26,* 546–553.

Baker, S. K., Kameenui, E. J., Simmons, D. C., & Stahl, S. A. (1994). Beginning reading: Educational tools for diverse learners. *School Psychology Review, 23*(3), 372–391.

Beck, I. L., Perfetti, C. A., & McKeown, M. G. (1982). Effects of long-term vocabulary instruction on lexical access and reading comprehension. *Journal of Educational Psychology, 74*(4), 506–521.

Benner, G. J., Nelson, J. R., & Epstein, M. H. (2002). The language skills of children with emotional and behavioral disorders: A review of the literature. *Journal of Emotional and Behavioral Disorders, 10,* 52–67.

Benner, G. J., Trout, A., Nordness, P. D., Nelson, J. R., Epstein, M. H., Knobel, M., Epstein, A., Maguire, K., & Birdsell, R. (2002). The effects of the *Language for Learning* program on the receptive language skills of kindergarten children. *Journal of Direct Instruction, 2*(2), 67–74.

Beveridge, M., & Jerrams, A. (1981). Parental involvement in language development: An evaluation of a school-based parental assistance plan. *British Journal of Educational Psychology, 51,* 259–269.

Blachman, B. (1991). Early intervention for children's reading problems: Clinical applications of the research in phonological awareness. *Topic in Language Disorders, 12*(1), 51–65.

Brett, A., Rothlein, L., & Hurley, M. (1996). Vocabulary acquisition from listening to stories and explanations of target words. *Elementary School Journal, 96*(4), 415–422.

Brinton, B., Fujiki, M., Spencer, J., & Robinson, L. (1997). The ability of children with specific language impairment to access and participate in an ongoing interaction. *Journal of Speech, Language, and Hearing Research, 40,* 1011–1025.

Catts, H. W. (1993). The relationship between speech-language impairments and reading disabilities. *Journal of Speech and Hearing Research, 36,* 948–958.

Cole, K. N., & Dale, P. S. (1986). Direct language instruction and interactive language instruction with language delayed preschool children: A comparison study. *Journal of Speech and Hearing Research, 29,* 206–217.

Cole, K. N., Dale, P. S., & Mills, P. (1991). Individual differences in language delayed children's responses to direct and interactive preschool instruction. *Topics in Early Childhood Special Education, 11,* 99–124.

Cole, K. N., Dale, P. S., Mills, P., & Jenkins, J. R. (1993). Interaction between early intervention curricula and student characteristics. *Exceptional Children, 60*(1), 17–28.

Craig, H. K. (1993). Social skills of children with specific language impairment: Peer relationships. *Language, Speech, and Hearing Services in Schools, 24,* 206–215.

Curtis, M. E. (1987). Vocabulary testing and vocabulary instruction. In M. G. McKeown & M. E. Curtis (Eds.), *The nature of vocabulary acquisition* (pp. 37–51). Hillsdale, NJ: Erlbaum.

Dale, P., & Cole, K. (1988). Comparison of academic and cognitive programs for young handicapped children. *Exceptional Children, 54,* 439–447.

Darch, C., Gersten, R., & Taylor, R. (1987). Evaluation of Williamsburg County Direct Instruction Program: Factors leading to success in rural elementary programs. *Research in Rural Education, 4,* 111–118.

Friedman, P., & Friedman, K. (1980). Accounting for individual differences when comparing the effectiveness of remedial language teaching methods. *Applied Psycholinguistics, 1,* 151–170.

Fujiki, M., Brinton, B., & Todd, C. (1996). Social skills of children with specific language impairment. *Language, Speech, and Hearing in Services in Schools, 27,* 195–202.

Gersten, R. M., & Maggs, A. (1982). Teaching the general case to moderately retarded children: Evaluation of a five-year project. *Analysis & Intervention in Developmental Disabilities, 2,* 329–343.

Gertner, B. L., Rice, M. L., & Hadley, P. A. (1994). Influence of communicative competence on peer preferences in a preschool classroom. *Journal of Speech and Hearing Research, 37,* 913–923.

Gray, B., & Ryan, B. (1973). *A language program for the nonlanguage child.* Champaign, IL: Research Press.

Griffith, P. L., Rogers-Adkinson, D. L., & Cusick, G. M. (1997). Comparing language disorders in two groups of students with behavioral disorders. *Behavioral Disorders, 22,* 160–166.

Hadley, P. A., & Rice, M. L. (1991). Conversational responsiveness of speech- and language-impaired preschoolers. *Journal of Speech and Hearing Research, 34,* 1308–1317.

Hall, P. K., & Tomblin, J. B. (1978). A follow-up study of children with articulation and language disorders. *Journal of Speech and Hearing Disorders, 63,* 227–241.

Hart, B., & Risley, T. R. (1995). *Meaningful differences in the everyday experience of young American children.* Baltimore: Brookes.

Hedge, M., Noll, M., & Pecora, R. (1979). A study of some factors affecting generalization of language training. *Journal of Speech and Hearing Disorders, 44,* 301–320.

Hinshaw, S. P. (1992). Externalizing behavior problems and academic underachievement in childhood and adolescence: Causal relationships and underlying mechanisms. *Psychological Bulletin, 111,* 127–155.

Institute of Child Health and Human Development. (2000). *Report of the National Reading Panel. Teaching children to read: an evidence-based assessment of the scientific research literature on reading and its implications for reading instruction* (NIH Publication No. 00-4769). Washington, DC: U.S. Government Printing Office.

Kaiser, A. P., & Hester, P. P. (1997). Prevention of conduct disorder through early intervention: A social-communicative perspective. *Behavioral Disorders, 22,* 117–130.

King, R. R., Jones, C., & Lasky, E. (1982). In retrospect: A fifteen-year follow-up report of speech-language-disordered children. *Language, Speech, and Hearing Services in Schools, 13,* 24–32.

Lloyd, J., Epstein, M. H., & Cullinan, D. (1981). Direct Instruction for learning disabilities. In J. Gottlieb & S. S. Strichart (Eds.), *Developmental theory and research in learning disabilities* (pp. 41–45). Baltimore: University Park Press.

Maggs, A., & Morath, P. (1976). Effects of direct verbal instruction on intellectual development of institutionalized moderately retarded children: A 2-year study. *Journal of Special Education, 10,* 357–364.

Medo, M. A., & Ryder, R. J. (1993). The effects of vocabulary instruction on readers' ability to make causal connections. *Reading Research and Instruction, 33*(2), 119–134.

Mitchell, M., Evans, C., & Bernard, J. (1978). Trainable children can learn adjectives, polars, and prepositions. *Language, Speech, and Hearing Services in the Schools, 8,* 181–187.

Osborn, J., & Becker, W. C. (1980). Direct Instruction language. *New Directions for Exceptional Children, 2,* 79–92.

Prelock, P., & Panagos, J. (1980). Mimicry versus imitative production in the speech of the retarded. *Journal of Psycholinguistic Research, 9,* 565–578.

Recht, D., & Leslie, L. (1988). Effects of prior knowledge on good and poor readers' memory of text. *Journal of Educational Psychology, 80*(1), 16–20.

Rescorla, L. (2002). Language and reading outcomes to age 9 in late-talking toddlers. *Journal of Speech, Language, and Hearing Research, 45*(2), 360–371.

Silva, P., Williams, S., & McGee, R. (1987). A longitudinal study of children with developmental language delay at age three: Later intelligence, reading, and behavior problems. *Developmental Medicine and Child Neurology, 29,* 630–640.

Snow, C. E., Burns, M. S., & Griffin, P. (1998). *Preventing reading difficulties in young children.* Washington, DC: National Academy Press.

Stanovich, K. E., Cunningham, A. E., & Cramer, B. B. (1984). Assessing phonological awareness in kindergarten children: Issues of task comparability. *Journal of Experimental Child Psychology, 38*(2), 175–190.

Stuart, M. (1999). Getting ready for reading: Early phoneme awareness and phonics teaching improves reading and spelling in inner-city second language learners. *British Journal of Educational Psychology, 69,* 587–605.

Tallal, P. (1988). Developmental language disorders. In J. F. Kananaugh & T. J. Truss, Jr. (Eds.), *Learning disabilities: Proceedings of the national conference* (pp. 181–272). Parkton, MD: York Press.

Tallal, P., Townsend, J., Curtiss, S., & Wulfeck, P. (1991). Phenotypic profiles of language-impaired children based on genetic/family history. *Brain & Language, 41,* 81–95.

Waldron-Soler, K. M., Martella, R. C., Marchand-Martella, N. E., Warner, D. A., Miller, D. E., & Tso, M. E. (2002). Effects of a 15-Week *Language for Learning* implementation with children in an integrated preschool. *Journal of Direct Instruction, 2*(2), 75–86.

Warren, S. F., & Gazdag, G. (1990). Facilitating early language development with milieu intervention procedures. *Journal of Early Intervention, 14,* 62–86.

Weiner, P. S. (1974). A language-delayed child at adolescence. *Journal of Speech and Hearing Disorders, 39,* 202–212.

CHAPTER FOUR

READING

MARCY STEIN AND DIANE KINDER
University of Washington–Tacoma

OBJECTIVES

After studying this chapter you should be able to:

1. explain why learning to read is important in today's society;
2. identify the five critical components addressed by the National Reading Panel;
3. define phonemic awareness and give examples of phonemic awareness instructional activities;
4. explain the difference between synthetic (explicit) and analytic (implicit) approaches to phonics instruction;
5. discuss the relationship between reading fluency and reading comprehension;
6. identify lesson events that are common to most Direct Instruction reading programs;
7. explain the ways in which word lists are constructed for most Direct Instruction reading programs;
8. explain the role decodable text plays in beginning and remedial reading instruction;
9. discuss how Direct Instruction reading programs promote the development of reading fluency;
10. explain how vocabulary is developed in *Reading Mastery;*
11. explain the features of explicit comprehension instruction using an example from one of the programs;
12. discuss how *Corrective Reading* addresses the five major topics identified in the National Reading Panel report;
13. summarize the evidence available to support the use of Direct Instruction reading programs.

Learning to read serves as the foundation not only for success in school but also for productive employment and active participation in a democratic society. The consequences of reading failure are pervasive. Students who fail to acquire early reading skills are less likely to graduate from high school, be gainfully employed, and function as active citizens in their communities.

In the past twenty-five years, a considerable amount of research on reading and reading instruction has been conducted, summarized, and made available to those interested in improving the reading performance of all students. After a brief discussion of the importance of reading, this chapter summarizes key findings from that body of research. Following the research summary, three Direct Instruction reading programs are discussed with respect to how the instruction in each program reflects the implications from that research. After reading this chapter, readers will understand the differences among these Direct Instruction programs as well as their common features. In addition to those reading programs, the chapter discusses Direct Instruction reading programs for nonschool use that can serve as a resource to parents.

This chapter also provides specific examples of how Direct Instruction teaching techniques, such as signals and error corrections, are incorporated into the Direct Instruction reading programs. For example, the chapter highlights signals that are particularly helpful when teaching students to sound out words. Recommendations for monitoring student progress along with suggestions for identifying and solving common instructional problems are presented. Instructional materials that complement the use of Direct Instruction reading programs are briefly discussed as extensions and adaptations. Finally, a summary of comparative and evaluation research conducted on each of the programs is provided.

IMPORTANCE OF READING

The number of nationally sponsored reading reports generated during the last quarter century underscores the prominent role that reading plays in the academic achievement of all students (Adams, 1990; Anderson, Hiebert, Scott, & Wilkinson, 1985; Chall, 1975; National Reading Panel, 2000; Snow, Burns, & Griffin, 1998). In *Becoming a Nation of Readers* (Anderson et al., 1985), one of the earliest of these reports, the Commission on Reading conveyed the importance of reading this way:

> Reading is a basic life skill. Reading is important for the society as well as the individual. Economics research has established that schooling is an investment that forms human capital—that is knowledge, skills, and problem-solving ability that have enduring value. While a country receives a good return on investment in education at all levels from nursery school and kindergarten through college, the research reveals that the returns are highest from the early years of schooling when children are first learning to read (p. 1).

As the Commission implied, the impact of learning to read extends beyond academic achievement to an impact on the economic growth and social well-being of our nation. Evidence suggests that high school graduation can be predicted based on reading skill at the end of third grade (Slavin, Karweit, Wasik, Madden, & Dolan, 1994). Not surprisingly, failure to graduate from high school is associated with lack of success in society (Simmons & Kameenui, 1998). In 2000, the United States Department of Labor reported that dropouts were unemployed at twice the rate of those who only completed high school. In 1997, the Employment Policies Institute reported that one-third of welfare recipients were functionally illiterate. If employed, those with limited literacy skills were in lower-paying jobs (Pryor & Schaffer, 1997) increasing the need for assistance. Adjudication also is associated with illiteracy and failure to complete high school (Cornwall & Bawden, 1992). Many incarcerated youth are reading below fourth-grade level—that is, they are functionally illiterate (Hodges, Giuliotti, & Porpotage, 1994).

Since 1969, the National Assessment of Educational Progress (NAEP), often referred to as the Nation's Report Card, has been used to monitor achievement in key academic areas. Because the reading assessment has been given in its current form since 1992, it not only provides an assessment of current student achievement but also allows for comparisons of achievement over time. The results of the 2000 assessment of reading (National Assessment of Educational Progress, 2001) were not significantly different from previous results. The most recent assessment revealed that only 32 percent of participating students in fourth grade were reading at or above the proficient level. Further, the results showed that the gap between higher- and lower-performing students has increased since 1992. In 2000, the scores of the lowest-performing students decreased compared to the scores of the lowest-performing students in 1992, while the scores of the highest-performing students increased compared to the scores of the highest-performing students in 1992. While these results seem discouraging, there is a growing body of research in the area of reading and reading instruction that suggests that curricular and instructional interventions can offset even the difficulties encountered by the lowest-performing students.

As of this writing, the most recent comprehensive review of research on the reading process and reading instruction is the *Report of the National Reading Panel: Teaching Children to Read* (2000). The National Reading Panel consisted of fourteen experts who, working with subgroups, screened approximately 15,000 research studies published prior to 1966 and approximately 100,000 research studies published between 1966 and 1998. Only studies that met the highest standards of scientific evidence were considered in the review. Based on an analysis of the research, the final report represents a consensus of these experts on what is known about the reading process and subsequent instructional implications.

To make the findings from the report more accessible to a wider audience, Armbruster, Lehr, and Osborn (2001) wrote *Put Reading First,* a guide based on the National Panel's report. The guide offers educators clear definitions of important reading concepts, summarizes major findings from the report, and, most importantly, discusses the implications those findings have for designing and delivering research-based reading instruction.

CRITICAL COMPONENTS OF READING PROGRAMS

The *Report of the National Reading Panel* and *Put Reading First* address five critical components for effective reading programs: phonemic awareness, phonics, fluency, vocabulary, and text comprehension. What follows is a brief description of the panel's findings for each component.

Phonemic Awareness

Phonemic awareness refers to the ability to identify and manipulate individual sounds in *spoken* words (not to be confused with phonics, which focuses on the relationship between letters and sounds in *written* words). An easy way of discriminating phonemic awareness activities from phonics activities is to ask the question, "Can students do the activity in the dark?" If they can, then it is a phonemic awareness activity; if they can't, it is probably a phonics activity.

Research suggests that phonemic awareness and letter knowledge are among the strongest predictors of success in learning to read and that, subsequently, the absence of phonemic awareness is a consistent characteristic of poor readers. Some evidence suggests that about one in five children do not develop phonemic awareness without instruction (Smith, Simmons, & Kameenui, 1998).

Fortunately, there is considerable evidence that phonemic awareness can be taught. Specifically, teaching the phonemic awareness skills of blending and segmenting appears to increase not only reading performance but achievement in spelling and reading comprehension as well.

Phonics

While phonemic awareness is important for learning to read, it is not sufficient. The research literature, as summarized by the National Reading Panel, provides clear support for the use of systematic phonics instruction. The Panel found that phonics instruction:

1. was most effective when it began in kindergarten or first grade—that is, before students learned to read independently;
2. improved the reading performance of first graders who were identified to be at-risk for reading failure and for older, disabled readers (those with average IQs but limited reading skills);
3. improved students' ability to decode regularly spelled words (those in which the letters produced their most common sounds) and to decode regular nonsense or "pseudo-words";
4. improved students' ability to decode irregular words (those containing letters that did not correspond to their most common sound);
5. produced significant gains in comprehension for young readers and for disabled readers when compared to nonphonics instruction.

The Panel outlined the major phonics instructional approaches and identified two as most common: synthetic (explicit) phonics instruction and analytic (implicit) phonics instruction. Teachers using synthetic phonics instruction teach students to pronounce the sounds for individual letters in isolation and then blend the sounds to form words (i.e., sounding out). Teachers using analytic phonics instruction do not teach students to produce sounds in isolation but rather to associate sounds with letters after the word is identified. For some readers, synthetic programs, because of their explicitness, result in better reading achievement than nonphonics or analytic phonics programs. Research findings suggest that synthetic phonics programs are particularly effective for younger students who are at-risk for reading failure.

The National Reading Panel identified the use of decodable texts, books designed to include words that are comprised of the letter–sound correspondences previously taught, as a topic neglected by researchers. Logic suggests that decodable texts provide students with valuable practice in applying their knowledge of phonics to reading connected text. Without this practice, it has been suggested that some students fail to use their phonics knowledge when they read text. These students tend to rely on less reliable strategies, such as using context and pictures.

In an analysis of the text selections in reading programs adopted in California in 1996, Stein, Johnson, and Gutlohn (1999) found that, in many of the approved programs, students were routinely given text selections to read for which they had been taught fewer than 50 percent of the words they encountered. This discrepancy between what is taught and what is read is thought to be problematic for students who are at-risk for reading failure. Although the research support for the use of decodable texts is minimal, reading researchers agree that the use of such texts should be the topic of further study.

Fluency

Fluency is the ability to read quickly, accurately, and with expression. Fluency is thought to be the connection between accurate word recognition and comprehension because fluent readers, those with well-developed decoding skills, appear better able to focus their attention on the meaning of the text they are reading. The National Reading Panel reviewed research on two common approaches to fluency building: oral reading and silent reading.

Traditionally, oral reading practice consists of round-robin reading, in which individuals are called on to read small selections aloud. Research suggests that there is little relationship between round-robin reading and reading achievement, most likely due to the limited amount of practice individuals receive during this activity.

The Panel found that more effective fluency-building activities involve having students practice reading a passage repeatedly until they have reached a specified level of proficiency. This practice may take the form of partner reading, choral reading, tape-assisted reading, or simply one-to-one reading with an adult. These fluency-building activities have been shown to be effective with students through the fifth grade and for older students with reading difficulties.

In contrast to research support for oral repeated reading, the Panel found no research supporting the use of silent reading practice to promote fluency.

Vocabulary

Vocabulary knowledge plays an important role in comprehension of text materials. Vocabulary deficiencies have been identified as a primary cause of academic failure from third grade through high school. However, it is important to note that the number of experimental studies addressing the relationship between vocabulary and reading comprehension is small and that few of the studies in the area of vocabulary have been conducted with students outside of the third- to eighth-grade range. Nonetheless, the Panel found "important and interesting trends" worth noting.

First, research suggests that no single method of vocabulary instruction is best; rather both indirect and direct methods for increasing vocabulary benefit students. The magnitude of vocabulary growth documented for school-age students implies that they acquire much of their vocabulary not from explicit instruction, but from daily interactions with oral and written language. The implications of this research are simply that students need exposure to rich oral language through interacting with adults, listening to adults read, and reading extensively on their own.

In addition to indirect methods, research also supports direct methods of vocabulary instruction, indicating that specific word instruction prior to text reading assists students not only with the acquisition of new vocabulary, but also with text comprehension. Multiple exposures to vocabulary words also are found to improve word learning.

Finally, research suggests that students benefit from learning how to independently determine the meaning of new words. Word-learning strategies that promote this type of independence include learning to use dictionaries and other reference materials, as well as learning to use word parts and context to determine word meanings.

In summary, vocabulary instruction appears essential to academic success. The relationship between reading comprehension and vocabulary is strong. Student differences in word knowledge have been identified as early as kindergarten, and the gap increases throughout school. Therefore, teachers must not only teach vocabulary directly, but also engage students in many oral language activities.

Text Comprehension

Only in the last thirty years has the comprehension process received much scientific attention. Current research in this area suggests that, while once thought of as a passive process, reading comprehension is now regarded as an interaction between reader and text. During this interaction, readers draw on their background knowledge as a basis for understanding what they read. Poor readers often demonstrate deficiencies in the structure and extent of their background knowledge, thereby making the comprehension process difficult for them (Weaver & Kintsch, 1991).

Much of the research on reading comprehension included in the National Reading Panel's report was conducted with students in third through sixth grade. Based on the available evidence, the Panel concluded that:

> teaching a variety of reading comprehension strategies leads to increased learning of the strategies, to specific transfer of learning, to increased memory and understanding of new passages, and, in some cases, to general improvements in comprehension (pp. 4–51).

The comprehension strategies supported by this research literature include: comprehension monitoring, using graphic organizers, answering questions, generating questions, understanding story structure, and summarizing.

OVERVIEW OF DIRECT INSTRUCTION READING PROGRAMS

Three major Direct Instruction reading programs are discussed in this chapter: *Reading Mastery, Horizons,* and *Corrective Reading.* The next section describes critical features and lesson events common to all Direct Instruction reading programs, followed by individual program descriptions.

Critical Features

All Direct Instruction reading programs share critical features. All of the reading programs have a placement test to ensure appropriate placement of students in the material. Some placement tests provide multiple entry points within a given level (e.g., *Reading Mastery* Level I); other placement tests provide recommendations for placement into the appropriate level (e.g., *Corrective Reading*). The programs also contain in-program tests to monitor student progress. Additional in-program tests provide teachers with information regarding the development of reading fluency for each student. All in-program tests are accompanied by suggestions for remediation based on student test performance.

Another critical feature of Direct Instruction reading programs is the use of an explicit phonics approach. While the approach remains consistent across the programs, the specific phonics strategies vary somewhat by program. These strategies are described in the program descriptions found later in this chapter.

Two final features common to all Direct Instruction reading programs are careful sequencing of concepts and skills and cumulative review of previously taught material. An example of careful sequencing is teaching prerequisite or component skills required by a particular strategy *prior* to the introduction of that strategy. For example, in *Reading Mastery,* before students are asked to sound out words, they are taught oral blending and segmenting skills, as well as the individual letter–sound correspondences that are contained in those words.

An example of cumulative review is easily seen in the introduction and review of letter–sound correspondences. Once a correspondence is introduced, it consistently appears in isolated sounds activities. These activities are designed to provide practice for students in discriminating between previously and newly introduced sounds. Additional practice with newly introduced sounds occurs in word-reading activities and subsequently in reading text selections.

Lesson Events

In addition to the critical features mentioned above, Direct Instruction reading programs also contain common lesson events. These events include: word study, vocabulary development, text selection reading, fluency building, comprehension strategy instruction, and independent work. Depending on the level of the program, word study consists of phonemic awareness instruction; introduction and review of phonics elements (i.e., individual letter–sound correspondences, letter combinations, and affixes); and word list reading. Vocabulary development usually occurs in conjunction with word study. In addition to learning how to decode new words, the meanings of those words are often introduced. It is important to note that word meanings are always taught prior to students' encountering those words in their text selections and independent work.

Reading of the main text selection is a critical lesson event in all Direct Instruction reading programs. In the beginning levels, decodable text selections give students the opportunity to practice and apply the phonics they have been taught to the text selections they read. Once students have mastered basic decoding skills, the focus of the text selections changes to learning from informational text and developing an appreciation of literature. Reading fluency is developed through multiple readings of text selections, additional partner practice, and through the careful monitoring of students' rate and accuracy.

Comprehension strategies are explicitly taught in every Direct Instruction reading program. These strategies include developing reasoning skills, interpreting figurative language, and analyzing characters and settings. Once these strategies are taught, students are required to apply them when reading their text selections and completing independent work activities. For example, after students are explicitly taught about similes, they then are asked to identify and interpret similes in their text selections and complete independent work activities that require application of this knowledge. Independent work activities not only provide practice applying comprehension strategies but also previously introduced decoding strategies.

Program Descriptions

The three major Direct Instruction reading programs are: *Reading Mastery, Horizons,* and *Corrective Reading. Reading Mastery* and *Horizons* are designed for elementary students. Two Direct Instruction *integrated* reading and language arts programs also are available to accommodate states that adopt only integrated programs. The integrated program based on *Reading Mastery* is *Reading Mastery Plus*; the integrated program based on *Horizons* is *Journeys.* Figure 4.1 captures the relationships among the reading programs and the reading/language arts programs.

Both *Reading Mastery* and *Horizons* also have condensed versions of their two earliest levels. The condensed versions essentially cover the same content but in fewer lessons. *Reading Mastery Fast Cycle* is the condensed version of the first two levels of *Reading Mastery*; *Horizons Fast Track A/B* is the condensed version of *Horizons Levels A and B.* This chapter will discuss only the complete reading programs, *Reading Mastery* and *Horizons.*

Corrective Reading is designed for struggling readers in grades three through twelve. Recently, *Corrective Reading* has been incorporated into a remedial program called the *Reach System.* In this system, *Corrective Reading* is used as the primary reading program in conjunction with *Reasoning and Writing* and *Spelling Through Morphographs* to create a comprehensive language arts program for students in grades four to eight who are performing significantly below grade level.

An overview of the goals and content of each of the three major Direct Instruction reading programs is presented in the next sections. At the beginning of each individual program description, a table is provided that outlines the different levels in each program, the number of lessons per level, and the major instructional focus of each level.

Reading Mastery. Originally named *DISTAR* (Direct Instruction System for Teaching Arithmetic and Reading), *Reading Mastery* was renamed when *Levels 3–6* were added to

	Grade						
	K	1	2	3	4	5	6
Reading Programs							
Reading Mastery	Level I	Level II					
Reading Mastery Plus			Level 3	Level 4	Level 5	Level 6	
Horizons	Level A	Level B					
Reading/Language Arts Programs							
Reading Mastery Plus	Level K	Level I	Level 2	Level 3	Level 4	Level 5	Level 6
Journeys	Level K	Level I	Level 2	Level 3			

Program Sequences

FIGURE 4.1   Relationships among Direct Instruction Reading and Reading/Language Arts Programs. Reprinted with permission from the SRA/McGraw-Hill Catalog.

the program. *Levels I* and *II* (represented in Roman numerals) are sometimes referred to as *Reading Mastery Classic.* As mentioned earlier, to create an integrated reading and language arts program, language instruction was added to *Reading Mastery.* This integrated program, called *Reading Mastery Plus,* contains *Levels K–6* (levels designated by Arabic numerals 1–6). For purposes of this chapter, only the reading instruction represented in *Reading Mastery Plus* is discussed. For more information about the language component of *Reading Mastery Plus,* see Chapter 3 on Direct Instruction language programs. While all levels of *Reading Mastery* provide instruction in both decoding and comprehension skills, each level is designed with a major focus (see Table 4.1).

   Levels K, 1, and *2* of *Reading Mastery* are designed to teach students the decoding skills they need to become accurate and fluent readers. These levels are designed with the assumption that students who enter the program have little or no prior knowledge of reading. The program assumes that students do not know the alphabet, letter names, or high-frequency sight words, such as *stop* or *go.*

   While *Levels 3* and *4* continue to emphasize accurate and fluent decoding, the primary focus of these levels is to teach students how to "read to learn." That is, students are taught the skills necessary to read, comprehend, and learn from informational text. While these levels also contain fictional selections, the emphasis is on reading and understanding nonfiction. The focus of *Levels 5* and *6* is literature. Students are taught how to interpret figurative language, such as similes and metaphors, as well as how to think critically about what they are reading. The following sections outline how the program addresses each of the five topics identified by the National Reading Panel.

Horizons.   Table 4.2 provides details about the *Horizons* program, which was written to address some of the criticisms of *Reading Mastery.* These criticisms include the modified

TABLE 4.1   Reading Mastery

LEVELS	NUMBER OF LESSONS	MAJOR EMPHASIS
Reading Mastery Plus: Levels K, 1, and 2 (Same as *Reading Mastery Classic:* Levels I and II)	100 lessons (K) 160 lessons each (1 and 2)	Learning to Read: Decoding Skills
Reading Mastery Fast Cycle: Levels I and II	170 lessons total (I and II)	
Reading Mastery Plus: Levels 3 and 4	145 lessons each	Reading to Learn: Content Area Skills
Reading Mastery Plus: Levels 5 and 6	120 lessons each	Learning through Literature
Reading Mastery Plus: Levels 5 and 6	120 lessons	Learning through Literature

orthography, difficulty in accommodating students who enter school midyear, and the late introduction of capital letters and spelling. *Horizons* does not use the same type of altered orthography, introduces both capital letters and spelling earlier, and better accommodates students who enter midyear.

Level A of the *Horizons* program is taught in three phases: the Pre-Reading Phase, the Highly Prompted Phase, and the Less Prompted Phase. *Level B* builds on the skills taught in *Level A* and is divided into a Prompted Phase and Unprompted Phase. *Level C/D* is an accelerated version of *Reading Mastery Levels 3* and *4.* For the purposes of brevity, *Levels A* and *B* will be discussed together.

Corrective Reading.   *Corrective Reading* is designed as a remedial reading program for students in grades three to twelve who have difficulty with decoding, comprehension, or

TABLE 4.2   Horizons

LEVELS	NUMBER OF LESSONS	MAJOR EMPHASIS
Level A	155 lessons	Decoding Skills
Level B	140 lessons	Decoding Skills
Level A–B Fast Track	Equivalent of Levels A and B in 150 lessons	Accelerated Decoding
Level C–D	Equivalent of *Reading Mastery* Levels 3 and 4 in one year	Text Comprehension: Reading to Learn

TABLE 4.3   Corrective Reading

DECODING	NUMBER OF LESSONS	MAJOR EMPHASIS
Level A	65 lessons	Word attack skills for nonreaders
Levels B	B1—65 lessons	More complex decoding skills
	B2—65 lessons	emphasizing rate and accuracy
Level C	125 lessons	Multisyllabic words and the application to content area texts

COMPREHENSION	NUMBER OF LESSONS	MAJOR EMPHASIS
Level A	60 lessons	Basic thinking skills, including vocabulary, true/false, and analogies
Level B	B1—60 lessons	More advanced reasoning skills
	B2—65 lessons	
Level C	140 lessons	Application of higher order thinking skills to text

both. The program contains two independent components, *Decoding* and *Comprehension,* with three levels for each component (see Table 4.3). The components can be taught separately (a single-strand sequence) or together (a double-strand sequence).

CONTENT ANALYSIS AND FORMAT FEATURES

The following section provides content analyses of *Reading Mastery, Horizons,* and *Corrective Reading.* The content analysis describes specifically how each reading program addresses each of the five major topics discussed by the National Reading Panel: phonemic awareness, phonics, fluency, vocabulary, and text comprehension. As part of the content analysis, the major teaching strategies in each program are summarized and illustrated with examples of instructional formats found in the programs.

Reading Mastery

Reading Mastery is a developmental reading program for students in grades K–6. In *Levels K, 1,* and *2,* the emphasis is on the development of the acquisition of accurate and fluent decoding skills; in *Levels 3–6,* the focus changes to an emphasis on the development of comprehension and vocabulary. Below is a description of how *Reading Mastery* reflects the major findings of the National Reading Panel with specific program examples included.

Phonemic Awareness.   *Reading Mastery* begins instruction in phonemic awareness with Lesson 1 of the first level and continues that instruction until several lessons after students begin reading words and sentences. The two primary phonemic awareness skills taught are oral segmenting (Say the Sounds) and oral blending (Say It Fast).

SAY THE SOUNDS—SAY IT FAST
Lesson 8
Task 11—Children say the word slowly, then say it fast

a. First, you're going to say a word slowly without stopping
   between the sounds.
   Then you're going to say the word fast.
b. Listen. (Hold up a finger for each sound.)
   Say (pause) **mmmēēē.** Get ready. Hold up a finger
   for each sound. *Mmmēēē.* Again. Get ready.
   Hold up a finger for each sound. *Mmmēēē.*
   Say it fast. (Signal.) *Me.*
   Yes, **me.**
c. Listen. Hold up a finger for each sound.
   Say (pause) **rrraaannn.** Get ready. Hold up a finger
   for each sound. *Rrraaannn.* Again. Get ready.
   Hold up a finger for each sound. *Rrraaannn.*
   Say it fast. (Signal.) *Ran.*
   Yes, **ran.**
d. Listen. Hold up a finger for each sound.
   Say (pause) **ooonnn.** Get ready. Hold up a finger
   for each sound. *Ooonnn.* Again. Get ready.
   Hold up a finger for each sound. *Ooonnn.*
   Say it fast. (Signal.) *On.*
   Yes, **on.**
e. Repeat *b* through *d* until firm.
f. Call on different children to do *b, c,* or *d.*

FIGURE 4.2 *Reading Mastery Classic Level I,* **Lesson 8,**
Task 11. Reprinted with permission of the McGraw-Hill
Companies.

The purpose of the segmenting activity is to teach students that words are comprised of various individual sounds. Moreover, the segmenting activities are used to teach students how to combine the sounds without stopping between them. For many students, identifying a word is easier when the sounds are combined without stopping.

In the oral blending format, the teacher says a word slowly, "mmmmmēēēēē," and then asks students to say it at a normal rate, "me." The oral segmenting and blending skills are introduced separately. However, soon after their introduction, a format is introduced that requires students to combine both segmenting and blending. Figure 4.2 represents the first time students are asked to combine both phonemic-awareness skills.

The final phonemic-awareness activity taught in *Level I* of *Reading Mastery* is rhyming. Students are taught to rhyme by combining an onset (initial sound) and a rime (all sounds past the initial sound). The teacher models how to combine the initial sound with the remaining part of the word (e.g., /m/ plus /at/ is pronounced "mat"). Figure 4.3 shows an example of how students are introduced to oral rhyming.

SAY IT FAST—RHYMING
Lesson 16
This is an oral task.
Task 10—Children say word parts slowly

a. My turn to say a word slowly. First I'll say (pause)
   mmm. Then I'll say (pause) **at.** Listen again.
   First I'll say (pause) **mmm.**
   Then I'll say (pause) **at.**
   Here I go. (Hold up one finger.) **mmm.**
   (Hold up a second finger.) (**mmm**) **at.**
b. Do it with me. (Hold up one finger.) First you'll
   say (pause) **mmm.** (Hold up second finger.)
   Then you'll say (pause) **at.**
   Get ready. (Say mmmat with the children as you
   hold up a finger for each part.)
c. Again. (Hold up one finger.) First you'll say (pause)
   mmm. (Hold up second finger.) Then you'll say
   (pause) **at.**
   Get ready. (Say mmmat with the children as you
   hold up a finger for each part.)
d. Repeat c until firm.
e. All by yourself. (Hold up one finger.) First you'll
   say (pause) **mmm.** (Hold up second finger.)
   Then you'll say (pause) **at.**
   Get ready. (Hold up one finger, then
   second finger as the children say *mmmat.*)
f. Again. (Repeat e until firm.)

FIGURE 4.3   *Reading Mastery Classic Level I,* **Lesson 16,**
Task 10. Reprinted with permission of the McGraw-Hill
Companies.

Phonics.   *Levels K, 1,* and *2* of *Reading Mastery* emphasize the acquisition of accurate and fluent decoding skills through explicit and systematic phonics instruction. This involves the coordination of instruction in several different skill tracks: letter–sound correspondences, regular words, irregular words, and text selections.

Letter–Sound Correspondences.   *Level 1* uses a specially designed orthography as a prompt to help students learn individual letter–sound correspondences. The goal of using this orthography is to regularize the reading code so that students can apply phonics knowledge to a greater number of words. In the *Reading Mastery* orthography, the letters in the diphthongs /ch/, /sh/, /th/, and /wh/ are joined and students are taught one sound for the joined symbol. Similarly, students are taught long vowels by introducing the letters with macrons ($\bar{a}$, $\bar{e}$, $\bar{i}$, $\bar{o}$, $\bar{u}$). Short vowels are taught as traditional letters. A final orthographic convention is the use of small letters to indicate silent letters (e.g., mād$_e$). By utilizing this orthography, students are able to sound out more words without learning lengthy phonics rules. They simply sound out the full-sized symbols to identify the word. The orthography is gradually and completely faded by the middle of *Level 2.*

The introduction of letter–sound correspondences and letter combinations adheres to the following sequencing guidelines:

1. Skills or elements that are likely to be confused with one another are separated in the instructional sequence. For example, vowels and other letters that look and sound alike are separated (e.g., a/e, b/d, m/n, r/n).

2. Skills that are consistent with a strategy or occur more frequently are introduced before others. For example, *Reading Mastery I* teaches only the hard sounds for /c/ and /g/ (as in *cat* and *goat*). The soft sounds (/c/ as in *since;* /g/ as in *edge*) occur less frequently in the English language and are, therefore, taught later.

3. Finally, more useful skills are introduced before less useful skills, for example, /x/ and /z/ are introduced later in the instructional sequence than /d/ and /r/ for that reason.

Figure 4.4 shows the pronunciation guide for the sounds taught in the program; the orthography used in the early levels of the program is illustrated under Symbols. The sequencing guidelines outlined above are reflected in the order of letter–sound introduction also in the guide.

In *Level 2,* decoding continues to be emphasized. Students move from a phonic analysis to a more structural analysis. Instead of letter-by-letter reading, the students are introduced to letter combinations (e.g., /ar/, /ai/, /ea/) and are directed to attend to word parts (i.e., prefixes and suffixes) in order to help them read multisyllabic words.

Regular Words.   To be considered a regular word in *Reading Mastery,* the word must meet two criteria. First, it must contain letters that represent their most common sounds. Second, the word must contain only those letter–sound correspondences that have been previously taught. For example, the word *man* would be considered regular only because each of the letter correspondences (i.e., /m/ /a/ /n/) makes its most common sound *and* only when the individual correspondences had been previously taught.

As mentioned earlier, the decoding strategy in the program is an explicit phonics strategy: the predominant strategy for word reading is sounding out, which requires students to combine their segmenting and blending skills with their knowledge of letter–sound correspondences to decode a word. Figure 4.5 illustrates how students are taught to sound out *am.*

The introduction of regular words is sequenced according to level of difficulty. First students are taught how to sound out vowel/consonant (VC) words such as *am* and *at.* Then they are introduced to different word types gradually and in the following sequence: CVC (e.g., *mad, cat*) CVCC (e.g., *sand*), CCVC (e.g., *clap*), and CCVCC (e.g., *stand*).

Sight-reading (or Reading the Fast Way) involves reading words without first sounding them out. When students begin reading words by sight, the program encourages the teacher to use sounding out as an error correction when students misread a word.

PRONUNCIATION GUIDE

Symbol	Pronounced	As in	Voiced or Unvoiced*	Introduced in Lesson
a	aaa	and	v	1, 12
m	mmm	ram	v	4, 11
s	sss	bus	uv	9, 16
ē	ēēē	eat	v	19
r	rrr	bar	v	23
d	d	mad	v	27
f	fff	stuff	uv	31
i	iii	if	v	34
th	ththth	this and bathe (not thing)	v	38
t	t	cat	uv	41
n	nnn	pan	v	44
c	c	tack	uv	48
o	ooo	ox	v	51
ā	āāā	ate	v	58
h	h	hat	uv	61
u	uuu	under	v	64
g	g	tag	v	68
l	lll	pal	v	72
w	www	wow	v	76
sh	shshsh	wish	uv	80

Symbol	Pronounced	As in	Voiced or Unvoiced*	Introduced in Lesson
I	(the word I)		v	88
k	k	tack	uv	92
ō	ōōō	over	v	98
v	vvv	love	v	102
p	p	sap	uv	108
ch	ch	touch	uv	113
e	eee	end	v	118
b	b	grab	v	121
ing	iiing	sing	v	124
ī	īīī	ice	v	127
y	yyy	yard	v	131
er	urrr/errr	brother	v	135
x	ksss	ox	uv	139
oo	oooo	moon (not look)	v	142
J	j	judge	v	145
ȳ	īīī/ȳȳȳ	my	v	149
wh	www or wh	why	v or uv	152
qu	kwww (or koo)	quick	v	154
z	zzz	buzz	v	156
ū	ūūū	use	v	158

*Voiced sounds are sounds you make by vibrating your vocal chords. You do not use your vocal chords for unvoiced sounds—you use air only. To feel the difference between voiced and unvoiced sounds, hold your throat lightly and say the sound *vvv*. You will feel your vocal chords vibrating. Then, without pausing, change the sound to *fff*. The vibrations will stop. The only difference between the sounds is that the *vvv* is voiced and the *fff* is not.

FIGURE 4.4 *Reading Mastery Classic Level I,* **Pronunciation Guide. Reprinted with permission of the McGraw-Hill Companies.**

CHILDREN SAY THE SOUNDS, THEN SOUND OUT THE WORD
Lesson 28, Task 6—Children say the sounds, then sound out the word

a. (Point to the first ball of the arrow for **am.**)
   This is the word (pause) **am.** What word?
   (Touch the first ball.) *Am.*
   Yes, **am.**
b. (Point to the ball for **a.**) When you sound out (pause)
   am, what sound do you say first?
   (Touch the ball for a.) *aaa.* Yes, **aaa.**
   (Point to the ball for m.) What sound do you
   say next? (Touch the ball for **m.**) *mmm.*
   Yes, **mmm.**
c. (Repeat *b* until firm.)
d. (Return to the first ball.) You're going to sound it
   out, then say it fast. Everybody, sound it out.
   Get ready. (Move under each sound. Hold under
   each sound for two seconds.) *Aaammm.*
e. (Return to the first ball.) Again. Sound it out.
   Get ready. (Move under each sound. Hold under
   each sound for two seconds.)
   Aaammm.
f. (Repeat *e* until firm.)
g. (Return to the first ball.) Say it fast. (Slash to the end
   of the arrow.) *Am.*
   Yes, **am.** You read the word (pause) **am.**
   I (pause) **am** (pause) happy.
h. (Call on different children to do *e* and *g*.)

FIGURE 4.5 *Reading Mastery Classic Level I,* **Lesson 28, Task 6. Reprinted with permission of the McGraw-Hill Companies.**

Irregular Words.   Irregular words in the program are those words for which students have not been taught the individual letter–sound correspondences or are those words made up of some letters that do not make their most common sounds. Many high-frequency sight words are irregular words (e.g., *was, walk*). The program introduces students to irregular words by reminding students that *all* words can be sounded out. However, as part of the irregular word strategy, students are taught that they don't always *say* the word the same way they sound it out. The purpose of teaching this irregular word strategy is to emphasize to students that they should *always* examine letter–sound correspondences when reading. Figure 4.6 illustrates how students are taught to read the word *said.*

CHILDREN SOUND OUT AN IRREGULAR WORD
Lesson 89
Task 8—Children sound out an irregular word (said)

---

a. (Touch the ball for **said**.) Sound it out.
b. Get ready. (Quickly touch each sound as the children say *sssaaaiiid*.)

To correct	If the children sound out the word as **ssseeed** 1. Say: You've got to say the sounds I touch. 2. Repeat *a* and *b* until firm.

c. Again. (Repeat *b* until firm.)
d. That's how we <u>sound out</u> the word. Here's how we <u>say</u> the word.
    Said. How do we <u>say</u> the word? (Signal.) *Said.*
e. Now you're going to <u>sound out</u> the word. Get ready.
        (Touch each sound as the children say *sssaaaiiid*.)
f. Now you're going to say the word. Get ready. (Signal.) *Said.*
g. (Repeat *e* and *f* until firm.)
h. Yes, this word is **said**. She **said,** "Hello."

said

FIGURE 4.6   *Reading Mastery Classic Level I,* Lesson 89, Task 8.
Reprinted with permission of the McGraw-Hill Companies.

In *Level 2* of the program, when students have demonstrated that they consistently use letter–sound correspondences to decode new words, instruction in irregular words is modified. At that time, students are told that they only need to remember some difficult words and a memorization strategy is substituted for sounding out the irregular words.

In *Levels 3–6*, students are taught to read new words, both regular and irregular, through a three-step process. The teacher (1) models how to pronounce the word, (2) has the students say and then spell the word, and (3) has the students read the list again. Students are told to spell words when they are first introduced because spelling requires students to attend to the letter sequences in that word and remember the pronunciation. Repeating a word without spelling it first requires far less student engagement and memory. The goal of using spelling is not to teach spelling per se but to increase student attention to the word being introduced.

Text Selections.   The goal of all phonics instruction is the application of that instruction to reading connected text. Initially in *Reading Mastery* the selections are no longer than a single word. Gradually, however, the selections become more complex. In *Levels K, 1,* and *2* of the program, no words appear in a text selection without having been first introduced and practiced in a preceding word list activity.

QUOTATION FINDING
Lesson 94
Task 24—Quotation finding

---

a. (Pass out Storybook 1.)
b. Open your book to page 7.
c. (Point to the quotation marks around the word **wow** in the second
                 sentence.) These marks show that somebody is saying
                something. He's saying the word between these marks.
d. (Point to the quotation marks around **that fat fish is mom** in
             the last sentence.) These marks show that somebody is saying
             something. He's saying all the words between these marks.
e. (Point to the quotation marks around **wow**.) Everybody, touch these
         marks in your story. (Check children's responses.) Somebody
                 is saying the word between those marks.
f. (Point to the quotation marks around **that fat fish is mom.**)
                   Everybody, touch these marks in your story.
                       (Check children's responses.)
            Somebody is saying all the words between those marks.
e. (Repeat *e* and *f* until firm.)

FIGURE 4.7   *Reading Mastery Classic Level I,* **Lesson 94, Task 24.**
Reprinted with permission of the McGraw-Hill Companies.

In the earliest text selections, students are asked to sound out every word. Shortly after they are introduced to sight-reading words in lists, they begin sight-reading their text selections as well.

In addition to learning how to decode text selections, the program also introduces students to a set of additional skills designed to help them become fluent readers. For example, students are taught to identify end punctuation (e.g., periods, question marks) and quotation marks prior to reading text selections that include these features. Figure 4.7 shows how students are introduced to quotation marks.

Fluency.   Reading fluently and accurately is emphasized in all levels of *Reading Mastery.* Fluency is encouraged in two ways. First, the program provides teachers with activities that promote reading fluency. Second, the program provides for systematic monitoring of students' reading fluency through the use of reading checkouts and in-program mastery tests.

In *Level 1,* teachers are encouraged to monitor fluency rates after students have learned to sight-read their text selections. At that point reading checkouts appear in every fifth lesson. In a reading checkout, students are asked individually to read a passage within a specified amount of time. Criteria for passing the checkout are specified along with recommendations for remediation, if needed. In *Level 2,* similar decoding checkouts appear in every fifth lesson.

In *Levels 3* and *4,* reading checkouts also occur during every fifth lesson. In order to pass a reading checkout, the students must read the designated passage in one minute with fewer than two errors. In *Levels 5* and *6,* reading checkouts occur every tenth lesson. In addition to the lesson checkouts, reading fluency is monitored through the use of in-program tests.

To develop reading fluency, teachers are advised to have their students read the text selections multiple times. In the beginning levels, teachers are encouraged to model reading fluently, paying close attention to punctuation marks and phrasing. In the later levels, the program recommends that teachers have students practice their oral reading with partners. Specific directions for conducting effective paired practice are provided in several of the teacher guides.

Vocabulary.   Beginning in *Level 3* students are introduced to new vocabulary both directly and indirectly. One direct strategy for teaching vocabulary uses model sentences that contain two to three key words. Each model sentence goes through an eight-step cycle that begins with the teacher introducing it to students (e.g., "They waded into the stream to remove tadpoles"), and ends with the assessment of student mastery of the new vocabulary (e.g., "What is the name for baby frogs or toads?"). Throughout this cycle, students encounter the new vocabulary in daily lessons and in their independent work.

Another method of teaching vocabulary in the program is direct teaching of definitions, along with word substitution. Teachers give students the meanings of a target word and then ask them to substitute the target word for a known word in a sentence. Figure 4.8 shows how this strategy is used to teach the meaning of *explain*.

Finally, an additional vocabulary strategy, found primarily in *Levels 5* and *6,* involves first teaching students to use surrounding context to determine the meaning of an unknown word and then using the dictionary to check if they are correct. The purpose of this strategy is to teach students to use multiple sources of information to expand their vocabulary knowledge and become more independent word learners.

Text Comprehension.   In *Levels K, 1,* and *2,* instruction in reading comprehension primarily involves picture comprehension exercises and oral and written questions about a given

---

VOCABULARY—Lesson 71

1. explain	4. crude
2. insist	5. fifth
3. honest	

a. Word 1. What word? (Signal.) *Explain.*
- When you **explain** something, you **tell** about it.
  Here's another way of saying **She told about her talent: She explained her talent.**
b. Your turn. What's another way of saying **She told about her talent?** (Signal.) *She explained her talent.*
- (Repeat step *a* until firm.)

FIGURE 4.8   *Reading Mastery Plus Level 3,* Lesson 71, Exercise 2. Reprinted with permission of the McGraw-Hill Companies.

text selection. The picture comprehension exercises give students practice with prediction. These activities require students to predict what an upcoming picture might show based on the text selection they have just read.

Comprehension questions related to the text selections occur before, during, and after students read the selections. These questions provide a purpose for reading, focus student attention on critical information in the selection, and encourage them to monitor their comprehension and integrate new knowledge from the selection with their own background knowledge.

Levels 3 and *4* emphasize two types of literal and interpretive reading comprehension: comprehension of facts, rules, and perspectives, and more general comprehension skills such as main idea, sequencing, and fact versus opinion. All comprehension instruction follows a similar sequence:

1. Background information (i.e., facts, rules, perspectives) or initial instruction in a given strategy (e.g., main idea) is presented in a comprehension passage;
2. Within two lessons of introducing the comprehension passage, the information appears in the text selection;
3. A variation of that information also appears in student independent activities;
4. The information is reviewed in subsequent lessons and integrated with previously introduced information or strategies;
5. The in-program mastery tests assess students' understanding of the material presented.

In addition to teaching more traditional types of comprehension skills, *Levels 5* and *6* emphasize three other categories of comprehension: reasoning skills, analyzing characters and setting, and literary devices. Instruction in reasoning skills includes teaching students seven rules for identifying logical fallacies (e.g., Just because you know about a part doesn't mean you know about the whole thing). Once students can identify these fallacies they are asked to apply the rules to text selections to determine whether a text violates one of the logic rules.

Another example of instruction in reasoning involves teaching students about contradictions. *Reading Mastery* is one of few comprehensive reading programs that explicitly teaches such complex reasoning skills. Figure 4.9 illustrates two exercises that give students practice in logical reasoning. Figure 4.9a teaches students the following rule of logic in Lesson 94: *Just because two events happen around the same time doesn't mean one event causes the other event.* Figure 4.9b teaches students how to find a contradiction in a passage.

Instruction in literary devices teaches students to understand similes, metaphors, exaggeration, sarcasm, and irony. Not only are students taught how to interpret literary text, but they are also taught how to discriminate these devices from one another. Figure 4.10 provides an example of how irony is taught.

Horizons

Horizons is a developmental reading program for students in grades K–4. In *Levels A* and *B* and *Fast Track A-B,* the program focuses on teaching accurate and fluent decoding skills; *Fast Track Levels C-D* combines the lessons of *Reading Mastery 3* and *4* into a year-long program with a focus on the development of comprehension and vocabulary. Below is a

---

D   **LOGIC**

Write the answers for items 1 and 2.

Here's one rule of logic: *Just because two events happen around the same time doesn't mean one event causes the other event.*

The following statement by a writer breaks that rule: "The last five times Sally tapped home plate, she hit a home run. She should always remember to tap home plate when she goes up to bat."

1. What two events happen around the same time?
2. What event does the writer think causes the home run?

FIGURE 4.9a   *Reading Mastery Plus Level 6,* Lesson 94, Exercise 5. Reprinted with permission of the McGraw-Hill Companies.

description of how *Horizons* reflects the major findings of the National Reading Panel with specific program examples included.

Phonemic Awareness.   Two basic phonemic-awareness activities are introduced in the Pre-Reading Phase of *Level A*: blending (Say It Fast) and segmenting (Saying Word Parts). All examples used in these activities are presented in a sequence that reflects an increasing difficulty level. For example, in both Say It Fast and Saying Word Parts activities, students initially work with compound words and later with individual letters. Figure 4.11 gives an example of Saying Word Parts using the words *an* and *ear.*

Phonics.   *Horizons* teaches beginning reading skills using three orthographic prompts that enable students to sound out many words in standard print. Unlike the special orthographic

---

E   **CONTRADICTIONS**

Write the answers to items 1–3.

Here's how to find a contradiction in a passage:
- Assume that what the writer says first is true.
- Read until you find a contradiction.
- Make up an if-then statement that explains the contradiction.

There are no underlined statements in the passage below. Read the passage and find a statement that contradicts an earlier statement.

Bert was getting ready for his camping trip. At six in the morning, he started filling his backpack. He put in three shirts, an extra pair of pants, and some socks. When he left a few minutes later, the sunset was turning the sky red. Bert looked forward to his trip.

1. Write the statement you assume to be true.
2. Write the contradiction.
3. Write an if-then statement that explains the contradiction.

FIGURE 4.9b   *Reading Mastery Plus Level 6, Teacher's Guide.* Reprinted with permission of the McGraw-Hill Companies.

_E_   IRONY

Write the answers for items 1–3.
  Here's how irony works:
- A character believes something.
- The character acts in a certain way because of his or her belief.
- Later, the character finds out the belief was mistaken.

Here's an example of irony from "The Necklace."

1. Matilda had a mistaken belief about the necklace. What was that belief?
2. Matilda did something because of her belief. What did she do?
3. What would Matilda have done if she had known the truth about the necklace?

FIGURE 4.10   _Reading Mastery Plus Level 6, Teacher's Guide._ Reprinted with permission of the McGraw-Hill Companies.

prompts in _Reading Mastery,_ the prompts in _Horizons_ are not sound-specific. That is, the prompts do not specify how to pronounce specific letters or sound combinations. The prompts show students _when_ to use a pronunciation strategy. For example, the first prompt is underlining. In the _Horizons_ text, all letter combinations are underlined to indicate that those letters make a single sound.

The second prompt is the squiggled underline. The squiggled underline appears in irregular words, those words that contain letters that do not make their most common sound (e.g., _was, said_). The final prompt is the blue letter. A blue letter indicates that the letter is

---

SAYING WORD PARTS

a. You're going to say words a sound at a time.
- The first word is **an.**
- What word? (Signal.) _An._
- **An** has two sounds. Listen: **aaa . . . nnn.**
- Your turn: Say **an** a sound at a time. Get ready.
  (Tap) _aaa_ (tap) _nnn._
b. New word: **ear.**
- What word? (Signal.) _Ear._
- Listen: **EEE . . . rrr.**
- Say **ear** a sound at a time. Get ready.
  (Tap) _EEE_ (tap) _rrr._

FIGURE 4.11   _Horizons Level A,_ Lesson 23, Exercise 6. (Note: Horizons scripts use capital letters to show long vowel sounds.) Reprinted with permission of the McGraw-Hill Companies.

SOUNDS FROM LETTER NAMES

a. (Write on the board:)

m   s

b. (Point to **m.**) Everybody, what letter? (Touch.) *M.*
- I can say **M** a part at a time. Listen: **eee . . . mmm.**
- Your turn. Say **M** a part at a time. Get ready.
  (Tap) *eee* (tap) *mmm.*
c. Listen: When you read words, you don't say the names
  of the letters. You say the **sounds.**
- The sound that **M** makes is the last part of the letter name.
  It's **mmm.**
- Everybody, say the sound that **M** makes. (Signal.) *mmm.*

**FIGURE 4.12   *Horizons Level A,* Lesson 19, Exercise 4.
Reprinted with permission of the McGraw-Hill Companies.**

silent and that some other letter in the word will say its name. Examples of blue letters include the final *e* in words such as *make* and *time.* A blue letter also may represent a silent letter that is part of a sound combination (e.g., *ai/paid,* where *i* is blue; *oa/boat* where *a* is blue).

Once students learn these three prompts, they are introduced to an explicit phonics strategy that allows them to sound out and read many words. These prompts are gradually faded in *Level B* of the program. More than 25 percent of the words students read in the Prompted Phase of *Level B* contain an orthographic prompt (i.e., blue letters, underlined letters, or letters with squiggle underlines). By the time students reach the Unprompted Phase of the program, however, only about 8 percent of the words are prompted. The remaining prompts are faded by the end of *Level B.*

Letter–Sound Correspondences.   In *Level A* of the program, students are taught a strategy for identifying sounds for individual letters based on their knowledge of letter names. The letters are taught in families that are organized around three specific patterns. The first family of letters taught in the program includes the letters *f, l, m, n, r,* and *s.* The sound of each of those letters is the last part of the letter name (e.g., the sound for *f* is the last part of its name, "eeeeFFFFF"). The students are taught to say the letter name a sound at a time and then taught a rule: The second part of the name is the sound these letters make in words.

The next family consists of letters whose sound is the first part of the letter name (e.g., *d* is the first part of "Deeeeee"). The final family consists of irregular sounds such as /c/, /g/, /h/, and /w/, which are introduced in the context of words as needed. Figure 4.12 provides an example of how *Horizons* teaches letter–sound correspondences.

Regular Words.   In contrast to the blending strategy in *Reading Mastery, Horizons* teaches students to blend the letters *with* stopping between the sounds. The reason for doing this is because in the *Horizons* program, reading and spelling are more closely integrated than in *Reading Mastery.* (While *Reading Mastery* contains spelling instruction, spelling is an

---

READING WORDS

a. Find the red balloon. ✓
● (Teacher reference:)

> 1. expl<u>ai</u>n
> 2. p<u>aw</u>
> 3. par<u>ty</u>
> 4. ed<u>ge</u>
> 5. p<u>ai</u>nting

b. A combination is underlined in each word. You'll tell me the sound for the combination, then tell me the whole word.

FIGURE 4.13 *Horizons Level B, Teacher's Guide.* **Reprinted with permission of the McGraw-Hill Companies.**

optional component.) When students spell, they pause between the letters of the word in order to write them. Therefore, the blending strategy in *Horizons* better prepares students for spelling by allowing them to pause when reading words as well.

In addition to sounding out words, a word-reading strategy used frequently in *Level B* is that of reading part of the word first, then reading the entire word. The part read first is always underlined. Reading words in parts helps students focus on difficult endings, letter combinations, or syllables. By the end of *Level B,* students are able to read over 2000 words and spell more than 300 words. Figure 4.13 illustrates an instructional task that gives students practice in reading words with letter–sound combinations.

Text Selections.   The text selections in *Horizons* are designed to provide students with practice in the application of phonics skills and comprehension strategies. All text selections in the program are read twice. The purpose of the first reading is to focus on decoding accuracy. Once students have achieved a specified accuracy criterion during the first reading (i.e., met an error limit), they reread the story in order to develop meaning. As in *Reading Mastery,* no word appears in a text selection that has not been first introduced and previously practiced in a word list.

In *Level A,* during the Pre-Reading Phase, text selection reading is sequenced so that students are reading increasingly more text on their own. By the time the students enter the Less Prompted Phase, they are reading stories that contain 150–175 words. By the end of *Level B,* students will be reading text selections that contain approximately 400 words.

Fluency.   Reading fluency is developed in *Horizons* much as it is in *Reading Mastery.* To develop reading fluency, the teacher is directed to model fluent reading, provide at least two readings of the text selections, and provide opportunities for partner reading.

As in *Reading Mastery,* fluency is monitored through use of the in-program mastery tests. These tests are available every tenth lesson. Each test contains two sections: a group-administered section and an individually administered section or checkout. Each checkout specifies the section of text to be read by the student and the time allotment for reading that section. If students do not meet the criterion for the checkout, specific remedial activities are recommended.

Vocabulary. Because explicit teaching of vocabulary does not occur in *Horizons* until *Level C/D* and, because *Level C/D* is a condensed version of *Reading Mastery Levels 3* and *4,* the readers are directed to the vocabulary section under *Reading Mastery.*

Text Comprehension. Text comprehension in *Horizons* is taught primarily through direct teacher questioning. The questions range from literal comprehension questions to predictive questions, to inferential questions focused on elements of story grammar (i.e., characters, setting, plot, etc.). Practice comprehension activities are included in all independent work. The most focused and specific instruction in text comprehension occurs in *Level C/D.* As with vocabulary, the reader is directed to examine the text comprehension section for *Reading Mastery* described above.

Corrective Reading

Corrective Reading is a program designed for struggling readers in grades 3–12. The program contains two major strands: *Decoding* and *Comprehension. Decoding Levels A, B,* and *C* address basic decoding skills, reading fluency, and the ability to read informational text. *Comprehension Levels A, B,* and *C* teach literal and inferential comprehension as well as critical reading skills and organizing information. Below is a description of how *Corrective Reading* reflects the major findings of the National Reading Panel with specific program examples included.

Phonemic Awareness (Decoding). The phonemic awareness activities in *Corrective Reading* are found in *Decoding Level A.* In that level, students practice saying words that are similar but differ in a single phonic element. For example, students are asked to pronounce words with and without endings (*show/showed*), similar words with different vowels (*pen, pin*), and words with consonant blends (*flip, cast*). Figure 4.14 illustrates an example of how students are taught to pronounce words with different endings (Task A) and different middle sounds (Task B).

Phonics (Decoding). The phonics instruction in *Corrective Reading* is designed to improve the reading of those students who had been previously taught ineffective reading strategies, such as looking at the first letter in a word and guessing. The word identification strategies emphasized in this program are phonics-based. In each level of *Decoding,* students are systematically introduced to letter–sound correspondences, letter combinations, and carefully constructed word lists and text selections.

Letter–Sound Correspondences. In *Decoding Level A,* the sounds associated with all of the consonants and vowels are reviewed and the letter combinations /th/, /wh/, /sh/, and /ch/ are emphasized. In *Decoding Level B1* and *B2,* students are taught approximately thirty-two

PRONUNCIATIONS

> **Note: Do not write the words on the board. This is an oral exercise.**

Task A
1. Listen: **chances.** Say it. (Signal.) *Chances.*
2. Next word: **casts.** Say it. (Signal.) *Casts.*
3. (Repeat step 2 for **stopped, fished.**)
4. (Repeat the words until firm.)

Task B Slum, slim, slam
1. Listen: **slum, slim, slam.** Say those words. (Signal.) *Slum, slim, slam.* (Repeat until firm.)

2. One of those words has the middle sound **ĭĭ.** I'll say the words again: **slum, slim, slam.**
3. Which word has the middle sound **ĭĭ?** (Signal.) *Slim.* Yes, **slim.** Which word has the middle sound **ăăă?** (Signal.) *Slam.* Yes, **slam.** Which word has the middle sound **ŭŭŭ?** (Signal.) *Slum.* Yes, **slum.**
4. Listen: **slŭŭŭm.** What's the middle sound in the word **slum?** (Signal.) *ŭŭŭ.* Yes, **ŭŭŭ.** Listen: **slĭĭĭm.** What's the middle sound in the word **slim?** (Signal.) *ĭĭĭ.* Yes, **ĭĭĭ.** Listen: **slăăăm.** What's the middle sound in the word **slam?** (Signal.) *ăăă.* Yes, **ăăă.**
5. (Repeat step 4 until firm.) Good job.

FIGURE 4.14 *Corrective Reading, Decoding A,* **Lesson 61, Exercise 2. Reprinted with permission of the McGraw-Hill Companies.**

additional letter combinations. *Decoding Level C* reviews the letter combinations previously introduced and introduces the less frequent letter combinations of /ure/, /aw/, /au/, /tial/, and /cial/. During this level, students are introduced to eleven affixes (e.g., *re, dis, pre*) as a prerequisite for reading multisyllabic words. Figure 4.15 provides an example of teaching the prefix *ex.*

Regular and Irregular Words. As with all of the Direct Instruction reading programs, once students have been introduced to individual letter–sound correspondences or letter combinations, they are given word lists that provide practice in reading words with those phonic

AFFIX: ex

1. Print on the board: **tend, cite, ample, plain, pose.**
2. For each word:
   (Point to the word.) What word? (Signal.)
3. (Add **e-x** to the beginning of each word:
   extend, excite, example, explain, expose.)
4. For each word:
   (Point to the word.) What word? (Signal.)
5. (Repeat the list until firm.)

FIGURE 4.15 *Corrective Reading, Decoding C,* **Lesson 26, Exercise 1. Reprinted with permission of the McGraw-Hill Companies.**

```
1. ranch   faster   chopped
   goats   checked   horses
   bent   slap   leave   heels
   loafers   swam   swim   jab

2. rode   named   rider   safe
   makes   side   tame   time

3. Emma   anyone   nobody   good
   because   let's   boss   didn't
   ready   their   Flop   woman
   women   milked   herself   station
   question   biggest   stayed   Branch
```

FIGURE 4.16   *Corrective Reading, Decoding B1,* **Lesson 26, Parts 1–3. Reprinted with permission of the McGraw-Hill Companies.**

elements. At the beginning of *Decoding Level A,* students are encouraged to sound out the words in the lists. Later in the program, it is suggested that teachers use sounding out primarily as an error correction.

In addition to providing practice in reading words with phonic elements, the word lists also provide practice in reading compound words (e.g., *greenhouse*), words with endings (e.g., *taped*), difficult blends (e.g., *splash*), spelling irregularities (e.g., *league*), and with prefixes as well as suffixes (e.g., *predict, carelessness*). The construction of each word list is targeted to provide practice either on a specific phonic element, on sight words, or on difficult words that students will encounter in the corresponding text selections. Figure 4.16 provides an example from *Decoding B1* of carefully constructed word lists that appear in student books.

Text Selections.   The text selections in *Corrective Reading* are designed to move from highly decodable and simple texts (*Decoding Level A*) to more informational types of text (*Decoding Level C*). The selections increase in length, difficulty, and interest. The earlier texts are written to decrease the probability that a student could read the text simply by guessing correctly. The later texts are written to provide more systematic instruction on the type of selections more typically found in textbooks. By *Level C,* students are reading sophisticated text that includes more complex syntax (e.g., multiclause sentences, passive voice) as well as a higher percentage of new words and difficult vocabulary. In *Decoding Level C,* selections are derived from magazines, newspapers, and other sources.

Fluency (Decoding).   In *Corrective Reading,* reading fluency is promoted through multiple readings of the text selection both within the teacher-directed lesson and through partner reading activities. Both accuracy and fluency are monitored in the *Decoding* programs. Reading checkouts are designed to monitor student progress and to provide feedback to them regarding their progress. Table 4.4 provides the reading fluency criteria for *Decoding Levels*

TABLE 4.4   Corrective Reading Fluency Criteria

DECODING A	DECODING B1	DECODING B2	DECODING C
60 wpm	90 wpm	120 wpm	Over 150 wpm
98% accuracy	98% accuracy	98% accuracy	98% accuracy
2.5 grade level	3.9 grade level	4.9 grade level	7.0 grade level

A–C. It should be noted that the fluency criteria in *Corrective Reading* are considered to be minimal criteria.

Vocabulary (Comprehension).   Vocabulary is taught using a variety of methods in all levels of *Corrective Reading Comprehension* in which students are taught certain systems of facts (e.g., body systems: skeletal, muscular, circulatory, etc.) and simultaneously are taught related vocabulary. In *Levels B1* and *B2,* students also are taught vocabulary through parts of speech (e.g., *select, selective, selection*). In *Level C,* students are taught the meanings of affixes and how to use an affix to determine the meaning of a word (e.g., "If *re* means again, than *recount* means to count again"). Dictionary skills also are introduced in this level.

Finally, at all levels, students are taught some vocabulary using simple definitions. Once a vocabulary word or phrase is introduced in the program, students encounter that word or phrase many times in text selections and independent workbook exercises. Figure 4.17 gives an example of vocabulary instruction that involves different parts of speech (i.e., *select, selected,* and *selecting*) in *Comprehension Level B1.*

Text Comprehension (Comprehension).   Table 4.5 outlines the major comprehension skill tracks and strategies taught in each level of *Comprehension.*

DEFINITIONS

1. Complete each sentence by saying **select, selected,** or **selecting.**
2. Listen. The man will **blank** a shirt. What word? (Signal.) *Select.* Say the sentence. (Signal.) *The man will select a shirt.*
3. Listen. The man has **blank** a shirt. What word? (Signal.) *Selected.* Say the sentence. (Signal.) *The man has selected a shirt.*
4. Listen. The man has to **blank** a shirt. What word? (Signal.) *Select.* Say the sentence. (Signal.) *The man has to select a shirt.*
5. Listen. You must **blank** a shirt. What word? (Signal.) *Select.* Say the sentence. (Signal.) *You must select a shirt.*
6. Listen. They are **blank** a shirt. What word? (Signal.) *Selecting.* Say the sentence. (Signal.) *They are selecting a shirt.*
7. Listen. They are not **blank** a shirt. What word? (Signal.) *Selecting.* Say the sentence. (Signal.) *They are not selecting a shirt.*
8. (Repeat steps 1–7 until firm.)

FIGURE 4.17   *Corrective Reading, Comprehension B1,* **Lesson 13, Exercise 1. Reprinted with permission of the McGraw-Hill Companies.**

TABLE 4.5 Corrective Reading Comprehension

LEVEL	MAJOR SKILL TRACKS	SAMPLE INSTRUCTIONAL STRATEGIES IN EACH TRACK
Level A	Thinking Operations	Analogies Deductions Statement Inference
	Information	Calendar Poems Animals: Mammals; Reptiles
Level B1 and B2	Reasoning Skills	Deductions Basic Evidence Contradictions
	Information Skills	Classification Body Systems Economic Rules
	Sentence/Writing Skills	Parts of Speech Sentence Combinations Writing Directions Editing Writing Stories
Level C	Organizing Information	Main Idea/Outlining
	Operating on Information	Deductions Argument Rules Contradictions
	Using Sources of Information	Maps/Graphs Supporting Evidence Filling Out Forms
	Using Information for Directions	Writing Directions
	Communicating Information	Combining Sentences Editing Meaning from Context

The skills taught in *Comprehension Level A* form a framework for learning information. Students are taught thinking operations they can use to solve problems and learn how to organize information to make inferences about what they read. The focus of *Level B* is on comprehension skills and strategies that will allow students to learn from their content area textbooks. The skills build on the foundation established in *Level A* but include the introduction to reasoning and analysis skills that are applicable to many content areas. Finally, in *Level C,* students are introduced to critical thinking skills that include analyzing basic evidence and identifying contradictions and faulty arguments. Unlike the previous levels,

Here's an argument:

> **The last two times Joe tapped home plate, he hit a home run. He should always remember to tap home plate when he goes up to bat.**

What does the writer want us to conclude? (G)
Why does the writer think that tapping home plate will cause Joe to hit a home run? (H)
Say the rule the argument breaks. (I)

Here's how you could prove that tapping home plate doesn't cause Joe to hit a home run. Make Joe tap home plate every time he goes up to bat. If he doesn't hit a home run **every time** he taps home plate, then tapping home plate doesn't cause him to hit a home run.

FIGURE 4.18   *Corrective Reading, Comprehension C,* **Lesson 45, Part B. Reprinted with permission of the McGraw-Hill Companies.**

Level C also emphasizes written communication and the development of greater independent learning strategies. Figure 4.18 illustrates how students are taught to apply critical reading skills to a passage containing a faulty argument.

OTHER DIRECT INSTRUCTION READING PROGRAMS

Two reading programs based on a Direct Instruction approach to beginning reading designed specifically for use in nonschool settings are *Teach Your Child to Read in 100 Easy Lessons* and *Funnix. Teach Your Child to Read in 100 Easy Lessons* is a book that contains short lessons designed for beginning readers, adapted from *Reading Mastery.* The orthography and sequence of introduction for letter–sound correspondences used in the book are identical to those found in *Reading Mastery.* A primary difference between *Reading Mastery* and *Teach Your Child to Read* is in the rate of introduction. After completing one hundred lessons from this book, students are estimated to read on a second-grade level. The authors also provide parents with recommended reading for their children who are completing these lessons.

Funnix is a CD program with graphics and animation designed to teach beginning reading skills to young children and adult nonreaders. The program contains two components*: Funnix Beginning Reading* and *Funnix 2. Funnix Beginning Reading* is a 120-lesson adaptation of *Horizons.* The same orthographic prompts used in *Horizons* are used in *Funnix. Funnix 2* is a second-grade reading sequence designed for students who complete *Funnix Beginning Reading* or *Teach Your Child to Read in 100 Easy Lessons.*

TEACHING TECHNIQUES

Chapter 2 provides an overview of teaching techniques unique to Direct Instruction. Many of these techniques, such as the use of brisk pacing, signals, and error correction procedures, are found in all Direct Instruction programs. However, Direct Instruction reading programs also contain signals and error corrections that are unique to these programs. These teaching techniques are discussed in the following section.

Signals

Unique signals are used in the early levels of *Reading Mastery* and *Corrective Reading, Decoding* primarily for teaching letter–sound correspondences and sounding out words. Letter–sound correspondences can be classified as either continuous or stop sounds. Continuous sounds are those that can be said as long as the person has breath to say them (e.g., /s/, /m/, /a/). Stop sounds are quick sounds and cannot be held without distorting the sound (e.g., /d/, /b/, /p/). In teaching students to identify both continuous and stop sounds, *Reading Mastery* encourages teachers to signal differently during the teaching presentation. Teachers are to tap the sound when asking students to identify a stop sound and point and hold under the sound to indicate how long students should say continuous sounds.

Reading Mastery also utilizes visual prompts to help both teachers and students remember when to hold a sound and when to say the sound quickly. All letters are introduced on arrows. On the arrow under the letter is either a dot (•) or an arrowhead (➤). The dot signifies that the sound for that letter is continuous and should be said for as long as the teacher touches the dot. The arrowhead signifies that the letter is a stop sound and that students should say the sound quickly as the teacher signals along the arrow.

The procedure for identifying continuous sounds (in unison) is for the teacher to say, "Get ready," pause for one second, and quickly move her finger to the dot under the sound and hold it there for approximately two seconds while all of the students say the sound. The signal for stop sounds involves the teacher saying, "Say it fast," pausing for one second, and quickly moving her finger along the arrow, past the arrowhead, to the end of the arrow. The students are to say the sound quickly. In *Corrective Reading, Decoding,* teachers follow these same procedures when signaling for continuous and stop sounds; however, the arrow with the arrowhead or dot is not used.

The "sound it out signal," used to teach students to decode words in the early levels of *Reading Mastery* and *Corrective Reading (Decoding),* is similar to the individual letter–sound correspondence signal. Like individual letters, the words in these levels are printed on arrows. In *Reading Mastery* the teacher is prompted by a dot under each continuous sound and an arrowhead under the stop sounds. The signal in both programs consists of teachers pointing to the beginning of the arrow and saying, "sound it out," quickly moving their finger under the first continuous sound, and holding it for at least one second before moving quickly to the next sound. If the word contains a stop sound, teachers move quickly over the arrowhead and on to the continuous sound that is held for at least one second. Figure 4.19a and 4.19b illustrate the signals recommended for teaching individual letter–sound correspondences and sounding out words, respectively.

Error Corrections

The recommended procedures for error corrections in Direct Instruction reading programs are quite similar to the error correction procedures in most Direct Instruction programs. Generally, when students make errors, teachers model the answer or highlight the component skill or steps in the strategy that were missed (model), have students repeat the task (test),

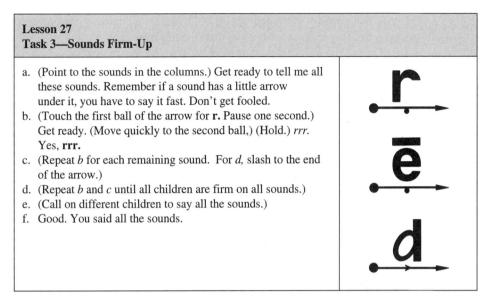

Lesson 27
Task 3—Sounds Firm-Up

a. (Point to the sounds in the columns.) Get ready to tell me all these sounds. Remember if a sound has a little arrow under it, you have to say it fast. Don't get fooled.
b. (Touch the first ball of the arrow for **r.** Pause one second.) Get ready. (Move quickly to the second ball,) (Hold.) *rrr.* Yes, **rrr.**
c. (Repeat *b* for each remaining sound. For *d,* slash to the end of the arrow.)
d. (Repeat *b* and *c* until all children are firm on all sounds.)
e. (Call on different children to say all the sounds.)
f. Good. You said all the sounds.

FIGURE 4.19a *Reading Mastery Classic Level I,* **Lesson 27, Task 3. Reprinted with permission of the McGraw-Hill Companies.**

and continue on to another example and return later to the example that was missed (delayed test). For example, when teachers hear students misidentify a sound, the teachers immediately model the correct sound ("This sound is /aaaaa/"), test students by asking them to

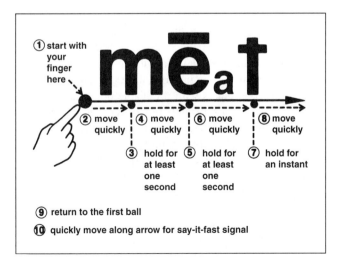

FIGURE 4.19b *Reading Mastery Classic Level I,* **Lesson 46, Task 9. Reprinted with permission of the McGraw-Hill Companies.**

identify that sound ("What sound is this?"), and then continue practice on other sounds, making sure they return to the sound that students missed.

The goal of well-designed phonics programs is for students to use their knowledge of phonics to decode text. Because all Direct Instruction reading programs teach phonics strategies, when students misidentify words teachers are encouraged to have them correct their errors by sounding out the word. Using sounding out as an error-correction procedure is essential for teaching students how to apply their phonics knowledge during reading, especially in beginning and remedial reading programs.

ASSESSMENT AND TROUBLESHOOTING

This section includes recommendations for assessing student progress and information on troubleshooting common reading errors so that teachers can prevent or remedy these errors before they become chronic problems.

Assessment

The teacher's guide for each of the three Direct Instruction reading programs discussed in this chapter includes individually administered placement tests designed to help teachers place students in the appropriate level or lesson. The tests also help teachers more appropriately group students for instruction. The results of the *Reading Mastery* placement test allow the teacher to place students at Lesson 1, Lesson 11, or in the *Fast Cycle* program. The placement test for *Horizons* provides information that helps teachers determine whether to place students in *Horizons Fast Track, Reading Mastery,* or in *Horizons Level A.* The *Corrective Reading* teacher's guide includes separate tests for decoding and comprehension, with guidelines for placing students in *Levels A, B,* or *C* of *Corrective Reading Decoding* or *Comprehension.*

As mentioned previously, in addition to placement tests, a critical feature of all Direct Instruction reading programs is the systematic assessment of student performance through the use of in-program tests and daily work. Often this assessment is overlooked or not implemented fully. First and foremost, the in-program tests should be used carefully and consistently. These tests provide teachers with invaluable information regarding whether students have mastered the material most recently introduced. The results should be used to plan and implement supplemental and remedial activities.

In addition to the results from the in-program tests, teachers should use information derived from students' daily work. Student responses during teacher-directed lessons and performance on independent activities should be considered in planning supplemental and remedial activities. Daily monitoring of student performance is most useful when it is recorded. The record provides teachers with information over time that can be used to detect error patterns and prevent chronic problems.

Related to issues of monitoring student performance are issues related to maintaining a high performance criterion. Most Direct Instruction teacher guides recommend that students be "firm" on a task before the teacher introduces the next task. Unless the manual specifies a criterion (e.g., an error limit), being "firm" usually means completing the task with no errors. Because Direct Instruction programs provide significant amounts of practice and repetition, some teachers assume that students need not reach a high criterion *daily* because they are likely to encounter the same or similar examples the following day. When students are not required to become "firm" on daily work, they are likely to encounter considerable difficulties in later lessons when new content is introduced.

Troubleshooting

Four areas are likely to give students in Direct Instruction reading programs difficulty. First, many students in *Reading Mastery Level 1* have trouble blending sounds without stopping between them when sounding out words. This problem may result in misidentification of the word. One cause of the problem may be that the students were not firm on oral segmenting tasks before sounding out was introduced. Therefore, a common solution to the problem is for the teacher to return to oral segmenting tasks to provide additional practice. Moreover, teachers who experience this problem should assess whether they are providing a clear model of sounding out without stopping between the sounds. Often teachers are not aware that they are inadvertently contributing to the problem. Finally, teachers should always generate more and different words to provide additional practice in sounding out.

A second area that often needs troubleshooting is the discrimination of vowel sounds. Short vowels sound similar to one another and are likely to be confused. Therefore, teachers should recognize the need to more closely monitor student performance on the identification of isolated vowel sounds during oral practice. More individual turns and more practice both within and outside the formal lesson may be required to ensure mastery.

Balancing an emphasis on decoding accuracy and fluency has always been challenging for teachers, especially when working with low-performing students. Only recently has the role of fluency in reading proficiency been emphasized. As mentioned earlier, the relationship between reading fluency and reading comprehension is robust. It should be noted that the fluency criteria in Direct Instruction programs are considered to be minimal criteria. That is, most teachers using Direct Instruction reading programs should consider increasing those criteria. (See next section on Extensions and Adaptation for recommendations.)

Finally, students may have difficulty with reading comprehension, specifically, remembering critical content, including facts and rules. The problems are most noticeable in independent written work. Most comprehension problems can be addressed by increasing the amount and type of supplemental practice. Students should not be asked to complete independent work that they have not first mastered during oral practice.

EXTENSIONS AND ADAPTATIONS

Because a comprehensive reading program is not the only component of a reading curriculum, this section outlines supplementary instructional materials that complement Direct Instruction reading programs. The areas most frequently supplemented include phonics, fluency, and vocabulary.

Phonics

Teachers using Direct Instruction reading programs may find that supplementary materials are useful in providing additional practice in reading connected text. Several companies design materials to provide this practice in innovative ways. An example of such a product is available through J/P Associates. This product, *Reader's Club* (Dodds & Chislett, 1995), provides additional reading material for students in *Reading Mastery Level I*.

Teachers using *Corrective Reading* have found that supplementing the program with either *REWARDS* (Archer, Gleason, & Vachon, 2001), *REWARDS Plus* (Archer, Gleason, & Vachon, 2003), and/or *Spelling Through Morphographs* increases students' ability to decode multisyllabic words and expand their vocabulary. *REWARDS* is a program designed specifically to teach students how to read multisyllabic words. It is a twenty-lesson program that is often used preceding *Corrective Reading Decoding Level C. REWARDS Plus* is an extension of *REWARDS* that uses social studies content to practice the strategies taught in *REWARDS*.

Spelling Through Morphographs is an innovative spelling program that uses morphographs as the basis for teaching students to spell difficult words (see Chapter 6 on Direct Instruction Spelling). Because the program teaches affixes and their meanings, teachers who use *Spelling Through Morphographs* report that the program improves reading and vocabulary as well as spelling. The program can be used with *Reading Mastery* and with *Corrective Reading*.

Fluency

As mentioned earlier, the fluency criteria in most Direct Instruction reading programs are minimal. Many Direct Instruction teachers choose to increase the criteria and supplement the fluency practice in the reading programs with additional reading materials. Supplementary programs that can be used for increasing fluency include *Accelerated Reader* (Renaissance Learning, 2002a), *Fluent Reader* (Renaissance Learning, 2002b) and *Read Naturally* (Read Naturally, 2001). *Accelerated Reader* is a computer-based program designed to motivate students to read more literature. Students are encouraged to read books at their instructional level and then are required to take a test to assess their understanding of the book. While *Accelerated Reader* helps increase fluency indirectly by increasing reading practice in an appropriate range of reading materials, *Fluent Reader* is designed to directly increase reading fluency by providing timed practice on specified passages. *Read Naturally,* like *Fluent Reader,* is designed to increase reading fluency directly through the use of repeated and timed practice on selected passages.

Providing practice on reading materials outside the instructional programs not only encourages more accurate and fluent reading but also provides the necessary practice for students in applying their decoding skills to a wider range of texts.

Vocabulary

Vocabulary development for students in Direct Instruction programs can be enhanced in primarily two ways. For younger students, vocabulary development is promoted through the use of language-development programs. (See Chapter 3 on Direct Instruction Language.)

Several supplementary language programs written specifically for use with Direct Instruction reading programs are useful in developing vocabulary skills. One program designed for such use is *PALS-Performance-Based Activities & Literature Skills* (DeLuca, 2000). This program provides students in *Reading Mastery* with vocabulary activities that are directly related to each literature selection in the program.

The second way that vocabulary development can be encouraged is through the use of supplementary writing activities. For example, *Perfect Independent Practice* (Roach, 1998, 1999) and *The J/P POWER Series* (Dodds, Chislett, Dodds, & Dodds, 2002) are programs designed to provide additional practice on the vocabulary and content in *Corrective Reading*.

Comprehension

Reading Success (Dixon, Klau, Rosoff, & Conrad, 2002) is a recently published supplemental reading comprehension program for students who decode at a fourth-grade level or higher. The program contains eighty lessons that require fifteen to twenty minutes of instructional time. These lessons are designed to enhance the effectiveness of Direct Instruction reading programs as well as promote students' ability to transfer the skills those programs teach. *Reading Success* provides additional instruction in strategies designed to foster reading comprehension of both narrative and expository text. For example, the program provides instruction in figurative language as well as paraphrasing passages.

RESEARCH ON DIRECT INSTRUCTION READING

The previous discussion described the evidence supporting the use of Direct Instruction reading programs in terms of how each addresses the five topics identified by the National Reading Panel. Additional evidence to support the use of Direct Instruction reading programs is derived from comparative and evaluative research on the programs themselves.

Both *Reading Mastery* and *Corrective Reading* have been systematically investigated in a number of studies (Adams & Engelmann, 1996; Grossen, 1998; Schieffer, Marchand-Martella, Martella, Simonsen, & Waldron-Soler, 2002). A meta-analysis of Direct Instruction reading research (Adams & Engelmann, 1996) determined a .69 effect size for studies using Direct Instruction reading programs. This effect size is considered to be well above educational significance and approximately equivalent to a ten-point increase on an IQ scale. Adams and Engelmann compared this to the meta-analysis of whole language conducted by Stahl and Miller (1989) that resulted in an effect size of .09, one that is close to chance.

Most of the early research on Direct Instruction was conducted as part of the Follow Through Project. As mentioned in Chapter 2, the Direct Instruction program used in Follow Through was *DISTAR*. An independent evaluation of Follow Through conducted by ABT and Associates (Stebbins, St. Pierre, Proper, Anderson, & Cerva, 1977) found that, at the end of third grade, in reading, students in the Direct Instruction model of Follow Through outperformed comparable control students, as well as students in other Follow Through models.

Meyer (1984) examined the long-term effects of Follow Through by comparing Direct Instruction Follow Through students' ninth-grade reading performance to the reading performance of a similar group of students who had not been in Follow Through. Her results favored those students who had participated in the Direct Instruction Follow Through Model. Other studies (Becker & Gersten, 1982; Gersten, Darch, & Gleason, 1988; Gersten & Keating, 1987) found similar long-term effects from the implementation of Direct Instruction reading programs. (See Chapter 2 for a more detailed description of Follow Through.)

More recently, a number of studies have been conducted to evaluate the efficacy of *Reading Mastery, Horizons,* and *Corrective Reading.*

Reading Mastery

Recently, Schieffer et al. (2002) conducted a comprehensive review of twenty-five non-Follow Through studies comparing *Reading Mastery* to other reading curricula or evaluating the effects of the program across a range of participants. Eight studies included participants who were reading below their same-age peers but not receiving special-education services. Four studies compared *Reading Mastery* or *DISTAR* to other programs for general education students. A group of nine studies analyzed by Schieffer and her colleagues compared the achievement of special education students taught with *Reading Mastery* to those receiving reading instruction from other programs. Finally, Schieffer et al. considered four studies that investigated the effects of *Reading Mastery* or *DISTAR* without comparison to other programs. Schieffer and her colleagues concluded that the use of both programs has positive outcomes for all populations of students. The effects for *Reading Mastery* were most positive with struggling readers, those reading below their same-age peers but not receiving special education services.

Recently a number of comprehensive school reform models for educating at-risk urban students have implemented *Reading Mastery* (Kemper & MacIver, 2002). Although the evaluation of some of these models has shown positive results (Berkeley, 2002; Carlson & Francis, 2002), other implementations have had mixed results (MacIver & Kemper, 2002; O'Brien & Ware, 2002). These findings may be due to differences in the level of implementation.

Silbert (2002) reported that the failure of some comprehensive school-reform models is likely to be caused by poor implementation. These models typically lack initial support, adequate coaching, and sufficient instructional time. Not surprisingly, evidence suggests that high levels of teacher implementation are strongly related to student success (Carlson & Francis, 2002). Specifically, the relationship between teacher implementation and student performance seems particularly strong at the kindergarten level (Gersten et al., 1988; Silbert, 2002).

In summary, *Reading Mastery* has been the subject of a number of studies including evaluations of large-scale school-reform efforts. The effects of the program are clearest for struggling readers, although positive effects have been noted for general education and special-education students, as well. In reviewing this research, it is important to consider the quality of the *Reading Mastery* implementation when interpreting the results.

Horizons

Tobin (2003) conducted a carefully controlled school study comparing the effects of *Horizons Fast Track A/B* to the district-adopted basal reading curriculum. Four classes of first-grade students were initially matched to ensure that the groups were not significantly different at the beginning of the study. The results demonstrated that the *Horizons* groups performed significantly better on measures of reading fluency, reading accuracy, and nonsense word reading than the groups taught using the district-adopted basal reading program. More research on the efficacy of the program is needed.

Corrective Reading

The American Federations of Teachers (1999), as an outgrowth of its Task Force on Improving Low-Performing Schools, published a review of effective remedial reading interventions. To be listed in the review, the programs must have demonstrated: (1) evidence of effectiveness based on independent evaluations of student performance, (2) replication across a number of sites, and (3) evidence of available support for implementation. *Corrective Reading* was one of only five programs listed in this review.

Grossen (1998) reviewed all available research on the program, both controlled comparisons and school evaluations. Eight of the studies she examined evaluated only *Corrective Reading Decoding,* one evaluated only *Corrective Reading Comprehension,* and five addressed both components of the program. A wide range of participants was included in the studies: general education students, limited English-speaking students, and special education students with various identified disabilities.

Grossen (1998) reported that students in *Corrective Reading* progressed faster than expected and faster than students in the comparison groups in all but one of the studies. In the studies Grossen reviewed, reading improvement for students in the program was demonstrated across populations of students as well as across settings in the United States, England, Canada, and Australia.

Corrective Reading also has been investigated in a number of large-scale evaluation studies. One such study, conducted in Broward County, Florida, involved middle school Title I students. In that study, Ligas (2002) found that students who received thirty-five or more hours of instruction in *Corrective Reading* made greater gains than comparable students taught using other programs.

REFERENCES

Adams, M. J. (1990). *Beginning to read: Thinking and learning about print.* Cambridge, MA: MIT Press.

Adams, G. L., & Engelmann, S. (1996). *Research on Direct Instruction: 25 years beyond DISTAR.* Seattle, WA: Educational Achievement Systems.

American Federation of Teachers. (1999). *Building on the best: Learning from what works: Five promising reading intervention programs.* Washington, DC: Author.

Anderson, R. C., Hiebert, E. H., Scott, J. A., & Wilkinson, I.A.G. (1985). *Becoming a nation of readers: The report of the Commission on Reading.* Champaign, IL: Center for the Study of Reading and the National Academy of Education.

Archer, A. L., Gleason, M. M., & Vachon, V. (2001). *REWARDS.* Longmont, CO: Sopris West.

Archer, A. L., Gleason, M. M., & Vachon, V. (2003). *REWARDS Plus.* Longmont, CO: Sopris West.

Armbruster, B. B., Lehr, F., & Osborn, J. (2001). *Put reading first: The research building blocks for teaching children to read.* Jessup, MD: National Institute for Literacy.

Becker, W. C., & Gersten, R. (1982). Follow-up of Follow Through: The later effects of the Direct Instruction model on children in fifth and sixth grades. *American Educational Research Journal, 19,* 75–92.

Berkeley, M. (2002). The importance and difficulty of disciplined adherence to the educational reform mode. *Journal of Education for Students Placed At Risk, 7*(2), 221–240.

Carlson, C. D., & Francis, D. J. (2002). Increasing the reading achievement of at-risk children through Direct Instruction: Evaluation of the Rodeo Institute for Teaching Excellence (RITE). *Journal of Education for Students Placed At Risk, 7*(2), 141–166.

Chall, J. (1975). The reading problem: A diagnosis of the national reading problem; a national strategy for attacking the reading problem; legislative and administrative actions. In J. Carroll (Ed.), *Toward a literate society: The report of the committee on Reading of the National Academy of Education* (pp. 3–45). New York: The National Academy.

Cornwall, A., & Bawden, H. (1992). Reading disabilities and aggression: A critical review. *Journal of Learning Disabilities, 25,* 281–288.

DeLuca, K. (2000). *PALS-Performance-based activities & literature skills.* Valley Stream, NY: J/P Associates.

Dixon, R., Klau, K., Rosoff, A., & Conrad, L. (2002). *Reading success: Effective comprehension strategies.* Boston, MA: Classical Learning Universe.

Dodds, T., & Chislett, M. (1995). *Readers club.* Valley Stream, NY: J/P Associates.

Dodds, T., Chislett, M., Dodds, E., & Dodds, M. (2002). *J/P POWER series.* Valley Stream, NY: J/P Associates.

Employment Policies Institute. (1997, February). *From welfare to work: The transition of an illiterate population.* Retrieved July 10, 2002 from http://www.epionline.org/pubs.html

Gersten, R., Darch, C., & Gleason, M. (1988). Effectiveness of a Direct Instruction academic kindergarten for low-income students. *Elementary School Journal, 86,* 257–276.

Gersten, R., & Keating, T. (1987). Long-term benefits from Direct Instruction. *Educational Leadership, 44,* 28–31.

Grossen, B. (1998). *The research base for Corrective Reading, SRA.* Blacklick, OH: Science Research Associates.

Hodges, J., Giuliotti, N., & Porpotage, F. M. (1994, October). Improving literacy skills of juvenile detainees [Electronic version]. *Juvenile Justice Bulletin, U.S. Department of Justice,* Retrieved from http://www.ojjdp.ncjrs.org/

Kemper, E. A., & MacIver, M. A. (2002). Direct Instruction reading programs: Examining effectiveness for at-risk students in urban settings (Special Issue). *Journal of Education for Students Placed At Risk, 7*(2).

Ligas, M. R. (2002). Evaluation of Broward County Alliance of Quality Schools project. *Journal of Education for Students Placed at Risk, 7*(2), 117–139.

MacIver, M. A., & Kemper, E. (2002). The impact of Direct Instruction on elementary students' reading achievement in an urban school district. *Journal of Education for Students Placed At Risk, 7*(2), 197–220.

Meyer, L. A. (1984). Long-term academic effects of the direct instruction Project Follow Through. *Elementary School Journal, 84,* 389–394.

National Assessment of Educational Progress. (2001). *The nation's report card: Fourth-grade reading 2000.* Retrieved June 26, 2001 from http://nces.ed.gov/nationsreportcard/reading.avegscore.asp

National Reading Panel. (2000). *Report of the National Reading Panel: Teaching children to read: An evidence-based assessment of the scientific research literature on reading and its implications for reading instruction.* Jessup, MD: National Institute for Literacy.

O'Brien, D. M., & Ware, A. M (2002). Implementing research-based reading programs in Fort Worth Independent School District. *Journal of Education for Students Placed At Risk, 7*(2), 167–196.

Pryor, F. L., & Schaffer, D. (1997). Wages and the university educated: A paradox resolved [Electronic version]. *Monthly Labor Review,* 3–18.

Read Naturally. (2001). *Read Naturally.* Saint Paul, MN: Author.

Renaissance Learning. (2002a). *Accelerated Reader.* Wisconsin Rapids, WI: Author.

Renaissance Learning. (2002b). *Fluent Reader.* Wisconsin Rapids, WI: Author.

Roach, R. (1998). *Perfect independent practice (Level A).* Valley Stream, NY: J/P Associates.

Roach, R. (1999). *Perfect independent practice (Levels B1 & B2).* Valley Stream, NY: J/P Associates.

Schieffer, C., Marchand-Martella, N. E., Martella, R. C., Simonsen, F. L., & Waldron-Soler, K. M. (2002). An analysis of *Reading Mastery* program: Effective components and research review. *Journal of Direct Instruction, 2*(2), 87–119.

Silbert, J. (2002). Commentary. *Journal of Education for Students Placed At Risk, 7*(2), 265–272.

Simmons, D. C., & Kameenui, E. J. (1998). *What reading research tells us about children with diverse learning needs: Bases and basics.* Mahwah, NJ: Erlbaum.

Slavin, R. E., Karweit, N. L., Wasik, B. A., Madden, N. A., & Dolan, L. J. (1994). Success for all: A comprehensive approach to prevention and early intervention. In R. E. Slavin, N. L. Karweit, & B. A. Waskin. (Eds.), *Preventing Early School Failure.* Boston: Allyn and Bacon.

Smith, S. B., Simmons, D. C., & Kameeuni, E. J. (1998). Phonological awareness: Research bases. In D. C. Simmons & E. J. Kameenui (Eds.), *What reading research tells us about children with diverse leaning needs: Bases and basics* (pp. 61–109). Mahwah, NJ: Erlbaum.

Snow, C. E., Burns, M. S., & Griffin, P. (Eds.). (1998). *Preventing reading difficulties in young children.* Washington, DC: National Academy Press.

Stahl, S. A., & Miller, P. D. (1989). Whole language and language experience approaches for beginning reading: A quantitative research synthesis. *Review of Educational Research, 59,* 87–116.

Stebbins, L. B., St. Pierre, R. G., Proper, E. C., Anderson, R. B., & Cerva, T. R. (1977). *Education as experimentation: A planned variation model Vols. 4A, 4C. An evaluation of Follow Through.* Cambridge, MA: ABT.

Stein, M. L., Johnson, B., & Gutlohn, L. (1999). Analyzing beginning reading instructional materials: The relationship between instruction and text. *Remedial and Special Education, 20*(5), 275–287.

Tobin, K. G. (2003). The effect of Direct Instruction and prior phonological awareness training on the development of reading in first grade. *Journal of Direct Instruction.*

U.S. Department of Labor. (2000). *Report on the American workforce,* Bureau of Labor Statistics. Retrieved on August 6, 2002, from http://www.bls.gov/opub/rtaw/stattab6.htm

Weaver, C. A., & Kintsch, W. (1991). Expository text. In R. Barr, M. Kamil, P. Mosenthal, & P. D. Pearson (Eds.), *Handbook of reading research.* (Vol. 2, pp. 230–245). New York: Longman.

CHAPTER FIVE

WRITING

LAURA D. FREDRICK AND CANDACE STEVENTON
Georgia State University

OBJECTIVES

After studying this chapter you should be able to:

1. articulate the importance of writing in a literate society;
2. explain the importance of effective writing instruction;
3. describe the components of effective writing instruction;
4. explain how the six design principles are incorporated in Direct Instruction writing programs;
5. identify teaching formats in Direct Instruction writing programs that reflect the six design principles;
6. describe how Direct Instruction writing programs assess for placement and monitor progress;
7. explain how adaptations and extensions develop naturally from the Direct Instruction writing programs;
8. summarize the research that demonstrates the effectiveness of the Direct Instruction writing programs.

Writing is important for learning and for sharing what we know. The importance of writing begins at an early age and continues for a lifetime. As a literate society we rely on writing as an effective means of communication in all walks of life. Because we rely on writing as a major means of communication in our society, writing instruction is critical. This instruction should prepare students for the myriad of writing tasks they will encounter in school and beyond. Writing tasks are typically framed into standards that all students should meet. National writing standards for students continue to increase as we become more sophisticated in our assessment of the writing process. In many states students must demonstrate writing proficiency to earn an academic high school diploma, and by 2005 the SAT will include a writing portion that will account for one-third of the total SAT score. Coupled with these increased standards is evidence to suggest that most students will not learn to write effectively without writing instruction.

Unfortunately, not all writing instruction is equally effective. Effective writing instruction is grounded in six design principles that produce competent and confident writers. In the content analysis and format features that follow, we describe how those principles are incorporated in Direct Instruction writing programs.

These six design principles provide an excellent framework for the delivery of instruction that is responsive to a variety of learners. To be responsive to learners' needs we must place them at appropriate instructional levels and continually monitor their progress. If students do not make adequate progress, adaptations are available. Likewise, when students initially master skills they must continue to practice these skills in a variety of ways to show generalized skills in new situations. Direct Instruction writing extensions are available for this practice. We conclude our examination of the Direct Instruction writing programs by providing information about assessments, adaptations, and extensions before presenting the empirical evidence of the effectiveness of these writing programs.

In our discussion of the effectiveness of the Direct Instruction writing programs we examine research on teaching the reasoning and logic skills incorporated in the programs. In addition, we examine large implementations that include several Direct Instruction programs used in conjunction with the writing programs. Finally, we present the available research that specifically examines these writing programs and their impact on writing development.

IMPORTANCE OF WRITING

Children first experience the importance of writing when they learn to write their names. For most children, learning to write their names and letters of the alphabet occurs before any formal schooling. As soon as children begin their schooling they learn that the importance of being able to write their names is to communicate to teachers which paper is theirs. The handwriting may be slow and labored, but if it is legible teachers are happy and students are proud because the message has been communicated. This early need for writing quickly escalates as children are expected to write more often and for more reasons as they progress through school.

Early writing instruction is often focused on handwriting. However, compared to written language, handwriting has received very little attention as evidenced by the limited instructional time allocated for it (Bain, Bailet, & Moats, 1991). Yet failure to develop handwriting skills will hinder students' writing progress (Graham, 1999a). If handwriting cannot be deciphered it fails to communicate (Isaacson & Gleason, 1997). In addition, when writing is labored assignments take longer to complete and students may have difficulty keeping up with note taking (Graham, 1999b). In both cases students may become frustrated and stop trying.

Writing is important for learning. Students learn to take notes when teachers or other students are sharing information and when they are reading for information. To do this, students must be able to determine what is important, how the information is related to the big picture of the discussion or text, and how they can write it quickly in an abbreviated form so that they can keep up with the oral presentation of information and still have a permanent record to refer to at a later time. Students also use writing to practice what they are learning. They may write note cards to study definitions or foreign language vocabulary or conjugations; they may write outlines from memory to practice and test their understanding of some important events in history.

In addition to writing to learn, students "are asked to demonstrate their learning in different subjects through writing" (Strengthening the Second "R," 2002, p. 1). This writing may be on papers, tests, or homework. If a teacher is to evaluate content knowledge from what students write, the writing must be clear, complete, and well organized. If students' writing is disorganized or replete with grammatical errors, it is difficult for the teacher to determine what the students know. This demand for demonstrating learning through writing continues to increase in upper elementary, middle school, high school, and college (Harris & Graham, 1996).

Writing is important because of its relationship to reading. From an extensive review of the research on the relationship between reading and writing, Tierney and Shanahan (1991) found support for the theory that reading and writing are related. However, from the current research the nature of this relationship is not completely clear. What is clear, however, is that "students who have difficulties with written expression often have difficulties with reading" (Isaacson, 1994, p. 50). Students' reading influences their writing (Adams, 1990), and, through their writing, students learn that the purpose of writing is to share ideas. Reading and writing are interrelated literacy skills for communicating and understanding.

In addition to being linked to reading, writing is linked to thinking. Writing is "a power tool for the enhancement of thinking and learning. Writing and reading together engage learners in a greater variety of reasoning operations than when writing or reading are apart" (Tierney & Shanahan, 1991, p. 272). Writing helps us organize and clarify our thoughts and has an integrating effect on long-term learning. Students may read a portion of text that explains an event or a phenomenon and then write a description of this in their own words. To the extent that manipulating information helps us to understand and remember, writing helps us learn by prompting us to elaborate and manipulate. The more we manipulate the content, the more likely we are to understand and remember it (Tierney & Shanahan).

High-stakes testing often includes a writing component. Currently, twenty-six states require students to demonstrate writing competency to graduate from high school with an academic diploma. North Carolina and Delaware will soon join these states. Forty-nine of the fifty states require a measure of writing competency for high school graduation or include writing assessments as part of statewide testing. These assessments are often used to compare students with national norms, to promote students from one grade to the next, to monitor school performance, to improve teaching and learning, to maintain accreditation, and/or to award school and teacher bonuses (State Assessment Services—State Assessment Advisor, 2002). As previously noted, the College Board has approved the inclusion of a writing component on the SAT beginning in 2005. This writing component will "include a 25-minute essay and multiple-choice grammar usage questions" (Simmons, 2002, C1). It will be worth a maximum of 800 points, the same value given to the verbal section and to the math section, making the writing component one third of the total SAT score (Simmons).

The importance of writing does not end with graduation. In the workplace and in society at large the demand for writing continues. Writing is an important job-related skill

(Agnew, 1992). There are very few jobs that do not require some writing, from technical report writing to notes about a customer's electrical problem and how it was corrected. Consider how often we now send an E-mail rather than make a phone call. When we make phone calls only the person on the receiving end may have to write something—the message to be shared with someone else or a reminder to go or get something. Now, however, with our reliance on E-mail, a good bit of what we had previously communicated orally, we now communicate in writing. We can get our E-mail programs to check for spelling and grammar, but we can't get them to check for clarity and organization so that the E-mail delivers the intended message. Whether in the classroom, the workplace, or simply friend to friend, people are often judged by their writing (Bain et al., 1991). Writing is a literate behavior (Snow, Burns, & Griffin, 1998) and people who do not write in a way that clearly communicates a message to others are not considered literate.

IMPORTANCE OF WRITING INSTRUCTION

The primary reason for teaching writing is to enhance students' communication skills (Graham, 1999a). Young children often approach writing as if it were the same as talking except that they write it on paper. That is, to write a story, they write the words they would use to tell a story orally to a friend. Sentences may be very long. A story may be one sentence that continues for a half page or more. There is little to no planning or organization so that people and events may appear in the story without any introduction. An event important to the beginning of the story may be omitted initially. As young students are writing their story they may realize that they omitted the important event in the beginning of their story. However, instead of returning to the beginning of the story where the event should be introduced, they are likely to introduce the event into the story wherever they are in the story. Writing as a communication process, however, is different from conversation and serves as one of the first challenges that writing instruction teachers face (Isaacson, 1994).

Unfortunately, it appears many teachers are not teaching writing or are at least not teaching it well. Students often begin college and even graduate school ill-prepared to write (Stein, Dixon, & Barnard, 2001). The prevalence of writing centers on college campuses along with required developmental writing courses before beginning academic college courses is evidence of the importance of writing instruction as well as evidence that writing is not currently being taught well. College professors often blame the high school teachers when students are not prepared to write, while high school teachers blame middle school teachers (Stein et al., 2001). Students' difficulty with written expression is thought to be the result of inadequate instruction (Isaacson, 1994), poorly trained teachers, presenting writing too late in the curriculum, and not allocating enough time to write.

"Students probably will not become better writers if they do not spend a relatively substantial part of most school days engaged in productive writing activities" (Dixon, Isaacson, & Stein, 2002, p. 95). The importance of writing instruction is clearly seen in the call for allocating more time for writing instruction and practice (Dixon et al.; Isaacson, 1994; Snow et al., 1998). Graves (1985) found "that children need to write a minimum of 4 days a week to see any appreciable change in the quality of their writing" (p. 39).

Writing is a very demanding and complex process, possibly the most complex of the language skills (Bain et al., 1991; Hall, Salas, & Grimes, 1999; Harris, Schmidt, & Graham, 1997). Writers must take on two roles simultaneously, the author role and the secretary role (Dixon et al., 2002; Isaacson, 1994; Smith, 1982). Both of these roles must be taught explicitly (Isaacson & Gleason, 1997). According to Isaacson (1994), there was a time when we focused primarily on the secretary functions such as "spelling, punctuation, handwriting, and grammar" (p. 44). This focus was followed by an emphasis on the author role and the content to be communicated, but at the expense of the secretary role. Effective writing instruction includes instruction in both roles. Not only must students learn both roles, they need to become fluent in the tool skills of each role. "Tool skills are the most basic elements of more complex skills" (Johnson & Layng, 1992, p. 1479).

Handwriting is an important tool skill for the secretary role, a skill that is often neglected in today's schools. Students need to be fluent in handwriting (Graham, Harris, MacArthur, & Schwartz, 1991) so that they can focus their attention on the content of their writing. When the mechanics of handwriting demand too much attention, students may be unable to focus on the content of their writing (Graham, 1990).

In addition to interfering with text production, poor penmanship can affect the perceptions others have of quality writing (Graham, 1999a). Yet, handwriting instruction is not being stressed in our schools, possibly because teacher-preparation programs rarely include instruction in how to teach handwriting. Unfortunately, there is very little evidence that students will learn handwriting in some natural way by simply being immersed in a literacy-rich environment; rather, students need explicit instruction in handwriting. "The basic goals of handwriting instruction are to help students develop handwriting that is legible and that can be produced quickly with little conscious attention" (Graham, 1999a, p. 84).

SIX DESIGN PRINCIPLES OF EFFECTIVE INSTRUCTION

Writing instruction is critical for the development of many writing skills, and for students to become competent and confident writers, the instruction they receive must be carefully designed. "The first steps in learning to write are as important as the first steps in reading instruction. What the student learns at first will influence the student's approach to writing" (Engelmann & Silbert, 1983, p. 3). If students learn misconceptions about writing early in their education, these misconceptions will be difficult to correct later on. Writing instruction that incorporates the six design principles of effective instruction is recommended if the time and energy devoted to writing instruction is to result in high-level writing skills. The six design principles of effective instruction include: big ideas, conspicuous strategies, mediated scaffolding, strategic integration, primed background knowledge, and judicious review (Kameenui, Carnine, & Dixon, 2002). These design principles guide effective instructional delivery in writing instruction.

Big Ideas

Big Ideas are the important aspects of a content area. With each passing year there is more information to be learned and greater demands on teachers to facilitate that learning.

However, not all information is equally important. What makes information more or less important is the extent to which it promotes new learning or can be used to solve new problems. The big ideas are those concepts or ideas that are the most important because they provide knowledge and skills that students can use to further develop their expertise in a particular content area. Text structure, the way text is organized, is a big idea in writing instruction. Text structures provide patterns students can use to organize the important information they are trying to communicate with their writing. An example of a text structure is compare/contrast (Kameenui & Simmons, 1999). While there are several text structures that can be taught, it is more effective to teach just a couple of text structures each year and to teach them very well (Dixon et al., 2002).

Conspicuous Strategies

Conspicuous strategies are overt strategies students can use to facilitate their writing. Mature writers use strategies to engage in the processes of writing as they create text (Englert, Raphael, Anderson, Anthony, & Stevens, 1991). Students need to learn these strategies, and while some of these strategies may be learned relatively independently, "extensive empirical evidence suggests strongly that all students . . . benefit from having good strategies made conspicuous for them, as long as great care is taken to ensure that the strategies are designed to result in widely transferable knowledge of their application" (Kameenui et al., 2002, p. 11). An example of a conspicuous strategy in writing instruction is to simplify the problem. Here is an example many of us may use when we hesitate for just a second to decide if we want to write *friend and I* or *friend and me* in the sentence *George came with my friend and I/me.* To simplify, we write two sentences: *George came with my friend,* and *George came with me.* When we simplify the original sentence, it is easy to know the correct pronoun in the first sentence is *me: George came with my friend and me* (Dixon et al., 2002).

Mediated Scaffolding

Mediated scaffolding provides the support needed to help students master the big ideas and to be successful. Effective scaffolding essentially provides as much support as students need and, as soon as possible, fades that support while students remain successful until independent performance is demonstrated. Think sheets provide a type of scaffolding designed to support students' planning, drafting, revising, and editing. A think sheet asks students to provide specific information to help them get started with their writing. Students are asked to write the topic, the audience, their goal, and everything they know about the topic, and then to list possible ways to group their ideas (Dixon et al., 2002). Filling out the think sheets helps students plan and organize their writing (Englert et al., 1991). Initially these think sheets can be completed with teachers and peers modeling and discussing the process until, eventually, students can use the think sheets on their own.

Strategic Integration

Strategic integration is "the careful and systematic combining of essential information in ways that result in new and more complex knowledge" (Kameenui et al., 2002, p. 13).

Helping students see the relationships within and across content areas promotes higher-level learning in related content areas. The compare/contrast text structure is a big idea that can be integrated into reading and writing instruction as we teach both comprehension and composition (Kameenui & Simmons, 1999). Teaching "mechanical skills concurrently with composition, focusing upon big ideas such as sentence manipulation to learn usage or morphology for spelling" (Dixon et al., 2002, p. 112) is another example of strategic integration.

Primed Background Knowledge

Primed background knowledge is critical to new learning. It refers to any preexisting knowledge students have that will affect new learning. It is important to know students' background knowledge and to make them aware of the background knowledge they have that will help them learn the new skills. Often teachers know that students have demonstrated prior knowledge that will support new learning but they fail to make the students aware that they have this knowledge. When teaching students to include pronouns effectively in their writing, teachers may first remind students of what they know about nouns and how to use nouns in writing.

Judicious Review

Judicious review refers to "repeatedly considering material in sensible and well-advised ways" (Kameenui et al., 2002, p. 14). Judicious review enhances memory and builds fluency. According to Kameenui et al., the four critical dimensions of judicious review are that it is sufficient, distributed, cumulative, and varied. There must be enough review that students are able to "perform the task without hesitation," and the review "must be distributed over time" (p. 14). In addition "the review must snowball strategically into an integrated form, in which familiar information establishes the groundwork for new information, and both new and old information are melded over time" (p. 15). Finally, the practice needs to be varied to increase the probability of generalization of the newly learned content to new contexts or situations. Most commercial writing programs do not provide enough review and practice (Stein et al., 2001). For example, they may introduce many text structures in one school year, leaving students unprepared to write any one text structure very well. If, however, teachers provide adequate review of a text structure such as compare/contrast, the strategies may become less conspicuous, the need for scaffolding more diminished, the priming of background knowledge easier, and strategic integration obvious. The six design principles provide a means for structuring the teaching of both the author role and the secretary role in writing while also demonstrating the importance of providing writing instruction if students are to learn to write well.

If we want writing to be taught effectively we must use instructional strategies that have demonstrated effectiveness and we must continue to evaluate these strategies (Hillocks, 1984). In the 1990s many school districts adopted a "literature-based" approach to teaching reading and writing. The focus was on authentic literature as dictated by the "whole-language" approach. There was little, if any, direct teaching of reading or writing and the reading scores in many states began to decline (Carnine, Silbert, & Kameenui, 1997). It became evident that without direct explicit instruction it was very difficult for many, if not most, students to learn to read and write well. Good writing is not likely to develop by relying on "the student's natural development of writing abilities within authentic contexts" (Harris & Graham, 1996, p. x), or by simply allowing or requiring students to write without instruction. Teachers need to take an active role in directing writing instruction and this instruction needs to be explicit (Isaacson, 1994; Strengthening the Second "R", 2002).

The importance of writing instruction is seen in the benefits it provides all children. While many readily agree that students with learning problems, or students who are at-risk, may need explicit writing instruction, such instruction is not always considered necessary for other children. Yet there is evidence that effective writing instruction benefits all children including those with disabilities, those in general education, those who are high achievers (Strengthening the Second "R", 2002), and those we label as gifted (Ginn, Keel, & Fredrick, 2002).

OVERVIEW OF DIRECT INSTRUCTION WRITING PROGRAMS

Good writing has four core features: it is clear, expresses exactly what the writer wants to communicate, is efficient, and follows the basic rules of grammar. Direct Instruction writing programs integrate and build on these core features for reading and writing activities as students progress through school. Students become facile writers who view writing as both enjoyable and useful.

Direct Instruction writing programs are uniquely organized into teaching tracks rather than teaching units. Program lessons consist of multiple tracks that provide students ample opportunity to learn, practice, and apply skills and concepts that are necessary for understanding more complex writing skills and concepts. Table 5.1 provides a brief program description and a listing of the skills, concepts, and tracks found in the various programs.

In addition to the unique organization of these programs, big ideas and strategies are utilized to provide students with optimal learning. For instance, we can scan Table 5.1 and notice that a big idea in writing instruction, writer as author and secretary, is evident in the majority of the programs. Composition, mechanics, and editing are taught concurrently. The strategic integration of these basic writing processes produces competent and confident writers.

While Direct Instruction writing programs share many common design features, the programs differ in purpose and scope. *Cursive Writing* and *Reasoning and Writing* are intended for students who are working at or near grade level. *Basic Writing Skills* and *Expressive Writing* are remedial programs designed for older students who have not mastered basic writing skills. An overview of the individual programs follows. To allow for easy reference, the programs are discussed in the same order as they are listed in Table 5.1.

Cursive Writing

The *Cursive Writing* program builds on the student's prior knowledge of manuscript stroke formations. The program teaches cursive letters as simple extensions of manuscript letters. This format provides a "natural" transformation process. In addition, the program controls the sequence for converting manuscript letters to cursive letters and provides students with two general conversion rules for slant and joined letters. The controlled sequence and the generalizability of the conversion rules facilitate the most efficient and broad acquisition of cursive writing skills.

Strategies are employed to teach students basic letter formations. Conspicuous visual prompts are utilized and faded. Teachers provide heavy scaffolding of new skills. First, they model and talk through the strokes with the students. Then the students trace the letters one stroke at a time. Finally, the students practice writing the letters in isolation and writing the letters when they are joined with other letters. All learned letters are practiced regularly.

TABLE 5.1 Overview of Direct Instruction Writing Programs

PROGRAM SUMMARY	MAJOR CONCEPTS, SKILLS, TEACHING TRACKS
Cursive Writing • 140 lessons • For older students or third- and fourth-grade students who passed the placement test and have mastered basic manuscript	• Name, read, and write upper- and lower-case letters, letter combinations, and words • Copy letters, words, sentences, and paragraphs according to a rate criterion • Read questions in cursive and write cursive responses
Basic Writing Skills: Sentence Development • 31-lesson remedial program • Mastery quizzes and unit tests • For students in grades 6–12 who pass the placement test and demonstrate at least third-grade reading and spelling skills	• Recognize and write complete sentences • Expand simple sentences • Combine shorter sentences into longer sentences • Write compound and complex sentences

Basic Writing Skills: Capitalization and Punctuation
• 40-lesson remedial program
• Mastery quizzes and unit tests
• For students in grades 6–12 who pass the placement test and demonstrate at least third-grade reading and spelling skills
	• Edit and write sentences by utilizing 19 basic capitalization and punctuation rules that include
	  ○ Capitals of specific people, places, events
	  ○ Commas
	  ○ Apostrophes
	  ○ Question marks

Expressive Writing 1 • 50 lessons • For fourth- through eighth-grade students who have not mastered or have not been taught basic expressive writing skills and read on a third-grade reading level	• Follow basic rules of grammar, style, and punctuation • Translate observations into sentences • Edit and write paragraphs that do not deviate from a topic • Edit one's own work and the work of peers
Expressive Writing 2 • 10 preprogram lessons and 45 regular lessons • For fourth- through eighth-grade students who have been through Expressive Writing 1 or who pass the placement test; have beginning fourth-grade reading skills; read and write cursive; copy simple sentences at 15 words per minute; and possess basic language patterns	• Write in a clear manner • Write using a variety of sentences • Write passages that report on events and infer events not shown in pictures • Write what people say using appropriate paragraphing skills • Edit for clarity, punctuation, paragraph conventions, and sentence forms

TABLE 5.1   (Continued)

PROGRAM SUMMARY	MAJOR CONCEPTS, SKILLS, TEACHING TRACKS	
Reasoning and Writing: Level A • 70 lessons (including 7 test lessons) • For young students who pass the placement test, have basic language-comprehension skills, and are in a beginning reading program	• Following Directions • True/False • Sequencing • If-Then • All, Some, or None • Classification	• Right/Left • Questions and Clues • Data • Alternative Solutions • Story Grammar • Writing
Reasoning and Writing: Level B • 70 lessons (including 7 test lessons) • For young students who read on a beginning second-grade level	• Classification and Clues • Sentence Construction • Directions • Dialect • Deductions • Perspective • Spatial Orientation	• Temporal Sequencing • Clarity • Time, Rate, and Distance • Reporting and Inference • Correlated Events • Story Grammar
Reasoning and Writing: Level C • 110 lessons (including 10 test lessons) • For students who pass the placement test, read on at least a second-grade level, can follow instructions, can copy 10 words per minute, and can correctly spell copied words	• Deductions • Sentence Analysis • Mechanics • Editing • Reporting–based on Pictures	• Inferring–based on Pictures • Clarity–based on Pictures • Relevance • Expanded Writing Process
Reasoning and Writing: Level D • 110 lessons (including 11 test lessons) • For students who pass the placement test, read on at least a fourth-grade level, can copy 15 words per minute, and can write basic paragraphs	• Parts of Speech and Sentence Analysis • Clarity • Sentence Types • Inaccurate and Unclear Directions	• Misleading and Inaccurate Claims • Arguments • Passage Writing
Reasoning and Writing: Level E • 70 lessons (including 7 test lessons plus 10 additional projects) • For students who pass the placement test, are able to read on at least a fourth-grade level, can copy 15 words per minute, and can write basic paragraphs	• Retell • Parallel Construction • Parts of Speech/ Sentence Analysis • General/Specific	• Clarity • Vocabulary • Descriptions • Writing • Projects (Team Activities)
Reasoning and Writing: Level F • 100 lessons (including 7 test lessons) • For students who pass the placement test, read on a fourth-grade level, and can write basic paragraphs	• Retell • Grammar and Usage • General/Specific • Clarity of Meaning	• Deductions and Inferences • Writing • Writing Extensions

Teachers gradually fade their support but continue to monitor student performance and provide corrective feedback.

The *Cursive Writing Program* emphasizes application of cursive skills. Students are required to copy sentences, to read in cursive, and to write responses to questions in cursive. In addition, rate and accuracy criteria are used to promote writing fluency. By strategically integrating the mechanics of cursive handwriting with composition and requiring fluent skill performance, students begin to apply cursive skills to other writing activities.

Basic Writing Skills

There are two *Basic Writing Skills* programs: *Sentence Development* and *Capitalization and Punctuation.* Both programs are remedial and are intended for students in grades six through twelve.

Basic Writing Skills: Sentence Development.   *Basic Writing Skills: Sentence Development* teaches students to write a variety of well-constructed sentences. The instructional skill sequence requires students to master presented skills before moving on to new lessons. The program emphasis is on skill mastery and judicious cumulative review. Teachers provide scaffolding of newly presented rules, sentence manipulation procedures, and editing checks. Students learn the rules and procedures and then edit inaccurate sentence models. Finally, students compose sentences and edit their own work.

Basic Writing Skills: Capitalization and Punctuation.   *Basic Writing Skills: Capitalization and Punctuation* teaches capitalization and punctuation rules. It emphasizes mastery of newly learned skills before the introduction of additional skills. The teacher provides scaffolding and conspicuous strategies to teach the application of nineteen capitalization and punctuation rules. First, teachers employ modeling and questioning to teach new skills and review learned skills. Next, they provide inaccurate models that students are required to check and edit. Finally, teachers dictate sentences that students write and edit to show how well they can apply the rules and strategies.

Expressive Writing

There are two Expressive Writing programs: *Expressive Writing 1* and *Expressive Writing 2.* Both are remedial programs designed for students in grades six through twelve.

Expressive Writing 1.   *Expressive Writing 1* can meet the needs of a wide variety of learners who have not yet mastered beginning written expression skills. It concurrently introduces skills required of the writer as an author and a secretary through four major teaching tracks: (1) mechanics, (2) sentence writing, (3) paragraph writing, and (4) editing. The strategic integration of these four tracks allows students to learn a foundation of skills that build on one another and lead naturally to other skills.

The skills taught in the mechanics track include capitalizing the first word in a sentence and placing periods at the end of a sentence. Students also learn to indent the first word of a paragraph, copy accurately, and read passages written in cursive.

In the sentence-writing track, a declarative sentence structure of naming and telling more is taught. This basic sentence structure allows students to communicate ideas in an effective manner. By manipulating the word order in sentences, more elaborate sentences can be introduced. Students are shown that changes in mechanics relate to changes in sentence structures. This big idea teaches students that punctuation and grammar conventions are not arbitrary.

The paragraph-writing activities form the core of the program. Students are required to use all the skills taught in the other tracks. The paragraph structure is similar to the basic sentence structure of naming and telling more. It is an efficient format that involves pictures and requires students to report on what happened. It utilizes limited vocabulary and sentence types, thus reducing punctuation and spelling problems. In addition, it provides students with an effective template to understand and develop main ideas and supporting details.

Lessons include editing checks so that students reread their paragraphs four times. Students edit their own writing as well as the writing of their peers. The editing activities plus continuous teacher feedback minimize the development of bad writing habits. By the end of the program, students have mastered a paragraph writing structure and a basic battery of writing skills that allow them to learn about other writing genres and mechanical manipulations.

Expressive Writing 2.   *Expressive Writing 2* expands the four teaching tracks introduced in *Expressive Writing 1*. In addition to the mechanics taught in *Expressive Writing 1*, students are taught to punctuate sentences with a dependent clause, actions or names, and quotations, as well as sentences using the word *but*. Students learn to manipulate a variety of sentence types including sentences that begin with a dependent clause, sentences that contain a series, and compound sentences. Paragraph conventions are expanded to teach direct quotations. Passage writing and editing, the most important components of the program, provide students practice with the roles of author and secretary. Editing checks are expanded to include a broader range of writing skills such as pronoun clarity, commas and quotes, sentence types, and multiple paragraphs. Students read their passages orally to the class and teachers call on students to tell something good about the selection that relates to the editing requirements. All students are afforded an opportunity to fix their passages before turning in the final draft.

The writing process of planning, drafting, editing, revising, and publishing is evident in the careful sequencing and integration of the program's four teaching tracks. Students are able to report on and infer events, understand types of important detail, use mechanical skills for expressing ideas, and edit what they write. By the end of this program, students are transformed into competent beginning writers who understand and enjoy the writing process.

Reasoning and Writing

The *Reasoning and Writing* series is the newest of the Direct Instruction writing programs. This series is designed for students who are at or near grade level. The programs progress at one year of curriculum per school year and are intended for students who have not been previously exposed to the content. The *Reasoning and Writing* series includes six levels, A–F, that are designed to meet the needs of diverse learners in the elementary and middle grades. The program is a unique organization of higher-order thinking skills and design features that ensure great results and accelerated cognitive growth for all students. The cumulative and sequenced instructional tracks that emerge across all levels of the program are best understood through a level-by-level analysis.

Reasoning and Writing: Level A.   *Reasoning and Writing: Level A* prepares students for higher-order thinking skills that students will encounter in later grades. A big idea at this level is the story grammar that integrates what students learn. Story grammars use characters to teach students about story structure. The characters possess qualities that put them in problematic situations. Possible solutions are predicted based on information about the characters and details of the story. This unique, and highly engaging, story genre enables students to create parallel stories based on familiar story grammars and to extrapolate the details of model stories to create new stories with the same grammar. Major skill tracks taught at this level are related to stories. Skills are introduced through isolated instruction and are integrated into the stories later.

Three other big ideas introduced at this level are sequencing, classification, and basic reasoning. Students learn and apply these major concepts to help understand the stories and to create their own stories. Sequencing knowledge allows students to use symbols to create a sequence of events or to refer to symbols to reconstruct a series of events. Classification knowledge involves people, objects, and events. Reasoning knowledge includes the concepts of *if-then* statements, *all, some,* and *none,* direction words, clues to eliminate possibilities, and binary logic (a classification system that uses only two choices). Through story grammars and these major knowledge structures, students learn that words can be used to express ideas and that writing is a way to illustrate those ideas.

Reasoning and Writing: Level B.   *Reasoning and Writing: Level B* expands on what students have learned about story grammars. It teaches them to anticipate events and to relate those events to characters and situations. Students also learn temporal sequencing of events, a higher-order thinking skill that requires interpreting pictures and diagrams. Classification knowledge is expanded and requires students to manipulate subclasses that are within larger classes. Reasoning knowledge is expanded to include constructing deductions and drawing conclusions, following and writing instructions, and adopting different perspectives.

In the writing track, students work with sentences that name and tell more. This sentence format prepares the students for further sentence analysis skills. It also introduces students to inferences and to discrimination of sentences that do and do not accurately report what a picture shows. The writing track strategically integrates basic mechanics, grammar, and reasoning skills to prepare students for later writing.

Reasoning and Writing: Level C.   *Reasoning and Writing: Level C* focuses on the writing process that lays the foundation for narrative writing. At this level, the writing process involves strategic integration of pretaught skills and effective instructional sequences. Skill introduction is cumulative in nature and is practiced extensively throughout the remainder of the program. Big ideas are viewed as global strategies to create relationships between what students already know and what they are taught at this level.

The global strategies are major teaching tracks found within the program. Students are introduced to grammar skills through the understanding that grammar provides a communication link to the reader. Students learn to communicate details by organizing and writing basic passages that report on pictures. This writing format sets the stage for drawing inferences based on missing pictures and using picture details as evidence of what must have happened. Students are taught basic rules of clarity and organization. Exercises focus on the idea that what somebody writes may be perfectly clear to the writer, but not to the reader. In addition, students are taught editing as a system of checks used to reinforce the communication skills and mechanical skills. The editing activities are conspicuous strategies that relate what students learn to what they write.

Level C lays the groundwork for the writing process, a process that students must apply in later grades. Through careful integration and sequencing of skills, procedures, and strategies, students are able to look at the writing process as a communication process. They become writers who view the writing process as interconnected components necessary for effective communication.

Reasoning and Writing: Level D. *Reasoning and Writing: Level D* shifts the writing process focus from narrative writing to expository writing. At this level, most of the writing assignments involve examining sources of information, identifying problems of accuracy, and writing explanations to problems. Students learn to write about what others say by working with misleading claims, faulty arguments, and contradictory accounts.

The major vehicle that drives the higher-order thinking skills taught at this level is the outline diagram. Outline diagrams are conspicuous strategies that provide students with visual templates to construct various forms of sentence and passage writing. Students learn to use outline diagrams to respond to misleading claims and directions and to discriminate faulty arguments. Outline diagrams are introduced in a controlled instructional sequence. The teaching formats and activities provide scaffolded instruction. As a result of these design features, students who complete this level are practiced at approaching sources with specific questions they want answered. They can interpret information presented in a variety of forms. They can summarize and critique what they read. Most importantly, they have learned higher-order thinking skills that are necessary for reading and writing assignments in later grades.

Reasoning and Writing: Level E. *Reasoning and Writing: Level E* expands outline diagrams to incorporate a variety of expository writing formats. Several big ideas for writing responses are taught. Students learn to respond to arguments that have faulty conclusions. They learn about hypothesis testing by writing critiques of faulty conclusions based on experimental evidence. In addition, they learn to draft plans that require a series of decisions by following a complex outline diagram to explain which plan is practical and why alternatives are impractical.

One major instructional track introduced at this level is the retell. Retell activities provide for strategic integration of skills necessary for organizing information around different category headings, recalling details of what was presented, and reconstructing sentences that were presented orally. Students who master these skills become adept at note taking and reconstructing information.

Reasoning and Writing: Level F. Although *Reasoning and Writing: Level F* continues to develop specific skills in usage, grammar, and following formats for expressing ideas, the major focus is on critical thinking. Four big ideas included at this level are alternative explanations, parallelism, general versus specific, and the relationship between a large population and a sample of members. Students learn to discriminate faulty arguments and to write other possible conclusions. Parallelism is used to teach parts of speech as a general rule of grammar by showing that words holding the same position and function have the same part of speech. General versus specific is a key concept that students apply to the important skill of writing summaries, deductions, and directions. Finally, students learn that a sample population may provide a distorted view of the range of variation in a whole population. These big ideas provide students with a good beginning to understand the scientific method, to identify problems and write about them, to view conclusions skeptically, and to consider alternatives that are consistent with the evidence given. More importantly, students learn relevant skills that promote higher-order reasoning and writing required in later grades.

CONTENT ANALYSIS AND FORMAT FEATURES

Direct Instruction writing programs, particularly the *Reasoning and Writing* series, are organized to teach clear communication from writer to reader. Siegfried Engelmann stated:

> For writers, facility with perspectives means addressing not only the content they want to express but also any possible difficulties that a reader might have in understanding the details of their communication. . . . Readers and writers achieve flexible perspectives by learning how to analyze a communication for the significance of its details and by learning to place those details in the "big picture" (Science Research Associates/McGraw-Hill, 1983, p. 3).

While content varies across and within the Direct Instruction writing programs, the central purpose of teaching skills that result in clear written communication is continuous throughout all the programs. In Direct Instruction writing programs, the big picture is presented through big ideas and supported by the use of proven and effective curricular design principles.

Direct Instruction writing programs use formats to teach the big ideas and strategies that develop competent writers. These teaching formats follow Direct Instruction design and delivery principles. Excerpts of these formats are presented and summarized in this section. The excerpted formats are by no means a comprehensive list. Rather, they are snapshots that typify the basic design principles of good writing instruction.

Big Ideas

One big idea in writing instruction is the dual role of the writer as an author and as a secretary. The *Expressive Writing* programs integrate these two roles as students progress from sentence writing to passage writing. Figure 5.1 illustrates a lesson at the beginning of *Expressive Writing 1*. Students are to write a basic paragraph and make sure it complies with the editing checks listed below the picture. Prior to this lesson, students have practiced discriminating sentences that report on what happened, using pronouns to replace nouns, and punctuating simple declarative sentences.

Figure 5.2 shows a lesson from the end of *Expressive Writing 2* that requires students to write five paragraphs based on pictures and sentences and to follow editing criteria that

PART F

Instructions: Write a paragraph that reports on what Jill did. Copy the sentence that tells the main thing Jill did. Then make up at least two more sentences that tell what she did. Begin each new sentence with *she.*

| backwards | air | waved | ice cream cone | sidewalk | smiled |

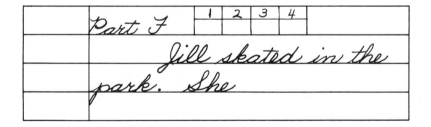

Check 1: Does each sentence begin with a capital and end with a period?

Check 2: Does each sentence tell what happened, not what is happening?

Check 3: Does each sentence report on what the picture shows?

Check 4: Does each new sentence you made up begin with *she?*

FIGURE 5.1 *Expressive Writing 1,* **Student Workbook, Lesson 9, Part F. Reprinted with permission of the McGraw-Hill Companies.**

PART D

Bill lost his balance as he climbed up a tall tree.

What was in the truck?
How did Bill get down from the tree?
Why didn't Bill get hurt?
What did Bill say to his friends after they helped him?

mattresses	piled	yelled	telephone booth
scared	tightly	grip	dangled

Check 1: Is each sentence punctuated correctly?
Check 2: Are there any unclear words in your paragraphs?
Check 3: Did you tell all the important things that must have happened?
Check 4: Did you write at least five paragraphs?

Workbook	Paragraph				Bonus	Total
	Check 1	Check 2	Check 3	Check 4		

FIGURE 5.2 *Expressive Writing 2,* **Student Workbook, Lesson 40, Part D.
Reprinted with permission of the McGraw-Hill Companies.**

D.

FIGURE 5.3   *Reasoning and Writing: Level A,* **Student Workbook, Lesson 13, Part D. Reprinted with permission of the McGraw-Hill Companies.**

are more sophisticated. In the last five lessons of the program, students are asked to write an interesting story. They are given a template with four blank picture boxes and editing criteria. By integrating editing with writing, students quickly learn their dual roles as secretaries and authors.

Another big idea in writing is the use of text structures to teach writing genres. *Reasoning and Writing: Level A* first introduces students to story grammars. Students learn to anticipate and predict outcomes through story grammars. Figure 5.3 illustrates an activity that requires students to tell the story based on the picture of Paul, who in an earlier story, painted things purple. If Paul dripped paint on something near where he was painting, he solved the problem by painting that item purple. Students follow the basic story grammar for Paul using the *p-starting* words shown in the picture.

A third big idea is the writing process. *Reasoning and Writing: Level C* develops this process during the last twenty lessons of the program. Figure 5.4 shows the teaching format

EXERCISE 3—Passage Writing Endings

1. Everybody, pencils down. For the rest of the lessons in this program, you're going to spend more time writing. You have learned a lot of things. Now you'll get to use them. You're going to write letters. You're going to write make-believe stories. You're going to write long stories. And you're going to learn how to revise them after you've written them. You'll revise them to make them better. We may even make a book that has our better stories in it and put that book in the library.

2. Today I'm going to tell you the first part of a story. Then you're going to make up an interesting ending.

• Listen to the first part of the story:

> Barbara was very sad. Her little sister needed an operation. That operation cost hundreds and hundreds of dollars, but Barbara's parents didn't have enough money for the operation. Barbara couldn't help them out because all she had was 16 dollars.
>
> Two days after Barbara and her parents learned that Barbara's sister might die without the operation, Barbara was walking along the sidewalk a few blocks from her house. She was walking and thinking and worrying about her sister.
>
> Suddenly, she stopped. She saw something on the sidewalk. It was a wallet, and it had lots of money in it. She picked it up and counted the money—2 thousand dollars.
>
> She looked at the cards in the wallet. That wallet belonged to a person named Dave Smith.
>
> Barbara didn't know what to do. The wallet didn't belong to her and she was very honest. She didn't want to take money that belonged to Dave Smith. But Barbara didn't want her sister to die, either.
>
> At last, Barbara decided to ask somebody what she should do. She took the wallet and went to . . .

3. That's where the story stops. You have to write the rest of it. Remember the problem that Barbara had. She didn't want to take the money because it didn't belong to her. At the same time, she wanted her sister to have the operation.

4. Everybody, take out a sheet of lined paper and write your name on the top line. Raise your hand when you're finished.

• Everybody, open your textbook to lesson 91 and find part D.

That picture shows Barbara walking somewhere with the wallet.

• Touch what's written below the picture. It says: Barbara took the wallet and went to . . . Remember, she went to talk to somebody who could help her figure out what to do.

• You'll start your paragraph with what's already written. You'll complete that sentence. Then you'll write at least **three** paragraphs that make a nice ending to the story. You'll tell what Barbara did first and what she decided to do with the wallet. Remember to give a clear picture of what happened. Don't just say she went to a friend's house. **Name** the friend. Don't just say they talked. Tell what they **said.** Then give a clear picture of what Barbara did **after** she talked to the person she went to see. At least two sentences should begin with a part that tells when. Raise your hand when you're finished. You have 15 minutes.
(Observe students and give feedback.)

5. (After 15 minutes, say:) Stop writing. Now you'll check your ending. Make check boxes under your paragraphs.

FIGURE 5.4 *Reasoning and Writing: Level C,* **Lesson 91, Exercise 3. Reprinted with permission of the McGraw-Hill Companies.**

EXERCISE 3—Passage Writing Endings (Continued)	

- Here's check 1: Does each paragraph have no more than one person talking? Look over your paragraphs. If more than one person talks in a paragraph, fix it up. Make a **P** with a circle around it to show where the next paragraph should begin. Raise your hand when you're finished with check 1.
- ù Here's check 2: Did you write at least two sentences that begin with a part that tells when? Find those sentences. Make sure they're

punctuated correctly. Raise your hand when you're finished with check 2.
6. I'll mark your papers before the next lesson and tell you about any mistakes.

Note: **On the next lesson, students will revise and rewrite their stories. You will divide the class into teams of 3 students. Try to include a higher performer in each team. Team members will sit together.**

for introducing passage writing. In this format, teachers set the stage for writing by referring to skills students have learned thus far and to the types of stories students will be able to write and publish. Teachers provide the students with the first step in the writing process, prewriting. In addition, they set the editing criteria for the students' first drafts. After the students write their first drafts, teachers guide them through the editing process. During the next lesson, students work in teams to revise the endings they wrote.

Conspicuous Strategies

Conspicuous strategies are planning strategies that provide the framework for big ideas in writing. *Reasoning and Writing: Level D* develops X-boxes to support the big ideas of claims, directions, and arguments. Figure 5.5 shows a test item from Test 2 given after Lesson 20. Here, the X-box is used to provide a template for writing clear directions.

Later in the program, the X-box is modified and expanded to support responses to claims and arguments. Figure 5.6 displays all of the outline diagrams using X-boxes in Level D.

Part C

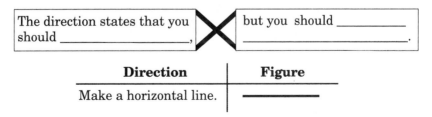

FIGURE 5.5 *Reasoning and Writing: Level D,* Student Textbook, Lesson 20, Test 2, Part C. Reprinted with permission of the McGraw-Hill Companies.

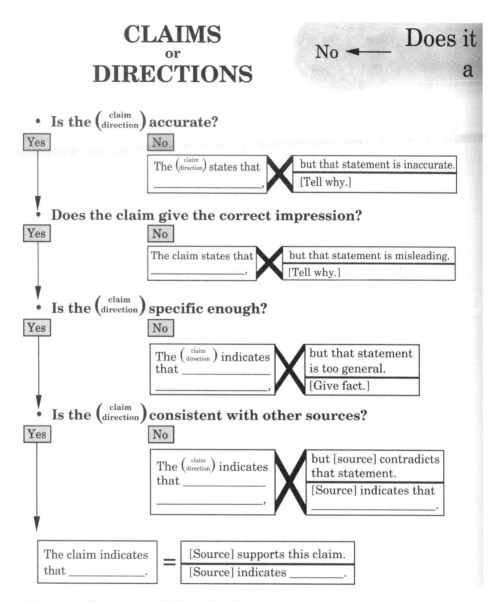

FIGURE 5.6 *Reasoning and Writing: Level D,* **Student Textbook, Outline Diagrams. Reprinted with permission of the McGraw-Hill Companies.**

Mediated Scaffolding

The *Cursive Writing* program relies on scaffolding to teach students how to write cursive letters, words, and sentences. Figure 5.7 is an excerpt from a portion of Lesson 1 of the student workbook and the teacher-presentation book. The format utilizes heavy scaffolding that is faded as students practice the various letter forms. As students become proficient in

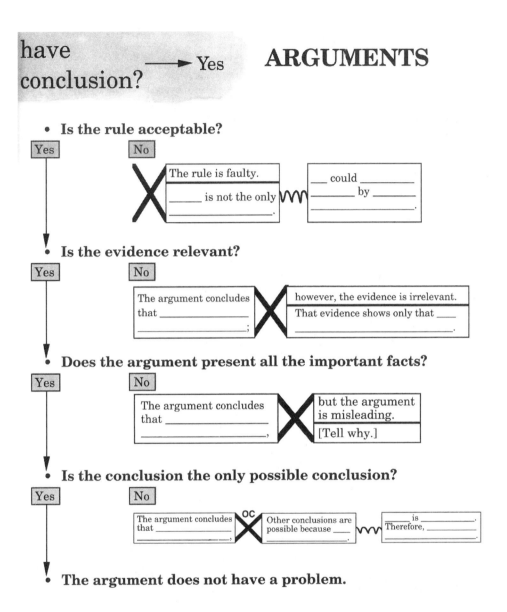

letter writing, teachers fade the modeling and questioning prompts. After practice with tracing the letter forms, students practice writing the letters without the tracing prompts. Students continue to practice the letters throughout the entire program.

Strategic Integration

Strategic integration combines a variety of previously learned skills and concepts to develop higher-order thinking processes. *Reasoning and Writing: Level E* uses team activities to

INTRODUCING BASIC FORMS—Lesson 1

EXERCISE 5—Form Introduction

1. You're going to learn how to make an i form.
   That's the letter **i** without a dot.
   First I'll say each stroke for the i form
   and then I'll make it.

2. Up to the half line.
   (Write that stroke on the
   board and stop.)
   Name that stroke.
   (Signal.) Up to the half line.
   To correct:
   a. (Repeat the stroke description.)
   b. Name that stroke. (Signal.)

3. Next stroke.
   Down to the baseline and tail.
   (Write that stroke on the board.)
   Name that stroke.
   (Signal.) Down to the baseline and tall.

4. (Repeat steps 2 and 3 for
   two more examples.)

5. Touch the arrow at the bottom
   of your worksheet. (Check.)
   This arrow shows which way
   your paper should face.

6. Turn your paper so the arrow points
   to the middle of your body. (Check.)

7. Your turn to trace some i forms.
   Touch line 4. (Check.)
   There's a bump on every slant bar
   right at the baseline.
   Put your pencil on the bump of the
   first slant bar. (Check.)
   Don't make the stroke until I tell you.

8. **Up to the half line.**
   Do it. (Check.)

9. Next stroke.
   Down to the baseline and tail.
   Do it. (Check.)

10. Get ready to trace the next i form faster.
    Put your pencil on the bump. (Check.)
    Don't lift your pencil from the paper.

11. Listen: Up to the half line.
    Do it. (Check.)

12. Next stroke.
    Down to the baseline and tail.
    Do it. (Check.)

13. Put your pencil on the next bump. (Check.)

14. Up to the half line.
    Do it. (Check.)

15. Next stroke. Down to the baseline and tail.
    Do it. (Check.)

16. Finish that line by tracing each i form.
    (Check.)

EXERCISE 6—Dotting the I Form

1. To make the letter **i** you make
   and **i** form with a dot.
   (Make an **i** form on the board
   and dot it.)

2. Touch line 5. (Check.)
   Trace the **i** forms on that line.
   After you trace each **i** form, dot it. (Check.)

FIGURE 5.7 *Cursive Writing Program,* **Lesson 1, Exercises 5 and 6, and Student Workbook Lesson 1, lines 4 and 5. Reprinted with permission of the McGraw-Hill Companies.**

Lesson (71) – Team Activity

- You've worked with outline diagrams that tell about problems with different kinds of arguments, but you've never made up arguments for these outline diagrams.

- Your team is going to construct an argument for the diagram below. Your argument won't be exactly like any of the arguments you've worked with, but it will be faulty, just like the other arguments.

- After your team makes up the argument, you'll explain the problems with the argument by following the outline diagram and writing a passage.

Outline diagram

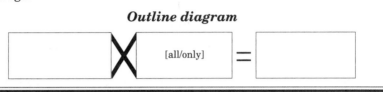

FIGURE 5.8 *Reasoning and Writing: Level E,* **Student Textbook, Lesson 71—Team Activity. Reprinted with permission of the McGraw-Hill Companies.**

incorporate what students have learned at this level. Figure 5.8 is the first team activity that is introduced. Each team is to write a faulty argument and a critique based on an outline diagram for inadequate evidence.

Additional team projects involve integration of other skills such as rewriting passages to obscure words, and constructing outline diagrams that have provisions for a summary, disagreement with a policy, and alternatives.

Primed Background Knowledge

Primed background knowledge is the last, but not the least important, of the six strategies covered in this section. Students' background knowledge affects their acquisition of new skills. Priming student knowledge of preskills required for acquisition of more sophisticated grammar and mechanical structures is crucial to the development of writers who are facile at communicating ideas in a clear and concise manner. *Reasoning and Writing: Level F* does not ignore this aspect. Figure 5.9 is an excellent example of how this program primes student knowledge of previously learned skills to teach a new skill. Students are reminded that they have learned various parts of speech and the procedure to figure out various parts of speech by their position in sentences. This previously learned knowledge is reviewed to introduce how these skills are needed to identify conjunctions, a more sophisticated part of speech.

Lesson 69

Part A

- You're going to do some projects that involve parts of speech. You've seen that words have different parts of speech in different sentences. You figure out the part of speech by seeing where the word is and what the word does.

- Sometimes the word **remaining** is a verb:

  The girls were remaining in the office.

- It's a verb because it tells what the girls were doing.

- Sometimes the same word is an adjective:

  We didn't eat the remaining fish.

- **Remaining** is an adjective because it comes before **fish** and tells what kind of fish.

- You've learned about joining words: **and, or** and **but.** These words are **conjunctions.**

- Other words can be conjunctions in some sentences.

- Here's how you test to see if a word is a conjunction:
  - ✔ If the words that follow it make a complete sentence, the word is a conjunction.

- The word **that** is a conjunction in some sentences.

- Here is one of those sentences:

  She argued that <u>her brother should help her clean the garage.</u>

- The words after the word **that** are underlined. They make up a complete sentence:

  Her brother should help her clean the garage.

- The word **that** is a conjunction in that sentence.

- The word **that** is not a conjunction in this sentence:

  He bought a car that <u>was red.</u>

- The words after **that** do not make up a complete sentence. So **that** is not a conjunction.

FIGURE 5.9 *Reasoning and Writing: Level F,* **Student Textbook, Lesson 69, Part A. Reprinted with permission of the McGraw-Hill Companies.**

PART C—Mastery Quiz

Directions: Read each group of words. Write an *S* next to each sentence. Write an *N* next to each group of words that is not a sentence. On the line, tell what is wrong.

___ 1. eats nuts and raisins on yogurt

_____

___ 2. a chicken with green wings flew through the window

_____

___ 3. on the beach, Carla and I find huge clam

_____

___ 4. the beautiful unicorn with the hurt hoof

_____

___ 5. after the test, the students walked to the theater

_____

FIGURE 5.10   *Basic Writing Skills: Sentence Development,* **Student Blackline Master, Lesson 6, Part C: Mastery Quiz. Reprinted with permission of the McGraw-Hill Companies.**

Judicious Review

Grammar skills require continuous review for students to become fluent writers and editors. *Basic Writing Skills: Sentence Development* is designed with built-in cumulative review of sentence-writing skills. Figure 5.10 shows the mastery quiz given at the end of Lesson 6. Students are required to discriminate complete from incomplete sentences. Prior to this quiz, students have learned and practiced identifying subjects and predicates in sentences. In addition, students have learned to identify a complete sentence by asking three questions: "Does it have a subject?" "Does it have a predicate?" "Does it make sense?" In subsequent lessons, students are required to use this learned information to edit sentences they compose.

TEACHING TECHNIQUES

When we teach any of the Direct Instruction writing programs, a basic rule is that teachers should not present from the front of the room unless they are showing something on the board. Teachers should present from somewhere in the middle of the room and move around to observe a good sample of their students. The flow and pace of the lessons are supported with use of efficient and effective signals and appropriate error-correction procedures.

Signals

Many of the Direct Instruction writing programs call for group responses. Group responses provide teachers with immediate feedback regarding student understanding of basic writing rules and procedures prior to the students' writing activities. Two main signals are used in Direct Instruction writing programs: hand-drop and auditory signals. First, if students' eyes are on the teacher, a hand-drop signal is typically used. For example, in *Reasoning and Writing: Level B,* the teacher would first put her hand in a focus position (similar to what a police officer would do to stop traffic) to tell students that they should listen carefully to her words. "Listen: This thing is in the class of girls. Everybody say that." When the teacher says the final word (*that*) in the aforementioned format, she should immediately drop her hand, being careful to not talk and move at the same time. An auditory signal such as a snap might be used at the "bottom" of the hand-drop signal. Again, this signal is used when students are looking at the teacher rather than at their books. As soon as students respond, the teacher immediately raises her hand in the focus position.

Another signal typical to Direct Instruction writing programs is the auditory signal. The auditory signal might involve the use of a snap, clap, or tap; some teachers choose to use voice inflection here. Say a teacher was presenting a lesson from *Reasoning and Writing: Level D* that involves textbook work. The students are to read from their textbook and write their responses on lined paper. After writing a response, the teacher has the students respond in unison with the correct answer (e.g., "Everybody, what's Item 5?"). At this point, the teacher should provide an auditory signal to cue students to respond together. The snap, clap, or tap would be provided immediately after saying "5" in the example.

If teachers choose to write on the board or on an overhead transparency, they may use a point-touch signal. If a sentence is written on the board, the teacher would point to the beginning of the sentence and say, "Read the sentence. Get ready." As soon as the teacher says the last word (*ready*), he should tap the board to evoke a unison oral response. Again, the teacher should be mindful not to talk and move at the same time. Remember, talk first, signal second!

Error Corrections

Direct Instruction writing programs use a simple but basic error-correction procedure for group responding when errors are made. When an error occurs, teachers should immediately correct the mistake. They should not wait for students to finish their response. The basic error-correction procedure is for teachers to (1) model the correct response, (2) ask the students to repeat the correct response, and (3) return to the beginning of the task sequence to check for understanding of the correct response. For example, in *Reasoning and Writing: Level C* the teacher asks students to touch a certain picture and name the person pictured. If the students respond incorrectly, the teacher would model the correct response, "That person is Jane," repeat the task, "Everybody, touch picture 2. Name that person," and start over at the beginning of the task. This "backing up" step is crucial. It allows teachers to check for the students' firm understanding of the correct response and affords the students another opportunity to practice the correct response. The repeat-until-firm procedure appears on the most critical parts of new teaching exercises and focuses on knowledge that is very important for later work. By firming the students' responses, we can reduce the amount of errors in students' written work.

Managing students' writing activities requires teachers to move from student to student and observe, check, and correct as many students as possible in the time allowed. Teachers should read passages as students are writing. They should focus positive comments to students who are working quickly and accurately and following all directions. When teachers observe students making errors, they should correct them by stating previously learned rules, procedures, or criteria for following directions to the class.

If students fail to apply learned rules and procedures, teachers should make frequent comments that focus on what students are doing well and the errors they are making. Teachers should provide comments such as, "I am seeing some good opening sentences that tell the main thing about what the group did" or "Watch how you punctuate the sentence that tells what Jim said." They should not provide a great deal of individual help. Instead, teachers should point to the problem area and say, "Look at the first word in your sentence."

Another correction procedure is to make a mark in the margin on any line that has a problem. This correction allows students to find and correct the problem on their own. For example, *Expressive Writing Programs 1* and *2* have built-in edit checks in the form of questions that students must answer to receive points for written work. Teachers refer to these edit checks as students are completing their writing assignments. For example, teachers simply ask, "Are there any run-on sentences in your paragraph?"

ASSESSMENT AND TROUBLESHOOTING

Most Direct Instruction writing programs contain placement tests, in-program mastery tests, and continuous assessments for troubleshooting purposes. These curriculum-based assessments pinpoint students' specific skill strengths and areas in need of improvement. Based on the assessment results, teachers can make informed decisions regarding grouping and scheduling for instruction.

Placement Tests

The majority of Direct Instruction writing programs contain placement tests. These tests are designed to assist the teacher in determining which students would benefit from the various programs. The *Basic Writing Skills* program placement tests are group administered and pinpoint the specific lesson where students should begin. The *Cursive Writing Program* placement test can be administered to individual students or to a group. The student is required to copy sixteen lowercase manuscript letters within three minutes. Teachers score the results by assigning each written letter a point value ranging from 0 to 5 based on letter formation criteria. Students must meet a minimum score of 55 out of 80 points for consideration to begin cursive handwriting. If the minimum score is not met, students should continue to practice manuscript letters before entering the *Cursive Writing Program.*

Although there is no placement test for the *Expressive Writing 1* program, students should be reading on a third-grade level and have not mastered basic expressive writing skills. The *Expressive Writing 2* program provides a placement test to determine whether students can place at this level. This test requires them to write a paragraph about a sequence of events based on two pictures. The first picture shows what took place at the beginning of the story and the second picture shows how the story ended. Teachers verbally model a possible story to explain what must have taken place. A word box is included with the picture prompts. Students must spell these words correctly if they use them in their stories. Students have a fifteen-minute time limit. The program provides examples of acceptable and unacceptable responses. As a general rule, if students demonstrate continuity and most of what they write can be improved with punctuation marks, then they are appropriate for the preprogram lessons within the *Expressive Writing 2* program.

When students complete the *Expressive Writing* programs, they can be placed in the *Reasoning and Writing* series. Those who have successfully completed *Expressive Writing 1* and 2 can begin *Reasoning and Writing: Level D*. The content of *Expressive Writing 1* and 2 is equivalent to the content of *Reasoning and Writing: Level C*.

Reasoning and Writing contains group-administered placement tests at all levels except *Level B*. The criterion for placement in *Level B* is successful completion of a first-year reading program or *Level A*. The placement tests at the lower levels of the program are timed. Students are required to follow directions and copy words accurately at an acceptable rate. In addition, all levels of the program require minimum reading levels for students to be successful. For example, *Reasoning and Writing: Level C* is appropriate for students who read at least on a second-grade level and can copy words accurately at a rate of ten words per minute. The placement test evaluates students' performance at copying and following directions. If students fail to meet minimum criteria, the program recommends that they work on developing the needed skills during the first few months of the school year.

Mastery Tests

Mastery tests and quizzes are spaced throughout the various Direct Instruction writing programs. This intermittent test schedule provides remediation opportunities. For example, *Reasoning and Writing: Level B* provides a chart with suggested test remedies (see Figure 5.11). The basic procedure is to repeat exercises from previous lessons. After students are firm on the remedies, the tests or parts of the tests are readmininstered. The tests are embedded in the various levels of the *Reasoning and Writing* program as test lessons. This test-reteach-retest format remains consistent throughout all levels of the program.

The *Basic Writing Skills* program contains unit tests and mastery quizzes. Data sheets to record mastery test and quiz results are included with the programs. Students must meet the mastery/unit test criteria before moving on to new lessons. If 20 percent or more students make any errors on the mastery tests, teachers should reteach. If 20 percent or more students exceed the error limits for the unit tests, teachers should reteach. Review and reteaching procedures are specified and additional quiz items are provided for each mastery quiz.

Test	Test Part Failed	Lesson	To remedy, present: Book Exercise	Workbook Part
1	A	9	3	B
	B	3	2	B
	C	3	3	C
2	A	14	2	A
	B	19	2	B
3	A	27	1	A
	B	28	2	B
4	A	38	1	A
	B	34	4	C
	C	33	2	B
5	A	47	1	A
	B	48	1	A
6	A	57	4	C
	B	57	1	A
	C	55	4	D
7	A	69	1	A
	B	65	2	B
	C	64	4	C

FIGURE 5.11   *Reasoning and Writing: Level B,* Test Remedy Chart. Teacher's Guide. Reprinted with permission of the McGraw-Hill Companies.

Continuous Assessment for Troubleshooting

In addition to placement and mastery tests, the overall instructional design and teaching procedures found in Direct Instruction writing programs provide for ongoing informal assessments. These ongoing assessments provide teachers with immediate troubleshooting procedures. Some of the learning tasks call for unison responses. As discussed in the previous section on error corrections, teachers listen for and immediately correct errors. A repeat-until-firm procedure is incorporated for new or critical skills and can be used to remediate any areas in need of improvement that arise as the students progress through the program. By observing and providing positive or corrective feedback, teachers continuously assess student progress, thereby minimizing student errors.

Students who are not performing at suitable levels should have additional practice with those skills needed to produce firm responding. For instance, the *Cursive Writing* program provides a supplemental practice sheet that students use when they are having serious trouble writing a particular letter.

Direct Instruction writing programs demand a high degree of application of learned writing skills. The *Reasoning and Writing* program incorporates a sharing, revising, editing process that assists students with corrections prior to turning in their writing assignments. First, teachers call on a mixture of higher- and lower-performing students to read their written work. Other students attend to the passages and identify any problems. Teachers can model the behavior that students should follow as they note problems and praise those students who identify problems correctly. Next, the students revise and edit their papers before handing them in for a grade. Students use editing procedures such as a caret (^) to fix up minor errors. If students leave out a sentence, they write the sentence at the bottom of the paper. Students who require extensive revisions are assigned the fix-up as homework and instructed to rewrite the whole passage. In addition, teachers may employ a peer-checking procedure by assigning the higher performers to be "checkers" to lower-performing students. The role of these higher performers is to read corrected passages, identify possible problems, and provide their peers with immediate corrective feedback. While mastery tests and continuous assessments provide opportunities for remediation and troubleshooting, several extensions and adaptations are available to provide opportunities for student practice and application of learned writing skills.

EXTENSIONS AND ADAPTATIONS

Writing integrates thinking, language, reading, and spelling skills; therefore, teachers can extend writing activities to a wide range of content areas. Several extensions are available within the Direct Instruction writing programs and within supplemental programs. In addition, writing does not develop at the same rate for all learners. Adaptations to writing are necessary to accommodate the needs of diverse learners. Adaptations for accelerating students who require less practice to master skills and adaptations for students who need additional instruction and practice are provided in Direct Instruction writing programs.

Extensions

The *Basic Writing Skills, Cursive Writing,* and *Expressive Writing* programs are intended to be taught every day until the programs are completed. The *Reasoning and Writing* programs are designed to be taught two to three times per week since the content of these programs does not cover an entire language arts curriculum. Therefore, in-program extensions and supplemental programs should be used with the *Reasoning and Writing* programs to ensure that students are skilled with many writing genres.

In-Program Extensions.   All levels of the *Reasoning and Writing* program provide teachers with suggested extension activities for use at the completion of each program level. For example, *Reasoning and Writing: Level D* provides suggestions for further activities that include showcasing papers, conducting debates, and writing summaries and critiques. In addition, *Reasoning and Writing: Writing Extensions,* a set of blackline masters, including a teacher-presentation manual, were developed for each level of the program and are available through Science Research Associates. The extensions are not intended to replace the program lessons. Instead, they are introduced after students have learned the writing skills and concepts introduced within each level of the program. The main objectives of the *Writing Extensions* are for students to practice learned skills, to become fluent writers, and to personalize their writing. For example, *Level A* reinforces the editing and rewriting process. Students learn to use a caret (^) to show where words or word parts are to be inserted in revised text. Sentence pairs are presented, such as the following:

> We have dog.
> We have a dog.

The students must identify the correct sentence and insert a caret and the missing word above the caret as follows:

>   a
> We have ^ dog.

Checking for correctness and accuracy is continued with application of higher-order thinking skills through these extension materials. For example, *Level E* provides a valuable extension to the analysis skills taught in a *Reasoning and Writing: Level E* activity that targets reliable sources. In the extension activity, the students research these sources and check their accuracy. Next, they write about their findings using the same format taught in the *Reasoning and Writing* program.

Supplemental Program Extensions.   Several programs are available that provide effective supplemental activities and opportunities for independent practice of writing skills. The *Supplemental Writing & Extensions Activities for Reasoning & Writing A & B* program (McGlocklin, 1998) provides writing experiences for primary students in *Reasoning and Writing Levels A* and B. This program is intended for students who are fluent in the mechanics of handwriting and can copy from the board or overhead. The extensions reinforce students' independent functioning of mastered skills; therefore, they extend skills that have been mastered at the oral and auditory levels.

    Adventures in Language: Levels I and II (Dodds & Chislett, 1999) is appropriate for grades one to three and for all students who need basic language and grammar skill development. The program incorporates a game format to motivate students, and includes a teacher-presentation book, student workbooks, and blackline masters for homework. The program incorporates thirty-seven basic grammar usage skills. It can be used in conjunction with *Expressive Writing* and *Reasoning and Writing Levels A, B,* and *C.*

    Learning through Literature: Story Studies (Dodds & Goodfellow, 1990) is designed for primary classrooms when the students are not yet strong independent readers. *Story Studies* introduces students to basic literary structures such as problem-centered linear stories, fairy tales, folktales, and poetry. The teacher reads a new book to the students each week. The books are presented in an organized manner so that students develop a framework into which they can add new information and concepts. Each lesson directs the teacher to introduce the story to the students, read the story aloud, discuss the story and illustrations, and have the students recall information (Science Research Associates/McGraw-Hill, 1991b). Most lessons in the *Story Studies* program have integrated writing activities. Combining the early levels of *Reasoning and Writing* with *Story Studies* provides students with ongoing writing opportunities while they are developing the reasoning skills to become more powerful writers. One way to combine these programs is to teach *Reasoning and Writing* three times per week (Monday, Wednesday, and Friday) and to teach the *Story Studies* program twice a week (Tuesday and Thursday).

The *Learning through Literature: Novel Studies* (Dodds & Goodfellow, 1990) series introduces students to great literature through novel studies. Although the novels are not grade-specific, the themes of the novels are closely tied to themes studied in grades three to six (Science Research Associates, 1991a). Teachers familiar with the upper levels of *Reading Mastery* will see many parallels between *Reading Mastery* and *Novel Studies*. Each lesson in the *Novel Studies* program includes word practice, vocabulary instruction, activation of prior knowledge, information passages, guided story reading, and written comprehension questions. In addition, each lesson has varied writing activities that allow the students to integrate skills they are learning in *Reasoning and Writing*. For example, when reading the *Sign of the Beaver,* one of the writing activities is to compare and contrast the views of the two main characters on land ownership and construct an argument to defend their own opinion about land ownership. Students are taught how to construct arguments beginning in *Reasoning and Writing: Level D* and continue to practice this skill in *Levels E* and *F*. Students are taught how to write a compare and contrast paper in *Reasoning and Writing: Level F*. As mentioned previously, extensions are necessary when the *Reasoning and Writing* programs are taught three days per week. The extended writing assignments in the *Novel Studies* program offer teachers ample extension activities on the two days per week that *Reasoning and Writing* is not taught.

Readers & Writers: Becoming Authors through Genre Studies (Dodds & Goodfellow, 1993) exposes students to literary genres and provides opportunities for students to practice the steps of the writing process as they explore five literary genres: biographies, mysteries, science fiction, realistic animal stories, and sport stories. *Genre Studies* is designed for students in grades four to eight. The students read widely in each of the five genres, critically analyze what they have read, and become authors themselves in that genre (Goodfellow & Dodds, 1993). This program allows teachers to accommodate diverse reading abilities because the program does not require all the students to read the same book within each genre. For example, in the biography genre, students may choose any famous person to read and write about. The level of difficulty of the book they choose to read can be geared to their reading level. In fact, the authors of the program include a list of books within each genre that are designated as being at an easy, intermediate, or advanced reading level. As with the *Novel Studies* program, the extended writing assignments in the *Genre Studies* program offer teachers ample extension activities on the two days per week that *Reasoning and Writing* is not taught.

Adaptations

To adapt Direct Instruction writing programs to meet the needs of diverse learners, teachers may choose to either accelerate students within the programs or provide additional instruction and practice for students who have not mastered the skills being taught.

Acceleration.   *Reasoning and Writing* is highly adaptable and responsive to a variety of learners. For instance, *Level A* offers four different schedules for lower performers and higher performers in kindergarten and grade 1 that parallel the level of reading instruction. For average performers in grade 1, the program recommends conducting lessons two or three days per week. For higher performers, a schedule of five lessons per week is recommended. This schedule allows for higher performers to complete *Levels A* and *B* by the end of first grade.

The upper levels of *Reasoning and Writing* suggest scheduling lessons three days a week. Teachers should not rush through the program. Instead, it is better to incorporate additional firm-up time and to use higher performers as feedback coaches for lower-performing students. Finally, the teachers' use of writing extensions, content area writing exercises, and research projects for higher-performing students is recommended.

Providing Additional Instruction and Practice.   Pacing of lessons, mastering preskills, and opportunities for practice are important facets of planning for lower-performing students. In the early grades, consideration of the companion preskills of language, reading, and handwriting is necessary. For example, students must have a firm language foundation and possess first-grade reading skills in order to be successful in *Reasoning and Writing: Level A*. For kindergarten, three lessons per week are recommended once students demonstrate mastery of necessary preskills and can pass the placement test. For students in grade one who are not ready for *Level A* at the beginning of the school year, the program recommends conducting five lessons per week once students demonstrate the necessary preskills and pass the placement test.

At the upper levels of *Reasoning and Writing,* different scheduling options are suggested. For example, *Level D* suggests scheduling four lessons per week and using only three of them to teach new lessons. The fourth lesson becomes the "catch-up" lesson when teachers work with lower-performing students. Another option is to teach fewer lessons per week as tasks become more extensive and student responses require increased teacher feedback. The suggested schedule at *Level D* is to teach two lessons per week and schedule a third period during the week to provide feedback and allow students to listen to and respond to other students' work.

In addition to responsive scheduling and pacing of lessons, an effective and easy method for supporting lower performers is the class arrangement. Teachers should seat lower performers closest to the front of the classroom with the middle performers arranged around the low performers and the high performers on the periphery. This arrangement affords teachers easy access to lower-performing students.

Finally, additional time for review and practice is necessary for lower performers. The *Reasoning and Writing: Writing Extensions Blackline Masters* provide low-performing students with opportunities for review and practice of previously learned skills. Teachers could use the supplemental programs suggested in this chapter for homework assignments, thereby providing additional opportunities for these students to review and practice crucial writing skills necessary for continued progress.

RESEARCH ON DIRECT INSTRUCTION WRITING PROGRAMS

Research on the Direct Instruction writing programs is more limited than research on Direct Instruction reading and mathematics programs. The writing programs were developed later and were not a part of the initial Follow Through Project when a large body of the Direct Instruction research began. *Cursive Writing* was first published in 1980, *Basic Writing Skills* and *Expressive Writing 1* in 1983, *Expressive Writing 2* in 1985, and *Reasoning and Writing Levels A, B, C* in 1991, and *Levels D, E, F* in 1993, 1994, and 1995, respectively. Not only were the writing programs developed later, they have not been used as widely.

While the research is limited, what is available provides strong evidence of the effectiveness of the Direct Instruction writing programs for students in general education (Lenz & Schumaker, 1999), students who are high-risk (Cross, Rebarber, & Wilson, 2002; Grossen, in press), students with learning disabilities or behavior disorders (Anderson & Keel, 2002), and students who are gifted (Ginn, Keel, & Fredrick, 2002). Research is available for *Expressive Writing* and for *Reasoning and Writing*. To present this research, we introduce studies in which the researchers investigated the effectiveness of teaching reasoning skills (Collins & Carnine, 1988) and logic skills (Grossen & Carnine, 1990) as both are incorporated in the *Reasoning and Writing* program, research in which *Reasoning and Writing* and *Expressive Writing* were used in conjunction with other Direct Instruction programs as part of large school implementations (Cross et al., 2002; Grossen, in press), and two studies that investigated the effects of *Reasoning and Writing* (Anderson & Keel, 2002; Ginn et al, 2002).

Two important studies demonstrate the effectiveness of teaching reasoning and logic skills explicitly and support an important component of the *Reasoning and Writing* program. Working with ninth, tenth, and eleventh grade students in a resource room, Collins and Carnine (1988) investigated the effectiveness of a reasoning skills program based on *Theory of Instruction* (Engelmann & Carnine, 1982). After completing this reasoning skills program, students from the resource room performed better than teacher-education students performed on a drawing conclusions component of a reasoning skills test. Further, Grossen and Carnine (1990) required high school students with learning disabilities to draw diagrams while learning an explicit logic strategy. On a test of the students' skill in solving logical problems, Grossen and Carnine found that their participants performed as well as gifted high school students. Finally, after one year of instruction with *Reasoning and Writing,* students in general education showed an increase of more than two standard deviations on the Test of Written Language (Lenz & Schumaker, 1999).

Reasoning and Writing is often used along with other Direct Instruction programs in large-scale implementations. For example, Cross et al. (2002) used Direct Instruction language, reading, and spelling programs in conjunction with *Reasoning and Writing* and *Expressive Writing* across fourteen elementary schools in nine states and the District of

Columbia. Pre- and post-test data were available for 5,874 English-proficient students. First-year results across standardized reading and language measures for kindergarten through second grade were encouraging. While there were no specific measures of writing, and the writing programs were used in conjunction with other Direct Instruction language arts programs, gains in language, listening, and reading provided evidence of the effectiveness of the combined programs.

Additional research supports the effectiveness of Direct Instruction writing programs used in conjunction with other Direct Instruction programs (Grossen, in press). The comprehensive Direct Instruction model was assessed with seventh- and eighth-grade students in the poorest performing middle school located in one of the lowest-performing districts in California. Nearly half (48%) of the students read below the fourth-grade level. Among the Direct Instruction programs used in this school were *Reasoning and Writing* and *Expressive Writing*. As reported by Grossen, after one year the percentage of students reading at their approximate grade level (seventh grade or higher) more than doubled from 22 percent to 47 percent. In a separate analysis of English Language Learners (ELL), the percentage of students reading at their approximate grade level increased from 10 percent to 36 percent. After the second year, Grossen reported that students again made two years' gain on the MAST with one year of instruction.

While the research specific to Direct Instruction writing programs is limited, two published articles (Anderson & Keel, 2002; Ginn et al., 2002) specifically investigated the effectiveness of the *Reasoning and Writing* program. In the first, Anderson and Keel (2002) targeted ten students with learning disabilities (LD) and/or behavior disorders (BD). All students received services for written expression in a resource room where *Reasoning and Writing: Level C* was taught for thirty-five to fifty minutes each day for six weeks. Increases on the Test of Written Language-2nd edition (TOWL-2) were found after students received instruction in the program, with performance in several writing subtests determined to be statistically significant.

While many are familiar with the use of Direct Instruction programs with students who are at-risk or who have learning or other disabilities, very few realize the potential impact of these programs for students who are gifted. Ginn et al. (2002) investigated the effectiveness of *Reasoning and Writing: Level F* with seventy-four fifth-grade students in resource classes for the gifted across four schools. The four schools provided one experimental and three comparison groups all taught by experienced gifted-education teachers. Progress for all groups was measured using the Test of Written Language (3rd edition) and the New Jersey Test of Reasoning Skills (NJTRS). Students across groups made comparable gains.

REFERENCES

Adams, M. J. (1990). *Beginning to read: Thinking and learning about print.* Cambridge, MA: MIT Press.
Agnew, E. (1992). Basic writers in the workplace: Writing adequately for careers after college. *Journal of Basic Writing, 11*(2), 28–46.
Anderson, D. M., & Keel, M. C. (2002). Using *Reasoning and Writing* to teach writing skills to students with learning disabilities and behavioral disorders. *Journal of Direct Instruction, 2,* 49–55.

Bain, A. M., Bailet, L. L., & Moats, L. C. (1991). *Written language disorders: Theory into practice.* Austin, TX: Pro-Ed.

Carnine, D. W., Silbert, J., & Kameenui, E. J. (1997). *Direct Instruction reading* (3rd ed.). Upper Saddle River, NJ: Merrill.

Collins, M., & Carnine, D. (1988). Evaluating the field test revision process by comparing two versions of a reasoning skills CAI program. *Journal of Learning Disabilities, 21,* 375–379.

Cross, R. W., Rebarber, T., & Wilson, S. F. (2002). Student gains in a privately managed network of charter schools using Direct Instruction. *Journal of Direct Instruction, 2,* 3–21.

Dixon, R. C., Isaacson, S., & Stein, M. (2002). Effective strategies for teaching writing. In E. J. Kameenui, D. W. Carnine, R. C. Dixon, D. C. Simmons, & M. D. Coyne (Eds.), *Effective teaching strategies that accommodate diverse learners* (2nd ed., pp. 93–119). Upper Saddle River, NJ: Pearson Education.

Dodds, T., & Chislett, M. (1999). *Adventures in language I and II.* Valley Stream, NY: J/P Associates.

Dodds, T., & Goodfellow, F. (1990). *Learning through literature.* Columbus, OH: SRA/McGraw-Hill.

Dodds, T., & Goodfellow, F. (1993). *Readers & writers: Becoming authors through genre studies.* Columbus, OH: SRA/McGraw-Hill.

Engelmann, S., & Carnine, D. W. (1982). *Theory of instruction.* New York: Irvington.

Engelmann, S., & Davis, K. (2001). *Reasoning and writing: Level A.* Columbus, OH: SRA/McGraw-Hill.

Engelmann, S., & Silbert, J. (1983). *Expressive writing 1.* Columbus, OH: SRA/McGraw-Hill.

Englert, C. S., Raphael, T. E., Anderson, L. M., Anthony, H. M., & Stevens, D. D. (1991). Making strategies and self-talk visible: Writing instruction in regular and special education classrooms. *American Educational Research Journal, 28,* 337–372.

Ginn, P. V., Keel, M. C., & Fredrick, L. D. (2002). Using Reasoning and Writing with gifted fifth-grade students. *Journal of Direct Instruction, 2,* 41–47.

Goodfellow, F., & Dodds, T. (1993). *Readers & writers: Becoming authors through genre studies teacher's guide.* Columbus, OH: SRA/McGraw-Hill.

Graham, S. (1990). The role of production factors in learning disabled students' compositions. *Journal of Educational Psychology, 82,* 781–791.

Graham, S. (1999a). Handwriting and spelling instruction for students with learning disabilities: A review. *Learning Disability Quarterly, 22,* 78–98.

Graham, S. (1999b). The role of text production skills in writing development: A special issue—I. *Learning Disability Quarterly, 22,* 75–77.

Graham, S., Harris, K. R., MacArthur, C. A., & Schwartz, S. (1991). Writing and writing instruction for students with learning disabilities: Review of a research program. *Learning Disability Quarterly, 14,* 89–114.

Graves, D. H. (1985). All children can write. *Learning Disabilities Focus, 1*(1), 36-43.

Grossen, B. (in press). Success of a Direct Instruction model at a secondary level school with high-risk students. *Reading and Writing Quarterly.*

Grossen, B., & Carnine, D. (1990). Diagramming a logic strategy: Effects on difficult problem types and transfer. *Learning Disability Quarterly, 13,* 168–182.

Hall, J. K., Salas, B., & Grimes, A. E. (1999). *Evaluating and improving written expression: A practical guide for teachers* (3rd ed.). Austin, TX: Pro-Ed.

Harris, K. R., & Graham, S. (1985). Improving learning disabled students' composition skills: Self-Control strategy training. *Learning Disability Quarterly, 8,* 27–36.

Harris, K. R., & Graham, S. (1996). *Making the writing process work: Strategies for composition and self-regulation.* Cambridge, MA: Brookline.

Harris, K. R., Schmidt, T., & Graham, S. (1997). Every child can write: Strategies for composition and self-regulation in the writing process. In K. R. Harris, S. Graham, D. Deshler, & M. Pressley (Eds.), *Teaching every child every day* [Electronic version]. Cambridge, MA: Brookline.

Hillocks, G., Jr. (1984). What works in teaching composition: A meta-analysis of experimental treatment studies. *American Journal of Education, 93,* 133–170.

Isaacson, S. L. (1994). Integrating process, product, and purpose: The role of instruction. *Reading and Writing Quarterly, 10,* 39–62.

Isaacson, S. L., & Gleason, M. M. (1997). Mechanical obstacles to writing: What can teachers do to help students with learning problems? [Electronic version]. *Learning Disabilities Research and Practice, 12,* 188–194.

Johnson, K. R., & Layng, T. V. J. (1992). Breaking the structuralist barrier: Literacy and numeracy with fluency. *American Psychologist, 47,* 1475–1490.

Kameenui, E. J., Carnine, D. W., & Dixon, R. C. (2002). Introduction. In E. J. Kameenui, D. W. Carnine, R. C. Dixon, D. C. Simmons, & M. D. Coyne (Eds.), *Effective teaching strategies that accommodate diverse learners* (2nd ed., pp. 1–21). Upper Saddle River, NJ: Pearson Education.

Kameenui, E. J., & Simmons, D. C. (1999). *Adapting curricular materials: Vol. 1. An overview of materials adaptations. Toward successful inclusion of students with disabilities: The architecture of instruction.* Reston, VA: Council for Exceptional Children.

Lenz, K., & Schumaker, J. (1999). *Adapting language arts, social studies, and science materials for the inclusive classroom: Grades six through eight.* Reston, VA: Council for Exceptional Children.

McGlocklin, L. (1998). *Supplemental writing & extension activities for Reasoning & Writing A and B.* Eugene, OR: Association for Direct Instruction.

Science Research Associates/McGraw-Hill. (1983). *Reasoning and writing lesson sampler.* Columbus, OH: SRA/McGraw-Hill.

Science Research Associates/McGraw-Hill. (1991a). *Learning through literature lesson samples for novel studies.* Chicago, IL: Author.

Science Research Associates/McGraw-Hill. (1991b). *Learning through literature lesson samples for story studies.* Chicago, IL: Author.

Simmons, K. (2002, June 28). College entrance test due changes. *The Atlanta Journal Constitution,* pp. C1, C7.

Smith, F. (1982). *Writing and the writer.* New York: Holt.

Snow, C. E., Burns, M. S., & Griffin, P. (Eds.). (1998). *Preventing reading difficulties in young children.* Washington, DC: National Academy Press.

State Assessment Services—State Assessment Advisor. (June 16, 2002). http://www.homeroom.com/Irp/IN-DEX.asp

Stein, M., Dixon, R., & Barnard, S. (2001). What research tells us about writing instruction for students in the middle grades. *Journal of Direct Instruction, 1,* 107–116.

Strengthening the Second "R": Helping students with disabilities prepare well-written compositions. (2002, Winter). *Research Connections in Special Education, 10,* 1.

Tierney, R. J., & Shanahan, T. (1991). Research on the reading-writing relationship: Interactions, transactions, and outcomes. In R. Barr, M. Kamil, P. B. Mosenthal, & P. D. Pearson (Eds.), *Handbook of reading research* (Vol. 2, pp. 246–280). New York: Longman.

CHAPTER SIX

SPELLING

FLINT L. SIMONSEN
Eastern Washington University

ROBERT DIXON
Classical Learning Systems

OBJECTIVES

After studying this chapter you should be able to:

1. describe the importance of spelling and spelling instruction;
2. describe the relationship between spelling and other language arts;
3. describe the three instructional approaches used in the *Spelling Mastery* and *Spelling Through Morphographs* curricula;
4. provide examples of words that would be appropriate to teach using each instructional approach;
5. explain how to use informal assessments in the *Spelling Mastery* and *Spelling Through Morphographs* curricula;
6. describe strategies for adapting and troubleshooting the *Spelling Mastery* and *Spelling Through Morphographs* curricula;
7. describe extension activities for spelling instruction;
8. describe methods for adapting the *Spelling Mastery* and *Spelling Through Morphographs* curricula;
9. describe the key findings from the research on teaching spelling.

Teaching children to spell is often regarded as a relatively low priority in schools. Spelling instruction has been given so little attention in education that it has been described as a "forgotten basic" (Templeton & Morris, 1999). In many schools, teaching students to spell consumes few instructional minutes and frequently bears little resemblance to actual instruction. In this chapter, a direct and systematic approach to spelling instruction is described. Specifically, the essential components, instructional strategies, and appropriate use of two Direct Instruction spelling curricula (i.e., *Spelling Mastery* and *Spelling Through Morphographs*) are summarized. The features of three spelling instructional approaches (i.e., phonemic, whole-word, and morphemic) are described, as well as how each approach is used in Direct Instruction spelling programs. This chapter also will describe error-correction procedures and assessment methods (both formal and informal) specific to spelling instruction. Ways in which *Spelling Mastery* and *Spelling Through Morphographs* can be adapted to meet unique student needs, as well as extension activities that link spelling instruction to the development of other related skills in the language arts will be discussed. In addition, the research literature supporting the components of these curricula is presented.

IMPORTANCE OF SPELLING

Why should educators waste time teaching students to spell accurately? After all, the written English language has so many irregularities and "odd" rules that accurate spelling can be a frustrating and fruitless endeavor. Besides, "advocates of invented spelling claim that citizens of the twenty-first century won't need to spell because spell-checkers and spelling aids will do that for them" (Bender, 1994, p. 70). These ideas may represent the conventional wisdom regarding the importance of spelling and frequently reflect educational practice. Although spelling may be viewed with disregard and treated educationally with muted significance, there are important reasons to direct efforts to teach students to spell accurately.

In the "real world," accurate spelling is an essential component of successful writing. Transfer of spelling skills to writing arguably is the primary purpose of teaching spelling (Dixon & Engelmann, 1999). Accurate spelling alone does not characterize good writing but, nonetheless, is a necessary component of all high-quality written products.

> Spelling is not an end in itself, but it is an essential prerequisite for effective writing. Although students might be able to write creatively, they are frequently marked down if they misspell words. Furthermore, if students are not adept in spelling words they want to use, the laborious task of looking up words might prompt students to express themselves in terse and 'uncreative' ways. If they are adept at spelling words, on the other hand, they normally exhibit far more freedom in their written self-expression (Dixon & Engelmann, 2001, p. 8).

Although computers are available for many writing tasks, these tools do not uniformly benefit the language skills of their users. When a spell-checker is used to produce accurate spelling, the tool contributes nothing to learning to spell better. Rather, sole reliance on a spell-checker might contribute little to the improvement of spelling skills (Bender, 1994). Specifically, use of spell-checkers and other spelling aides does not necessarily teach any strategies for accurate spelling. In short, dependence on these tools may leave accurate spelling to chance in their absence.

In contrast, if a person has a strong, reliable strategy for learning to spell new words, then a spell-checker can be a tremendous resource by providing immediate feedback and reducing the likelihood of making the same errors in the future. Used as a tool rather than a crutch, an individual gradually can become less reliant on spell-checkers for accurate spelling.

In addition to written expression, spelling performance is positively related to other language arts. Good spellers also tend to be good readers (Institute of Child Health and Human Development, 2000). There is some evidence that teaching students to be good spellers may lead to better reading performance (Lum & Morton, 1984; Uhry & Shepherd, 1993). However, good spelling could just as well be the direct result of good reading instruction (Bruck & Waters, 1990). That possibility, though, seems unlikely given that "spelling-to-sound rules just plain do not work in reverse" (Adams, 1990, p. 100). In other words, producing letters in response to the sounds heard in spoken words (sound-to-spelling) is an unreliable strategy for producing accurate spelling (e.g., spelling /f-o-n/ for the spoken word *phone*).

Spelling may be held in low regard in education, yet the importance of accurate spelling is clear when the broader context of language development is considered (e.g., reading, vocabulary, written expression). Given the relationship of spelling performance to other areas of language use, spelling skills should be directly and systematically taught.

IMPORTANCE OF SPELLING INSTRUCTION

The traditional approach to spelling instruction used in nearly all public schools (if spelling is "taught" at all), requires students to memorize lists of spelling words dutifully for regurgitation on weekly spelling exams. Once completed, those spelling words are discarded and the teacher presents a new list to commit to memory for the following week. In many cases, words "passed" on an exam will never be seen or necessarily spelled by students in the future. In essence, retention of the memorized words is left to chance. This approach teaches children that accurate spelling is important only until the exam, after which time the words may be forgotten. More importantly, memorization of spelling words does not teach students a strategy for accurately spelling new words. Clearly, no one would argue that students should be required to memorize the entire contents of a dictionary, and yet reliance on this strategy does little to help students become accurate spellers. In short, memorization does not ensure that they will use the words that were covered in the instructional program during subsequent writing activities. Furthermore, memorization holds virtually no promise for helping students formulate a strategic approach to learning novel words.

In recognition of the inherent limitations of memorization, some common spelling instructional approaches attempt to teach students spelling strategies. Unfortunately, many spelling approaches teach faulty strategies that lead to spelling failures. For example, students in early primary elementary grades frequently are taught to spell all words phonetically (or the "kindergarten" or "first grade" way). Phonetically correct spellings, to be sure, are more desirable than phonetically impossible spellings. Although desirable for very young children to begin writing early and perhaps meritorious to allow "invented" phonetic misspellings during those early efforts (National Academy of Sciences, 1998), too often students are not directly encouraged to advance beyond phonetic to conventional spellings of words. Typically, invented spelling programs are designed on the assumption that students will "discover" the correct spelling of words on their own, at some point in the future. By contrast, the National Academy of Sciences has recommended that "conventionally correct spelling should be developed through focused instruction and practice" (p. 8). While some students might intuit spelling conventions through language "exposure" alone, many will not recognize the language patterns that lead to accurate and reliable spelling without explicit instruction. Given the conventional wisdom regarding the general difficulties surrounding spelling in the English language and lack of importance placed on accuracy in spelling, one should not be surprised that many children and adults reportedly have trouble with spelling (Dixon, 1993).

Although the field of education appears ambivalent about the importance of spelling (if not openly negative in many cases), this, like many other academic areas, can be explicitly and effectively taught. Students can be taught to recognize patterns in written and spoken language. They can learn to use spelling strategies that reliably lead to accurate spelling in their writing and reduce the need for memorization of words, and these skills can be maintained long after spelling instruction has ended.

Research in the area of spelling (e.g., Collins, 1983; Dixon, 1991; Graham, 1999) has led to the development of evidenced-based Direct Instruction spelling curricula (i.e., *Spelling Mastery* and *Spelling Through Morphographs*). In spite of the complexity of the English language, these curricula systematically teach students to spell accurately. By relying on research-based principles and practices, both programs have demonstrated substantial effects on the spelling development of children (e.g., Darch & Simpson, 1990). The remainder of this chapter will describe the components and appropriate use of these two spelling curricula.

INSTRUCTIONAL APPROACHES TO SPELLING

Three approaches to the teaching of spelling can be used to provide instruction to students: phonemic, whole-word, and morphemic.

Phonemic Approach

Successful reading and spelling performance are built on an understanding of the relationship between letters and their corresponding sounds. Research has demonstrated the important role the letter–sounds of words (or phonemics) play in the spelling skills of children as young as kindergarten age (Treiman, Cassar, & Zukowski, 1994). Moreover, children tend to have less difficulty spelling words that are based on predictable letter–sound relationships (Waters, Bruck, & Malus-Abramowitz, 1988).

In the language arts, close parallels are evident between the letter–sound correspondence tasks associated with reading and spelling. Within the context of reading, phonetics permits students to match the sounds that correspond to the written symbols (letters) in printed reading passages. For spelling, students identify the written letters that correspond to the spoken sounds. The National Reading Panel (NRP), at the direction of Congress, reviewed 1,962 research articles on phonemic awareness. The panel concluded that teaching phonemic awareness exerts "strong and significant effects" on children's reading and spelling skills, with those effects lasting well beyond the end of training. Further, the NRP found that systematic phonics instruction boosted the spelling skills of at-risk and typically developing readers as well as students from across the socioeconomic spectrum, from low to high SES (Institute of Child Health and Human Development, 2000). In short, letter–sound correspondence is a fundamental skill for promoting spelling accuracy.

Given that many words in the English language have regular phonemic patterns, a phonemic approach to spelling instruction allows students to spell regular words solely on the basis of their letter–sound relationships. For example, the word *dog* has three sounds /d/, /o/, and /g/ and can be correctly spelled using the three corresponding letters (*d, o,* and *g*) for each of those sounds.

Whole-Word Approach

While letter–sound correspondences can be used to spell a large number of regularly spelled words (i.e., words that are spelled just like they sound such as *map* and *ran*), not all words in the English language can be spelled correctly using a phonemic approach. Words that cannot be spelled correctly using letter–sound correspondence (i.e., by sounding them out) are irregularly spelled words. Examples of irregular words include *answer, of,* and *phone.* A different spelling strategy called the whole-word approach is required to teach these and many other irregularly spelled words.

As with the phonemic instructional approach, whole-word instructional methods are useful for some, but not all words in the English language. Although whole-word approaches work well for words that are considered irregular, many traditional whole-word approaches rely solely on rote memorization for all words. This practice ignores the advantages of using phonemic rules for words with regular spellings. "In typical whole-word spelling programs, words are grouped together in a list based on some similarity (e.g., similar beginning sound like /wh/ or /th/ or words belonging to a common theme like words related to states or countries)" (Simonsen & Gunter, 2001, p. 99). Students then memorize the words in preparation for the weekly spelling test. This heavy reliance on memorization strategies for spelling could be compared to requiring students to memorize the answers to all multidigit subtraction problems instead of teaching them the rule for borrowing (Dixon, 1993). Memorization is not the most efficient method for learning to spell all words but is advantageous for teaching the much smaller set of irregularly spelled words.

Together, the phonemic and whole-word approaches to spelling instruction are useful strategies for teaching a large but not exhaustive set of words in the English language. Thus, a third approach to the teaching of spelling is warranted.

Morphemic Approach

A morphograph is the smallest unit of identifiable meaning in written English. Morphographs include prefixes, suffixes, and bases or roots. Using a set of fourteen rules for combining morphographs, many words in written English can be created. For example, the word *container* is made from the prefix *con,* the base *tain,* and the suffix *er.* When consideration is given to the role of morphographs, the English language turns out to be far more predictable than the conventional wisdom regarding spelling would suggest. Morphemic principles govern the structure of many words in English. Through the morphemic approach, students are taught to spell morphographs rather than whole words and then learn the rules for combining morphographs into accurately spelled whole words. For example, using a morphemic approach, students would be taught that when a base ends in the letter *e* (e.g., *date*) and is to be combined with a suffix that begins with a vowel (e.g., the /ing/ suffix), the letter *e* is always dropped (*date* becomes *dating*). Adding the /ed/ suffix following the same combining rule turns *perceive* into *perceived.* Forget to drop the final *e* and one gets *perceiveed* (which even the most rudimentary spell-checker will identify as a careless mistake).

There are several advantages to using the morphemic approach to spelling instruction. First, the spelling of morphographs tends to be the same across different words, even when the *sounds* change. For example, the morphograph *sign* is spelled the same in the words *design, signal, signature, resigned,* and *ensign.* Second, when the spelling of a morphograph changes across words it does so in predictable ways. The morphograph *date* is spelled differently in the words *sedate* and *sedative,* but the change is governed by the rule for dropping the final *e.* Third, there are far fewer morphographs than the number of words in written English. Dixon (1993) estimated that teaching individuals to spell 750 carefully selected morphographs would allow the accurate spelling of between 12,000 to 15,000 words. Further, there are relatively few spelling principles for combining morphographs. Therefore, teaching students to spell a small number of morphographs and an even smaller number of rules for combining morphographs will yield far greater gains in spelling performance in a much shorter amount of time than requiring the memorization of those several thousand words.

An additional component of the morphemic approach is called morphographic analysis. In its simplest form, morphographic analysis is the process of identifying the component morphographs in a word. For example, the word *hopping* is composed of two component morphographs (*hop* and *ing*). Yet, even in this simple analysis, students must literally know their rules for combining morphographs forward and backward (i.e., both to construct words from component morphographs and deconstruct words into the smallest units of meaning from which they are made). The primary benefit of using morphographic analysis is that students gain the tools for learning new words on their own, long after formal instruction.

OVERVIEW OF DIRECT INSTRUCTION SPELLING PROGRAMS

This section describes two Direct Instruction spelling programs: *Spelling Mastery* and *Spelling Through Morphographs.*

Spelling Mastery

Spelling Mastery consists of six instructional levels (Levels A through F) and a total of 660 lessons. Lessons within each level are sequenced so students learn simple spelling strategies (e.g., letter–sound correspondence for predictably spelled words) before more complex spelling strategies (e.g., morphemic spelling rules) are introduced. In addition, within each lesson, introduction of new content is sequenced to minimize acquisition of misrules. For example, the letter *b* and *d* are introduced in separate lessons to avoid potential confusion between them.

Spelling Through Morphographs

The *Spelling Through Morphographs* curriculum is designed around the morphemic approach to spelling instruction. Briefly, a morphograph is the smallest unit of identifiable meaning in written English. *Spelling Through Morphographs* is composed of 140 lessons in which students are taught to spell several hundred morphographs and fourteen spelling rules for combining them into words. "When students complete the first half of *Spelling Through Morphographs,* they will have been taught only 252 morphographs, but with these the students can spell more than 3000 words and parts of thousands more" (Dixon & Engelmann, 2001, p. 7). The curriculum is designed for students between fourth through twelfth grade. Some students with disabilities or students with English as a second language can be placed appropriately in the *Spelling Through Morphographs* curriculum. In contrast to the *Spelling Mastery* curriculum, *Spelling Through Morphographs* can be used as an accelerated "fast cycle" for students who have the prerequisite skills for manipulating letters and their corresponding sounds.

CONTENT ANALYSIS AND FORMAT FEATURES

In this section, the major instructional content features of the *Spelling Mastery* and *Spelling Through Morphographs* curricula are described based on the three approaches to spelling instruction (i.e., phonemic, whole-word, and morphemic). Examples of lesson formats that illustrate the instructional content of the curricula also are provided.

Phonemic Approach

Spelling Mastery explicitly teaches the letter–sound relationships for high frequency regular words (i.e., words that occur at high rates in passages of written English and can be spelled phonetically). Early lessons in *Spelling Mastery* directly teach students letter–sound relationships. Following mastery of phonemics, the program continues to provide opportunities to practice those skills while introducing new and more challenging material.

Although *Spelling Through Morphographs* lessons do not explicitly teach students phonemics, the curriculum recognizes its importance by recommending that students pass an initial placement test to demonstrate mastery of letter–sound relationships prior to beginning the curriculum. This recommendation is supported in the research literature. Beers, Beers, and Grant (1977) argued for postponing spelling instruction until students had received a year of instruction in phonemics. Mastery of this foundational skill is important for students to become accurate spellers of high-frequency regular words.

Whether using *Spelling Mastery* or *Spelling Through Morphographs,* both curricula have addressed the importance of teaching letter–sound relationships. *Spelling Mastery* uses the phonemic instructional approach across all six levels of the program and places heavy emphasis on directly teaching letter–sound relationships within the first two curriculum levels (consisting of 180 lessons). Knowing letter–sound correspondences should be considered a prerequisite to entering the *Spelling Through Morphographs* curriculum. Poor performance on the placement test indicates the need to teach letter–sound correspondences explicitly. Following poor student performance on the placement test, a student could be placed in the *Spelling Mastery* curriculum to develop phonemic skills. "Rather than postponing spelling instruction, these curricula directly assess and teach letter–sound relationships. This instruction will enable them to spell many high frequency regular sound words" (Simonsen & Gunter, 2001, p. 99).

An important component of a phonemic approach to spelling is *phonemic awareness* in general, but, more specifically, one subcategory of phonemic awareness: phonemic segmentation. The ability to segment words orally into their component sounds does not always ensure accurate spelling. Rather, the great value of this skill is that of considerably reducing the number and types of *misspellings* that students typically make.

For example, many students transpose letters in words, writing something such as *s-r-t-i-p-e* for *stripe*. Some students leave out essential letters (e.g., *s-t-i-p-e*) while others add letters (e.g., *f-r-i-n-e-n-d*). Students who are proficient at segmenting words orally are not likely to make these types of errors. They still might spell a word like *street* as *s-t-r-e-a-t*, but at least they are phonemically representing all the sounds they hear.

Figure 6.1 illustrates how *Spelling Mastery* initially teaches beginning spellers to segment words orally. These phonemic segmentation exercises are called pronunciation exercises in the program.

In later lessons of both Level A and B of *Spelling Mastery,* there is less teacher guidance, and the exercises involve longer, more challenging words (see Figure 6.2).

EXERCISE 2—Pronunciation

1. Listen: **mat.**
   Say it. (Signal.) **Mat.**
2. I'll say the sounds in **mat:**
   /mm/ . . . /a/ . . . /t/.
   Say the sounds in **mat.**
   Get ready. (Signal for each sound.)
   /m/ . . . /a/ . . . /t/.
   TO CORRECT:
   (Return to step 1.)
3. What is the first sound in **mat?**
   (Signal.) /mm/.
   TO CORRECT:
   a. (Say the correct sound.)
   b. (Return to step 1.)
4. Next sound? (Signal.) /a/.
5. Next sound? (Signal.) /t/.
   Yes. Those are the sounds in **mat.**

6. Listen: **not.**
   Say it. (Signal.) *Not.*
7. I'll say the sounds in **not:**
   /nn/ . . . /o/ . . . /t/.
8. Say the sounds in **not.**
   Get ready. (Signal for each sound.)
   /nn/ . . . /o/ . . . /t/.
9. What is the first sound in **not?**
   (Signal.) /nn/.
10. Next sound? (Signal.) /o/.
11. Next sound? (Signal.) /t/.
    Yes. Those are the sounds in **not.**
12. (Repeat steps 6–11 for: *pit.*)
13. (Call on individual students to say the sounds in: **not, mat, pit.**)

FIGURE 6.1 *Spelling Mastery Level A,* **Lesson 1, Exercise 2. Reprinted with permission of the McGraw-Hill Companies.**

LESSON 76, EXERCISE 1—Pronunciation	

1. Listen: **split.**
    Say it. (Signal.) *Split.*
 2. What's the first sound? (Signal.) */ss/.*
 3. Next sound? (Signal.) */p/.*
 4. Next sound? (Signal.) */ll/.*
 5. Next sound? (Signal.) */i/.*
 6. Next sound? (Signal.) */t/.*
 7. Listen: **strike.**
    Say it. (Signal.) *Strike.*
 8. What's the first sound? (Signal.) */ss/.*
	9. Next sound? (Signal.) */t/.*
	 10. Next sound? (Signal.) */rr/.*
	 11. Next sound? (Signal.) */i/.*
	 12. Next sound? (Signal.) */k/.*
	 13. (Repeat steps 7–12 for: ***spray, scrape, about, around.***)
	 14. (Call on individual students to say the sounds in: ***strike, spray, scrape, about, around, split.***)

FIGURE 6.2 *Spelling Mastery Level B,* **Lesson 76, Exercise 1. Reprinted with permission of the McGraw-Hill Companies.**

Relative to reading, there are few sounds in English that can be spelled only one way. For example, there are many ways to spell most long vowel sounds, especially /ê/. Nonetheless, it is important for students to learn those sound-to-symbol correspondences that are reasonably predictable.

Figure 6.3 shows how students are taught to spell individual sounds that are predictable, especially in single syllable words. (Morphemic rules or principles often come into play in multisyllabic words.) The sounds that the students spell in the word *expel* are not always spelled the way indicated. They are, however, useful correspondences for beginning spellers.

Often, sounds in a *pattern* are more predictable than sounds in isolation. Figure 6.4 shows how students learn to spell the /l/ sound with two *l*'s in single-syllable words, following a short vowel sound. Note, however, that the exercise uses none of the specialized language in the previous sentence: short vowels, single syllables. The students who are working at this level of the program range mostly from preschool to first grade. As you can see, the spelling

LESSON 23, EXERCISE 2—Spelling Sounds	

1. My turn to spell a new sound.
 2. The sound **/ff/** is spelled with the letter: **f.**
    Everybody, spell **/ff/.** Get ready. (Signal.) *f.*
    (Repeat until firm.)
 3. (Call on individual students to spell */ff/.*)
 4. Your turn.
    I'll say sounds.
	You tell me the letter that spells each sound.
	 5. Spell **/shsh/.** Get ready. (Signal.) *s-h.*
	 6. Spell **/ff/.** Get ready. (Signal.) *f.*
	 7. Spell **/rr/.** Get ready. (Signal.) *r.*
	 8. Spell **/nn/.** Get ready. (Signal.) *n.*
	 9. Spell **/ff/.** Get ready. (Signal.) *f.*
	 10. Spell **/ss/.** Get ready. (Signal.) *s.*
	 11. (Repeat steps 5–10 until all students are firm.)

FIGURE 6.3 *Spelling Mastery Level A,* **Lesson 23, Exercise 2. Reprinted with permission of the McGraw-Hill Companies.**

LESSON 28, EXERCISE 1—Patterns	
1. Get ready to spell short words that end in the **/ll/** sound.	9. (Repeat step 8 for: **stall, hill, fall.**)
2. **Stall.** What word? (Signal.) *Stall.*	10. Check the words as we spell them together. Put an X by any word that is spelled wrong and write it correctly.
3. Spell **stall.** Get ready. (Signal.) *S-t-a-l-l.*	
4. **Hall.** What word? (Signal.) *Hall.*	11. Spell **hall.** Get ready. (Signal.) *H-a-l-l.* (Write the word on the board as the students spell it.)
5. Spell **hall.** Get ready. (Signal.) *H-a-l-l.*	
6. (Repeat steps 4 and 5 for: **fall, hill.**)	
7. Get ready to write those words on Part A of your worksheet.	12. (Repeat step 11 for: **stall, hill, fall.**)
8. Word 1 is **hall.** What word? (Signal.) *Hall.* Write it.	

FIGURE 6.4   *Spelling Mastery Level A,* **Lesson 28, Exercise 1. Reprinted with permission of the McGraw-Hill Companies.**

of the pattern is prompted at this stage: teachers tell the students how to spell the /l/ sound in the words that follow. Eventually, students internalize the pattern. This approach in Direct Instruction is called stipulation. Whenever an explicit rule or explanation is more complicated or involves more prerequisite knowledge than the thing being taught, Direct Instruction uses stipulation.

What actually constitutes an "irregular spelling" in English is something specialists in orthography could debate forever, but it is unusual to find an English spelling that is *completely* irregular. For instance, the word *ceilidh* is a Gaelic borrowing that is still considered English, but the pronunciation is: "KAY – lee." (The word is a noun and means "a visit.") Although it is fine and correct to say that most of the sounds in most words are spelled regularly, that gives students little hope until they learn which sounds are which. *Spelling Mastery* attacks this problem by initially prompting students on the difficult or unpredictable spellings of newly introduced words. In Figure 6.5 (i.e., an example from the

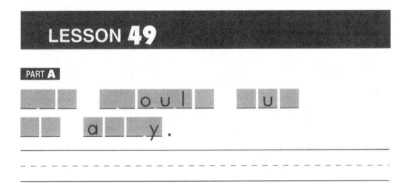

FIGURE 6.5   *Spelling Mastery Level B,* **Student Workbook, Lesson 49, Part A. Reprinted with permission of the McGraw-Hill Companies.**

student workbook), the lines represent a required letter, and the boxes indicate that one individual sound is being spelled with one, two, or more letters. The teacher dictates the sentence that corresponds to this illustration: *She should put it away.* In combination, the lines, the boxes, and the given letters are enough information for students to spell all the words in the sentence. Over many lessons, all the prompts are removed until students are spelling the words in the sentence with no prompting.

Whole-Word Approach

Commercially available whole-word spelling curricula may or may not use explicit teaching strategies for the development of accurate spelling. Explicit, whole-word approaches to spelling have been shown to produce highly accurate spellers (Larsen & McLaughlin, 1997; Pratt-Struthers, Struthers, & Williams, 1983). *Spelling Mastery* uses an explicit, whole-word spelling instructional approach to teach high-frequency, irregular words that cannot be spelled by applying phonemic rules. The program is unique among whole-word approaches in that it does not rely solely on memorization as the strategy for teaching irregular spellings. Rather, the program provides phonemically based scaffolding or prompting when students initially learn highly irregular words, and then systematically reduces the scaffolding over time. In effect, the curriculum judiciously combines explicit whole-word and phonemic instruction to support and facilitate learning irregular words.

For example, students are introduced to a sentence that contains irregular words (e.g., *I thought he was through*). At first the irregular letters or letter combinations are provided and students must fill in the missing letters (e.g., _ _ _ *ough* _ _ _ _ _ <u>a</u> _ _ _ _ _ *ough*). Presenting the words in this format highlights the predictable elements of irregular words. Gradually, the number of provided letters is decreased until students are able to spell all the words without visual prompts. Following mastery, sentence variations are presented using similar irregular words (e.g., *She thought about her homework throughout the night*). Notice how this progression promotes the gradual acquisition of accurate spelling without relying on memorization as the instructional strategy. Further, this explicit approach to whole-word spelling instruction facilitates the transfer of spelling to writing skills.

The critical element required for students to achieve long-term retention of words with greater than average phonemic irregularity is that of *review*: plenty of it, distributed, cumulative, and varied. In this example (see Figure 6.6), students write entire sentences made up of words that they initially learned through the strategy illustrated previously from Figure 6.5. This application is *varied* to the extent possible through the requirement that students spell words in new (or unfamiliar) sentences.

In addition to using sentences to teach spelling, *Spelling Mastery* also preteaches the spelling of some individual words prior to introducing them in other spelling exercises. Figure 6.7 illustrates a typical teaching format for this type of whole-word instruction.

Morphemic Approach

Spelling Through Morphographs explicitly teaches the use of morphographs. Students learn to spell morphographs rather than whole words. Once a small set of morphographs is mastered, students learn to combine these morphographs into multisyllabic words. At first, morphographs are combined to form words that do not require changes in spelling. In other

LESSON 88, EXERCISE 6—Sentence Variations	
1. Find Part D on your worksheet. 2. You are going to write a sentence made up of words you know how to spell. Remember to put the right end mark at the end of each sentence. 3. The sentence is: **He said that we should work.** Say the sentence. Get ready. (Signal.) He said that we should work. (Repeat until firm.) 4. Write it on the line. 5. Get ready to check your spelling. Put an X next to any word you missed. 6. Spell **He.** Get ready. (Signal.) *H-e.*	Write **He.** Check it. 7. Spell **said.** Get ready. (Signal.) *S-a-i-d.* Write **said.** Check it. 8. (Repeat step 7 for: **that, we, should, work.**) 9. What end mark did you put at the end of the sentence? Get ready. (Signal.) *A period.* Write a period. Check it. 10. Fix up any words you missed.

FIGURE 6.6 *Spelling Mastery Level B,* **Lesson 88, Exercise 6. Reprinted with permission of the McGraw-Hill Companies.**

words, early lessons do not require students to apply spelling combination rules. For example, students might learn to spell the morphographs *re + fresh + ing,* and combine them together to spell the word *refreshing.* More advanced lessons in the morphemic approach introduce additional spelling rules and principles (*Spelling Through Morphographs* teaches only fourteen spelling combination rules). For example, the doubling rule is applied when a short morphograph ending with a consonant – vowel – consonant (CVC) letter sequence is followed by a morphograph beginning with a vowel. When this pattern occurs, the final consonant is doubled (as in the case of the word *omitted*: o + mit + ed). These morphemic spelling rules provide a highly reliable strategy to avoid common spelling mistakes.

> Students who lack skills using morphographs might have difficulty spelling the words *hopping* and *hoping* (adding the /ing/ suffix to the words *hop* and *hope*). Using the rules for dropping the final *e* and for CVC consonant doubling, students will consistently and accurately spell these words (*hop* becomes *hopping* while *hope* becomes *hoping*) and many others that conform to the same morphemic rules (Simonsen & Gunter, 2001, pp. 101–102).

LESSON 47, EXERCISE 3—Vowel Patterns	
1. Get ready to spell some words that contain the sound /ē/ spelled with the letters **e-a.** 2. Spell **leave.** Get ready. (Signal.) *L-e-a-v-e.*	3. Spell **repeat.** Get ready. (Signal.) *R-e-p-e-a-t.* 4. (Repeat step 3 for: **speak, leader, year.**) 5. (Call on individual students to spell: **leader, speak, leave, repeat, year.**)

FIGURE 6.7 *Spelling Mastery* **Level B, Lesson 47, Exercise 3. Reprinted with permission of the McGraw-Hill Companies.**

Morphographic analysis is also utilized. More than simply breaking words into component parts, morphographic analysis allows students to understand the meaning of those word parts, combine them into new, accurately spelled words, and synthesize meaning for novel words. The Teacher's Guide for *Spelling Through Morphographs* (Dixon & Engelmann, 2001) includes the meaning of the morphographs taught in the curriculum. Gradually, students in both *Spelling Through Morphographs* and *Spelling Mastery* learn to conduct complex analyses of words using their knowledge of morphographs, morphograph combination rules, and morphograph meaning.

For example, the morphemic components of the word *exhilaration* are: *ex + hilar + ate + ion.* The prefix *ex* is the most obvious morphograph in this example. The non-word base, *hilar,* means 'merry' and occurs in other English words, is spelled the same way, and carries a similar meaning (e.g., *hilarity*). Again, recognizing the base *hilar* and its meaning helps students both to more accurately spell and to comprehend the spoken word *exhilaration.* The letter combination *tion* (and *cion, sion, cian,* etc.) is often incorrectly characterized as a suffix for the spoken sound /shun/ that occurs in many English words. In the present example, this type of error could lead students to guess at the spelling of the middle letters in the word. Students who have been taught the common suffix *ion* (instead of *tion*) are less likely to misspell this word.

The word *action* provides a clear illustration of the appropriate "break-point" in words that include the *tion* letter sequence. The word *action* is composed of two morphographs (i.e., the base *act* and the suffix *-ion*). As with the base *hilar* in *exhilaration,* recognizing the base *act* provides clues about the meaning of the word *action,* even if a student has never heard the word before. By contrast, if *action* is incorrectly broken into the base *ac + tion* (as is common practice in many schools when suffixes are introduced), the meaning of the word is lost. In short, skill in morphographic analysis can help students recognize the patterns in words, comprehend their meaning, and accurately spell them.

These examples demonstrate how morphographic analysis teaches students a strategy for understanding the meaning of related words within the context of reading comprehension. For example, the morphograph *spect* means 'look.' From this root, the words *inspect* ('to look over, or view closely'), *respect* ('the act of looking back, or to regard'), and *spectator* ('one who looks') can be created. More importantly, the relationships among these words can be understood.

Although sophisticated, this analysis allows fluent and accurate spelling and a far richer understanding of the English language. Morphographic analysis is embedded within the lessons of both *Spelling Mastery* and *Spelling Through Morphographs.*

Figure 6.8 illustrates basic morphograph combining at its simplest. Although this activity might appear to some—adults and students alike—as incredibly simple, it lays the groundwork for far more sophisticated and less obvious applications of morphemics.

The first complexity in an otherwise straightforward process arises when the spelling of one or more morphographs *does* change when the parts are added together. For the most part, such changes are predictable. Also, the rules governing such changes—in one form or another—are familiar ones to most adults. We know, for example, that something happens when we add the suffix *–ing* to the word *hop.*

Figure 6.9 illustrates the introduction of the doubling rule. Several critical prerequisites are taught prior to this introduction. First, students are taught to discriminate between *vowel*

LESSON 15, EXERCISE 6—Word Building	
Find part **C** on your worksheet. Get ready to spell some words that have more than one morphograph. 1. First word: **unsellable.** What is the first morphograph in **unsellable?** (Signal.) *un.* 2. What is the next morphograph in **unsellable?** (Signal.) *sell.* 3. What is the next morphograph in **unsellable?** (Signal.) *able.* 4. Write **unsellable.**	5. Next word: **misspend.** What is the first morphograph in **misspend?** (Signal.) *mis.* 6. What is the next morphograph in **misspend?** (Signal.) *spend.* 7. Write **misspend.** 8. (For **unhappy** and **authoring,** have the students identify each morphograph and spell each entire word.) 9. (Check spellings and have students rewrite any missed words.)

FIGURE 6.8   *Spelling Through Morphographs,* **Lesson 15, Exercise 6. Reprinted with permission of the McGraw-Hill Companies.**

letters and *consonant letters.* The rule is actually based on letters, not sounds. Also, students learn the convention of referring to *vowel letters* simply as *v,* and *consonant letters* as *c.* In addition, students are taught to discriminate single-syllable words ending in CVC (consonant letter-vowel letter-consonant letter) from words ending any other way. Finally, students are taught to spell all the words and suffixes used in this exercise before it is introduced. Therefore, students can focus solely on one new thing: the rule itself.

Notice that the level of prompting or scaffolding is extremely high when this rule is introduced (see Figure 6.9). As is the case with any topic in any Direct Instruction program, all of that help is gradually removed as students move closer and closer to applying the rule covertly and automatically, a process that takes place across several dozen lessons in both programs.

Many base morphographs are not stand-alone words. Such non-word bases, however, "behave" the same as base words. When students are taught the most frequently occurring non-word bases, they can use them in conjunction with prefixes and suffixes to accurately spell quite a vast quantity of words. Figure 6.10 illustrates the introduction of one useful non-word base.

Some teachers might elect to tie non-word bases into some instruction on etymology (i.e., tracing linguistic development over time and analyzing word parts), which is turn has some limited but useful application to vocabulary. For example, the non-word base *tain* derives from a Latin word meaning 'to hold,' which is fairly transparent in words such as *container, detain,* or *retain.*

Possibly the best thing we can do for students is not simply teach them to spell, but to extend the instruction in a way that almost guarantees that the students will learn how to learn how to spell. What should a student do when encountering a new, unfamiliar spelling, either outside of class, or even long after having received any formal spelling instruction? The way to achieve that ambitious goal is to teach students how to analyze words morphemically. That skill is basically the opposite of combining morphographs to form words. In

---

LESSON 24, EXERCISE 3—Doubling Rule

Note: It is absolutely necessary to repeat step 5 until all students are firm.

1. (Write on the board: double **c** when **cvc + v.** Point to the rule.)
    Here is a rule for changing the spelling of short words when you add a morphograph to the end of these words.
2. When a short word ends **CVC** and the next morphograph begins with a vowel letter, you must double this consonant.
    (Point to the final **c.**)
3. Listen again. (Repeat the rule.)
4. My turn: When do you double the final **C** in a short word? (Pause.)
    When the word ends **CVC** and the next morphograph begins with **V.**
5. Your turn: When do you double the final **C** in a short word? (S)
    When the word ends cvc and the next morphograph begins with v.
    (Repeat until firm.)
6. (Write **star** on the board.)
    Look at the last three letters in this word.
7. (Point to **t.**)
    Is this a **V** or a **C**? (S) *A c.*
    (Write **c** above the **t.**)
8. (Point to **a.**)
    Is this a **V** or a **C**? (S) *A v.*
    (Write **v** above the **a.**)
9. (Point to **r.**)
    Is this a **V** or a **C**? (S) *A c.*
    (Write **c** above the **r.**)
10. Is **star** a short **CVC** word? (S) *Yes.*

11. (Write **+ less** after **star.**)
    The next morphograph is **less.** Does **less** begin with a **V**? (S) *No.*
12. So do we double any letters? (S) *No.*

> **To correct:**
> a. You double the final **C** when the short word ends **CVC** and the next morphograph begins with **V.**
> b. (Repeat step 12.)

13. Why not? (S)
    Because less does not begin with v.
14. (Replace **less** with **ing.**)
    The next morphograph is **ing.** Does it begin with **V**? (S) *Yes.*
15. So do we double a letter? (S) *Yes.*
    What letter do we double? (S) *r.*
16. (Replace **ing** with **ed.**)
    The next morphograph is **e-d.**
    Does it begin with **V**? (S) *Yes.*
17. So do we double a letter? (S) *Yes.*
    What letter do we double? (S) *r.*
18. Everybody, spell **starred** with me.
    Remember to double the final **C.**
    Get ready.
    (Signal and say each letter with students.)
    S-t-a-r-r-e-d.
    (Repeat spelling until firm.)
19. (Replace **ed** with **ing.**)
    ing begins with **V.** Spell **starring.** Get ready (S)
20. (Replace **ing** with **less.**)
    Less does not begin with **V.** Spell **starless.**
    Get ready. (S)

FIGURE 6.9 *Spelling Through Morphographs,* **Lesson 24, Exercise 3. Reprinted with permission of the McGraw Hill Companies.**

analysis, students start with a word, and break it into its component morphographs (if, of course, the word is made up of more than one morphograph). In *Spelling Mastery* and *Spelling Through Morphographs,* the instruction on analysis starts out very simply. Students "undo" words that they have previously spelled by adding parts together. For instance, when given the word *refresh,* the students write the prefix *re-* and *fresh* in blanks that look like this: *refresh = _____ + _____ .*

LESSON 26, EXERCISE 4—Nonword Base	

1. (Write on the chalkboard: **reacting.** Point to it.)
   What word? (Signal.) Reacting.
   What's the first morphograph?
   (Signal.) *Re.*
   Next morphograph? (Signal.) *Act.*
   Next morphograph? (Signal.) *ing.*
2. Which morphograph in this word could stand alone?
   (Signal.) *Act.*
3. (Erase the morphograph **act.** Replace it with ject: **rejecting.**)
	(Point to **rejecting.**) What word?
	   (Signal.) *Rejecting.*
	   Tell me which morphograph in this word could stand alone. (Pause.)
	   Get ready. (Signal.) *None of them.*
	   Which morphograph takes the place of a morphograph that could stand alone?
	   (Signal.) *Ject.*
	4. Spell **ject.** Get ready. (Signal.)
	   Remember, ject is a morphograph that cannot stand alone.

FIGURE 6.10   *Spelling Mastery Level E,* **Lesson 26, Exercise 4, Steps 1–4. Reprinted with permission of the McGraw-Hill Companies.**

Next, in order to analyze words morphemically, students must literally learn the rules for combining morphographs *forward and backward* (see Figure 6.11). Students use the same strategy with words that illustrate other rules. For example, they analyze the word *hopping* into *hop* and the suffix *–ing,* as well as *hoping* into the word *hope* and the suffix *–ing.*

Eventually, the plus signs are removed, meaning that students are not given a cue about the number of morphographs they are looking for (see Figure 6.12). Eventually, this skill becomes very sophisticated, and it is practiced to the point where it would be very difficult—if not impossible—for a student to look at a word and *not* think about its morphemic components.

Morphographs can help demystify some aspects of English orthography that might otherwise seem completely irrational. For example, many people—students and adults alike—struggle with words having an unstressed ending that sounds like *ur.* One reality is that not every word like this ends with *a-r,* such as *scholar.* Sooner or later, a person just has to remember which words those are. The greater challenge seems to be the decision to use either *e-r* or *o-r* in these situations.

Spelling Mastery and *Spelling Through Morphographs* teach students that if a given word has an *ion* form, they use the *o-r* spelling when they add the sounds *ur.* For instance, the word protect has an *-ion* form (*protection*). Therefore, *protector* is spelled with *o-r.* Figure 6.13 shows a lesson in which students first write the *–ion* form of a word, if there is one. Then they write the word with either *e-r* or *o-r.*

TEACHING TECHNIQUES

In this section, teaching techniques (i.e., signals and error-correction procedures) specific to the *Spelling Mastery* and *Spelling Through Morphographs* curricula are described.

LESSON 24, EXERCISE 5—Morphograph Analysis	
Note: It is important that students write the morphographs as they are spelled before being put together: for instance, trace rather than trac.	What is the first morphograph in **careless?** (Signal.) *care.* Write it in the blank.
Find part **B** on your worksheet.	5. What is the next morphograph in **careless?** (Signal.) *less.* Write it in the next blank.
1. Number 1 says Blank plus blank equals **tracing.** What is the first morphograph in **tracing?** (Signal.) *trace.* Everybody, spell **trace.** Get ready. (Signal.)	6. Number 3 says: Blank plus blank equals **faced.** What is the first morphograph in **faced?** (Signal.) *face.* Write it in the blank.
2. Now write **trace** in the first blank. Don't forget to write the **e** at the end of **trace.**	7. What is the next morphograph in **faced?** (Signal.) *e-d.* Write it in the next blank.
3. What is the next morphograph in **tracing?** (Signal) *ing.* Write it in the next blank.	8. Fill in the rest of the blanks to show the morphographs in each word. (Check and correct.)
4. Number 2 says: Blank plus blank equals **careless.**	

FIGURE 6.11 *Spelling Through Morphographs,* **Lesson 24, Exercise 5. Reprinted with permission of the McGraw-Hill Companies.**

Signals

Signals are used to cue a group response so that all students respond together. Using signals provides teachers with feedback on student performance and gives students models of appropriate responding by their peers. The Teacher's Guide for *Spelling Through Morpho-*

LESSON **89**

PART E

Write the morphographs in each word.

1. experiment	5. universe
2. interruption	6. pleasant
3. fortunate	7. competent
4. bicycle	8. effortless

FIGURE 6.12 *Spelling Mastery Level F,* **Student Workbook, Lesson 89, Part E. Reprinted with permission of the McGraw-Hill Companies.**

LESSON **106**

PART C

	ion form?	**or** or **er** form?
1. dictate	_____	_____
2. consume	_____	_____
3. invent	_____	_____
4. instruct	_____	_____
5. stretch	_____	_____
6. contract	_____	_____

FIGURE 6.13   *Spelling Mastery Level E,* **Student Workbook, Lesson 106, Part C. Reprinted with permission of the McGraw-Hill Companies.**

graphs (Dixon & Engelman, 2001) provides the following guidelines on the use of signals in spelling instruction.

A point- or touch-signal should be used when students must respond to words or letters written on the board. The point-touch signal involves the following steps. First, the teacher should hold his finger an inch or so from the board, just below the beginning of the word (or letter). Next, he provides the question or cue for students to respond (e.g., "Spell *horse*. Get Ready"). After the teacher provides this question or cue, he quickly touches under the word (or letter), being sure not to talk and move at the same time. Students respond with the word *horse* as soon as the teacher's finger touches the board.

Following the same sequence, other signals could be used for the variety of tasks in the *Spelling Mastery* and *Spelling Through Morphographs* curricula that do not involve written words on the board. When students' eyes are on the teacher and they are responding to teacher-delivered cues such as, "Spell *mother*," a hand-drop signal may be appropriate. This signal may also be paired with an audible cue such as a snap at the end of the hand-drop. When students are responding to teacher-delivered cues as they look at their own workbooks (e.g., "What is the first morphograph in *tracing*?"), an audible signal such as a snap, tap, or clap would be more appropriate to cue students to respond together.

For the latter two tasks (i.e., tasks that require students to look at the teacher and tasks that require students to look at their own materials), the choice of signal generally is at the discretion of the teacher. The following suggestions should be considered for successful use of any signals, regardless of the program used. First, a signal should follow a teacher instruction by no less than one second. The signal (e.g., clap) should never overlap with the teacher instruction; thus, a teacher should not "talk and move" at the same time. Second, the teacher generally should not change the length of the pause between the instruction and the signal. Changing the pause interval can confuse students about when to respond (Dixon & Engelman, 2001).

Error Corrections

Spelling Mastery and *Spelling Through Morphographs* address error corrections through a series of structured, teacher-directed responses to student spelling errors. Error-correction procedures in these curricula combine (1) teacher demonstration (i.e., modeling) of correct responding with (2) guided opportunities for students to respond correctly (i.e., leading), and (3) assessment of student knowledge (i.e., testing). This generic error-correction sequence could be used for whole words and words containing more than one morphograph. An example error correction for each word type (i.e., *friend* and *receive*) from the *Spelling Through Morphographs* Teacher's Guide (Dixon & Engelmann, 2001) is illustrated in Table 6.1.

Spelling errors may also occur when a student has a problem with a spelling rule. For example, if a student makes an error through misapplication of a spelling rule, (i.e., misspelling *running* as *r-u-n-i-n-g*), the following error-correction sequence would be used.

TABLE 6.1   Error-Correction Strategies for Common Spelling Errors

	EXAMPLES	
Steps	*f-r-e for friend*	*r-e-c-i for receive*
1. MODEL the spelling of the missed morphograph by saying:	"Listen: **f-r-i-e-n-d.**"	"The second morphograph is **ceive; c-e-i-v-e**."
2. LEAD by spelling:	"With me, spell **friend.** Get ready."	"With me, spell **ceive.** Get ready."
3. TEST the students on the missed morphograph, saying	"Your turn. Spell friend. Get ready."	"Your turn. Spell **ceive.** Get ready."
4. TEST (VARIATIONS) Individual turns, saying: Test whole word saying:	"Let's see who can spell **friend.**" ———	——— "Now spell **receive.**"
5. DELAYED TEST by asking the students to spell the missed word or morphograph again, later in the exercise or even later during the lesson.	"Everybody spell **friend.**"	"Spell **receive.**" OR
Alternative: test on a different word containing the missed morphograph.	———	"Spell **deceiving.**"

First, the teacher states the rule, "name the rule that applies to *running*." Students respond with "the doubling rule." Second, he tests the rule, "when do you double the final consonant letter in a short word?" Students respond with, "when the word ends CVC and the next morphograph begins with V." Third, he tests the word, "spell *running*. Get ready." Students respond accordingly. Finally, the teacher provides a delayed test, having them spell the word *running*.

These structured teacher responses to errors prevent students from making repeated mistakes and provide instructional feedback that helps them become more accurate spellers.

ASSESSMENT AND TROUBLESHOOTING

In this section, the role of curriculum-based assessment is discussed. Specifically, use of the assessments built into *Spelling Mastery* and *Spelling Through Morphographs* are described. Further, general guidelines for troubleshooting student spelling problems in the curricula are provided.

Curriculum-Based Assessment

Deno (1987) defined curriculum-based assessment (CBA) as the "direct observation and recording of a student's performance in the local curriculum as a basis for gathering information to make instructional decisions" (p. 41). CBA is a broad term that includes a variety of measurement approaches (e.g., criterion-referenced tests, accuracy- and fluency-based assessment, curriculum-based measurement). Two types of curriculum-based assessment (i.e., placement tests and mastery tests) are built into the *Spelling Mastery* and *Spelling Through Morphographs* curricula. A description of each assessment procedure follows.

Placement Tests. The *Spelling Through Morphographs* placement test has two parts (A and B). Part A is used to determine whether students have the necessary phonemic foundation for entering the program. If *Spelling Through Morphographs* is too difficult, students likely would be placed in either Level A or B of *Spelling Mastery*. Part B of the placement test is used to determine whether a student's skills are too advanced for the curriculum. Generally, students who test out of *Spelling Through Morphographs* would placement test into Level F of *Spelling Mastery*. Students performing above the ceiling or below the floor of the *Spelling Through Morphographs* curriculum should complete the placement test for the *Spelling Mastery* curriculum to determine the appropriate level for beginning spelling instruction.

The placement test for *Spelling Mastery* is designed to determine which of the six instructional levels (Levels A through F) is the most appropriate place to begin spelling instruction. The program also assumes certain prerequisite skills. Those students who have not started to read and/or do not know the names of letters of the alphabet should not yet begin spelling instruction.

Ideally, teachers would use the placement tests from both programs to form spelling groups. In reality, teachers may not have the resources to place all students into homogeneous groups. Nonetheless, placement tests are the best tool for ensuring spelling instruction is appropriate and at the "just right" level for students.

Mastery Tests.   In addition to placement tests, criterion-referenced mastery tests are built into both *Spelling Mastery* and *Spelling Through Morphographs*. Mastery tests are used to assess the percentage of accurately spelled words at periodic intervals. The words tested are selected from the words taught in each respective curriculum. Beginning with Level C (and optionally for Levels A and B), *Spelling Mastery* includes mastery tests every fifth lesson. *Spelling Through Morphographs* includes built-in mastery tests every twenty lessons.

These tests serve several purposes. First, mastery tests provide students with feedback on how well they are doing on their spelling lessons. Given that teaching to mastery is an essential component of the Direct Instruction approach, results from mastery tests should reinforce student learning. Second, these assessments give teachers invaluable information on the effectiveness of instruction. If scores are *not* high on a mastery test, then students likely are not being "firmed" (i.e., brought to a high level of mastery) on all skills in the program.

In addition, mastery tests can be used by teachers to identify spelling error patterns. Perhaps students are having difficulty with high-frequency irregular words, (e.g., *many, friend, straight,* or *through*). Such a pattern would suggest the need for additional instruction with irregular words during the course of scheduled lessons or as unscheduled review to provide students with additional opportunities to practice.

Mastery tests represent a "valid" assessment of student progress. In contrast with typical weekly spelling tests, students are not told the words to be tested in advance. Approximately half of the words on any given mastery test come from the most recently completed ten to fifteen lessons, while the remaining words come from any previously completed lesson in the curricula. Therefore, even late in a school year, the mastery tests would assess retention of material taught during the early part of the year.

Placement and mastery tests provide a wealth of information about student spelling skills. Under some circumstances, other variations on CBA procedures may be necessary. For example, measuring the percentage of words correct may not be sensitive to the spelling progress of some students with disabilities. Further, percentage of words correct may not highlight particular student error patters. One assessment alternative is to measure the number or percentage of correct letter sequences (CLS) from the mastery test word lists or other content-driven word lists (White & Haring, 1980). Hall, Tindal, and Flick (1993) have provided the following illustration of this assessment procedure using the word *myself*:

$$^{\wedge}M^{\wedge}y^{\wedge}s^{\wedge}e^{\wedge}l^{\wedge}f^{\wedge} = 7 \text{ CLS} \qquad ^{\wedge}mis^{\wedge}e^{\wedge}l^{\wedge}f^{\wedge} = 5 \text{ CLS.}$$

When spelled correctly, *myself* has a total of seven correct letter sequences. The misspelling represented above would score five CLS.

Curriculum-based assessment is critical to placing students successfully and providing an appropriate pace for spelling instruction. Using assessment data can help teachers to maximize student success in the *Spelling Mastery* and *Spelling Through Morphographs* curricula.

Troubleshooting

Some sort of "trouble" during spelling instruction is not something that *might* happen; it is inevitable. That is, with any given group of students, one or more students are going to experience difficulty moving through the curriculum. The correction procedures outlined above are basic. They work well as additional instruction in many cases. Nonetheless, there will be times when one student or another struggles mightily with one word or concept or strategy in the program. On the one hand, such difficulties are undoubtedly challenging for teachers. On the other hand, overcoming them is a source of a great deal of personal satisfaction for teachers.

Our "intuitions" might tell us that if someone is having a lot of trouble, we should do something else to try to fix the problem. In reality, we should not do something else. A different approach usually ends up confusing students more than helping. What is most effective is to do more of the basic correction, more often.

The easiest way to modify the basic model-lead-test-delayed test procedure is to do two things. First, we should make each step *plural*: models, leads, tests, and delayed tests. The second thing is to *avoid* looking on those steps in terms of numerical order: if we do Step 1, then we have to do Step 2 before doing Step 3, and if we do Step 2, we can't go back to Step 1 until we've done Steps 3 and 4. The instructional sequence is not an invariant procedure, but rather a flexible framework for guiding instructional activities.

Teachers, therefore, must exercise judgment—informed by student performance—on how many times to repeat any given step, and on the order in which the steps ought to be followed. Say for example, that one student in a group misspells *friend* as *frend*. Assume further that the teacher models the correct spelling, and then that same student *spells it wrong again during the lead step*. That student has a problem: she can't spell the word correctly immediately after hearing the correct spelling, and with the considerable assistance of the teacher spelling it correctly along with her. In this case, it makes sense to model the correct spelling a few times, then to try leading again, and if that works, leading several times to help ensure that the student "gets it" during the test step, and moreover, the delayed test(s). In fact, it would be a good idea to do a lead two or three times before the first delayed test.

For the student described above with the problem spelling *friend,* it is possible that even more work will be required than doing steps more than once or doing steps in a different order. In particular, the lead step in the correction procedure is a type of *prompt.* Obviously, spelling a word orally as students spell it orally is a form of prompting, helping, or scaffolding. Additional prompting strategies also could be used.

Assuming that the "*friend* error" took place during oral practice, after the word had been introduced visually, a very strong prompt would be to write the word on the board and have students spell it as they are looking at it. If the teacher leads during that process, there is really a "double prompt": the word written on the board and the teacher spelling it with students. In the most stubborn cases, it is desirable to do even more prompting. If one student seems almost "hard-wired" to misspell *friend* as *frend,* then a verbal prompt can be added to the arsenal of prompts. In this case, the teacher might write the word on the board, then model spelling it, with an unusually strong verbal emphasis on the letter *i*: *f-r-I-e-n-d.*

Gradually, each prompt can be faded—possibly during the lesson, but even over the course of a few lessons if that is what it takes to solve the problem. Teachers unfamiliar with

Direct Instruction delivery often ask, "I'm doing that correction for the entire group, not just the student who made the error. Right? Won't everyone else tune out during the correction?" The fact is that, based on the vast experience of literally thousands of teachers, students will tolerate a lot more correcting than most adults think they might. That is especially true if the pacing during the correction is *very fast* (which allows for a large number of steps in a short period of time). It is also helpful if teachers explain to students how group corrections are going to work before starting to teach the program. It is a good idea to anticipate possible student complaints and then to address them before starting the program. When done quickly and positively, extensive corrections for stubborn problems demonstrate to all students just how committed the teacher is to helping every student learn.

EXTENSIONS AND ADAPTATIONS

Extensions to the *Spelling Mastery* and *Spelling Through Morphographs* programs include activities to transfer spelling skills to writing and practice activities to firm spelling skills. Adaptations include the acceleration or deceleration of students within the programs and equalizing (preparing for different learning rates by changing the groupings of students at set intervals).

Extensions: Writing

The most important extension of effective spelling instruction is the transfer of spelling to writing. Mastery of spelling skills is prerequisite to successful transfer to writing. Even when students do spell to a high level of mastery, there is no guarantee that they will transfer their skill to writing. Writing is a complex task requiring the simultaneous application of several skills (e.g., grammer, punctuation, word usage, organization). Therefore, during writing, students may not give spelling the same focus as during a spelling lesson. In addition, the likelihood of transferring accurate spelling to writing is in part dependent on the types of contingencies teachers place on accurate spelling during writing assignments.

Regarding the latter, two extreme views are practiced by teachers during writing activities. In one case, misspellings in writing are ignored. After all, as the title of one spelling text proudly proclaims, "You Kan Red This" (Wilde, 1992). This perspective does not encourage transfer of accurate spelling to writing. Like it or not, in the "real world," people expect to see educated writers spell correctly. The other extreme is the "old school" idea of marking every error judiciously and weighing spelling relatively heavily. This approach exaggerates the importance of spelling relative to all other aspects of writing.

There are a variety of ways of demonstrating to students that spelling is important in writing without discouraging the expression of ideas. For example, a teacher might hand back a writing assignment to a student with a note that says, "There are some spelling errors on this paper. When you find and correct any three of them, I'll change your grade from pencil to ink in my grade book." This approach says, in effect, that the assignment must be carried out to get credit for the project, but that the spelling won't influence the grade. This tactic places spelling in a reasonable perspective relative to other academic content.

Teachers can use such approaches flexibly. For example, one student might misspell five words in an assignment and be required to find two or three of them. Another might misspell twenty words and be required to find five or six of them. A temporary modification of this type of procedure for students who are really struggling hard with writing is to mark some misspellings, then simply require students to find the correct spellings for some of those marked. A judicious combination of effective and efficient spelling instruction, combined with reasonable contingencies for correct spelling, is the surest way to ensure the transfer of accurate spelling to writing.

Extensions: Practice Activities

While the *Spelling Mastery* and *Spelling Through Morphographs* curricula do not have assigned homework, there are several activities that could be used to create opportunities to practice spelling skills. Three spelling activities (i.e., Add-a-Word, Write-Say, and the Good-bye List) illustrate variations on practice activities for lists of spelling words.

Add-A-Word spelling is an explicit, whole-word approach to spelling instruction (Pratt-Struthers et al., 1983) in which students are given individualized spelling lists. Students study their lists by copying the words, covering them, writing the words, and then comparing (or checking) their work. When a student correctly spells the word for two or three consecutive days, the word is dropped from the list. Mastered words are retested five days after removal from the list and then once monthly. New words are added to replace the mastered words from the list.

The Write-Say approach (Kearney & Drabman, 1993) is a second example of teaching spelling that could be used to provide opportunities to practice spelling skills. Students using Write-Say touch each letter of a word while spelling the word out loud. The student then covers the word and writes it on a sheet of paper. As with Add-A-Word, the student then uncovers the correctly spelled word and checks his or her own word for accuracy.

The Good-bye List is a similar approach in which a list of words are studied and periodically tested. Once a student has correctly spelled any word on the list three times, it is dropped from the list. New words can be added to replace the words to which students have said "good-bye."

These approaches could be used for words that have yet to be mastered in the *Spelling Mastery* or *Spelling Through Morphographs* curricula or can be used as a method for cumulative review of words that students have already mastered.

Adaptations: Acceleration or Deceleration

The guideline of teaching approximately one lesson per day should be considered a general guideline, based on averages, rather than the performance of any given group of students. Teachers have an ethical obligation to pace lessons according to student performance (i.e., moving at a rate much faster than one lesson per day if students can handle a quicker pace, and moving at a slower pace when performance indicates the need to do so).

Instruction could be accelerated by skipping some content from the *Spelling Mastery* and *Spelling Through Morphographs* curricula. Skipping lessons is almost always a mistake. New or recently introduced material should never be skipped. Teachers could judiciously skip some activities or items that students already have had multiple opportunities to practice. For example, words appearing in the spelling review activities will have occurred in a fair number of previous lessons. If students are suppose to write ten words during a given spelling review activity, a teacher could instead ask them to spell just five of the words. A safe acceleration strategy would be to have students spell the five most difficult words. If successful, the students likely would have spelled the easier words correctly as well. On the other hand, if error rates begin to increase, then the teacher should discontinue the acceleration strategy.

The spelling performance of some students in *Spelling Mastery* or *Spelling Through Morphographs* suggests the need to proceed at an instructional pace of less than one lesson per day. If a teacher's pacing through all activities is fast, and if the teacher corrects every error and otherwise takes students to a high level of mastery, yet takes more than a day to teach each lesson, then the slower lesson pace is probably just right for those particular students.

Adaptations: Equalizing

A placement test provides information about where students should begin instruction but does not indicate the various rates at which students in a reasonably homogeneous group will learn. Students inevitably will learn at different rates. In the case of reading, many schools prepare in advance for different learning rates by planning to change the groupings of students at set intervals. This type of adjustment for *Spelling Mastery* or *Spelling Through Morphographs* may not be practical.

Spelling contests are one means for equalizing groups while maintaining instruction at the "just right" level for all students. An entire lesson can be dedicated to a spelling contest that takes place instead of the regularly scheduled lesson. A teacher should not skip a regularly scheduled lesson for this, but rather, should just postpone it until the next lesson period.

Spelling contests are not like spelling bees, where all students must embarrass themselves by missing a word before the whole thing is over. Instead, a spelling contest is between two teams (e.g., left and right halves of the class, front and back halves). The game rules are simple: the teacher dictates a word to the first team. Students raise their hands, but the teacher is free to call on someone whose hand is not raised, to ensure that everyone participates. If the student called on spells the word right, that team gets a point. If not, the teacher quickly runs the correction procedure for a misspelled word, and then dictates a different word to the other team.

Such contests, when quickly paced, not only are effective for getting a whole group to roughly the same level of achievement, but require virtually no teacher preparation time. The teacher simply puts a finger in the Teacher Presentation Book at the last successfully completed lesson, and then chooses *any* words from any review activities prior to that lesson.

Additional procedures will help ensure the greatest benefit for the time invested in a contest. A teacher can call on struggling students to spell easier words drawn from the teacher-presentation book. That allows the struggling students to contribute points to the team. When not responding, that student is sitting there, listening to correct spellings or participating in normal correction procedures. In addition, these contests are the most fun for students when the point totals are close. If one team is pulling too far ahead of the other, the teacher can begin to give harder words to the leading team. Students are likely to "see through" both of these strategies, but they are effective, nonetheless, if it is clear to everyone that the teacher is really trying to help everyone and make spelling enjoyable.

Furthermore, a teacher is not restricted to presenting *words* during contests. For example, the teacher might ask one team, "What are the morphographs in the word *infinitely*?" (in + fine + ite + ly), or "When do you double the final consonant in a short CVC word?" Any skill that appears to need work is potentially useful for spelling contests.

RESEARCH ON DIRECT INSTRUCTION SPELLING PROGRAMS

The advantages of using *Spelling Mastery* and *Spelling Through Morphographs* have been demonstrated for a variety of students, including (1) primary grade general education students (Burnette et al., 1999; McCormick & Fitzgerald, 1997; Vreeland, 1982), (2) middle school students (Earl, Wood, & Stennett, 1981; Hesse, Robinson, & Rankin, 1983; Robinson & Hesse, 1981), and (3) students with significant delays in the area of spelling (Maggs, McMillan, Patching, & Hawke, 1981).

Empirical research studies are scarce in the area of spelling instruction. Few studies have analyzed the components of *Spelling Mastery* and *Spelling Through Morphographs*. Therefore, the research literature does not suggest that one particular spelling approach (e.g., phonemic versus morphemic instruction) leads to superior spelling performance. Much of the research support for the components of these curricula comes by proxy from the validation research for the Direct Instruction model (e.g., error correction, review, and distributed practice). As the research support for those general Direct Instruction principles is described elsewhere in this book (see Chapter 2), the supporting research for components of *Spelling Mastery* and *Spelling Through Morphographs* are not described again here. While research specific to spelling instruction does not describe the unique effect of the instructional components of either program, several studies have evaluated both curricula as a whole (see Simonsen, Gunter, & Marchand-Martella, 2001). The following discussion will focus on the effects of these curricula relative to other spelling programs and relative to individual student progress over time.

Students taught to spell using *Spelling Mastery* and *Spelling Through Morphographs* (formally called *Corrective Spelling Through Morphographs*) were consistently more accurate than students taught to spell through other spelling curricula. Studies comparing either program with traditional basal spelling curricula have shown that students taught using the Direct Instruction spelling curricula made significantly greater gains in spelling performance, doing as much as twice as well as students receiving other spelling instruction (Earl et al., 1981; Vreeland, 1982). For example, Gettinger (1993) found that students accurately spelled more words following Direct Instruction spelling than students participating in a spelling program that encouraged them to use inventive spelling. In another study, students who received spelling instruction in *Spelling Mastery* outperformed students taught to use the cognitive strategy of imagining themselves correctly spelling words on a projection screen (Darch & Simpson, 1990).

Several investigations of the *Spelling Mastery* and *Spelling Through Morphographs* curricula have studied individual student spelling performance rather than compare performance across groups of students. These single-case research studies have demonstrated both improvement and maintenance in spelling performance following instruction with both curricula (e.g., Robinson & Hesse, 1981; Sommers, 1995). For example, McCormick and Fitzgerald (1997) used *Spelling Mastery* to raise the spelling skills of sixth-grade students more than one year above their grade level norms. Similar effects have been shown for *Spelling Through Morphographs* (and its previous versions). In one study, both general and special education students made fifteen-month and eleven-month gains, respectively, in spelling performance during an eight-month period following instruction using *Morphographic Spelling* (*Corrective Spelling Through Morphographs* was adapted from *Morphographic Spelling*) (Maggs et al., 1981). In addition, research has shown that the substantial gains in spelling performance following Direct Instruction spelling are maintained by students after spelling instruction has stopped (Hesse et al., 1983).

While the research base on spelling instruction is scarce, most of the published empirical research studies on spelling were directed at the evaluation of Direct Instruction spelling curricula. Together, those studies suggest that both programs have a substantial positive impact on student spelling performance.

REFERENCES

Adams, M. J. (1990). *Beginning to read: Thinking and learning about print: A summary.* Champaign-Urbana, IL: Center for the Study of Reading, University of Illinois.

Beers, J., Beers, C., & Grant, K. (1977). The logic behind children's spelling. *Elementary School Journal, 77,* 238–242.

Bender, R. (1994). Do word processors really make good spellers obsolete? *Effective School Practices, 13*(1), 70–71.

Bruck, M., & Waters, G. (1990). Effects of reading skill on component spelling skills. *Applied Psycholinguistics, 11,* 425–437.

Burnette, A., Bettis, D., Marchand-Martella, N. E., Martella, R. C., Tso, M., Ebey, T. L., McGlocklin, L., Hornor, S., & Cooke, B. (1999). A comparison of *Spelling Mastery* and a whole-word approach across elementary grades in a Title I school. *Effective School Practices, 18*(2), 8–15.

Collins, M. (1983). Teaching spelling: Current practices and effective instruction. *Direct Instruction News, 3*(1), 14–15.

Darch, C., & Simpson, R. G. (1990). Effectiveness of visual imagery versus rule-based strategies in teaching spelling to learning disabled students. *Research in Rural Education, 7*(1), 61–70.

Deno, S. L. (1987). Curriculum-based measurement. *Teaching Exceptional Children, 20,* 41.

Dixon, R. C. (1991). The application of sameness analysis to spelling. *Journal of Learning Disabilities, 24,* 285–291.

Dixon, R. C. (1993). *The surefire way to better spelling: A revolutionary new approach to turn poor spellers into pros.* New York: St. Martin's Press.

Dixon, R. C., & Engelmann, S. (1999). *Spelling Mastery: Series guide.* Columbus, OH: SRA/McGraw-Hill.

Dixon, R. C., & Engelmann, S. (2001). *Spelling Through Morphographs: Teacher's guide.* Columbus, OH: SRA/McGraw-Hill.

Earl, L. M., Wood, J., & Stennett, R. G. (1981). Morphographic spelling: A pilot study of its effectiveness with grade six students. *Special Education in Canada, 55*(4), 23–24.

Gettinger, M. (1993). Effects of invented spelling and Direct Instruction on spelling performance of second-grade boys. *Journal of Applied Behavior Analysis, 26,* 281–291.

Graham, S. (1999). Handwriting and spelling instruction for students with learning disabilities: A review. *Learning Disability Quarterly, 22,* 78–98.

Hall, T., Tindal, G., & Flick, D. (1993). *Portfolio assessment using curriculum-based measurement: A model for schools.* Eugene, OR: Research, Consultation, & Teaching Program: Behavioral Research and Teaching.

Hesse, K. D., Robinson, J. W., & Rankin, R. (1983). Retention and transfer from a morphemically based direct instruction spelling program in junior high. *Journal of Educational Research, 76,* 276–279.

Institute of Child Health and Human Development. (2000). *Report of the National Reading Panel: Teaching children to read: An evidence-based assessment of the scientific research literature on reading and its implications for reading instruction.* (NIH Publication No. 00-4769). Washington, DC: U.S. Government Printing Office.

Kearney, C. A., & Drabman, R. S. (1993). The Write-Say Method for improving spelling accuracy in children with learning disabilities. *Journal of Learning Disabilities, 26,* 52–56.

Larsen, D., & McLaughlin, T. F. (1997). The effects of cover, copy, and compare on spelling accuracy of a preschool child. *Reading Improvement, 34,* 189–192.

Lum, T., & Morton, L. L. (1984). Direct Instruction in spelling increases gains in spelling and reading skills. *Special Education in Canada, 58*(2), 41–45.

Maggs, A., McMillan, K., Patching, W., & Hawke, H. (1981). Accelerating spelling skills using morphographs. *Educational Psychology, 1,* 49–56.

McCormick, J., & Fitzgerald, M. (1997). School-wide application of Direct Instruction: *Spelling Mastery* at Yeshiva. *Effective School Practices, 16*(3), 39–47.

National Academy of Sciences. (1998). *Preventing reading difficulties in young children.* Washington, DC: National Academy Press.

Pratt-Struthers, J., Struthers, T. B., & Williams, R. L. (1983). The effects of the Add-A-Word Spelling Program on spelling accuracy during creative writing. *Education and Treatment of Children, 6,* 277–283.

Robinson, J. W., & Hesse, K. D. (1981). A morphemically based spelling program's effect on spelling skills and spelling performance of seventh grade students. *Journal of Educational Research, 75,* 56–62.

Simonsen, F. & Gunter, L. (2001). Best practices in spelling instruction: A research summary. *Journal of Direct Instruction, 1,* 97–105.

Simonsen, F., Gunter, L., & Marchand-Martella, N. (2001, January). *Spelling research: Research on teaching children to spell* (R80000549). DeSoto, TX: SRA/McGraw-Hill.

Sommers, J. (1995). Seven-year overview of Direct Instruction programs used in basic skills classes at Big Piney Middle School. *Effective School Practices, 14*(4), 29–32.

Templeton, S., & Morris, D. (1999). Questions teachers ask about spelling. *Reading Research Quarterly, 34,* 102–112.

Treiman, R., Cassar, M., & Zukowski, A. (1994). What types of linguistic information do children use in spelling? The case of flaps. *Child Development, 65,* 1318–1337.

Uhry, J., & Shepherd, M. (1993). Segmentation/spelling instruction as part of a first-grade reading program: Effects on several measures of reading. *Reading Research Quarterly, 28,* 218–233.

Vreeland, M. (1982). Corrective spelling program evaluated. *Direct Instruction News, 1*(2), 3.

Waters, G. S., Bruck, M., & Malus-Abramowitz, M. (1988). The role of linguistic and visual information in spelling: A developmental study. *Journal of Experimental Child Psychology, 45,* 400–421.

White, O. R., & Haring, N. G. (1980). *Exceptional teaching* (2nd ed.). Columbus, OH: Charles E. Merrill.

Wilde, S. (1992). *You kan red this!: Spelling and punctuation for whole language classrooms, K–6.* Portsmouth, NH: Heinemann Educational Books.

CHAPTER SEVEN

MATHEMATICS

VICKI E. SNIDER
University of Wisconsin—Eau Claire

DONALD CRAWFORD
Otter Creek Institute

OBJECTIVES

After studying this chapter you should be able to:

1. list two reasons why mathematics is important;

2. describe trends in mathematics achievement among students in the United States during the past decade;

3. explain why curriculum is important in mathematics education;

4. summarize the history of math education in the United States during the twentieth century;

5. explain the difference between implicit and explicit instruction and relate to teaching methods called "constructivism" and "Direct Instruction";

6. list the limitations of implicit instruction;

7. explain why the distinction between routine computational skills and conceptual mathematical understanding is not useful;

8. define "strand" curriculum;

9. list three Direct Instruction mathematics programs and identify their target audiences;

10. identify at least four big ideas in mathematics;

11. list four types of errors students make in math and indicate how to address each type of error;

12. summarize the research base to support Direct Instruction mathematics programs.

Mathematics influences our lives in many ways. The study of mathematics is important for both pragmatic and philosophical reasons. From a pragmatic perspective, mathematics opens the door to postsecondary education and to opportunities for well-paying jobs. From a philosophical viewpoint, mathematics affects our lives everyday, both directly and indirectly. Understanding basic mathematical concepts allows individuals to exercise some control over the increasing amount of information that floods our lives. Ultimately, mathematics is the catalyst for advances in technology and civilization.

Unfortunately, national and international tests suggest that American children lack fundamental mathematical skills. The National Assessment of Educational Progress (NAEP) was administered to fourth, eighth, and twelfth graders in the United States in 1996 and 2000 (U.S. Department of Education, 2000b). Results of the NAEP indicated that scores have steadily increased over the past twenty years. However, the gains for fourth graders are much higher than the gains for eighth- or twelfth-grade students. Although modest achievement gains occurred in fourth and eighth grade, twelfth graders' performance declined slightly since 1996 (U.S. Department of Education, 2001a). It appears that a slump in math achievement begins shortly after fourth grade and continues into high school. Further, the Third International Mathematics and Science Study (TIMSS) was administered in 1995 to more than 500,000 students in forty-one countries at three age levels (Masini & Taylor, 2000) and again to eighth graders in 1999 (U.S. Department of Education, 2000a). International comparisons confirm that no other country has a sharper drop in math ranking than American children (Loveless & DiPerna, 2000).

This chapter describes three Direct Instruction mathematics programs: *DISTAR Arithmetic, Corrective Mathematics,* and *Connecting Math Concepts.* Direct Instruction mathematics curricula are presented in the context of the current data on achievement in mathematics and the historically divisive controversies about the best method and most appropriate content to teach in mathematics. The three programs are described including an overview, content analysis, and description of format features. Teaching techniques and suggestions for assessment and troubleshooting are given. Finally, research that supports the efficacy of Direct Instruction mathematics programs is also presented.

IMPORTANCE OF MATHEMATICS

Competence in mathematics at an eighth-grade level sets the stage for higher-level math courses necessary for success later in life. There appears to be a strong relationship between completing mathematics courses in middle and high school and entering postsecondary education. This relationship is true for both two- and four-year colleges (Mathematics Equals Opportunity, 1997). Eighty-three percent of students who took Algebra I and geometry went on to college within two years of their graduation, whereas only 36 percent of students who did not take those courses went on to higher education. This correlation was especially striking among low-income students. Low-income students who took Algebra I and geometry were almost three times more likely to attend college as those who did not.

Students with strong math and science skills are more likely to be employed and generally earn more than workers with lower achievement, even if they have not gone to college. For example, high school graduates who scored in the top quartile of the Armed

Services Vocational Aptitude Battery earned 38 percent more per hour than similar graduates who scored in the lowest quartile (Mathematics Equals Opportunity, 1997). Some firms already require workers to pass a basic skills test in math and reading, and jobs that do not require a college education require math competence at the ninth-grade level (Murnane & Levy, 1996). The need for workers with skills in mathematics is likely to increase in the future. Projections from the Occupational Outlook Handbook (Bureau of Labor Statistics, 2002–03) indicate that between 2000–2001, jobs that require bachelor's or other postsecondary degrees accounted for 42 percent of new job growth compared to only 29 percent of all jobs in 2000.

Every job requires some understanding of mathematics. Adults routinely compute and use graphs and tables. They approximate, estimate, interpolate, extrapolate, and generalize. People who are not mathematicians use probabilities, identify the limits of an analysis, discover relationships, use variables and functions, analyze and compare data, interpret models, and test hypotheses. People use mathematics directly at home for cooking, home maintenance, building, and finances. People in business routinely convert a business question into a mathematical one. A business considering expansion uses mathematics to conduct consumer surveys, compute specifications for a new store or office, project start-up costs, sales volume, production costs, and trends (Fessenden, 1998).

People also use mathematics indirectly. Mathematics makes DNA testing available; it allows weathermen to project weather patterns and computers to run software. Mathematics permits development and improvement of technology, defense, economics, machinery, and health care. Mathematics is increasingly important in our information age. The volume of information has increased as well as speed of access to that information. More information increases the risk of misuse of that information, which makes it increasingly important that people know where numbers come from and how to interpret them. "Learning to think and reason mathematically is the only way our children can be sure that they are in control, not being controlled" (Miller, 1998, p. 9).

IMPORTANCE OF MATHEMATICS INSTRUCTION

The 1995 TIMSS revealed that children and youth in the United States performed as well as students in other countries in fourth grade but lost ground as they continued in school, until by twelfth grade they scored below the international average and among the lowest of the TIMSS nations (U.S. Department of Education, 2001b). A British weekly, *The Economist,* noted that, "The longer children stay in American schools, the worse they seem to get" (America's Education Choice, 2000, p. 17). The 1999 TIMSS, which was conducted only with eighth-grade students, indicated that students in the United States performed below the international average in mathematics. This finding was disheartening because only four years earlier, when those eighth-grade students were in fourth grade, they had fared well in international comparisons (U.S. Department of Education, 2000a). American students do not start out behind but fall behind during the middle school years.

These data suggest that curriculum and instruction do shape mathematics achievement. Following the 1996 assessment, TIMSS researchers concluded that poor student performance was a result of the "unfocused" curriculum (Valverde & Schmidt, 1997). A later analysis suggested that there was a strong relationship between curriculum factors and higher achievement (Schmidt et al., 2001). An analysis of mathematical concepts considered essential in grades one to eight revealed interesting differences between the top-achieving countries and the United States. Schmidt, Houang, and Cogan (2002) found that top-achieving countries covered a limited number of topics at each grade level and covered them for about three years. Foundation topics, such as whole-number concepts, were introduced in the early grades, and more sophisticated mathematical topics were gradually covered in the later grades. No such logical progression was apparent in the United States. Prerequisite knowledge was not necessarily introduced first. Many more topics were considered essential at each grade level, and the average duration of each topic was six years. This analysis suggests that in the United States topics are covered superficially over a longer period of time. A drawback to this lack of coherence in curriculum is that it exacerbates inequities in education. Those who are advantaged do well; others do not. The increasing discrepancy between the "haves" and "have-nots" in mathematical skill is similar to the Matthew effects in reading, as noted in Chapter 1. Socioeconomic status accounted for 40 percent of the variance in scores of children in the United States but only 20 percent of the variation across all the participating TIMSS countries (Schmidt et al., 2002). Similarly, socioeconomic status accounted for about 60 percent of the difference in NAEP scores (Masini & Taylor, 2000). Well-designed mathematics curricula are important because they promote equity.

It appears that mathematics instruction does play a critical role in mathematics achievement. Unfortunately, current practice seems to have a negative, rather than a positive, influence on reaching goals promoted by math educators. The underlying assumption of all Direct Instruction programs is that all students can learn to think mathematically when carefully taught.

Goals

It is hard to disagree with the goals outlined in standards published by the National Council of Teachers of Mathematics (NCTM) (1989). They include the following broad goals:

1. To value mathematics.
2. To become confident in their ability to do mathematics.
3. To become mathematical problem solvers.
4. To communicate mathematically.
5. To reason mathematically.

The NCTM *Standards,* which arguably precipitated a decade of "math wars," were considered groundbreaking among math educators because they reinforced student-centered, discovery learning called constructivism. However, the goals themselves bear many similarities to the broad goals of education throughout the twentieth century. A brief history of math education in the United States during the twentieth century brings curricular issues in mathematics into perspective and provides a lens for viewing the unique contribution of Direct Instruction programs to mathematics education.

History

Rappaport (1975) identified three distinct periods in math education up to 1975. Teachers stressed traditional skills for daily problem solving from the beginning of the twentieth century until about 1935. Math was considered a "tool" subject, to be applied rather than studied for its own sake. During the next period, which lasted into the 1950s, teaching *methods* began to emphasize "meaningful arithmetic," but the actual content of math instruction did not change. There was an increased emphasis on conceptual understanding of the base ten number system, and problem solving was emphasized at all levels.

The third period began after the humiliating launch of Sputnik by the former Soviet Union in 1957, which caused Americans to question whether math and science instruction in the public schools was sufficiently rigorous. Congressional initiatives prompted mathematicians and math educators to form committees to study curricular issues (Klein, 2001). The result was *new math,* which emphasized significant changes in the *content* of math curricula to prepare students to think mathematically. Math was no longer viewed as a tool subject but as an intellectual exercise. Kindergartners were introduced to set theory and upper elementary students worked problems in base three. Although many math educators defended new math, critics wondered what kind of mathematical understanding students had when they could not add, subtract, multiply, or divide (Martin, 1973).

By the 1970s, new math was abandoned and a *back-to-basics* movement had taken its place. Some concluded that the failure of new math was inevitable because only about 40 percent of students in the public schools were actually capable of understanding mathematics anyway (Rappaport, 1975). Others concluded that the reason it failed was that teachers did not understand mathematical concepts very well themselves. However, the back-to-basics movement did not last long. A decade later, renewed criticism that mindless rote recitation did not promote conceptual understanding of math concepts led the NCTM to design and promote the standards that provided the foundation for a philosophy of math instruction called constructivism. Constructivism reflected teaching *methods* that emphasized discovery and group learning and *content* that emphasized conceptual understanding, often to the exclusion of traditional algorithms and calculation.

An important idea that emerges from this brief summary of math instruction during the twentieth century is the distinction between methods and content. Many educators equate child-centered, implicit methods (i.e., discovery learning or constructivism) with content that promotes understanding and teacher-directed, explicit methods with content that promotes rote learning and mindless computation. This view promotes a false dichotomy between routine basic skills and conceptual understanding. However, sophisticated mathematical content can be taught using teacher-directed methods such as Direct Instruction. In fact, there are limitations of implicit instruction. Furthermore, higher-level concepts and basic skills do not represent irreconcilable opposites but intertwined components of mathematical thinking.

Implicit versus Explicit Instruction

Implicit instruction refers to constructivist methods of teaching: teachers set up situations that encourage students to discover important concepts. This approach is problematic for many reasons. First, some mathematics concepts do not lend themselves to discovery

(Carnine, 1990). For example, dividing fractions beyond the most elementary examples is not easily conveyed with manipulatives or activities.

Many students, particularly low-performing students, learn more quickly from a clear, concise explanation of what to do and how to do it (Carnine, 1990). When explicit strategies are not provided, students often make up their own creative, but incorrect, mathematical rules. A common example of this is representing fractions by putting the larger number on the bottom and the smaller number on top regardless of whether or not the fraction is more or less than one. Students learn the misrule that the top number is the number of parts shaded and the bottom number is the number of *total parts,* not the number of *parts in the whole.* This misconception leads to the mistaken belief that all fractions are less than one. This misrule could be avoided by stating an explicit rule (e.g., "the bottom number tells how many parts in each whole group") and by providing examples that include improper fractions early in the instructional sequence.

Another drawback to implicit instruction is that it does not provide for a gradual transition from structured to independent work. Students work in groups semi-independently from the beginning. Guided practice has been found to be an effective teaching technique (Good & Grouws, 1979). During guided practice, the teacher asks questions that prompt students to apply the new concept successfully. The teacher provides scaffolding, which is gradually reduced as students gain confidence in applying the new concept independently.

A final problem associated with implicit instruction is that the teacher's explanations are often confusing. The teacher's manual that accompanies implicit approaches contains general directions for the teacher using terms such as *explain* or *discuss* rather than providing specific advice on how to present skills. In addition, teacher's manuals do not provide wording for correcting student errors or reteaching procedures for chronic errors (Stein, Silbert, & Carnine, 1997).

As a result of all these problems, students acquire numerous mathematics misconceptions. These misconceptions are not unique to students who are low-performing; they are common among large numbers of students (Resnick & Omanson, 1987). Common errors include subtracting the larger number from a smaller one regardless of location (e.g., $82 - 29 = 67$) (Resnick & Omanson); subtracting incorrectly with regrouping when there are zeros in the subtrahend (e.g., $502 - 34 = 478$) (Trafton, 1984); confusing algorithms for adding and multiplying fractions

$$\left(\frac{2}{3} + \frac{3}{5} = \frac{5}{8} \right)$$

(Trafton, 1984); and ordering decimals (e.g., 12.10, 12.09, 13.00) (Zawojewski, 1983). Misconceptions and apprehensions about solving word problems abound (Lewis & Mayer, 1987). These errors are not inevitable but are the result of haphazard instruction that relies on discovery.

Basic Skills versus Conceptual Understanding

Wu (1999) noted that education is plagued by false dichotomies. Many math education reformers want to eliminate routine pencil-and-paper computation algorithms from the curriculum in favor of mathematical thinking. However, knowledge of basic skills cannot be separated from conceptual understanding. Precision and fluency in basic skills form the basis for conceptual understanding (Wu). The same dichotomy exists in other academic subjects. Issaacson (1987) pointed out that learning to write requires both mechanical skills and creative expression just as learning to play the piano involves practice and repetition of scales and fingering exercises as well as recitals and improvisation. Similarly, the reading wars pitted phonics approaches against meaning approaches, when in fact the two are inextricably linked. As noted in Chapter 4, explicit, systematic phonics instruction provides the basis for fluent decoding, which is a prerequisite to getting meaning from text.

For any curriculum to be complete, it must include attention to basic skills for two reasons. First, basic skills provide the foundation for higher-level skills. They are a stepping stone, never an end in themselves. Some basic skills are indispensable preskills to more complex endeavors. Second, rapid and effortless performance of basic skills frees attention for thinking about complex operations whether it be mathematics, reading, writing, or playing the piano. When students have a firm foundation in mathematics, they are more likely to achieve the goals of the NCTM: to value mathematics and develop confidence; to reason and communicate mathematically; and to solve problems. Direct Instruction mathematics curricula achieve these goals by organizing the content around strands (described below). Basic skills are systematically woven into increasingly complex thinking operations that build over time.

DESIGN FEATURES OF EFFECTIVE MATHEMATICS PROGRAMS

Effective mathematics programs have two unique design features. First, they are designed within an integrated strand curriculum. That is, each lesson is organized around multiple skills or topics rather than around a single skill or topic. A second unique design feature is the use of big ideas that connect multiple math concepts and strategies or teaching procedures that make the big ideas explicit.

Integrated Strand Curriculum

In a strand curriculum, each skill/topic is addressed for only five- to ten-minutes in any given day's lesson but is revisited day after day for many lessons. An important advantage of strand organization is that it promotes mastery rather than teaching for exposure. This design offers an alternative to the spiral curriculum. Figure 7.1 illustrates the difference between a strand curriculum and a spiral one.

Spiral Curriculum.   Although there appears to be nothing "spiral" about the spiral curriculum, it has a spiral organization because units are revisited year after year. For example, traditional textbooks treat place value, addition, subtraction, multiplication as separate units and each unit "spirals around" every year.

Although the intent of the spiral design is to treat each concept with increasing depth at successive grade levels, the functional result is that students acquire a superficial understanding of math concepts. Teaching for exposure means that many topics are covered but only briefly. On average, teachers devote less than thirty minutes of instructional time

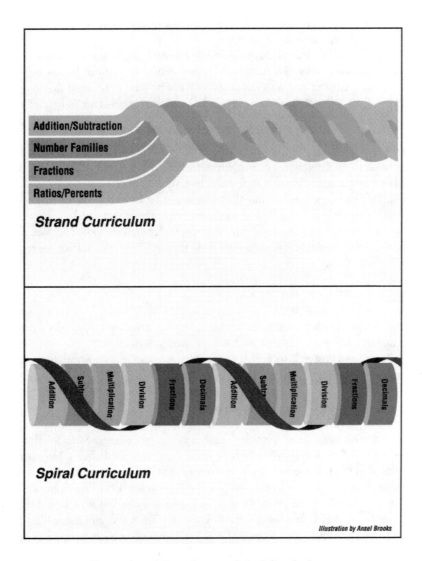

FIGURE 7.1   Illustration of Strand versus Spiral Curriculum

across the entire year to 70 percent of the topics they cover (Porter, 1989). This spiral design was apparent in the TIMSS analysis that found standards and textbooks in the United States to be a "mile wide, an inch deep" (Schmidt et al., 2002, p. 13).

Another problem with the spiral design is that the rate for introducing new concepts is often either too fast or too slow. Units are approximately the same length and each topic within a unit is one day's lesson. For example, exactly the same amount of time may be given to addition of fractions with the same denominators and addition with different denominators. Assuming the math period is the same length of time, some days there will be too much time (leading to wasted instructional time) and some days there will not be enough time to introduce, let alone master, the concept.

The spiral design also leads to insufficient review once units are completed. There may be some review of previously introduced topics within the chapter, but once students move on to the next chapter previous concepts may not be seen again until they are covered the next year. Even when there is some review in later chapters, it is not integrated review. Lack of practice during the interim may turn review into reteaching.

Strand Curriculum. In the strand curriculum topics are intertwined over time, strengthening students' understanding of mathematical concepts, much as fibers in a rope are woven together for strength. Organizing lessons into strands makes sequencing and cumulative introduction of skills feasible and allows topics to be treated in depth. Strands also allow concepts to be arranged in a logical scope and sequence so that several topics can appear in one lesson. Preskills can be taught prior to being integrated into more complex mathematical concepts. For example, before students are taught to find equivalent fractions by multiplying by a fraction of one

$$\left(\text{e.g.,}\ \frac{3}{4}\times\frac{2}{2}=\frac{6}{8}\right),$$

students learn necessary multiplication facts, they learn that multiplying by 1 doesn't change the value of a number and that 1 can be expressed as a fraction.

The strand design also avoids the problems associated with variability in the appropriate rate of introduction of concepts. Because more than one topic is covered in each lesson, the rate of introduction is easily adjusted by the number of minutes and the number of consecutive days that are spent on a concept.

Finally, cumulative introduction allows systematic review of concepts until they are integrated with other more complex mathematical procedures. Strands allow distributed review of skills in which only a few problems are presented over a long period of time allowing students to become both accurate and rapid in their responses. Distributed practice facilitates mastery better than massed practice (Dempster, 1991; Willingham, 2002), and it is easy to schedule when lessons are designed in strands. Within a strand the amount of structure is gradually decreased each day moving from the initial teaching presentation through guided practice to independent practice. Because each lesson contains many strands, a balance between new learning and practice is maintained.

Big Ideas and Strategies

An important goal in the design of high-quality curricula is identification of big ideas and the use of conspicuous strategies (Kameenui, Carnine, & Dixon, 2002). Big ideas connect multiple math concepts that are often perceived by students as disparate, unrelated facts that must be memorized without understanding. As Carnine, Dixon, and Silbert (1998) noted, the use of big ideas "enhances understanding while simultaneously reducing the quantity of content to be learned, remembered, and applied" (p. 95). Strategies are the teaching procedures that make the big ideas explicit. Experts often use covert cognitive strategies to solve mathematical problems. Conspicuous strategies make those strategies overt so that naïve learners can learn to use them. An important characteristic of effective strategies is that they are neither too narrow nor too broad. For example, teaching the rule "invert the divisor and multiply" to solve division with fractions is too narrow and does not promote understanding. On the other hand, telling students to visualize or draw a picture of the problem is too broad and has limited generalizability for solving problems like $2/97 \div 16/58$. Furthermore, most math textbooks lack the coherent vision to make consistent use of any strategies they do develop, which is unfortunate because an effective and efficient way to provide cumulative review is to use previously learned math strategies in new applications.

OVERVIEW OF DIRECT INSTRUCTION MATHEMATICS PROGRAMS

There are three Direct Instruction mathematics programs: (1) *DISTAR Arithmetic, Levels I and II*, (2) *Corrective Mathematics* in *Addition, Subtraction, Multiplication*, and *Division; Mathematics Modules in Basic Fractions; Fractions, Decimals, Percents;* and *Ratios and Equations*, and (3) *Connecting Math Concepts (CMC), Levels A, B, C, D, E, Bridge*, and *F.*

DISTAR Arithmetic

DISTAR Arithmetic was first published in 1970 and was the prototype of Direct Instruction mathematics programs. *DISTAR Arithmetic I* consists of 160 lessons that are designed for students in kindergarten or for students who are low-performing. In *DISTAR Arithmetic I* "students acquire strategies for analyzing and solving addition, subtraction, and algebra addition" (Adams & Engelmann, 1996, p. 118). *DISTAR Arithmetic I* takes nothing for granted and provides step-by-step procedures that show even the most naïve learners can solve increasingly complex story problems. A single strategy is applied to a wide range of problems to emphasize understanding before memorization. *DISTAR Arithmetic II* consists of 160 lessons that review the content of *DISTAR Arithmetic I* and then move on to new objectives. *DISTAR Arithmetic II* helps "students acquire strategies for handling multiplica-tion, operations with fractions, and problems in columns" (Adams & Engelmann, 1996, p. 118).

Corrective Mathematics

Corrective Mathematics is a remedial math program designed for students in grades three through postsecondary. The *Corrective Mathematics* series includes four separate modules (i.e., *Addition, Subtraction, Multiplication*, and *Division*) that can be used developmentally for students in grades three and four; however, it is most frequently used with older students who have previously experienced failure in mathematics. Each module includes sixty-five lessons.

There are also three additional modules in the *Mathematics Modules* series that are designed to teach advanced mathematical skills. These modules include: *Basic Fractions; Fractions, Decimals, Percents*; and *Ratios and Equations*. These modules build on each other and are designed for students in fourth grade through postsecondary. The *Basic Fractions* module includes fifty-five lessons; the *Fractions, Decimals, Percents* module includes seventy lessons; and the *Ratios and Equations* module includes sixty lessons.

Connecting Math Concepts

Connecting Math Concepts (CMC) is a complete developmental mathematics program designed to teach average-achieving youngsters to compute, solve problems, and think mathematically. *CMC Level A* is a first-grade level and the other levels roughly correspond to subsequent grade levels. *CMC Levels A–D* each contain 120 lessons. *CMC Level E* contains 125 lessons, the *CMC Bridge* has 70 lessons, and *CMC Level F* has 100 lessons. The *CMC Bridge to Level F* provides a shortened version of *CMC Level E* so that students can complete the bridge and much of *CMC Level F* in one year. By the time students have completed all levels of *CMC,* they should be ready for algebra.

CONTENT ANALYSIS AND FORMAT FEATURES

Direct Instruction mathematics programs organize key mathematical skills and concepts into strands and include big ideas and strategies. In the next section we provide a content analysis of how *DISTAR Arithmetic, Corrective Mathematics,* and *Connecting Math Concepts* include these important features in their curricular design. Next we will illustrate important content features with specific program format examples.

DISTAR Arithmetic

Strand Curriculum. Table 7.1 organizes the content of *DISTAR Arithmetic I and II* and describes the culminating skills in each strand. Some strands may develop over the entire 160 lessons, and others can be covered in a much shorter time. Because the tasks are structured simply, sequenced logically, and include sufficient practice, students can be expected to master the stated skills at the end of 160 lessons. Independent practice is provided in the form of "take-homes." A structured teacher presentation accompanies one or more problems on the take-home and enough problems for keeping students busy for twenty to thirty minutes.

Big Ideas and Strategies. The single most important big idea in *DISTAR Arithmetic I* is the equality rule (Engelmann & Carnine, 1982). Application of the equality rule enables students to solve a wide range of problems. The equality rule states that "You must end up with same number on this side and on the other side" (Engelmann & Carnine, 1982, p. 48). Most math curricula encourage students to use manipulatives to count until they memorize basic addition facts. However, if they do not understand equality, they will experience difficulty with more complex arithmetic operations, especially algebra addition. Equality is introduced in Lesson 50. In this lesson, previously introduced strands are braided together into a new strand.

The format for teaching the equality rule is presented in Figure 7.2. In Step b students read the problem (symbol identification and equality). In Steps c and d, students read what

TABLE 7.1 Scope and Sequence of Major Strands in *DISTAR Arithmetic Levels I & II*

	DISTAR I	DISTAR II
Symbol identification/ writing	Copy any numeral from 1 through 100 and the symbols =, +, −, and ☐	Review
Rote counting	Say the numbers in any counting sequence between 1 and 100 forward or backwards.	Review
Rationale counting	Touch and count a group of lines.	N/A
Number relationships	Write the more-less or equal symbol to compare numerals or groups of objects or lines.	Review
Addition (whole numbers)	Solve 2-term addition (4 + 2 = ☐) and algebra-addition problems (4 + ☐ = 7).	Solve 2- and 3-term column addition problems that don't involve carrying and 2-term problems that do.
Subtraction (whole numbers)	Solve subtraction problems (6 − 4 = ☐) by counting backward.	Solve 2-digit column subtraction problems that don't involve borrowing.
Place value	Express 2-digit numbers as addition facts (43 = 40 + 3).	Rewrite a row problem (42 + 6 + 149) in a column with tens and ones appropriately aligned.
Facts	Respond quickly to certain addition facts orally.	Respond quickly orally and in writing to selected addition, algebra-addition, and subtraction facts.
Problem solving	Read a word problem, orally translate the problem into an arithmetic statement, write the appropriate symbols, and solve the problem.	Read, write, and solve the following types of story problems: addition and subtraction classification, multiplication, algebra multiplication, fraction multiplication.
Multiplication (whole numbers)	N/A	Solve single-digit multiplication and algebra multiplication problems.
Fractions	N/A	Represent simple fractions, determine the value of fractions, reduce fractions, and multiply fractions.
Measurement	N/A	Construct length of a centimeter, meter, inch, and foot; state equivalencies and compare the length or weight of objects to a given length or weight.
Applications (money and time)	N/A	Figure out the value of a mixed group of coins and tell time when the minute hand is pointing at the hour.

LESSON 50, TASK 4—EQUALITY   Teaching the Equality Rule

Touch with a definite motion just below the symbol.
Words spelled with extra letters should be held when they are said. Emphasize words in **boldface.**

a. (Write this problem on the board.)

$$\left(\begin{array}{c} 4 + 2 \\ |||| \;\; || \end{array} \right) = \square$$

b. I'll touch and you read. (As you touch each symbol, the children read:) *4 plus 2 equals how many?*
c. (Ring 4 + 2 with your finger.) Read everything on this side of the equals. (Signal.) *4 plus 2.*
d. (Continue to ring 4 + 2.) Read everything on the other side of the equals. (Pause.) Get ready. (Signal.) *How many?*
e. Remember the rule about equals. (Ring 4 + 2.) You **must** end up with the same number on this side **aaannnd** on the other side.
f. (Ring 4 + 2.) Get ready to tell me about the other side. You must end up with the same number on this side **aaannnd** (signal) *on the other side.* (Repeat until firm.)
g. Let's make the sides equal.
h. (Ring 4 + 2.) We have to count all the lines on this side. I'll touch the lines and you count. (As you touch each line, the children count:) *1, 2, 3, 4, 5, 6.*
   What number did we end up with on this side? (Signal.) *6.*
i. We must end up with the same number on this side and on the other side. We ended up with six on this side. What's the same number as six? (Signal.) *6.*
   So what number must we end up with on the other side? (Signal.) *6.* Yes, six.
j. I'll draw the lines. You count and tell me when to stop. (Draw the lines under the box as the children count:) *1, 2, 3, 4, 5, 6. Stop.*

To correct	(If the children don't tell you to stop after 6, keep drawing lines. Then say:) I fooled you. We were supposed to end up with six. You have to tell me when to stop. (Repeat from *h*.)

k. The lines under a box always tell what numeral goes in that box. How many lines are under the box? (Pause and signal.) *6.*
l. So what numeral goes in the box? (Signal.) *6.* (Write 6 in the box.) We made the sides equal.
m. (Ring 4 + 2.) Think big. What number did we end up with on this side? (Pause and signal.) *6.*

To correct	I'll touch and you count. (As you touch the lines, the children count:) *1, 2, 3, 4, 5, 6.* What number did we end up with on this side? (Signal.) *6.*

n. (Continue to ring 4 + 2.) Did we end up with the same number on the other side? (Signal.) *Yes.* What number? (Signal.) *6.*
o. We made the sides equal. (Ring 4 + 2.) We ended up with the same number on this side aaannnd (signal) *on the other side.*
   (Repeat from *m* if the children need practice.)

FIGURE 7.2   *DISTAR Arithmetic I,* Lesson 50, Task 4. Reprinted with permission of the McGraw-Hill Companies.

is on *this side* and the *other side* of the equation (equality). In Steps e and f, the rule is presented and students practice it. In Steps g through l the rule is applied to solve the problem (rote counting, counting events and objects, equality) and then indicate the number they must end up with on the other side (equality, rote counting, numerals and lines).

The equality rule gives students a strategy for solving addition problems such as 3 + 5 = ☐ as well as 3 + ☐ = 8. In Lesson 80, shown in Figure 7.3, students learn how to work an algebra addition problem. They find the box and tell why counting can't start on the side with the box (because the box doesn't tell how many lines to draw), so they circle the side without the box (to remind them that's where to start counting). Then students tell how many they must end up with. They learn that they have to start counting until they end up with that number. Because they have already learned that the lines under a box tell what numeral goes in the box, they are able to write the missing addend.

Corrective Mathematics

Strand Curriculum.   Table 7.2 describes the major activities in each strand of the *Addition, Subtraction, Multiplication* and *Division* modules of the *Corrective Mathematics* series. The modules can be presented in order (addition, subtraction, multiplication, division) or the teacher can elect to present only one module. For example, if students already know how to add and subtract, instruction would begin with the multiplication module. Each module covers a single topic but is designed around strands that are interwoven over 65 lessons. Strands in the addition, subtraction, multiplication, and division modules include facts, place value, operations, and story problems.

Big Ideas and Strategies.   Each lesson includes practice on math facts, and students learn math facts through fact number families. The fact family includes two small numbers and a big number in a format from the Addition module that is shown in Figure 7.4 on page 222.

In the *Addition module,* each family generates two facts (e.g., 9 + 5 = 14 and 5 + 9 = 14). In the *Subtraction module,* students can use number families to generate four facts (e.g., 9 + 5 = 14, 5 + 9 = 14, 14 − 5 = 9, 14 − 5 = 9). In the *Multiplication module,* the relationship between multiplication and division is stressed as shown in Figure 7.5 on page 222.

The place value strand provides preskills for introducing increasingly complex number operations. The story problems strand uses previously taught operations to solve increasingly complex problems. Story problems are introduced about halfway through each module.

Connecting Math Concepts

Strand Curriculum.   Table 7.3 on pages 224–227 provides an overview of *some* of the important skill strands that develop over grades one to six in *Connecting Math Concepts.* It is important to note that Table 7.3 omits several skill strands including symbol identification, mental arithmetic, estimation, calculator skills, and ratio and proportions. Instead, focus is placed on counting, operations with whole numbers, number relationships, facts, number families, place value, problem solving, applications, geometry, fractions, decimals and percents, and pre-algebra.

LESSON 80, TASK 3—ALGEBRA ADDITION   How to Work a Problem

Emphasize words in **boldface.**

Group Activity
a. (Write $3 + \square = 5$ on the board.)
b. This is a tough problem. I'll touch and you read. (Pause.) Get ready. (Touch each symbol as the children read:) *3 plus how many equals 5?*
c. There's a box in this problem, so what do we have to do? (Signal.) *Start counting on the other side.* Yes, start counting on the other side.
d. Who can find the box for me? (Call on a child to go to the board and touch $\square$.)
e. (Point to $\square$.) Everybody, why can't we start counting on the side with a box? (Signal.) *A box doesn't tell you how many lines to draw.* Right. We don't know how many lines to draw on the side with a box. That's why we have to start counting on the other side.
f. (Point to $\square$.) Everybody, I want to draw a ring around the side we start counting on. Read everything on the side we start counting on. Get ready. (Signal.) *5.*
g. We start counting on the side with five, so I'll draw a ring around that side. (Ring 5 with your chalk.)

$$3 + \square = \boxed{5}$$

h. (Point to 5.) What number do we end up with on this side? (Signal.) *5.* Yes, five. So what number **must** we end up with on the other side? (Signal.) *5.* Yes, five.
i. (Point to 3.) Everybody, do we end up with five in the first group? (Signal.) *No.* So we'll have to count until we end up with five.
j. How many are in the first group? (Signal.) *3.* Get it going. (Raise your hand. When *threeee* is firm, drop your hand. Draw lines under $\square$ as the children count:) *4, 5, Stop.*

To correct	(If the children don't tell you to stop, continue drawing lines.) You didn't tell me when to stop. What number must we end up with on the side with three plus how many? (Signal.) *5.* (Repeat *i* and *j*.)

What number did you end up with on the side with three plus how many? (Signal.) *5.* Yes, five.
k. Are you going to write five in the box? (Signal.) *No.*

To correct	(If the children say *yes*, say:) I fooled you. There aren't five lines under the box.

l. Everybody, the lines under a box always tell what numeral goes in that box. Get ready to tell me what numeral goes in the box. (Pause for two seconds.) What numeral? (Signal.) *2.* (Write 2 in $\square$.)

$$3 + \boxed{2} = \boxed{5}$$

m. Everybody, three plus **how many** equals five? (Signal.) *2.* Say the statement. (Signal.) *3 plus 2 equals 5.* (Repeat *m* until the response is firm.)

FIGURE 7.3   *DISTAR Arithmetic I,* Lesson 80, Task 3. Reprinted with permission of the McGraw-Hill Companies.

TABLE 7.2   Scope and Sequence of *Corrective Mathematics* (4 of 7 modules shown)

	ADDITION	SUBTRACTION	MULTIPLICATION	DIVISION
Facts	Determine the sum of numbers under 20, write two facts for any given two 1-digit numbers (e.g., $2 + 4 = 6$ and $4 + 2 = 6$) and determine complex addition facts such as $14 + 8 = 22$.	Determine the 1-digit difference of numbers under 20 and write two facts for any given 1- or 2-digit number (e.g., $6 - 2 = 4$ and $6 - 4 = 2$).	Determine product of two 1-digit numbers and write two multiplication fact statements (e.g., $2 \times 4 = 8$ and $4 \times 2 = 8$) even when 1 is zero. Determine the sum of a 2-digit and 1-digit number.	Determine the 1-digit quotient of a 1- or 2-digit dividend and a 1-digit divisor and write two division facts for any 1- or 2-digit dividend.
Place value	Say and write the numeral for any 2-, 3-, or 4-digit number.	Say and write the numeral for any 2-, 3-, or 4-digit number.	Say the number of a 3-, 4-, or 5-digit numeral and say the number in each column of a 2-digit numeral.	Determine the approximation of a 2-digit number to the nearest ten and of a 3-digit number to the nearest hundred.
Operations	Determine the sum of up to three or four 1-, 2-, 3-, or 4-digit numbers.	Determine the difference of two numbers less than 10,000, regrouping required.	Determine the product of 1-, 2-, or 3-digit numbers with and without regrouping.	Determine the 3-digit quotient and remainder resulting from the division of a 4-digit number by a 2-digit number.
Story problems	Determine the sum in story problems with extraneous information.	Determine the difference or sum in problems in which the verbs signify the operation, problems which have the words *not, and,* classification and comparison problems.	Determine the product, sum, or difference in a story problem with two numbers.	Determine the quotient, product, sum, or difference in story problems with two numbers.

FIGURE 7.4 *Corrective Mathematics
Addition,* **Student's Book, Lesson 30,
Part 2. Reprinted with permission of
the McGraw-Hill Companies.**

Big Ideas and Strategies.   *Connecting Math Concepts* is integrated across levels so that
big ideas and strategies taught at one level are reinforced and applied at later levels providing
consistent instruction that is rare in a math series. Because it is a complete developmental
mathematics series intended for use in grades one to six, numerous big mathematical ideas
are taught. This section will present six big ideas from *CMC.*

Number Families.   Like *Corrective Mathematics,* number families are used as the main
vehicle for teaching addition and subtraction facts and relationships, but *CMC* presents
number families as three numbers written on an arrow as shown in Figure 7.6. In this number
family 1 and 7 are the "small numbers" and 8 is the "big number."
    Each number family generates four facts. In this case, $1 + 7 = 8$, $7 + 1 = 8$, $8 - 7 = 1$,
and $8 - 1 = 7$. Students who have learned the fifty-five number families in *CMC* can figure
out all 200 basic addition and subtraction facts. So in *CMC,* students work to memorize
fifty-five number families and practice with all four of the facts generated from each number
family as a set. This strategy, of course, also helps students comprehend the inter-relatedness
of addition and subtraction at a much deeper level.

Word Problems.   A related big idea in *CMC* is that the best strategy for solving word
problems is to map the problem information onto the arrow of a number family. Once students
understand number families, *CMC* uses the number families as the foundation of all the word
problem strategies throughout the six levels of the program. Students learn several strategies

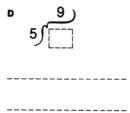

FIGURE 7.5   *Corrective Mathematics
Multiplication,* **Student's Book,
Lesson 13, Part 7. Reprinted with
permission of the McGraw-Hill
Companies.**

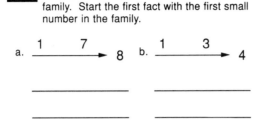

Part 3 Write the two addition facts for each number family. Start the first fact with the first small number in the family.

FIGURE 7.6 *Connecting Math Concepts Level B,* **Student Workbook, Lesson 20, Part 3. Reprinted with permission of the McGraw-Hill Companies.**

for transferring the information in the written word problem into number families on arrows systematically. Then, if one of the "small numbers on the arrow" is the unknown, students know to subtract. If the "big number at the end of the arrow" is the unknown, then students know to add to solve the problem.

In comparison problems (e.g., Alan drove 42 miles to work. Betty drove 26 less miles to work than Alan. How many miles did Betty drive to work?), the difference between the two things being compared plus the smaller of the two equals the larger of the two. In *CMC,* students learn that the difference between the two things being compared and the smaller of the two are the "small numbers" and go "on the arrow" in the comparison problem number family. The larger of the two things being compared is the "big number" and goes "at the end of the arrow." For example, in Lesson 38 of *CMC Level C,* students are introduced to comparison problems using letters. Students read the following problem in their textbook: "S is 15 more than B. B is 77. What number is S?" The teacher guides students in making a number family for the first sentence by placing two variables on the arrow. The second sentence gives the value for one of the variables, so students replace the variable with the number, which leaves only one variable. Students can then solve the problem. The teacher script for the first problem is shown in Figure 7.7 on page 228. In Lesson 40, students work comparison problems that involve names. For example, "Fran was 14 years older than Ann. Ann was 13 years old. How many years old was Fran?" By Lesson 44, a new variation is presented in which the comparative reference is in the question rather than the first statement. For example, "Henry weights 89 pounds. Dan weights 76 pounds. How many pounds heavier is Henry than Dan?"

One feature in *CMC* is that new topics and explanations are also included in the student book in a block. Making these explanations visible to students allows them the opportunity to read along with the initial presentation of a concept or strategy as well as the chance to turn back and revisit that explanation on subsequent days. The example below in Figure 7.8 on page 229 shows how one type of comparison problem is explained in *CMC Level C,* in language simplified enough for third-grade readers.

In all the word problem strategies in *CMC,* including classification, gain and loss, as well as comparison, students learn to read the problems, find out what information is given, place it in the correct place on a number family arrow, and then solve for the unknown. Thus,

TABLE 7.3   Scope and Sequence of Selected Tracks in *Connecting Math Concepts Levels A–F*

	LEVEL A	LEVEL B	LEVEL C
Counting	Rote count to 100; count from ___ to ___ , count objects and events, count backwards, count ordinals, count by 10	Count by 2, 5, 10, 25, 100, 9, 4; count ordinal numbers	
Operations with whole numbers	Solve single-digit addition and substraction, algebra addition, 2-digit addition without carrying, and add tens numbers	Carry in addition with 1-, 2-, and 3-digit numbers. Subtraction with and without regrouping	Column addition and subtraction; column multiplication with single-digit divisors; division with a single-digit quotient with remainder
Number relationships	Compare two numerals, lines, or groups of objects (more than, less than, or equal)	Use <, =, > signs; write numerals in order	Use <, =, > signs; write multiplication as addition; check subtraction by adding; find number families with the same big number
Facts		+0, +1, +2, +9, +3, +doubles; –0, –1, –2, –10, –9	+6, +4, +5, +7, +8; –4, –6, –3, –5, –7; count by 5
Number families		Write 4 facts for each number family; find missing number in a fact family	Make number families for 1-, 2-, and 3-digit numerals; analyze data with 2-by-2 tables
Place value	Say and write numerals up to 100	Read and write numerals up to 100	Read and write numerals up to 100,000; express numbers as tens or hundreds (e.g., 3200 is 32 tens)
Problem solving	Orally solve action, comparison, "joining," and "all but" problems	Write number problems for 1- or 2-digit story problems using number families; solve problems by refering to a calender	Solve comparison, action, and classification word problems by using number families; set up simple multiplication and division word problems

Note: Table 7.3 omits several skill strands including symbol identification, mental arithmetic, estimation, calculator skills, and ratio and proportions.

LEVEL D	LEVEL E	LEVEL F
Borrow across zeros; solve operations with money values; column multiplication with 1- or 2-digit multipliers; division with 1-digit divisor	Calculate short and long division problems with 1- and 2-digit divisors	Compute long division with zeros in the divisor and dividend; use calculator to work division problems that do not have a whole-number answer
Complete equations involving the relationship between multiplication, division, and fractions	Solve problems that show relationship between fractions/whole numbers and fractions/decimals/ mixed numbers; use inverse operations to check and solve equations	Convert a fraction into a percent value
Multiplication and division facts		
Use logic of number families to complete 3-by-3 tables	Make fraction number families and complex number families; use number families to solve equations with an unknown	Write number families for decimal and percent values and number families that compare two values
Read and write thousands, numerals that have 4, 5, or 6 digits; round to nearest hundred or thousand; place value addition (36 = 30 + 6)	Round to nearest ten, hundred, or thousands; identify place value through millions; express numbers that are multiples of 10, 100, or 1000 as factors	Review
Solve money and "price-tag" problems using number families; mixed sets of number-family word problems; write fraction number families; work multistep and ratio word problems including measurement problems	Set up and solve addition/ subtraction problems using number-family tables and multistep problems	Set up and solve ratio equations and tables, probability, multiplication, and mixed-number problems, multistep problems that involve inverse operations; time, coins, and money amounts, measurement, circle graphs, and averages

TABLE 7.3 (Continued)

	LEVEL A	LEVEL B	LEVEL C
Applications	Measure inches; write value of a nickel, dime, or quarter and pennies	Tell time when minute hand is pointing to a number; write value of dollar and mixed coin amounts; answer calendar questions	Tell time to the minute; solve addition and subtraction problems involving time; read, write, round off, and solve word problems with money
Geometry		Identify triangles, circles, rectangles; find perimeter	Find area of rectangle and volume of boxes
Fractions			Read and write fractions; analyze fraction values; add and subtract fractions with like denominators; relate fractions to division
Decimals and percents			
Pre-algebra			Find points on a coordinate system for x and y

the big idea of number families provides the basis for the big idea that is a common foundation for all the word problem strategies.

Tables. Another big idea in *CMC* is closely related to the number family arrow. The big idea of representing data in tables is used in a powerful way in *CMC*. Rather than simply having students read data from tables, *CMC* has them work with some of the data in a table to figure out missing information in the table. Work with tables begins in *CMC Level C*,

LEVEL D	LEVEL E	LEVEL F
Find area and perimeter of polygons, length of unknown sides; volume of a box; identify lines that intersect and are parallel	Solve problems involving two- and three-dimensional figures, and angles and lines	Work with complex shapes (e.g., areas that have holes); volume of prisms, pyramids, and cones
Find fractions equivalent to other fractions, whole numbers, and decimals; add, subtract, and multiply fractions and mixed numbers with like and unlike denominators; use fractions to express ratios and proportions	Compute fractions and mixed numbers; find equivalent fractions when denominator is large; compare value of fractions; simplify fractions	Work multiplication problems by crossing out zeros or fractions equal to one; work problems involving reciprocals; solve mixed number problems
Read and write decimal numbers to hundredths; order decimal and whole numbers; write decimals as mixed numbers	Add, subtract, and multiply decimal values	Divide decimal values; decimal fractions
Plot points on a coordinate system; figure out the "function" of x; use information about a "sequence" to determine a function; plot lines and relate lines to equivalent fractions	Relate a line on the coordinate system to values in a table; complete function table	Use the distributive principle to solve problems; combine + and – numbers that are added or subtracted; work problems with exponents; use lines to understand ratio relationships

where three types of table problems are introduced: addition/subtraction, multiplication/division, and graphs. To solve for missing data in a table, *CMC* treats rows and columns of tables as number families. Initially tables have only three rows and columns, two for the "small numbers" and one total column and row for the "big number" of the number families. If the table gives the total row or column, students use the same strategies they used in number families to solve for the unknown in the table. If the table does not give the total, then students add to get the total. Thus, the big idea in *CMC* is that tables are simply extensions of number

LESSON 38
Student Textbook

Part 2
Make the number family.
Then write the addition problem or subtraction problem.
Then answer the question the problem asks about.

a. S is 15 more than B. B is 77. What number is S?
b. F is 66 less than T. F is 399. What number is T?
c. J is 185 more than M. J is 276. What number is M?
d. L is 207 less than R. R is 288. What number is L?

Teacher Presentation Book

a. Find part 2 in your textbook.
   These are really hard problems because they have two letters. You're going to figure out the number for one of those letters.
b. Touch problem A.
   Listen to the whole problem: S is 15 more than B. B is 77. What number is S?
   • Listen to the first sentence again: S is 15 more than B.
   • Your turn: Make the number family for that sentence.
   Raise your hand when you're finished. (Observe students and give feedback.)
c. (Write on the board:)

$$\xrightarrow{\quad 15 \qquad B \quad} S$$

   • Here's what you should have for the first sentence. It shows that S is 15 more than B.
d. The next sentence in the problem says: B is 77.
   If B is 77, I can cross out B and write 77. Watch. (Write to show:)

$$\xrightarrow{\quad 15 \qquad \overset{77}{\cancel{B}} \quad} S$$

   • The last sentence in the problem says: What number is S? That's the number we don't know.
   • Now we can work the problem and figure out what number S is.
   • Your turn: Fix up your number family with the number for B. Then work the problem and figure out what number S is. Raise your hand when you're finished.
     (Observe students and give feedback.
e. Check your work.
   • Eveybody, what number is S? (Signal.) *92.*
   • (Write to show:)

$$\xrightarrow{\quad 15 \qquad \overset{77}{\cancel{B}} \qquad \overset{92}{\cancel{S}} \quad}$$

FIGURE 7.7   *Connecting Math Concepts Level C,* Textbook, Lesson 38, Part 2 and Lesson 38, Exercise 2. Reprinted with permission of the McGraw-Hill Companies.

PART 4

- Here's how to work the problems:

1. Read the first sentence and make the number family with two letters and a number.
2. Then read the next sentence. That sentence gives a number for one of the letters. Cross out the letter and write the number.
3. Figure out the number for the other letter.
4. Write the number problem and the answer.

- **Fran was 14 years older than Ann.**

- **Ann was 13 years old.**

- **How many years old was Fran?**

$$\xrightarrow[\quad 14 \quad]{A} F$$

$$\xrightarrow[\quad 14 \quad]{\overset{13}{\cancel{A}}} F$$

$$\xrightarrow[\quad 14 \quad]{\overset{13}{\cancel{A}} \quad 27} \cancel{F}$$

$$\begin{array}{r} 14 \\ +13 \\ \hline 27 \end{array}$$

FIGURE 7.8   *Connecting Math Concepts Level C,* **Textbook, Lesson 43, Part 4. Reprinted with permission of the McGraw-Hill Companies.**

families and the same strategies used in word problems are applicable to tables. Figure 7.9 shows a table from *CMC Level C* and the questions that are asked of students.

Students can use the big idea of number families to figure out how many small fish are in Pond B to answer the question, "Are there more small fish in Pond A or in Pond B?"

Part 5

	Pond A	Pond B	Total for both ponds
Big fish			
Small fish	200		640
Total fish			780

Fact 1: There are 50 big fish in pond B.

Fact 2: In pond A, there are 110 more small fish than big fish.

a. How many big fish are in Pond B?

b. Are there more small fish in Pond A or in Pond B?

c. What's the total number of fish in Pond A?

d. Which Pond has more big fish?

e. If you wanted to go fishing for big fish, which Pond would you fish in?

FIGURE 7.9   *Connecting Math Concepts Level C,* **Textbook, Lesson 93, Part 5. Reprinted with permission of the McGraw-Hill Companies.**

In the row for small fish, students see that they have a number family: $200 + ? = 640$. They solve for the unknown by subtraction to find out there are 440 big fish in Pond B. Now they can determine that there are more small fish in Pond B.

The more complicated step comes when the students need to figure out how many total fish are in Pond A. The table shows there are 200 small fish in Pond A and students are then given comparison information. Fact 2 tells the students that there are 110 *more* small fish than big fish in Pond A. Armed with this information the students must use the comparison word problem strategy: difference + smaller quantity being compared = big number. So 110, the difference, plus the unknown, but smaller, number of big fish add together to equal 200 small fish. The students use the number family concept of $110 + ?$ $=200$, and subtract to find out there are 90 big fish in Pond B. Then they have a vertical number family $90 + 200 = ?$, which they must solve to find out the total number of fish in Pond A. Can you figure out the rest of the missing data in the table, and answer the five questions below the table? The third-grade students studying from *CMC* can! The table problem strategies are used in ever more sophisticated ways through *CMC Level F.*

Volume of a Solid.   Another example of how the instructional design in *CMC* uses a big idea to simplify learning at the same time deepening understanding for students comes from *CMC Levels E and F* when students learn how to compute the volume of a solid.

In geometry students are typically expected to learn seven formulas to calculate the volume of seven three-dimensional figures:

Rectangular prism: $1 \cdot w \cdot h = v$

Wedge: $\frac{1}{2} \cdot 1 \cdot w \cdot h = v$

Triangular pyramid: $\frac{1}{6} \cdot 1 \cdot w \cdot h = v$

Cylinder: $\pi \cdot r^2 \cdot h = v$

Rectangular pyramid: $\frac{1}{3} \cdot 1 \cdot w \cdot h = v$

Cone: $\frac{1}{3} \cdot \pi \cdot r^2 \cdot h = v$

Sphere: $\frac{4}{3} \cdot \pi \cdot r^3 \cdot = v$

These equations emphasize rote formulas rather than big ideas. An analysis based on big ideas reduces the number of formulas students must learn from seven to slight variations of a single formula: area of the base times the height $(b \cdot h)$ (Carnine et al., 1998, p. 95).

Use of big ideas such as the meta-formula for volume (the single formula of area of the base times the height) helps students connect math concepts to each other while reducing the number of seemingly disparate facts they have to remember.

Fractions Equal to One.   Another big idea in *CMC* is the concept of "fractions equal to one." Connecting the procedure for finding equivalent fractions to the concept of fractions equal to one is typically one of the most difficult topics to teach. For example, beginning in *Level C of CMC,* students are taught that fractions consist of the bottom number that tells how many parts are in a whole, and a top number that tells how many parts are used. From

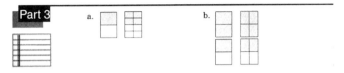

FIGURE 7.10   *Connecting Math Concepts Level D,* **Textbook, Lesson 67, Part 3. Reprinted with permission of the McGraw-Hill Companies.**

the earliest examples, students learn the concept that fractions can be greater than one (thereby neatly preventing a common misconception that fractions are always less than one), less than one, or they can be "fractions equal to one." Students are taught how to apply the concept through the skill of writing "fractions equal to one"

$$\left(\text{e.g., } \frac{4}{4} \text{ or } \frac{7}{7}\right).$$

After practicing this skill throughout *CMC Level C and D,* this big idea is integrated with another concept—that numbers multiplied by one give you an equivalent value—to provide an explicit strategy for finding equivalent fractions. Through explanation and pictures of fractions, students extend their previous learning to the idea that a fraction multiplied by a "fraction equal to one" gives a fraction of equivalent value. After developing this idea in a strand woven through a dozen lessons, in *CMC Level D* students are then introduced to the procedure for how to find equivalent fractions. They see the fraction pictures shown in Figure 7.10.

Students write the equation

$$\frac{1}{2} \times \left(\ \right) = \frac{4}{8}.$$

They learn that "to find the fraction that equals one, you say the multiplication problem for the bottom and for the top" (Engelmann, Engelmann, & Carnine, 1993, p. 19). The pictures are gradually faded and students learn to solve equivalent fractions by finding the missing fraction that equals one as shown in Figure 7.11.

Students solve the problems independently by using a strategy to find the fraction of one. They ask, "Two times what number equals 8?" Because the denominator is 4, the fraction equal to one is

$$\frac{4}{4}.$$

Students multiply 1 times 4 to get 4 as the numerator of the equivalent fraction. Not only have students been taught the explicit procedural knowledge, they also have the conceptual understanding of what they are doing. Students can explain that

$$\frac{1}{3} \text{ is equivalent to } \frac{4}{12}$$

because it is multiplied by a fraction equal to one, which always yields an equivalent value.

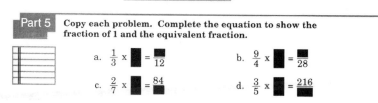

FIGURE 7.11   *Connecting Math Concepts Level D,* **Textbook, Lesson 74, Part 5. Reprinted with permission of the McGraw-Hill Companies.**

The consistency of the above sequence over two years sets *CMC* apart from most other math programs. However, this is only the beginning of the application of the strategy of multiplying by a fraction equal to one. In *CMC Level E* when students add and subtract unlike fractions they use fractions equal to one to convert the two unlike fractions into equivalent fractions with common denominators. During the initial presentation of this concept, the teacher-presentation book provides a detailed script for finding the least common denominator so that consistency is maintained in presenting the strategy. The student textbook provides simple prompts that provide scaffolding until students master this difficult procedure as shown in Figure 7.12.

CMC continues to apply this big idea of multiplying by a fraction equal to one in other areas as well. In *CMC Level E,* students use this same strategy to solve ratio problems. First, students learn to solve ratio problems that compare one thing. For example, "There were 9 bees for every 2 flowers. There were 20 flowers. How many bees were there?" Students set up a ratio of bees to flowers and solve by finding the fraction "equal-to-one" by which they will multiply as show in Figure 7.13.

Part 5

- Remember the steps:

  ✔ Find the first common number you reach when you count by the number in each denominator.

  ✔ Write the first common number as the denominator for **both fractions.**

  ✔ Work equivalent-fraction problems to figure out the numerators.

  ✔ Then add or subtract.

$$\frac{7}{8}\left(\blacksquare\right)=\blacksquare$$
$$+\frac{5}{6}\left(\blacksquare\right)=+\blacksquare$$

FIGURE 7.12   *Connecting Math Concepts Level E,* **Textbook, Lesson 67, Part 5. Reprinted with permission of the McGraw-Hill Companies.**

Lesson 61
EXERCISE 5   Problem Solving
Proportions

a. Find part 4.
• These are ratio problems. To work some of them, you can use a simple fraction that equals 1. For other problems, you'll use a fraction over the same fraction.
b. Problem A: There were 9 bees for every 2 flowers. There were 20 flowers. How many bees were there?
• Write the names, the equation, and figure out the answer. Remember, you say the problem on top or on the bottom. If the answer is a whole number, you write the whole number. If the answer is not a whole number, write the fraction. Raise your hand when you've worked the problem and boxed the answer.
(Observe students and give feedback.
• (Write on the board:)

$$\text{a.} \quad \frac{\text{bees}}{\text{flowers}} \quad \frac{9}{2} \left(\frac{10}{10}\right) = \frac{\boxed{90}}{20}$$

• Here's what you should have. The fraction that equals 1 is 10/10. Listen: After problem A, write the whole answer—90 bees—and box it.
• (Write to show:)

$$\text{a.} \quad \frac{\text{bees}}{\text{flowers}} \quad \frac{9}{2} \left(\frac{10}{10}\right) = \frac{\boxed{90}}{20} \boxed{90 \text{ bees}}$$

FIGURE 7.13   *Connecting Math Concepts Level E,* **Lesson 61, Exercise 5. Reprinted with permission of the McGraw-Hill Companies.**

Twenty lessons later, students learn to solve ratio-table problems that compare two things. Now students have the preskills to make a connection between fraction number families in comparison word problems and the ratio table. Students have already learned to solve comparison problems, but this time the comparison involves fractions. The student textbook activity is shown in Figure 7.14.

Difference comes first on the number arrow, but isn't known yet. The sand weighed

$$\frac{2}{5}$$

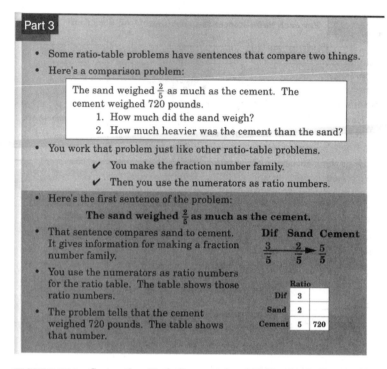

FIGURE 7.14   *Connecting Math Concepts Level E,* **Textbook, Lesson 82, Part 3. Reprinted with permission of the McGraw-Hill Companies.**

as much as the cement. Sand is

$$\frac{2}{5}$$

and cement is a fraction equal to one because that is what sand is being compared to. So cement is

$$\frac{5}{5}.$$

Students easily figure out that the difference is

$$\frac{3}{5}.$$

CMC teaches students they can arrange a number family vertically in a ratio table using only the numerators to show the relationship (because the denominators reduce). Students enter the actual numbers into the table in order to figure out the other quantities. To find how much the sand weighed, students use the numerators derived from the comparison number family in the table. The problem tells that the cement weighed 720 pounds. Then they solve to find out how much the sand weighed by finding the fraction of one

$$\left(\frac{144}{144}\right)$$

for the fraction problem

$$\frac{2}{5} = \frac{?}{720}.$$

The sand weighed 288 pounds. With this information, students can make a number family to figure out how much heavier the cement was than the sand (720 – 288 = ?) to find that the difference was 432 pounds.

Once the strategy is learned, then *CMC* adds numbers that are more challenging to the students' developing computational skills. Later in *CMC Level E* and throughout *CMC Level F* these ratio tables employ both mixed fractions and percentages to solve problems that stump many adults.

TEACHING TECHNIQUES

Direct Instruction mathematics programs include the use of signals and effective error corrections.

Signals

The purpose of using a signal is to promote unison responding. Signals let students know when to answer so they can initiate their own response rather than just following the lead voice. Unison responding is an efficient way for teachers to get information about whether or not students understand new concepts. Unison responses give teachers information about student understanding before students are forced to fail on the paper-and-pencil tasks, which can lead to frustration and lack of motivation.

In *DISTAR Arithmetic* I teachers use a point-touch signal when students are looking at a symbol or numeral on the page of the presentation book. This signal is used frequently when students are learning to identify numerals. Teachers hold their finger about an inch from the page taking care that the students can see the symbol/numeral on the page of the presentation book. Teachers point, pause for a minimum of one second to give students a chance to think, and then say "get ready" and touch under the symbol/numeral. An exercise for identifying the numeral 2 might look like this. Students look at the numeral on the page of the presentation book or on the board and the teacher says, "When I touch it, tell me what it is." Then the teacher pauses briefly, says "Get ready," then touches just below the symbol. Students respond with "2" right at the point-touch signal.

Another signal that is used in Direct Instruction mathematics programs is the hand-drop signal. This signal is given to evoke a verbal unison response while students are looking at the teacher. This signal is commonly used during counting exercises. Teachers should raise their arm at the beginning of the task with their hand in a focus position like a person stopping traffic. After the question is asked, teachers should pause one second and drop their hand quickly. A "Get Ready" prompt might be used before the hand-drop signal. An audible prompt such as a snap may be used at the end of the hand-drop signal; thus, the hand stays in a focus until teachers want the students to respond. At this point, teachers may say, "Get Ready" followed by a drop of the hand and a snap (the latter serving as an auditory cue for students to come in together). The hand-drop signal might sound like this. "You're going to start with 12 and end up with 16." (Pause.) "Get ready." (The response 12, 13, 14, 15, 16 comes immediately after "Get Ready.")

The most frequently used signal in Direct Instruction mathematics programs is the auditory signal. An auditory signal is used when students cannot look at the teacher because they are looking at their own worksheet, workbook, or textbook, or giving a written response. An auditory signal can be anything (snap, clap, tap) that lets students know when to respond. The procedure is very similar to the other two signals. Teachers ask a question or make a request, pause at least one second to give students time to think, say "Get ready," and snap, clap, or tap. It might sound like this if students were reading a problem. "Everybody, you're going to touch and read the next problem." (Pause.) "Get ready."

When a signal is effective, teachers (1) talk first, pause about one second to give students "think time," and then signal, (2) require students to answer in a reasonable speaking voice rather than a slow, droney voice, and (3) refrain from mouthing the correct answer or giving unnecessary clues or prompts (Engelmann & Carnine, 1992).

Error Corrections

When students make errors, it is the responsibility of teachers to diagnose those errors to make an appropriate correction. Corrections are easier to do when instruction is explicit than when it is implicit. When an explicit strategy or rule has been taught, reteaching is relatively simple. However, if students have made up their own strategies or developed misrules, teachers must ask many questions to figure out students' thinking errors. Questioning is a time-consuming process for which teachers seldom have time. Generally, errors in mathematics fall into three categories: component skill errors, strategy errors, and fact errors.

Component Skill Errors.   Component skill errors can be thought of as errors caused by deficits in the components of a strategy (Stein et al., 1997); in other words, they indicate missing preskills. For example, if a student in *DISTAR Arithmetic I* who wrote 8 in the box for the problem, $3 + \square = 5$, has not mastered the component skill that lines under a box always tell what numeral goes in that box, an immediate correction would be to say, "I fooled you. There aren't eight lines under the box" (Engelmann & Carnine, 1976b, p. 60). The teacher would repeat the task that was missed. Then she would repeat the entire part of the lesson where the mistake was made to ensure firm responding.

If a component skill error is chronic, teachers should look back to the lesson in which the preskill was first taught to find an error correction. In this case, the teacher could find the correction eight lessons earlier, in Lesson 72. In this example, the correction would be:

I fooled you. The lines under a box always tell what numeral goes in that box. Count the lines under the box. (Signal) 1, 2, 3. How many lines are under the box? (Signal). 3. So what numeral goes in the box? (Signal) 3. Let's try that again (Engelmann & Carnine, 1976a, p. 96).

Strategy Errors.   Strategy errors indicate a fundamental lack of understanding of how to do a mathematical procedure, and they are often the result of omitting one or more steps in a procedure (Stein et al., 1997). The correction procedure for strategy errors is to reteach the entire procedure. The correction does not necessarily mean reteaching an entire lesson, only the tasks related to the strand in which the student experiences difficulty. For example, a student in *DISTAR Arithmetic I* might forget to start the problem, $3 + \square = 5$, by circling the side to start counting on (the side without the unknown quantity or box). This error is a failure to apply the first step in the procedure for solving addition problems. The correction for strategy errors is to provide prompts that remind students of the steps in the procedure and provide sufficient practice until they can perform the operation independently. In this case, a prompt that would remind students of the procedure is, "First you're going to ring the side that you start counting on. Then you're going to end up with the same number on the other side" (Engelmann & Carnine, 1976a, p. 201). Before the student continues to work the problem, the teacher should check for understanding by asking, "What are you going to do first?" If the student responds correctly, then she should be encouraged to go ahead and solve the problem. Firming might involve a precorrection on the next problem. For example, "Be careful. What do you do first to solve this problem?"

Fact Errors.   Fact errors are errors in complex computation caused by errors in basic facts such as $9 + 8$ or $17 - 8$. If fact errors are infrequent or random, teachers simply need to provide additional motivation for accuracy. If students make fact errors during the teacher-directed presentation, the correction is simply to state the correct fact and test for accuracy. For example, if students said that $9 + 8 = 15$, the teacher would immediately respond, "$9 + 8 = 17$. What is $9 + 8$? Say the whole thing." If errors are frequent or systematic, then teachers need to implement systematic instruction to promote mastery of math facts. It is important to note that no commercial mathematics program can provide sufficient practice in math facts for all students to attain mastery, and teachers should plan to provide supplemental instruction to low-performing students. Supplementary programs for teaching math facts are described below.

ASSESSMENT AND TROUBLESHOOTING

All the Direct Instruction mathematics programs include specific procedures for placement in a program and assessment of student mastery.

Placement

Placement tests indicate whether students possess the necessary preskills to experience success and may also provide information about how to group for instruction. It is critical to place students at an appropriate instructional level so that they can experience both success and academic challenge. Direct Instruction mathematics programs include placement tests. For example, the *Corrective Mathematics* and *Mathematics Modules* programs include a comprehensive placement test that places students in the correct program and lesson (e.g., 6, 7, or 8 errors on Part A of Basic Fractions places a student in Lesson 1 of the module; 4 or 5 errors in Part A places a student in Lesson 19 of this module). Beside the comprehensive placement test there are also preskills (necessary skills to be mastered for a particular module) assessments and placement tests for each specific module. *DISTAR Arithmetic I and II* and *Connecting Math Concepts* (*CMC Levels A–E,* including the *Bridge,* with the exception of *CMC Level F*) also include placement tests.

Mastery

It is also critical for teachers to monitor mastery. There are three ways to monitor mastery; teachers must do all three. First, teachers must observe student behavior during the lessons. Every student response provides important diagnostic information. Second, teachers should monitor performance on daily, written, independent work to determine if students are firm. If students are firm, they can perform a skill independently with high levels of accuracy. Teachers should carefully monitor accuracy on independent work and if they notice a serious problem that is not unique to only the lower performing students in the class, they should stop and repeat the part of the lesson that gave students trouble. No more than 30 percent of the students should make mistakes on any independent work. It is absolutely critical that students are firm on each lesson because success with each lesson depends on mastery of the skills in previous lessons.

A third way to check for mastery is with the mastery tests that are provided with all Direct Instruction mathematics programs. *DISTAR Arithmetic I* has seventy-two in-program mastery tests and *DISTAR Arithmetic II* has fifteen in-program mastery tests. Each *Corrective Mathematics* module has a minimum of fifteen mastery tests. In *CMC,* mastery tests are included every tenth lesson. Teachers must give these mastery tests and *use* the results to make sure that students are reaching mastery criteria. For example, if students fail to master the equality rule in Lesson 50 of *DISTAR Arithmetic I,* they will fail to grasp addition in Lesson 61 and algebra addition in Lesson 80. Without complete mastery of the subskills, students will begin to fail through no fault of their own. Although the programs are designed to provide the best chance for student success, different students will need different amounts of practice to reach mastery. It is the teacher's responsibility to use information from students' oral and written responses to ensure success.

One key advantage of Direct Instruction mathematics programs is that the procedures and strategies students must employ are all explicitly taught in the program, and teachers know that students have been presented an effective strategy for solving any problem they encounter. Problems are carefully chosen so that they can be solved by the procedures previously taught. If students are unable to complete some work, the correction procedure is to reteach using the *same strategies* and the *same wording.*

Their problem is that they didn't attend to or couldn't perform on some detail that you covered in your initial presentation. So tell them what they didn't attend to and repeat the activity (or the step) that gives them the information they need. This approach shows them how to process the information you already presented. A different demonstration or explanation, however, may not show them how to link what you said originally with the new demonstration (Engelmann, Kelly, & Carnine, 1994, p. 20).

When teachers are able to solve any student problem by simply repeating prior instruction, the textbook is effective.

Teachers new to *CMC* sometimes have difficulty presenting guided practice on a procedure or set of steps quickly enough to maintain continuity. If the pace is too slow, or the teacher digresses from the steps, students lose track of the explanation. Only if teachers move quickly through the minimal wording provided by the script, avoiding interruptions or additional explanations, will students be able to follow the sequence of the steps in the procedure.

Another issue in guided practice comes when students are slow in completing the small amounts of written work that are followed by immediate "workchecks." Teachers should always move on to the workcheck after a reasonable period of time, even if some students haven't finished. If students learn that the teacher will wait forever for them to finish they have no incentive to hurry, and will become slower and dawdle even more. Conversely, moving on before everyone has finished gives a clear message that students must work quickly, and will reduce the time students must sit waiting and will greatly speed up lesson completion.

EXTENSIONS AND ADAPTATIONS

Although all the Direct Instruction mathematics programs are comprehensive, some students may still need additional practice. Math facts and fluency as well as word problems frequently present special problems for students. Interactive videodisc programs can be useful when remedial instruction on a specific math skill is desired.

Math Facts and Fluency

CMC provides practice in math facts using number families, which reduces the number of facts needed to be learned. *Levels B, C,* and *D* of *CMC* gradually introduce sets of facts and then provide practice in a variety of formats.

Fluency errors can typically be attributed to insufficient knowledge of math facts. Students may have an accurate, but time-consuming, or other strategy (e.g., finger counting) for figuring out facts. Lack of speed with math facts is a symptom of a mentally demanding strategy for calculating facts that will interfere with attention to higher-level math operations. This problem is analogous to problems with reading fluently. Students who struggle to decode common words and students who struggle to compute basic facts both devote most of their attention to the basic skill, preventing attention to the higher goals of the activity. Struggling readers cannot attend to the meaning of what they are decoding. Students who struggle with facts cannot attend to the procedures or reasoning involved in the problem they are trying to solve. Slow and painful math fact calculations can also decrease student motivation. It is hard to be motivated when simple computation rather than interesting problem solving consumes all of one's attention.

Teachers who find that students need additional practice may want to consider a supplemental program of practice on math facts. Stein et al. (1997, p. 87) recommend that a program should include the following components to promote fast fact memorization:

1. a specific performance criterion for introducing new facts;
2. intensive practice on newly introduced facts;
3. systematic practice on previously introduced facts;
4. adequate allotted time;
5. a record-keeping system;
6. a motivation system.

One commercially available program designed specifically in accordance with these recommendations is *Mastering Math Facts* (Crawford, 1998). *Mastering Math Facts* is a structured program for sequential practice of math facts. The program is structured the same way for all four operations so teachers can implement a simple daily routine and allow quick learners to master higher operations while slower students proceed at their own rate. Each day's routine practice should take no more than six or seven minutes of class time.

The program's daily component consists of one-page practice sheets, lettered A–Z. The top half of each page gives practice focused on two facts and their inverses. For example, Set L is $2 + 7 = 9, 7 + 2 = 9; 7 + 4 = 11$, and $4 + 7 = 11$. The recommended method of practice is in student-pairs, with one student checking with an answer key (provided) while the practicing student states the facts and the answers aloud. After two minutes of practice, the students switch roles. Then the students take a timed test on the bottom half of the sheet, which includes all facts learned thus far. If students answer all forty facts correctly in one minute, they move on to the next set. If they do not, they repeat the same page again the next day. Students color in a letter square on a rocket chart as they pass each set.

The program includes placement tests for accelerating students into an operation in which they already have some proficiency. There are tests of writing speed so that adjusted goals can be created for students who can't write fast enough to answer forty problems in one minute. Students with such adjusted goals are expected to always meet or beat their previous best to pass. Within each operation there are also ten progress-monitoring tests (two-minute timings of all the facts in the operation). Every week or two students take these two-minute tests and graph the results on blank graph forms provided. This graphing enables the teacher and students to keep track of their progress.

Word Problems

Stein et al. (1997) recommend, "generalizable problem-solving strategies that are useful and efficient" (p. 219). *CMC* integrates problem-solving strategies with computational strategies in an efficient and effective fashion. Another commercially available program for grades one through six that teaches similarly direct problem-solving strategies is *Word Problems Made Easy* (Crawford, 2002).

Word Problems Made Easy is a supplemental program that teaches explicit strategies for solving common types of word problems. Each level corresponds to a grade level and has at least 160 daily ten-minute lessons. A minimum of twelve days of practice is provided for each strategy introduced. The strategies are based on formulas students learn for common problems, such as "less + difference = more" for comparing problems or "groups X things per group = things" for multiplication and division problems. Teacher prompts are provided for at least six days. The structure employs a basic concept from algebra. Students should set up the problem the same way each time then choose the appropriate arithmetic operations based on where the unknown is in the number sentence. Along with the step-by-step procedures available on the page, considerable scaffolding is provided in the early days of each strategy to help the students organize and write out the solution to the problem. After a number of days of teacher-led guided practice, when these supports fade away students are expected to do the problems entirely on their own. Each strategy also has three model explanations to show students how to communicate their solution process in writing.

Videodisc

Curricula that may be particularly valuable for older remedial students or students in alternative educational settings are the *Core Concepts* videodisc programs in mathematics developed by Hofmeister, Engelmann, and Carnine (1989). Eight programs have been developed and field-tested including: *Mastering Fractions; Mastering Informal Geometry; Mastering Decimals and Percents; Mastering Ratios and Word Problem Strategies; Mastering Equations, Roots, and Exponents; Problem Solving with Addition and Subtraction; Problem Solving with Multiplication and Division*; and *Problem Solving with Tables, Graphs, and Statistics*. The *Core Concepts* videodisc programs incorporate many of the same design features as the other Direct Instruction programs. They are designed around strands in carefully sequenced steps that provide opportunities for review and integration. These programs have four advantages over traditional programs: (1) they explicitly teach higher-level math skills that go beyond the elementary level; (2) the videodisc format incorporates interesting visual graphics; (3) it is easy to review or make up lessons missed due to absence; and (4) because the lessons are presented on videodisc, teachers are free to circulate around the room and monitor student progress and behavior. Research has shown very promising results with the videodisc programs compared to traditional basals for teaching fractions (Kelly, Carnine, Gersten, & Grossen, 1986; Kelly, Gersten, & Carnine, 1990), ratios and proportions (Moore & Carnine, 1989), algebra (Kitz & Thorpe, 1995), and geometry (Fischer, Kitz, & Tarver, 1996).

RESEARCH ON DIRECT INSTRUCTION MATHEMATICS PROGRAMS

Unlike traditional basals, Direct Instruction mathematics programs have undergone extensive field-testing prior to being marketed (Engelmann et al., 1993). Adams and Engelmann (1996) conducted a meta-analysis of all Direct Instruction programs including *DISTAR Arithmetic I and II, Corrective Mathematics,* and *Connecting Math Concepts*. They found an effect size of 1.11 in favor of Direct Instruction mathematics programs in the thirty-three comparisons that included a math component. It is important to note that an effect size of between .3 and .6 are considered promising in educational research (Forness, Kavale, Blum, & Lloyd, 1997) and anything over .75 is extremely rare (Adams & Engelmann, 1996).

A more recent review of the research also found favorable outcomes for Direct Instruction mathematics programs. Przychodzin-Havis, Marchand-Martella, Martella, and Azim (in press) reviewed twelve studies (including the above mentioned meta-analysis) published since 1990. These studies are summarized below.

One study was found using *DISTAR Arithmetic.* Young, Baker, and Martin (1990) investigated the effects of DISTAR and an adaptation to the program (an added discrimination learning theory or DLT phase). Participants included five students with intellectual disabilities; each scored between 35–54 on the Wechsler Intelligence Scale for Children-Revised (WISC-R). All participants had articulation problems. The authors concluded that the match-to-sample format of the added discrimination learning theory (DLT) phase coupled with *DISTAR Arithmetic* was effective in teaching math skills to students with articulation problems and low intellectual abilities.

Three studies were found using the *Corrective Mathematics* program. First, Parsons, Marchand-Martella, Waldron-Soler, Martella, and Lignugaris/Kraft (in press) examined the use of *Corrective Mathematics* in a secondary general education classroom for students struggling in math as delivered by peer tutors. After sixty instructional days, the authors found that both learners and peer tutors experienced post-test gains in one or both math subtests on a standardized academic achievement test. Second, Glang, Singer, Cooley, and Tish (1991) assessed the efficacy of *Corrective Mathematics* in teaching math skills to an eight-year-old student with traumatic brain injury. In this study, the student was also instructed using *Corrective Reading Comprehension A* to improve his reasoning skills. Instruction took place twice a week over a period of six weeks. After twelve hours of instruction, the authors found that the student's math fact rate and story problem accuracy improved. Finally, Sommers (1991) examined the effects of *Corrective Mathematics* and other Direct Instruction programs in improving the overall performance of at-risk middle school students over a two-year period. On math measures, students made average gains of 1.2 months per month of instruction (as noted by the author).

Six studies were found using *CMC.* First, Snider and Crawford (1996) included forty-six fourth graders who were randomly assigned to two general education classrooms. One classroom used *CMC Level D,* the other used *Invitation to Mathematics (SF)* by Scott Foresman. *CMC* students typically scored higher than the *SF* group on various math assessments used in the investigation.

Second, in a follow-up study by Crawford and Snider (2000) both teachers used *CMC.* After one year of using *CMC,* the teacher who had used *SF* had students who made greater gains than the previous year on both the multiplication facts tests and on both curriculum-based measures. No significant post-test differences were noted on the NAT subtests or Total Test scores. The authors cited several possible reasons for the lack of significant pre- to post-test gains. Some of these included: (1) less than optional implementation of *CMC,* (2) lack of alignment between NAT Concepts and Problem Solving subtests and either curriculum, and (3) performance on norm-referenced tests are more highly correlated to reading comprehension scores than with computation scores. Although the NAT results did not reach significance, the positive results shown by the remaining data prompted the districtwide implementation of *CMC.*

Third, Tarver and Jung (1995) compared *CMC* to a program that combined *Math Their Way (MTW)* and Cognitively Guided Instruction (CGI). One-hundred-nineteen students entering first grade were assigned to five classrooms. One experimental classroom used *CMC,* while four control classrooms used *MTW*/CGI. The study took place over two years. At the end of second grade, *CMC* students scored higher than the control group on all post-test measures as well as on an experimenter-constructed math attitudes survey (results were mixed at the end of first grade, however). Fourth, Brent and DiObilda (1993) compared the effects of Direct Instruction curricula to those of a traditional basal curriculum, the *Holt Math Series.* Students who received instruction in CMC generally scored higher than the control groups on a standardized academic achievement test.

Fifth, a prepublication investigation (McKenzie, Marchand-Martella, Tso, & Martella, in press) of the kindergarten level of *CMC* found that preschool children with and without disabilities improved cognitive and math skills over a six-week period. Sixth, Vreeland et al. (1994) compared *CMC* to the *Addison-Wesley Mathematics* program. Participants included five third-grade classrooms and four fifth-grade classrooms. *CMC* third and fifth graders scored higher than the control group on curriculum-based post-test measures, based on *CMC* and *Addison-Wesley.* Overall, results were positive enough to guide the school officials' decision to use *CMC* in almost all of its first- through sixth-grade classrooms. Finally, Wellington (1994) examined the effectiveness of *CMC* for a period of one year in a socioeconomically and ethnologically diverse school district. All eight of the district's elementary schools participated in the study. Results of the post-test showed statistically significant differences for two out of the eight first-grade groups: one in favor of the *CMC* group and one in favor of the control group. Fourth grade results showed statistically significant differences in favor of six out of the eight *CMC* groups.

In summary, empirical data supporting the effectiveness of Direct Instruction mathematics programs continue to accumulate.

REFERENCES

Adams, G .L., & Engelmann, S. (1996). *Research on Direct Instruction: 25 years beyond DISTAR.* Seattle, WA: Educational Achievement Systems.

America's Education Choice. (2000, April 1). *The Economist,* p. 17.

Brent, G., & DiObilda, N. (1993). Curriculum alignment versus direct instruction: Effects on stable and mobile urban children. *Journal of Educational Research, 86*(6), 333–338.

Bureau of Labor Statistics. (2002–03). *BLS releases 2000–2010 employment projections.* Retrieved May 22, 2002 from http://www.bls.gov/emp

Carnine, D. W. (1990). Reforming mathematics instruction. *ADI News, 10*(4), 1–4.

Carnine, D. W., Dixon, R. C., & Silbert, J. (1998). Effective strategies for teaching mathematics. In E. J. Kameenui & D. W. Carnine (Eds), *Effective teaching strategies that accommodate diverse learners* (pp. 93–112). Upper Saddle River, NJ: Prentice-Hall.

Crawford, D. (1998). *Mastering math facts.* Eau Claire, WI: Otter Creek Institute. Available at http://www.oci-sems.com/

Crawford, D. (2002) *Word problems made easy.* Eau Claire, WI: Otter Creek Institute. Available at http://www.oci-sems.com/

Crawford, D., & Snider, V. (2000). Effective mathematics instruction: The importance of curriculum. *Education and Treatment of Children, 23,* 122–142.

Dempster, F. N. (1991). Synthesis of research on reviews and tests. *Educational Leadership, 48*(7), 71–76.

Engelmann, S., & Carnine, D. (1976a). *DISTAR Arithmetic*. Chicago, IL: Science Research Associates.

Engelmann, S., & Carnine, D. (1976b). *DISTAR Arithmetic teacher's guide*. Chicago, IL: Science Research Associates.

Engelmann, S., & Carnine, D. (1982). *Corrective Mathematics*. Chicago, IL: SRA–Macmillan/McGraw-Hill.

Engelmann, S., & Carnine, D. (1992). *Connecting Math Concepts, Levels A, B, C*. Chicago, IL: SRA–McGraw-Hill.

Engelmann, S., Engelmann, O., & Carnine, D. (1993). *Connecting Math Concepts, Level D*. Chicago, IL: SRA–McGraw-Hill.

Engelmann, S., Kelly, B., & Carnine, D. (1994). *Connecting Math Concepts: Level E*. Chicago, IL: SRA–Macmillan/McGraw-Hill.

Fessenden, R. (1998). Market launch. In National Academy of Sciences (Eds.), *High school mathematics at work: Essays and examples for the education of all students* (pp. 18–23). Washington, DC: National Research Council. (ERIC Document Reproduction Service No. ED 425934.)

Fischer, T. A., Kitz, W. R., & Tarver, S. (1996). Effects of videodisc instruction on geometry achievement in a mainstreamed Native American high school class. *Effective School Practices, 15*(4), 39–49.

Forness, S. R., Kavale, K. A., Blum, I. M., & Lloyd, J. W. (1997). Mega-analysis of meta-analysis. *Teaching Exceptional Children, 29*(6), 4–9.

Glang, A., Singer, G., Cooley, E., & Tish, N. (1991). Using Direct Instruction with brain injured students. *Direct Instruction News, 11*(1), 23–28.

Good, T. L., & Gouws, D. A. (1979). The Missouri mathematics effectiveness project: An experimental study in fourth-grade classrooms. *Journal of Educational Psychology, 71,* 143–155.

Hofmeister, A. M., Engelmann, S., & Carnine, D. (1989). Developing and validating science education videodics. *Journal of Research in Science Teaching, 26,* 665–677.

Isaacson, S. (1987). Effective instruction in written language. *Focus on Exceptional Children, 19*(6), 1–12.

Kameenui, E. J., Carnine, D. W., & Dixon, R. C. (2002). Introduction. In E. J. Kameenui, D. W. Carnine, R. C. Dixon, D. C. Simmons, & M. D. Coyne (Eds.), *Effective teaching strategies that accommodate diverse learners* (pp. 1–21). Upper Saddle River, NJ: Prentice-Hall.

Kelly, B., Carnine, D., Gersten, R., & Grossen, B. (1986). The effectiveness of videodisc instruction in teaching fractions to learning-disabled and remedial high school students. *Journal of Special Education Technology, 8*(2), 5–17.

Kelly, B., Gersten, R., & Carnine, D. (1990). Student error patterns as a function of curriculum design: Teaching fractions to remedial high school students and high school students with learning disabilities. *Journal of Learning Disabilities, 23*(1), 23–29.

Kitz, W. R., & Thorpe, H. (1995). Comparing the effectiveness of videodisc and traditional algebra instruction with college-aged students with learning disabilities. *Remedial and Special Education, 16,* 295–306.

Klein, D. (2001). *A brief history of American K–12 mathematics education in the 20th century*. Retrieved March 28, 2002 from http://www.csun.edu/-vcmth00m/AHistory.html

Lewis, A. B., & Mayer, R. E. (1987). Students' miscomprehension of relational statements in arithmetic word problems. *Journal of Educational Psychology, 79,* 363–371.

Loveless, T., & DiPerna, P. (2000). *The Brown Center Report on American Education: 2000. How well are American students learning?* The Brookings Institute. Retrieved on March 28, 2002 from http://brookings.org/dybdocroot/gs/brown/bc_report/2000/achieve1.htm

Martin, R. (1973, June 4). New math just doesn't add up. *Chicago Daily News*, p. 5.

Masini, B., & Taylor, J. (2000). New evidence links curricula and instruction to mathematics achievement. (*Policy Issues, 7,* 2–8). Oak Brook, IL: North Central Regional Educational Lab. (ERIC Document Reproduction Service No. ED 455 110.)

Mathematics Equals Opportunity. (1997). *White paper prepared for U.S. Secretary of Education Richard W. Riley*. Retrieved March 28, 2002 from http://www.ed.gov/pubs/math/index.html#toc

McKenzie, M. A., Marchand-Martella, N., Tso, M., & Martella, R. C. (in press). Teaching basic math skills to preschoolers using *Connecting Math Concepts* Level K. *Journal of Direct Instruction*.

Miller, Z. (1998). Foreword: Mathematics for a modern age. In National Academy of Sciences (Eds.), *High school mathematics at work: Essays and examples for the education of all students* (p. 9). Washington, DC: National Research Council. (ERIC Document Reproduction Service No. ED 425934.)

Moore, L. J., & Carnine, D. (1989). Evaluating curriculum design in the context of active teaching. *Remedial and Special Education, 10*(4), 28–43.

Murnane, F., & Levy, F. (1996). *Teaching the new basic skills.* New York: Free Press.

National Council of Teachers of Mathematics. (1989). *Curriculum and evaluation standards for school mathematics.* Reston, VA: Author.

Parsons, J. L., Marchand-Martella, N., Waldron-Soler, K., Martella, R., & Lignugaris/Kraft, B. (in press). Effects of a high school-based peer-delivered Corrective Mathematics program. *Journal of Direct Instruction.*

Porter, A. (1989). A curriculum out of balance: The case of elementary school mathematics. *Educational Researcher, 18*(5), 9–15.

Przychodzin-Havis, A., Marchand-Martella, N., Martella, R. C., & Azim, D. (in press). Direct Instruction mathematics programs: An overview and research summary. *Journal of Direct Instruction.*

Rappaport, D. (1975). The new math and its aftermath. *School Science and Mathematics, 76*(7), 338–344.

Resnick, L. B., & Omanson, S. F. (1987). Learning to understand arithmetic. In R. Glaer (Ed.), *Advances in instructional psychology* (pp. 41–95). Hillsdale, NJ: Erlbaum.

Schmidt, W., Houang, R., & Cogan, L. (2002). A coherent curriculum: The case of mathematics. *American Educator, 26*(2), 10–26.

Schmidt, W., McKnight, C. C., Houang, R., HsingChi, W., Wiley, D. E., Cogan, L. S., & Wolfe, R. G. (2001). *Why schools matter.* New York: Jossey-Bass.

Snider, V., & Crawford, D. (1996). Action research: Implementing Connecting Math Concepts. *Effective School Practices, 15*(2), 17–26.

Sommers, J. (1991). Direct Instruction programs produce significant gains with at-risk middle school students. *ADI News, 11*(1), 7–14.

Stein, M., Silbert, J., & Carnine, D. (1997). *Designing effective mathematics instruction.* Columbus, OH: Merrill.

Tarver, S., & Jung, J. (1995). A comparison of mathematics achievement and mathematics attitudes of first and second graders instructed with either a discovery-learning mathematics curriculum or a direct instruction curriculum. *Effective School Practices, 14*(1), 49–57.

Trafton, P. R. (1984). Toward more effective, efficient instruction in mathematics. *Elementary School Journal, 84,* 514–530.

U.S. Department of Education. (2001a). *Highlights from the Third International Mathematics and Science Study-Repeat* (TIMSS-R). Office of Educational Research and Improvement (NCES 2001-027). Washington, DC: U.S. Government Printing Office.

U.S. Department of Education. (2001b). *Mathematics highlights 2000.* Office of Educational Research and Improvement (NCES 2001-518). Washington, DC: U.S. Government Printing Office.

Valverde, G. A., & Schmidt, W. H. (1997, Winter). Refocusing U.S. math and science education. *Issues in Science and Technology.* Retrieved May 20, 2002 from http://www.nap.edu/iddues/14.2/schmid.htm

Vreeland, M., Vail, J., Bradley, L., Buetow, C., Cipriano, K., Green, C., Henshaw, P., & Huth, E. (1994). Accelerating cognitive growth: The Edison School Math Project. *Effective School Practices, 13*(2), 64–69.

Wellington, J. (1994). Evaluating a mathematics program for adoption: Connecting Math Concepts. *Effective School Practices, 13*(2), 70–75.

Willingham, D.T. (2002) Allocating student study time. *American Educator, 26*(2), 37–38, 47.

Wu, H. (1999). Basic skills versus conceptual understanding. *American Educator, 23*(3), 14–19, 50–52.

Young, M., Baker, J., & Martin, M. (1990). Teaching basic number skills to students with a moderate intellectual disability. *Education and Training in Mental Retardation, 25,* 83–93.

Zawojewski, J. (1983). Initial decimal concepts: Are they really so easy? *Arithmetic Teacher, 30*(7), 52–56.

CHAPTER EIGHT

CONTENT AREAS

MARK HARNISS
University of Washington

KEITH HOLLENBECK
University of Oregon

SHIRLEY DICKSON
Education Commission of the States

OBJECTIVES

After studying this chapter you should be able to:

1. characterize student performance in content areas as measured by national assessments;
2. describe how Direct Instruction content area curricula are similar and different from skill-based Direct Instruction programs;
3. list the Direct Instruction programs that have been developed in the content areas;
4. explain why content area instruction is important;
5. list and define the six principles of effective curricular design;
6. identify some of the "big ideas" in the science and history programs;
7. describe how Direct Instruction programs in the content areas guide teachers instructionally;
8. describe techniques for assessing student performance in Direct Instruction content area programs;
9. describe the generic procedure for integrating reading and writing in Direct Instruction content area programs;
10. explain the research conducted on Direct Instruction content area programs.

The content areas (e.g., science, history, geography, biology, physics) comprise a diverse and multifaceted collection of factual, conceptual, and rule-based knowledge. Although they have been typically defined within the context of disciplines, rich interdisciplinary relationships exist that add not only to the complexity but also to the utility and value of this knowledge. In addition, content areas are noted for their breadth (i.e., the amount of information "owned" by a discipline) and depth (i.e., the level of detail and accuracy needed to understand content information adequately). The complexity, breadth, and depth of content areas pose a significant challenge to teachers and students. Given the time constraints of the school day and school year, teachers must decide between covering a large number of topics, thereby devoting little time to helping their students develop deep knowledge or teaching fewer topics in depth.

Content area curricula have been critiqued as heavily textbook-oriented with little emphasis on big ideas or important themes. Curricula tend to focus on disconnected facts rather than principles or rule relationships. (Haas, 1991; Nolet, Tindal, & Blake 1993; Siler, 1989–1990). As McKeown and Beck (1994) have noted, textbooks have come under attack because they are "not oriented toward developing a coherent chain of events" and they "lack the coherence needed to enable students to draw connections between events and ideas" (p. 5).

The result is that students perform poorly in the content areas. National assessments seem to support the notion that many students struggle in the content areas. For example, on the National Assessment of Education Progress (NAEP) as reported in *What Do Our 17-Year-Olds Know?* (Ravitch & Finn, 1987), many students failed to answer correctly even simple multiple-choice questions about history. Students correctly answered only 54 percent of the questions on average. Three-fourths of the students did not know when Lincoln was president and one-third of the students did not know that "life, liberty, and the pursuit of happiness" came from the Declaration of Independence. In 1994, the test was revised and administered to fourth-grade, eighth-grade, and twelfth-grade students. Only 17 percent of the fourth graders, 14 percent of the eighth graders, and 11 percent of the twelfth graders achieved the "proficient level" (defined as solid academic performance). In addition, only 41 percent of the eighth graders associated the dropping of the atomic bomb with World War II, 45 percent of the fourth graders identified the purpose of the Bill of Rights, and 12 percent of the twelfth graders explained the effects of economic and technological changes on farming (National Center for Educational Statistics, 1996).

In the 2001 NAEP, a majority of all students again proved nonproficient in history (Manzo, 2002). Manzo reported that for the 11,300 eighth graders tested, 48 percent scored at the basic level and 17 percent attained a proficient or advanced rating. For the 11,300 twelfth graders tested, 11 percent were proficient or advanced, but 57 percent were not even rated at the basic level.

Concerns about student performance in content areas are not limited to history. Since the 1960s, students in the United States have taken part in five international assessments of mathematics and science achievement utilizing the International Mathematics and Science Study (Phelps, 2001). In the early 1980s, students were assessed using the Second International Mathematics and Science Study (SIMSS). During the 1994–1995 school year, U.S. students again participated in the testing. This time the assessment was the Third International Mathematics and Science Study (TIMSS). The TIMSS was readministered during the

1999–2000 school year and was called the TIMSS-R (for repeat) (Holden, 2000). Holden stated that "compared to the 16 other countries that were in the TIMSS both years, the U.S. cohort is the only country to show a significant drop in both science and math achievement. Whereas in 1995 U.S. fourth graders tied with Austria for third place in science and were above average in math, they had slipped to below average in both subjects by the time they reached eighth grade" (p. 1866). "The unfortunate trend in . . . student performance continued downward through the upper secondary years [twelfth grade]" (Phelps, 2001, p. 394).

Despite the difficulties of teaching and learning in the content areas, there are methods that can be used to increase the efficacy of content area instruction. In this chapter we describe how designers of Direct Instruction programs have addressed the complexity of teaching and learning in the content areas. Specifically, we begin with a rationale for why the content areas are important. Next, we provide a rationale for why content area instruction and high-quality curriculum are important in improving student performance in the content areas. We further provide an overview of Direct Instruction programs in the content areas (specifically, history/social studies and science). We focus on a six-point analysis of an effective curriculum and describe how the Direct Instruction programs meet these six criteria. We also describe assessment and troubleshooting techniques used in these programs. Finally, we address teaching techniques and conclude with a description of extensions and adaptations for these programs.

IMPORTANCE OF CONTENT AREAS

State and national standards draw attention to the importance of the content areas. Increasingly states are defining what students should know and be able to do within each of the content areas. Additionally, the importance of content areas has been described in many reports by standards-setting organizations. For example, the National Center for History in the Schools (1995) states

> knowledge of history is the precondition of political intelligence. Without history, a society shares no common memory of where it has been, of what its core values are, or of what decisions of the past account for present circumstances. Without history, one cannot undertake any sensible inquiry into the political, social, or moral issues in society. And without historical knowledge and the inquiry it supports, one cannot move to the informed, discriminating citizenship essential to effective participation in the democratic processes of governance and the fulfillment for all our citizens of the nation's democratic ideals (p. 1).

In the National Science Education Standards (National Academy of Sciences, 1995), educators argue that science is important because

1. understanding science offers personal fulfillment and excitement;
2. citizens need scientific information and scientific ways of thinking in order to make informed decisions;
3. business and industry need entry-level workers with the ability to learn, reason, think creatively, make decisions, and solve problems;

4. strong science and mathematics education can help our nation and individual citizens improve and maintain their economic productivity (p. 2).

Rutherford and Ahlgren (1991) provide a more dramatic statement in their document *Science for All Americans (Online):*

> What the future holds in store for individual human beings, the nation, and the world depends largely on the wisdom with which humans use science and technology. And that, in turn, depends on the character, distribution, and effectiveness of the education that people receive (p. 1).

States have increasingly participated in this move toward standards in the content areas. For example, in Oregon, students are expected to (1) "use understanding of the chronological flow of human history to identify patterns, ideas and events over time," and (2) "identify and analyze causal relationships among events, describing how different perspectives affect interpretation of those events" (Oregon Department of Education, 1995, p. 8). In Washington, science standards are being developed that require students to (1) understand and use scientific concepts and principles, (2) know and apply the skills and processes of science and technology, and (3) understand the nature and contexts of science and technology (Office of the State Superintendent of Public Instruction, 2002).

The development of high standards, and its associated high-stakes testing, has advocates both within and outside of the field of education (Donlevy, 2000). The goal of these high standards is to provide students with the opportunity for future productive employment. The basic skills and general knowledge, as mandated in these high standards, provide students with those skills necessary to access higher education, postsecondary training, and/or the job market (Donlevy, 2000; Fox, Wandry, Pruitt, & Anderson, 1998). However, as noted earlier, these standards presume a high level of secondary curricular material that simply does not exist (Donlevy, 2000).

IMPORTANCE OF CONTENT AREA INSTRUCTION

Even as states develop more rigorous standards in social studies and science, there remains a disconnect between what teachers are expected to teach and how students perform on national assessments. If we are to see improvements in student performance in the content areas, we must work in two directions simultaneously. First, teachers must be better prepared to teach in the content areas. Second, curriculum must be developed to support teachers and students in the learning process.

Teacher Preparation

A school's capacity to improve the aforementioned problems in achievement is related to the knowledge base of its teachers (Youngs, 2001). Teachers' skills in teaching specific content are influenced by their pedagogical content knowledge (Llinares, 2000). Wayne (2002) declared, "student learning is a function of teacher quality" (p. 2). For example, Borko et al. (2000) suggested that teachers with high degrees of subject-matter knowledge emphasized conceptual, problem-solving, and inquiry aspects, while less knowledgeable teachers emphasized facts. Thus, not all students receive the same opportunity to learn and use subject matter in sophisticated ways.

A study by Stevens and Wenner (1996) showed that preservice teachers generally have a poor science and mathematics knowledge base. This trend was especially true for elementary teachers who had "generally low level conceptual and factual knowledge as well as inadequate skills" (p. 2) in both science and math. Shealy, Arvold, Zheng, and Cooney (1994) and Steele (1994) demonstrated a consistent relationship between math and science preparation for preservice teachers and student learning. Unfortunately, preservice teachers may not recognize their deficits. Stevens and Wenner found a negative relationship existed between personal teaching beliefs in ability to teach and actual knowledge base for entry-level teachers.

Concept-Based Instruction

The weak knowledge base of some teachers is problematic as it leaves teachers poorly prepared to teach the students with the greatest academic needs, particularly the students who read significantly below grade level. Far too many students come to middle and secondary content area classes reading significantly below grade level, which results in teachers focusing on decoding text at the expense of comprehending the material (Jitendra et al., 2001). When students move from the early elementary school to later grades, a fundamental curriculum shift occurs. No longer are they expected to "learn to read" but rather to "read to learn" (see Chapter 4 for further details on reading). Carnine, Silbert, and Kameenui (1990) state that in content area reading, "The reader is expected to extract, integrate, and retain significant main ideas and details presented in the material" (p. 339). Students are expected to have a solid skill base (e.g., reading, writing, and arithmetic), and the focus of instruction is on content area material (e.g., science, history, geography, and civics). As textbooks are commonly dominant features of content classes, these struggling readers face serious difficulties as they attempt to acquire information from the material. While reading instruction and interventions may be necessary to overcome underlying reading difficulties, students must still understand the discipline-specific content.

Research has shown that many students at-risk in general education classrooms have difficulty learning important information like concepts and principles within a text (Bryant, Ugel, Thompson, & Hamff, 1999; Garner, Gillingham, & White, 1989; Tindal, Nolet, & Blake, 1992). Often, students are distracted by seductive details that, although interesting, are not instructionally important. To add to this difficulty, researchers have noted that the majority of information found in textbooks is purely factual and is not structured to show how these discrete facts can be linked together to form complex knowledge (Jitendra et al., 2001). This shortcoming among textbooks leaves the responsibility for drawing these connections either to the teachers or the students themselves.

If most students cannot link facts to concepts, then classroom teachers must take responsibility for this task within the curriculum. If teachers also possess a weak knowledge structure, then the curriculum must support this endeavor (Erickson, 1998; Roid & Haladyna, 1982).

PRINCIPLES OF CURRICULAR DESIGN

Six principles of curricular design articulated by the National Center to Improve the Tools of Educators (NCITE) (Kameenui & Carnine, 1998) are useful in describing the components of the Direct Instruction content area curricula. They are: (1) big ideas, (2) strategic integration, (3) conspicuous strategies, (4) mediated scaffolding, (5) primed background knowledge, and (6) judicious review. These principles have been described in greater depth elsewhere (Carnine, 1991; Carnine, Caros, Crawford, Hollenbeck, & Harniss, 1996; Carnine, Crawford, Harniss, Hollenbeck, & Miller, 1998; Carnine, Miller, Bean, & Zigmond, 1994; Harniss, Hollenbeck, Crawford, & Carnine, 1994).

Big Ideas

Important principles that enable learners to organize and interrelate information are referred to as big ideas (as noted in Chapter 5). Big ideas are essential to help learners understand connections among facts and concepts they learn in history or science. As Rosenshine (1995) notes, "without [knowledge structures], new knowledge tends to be fragmented and not readily available for recall and use" (p. 263). In fact, Rosenshine argues that a primary goal of education is to ensure that students develop knowledge structures in which "the parts are well-organized, the pieces well connected, and the bonds between the connections are strong" (p. 267).

The advantage of using big ideas is that they create a manageable framework for all students to learn. Big ideas can help average and above average students learn content and at the same time engage those students who have been previously excluded from this type of thinking. By focusing on big ideas students can concentrate on critical content and organize it in a logical way.

Strategic Integration

Strategic integration refers to the integration of knowledge both within and outside of a content area. For students to integrate content area knowledge meaningfully within their lives, the curriculum must begin that process of integration for them. First, the curriculum must offer students an opportunity to integrate information from multiple contexts successfully. This integration is facilitated by the use of big ideas, which can be integrated with each other. Second, big ideas learned in one context should be explicitly applied in multiple contexts. This strategic integration of content within the curriculum can help students learn when to use specific knowledge.

Conspicuous Strategies

A strategy is a general framework used to solve problems and analyze content. Strategies become conspicuous when we make them more obvious by teaching them directly to students. In the content areas, conspicuous strategies are often simply the explicit application of big ideas to specific content. The purpose of explicitness is to ensure that all students learn strategies that lead to success in solving problems and understanding content.

Scaffolding

Scaffolding is a teaching procedure where teachers initially provide high levels of structure and support to naive students but over time reduce the structure and support they provide until students are able to perform tasks independently. Content area instruction should provide students with temporary support until their learning becomes self-regulated.

Primed Background Knowledge

Many studies have shown that simplifying, adding, or clarifying background information in textbook passages dramatically improves student comprehension and recall (Beck, Mc-Keown, & Gromoll, 1989; Beck, McKeown, Sinatra, & Loxterman, 1991; Britton, Van Dusen, Gulgoz, & Glynn, 1989; Duffy et al., 1989; Graves et al., 1991; McKeown & Beck, 1990; McKeown, Beck, Sinatra, & Loxterman, 1992). The procedure of simplifying, adding, or clarifying information for students is referred to as "priming" background knowledge.

Judicious Review

Many curricula provide limited opportunities for review, frequently at the end of each chapter or unit. Yet, review is known to be important for students' retention of information. Teachers should plan review that is sufficient (i.e., adequate to learn the content information initially), distributed (i.e., integrated over time so students do not learn something only to forget it), cumulative (i.e., new information builds on previously learned information), and varied (i.e., information learned in one context is eventually applied in another context) (Kameenui & Carnine, 1998).

OVERVIEW OF DIRECT INSTRUCTION CONTENT AREA PROGRAMS

Direct Instruction content area programs are designed to address many of the problems in typical content area classrooms. They address these problems by continuing the careful design of other Direct Instruction programs while addressing the more complex issues of content, older students, and teachers who may lack deep content knowledge.

Direct Instruction program design in the content areas mirrors the design of programs in skill areas such as reading and mathematics in many ways. One way that content area programs mirror skill programs is by carefully organizing and linking information (i.e., they focus on the big ideas within each content area). Additionally, Direct Instruction content area programs support and guide students in their initial use of this information. Finally, content area programs provide students with appropriate review and practice.

In addition to mirroring program design, Direct Instruction content areas programs also mimic earlier skill-based programs in their presentation delivery. They provide frequent opportunities to respond, include checks for understanding, and often maintain fast pacing.

Despite these similarities, Direct Instruction content area programs differ in several other ways from skill area programs. Specifically, content area programs focus on older grades where some presentation strategies used in early skill programs (e.g., group, oral responding) are less appropriate. In addition, prescriptive teaching formats are either embedded in the curriculum (i.e., within the *Earth Sciences videodisc*) or nonexistent (e.g., within *Understanding United States History*). In the science discs, the professional actors who are shown on the videodisc present the formats. In the history text, the expectation is that the text will be used in general education classrooms and teachers will present content in more traditional ways. Despite this, the curricula do include suggestions for teaching and have embedded instructional activities. Finally, programs are designed primarily for large-group instruction in general education classrooms rather than small-group instruction in special education resource room settings, for example.

Direct Instruction programs have been designed in history/social studies and in science.

1. History/Social Studies
   a. *Understanding U.S. History: Volume I*
   b. *Understanding U.S. History: Volume II*
2. Science
   a. *Understanding Chemistry and Energy*
   b. *Earth Sciences*
   c. *Earth Science [Videodisc]*
   d. *Chemistry and Energy [Videodisc]*
   e. *Understanding Life Sciences*

History/Social Studies

Understanding U.S. History: Volume I covers Early Native American culture to American expansion and international politics of 1914. The authors explain that United States history is very complicated, with many important people and events. "This book was written to enable you [the reader] to understand the ideas that link these important events. These ideas help explain what happened in the past, what is happening now, and what may happen in the future" (Carnine, Crawford, Harniss, Hollenbeck, & Steely, 1999, p. i). The text was developed at the University of Oregon. An instructional design team composed of four individuals designed, wrote, field-tested, and modified instructional chapters in the text. Using an instructional product verification procedure (Thiagarajan, 1978), chapters were developed and then subjected to expert and learner verification. A history expert evaluated the accuracy of the information included in the text. In addition, the materials were field-tested with age-appropriate learners in multiple settings. Based on feedback from these sources, the instructional design of the text was modified.

Science

The *Earth Science [Videodisc]* program and the *Chemistry and Energy [Videodisc]* program were designed and field-tested for use in junior high. The *Earth Science* and *Chemistry and Energy* videodiscs cover content typically taught in junior high physical science courses as well as earth science courses. For example, in physical science the concepts of mass, density, and pressure are introduced, taught, and applied in a wide range of meaningful contents. The *Chemistry and Energy* videodisc includes extensive examples of the application of physical science to biology.

The thirteen conceptual areas of the *Understanding Chemistry and Energy* program are: (1) atomic structure, protons, neutrons, and electrons; (2) molecules; (3) energy forms and conversions; (4) chemical energy; (5) covalent, ionic, and hydrogen bonding; (6) ions; (7) organic compounds; (8) equilibrium; (9) chemical reactions; (10) energy of activation and catalysts; (11) water; (12) diffusion; and (13) chemical formulas and equations.

The eight conceptual areas from *Earth Sciences* are: (1) temperature and matter; (2) the earth landmarks, movement (seasons/day/night), internal structure, landforms, and earthquake waves; (3) density (mass and volume); (4) forces (dynamic pressure, gravity, weathering, and static pressure); (5) convection (convection cells in the atmosphere, in the mantle, and in the ocean); (6) cycles (water and rock); (7) currents (ocean surfaces, sea breezes, and tides); and (8) weather (relative humidity, air masses, and high and low pressure areas).

CONTENT ANALYSIS AND FORMAT FEATURES

The six principles of curricular design are described for the history and science programs. In addition, format examples are provided to illustrate important content features.

Big Ideas from History

Understanding U.S. History was designed as a causal approach to history. It describes problems people have encountered in the past, how they solved those problems, and the effect of their solutions. The causal structure of the text is enhanced by explicitly teaching a problem-solution-effect (PSE) text structure at the beginning of the text and then using the PSE language throughout the text. PSE can be considered one of the main big ideas in the history text because PSE is reiterated in textual passages, graphics, and in many different questioning situations. In addition to PSE, other big ideas are used to assist student comprehension and retention including the Stages of Cooperation and the Four Factors of Group Success.

Problem, Solution, Effect.   PSE is introduced to students in the first chapter of the history text and is used consistently throughout. Students are taught that in history they will learn about problems people have faced over time, the ways they solved their problems, and the effect of those solutions. Specifically, they are taught that there are two kinds of problems (i.e., economic and people's rights), five kinds of solutions (i.e., accommodating, dominating, moving, inventing, and tolerating), and at least three possible effects of these solutions (i.e., end of problem, continuing problem, or new problem). The five solution types can be remembered using the mnemonic ADMIT, where the first letter of each solution forms a letter in the mnemonic (i.e., Accommodate, Dominate, Move, Invent, and Tolerate). Figure 8.1 graphically displays the Problem-Solution-Effect sequence.

Students learn this structure in the first chapter within the context of generic, nonhistory-related problems. They also learn to apply the structure in more complex ways. For example, they learn that one group's solution to a problem may cause a problem for another group, thus showing that there can be multiple perspectives on the same event.

After the Revolutionary War, the new United States government faced many problems, the greatest being economic. The federal government lacked taxing power to raise money to repay Revolutionary War debts and to fight off continuing British attacks. In addition, Britain was limiting United States trade. There were also trade barriers between states, and inflation was rampant. Farmers, the main economic force within the new United States, were going bankrupt. Those economic problems and a new federal tax caused Shays' Rebellion, a rebellion against a new central government tax.

Because the new United States government was about to collapse economically, the colonial leaders were forced to solve the problem by inventing a new form of government with a new constitution. This new government had legally binding cooperation and created a stronger federal government. The effect of this new legally binding cooperation was the U.S. Constitution and our current system of state and federal powers.

Stages of Cooperation.   When students learn about the Stages of Cooperation, they discover that when groups or individuals agree to cooperate they often move through a set

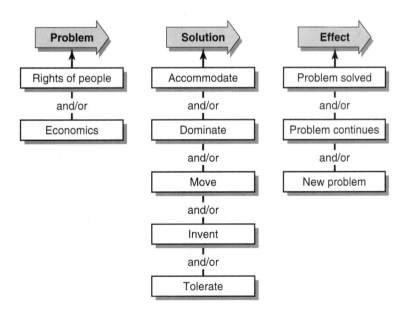

FIGURE 8.1   Problem-Solution-Effect. Adapted from *Understanding U.S. History: Volume I—Through 1914.*

Stages of Cooperation

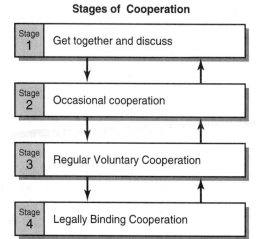

FIGURE 8.2   Stages of Cooperation. Adapted from *Understanding U.S. History: Volume I–Through 1914.*

of four stages. The first stage of cooperation involves getting together and discussing or complaining about a problem. The second stage is occasional cooperation. The key here is that cooperation is successful and thereby encourages continued cooperation. The third stage is regular voluntary cooperation. The fourth stage is legally binding cooperation. Figure 8.2 shows the Stages of Cooperation.

An example of the first stage was the Albany Plan of Union. During the French and Indian War, Ben Franklin and other colonial leaders met in Albany, New York, to do something about the problem of Britain losing the war against the French. Franklin wanted the delegates to develop some sort of collaborative, centralized government structure. Franklin's plan failed because it was a Stage 4 solution to a Stage 1 situation. The colonial leaders got together and discussed their problem but did not move toward the next stage, occasional cooperation.

The second stage is occasional cooperation. Students need to know that when cooperation is successful it often encourages continued cooperation. Individuals and groups move up or down through the stages of cooperation based on the level of success they experience at each level. An example of this stage was the Stamp Act Congress. Before the Revolutionary War, the Stamp Tax was passed by Britain to raise revenue. Through organized boycotts and other acts, the colonists managed to get it repealed. The colonists across colonial regions were not required to cooperate; they did so voluntarily and continued to cooperate until this economic problem was solved.

The third stage is regular voluntary cooperation. Because Stage 2 was successful prior to the Revolutionary War, the colonists progressed to Stage 3 during the Revolutionary War to solve the problem of how to manage the war. The Continental Congress and the Articles of Confederation, which gave almost no power to the central government and relied on voluntary cooperation instead, illustrate this stage.

The fourth stage is legally binding cooperation. After winning the Revolutionary War, this stage was *not* desirable to the colonial leaders. Because the United States had won the war with a Stage 3 form of government, the Second Continental Congress, there was no need to progress toward legally binding cooperation in government. The fact that no one wanted a strong federal government is reflected in the Articles of Confederation. The Articles were not a failed attempt at a government or a "stop-gap" government between the Revolutionary War and the Constitution; rather, America's leaders were still in Stage 3 of cooperation when they wrote the Articles of Confederation, with no need to progress to Stage 4.

As a general rule, people or groups do not want to relinquish their power and independence until it is necessary. It was only after severe economic problems (interstate taxation strangling trade, war debts, the cost of a peace-time navy, and so forth) that the founding fathers progressed toward a stronger form of government.

Four Factors of Group Success.   In the history text, students are taught that there are four factors that affect the outcome of a problem for a group or a conflict between groups. The four factors are (1) capability (what a group of people know how to do and what they are able to do); (2) resources (how many people or things a group has available to use in reaching its goals); (3) leadership (the skillfulness or expertise of a group's leaders); and (4) motivation (a group's desire to succeed). Figure 8.3 shows the four factors of group success. Students learn that evaluating the degree to which a group or groups possess these factors enables students to predict the outcome of an event.

The four factors of group success help explain the relative strengths and weaknesses of conflicting groups, which group may prevail, and what action must be taken so that a group can be strong enough to prevail. Using the example of the ratification of the United States Constitution, the four factors of group success help explain why the Federalists were successful against the anti-Federalists in getting a strong form of government. The Federalists were part of a rich aristocracy who did not want the new Constitution with a strong central government until severe economic problems threatened their fortunes and the future of the new country. With these fears, the Federalists had great *motivation* to solve the economic problems. Both groups had strong *leaders,* but because the Federalists were

Four Factors of Group Success

FIGURE 8.3   Four Factors of Group Success. Adapted from *Understanding U.S. History: Volume I–Through 1914.*

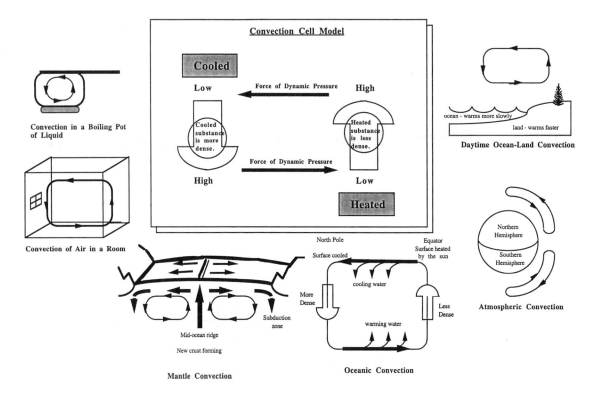

FIGURE 8.4 How Convection Applies to Various Sciences

wealthier than the anti-Federalists, they had the advantage in *resources*. Finally, because the Federalists controlled or owned most of the newspapers and the print shops, they were able to get their message out. They had the advantage in *capability*. Using the four factors, students can predict that the Federalists should win and the Constitution should be adopted.

Big Ideas from Science

Science content areas are complex and multifaceted. Direct Instruction content area programs provide students with a more manageable set of information organized by content-specific big ideas. In the following section, we describe one big idea from each program.

Earth Science Videodisc.   Too often earth science is taught as a series of segregated topics such as weather science, oceanography, and geology. In the videodisc program these topics are linked with the big idea of convection. Convection has the broad explanatory value that can provide a basis for causal discourse and an opportunity to demonstrate the interconnections among weather science, oceanography, and geology. The concept of the convection cell explains such seemingly disparate events such as sea breezes and continental drift. Figure 8.4 shows how the big idea of convection applies to the various sciences.

Understanding Life Sciences.   The *Understanding Life Sciences* book utilizes four unifying principles to cover big ideas that convey four key concepts around force. Figure 8.5 lists the big ideas for the first few chapters of the book.

The big ideas for the first five chapters are: (1) motion; (2) forces; (3) gravity, friction, and pressure; (4) energy, work, and power; and (5) mechanics. In Chapter 2 the big idea of forces is emphasized. Chapter 2 characterizes forces as those that change the motion of objects in predictable ways.

Strategic Integration in History

In the *Understanding U.S. History* textbook, strategic integration was accomplished by looking at how big ideas (i.e., PSE, stages of cooperation, and factors of group success) fit together to make sense out of a specific historical event (e.g., the ratification of the United States Constitution). Furthermore, big ideas learned in one context should be explicitly applied in multiple contexts. For example, the four factors of group success can be used in understanding many events including the establishment of the thirteen Colonies.

Big ideas can also be integrated over time by having students answer questions that integrate what they know from history with what they know about current events. For instance, the four factors are applicable to current events surrounding the unification of Europe. The stages of cooperation allow us to analyze why the United Nations succeeded and the League of Nations failed.

Strategic Integration in Science

In the *Understanding Life Sciences* text, students are taught the big idea of force and the definition that force changes motion in predictable ways. Using Chapter 2—Forces, students are first taught Section 2.1 that says forces change motion. Students are then taught two rules: (1) a force is a push or a pull, and (2) according to Newton's first law of inertia, objects remain at rest and objects remain in motion unless acted on by an unbalanced force. To reinforce this learning, students then complete lab exercises that explore motion. In these labs, students explore motion by experimenting with changing the motion of different objects.

Conspicuous Strategies in History

Strategies are made conspicuous (or explicit) in the history text by directly showing students how the big idea applies to a certain time in the past. As students learn about different big ideas, they also learn to apply them to content. For example, when students learn about the four factors of group success for the first time in the section on European exploration, they are initially quizzed on the definitions of the factors and asked to apply the factors to content. After learning the definition of resources, an interspersed question asks students to answer, "What are resources?" The next paragraph tells students something about the Jamestown colony and its resources followed by an interspersed question asking, "What advantage in resources did the Jamestown colony have over earlier attempts at colonization?" After

Physical Science
Unifying Principles

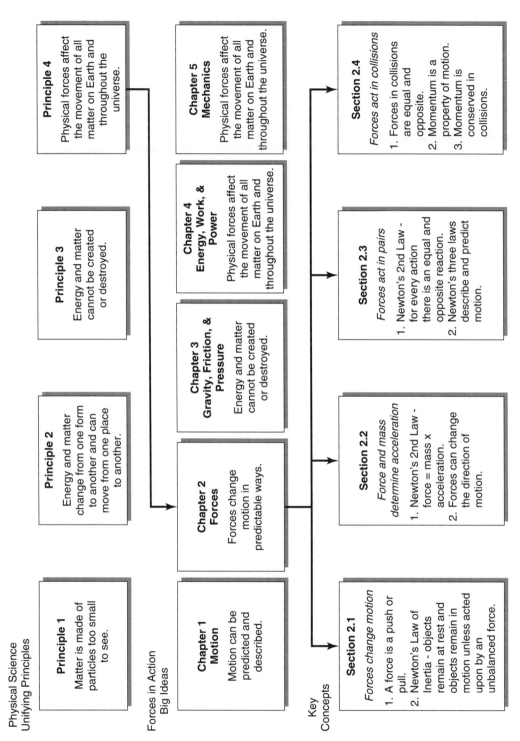

Principle 1

Matter is made of particles too small to see.

Principle 2

Energy and matter change from one form to another and can move from one place to another.

Principle 3

Energy and matter cannot be created or destroyed.

Principle 4

Physical forces affect the movement of all matter on Earth and throughout the universe.

Forces in Action
Big Ideas

**Chapter 1
Motion**

Motion can be predicted and described.

**Chapter 2
Forces**

Forces change motion in predictable ways.

**Chapter 3
Gravity, Friction, & Pressure**

Energy and matter cannot be created or destroyed.

**Chapter 4
Energy, Work, & Power**

Physical forces affect the movement of all matter on Earth and throughout the universe.

**Chapter 5
Mechanics**

Physical forces affect the movement of all matter on Earth and throughout the universe.

Key
Concepts

Section 2.1

Forces change motion

1. A force is a push or pull.
2. Newton's Law of Inertia - objects remain at rest and objects remain in motion unless acted upon by an unbalanced force.

Section 2.2

Force and mass determine acceleration

1. Newton's 2nd Law - force = mass x acceleration.
2. Forces can change the direction of motion.

Section 2.3

Forces act in pairs

1. Newton's 2nd Law - for every action there is an equal and opposite reaction.
2. Newton's three laws describe and predict motion.

Section 2.4

Forces act in collisions

1. Forces in collisions are equal and opposite.
2. Momentum is a property of motion.
3. Momentum is conserved in collisions.

FIGURE 8.5   Four Unifying Principles to Cover Big Ideas That Convey Four Key Concepts Around Force

students learn about all four factors, they encounter a test question that asks them to, "Use the four factors of group success to explain why the Jamestown colony survived. Begin with a general statement." These big ideas can then be used as organizational structures for writing essay answers to important history questions. For example, after students have read and practiced using the four factors of group success to interpret the Revolutionary War, they would be ready to explain how the four factors of group success in the Revolutionary War changed after the French became allies with the thirteen Colonies. By using the strategy of applying the big idea to the content, they should be able to answer this fairly complex question.

Students receive multiple opportunities across the curriculum to use the big ideas and apply them to new information. PSE sequences are used throughout the text. Every chapter highlights important PSE sequences. The four factors of group success are also used across the text to provide students with a way to understand the outcomes of important conflicts such as the French-Indian War and the many battles in the Revolutionary and Civil Wars. Once students learn how to apply PSE or the four factors to content, they have a strategy for organizing and understanding information.

Conspicuous Strategies in Science

In the *Understanding Life Sciences* text, students are expected to apply their understanding of the big idea of force. Students are asked to look at a photograph in the text that shows five students pushing on the back of a school bus. First, students are told to look at the photo and describe the scene. Then students are asked a series of five questions to guide their thinking. The questions are: (1) Why is the bus so hard to move? (2) Why might adding more students make the job easier? (3) How do you know the bus will move forward and not sideways? (4) What do you think of when you hear the word *force*? and (5) What role does force play in the picture?

Scaffolding in History

In the history text, scaffolding is accomplished through questioning strategies and graphic organizers. The interspersed questions, discussion questions, and test questions described earlier support students in learning and remembering the most important information in the text. For example, in the section on European exploration, students answer interspersed questions that prompt important factual information such as, "Who controlled the land routes between Europe and Asia?" and "What did Columbus not know about the earth when he sailed west to find Asia?" The use of interspersed questions during the reading of a text allows teachers to stop and check for student understanding (Rosenshine, 1986).

Interspersed questions have been shown to influence text processing in positive ways (Andre, 1979; Duchastel & Nungester, 1984; Faw & Waller, 1976; Gall, 1984; Gall et al., 1978; Richards & McCormick, 1988; Rothkopf, 1966; Rothkopf & Bisbicos, 1967; Tobias, 1987). Questions allow teachers to enhance recall of important information and to provide immediate feedback, both of which are critical components of efficient learning (Guskey & Gates, 1986; Henson, 1979; Slavin, 1989). Interspersed questions should require students to focus on those critical pieces of information that are needed for conceptual understanding

(Andre, 1979; Kameenui & Simmons, 1990). When teachers ask text-based questions that are "off-the-cuff" (i.e., with no advance planning), they are seldom as effective as planned questions (Good & Brophy, 1987). Designing appropriate interspersed questions helps students focus on critical concepts and principles.

In addition to more factually oriented interspersed questions, the history text combines some of students' background knowledge with information they have learned in the text to answer discussion questions such as, "What inventions make travel and trade easier today?" and "What might have happened in the Age of Exploration if da Gama discovered the south sea route before Columbus planned his voyage?" These questions allow students to integrate newly learned information with their own knowledge base.

Finally, students answer test questions that integrate information in complex ways, usually in the form of a big idea. Examples of these types of questions include, "Describe how Spain tried to gain wealth by looking for a new trade route to Asia. Begin with a general statement; then give the problem, solution, and effect" and "Describe how Spain tried to gain wealth in the 1500s from its discovery of Central and South America. Begin with a general statement; then give the problem, solution, and effect." Immediately after each initial introduction of a question, students are presented two example answers: a basic answer and an exemplary answer. In this way, students are supported in understanding the framework of an appropriate answer. These test questions are reintroduced in later sections and students are required to answer them without the benefit of an answer prompt. In this way, critical information is reviewed and kept current.

In addition to these questioning strategies, students are provided with graphic organizers that organize complex information in a visual format. For example, at the end of each chapter, students are provided with a graphic organizer that combines all of the important content in the form of big ideas from the chapter. In this way, students are shown a summary of the most important content from the chapter organized by big ideas (e.g., PSE, four factors of group success) and the relationship between the big ideas. For example, in the section dealing with the European exploration, students are presented a graphic organizer like the one in Figure 8.6.

This graphic organizer shows each of the big ideas from the chapter and organizes them geographically to show where each event occurred and whom it impacted. Students might initially be given graphic organizers in which content information has already been added. Later, they might fill in graphic organizers with teacher support. Eventually, students would fill them in by themselves.

Scaffolding in Science

In the *Understanding Life Sciences* text, before students are asked to learn the complex concept [big idea] of force, teachers take students through a series of inquiry-based activities to introduce them to the chapter concepts. Students can perform the activities either at home or as a supplement to classroom instruction. After teaching the appropriate sections, it is suggested that teachers revisit the results of those activities. For example, before Chapter 2 is undertaken students are introduced to the concept of action/reaction force pairs. Students are to observe what happens to a balloon taped atop a toy car. The action force of a balloon pushing air out is contrasted to the reaction force of the air pushing on the balloon and moving

	Geography and Climate affect Agriculture			Natural Resources affect Manufacturing		Agriculture and Manufacturing affect Trade
	Geography	Climate	Agriculture	Natural Resources	Manufacturing	Trade
The New England Colonies	hills with rocky soil	harsh winters and short growing season	not developed because of climate and geography	fish, whales, and trees	ships, naval products, and rum	exporting manufactured products/ importing agricultural products
The Middle Colonies	some hills and some flat land with good soil	moderate winters and average growing seasons	cash crops of grain and livestock	iron ore and farmland	iron and metal products	exporting grains, livestock, and iron products/ importing manufactured goods
The Southern Colonies	flat land with rich soil	mild winters and long growing seasons	cash crops of tobacco, rice, and cotton	other than farmland, not developed	not developed because of agriculture	exported agricultural products/ importing manufactured products and slaves

How New England and Southern Colonies were different

New England
Poor agriculture, because of geography and climate, caused the colonists to develop their natural resources for manufacturing

South
Excellent agriculture, because the geography and the climate, caused the colonists to not develop their natural resources for manufacturing

FIGURE 8.6 Graphic Organizer of the Development of the Thirteen Colonies

the car forward. From these examples and others, students learn that abstract concepts such as force name many situations or things, not just one. To assist with this learning, students are asked to provide nontextbook examples. The examples allow students to visualize each abstract concept in a concrete image and to understand its meaning in science.

Primed Background Knowledge in History

McKeown and Beck's (1990) analysis of history textbooks showed that textbooks assume unrealistic levels of students' prior knowledge, and these unrealistic levels negatively influenced student understanding. Many history instructional materials assume students have a great deal of prior knowledge and that students enter the study of history with much of the historical understanding already in place (Sinatra, Beck, & McKeown, 1992). However, McKeown and Beck's research findings labeled students' historical knowledge prior to instruction as "Spartan," lacking in connections, and displaying misunderstandings and confusion. Furthermore, research has shown that students with diverse learning needs have less background knowledge of social studies content than their normally achieving peers (Lenz & Alley, 1983).

For example, to understand the following primary source material about the Wintu Indians of California, students must have prior knowledge about the Wintu's worldviews and Native American worldviews in general.

> The Indians never hurt anything, but the White people destroy all. They blast rocks and scatter them on the ground. The rock says, "Don't. You are hurting me." But the White people pay no attention.... How can the spirit of the earth like the White man? . . . Everywhere the White man has touched, it is sore (McLuhan, 1971, p. 15).

To understand this passage, students need to know that Native Americans had a complex set of beliefs about the relationship between human beings and the environment. They believed that, when they acted in harmony with their beliefs, the world provided abundant natural resources, but when they acted against their beliefs, the environment might no longer provide them with what they needed.

This background knowledge would enable students to apply the big idea of PSE to comprehend the deeper meaning of the primary source material. Having learned the big idea of accommodating versus dominating as competing choices for solutions, students are prepared to apply that knowledge to a fundamental difference between how Native Americans and Western culture relate to the environment (e.g., accommodate and dominate, respectively). This knowledge is then relevant in studying humankind's place in the ecological system and the impact of our cultural assumptions. Students can grasp the environmental movement's call for us to accommodate to our environment instead of assuming we can dominate it.

In *Understanding U.S. History,* background knowledge is primed by providing definitions for important vocabulary content, showing students geographical information on maps, demonstrating when in time an event(s) took place, and by ensuring that all parts of a big idea are presented clearly and in order, if appropriate (i.e., PSE follows a sequence, whereas the four factors do not). For example, in the section on European exploration, students learn in the second paragraph that trade is the buying, selling, and transporting of products and goods. In addition, they learn that traders are people who engage in trade and accumulate wealth by buying items from one group of people at a low price and selling those things to other people at higher prices. This basic understanding of trade sets the stage for understanding Europe's desire to circumvent the land route to Asia in favor of a sea route.

In the same paragraph, they are directed to a world map that shows the geographic location of Europe. This activity sets the stage for understanding Columbus's misunderstanding about the world (i.e., that it was bigger than he imagined and there was another continent between Europe and Asia).

In the previous paragraph, students are told, "This chapter discusses Europe's Age of Exploration and gives reasons why many European countries started exploring the Americas. The time line shows when Portugal, Spain, and England started their exploration of the world," and provides students with an understanding of the progression of events over time.

Finally, ensuring that all big idea components are initially taught explicitly and then are introduced clearly and in sequence helps students understand important relationships without needing to infer missing parts. For example, all PSE sequences are presented in order so that students first learn the problem, then the solution, and finally the effects. The four factors of group success do not require a sequential presentation, but when the big idea is used all four factors are presented even in cases when one of the factors may not add much to the explanation (e.g., both groups have equal motivation).

Primed Background Knowledge in Science

Before students are asked to learn the new big idea of force, teachers review three key concepts and four vocabulary words. The key concepts for review are: (1) all motion is relative to the observer; (2) an object's motion is described by position, direction, speed, and acceleration; and (3) velocity and acceleration can be measured. The four review vocabulary words are: (1) *mass,* (2) *velocity,* (3) *acceleration,* and (4) *vector.* These key concepts and vocabulary set the stage for introducing the big idea of force.

Judicious Review in History

Providing sufficient review is accomplished in the history text by massing review soon after initial information is presented so that students have many opportunities to practice newly learned knowledge. In the text, for example, students are asked interspersed questions immediately after learning the information. Review is also distributed over time so students do not forget information they have been taught. In the text, students also review important information at the end of a section, end of chapter, and, in cases of very important information, across chapters. Review is also cumulative; that is, newly learned knowledge is integrated with previously learned knowledge. For example, previously learned big ideas are integrated with newly learned big ideas. Finally, review is varied. Students are provided opportunities to practice information in varied contexts to facilitate generalization and transfer. Big ideas are especially useful for creating varied review. Once a big idea such as PSE is learned, it can be applied in many different settings.

Judicious Review in Science

At the end of every section is a built-in review. For example, in Chapter 2, Section 2.1, students are given three problems: (1) Explain the difference between balanced and unbalanced forces, (2) What is the relationship between force and motion described by Newton's first law? and (3) What is inertia? How is the inertia of an object related to its mass?

At the end of each science chapter students are asked to (1) complete vocabulary exercises (i.e., given the word *acceleration,* students must provide an example from real life); (2) review key concepts through fill-in-the-blank, multiple-choice, and short answer questions; (3) apply concepts (i.e., given a cause—balanced forces act on an object—students must provide the effect); (4) use math skills in science (i.e., What force should Lori apply to a 5 kg box to give it an acceleration of 2 m/s^2?) (5) complete critical thinking exercises (i.e., A baseball is three times more massive than a tennis ball. If the baseball and the tennis ball are accelerating equally, what can you determine about the new force on each?); and (6) perform big idea activities (i.e., Pick an activity you enjoy, such as jumping on a trampoline or riding a scooter, and describe how Newton's laws apply to that activity).

ANOTHER DIRECT INSTRUCTION CONTENT AREA PROGRAM

Your World of Facts (Volumes I and II) is a program designed to preteach students key facts and relationships. The assumption underlying the program is that, once students have mastered the key facts presented in the curriculum, they will be in a better position to understand and comprehend content area textbooks. While students may know various facts, they are typically weak in understanding *systems* of facts. To understand a system of facts, students must learn how all the facts work together. *Your World of Facts Volumes I and II* uses several formats to increase student motivation and interest including games and graphic organizers. *Your World of Facts Volume I* addresses facts in the areas of plants, machines, geography, and the body. *Your World of Facts Volume II* covers vertebrates, animal life, vegetation, climate, and various industries around the world.

Teachers who want to use *Your World of Facts Volumes I and II* also have access to a student workbook and a teacher's guide. Teacher's guides contain scripted lessons and descriptions of the games and the rules for playing them. It also includes additional facts that can be used to extend the lessons. The student workbooks include the diagrams and question sheets needed to practice various fact relationships.

TEACHING TECHNIQUES

Teaching techniques in Direct Instruction content area programs are significantly less detailed than those found in skills-based or remedial Direct Instruction programs. For example, there are no teacher formats in the history or science programs. However, both programs do have teachers' guides that provide some guidance about teaching. The science teacher's guides are quite detailed and give teachers information about the philosophy of the program, the schedule of review, and approaches to achieve mastery. In contrast, the history teacher's guide primarily provides answers to interspersed questions and end-of-chapter questions.

In addition to less structured formats, there are differences with regard to other teaching techniques used in Direct Instruction content area programs. These include unison responding and signals as well as error corrections.

Unison Responding and Signals

Unison responding prompted with signals is more difficult to use in content areas programs because the answers to questions tend to be complex and not amenable to group responding (i.e., there are many possible correct responses to questions). In fact, unison responding is not used at all in the history text. Rather, questions are targeted to individual students. The teacher's guide does suggest that teachers use a strategy for ensuring that all students get an opportunity to respond and that students who are struggling get even more frequent opportunities to answer questions.

In contrast, the science videodiscs use a voice prompt (i.e., vocal inflection) as a signal for choral responding. Students are taught to respond out loud to questions that are delivered by the narrators. Teachers can then monitor the group to see whether all students are responding and can listen to hear if students are responding accurately.

Error Corrections

In history, there are no program-designed error-correction procedures. However, because interspersed questions are placed immediately after the paragraph where the content is presented, teachers can remediate by having students reread the previous section and provide the correct response. For example, the textbook reads:

> An economic problem involves difficulty in getting and keeping things that people need or want. For example, people need three basic things: (a) food to eat, (b) shelter to keep them dry and to protect them from the weather, and (c) clothing to keep them warm. People want things such as televisions or fancy clothes. When people can't get or keep what they need or want, they have an economic problem (Carnine, Steely, Crawford, Harniss, & Hollenbeck, 1999, p. 1).

The interspersed question reads as follows, "When do people have an economic problem?" If the student answered, "When they can't get televisions or fancy clothes," the teacher might say, "That is an *example* of an economic problem, but it doesn't answer the question, When do people have an economic problem? Find the sentence that specifically tells about when people have an economic problem." The student could then reread the paragraph and point to the line that says, "When people can't get or keep what they need or want, they have an economic problem." After checking where the student has pointed, the teacher might say, "That is correct. Please read the sentence." The teacher could also reinforce the correct answer by saying, "Yes, when people can't get or keep what they need or want, they have an economic problem."

In science, when students make errors in oral responding, teachers can model, lead, and retest the question. Teachers also have the option to replay the section of the videodisc where the information was presented. Built into the design of the videodiscs are short quizzes every few minutes. The quizzes require students to write answers to questions that are written on the screen. Then teachers move to the next screen where the answers are given. After several questions teachers ask students to self-report their accuracy. Based on the students' response, teachers can either continue to the next section or remediate by following the suggestions given on the video screen.

ASSESSMENT AND TROUBLESHOOTING

Both the history and science programs provide multiple opportunities for teachers to collect data about student performance. These data are critical for making decisions about student mastery of the content.

History

Assessment. The history text does not have a placement test nor does it provide guidelines for how mastery should be assessed. Teachers determine those guidelines. However, the history text does provide multiple opportunities for students to demonstrate their learning and for teachers to assess mastery. First, while reading the text, students answer interspersed questions after every one to two paragraphs. These questions are intended to highlight important information and ensure students are actively engaged in learning the content. They are primarily factual and require students to reiterate information learned in the previous section. In addition to interspersed questions, students answer frequent imbedded discussion questions that require them to go beyond merely reiterating factual information to combining previously learned information with new information. Finally, as students read they encounter critical information in the form of test questions. These questions require students to remember complex, interrelated information, often in the form of big ideas. The test questions embedded in the text contain a question prompt and two types of answers. The first type of answer is one that is considered adequate; the second type of answer is considered exemplary. Students have the opportunity to link the question to an appropriate response. Later in the section these questions are reviewed without the answers and students are required to generate their own answers based on the text's answers. Table 8.1 shows an example of a test question.

Within each chapter there are three to six sections. At the end of each section there are several types of activities that require students to remember vocabulary, important factual information, and critical information highlighted by test questions. At the end of a chapter, there are additional activities that students might complete. These include activities similar to those found at the end of a section (vocabulary, fact-based, and critical information) as well as activities that extend students' learning such as evaluating primary source documents, writing about the relationship between historical problems and modern problems, and various enrichment activities when students gather information from outside sources to answer a question.

TABLE 8.1 Test Question

Test Question 2: Describe how Spain tried to gain wealth in the 1500s from its discovery of Central and South America. Begin with a general statement; then give the problem, solution, and effect.

Basic Answer: *Spain wanted to gain wealth from its discovery of Central and South America.* The **problem** was that Spain still needed wealth. As a **solution,** Spain sent conquistadors to take the Native American's land, gold, and silver. The **effect** was that Spain became wealthy.

Exemplary Answer: *Spain wanted to gain wealth from its discovery of Central and South America.* The **problem** was that Spain still needed wealth to economically compete with its rivals. As a **solution,** Spain dominated Central and South America by sending Spanish conquistadors to take Native Americans' land, gold, and silver. They also enslaved Native Americans. The **effect** was that Spain became the wealthiest, most powerful country in the world. The **effects** of the conquests of the Aztecs and Incas were severe economic and people's rights problems.

Source: Adapted from Carnine, D., Crawford, D. B., Harniss, M. K., Hollenbeck, K. L., & Steely, D. (1999). *Understanding U.S. History: Volume I–Through 1914.* Eugene, OR: University of Oregon.

Troubleshooting. Because the material is cumulative and the assessments build from simple questions to complex, integrative questions, there are several points at which teachers can determine whether students are having trouble. Teachers can troubleshoot initial comprehension by having students write the answers to interspersed and discussion questions and then either grading them or having students correct and turn them in for analysis. These questions can also be practiced orally in large or small groups or even study pairs. Teachers should pay particular attention to student performance on the test questions. Because these questions represent the most important content for students to learn, all students must be able to at least answer test questions with a basic response. Ideally, students will be able to generate even more sophisticated responses.

Science

Assessment. Using videodiscs, student performance in the science curriculum is monitored and assessed in five ways: (1) students' oral responses during the videodisc presentation, (2) their written responses during the videodisc presentation, (3) students' performance on their independent work in the Student Response Booklet, (4) their performance on the lesson quizzes, and (5) mastery tests that occur every five lessons.

Besides giving assessment information, the videodisc teacher's guides provide remedies for low performers at each of those five assessment procedures. For example in the *Earth Science* Instructor's Manual (Core Concepts in Science and Mathematics, 1987), teachers are told that if students are not responding aloud after the narrator asks questions they are to tell them something like, "Answer the questions. You'll find this material a lot easier if you answer out loud. Praise students for good responses, 'That's good answering'" (p. 60).

The manual also provides suggestions for students who exhibit weak responses. For example, "The simplest remedy for a series of weak responses is to repeat the part of the lesson in which the weak responses occurred. Tell students, 'Let's go over that part once more.' Move backwards to the appropriate part and respond with the students. Praise students for accurate responses, 'That was a lot better'" (p. 61).

Specific to assessment, the videodisc series presents tests after every fifth lesson from Lesson 5–35. The purpose of these tests is to give students feedback as to what they have learned during the preceding four lessons. The tests also provide teachers a way to monitor the effectiveness of instruction as well as remedies. The test can be presented in videodisc format or in a paper-and-pencil format. The remedies specified for the five-lesson tests involve reteaching of earlier-taught segments. An example from the Lesson 5 test is shown in Figure 8.7.

In addition to the five-lesson tests, the *Earth Science* videodiscs also make use of daily facts quizzes and chart quizzes. The chart quizzes monitors students' mastery of chart wording. The chart quizzes require students to fill in the missing wording on the blank version of the chart (lesson graphic organizers).

Finally, a mastery test covers concepts taught in the entire *Earth Science* course. This paper-and-pencil test consists of seventy-eight items organized into twenty-eight groups. The mastery test can be used as both a pretest and a post-test. Each group of items has a remedy. Instructions for each remedy appear in the mastery test summary included in the instructor's manual. Figure 8.8 shows parts of the *Earth Science* mastery test.

Troubleshooting.   At any stage in the assessment procedures noted above, teachers can identify whether students are having difficulty. In particular, teachers should listen carefully during the oral responding period. This period of time is the best time to correct misconceptions and ensure students' initial learning is accurate. Further, teachers should pay careful attention to student performance on the quizzes offered after every fifth lesson. These assessments provide teachers with information about the extent to which students have learned and retained previously presented information. Teachers can then remediate if students are not performing at criterion.

EXTENSIONS AND ADAPTATIONS

Extending content area instruction to other areas helps students generalize and apply their new knowledge across other domains. For struggling learners, extending content to other areas provides additional practice.

One extension of content area instruction is to integrate reading and writing. Integrating reading and writing benefits both content knowledge and writing achievement. Manipulating content by writing about it appears to (1) engage students in a wider variety of reasoning operations than would reading or writing alone (Langer & Applebee, 1987); (2) improve comprehension, including how to discern important from unimportant information, summarize, infer, generate questions, and monitor comprehension (Dole, Duffy, Roehler, & Pearson, 1991; Langer & Applebee, 1987); and (3) focus on key concepts or larger issues or topics and extend the content beyond the text (Langer & Applebee, 1987;

Lesson 5 Test   **Name:**

Part A : *Write all the words that go in each cell*

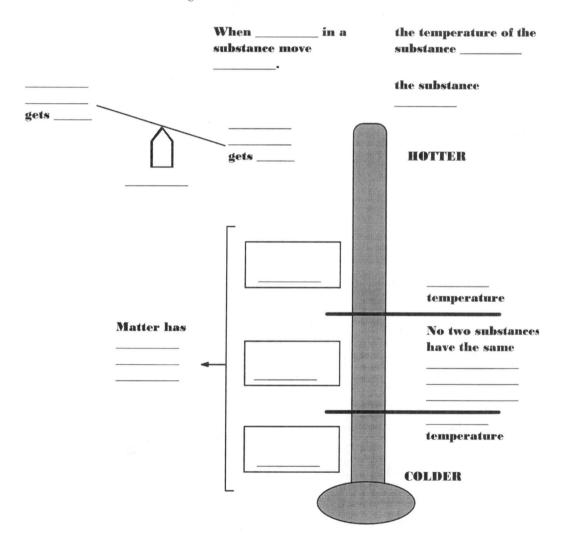

FIGURE 8.7   Compare/Contrast Graphic Organizer. Adapted from *Core Concepts in Science and Mathematics, Earth Sciences: Instructor's Manual.*

Name: _____   ☐ Pretest   Start Time:_____

Date: _____   ☐ Posttest   Finish Time: _____

Teacher: _____   Total Time: _____

School: _____

_____

The temperatures are shown on the rocks:

1. Which rock has the fastest-moving
    molecules?

    60° 45° 75°
    A   B   C

2. Which rock has the slowest-moving
    molecules?

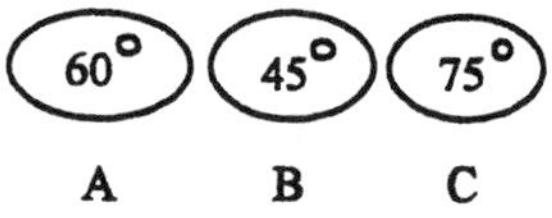

An object changed from size A to size B

9. Did it expand or did it contract?

10. Did the density increase or did it
    decrease?

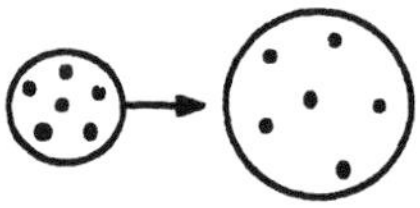

20. Write the letter for the side of this
    convection cell that is less dense.

    _____

These containers show the relative humidity of three air masses.

53. Which air mass has the lowest relative
    humidity? _____

54. Which air mass has the highest relative
    humidity? _____

    A   B   C

55. Which air mass is the coldest? _____

56. Which air mass is the hottest? _____

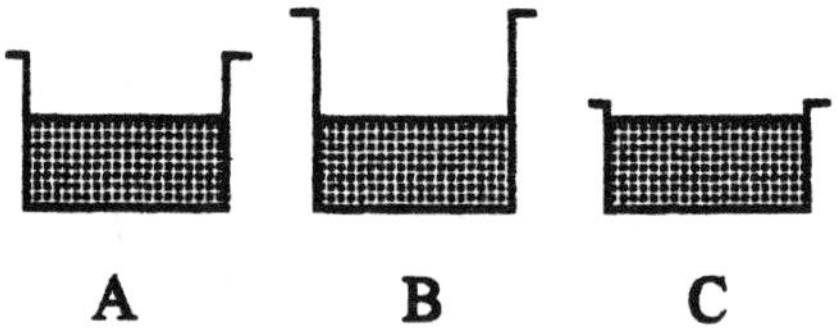

FIGURE 8.8   Parts of *Earth Science* Mastery Test. Adapted from *Core Concepts in Science and Mathematics, Earth Sciences: Instructor's Manual.*

Tierney & Shanahan, 1991). If students read content that is unfamiliar to them, writing about that content helps them recall more information than reading alone (Langer & Applebee, 1987). Because writing helps comprehension, integration of reading and writing also becomes an adaptation for struggling learners, helping them to comprehend history and science.

Reading with writing prompts more thoughtful consideration of ideas than writing or reading alone (Tierney, Soter, O'Flahavan, & McGuinley, 1989). Reading first also helps poor writers because what they read provides content for their written compositions (Newcomer & Barenbaum, 1991). Hence, integrating reading and writing becomes an adaptation for struggling learners as it provides content for their compositions. In the sections that follow, we describe the integration of reading and writing extension based on the six principles of curricular design articulated by the National Center to Improve the Tools of Educators (NCITE) (Kameenui & Carnine, 1998).

Big Ideas and Writing

There are several ways that teachers can integrate reading and writing around a big idea. After learning the Four Factors for Group Success and applying it to the success of Jamestown or to the Revolutionary War, students can apply these four factors to a persuasive essay on a predicted outcome for a current conflict between two countries or groups within a country. Students could also apply these four factors to a persuasive composition about an election or new project. They can apply Stages of Cooperation to a composition exploring the rebuilding of a country after war such as Afghanistan. After they have read about the events before, during, and after the Civil War, they can write a composition about the Civil War using the PSE text structure. Convection, learned in science, becomes a main idea to connect details in essays in which students propose ideas for heating and cooling homes that do not require electricity.

Strategic Integration and Writing

Writing compositions during content instruction is an extension of strategic integration. Writing helps students integrate facts and big ideas, apply content knowledge in the language arts, and integrate text structures in text and in writing. One example of writing serving as an extension of strategic integration is first teaching students the big idea of PSE, then having them read about the Civil Rights Movement and linking the facts of the Civil Rights Movement with the big idea PSE. Finally, they can write about one issue in the Civil Rights Movement using PSE as a text structure for organizing their compositions. One strategic integration across content instruction and language arts is having students read a novel related to the history content (e.g., *My Brother Sam is Dead* [Collier & Collier, 1974] and the Revolutionary War) and having students connect the two through writing (e.g., compare the father's initial attitudes toward the Revolutionary War with the events that led to the Revolutionary War). In science, students can apply what they learn to current problems through writing or to their personal lives. In both history and science, they are often required to read information from multiple sources. Writing helps students discern important from unimportant information in the various sources, connect information drawn from multiple sources, organize information, and finally manipulate the pertinent information from multiple sources to draw conclusions or make inferences.

Conspicuous Strategies and Writing

The application of content to writing extends conspicuous strategies. Students use big ideas or concepts as a strategy for planning and organizing their compositions. After they learn compare/contrast text structure for writing, they can use compare/contrast as an organizational strategy while reading science or social studies. For example, science books typically present a string of facts without organizing them into an overt text structure. Many science books describe the characteristics of mammals, reptiles, birds, and insects without linking the information between the various descriptions. Students, who have learned compare/contrast text structure for compositions, use compare/text structure as a strategy as they read, finding similarities and differences between each animal group. Science teachers can teach compare/contrast as a conspicuous strategy by teaching students to use a graphic organizer to record and link similarities and differences between the animal groups. The graphic organizer then becomes an organizing strategy for writing.

Scaffolding and Writing

Content and big ideas become the scaffolding for writing, and learned text structures for writing become scaffolding for learning content. As already noted, history and science textbooks tend to be poorly organized with no obvious text structures or links between facts and concepts. Learning text structures for organizing writing helps students apply the text structure to poorly organized textbooks, helping them to link facts and concepts. For example, in a chapter about Native Americans, a social studies text might present a series of facts about Native Americans in the Plains, the Northwest, and the Woodlands. This information may contain many facts to memorize. If the students had learned compare/contrast text structure for writing and were able to apply the compare/contrast text structure to the social studies text, then they could use a graphic organizer to link facts and to see similarities and differences between the groups. As they saw the differences, they would also see the differing effects of the environment on the housing, transportation, and food of the various groups of Native Americans. Finally, writing provides scaffolding for learning content, particularly content that was previously unfamiliar to students. As previously stated, writing about unfamiliar content helps them recall more of the content.

Background Knowledge and Writing

When integrating reading and writing, the learned content knowledge becomes the primed *background knowledge* for the composition. For example, once students have learned about the big idea of convection in science, they can write a composition integrating their new knowledge about magma with their prior knowledge about convection. Once they have learned about the effect of heat on molecules, students can again, through writing, integrate their new knowledge with their background knowledge of convection. Likewise, learned text structures become background knowledge that students can apply while reading to organizing poorly organized textbooks.

Judicious Review and Writing

Writing about content provides judicious review. Writing provides (1) a means of reviewing new information immediately by writing a few paragraphs linking the new knowledge to a concept (e.g., applying the facts of rebuilding the United States after the Civil War to the big idea of Stages of Cooperation) or (2) cumulative review (e.g., integrating newly learned information about the Civil War with previously learned knowledge about the Revolutionary War and linking those to the big idea of Four Factors of Group Success).

RESEARCH ON DIRECT INSTRUCTION CONTENT AREA PROGRAMS

Direct Instruction content area programs have not been researched as completely or as rigorously as other Direct Instruction programs such as reading or mathematics. Several studies, however, do support the efficacy of the content area programs.

History

Carnine et al. (1996) describe a series of field studies supporting the efficacy of the *Understanding U.S. History* text in comparison to more traditional texts. It is important to note that the following field studies were unpublished research investigations; further investigations using the *Understanding U.S. History* textbook are needed to provide increased support for this program.

The first two investigations were oriented toward formative evaluation and field-testing of the experimental textbook (Crawford & Carnine, 1994; Crawford, 1994). Feedback from these field-testing efforts was integrated into the textbook that was then evaluated in three additional field studies conducted the following year (Caros, 1996; Harniss, 1996; Hollenbeck, 1996). These studies investigated history knowledge measured through writing, multiple-choice and short-answer tests, and curriculum-based vocabulary probes. One of these studies (i.e., Harniss, 1996) also included an observational component that measured students' engagement and accuracy. The Crawford (1994) study showed that students using the conceptually organized textbook learned more about history, even when measured by tests drawn on the competing curriculum. Even with the same teacher, the classes of students who used this textbook learned more.

More information on the acquisition of organized knowledge was provided in the Hollenbeck (1996) study. In this investigation, the big ideas in the history text were used by all levels of students in their essays, although the lower-performing students could not remember as many of the facts. Students organized the chapter material using the big ideas; they were able to use the chapter's big ideas as a way to structure their own writing and, presumably, their thinking.

Findings from the Harniss (1996) investigation suggested that students with learning disabilities, behavioral disorders, and students who are at-risk for school failure were able to understand and use the history knowledge that had been organized by the big ideas. The increased engagement and decreased task-avoidance of these students when using the experimental textbook provided support for the notion that better-organized knowledge is more accessible to learners (Prawat, 1989).

Finally, the progress-monitoring approach of the Caros (1996) investigation found rapid growth in vocabulary learning in two very diverse populations. At the same time, comparison groups made little or no gains on vocabulary knowledge in a traditional curriculum.

Again, these studies provide support for the Direct Instruction history program; however, further studies published in scientific journals are needed.

Science Videodisc Programs

At the middle school level, studies have shown that students perform significantly better on measures of content knowledge and problem solving when they learn from the *Earth Science videodisc* than from other curricula. (Niedelman, 1991; Woodward, 1994) They were also more confident about their science problem-solving skills.

In high school, the videodisc interventions continued to show impressive gains. At-risk high school students who completed the *Understanding Chemistry and Energy videodisc* performed as well as their advanced placement peers (Hofmeister, Engelmann, & Carnine, 1989). Finally, when adult elementary education majors were taught using the videodiscs, they scored significantly higher than those who did not and had more positive attitudes to teaching science and confidence in science-teaching skills (Vitale & Romance, 1992). Further investigations are needed for the various Direct Instruction science programs.

REFERENCES

Andre, T. (1979). Does answering higher-level questions while reading facilitate productive learning? *Review of Educational Research, 49*(2), 280–318.

Beck, I. L., McKeown, M. G., & Gromoll, E. W. (1989). Learning from social studies texts. *Cognition and Instruction, 6*(2), 99–158.

Beck, I. L., McKeown, M. G., Sinatra, G. M., & Loxterman, J. A. (1991). Revising social studies text from a text-processing perspective: Evidence of improved comprehensibility. *Reading Research Quarterly, 26*(3), 252–276.

Borko, H., Peressini, D., Romagnano, L., Knuth, E., Willis-Yorker, C., Wooley, C., Hovermill, J., & Masarik, K. (2000). Teacher education does matter: A situative view of learning to teach secondary mathematics. *Educational Psychologist, 35*(3), 193–206.

Britton, B. K., Van Dusen, L., Gulgoz, S., & Glynn, S. M. (1989). Instructional texts rewritten by five expert teams: Revision and retention improvement. *Journal of Educational Psychology, 81,* 226–239.

Brophy, J. (1990). Teaching social studies for understanding and higher-order applications. *Elementary School Journal, 90*(4), 367–417.

Bryant, D. P., Ugel, N., Thompson, S., & Hamff, A. (1999). Instructional strategies for content-area reading instruction. *Intervention in School and Clinic, 34*(5), 293–302.

Carnine, D. (1991). Curricular interventions for teaching higher order thinking to all students: Introduction to the special series. *Journal of Learning Disabilities, 24*(5), 261–269.

Carnine, D. W., Caros, J., Crawford, D., Hollenbeck, K., & Harniss, M. K. (1996). Designing effective United States history curricula for all students. In J. Brophy (Ed.) *Advances in research on teaching: Vol. 6: History teaching and learning* (pp. 207–256). Greenwich, CT: JAI Press.

Carnine, D., Crawford, D. B., Harniss, M. K., Hollenbeck, K. L., & Miller, S. (1998). Effective strategies for teaching social studies to diverse learners. In D. Carnine & E. Kameenui (Eds.), *Effective strategies for teaching students with diverse learning and curricular needs* (pp. 177–202). Columbus, OH: Merrill.

Carnine, D., Crawford, D. B., Harniss, M. K., Hollenbeck, K. L., & Steely, D. (1999). *Understanding U.S. history: Volume I–through 1914.* Eugene, OR: University of Oregon.

Carnine, D., Miller, S., Bean, R., & Zigmond, N. (1994). Social studies: Educational tools for diverse learners. *School Psychology Review, 23*(3), 428–441.

Carnine, D., Silbert, J., & Kameenui, E. J. (1990). *Direct Instruction reading* (2nd ed.). Columbus, OH: Merrill.

Carnine, D., Steely, D., Crawford, D. B., Harniss, M. K., & Hollenbeck, K. L. (1999). *Understanding U.S. history: Volume II–Reconstruction to world leadership.* Eugene, OR: University of Oregon.

Caros, J. (1996). *Curriculum-based analysis of students' vocabulary acquisition within an experimental eighth-grade history text.* Unpublished manuscript. Eugene, OR: University of Oregon.

Collier, J. L., & Collier, C. (1974). *My brother Sam is dead.* New York: Scholastic.

Core Concepts in Science and Mathematics. (1987). *Earth sciences: Instructor's manual.* Gaithersburg, MD: Systems Impact.

Crawford, D. B. (1994). *An experiment comparing the effects of topically organized and causally organized textbooks in eighth grade U.S. History.* Unpublished doctoral dissertation. Eugene, OR: University of Oregon.

Crawford, D. B., & Carnine, D. (1994). *Promoting and assessing higher order thinking in U.S. History: Use of performance assessment to evaluate the effects of instruction.* Unpublished manuscript. Eugene, OR: University of Oregon.

Creemers, B. P. M. (1994). Effective instruction: An empirical basis for a theory of educational effectiveness. In D. Reynolds, B. P. M. Creemers, P. S. Nesselrodt, E. C. Schaffer, S. Stringfield, & C. Teddlie (Eds.), *Advances in school effectiveness research and practice* (pp. 189–205). Tarrytown, NY: Pergamon.

Dole, J. A., Duffy, G. G., Roehler, L. R., & Pearson, P. D. (1991). Moving from the old to the new: Research on reading comprehension instruction. *Review of Educational Research, 61,* 239–264.

Donlevy, J. (2000). The dilemma of high-stakes testing: What is school for? *International Journal of Instructional Media, 27,* 331–337.

Duchastel, P. C., & Nungester, R. J. (1984). Adjunct question effects with review. *Contemporary Educational Psychology, 9*(2), 97–103.

Duffy, T. M., Higgins, L., Mehlenbacher, B., Cochran, C., Wallace, D., Hill, C., Hangen, D., McCaffrey, M., Burnett, R., Sloane, S., & Smith, S. (1989). Models for the design of instructional text. *Reading Research Quarterly, 24,* 434–457.

Erickson, H. L. (1998). *Concept-based curriculum and instruction: Teaching beyond the facts.* Thousand Oaks, CA: Corwin.

Faw, H. W., & Waller, T. G. (1976). Mathemagenic behaviors and efficiency in learning from prose materials: Review, critique, recommendations. *Review of Educational Research, 46*(4), 691–720.

Fox, R. W., Wandry, D., Pruitt, P., & Anderson, G. (1998). School to adult life transitions for students with disabilities: Forging a new alliance. *Professional School Counseling, 1,* 48–52.

Gall, M. (1984). Synthesis of research on teachers' questioning. *Educational Leadership, 42*(2), 40–47.

Gall, M., Ward, B., Berliner, D., Cahen L., Winne, P., Elashoff, J., & Stanton, G. (1978). Effects of questioning techniques and recitation on student learning. *American Educational Research Journal, 15*(2), 175–199.

Garner, R., Gillingham, M. G., & White, C. S. (1989). Effects of 'seductive details' on macroprocessing and microprocessing in adults and children. *Cognition and Instruction 6*(1), 41–57.

Good, T. L., & Brophy J. E. (1987). *Looking in classrooms* (4th ed.). New York: Harper & Row.

Graves, M. F., Prenn, M. C., Earle, J., Thompson, M., Thompson, V., & Slater, W. H. (1991). Improving instructional text: Some lessons learned. *Reading Research Quarterly, 26*(2), 110–122.

Guskey, T. R., & Gates, S. L. (1986) Synthesis of research on the effects of mastery learning in elementary and secondary classrooms. *Educational Leadership, 43*(8), 73–80.

Haas, M. E. (1991). An analysis of the social science and history concepts in elementary social studies textbooks, grade 1–4. *Theory and Research in Social Education, 19,* 211–220.

Harniss, M. K. (1996). *Task requirements of content area textbooks: Effects on the academic achievement and engagement of middle-level students.* Unpublished manuscript. Eugene, OR: University of Oregon.

Harniss, M. K., Hollenbeck, K. L., Crawford, D. B., & Carnine, D. (1994). Content organization and instructional design issues in the development of history texts. *Learning Disability Quarterly, 17*(3), 235–248.

Henson, K. T. (1979). Questioning as a mode of instruction. *The Clearing House, 53*(1), 13–16.

Hofmeister, A., Engelmann, S., & Carnine, D. (1989). Developing and validating science education video-discs. *Journal of Research in Science Teaching, 26,* 665–677.

Holden, C. (2000). Asia stays on top, U.S. in middle in new global rankings. *Science, 290,* 1866.

Hollenbeck, K. (1996). *An observational study of between group differences in an eighth grade experimental US history textbook implementation project.* Unpublished dissertation. Eugene, OR: University of Oregon.

Jitendra, A. K., Nolet, V., Xin, Y.P., Gomez, O., Renouf, K., & Iskold, L. (2001). An analysis of middle school geography textbooks: Implications for students with learning problems. *Reading & Writing Quarterly, 17,* 151–173.

Kameenui, E. J., & Carnine, D. W. (Eds.). (1998). *Effective teaching strategies that accommodate diverse learners.* Upper Saddle River, NJ: Merrill.

Kameenui, E., & Simmons, D. (1990). *Designing instructional strategies: The prevention of academic learning problems.* Columbus, OH: Merrill.

Langer, J. S., & Applebee, A. N. (1987). *How writing shapes thinking.* Urbana, IL: National Council of Teachers of English.

Lenz, B. K., & Alley, G. R. (1983). *The effects of advance organizers on the learning and retention of learning disabled adolescents within the context of a cooperative planning model.* Final research report submitted to the U.S. Department of Education, Office of Special Education, Washington, DC.

Llinares, S. (2000). Secondary school mathematics teacher's professional knowledge: A case from the teaching of the concept of function. *Teachers and Teaching: Theory and Practice, 6*(1), 41–62.

Manzo, K. K. (2002). U.S. history again stumps senior class. *Education Week, 21*(36), 1.

McKeown, M. G., & Beck, I. L. (1990). The assessment and characterization of young learners' knowledge of a topic in history. *American Educational Research Journal, 27*(4), 688–726.

McKeown, M. G., & Beck, I. L. (1994). Making sense of accounts of history: Why young students don't and how they might. In G. Leinhardt, I. L. Beck, & C. Stainton (Eds.), *Teaching and Learning in History* (pp. 1–26). Hillsdale, NJ: Earlbaum.

McKeown, M. G., Beck, I. L., Sinatra, G. M., & Loxterman, J. A. (1992). The contribution of prior knowledge and coherent text to comprehension. *Reading Research Quarterly, 27,* 78–93.

McLuhan, T. C. (1971). *Touch the earth: A self-portrait of Indian existence.* New York: Promontory.

National Academy of Sciences. (1995). *Introducing the National Science Education Standards.* Downloaded July 31, 2002, from http://stills.nap.edu/readingroom/ books/intronses/

National Center for Educational Statistics. (1996). *Issue brief: Results from the NAEP 1994 U.S. history assessment—at a glance.* (NCES 96-869). Washington, DC: Author.

National Center for History in the Schools. (1995). *United States history: Exploring the American Experience.* Los Angeles, CA: Author.

Newcomer, P. L., & Barenbaum, E. M. (1991). The written composing ability of children with learning disabilities: A review of the literature from 1980 to 1990. *Journal of Learning Disabilities, 24,* 578–593.

Newmann, F. (1990). Higher order thinking in teaching social studies: A rationale for the assessment of classroom thoughtfulness. *Journal of Curriculum Studies, 22*(1), 41–56.

Niedelman, M. (1991). Problem solving and transfer. *Journal of Learning Disabilities, 24,* 322–329.

Nolet, V. W., Tindal, G., & Blake, G. (1993). *Focus on assessment and learning in content classes* (Training Module No. 4). Eugene, OR: University of Oregon, Research, Consultation, and Teaching Program.

Office of the State Superintendent for Public Instruction (OSPI). (2002). *EALRS for Science.* Retrieved December 18, 2002, from http://www.k12.wa.us/curriculumInstruct/science/EALR.asp

Oregon Department of Education. (1995). *Education for the 21st Century: Oregon academic content standards & benchmarks.* Salem, OR: Author.

Phelps, R. P. (2001). Benchmarking to the world's best in mathematics: Quality control in curriculum and instruction among the top performers in the TIMSS. *Evaluation Review, 25,* 391–439.

Prawat, R. (1989). Promoting access to knowledge, strategy, and disposition in students: A research synthesis. *Review of Educational Research, 59*(1), 1–42.

Ravitch, D., & Finn, C. (1987). *What do our 17-year-olds know?* New York: Harper & Row.

Richards, J. P., & McCormick, C. B. (1988). Effect of interspersed conceptual prequestions on note-taking in listening comprehension. *Journal of Educational Psychology, 80*(4), 592–594.

Roid, G. H., & Haladyna, T. M. (1982). The emergence of an item-writing technology. *Review of Educational Research, 50,* 293–314.

Rosenshine, B. V. (1986). Synthesis of research on explicit teaching. *Educational Leadership, 43*(7), 60–69.

Rosenshine, B. (1995). Advances in research on instruction. *Journal of Educational Research, 88*(5), 262–268.

Rothkopf, E. Z. (1966). Learning from written instructive materials: An exploration of the control of inspection behavior by test-like events. *American Educational Research Journal, 3*(4), 241–249.

Rothkopf, E. Z., & Bisbicos, E. E. (1967). Selective facilitative effects of interspersed questions on learning from written materials. *Journal of Educational Psychology, 58*(1), 56–61.

Rutherford, F. J., & Ahlgren, A. (1991). *Science for All Americans-Online* (Introduction). American Association for the Advancement of Science. Retrieved on December 18, 2001, from http://www.project2061.org/tools/sfaaol/Intro.htm

Shealy, B., Arvold, B., Zheng, T., & Cooney, T. J. (1994). *Persistence and evolution of five preservice secondary mathematics teachers' beliefs.* Paper presented at the AERA annual meeting, New Orleans.

Siler, C. R. (1989–1990). United States history textbooks: Cloned mediocrity. *International Journal of Social Education, 4*(3), 10–31.

Sinatra, G. M., Beck, I. L., & McKeown, M. G. (1992). A longitudinal characterization of young students' knowledge of their country's government. *American Educational Research Journal, 29*(3), 633–661.

Slavin, R. E. (1989). On mastery learning and mastery teaching. *Educational Leadership, 46*(7), 77–79.

Steele, D. F. (1994). *Helping preservice teachers confront their conceptions about mathematics content, teaching, and learning.* Paper presented at the AERA annual meeting, New Orleans.

Stevens, C., & Wenner, G. (1996). Elementary preservice teacher's knowledge and beliefs regarding science and mathematics. *School Science & Mathematics, 96*(1), 2–9.

Thiagarajan, S. (1978). Instructional product verification and revision: 20 questions and 200 speculations. *Educational Communications and Technology, 26*(2), 133–141.

Tierney, R. J., & Shanahan, T. (1991). Research in the reading-writing relationship: Interactions, transactions, and outcomes. In R. Barr, M. Kamil, P. B. Mosenthal, & P. Pearson (Eds.), *Handbook of reading research* (Vol. 2, pp. 246–280). New York: Longman.

Tierney, R. J., Soter, A., O'Flahavan, J. F., & McGuinley, W. (1989). The effects of reading and writing upon thinking critically. *Reading Research Quarterly, 24,* 134–173.

Tindal, G., Nolet, V. W., & Blake, G. (1992). *Focus on teaching and learning in content classes (Training module No. 3).* Eugene, OR: Research, Consultation, and Teaching Program, University of Oregon.

Tobias, S. (1987). Mandatory text review and interaction with student characteristics. *Journal of Educational Psychology, 79*(2), 154–161.

Vitale, M., & Romance, N. (1992). Using videodisc instruction in an elementary science methods course. *Journal of Research in Science Teaching, 29,* 915–928.

Wayne, A. J. (2002). Teacher inequality: New evidence on disparities in teachers' academic skills. *Education Policy Analysis Archives, 10*(30), 1–11.

Woodward, J. (1994). Effects of curriculum discourse style on eighth graders' recall and problem solving in earth science. *Elementary School Journal, 94,* 299–314.

Youngs, P. (2001). District and state policy influences on professional development and school capacity. *Educational Policy, 15*(2), 278–301.

■ ■ ■ ■ ■

CHAPTER NINE

APPLYING DIRECT INSTRUCTION PRINCIPLES TO NEW CONTENT

BENJAMIN LIGNUGARIS/KRAFT

Utah State University

OBJECTIVES

After studying this chapter you should be able to:

1. describe the three phases of effective curriculum development and teaching;
2. define "big ideas";
3. explain why using big ideas is important in curriculum planning;
4. describe the steps in the lesson delivery cycle;
5. describe the elements that characterize activities during each step in the lesson delivery cycle;
6. describe the instructional practices that characterize effective teacher/student interactions;
7. describe three different ways that lessons should be evaluated.

Schools are expected to teach a wide range of content to students. The previous chapters in this book testify to the breadth of curriculum that schools must address. However, the body of content that schools must teach is even greater than suggested thus far in this book. Curriculum is determined at state and local levels. Each state articulates its expectations in a set of standards and objectives sometimes referred to as the state's core curriculum. Each state also mandates tests to assess student progress on the core curriculum. This system of state and local control means that there will always be standards that cannot be addressed by nationally published programs. For example, each state has standards that relate to its own history, and some local areas even have local history standards. In addition, even when the broad outlines of the curriculum is similar across states, important specifics may vary. For example, some states may emphasize the science concept of ecological niche at the third-grade level, some at the fifth-grade level, and some not at all. The result of this variety of learning standards is that published Direct Instruction programs cannot address every objective that schools target for instruction. Thus, there is a need to be able to develop extensions and small-scale instructional programs on the local level.

Direct Instruction programs address most state core standards and objectives. In some cases, extensions are necessary to make the link from the skills taught in Direct Instruction programs to the specific standards and objectives in a particular state. For example, a state may have a standard regarding biographical writing at the fifth-grade level. The *Reasoning and Writing* program does not specifically address biography, but it does teach all the general writing skills that students need to "take on" this genre. An extension of the *Reasoning and Writing* program can be developed to give students experience using their general writing skills within the genre of biography.

Most states also have standards that cannot be addressed by extending skills that are taught in Direct Instruction programs. For example, most states include their state's history as an important area of study. In addition, there are many content areas that are not addressed by Direct Instruction programs at the elementary level. For example, health, social studies, and science are not addressed extensively at the elementary level.

To be sure, Direct Instruction programs do provide the broad skills that provide tools for learning in any area. For example, learning elementary social studies is built on foundations of language skills taught in the language series, reading skills taught in *Reading Mastery* and other reading programs, and writing skills taught in *Reasoning and Writing* and other writing programs. In addition, *Reading Mastery* includes important ideas from science, social studies, and other content areas in nonfiction passages. However, if we aspire to provide excellent instruction in all areas, there is a need for teachers and others to develop small instructional programs in specialized areas.

Direct Instruction programs are built on a foundation of *content analysis*—the process of identifying or constructing big ideas that coordinate specific facts, concepts, and skills into a coherent whole (Kameenui & Simmons, 1999; see Chapter 2 for more details). This content analysis is followed by an *analysis of communications* that results in clear communication of the big ideas and supporting ideas to the students so that students learn the *general case*. Direct Instruction teaches the general case by juxtaposing (or combining) examples and nonexamples and carefully constructed sequences of teacher questions and student answers. This plan is further developed by specifying how instruction is to be organized, for example, with sufficient instructional time devoted to teaching in small, same-skill groups with ongoing progress monitoring. Finally, the specific student–teacher interaction techniques are constructed for the lessons. The purpose of this chapter is to describe a system for developing, delivering, and evaluating small-scale instructional units that include some of the most important strengths of Direct Instruction.

OVERVIEW OF DESIGNING EFFECTIVE INSTRUCTION

The process of developing and delivering effective lessons can be divided into three steps: (1) unit planning, (2) lesson planning and delivery, and (3) evaluation (see Figure 9.1). During unit planning (Step I), teachers describe the content they will teach, how they will organize the content, and their sequence for introducing and practicing the targeted content. In addition, the unit planning step includes identifying instructional strategies and formats that are to be used in the unit.

In Step II, teachers develop lesson plans that describe the specific activities they will use to teach the content, how they will structure those activities, and how much time they will spend on each part of the lesson. Lessons are organized around a generic lesson structure of (1) learning set, (2) new material and guided practice, and (3) independent practice.

The primary focus of lesson delivery is effectively and efficiently interacting with students and presenting an array of activities that result in acquisition of the learning objectives. Teachers deliver lessons with techniques that are correlated with high student achievement such as providing numerous opportunities for student responding with feedback (Delquadri, Greenwood, Whorton, Carta, & Hall, 1986; Greenwood, Delquadri, & Hall, 1984; Sainato, Strain, & Lyon, 1987), conducting lessons at a brisk pace, providing corrective and positive feedback, and actively monitoring student performance (Christenson, Ysseldyke, & Thurlow, 1989; Hudson, 1996, 1997; Hudson, Lignugaris/Kraft, & Miller, 1993; Rosenshine, 1986; Sikorski, Niemiec, & Walberg, 1996).

Finally, in the evaluation step (Step III), teachers assess and evaluate three aspects of their curriculum. First, teachers should assess students to determine whether they acquired the objectives targeted in the curriculum. Second, they should evaluate their instructional delivery after each lesson to determine if changes might improve learning efficiency or

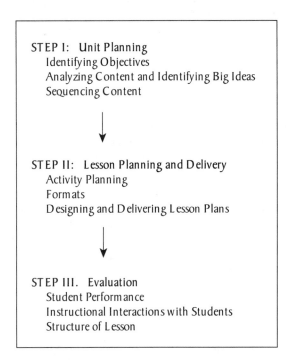

FIGURE 9.1 Process of Unit Planning, Lesson Planning and Delivery, and Evaluation.

increase student performance. The third aspect of the curriculum that they should examine is how lesson activities are designed. Inadequate student performance or inefficient lesson delivery might be remedied by modifying how lesson activities are designed. Teachers should examine each of their activities to determine if they supported and adequately addressed the targeted curriculum goal or objective.

PLANNING UNITS AND GENERAL STRATEGIES

In unit planning teachers specify the scope of the instructional unit by identifying learning objectives, analyze the content to determine the most efficient and effective way to organize information, determine how to sequence the content, and identify the formats that will be used to interact with students efficiently.

Identifying Objectives

Unit objectives are broad descriptions of the critical knowledge and skills that students should gain from instruction. They may describe specific skills or knowledge that are addressed inadequately in the adopted school curriculum. Unit objectives may also be based on state core curriculum descriptions or may be derived from an analysis of items on core content tests. For example, students in elementary schools typically learn about local communities and other communities in the world in social studies. Typical core social studies objectives address how communities are established and what factors influence how communities change over time; Figure 9.2 provides a typical core curriculum standard and four associated objectives.

Analyzing the Content and Identifying Big Ideas

In reviewing the targeted content, teachers should try to identify "big ideas" that tie the targeted content together and are most critical for students to learn (Kameenui & Simmons, 1999). Kameenui and Carnine (1998) define big ideas as "concepts, principles, or heuristics that facilitate the most efficient and broadest acquisition of knowledge" (p. 8). In content instruction such as social studies or science, big ideas form the conceptual framework that links specific facts into a coherent whole. The big idea describes the "sameness," the thing that is the same among the seemingly disparate pieces of information (see Chapters 2, 5, and 8).

These big ideas are the foundation of all the subsequent planning and lesson delivery activities. In some cases, teachers must develop big ideas on their own, other times they may find big ideas in a well-designed curriculum such as Direct Instruction. Teachers who were developing big ideas related to the social studies standard shown in Figure 9.2 could adapt a big idea from the Direct Instruction program, *Understanding U.S. History*. As described in Chapter 8, one big idea in social studies is problem-solution-effect. This big idea, diagrammed in Figure 9.3, may be readily applied to the core social studies objectives. Initially, students learn what characterizes a community and the various public institutions within their community such as police and fire departments, public works, and libraries.

STATE CURRICULUM STANDARD—Elementary Social Studies

Objective 1
Describe the characteristics of a community
    a. Identify the prominent institutions in your community.
    b. Describe the roles of various community workers.

Objective 2
Recognize the sequence of change in communities over time.
    a. Identify factors that contribute to the establishment of communities (e.g., location, natural resources, climate).
    b. Identify factors that contribute to the growth of communities (e.g., agriculture, industry, resources, transportation).
    c. Describe the development of various communities (e.g., village, town, city, megalopolis).

Objective 3
Trace the development of your local community.
    a. Identify the first inhabitants of the community.
    b. Identify the factors that contributed to the establishment of the community.
    c. Identify important historical sites and noted historical figures.

Objective 4
Predict future changes based on history and development of the local community.
    a. Identify factors that may have an impact on the future growth of the community.
    b. Trace changes in transportation over time.

FIGURE 9.2 Community Curriculum Standard for Elementary Level Social Studies

Students might also compare these characteristics with communities in Africa and Europe and determine community characteristics that are similar and those that are different. Why communities are established and how communities change over time are addressed within a problem-solution-effect framework. Simply, communities are established and individuals join communities to improve an economic condition or to improve their human rights.

Four factors will affect which solutions are applied to these community problems: (1) the group's capability; (2) the group's available resources; (3) leadership; and (4) motivation and persistence of the group. Generally, two types of solutions might be readily applied to why new communities form and understanding how they change over time. First, new communities are formed when people with common problems move to a new place. For example, individuals with a common economic desire to "get rich quick" established the mining communities in the western United States and Alaska. In other situations, individuals may solve their problem by forming a smaller, cohesive neighborhood or village within a larger community. Examples of these include the various ethnic quarters found in cities throughout the world. The people who live in these communities are tied by common beliefs, customs, and heritage.

PROBLEM
Why are new communities established?
 1. Economic Hardships
 2. Human Rights

SOLUTION
What kind of solutions result in a new community?
 1. Move and establish a new community
 2. Dominate the oppressors
 3. Tolerate and create supportive communities within the larger group

EFFECT
What happens when the solution is implemented?
 1. Community thrives
 2. Community is eradicated
 3. Community faces new problems

FIGURE 9.3   Problem-Solution-Effect Big Idea Applied to Community
Curriculum Standards

For all solutions there are effects. Communities may thrive initially, but economic and human rights conditions change over time creating new problems. Communities that adapt and develop solutions to these problems thrive and grow while communities that do not adapt and develop solutions disappear (e.g., deserted mining towns of the American West). The group's knowledge and skills, and their resources, leadership, and motivation are factors that contribute to how the community solves their problems and whether they survive over time.

Applying big ideas to the elementary core social studies unit will help create a richer instructional unit and provide a framework for students to understand information presented in social studies textbooks. In addition, this big idea introduces students to a generalizable structure for analyzing historical events. Finally, these big ideas taught in the elementary core curriculum lay the foundation for returning to these topics with increasing complexity in later grades. For example, the problem-solution-effect big idea may be used to analyze why countries have military conflicts and as a basis for analyzing the causes and effects of wars throughout history. In Chapter 8 the problem-solution-effect big idea is applied to the Revolutionary War era in U.S. History. This discussion of developing a big idea in social studies illustrates the broader idea that a careful analysis of the content is a necessary first step to developing instruction in any area. We cannot overemphasize the importance of this content analysis that results in big ideas: big ideas are the basis for instruction that teaches strategically.

Sequencing Content

After identifying the central big ideas, teachers decide on the order in which the individual concepts within the big idea will be taught. Carnine, Silbert, and Kameenui (1997) suggest that (1) prerequisite skills and foundational knowledge should be taught before more complex skills, (2) high-utility skills and important knowledge should be taught before lower-utility skills and less important facts, (3) easy skills and concepts should be taught before more difficult skills, and (4) concepts and information that are likely to be confused should be separated.

Three concerns must be brought together to sequence the content. The sequence must integrate the big ideas, the specific objectives (e.g., from the state core curriculum), and the guidelines for sequencing described above. Figure 9.4 shows a scope and sequence chart for teaching about communities (the objectives from the core shown in Figure 9.2) organized around the big idea of problem-solution-effect and using the sequencing guidelines.

The scope and sequence chart in Figure 9.4 provides a basis for designing specific lessons to teach students about the institutions in communities and how communities evolve through the problem-solution-effect big idea. Foundational knowledge about the community is taught initially and linked to a basic understanding of problem-solution-effect. The problem-solution-effect big idea is then developed with increasing complexity. For each critical concept teachers should allow at least one introductory lesson and two or more lessons to review critical concepts and integrate concept applications into the big idea. Each concept is addressed individually and then integrated into one or more applications. For example, government, police and fire departments, and public works are introduced individually and exemplified within students' local community (Lessons 3–8). These are also applied to a model community that students design in their classroom and compared and contrasted with example communities in Italy and Africa. The tracks in this scope and sequence are designed so that lessons include activities from several tracks. Thus, lessons address more than one objective. The advantage of this design is that information from various lessons is easily linked as students' knowledge increases in sophistication over a number of lessons. In addition, knowledge and skills are practiced repeatedly over time with cumulative reviews to enhance retention (Becker, 1986; Carnine, 1989).

LESSON PLANNING AND DELIVERY

Daily activities that address learning objectives are described in lesson plans. Lesson plans must be explicit in terms of the sequence of activities, what students are expected to do and accomplish in each activity, and how activities relate to each other and to the content studied in previous lessons. In the lesson plan structure described in Figure 9.5, teachers describe each task or activity and what students are expected to do.

The lesson plan is divided into three phases that include interrelated sets of activities. First are learning set activities. The purpose of learning set activities (Hudson et al., 1993)

Strands	1	2	3	4	5	6	7	8	9	10	11	12	13	14
Define community														▓
Definition of community	▓	▓	▓											▓
Explore local community														▓
Government, Police, Fire, Libraries	▓													▓
Public Works, places people live, work, and play				▓										▓
Design a community			▓	▓										▓
Compare to Italian community						▓								▓
Compare to African community								▓	▓					▓
How communities evolve														▓
Problem				▓	▓	▓	▓	▓	▓					▓
Economic hardships						▓								▓
Human rights						▓								▓
Problems faced by local community, Italian community, and African community								▓	▓	▓	▓			▓
Solution				▓	▓	▓	▓							▓
Move							▓							▓
Dominate							▓							▓
Tolerate							▓							▓
Solutions that changed local community, Italian community, and African community										▓	▓	▓		▓
Effect				▓	▓	▓	▓							▓
Problem solved								▓	▓	▓				▓
Problem changes or grows larger								▓	▓					▓
Problem disappears								▓	▓					▓
Historical artifacts of local community			▓	▓	▓	▓	▓	▓	▓	▓	▓			▓

(Column 14 is labeled *Cumulative Review*.)

FIGURE 9.4 A Community Curriculum Scope and Sequence That Employs the Problem-Solution-Effect Big Idea

Learning Set (Prerequisite Skills, Review, and/or Maintenance Check): (Time)
1. Activity: _____ (Obj, Instructional format)
   a. Introduction (1 or 2 sentences)
   b. Content Outline
2. Activity: _____ (Obj, Instructional format)
   a. Introduction (1 or 2 sentences)
   b. Content Outline

New Material and Guided Practice (Time)
1. Activity: _____ (Obj, Instructional format)
   a. Introduction (1 or 2 sentences)
   b. Content Outline
2. Activity: _____ (Obj, Instructional format)
   a. Introduction (1 or 2 sentences)
   b. Content Outline

Independent Practice: (Time)
1. Activity: _____ (Obj, Instructional format)
   a. Provide directions and check student understanding
2. Activity: _____ (Obj, Instructional format)
   a. Provide directions and check student understanding

FIGURE 9.5   A General Lesson Plan That Synthesizes the Suggestions of Several Researchers

is to get students ready for learning by previewing familiar material that is less demanding. This phase of the lesson sets a framework for the rest of the lesson (Rosenshine & Stevens, 1986) and provides opportunities for positive academic interactions between teachers and students. By confirming prerequisite skills or by reviewing material previously presented, teachers check on maintenance of skills and reduce the probability of student errors on related new material and guided practice activities (Christenson et al., 1989; Hofmeister & Lubke, 1990; Hudson, 1996; Hudson et al., 1993; Hunter, 1984; Rosenshine & Stevens, 1986; Test, Browder, Karvonen, Wood, & Algozzine, 2002).

Second are new material and guided practice activities. These activities are designed to present new content and to provide students with structured opportunities to practice this content. Because the material is new, it is likely to be more difficult or more demanding for students than the learning set material. These activities usually include numerous practice examples and frequent opportunities for student responding with teacher feedback (Hofmeister & Lubke, 1990; Hudson, 1997; Hudson et al., 1993; Hunter, 1984; Rosenshine & Stevens, 1986).

Third are independent practice activities. In independent practice activities, students practice skills to develop fluency and apply their knowledge in a broadening array of instructional situations (Englert, 1984; Hudson et al., 1993; Rosenshine & Stevens, 1986).

This lesson plan framework relates activities to each other and to content studied in previous lessons. This sequence of activities is often pictured as a recurring effective teaching cycle (see Figure 9.6). In a simple implementation of these three kinds of activities, teachers conduct the learning set activities followed by new material with guided practice and independent practice activities. Other variations are possible as well. Teachers may want more variation in task difficulty to increase students' persistence and attention to difficult tasks (Horner & Rose, 1989). To accomplish this, teachers begin the lesson with a learning set activity followed by more demanding new material with guided practice activity, and finally an independent practice activity. Teachers may then repeat this sequence one or more times during the lesson. For each lesson teachers decide how much time to spend reviewing previously learned information, teaching new information, and practicing information to consolidate learning. While activities within the learning set, new material and guided practice, and independent practice phases have different purposes, the activity planning process is similar across these lesson delivery phases.

Activity Planning

In designing the activities within each lesson phase, teachers decide how many practice examples should be included in the activity, how to sequence practice examples, and whether to structure the activity for the whole class, small groups, or individuals. Each activity in the lesson plan should be referenced to an objective and the instructional procedures or formats that will be used in the activity. In addition, teachers should provide the information essential for implementing the activity.

The principles used to organize information or skills for lesson activities are similar to those used to determine the sequence of content in the instructional unit. First, founda-

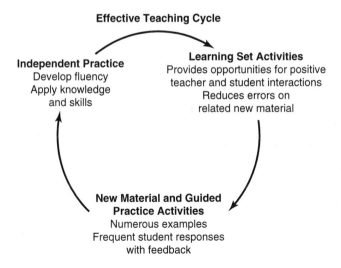

Effective Teaching Cycle

Independent Practice
Develop fluency
Apply knowledge
and skills

Learning Set Activities
Provides opportunities for positive
teacher and student interactions
Reduces errors on
related new material

**New Material and Guided
Practice Activities**
Numerous examples
Frequent student responses
with feedback

FIGURE 9.6   Lesson Planning Phases in an Effective Teaching Cycle

tional vocabulary that will be integrated into more complex knowledge such as stories, knowledge systems, or problem-solving strategies should be taught or reviewed early in the activity. Second, information or skills that students already have in their repertoire should be introduced early and more difficult skills and concepts should be integrated later in the activity. Third, information should be organized so there is a clear relationship between the critical pieces of knowledge. For example, visual displays are effective tools for showing relationships among pieces of information whether that be a process, sequencing events, comparing and contrasting points of view, or describing critical features (Cibrowski, 1998; Hudson et al., 1993). If the purpose of the activity is to establish these types of relationships, then a visual display can be used as the central organizing feature. Fourth, information that is likely to be confused within an activity should be introduced late in the activity or integrated into later activities.

Figure 9.7 shows the critical characteristics of a community. This visual display presents basic community vocabulary and shows relationships among the elements of a community. It could be used as the framework for various activities during a lesson. In the learning set it may be used to review the critical features of communities or to preview text reading on specific communities. In new material and guided practice, it may be used while students are reading to make sure the critical relationships among community elements are clear. Finally, the display may be used in a game format during independent practice or the learning set.

Formats

The teaching procedures for these activities are described in formats. In general, formats provide specific details about (1) how teachers present explanations and examples, (2) how

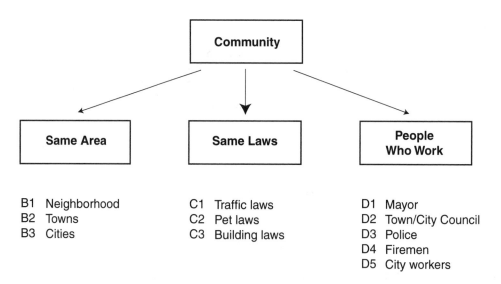

FIGURE 9.7   A Visual Display Depicting the Critical Characteristics of a Community

students respond (e.g., verbally, in writing, demonstrate) and (3) the basis for movement to the next example or lesson activity (e.g., three consecutive correct examples, repeat until firm). Figure 9.8 describes the key elements that should be included in effective and efficient instructional formats using the mnemonic *TESE*: Teacher action; Easy to hard demand on the student; Specify the expected type of response; and Evaluate. Formats should provide numerous opportunities for student responding, active monitoring of student performance, corrective and positive feedback, and support a brisk pace (Christenson et al., 1989; Hudson, 1996, 1997; Hudson et al., 1993; Rosenshine, 1986; Sikorski et al., 1996).

There are many possible formats for teaching vocabulary. Several formats are shown in Figure 9.9. Each of these include clear and logical teacher actions, easy to hard demands on students (e.g., examples are demonstrated or vocabulary is defined before students are asked to respond), the type of response (e.g., unison, individual or group verbal, or other form of response), and the basis for movement to the next vocabulary word. Selection of a format depends on the specific vocabulary to be taught. It is important to remember that students might be confused if too many different formats are employed within a short period of time. In general, a narrow range of formats should be used with naïve students. As these students learn how to work with various formats, the range of formats in an individual lesson can increase.

A format for a fact game based on a visual display from *Your World of Facts Volume I* (Engelmann, Davis, & Davis, 1981) is provided in Figure 9.10. This game may be used to provide practice on a visual display such as the one shown in Figure 9.7. Other, more complex, instructional formats include visual display formats used to teach fact systems (Engelmann & Carnine, 1982), reciprocal teaching formats used in content reading (Carnine, Silbert, & Kameenui, 1997; Palinscar, 1984; Palinscar & Brown, 1986), and math formats used to teach such skills as basic calculations, fractions, and story problems (Stein, Silbert, & Carnine, 1997).

Teacher Action
The presentation and questioning strategy is logical and aligned to the purpose of the activity.

Easy to Hard Demand on the Learner
Use a say-then-write response sequence.
Teach component skills, steps, and knowledge prior to teaching strategies.

Specify the Expected Type of Response
If possible use unison responding prior to individual responding.
Specify the mode of responding (e.g., say, write, show).

Evaluate
Indicate how to determine when to move to the next example or next activity.

FIGURE 9.8 Key Elements That Should Be Included in Instructional Formats

Example—Nonexample
1. Teacher: *This word is "x."*
   What word? Unison response.
2. Teacher: *This is an "x."*
3. Repeat with several examples and nonexamples.
4. Students discriminate examples from nonexamples.
   Is this "x" or "not x"? Unison response.
   Students generate examples.
   Name an "x" or *Give me an example of "x."* Individual responses.
5. Repeat Step 4 for each example and with several students until firm.

Demonstrating Meaning
1. Teacher: *This word is "x."*
   What word? Unison response.
2. Teacher: *"x" means* (definition or synonyms).
   What does "x" mean? Unison response.
3. Teacher: *Show me how you do "x."* Individual or unison response.
4. Repeat Step 3 for multiple students until firm.

Using a Word in a Sentence
1. Teacher: *This word is "x."*
   What word? Unison response.
2. Teacher: *"x" means* (definition or synonyms).
   What does "x" mean? Unison response.
3. Substitute target word for synonym.
   What's another way of saying (sentence with definition or synonym)?
   Group or individuals say the sentence using the target word for
   the definition or synonym.
   Generate a sentence.
   Use "x" in a sentence. Individual response.
4. Repeat Step 3 with at least three sentences and with multiple students until firm.

FIGURE 9.9   Several Formats for Teaching Vocabulary

In published Direct Instruction programs, formats are integrated into the teacher presentation scripts. For example, in *Reading Mastery Plus Level I,* the script uses a consistent format for sounding out new words. Whenever students are to sound out a new word, teachers lead them through the same sequence of steps. When teachers develop instruction, writing fully developed scripts can be time-consuming. Instead, we can write the format once and use it whenever that sequence of instruction is needed.

Fact Game
1. Divide students into groups with four players and one monitor (give the person the answer key)
2. Student rolls the 3 die, adds the numbers, and reads the corresponding question: *What goes in box A?*
3. Student answers the question: *Community*
4. Correct answer: Monitor marks a point on the student's scorecard.
   Incorrect answer:
          Monitor: (state the question with the answer): *What goes in box A?*
          Community
          (repeat the question): *What goes in box A?*
        Student: *Community*
5. Each student except the monitor takes a turn.
   Repeat questions until firm.
Teacher awards bonus points to groups running smoothly.

FIGURE 9.10 A Format for Playing the Fact Game

Designing and Delivering Lesson Plans

Effective lesson plans involve the design and delivery of learning sets, new material and guided practice, and independent practice.

Designing and Delivering the Learning Set.   The purposes of the learning set (Hudson et al., 1993) are to: (1) motivate students by providing numerous opportunities for success and reinforcement (Hudson, 1996; Kindsvater, Wilen, & Ishler, 1988); (2) preview material that sets a framework for the new material (Rosenshine & Stevens, 1986) and (3) ensure students have the necessary knowledge and skills to engage in the lesson successfully.

Learning set activities commonly include oral review with rapid paced questions and answers, fluency-building activities such as timings, peer tutoring, computer simulations, instructional games, and other formats. In addition, Heward et al. (1996) demonstrated that response cards may be used to enable all students to participate actively. The learning set activities should include group and individual responding. The mixture of group and individual responding is an effective strategy for monitoring all students in the group while maintaining student attention (Stevens & Rosenshine, 1981). When lessons begin with familiar review material, students are highly successful and teachers have opportunities to praise student accuracy and attention to the learning task. This initial success and early praise creates a positive motivational context and sets a positive tone for the lesson. Throughout the learning set, teachers check prior knowledge and reteach material as needed. This checking and reteaching strengthens prerequisites, supports success on related new material, and sets the stage to integrate previous material with new learning.

The learning set may include review material that is important to the current lesson or review material that is within the same content domain (e.g., math, science, social studies) and was mastered previously, but is not directly related to the day's lesson. Review material that is directly applicable to the day's lesson is included when the content is a prerequisite for the new material that will be addressed. Review material that is not directly applicable to the day's lesson may be included when students need additional practice to achieve mastery or to recheck student mastery on information that was previously mastered. In either case, the learning set activities provide a context for knowledge integration (Kameenui & Carnine, 1998). That is, the juxtaposition of mastered content in a domain with the new content that is to come sets the context for interrelating the concepts and ideas to create a new and more complex knowledge fabric.

A good strategy for designing these activities is to divide the activity into three parts. Part 1 includes questions or problems that address mastered content (e.g., definition and examples of different communities). This section provides assurance that students are firm on material that has already been taught. Part 2 includes problems or questions on content that students studied recently (e.g., types of laws, and people who work in the community). This section sets the stage for Part 3, a mixed set of questions or problems (e.g., review laws in the communities that students designed). By using this strategy teachers may confirm students' performance on content in isolation and when integrated into an increasingly complex instructional context.

The learning set not only sets the stage for integrating previously learned material with the new material but also contributes to the variety of instructional activities. Several researchers have demonstrated that the task variety achieved by mixing mastered and more complex material increases student interest and attention to task, particularly with low-performing students (Horner & Rose, 1989; Kameenui & Darch, 1995; Skinner, in press). In most classrooms, the learning set should take approximately 25 percent of the time allocated for the lesson (Hofmeister & Lubke, 1990).

The learning set phase of Lesson 4 in the community curriculum is presented in Figure 9.11. This learning set includes two activities that promote active student responding. The first activity is a whole-group teacher-directed activity in which students review basic concepts and vocabulary about communities. The second activity is a fact game that uses the visual display depicting the critical characteristics of a community (Figure 9.7). The fact game gives teachers an opportunity to check how well students understand the critical elements of a community and sets the stage for introducing how communities change and the basic problem-solution-effect big idea.

When teachers deliver learning set activities they should remain aware of the purposes of the learning set. The mixture of group and individual responding is an effective instructional management technique and gives teachers an opportunity to check student understanding of critical prerequisite knowledge. Because it is likely that students have a reasonably good understanding of the learning set material, they are likely to respond correctly at a high rate. Teachers may take advantage of this by providing positive feedback and quickly correcting student errors. If students make errors during the group-response activity, teachers may correct students as a group, creating a cohesive positive atmosphere to begin the lesson's activities. When fluency timings on important vocabulary or instructional games and worksheets are also included in the learning set, effective teachers

Lesson 4 of Community Unit Learning Set from Lesson Plan	
Learning Set (Prerequisite Skills, Review, and/or Maintenance Check):	

1. Activity: Oral questions: Communities
   a. Introduction: In social studies we have been studying communities.
   b. Content questions:
     What is community?
     What are some examples of communities?
	(Core Objective 1)

2. Activity: Fact Game with Community Visual Display (Figure 9.7); questions attached.	(Core Objective 1, Fact game format)

Questions for Fact Game	
Number on dice	Question
3.	What goes in box A?
4.	What goes in box B?
5.	What goes in box C?
6.	What goes in box D?
7.	These people enforce laws in the community.
8.	These people help protect our property when there is a disaster.
9.	These people help take care of roads.
10.	These people help pick up trash each week.
11.	This person is the head of the town or city.
12.	These people make town or city laws.
13.	What kinds of laws govern where cars can go and where stop signs are placed?
14.	What kinds of laws govern how dogs and cats should be treated?
15.	What kinds of laws govern how you should build houses?
16.	People who live near one another are in the same _____ .
17.	What is a large community usually governed by a mayor?
18.	What is a populated area that is smaller than a city, but larger than a neighborhood?

FIGURE 9.11   Learning Set from Lesson Plan for Lesson 4 of Community Unit

move around the classroom noting students' accurate performance and providing corrective feedback as needed (Gunter, Shores, Jack, Rasmussen, & Flowers, 1995; Hofmeister & Lubke, 1990). Throughout the learning set teachers should take advantage of high-rate correct responding by praising students' content knowledge and attention to task.

New Material and Guided Practice.   New material and guided practice activities are designed to present new concepts and skills and to provide practice using those concepts and skills. Acquisition of new material is facilitated by organizing learning activities in small instructional tasks. Each activity should include a brief presentation that clearly illustrates the critical feature(s) of the concept or skill and numerous examples for practice and feedback. Following an initial activity, teachers may include additional tasks that carefully extend concepts or skills to a broader array of applications. By carefully scaffolding (Kameenui & Carnine, 1998) or supporting the activity sequence, teachers increase the probability that all students will learn how to apply the critical concepts and rules in an increasingly broad array of contexts.

During the new material and guided practice phase, students should answer frequent questions and teachers should provide feedback after each answer. Keeping students active maintains an instructional focus. Frequent feedback helps students learn the critical information and supports motivation. Activities that combine oral and written responding might be included in the middle and latter part of guided practice. When written responding comes after a correct oral response, there is a high probability that students' written responses will be correct. Guided practice activities should include extensive teacher monitoring and feedback (Hofmeister & Lubke, 1990). Teachers might accomplish this by working with their whole class and mixing whole-class, small-group, and individual responses throughout an activity or by dividing students into small groups and moving around the classroom noting students' accurate performance and providing corrective feedback as needed.

Initial activities during new material and guided practice should be teacher-directed group activities to support initial acquisition of knowledge. These activities should include many examples of critical vocabulary, concepts and rules, and numerous structured opportunities for teacher and student interaction. Visual displays are effective tools for organizing activities where the purpose is to show relationships between important ideas or to link key vocabulary to a larger organizational structure (Engelmann & Carnine, 1982; Engelmann et al., 1981; Hudson et al., 1993). Activities with less support and scaffolding are included in the middle and latter part of guided practice. These activities include reading textbooks that elaborate on the facts and relationships, using games in which students take turns answering questions (see Engelmann et al., 1981 for examples of visual displays and related instructional games), and written exercises or study guides designed to expand the critical vocabulary and relationships learned in the initial activity. In most classrooms, approximately 50 percent of the time allocated for a lesson should be devoted to new material and guided practice (Hofmeister & Lubke, 1990).

The new material and guided practice phase of the community lesson plan is shown in Figure 9.12. In the first activity, frequent responding and feedback is accomplished by engaging students in an active discussion about how and why communities change. This discussion is organized around the problem-solution-effect visual display (see Figure 9.3). This visual display is used to link the problem-solution-effect big idea to experiences students have had designing their own communities in previous lessons. The second activity uses vocabulary formats to teach key vocabulary for an upcoming reading activity. By using these predesigned vocabulary formats, teachers avoid the labor of recreating formats for each day's vocabulary lesson. The vocabulary activities are followed by a guided reading activity with oral comprehension questions. The comprehension questions apply the problem-solution-effect big idea to the particular events in this chapter. In addition to helping students understand the chapter, this activity exemplifies and elaborates on the central big idea.

Lesson 4 of Community Unit New Material and Guided Practice from Lesson Plan	

1. Activity: Changing Communities
  a. Introduction: The community you started to build in class started small. After you "discovered the land," what did you do? Answer: Built houses
  b. Then what did you do? Answer: Built shops, farms, roads
  c. Do communities stay the same? Answer: No
  d. So communities change over time. What do communities do? Answer: Change over time
  e. Communities change when faced with problems (show problem, solution, effect visual display [Figure 9.3]). After you "discovered land" you needed a place to live. That was the problem.
  f. What solution did you think of for that problem? Answer: Chopped down trees and built houses
  g. Finally, what was the effect of the solution? How did the community change? Answer: We had houses and room to grow food.
  h. What are some other problems, solutions, and effects you faced in starting your community? Answer: Students generate list of problems, solutions, and effects. Write on visual display
	(Core Objective 2, Visual display format)

2. Activity We are going to continue reading about Sarah Noble and her father. Let's see if we can identify some of the problems they faced, how they solved their problems, and what effect those solutions had on them (Dalgliesh, A. [1954]. *The Courage of Sarah Noble.* New York: Charles Scribners & Son). Here are some important words you will read in the story today: Milford plots hollowed beyond johnny cake bean porridge courage pleasant comforting pattern	(Vocabulary formats)

3. Activity: Read story. Ask comprehensive questions.
Comprehensive questions
  1. (p.19) When Sarah and her father reached the land where they would build their home what problem did they face? (*where they would live while they built their home*)
  2. (p.19) What was their solution for this problem? (*live in a cave temporarily*)
  3. (p.19) What effect did this solution have on Sarah? (*at first she was lonely; then she got to know the Indian children who visited her*)
  4. (p.20) What did Sarah make her father for dinner? (*bean porridge*)
  5. (p.20) What problem did Sarah face at night? (*she was afraid of the night sounds*)
  6. (p.22) How did she solve this problem? (*talk to her father; talk to herself*)
  7. (p.22) What effect did this solution have on her? (*calmed her down; the night sounds became a comfortable pattern*)
	(Core Objective 2, Reading formats)

FIGURE 9.12 New Material and Guided Practice from Lesson Plan for Lesson 4 of Community Unit

Independent Practice.   Activities included in independent practice are designed to develop skill fluency and to consolidate knowledge (Hofmeister & Lubke, 1990). Independent practice activities should promote extended practice with concepts and skills acquired during new material and guided practice, and promote integration of this new learning with previously learned content. Independent practice activities may include fluency activities, worksheets, and study guides completed by groups or individual students, instructional games, computer games and simulations designed to integrate previously presented content (e.g., Horton, Lovitt, & Slocum, 1989; Woodward, Carnine, & Gersten, 1988), peer tutoring, and mastery tests.

Including activities from previous lessons in independent practice creates an overlap that helps integrate newer material with previously acquired skills and concepts. Several techniques may be used to design a sequence of activities to create an integrated fabric of knowledge. First, previously mastered, but related, activities may be juxtaposed with activities that address the new material presented during the current lesson. Second, the previously mastered material may be interspersed within the practice material for the current lesson (Skinner, in press). The third approach employs a combination of both strategies in which three activities are designed: a long activity that provides practice with current skills or concepts, a second, shorter activity that addresses previously mastered material, and a third short activity that provides interspersed practice. In most classrooms, approximately 25 percent of the allocated instructional time should be devoted to independent practice, although more time may be allocated near the end of a unit for cumulative review and practice (Hofmeister & Lubke, 1990).

The independent practice phase of the community lesson is shown in Figure 9.13. In the first independent practice activity, students interview their local police chief in their classroom. This activity expands students' understanding of local community leaders and uses interview skills that they learned in earlier lessons. In the second activity, students complete a comprehension exercise that links the problem-solution-effect big idea to the story they read in class.

Lesson 4 of Community Unit Independent Practice from Lesson Plan	
1. Activity: Continue interviews of "People who make our community work."— Police Chief a. Use interview form.	(Core Objective 1)
2. Activity: Comprehensive exercise using **Problem, Solution, Effect** visual display. a. Students work in groups of three. The monitor writes information on display. b. Group identifies **Problems, Solutions,** and **Effects** Sarah faced in today's chapter and in earlier chapters.	(Core Objective 2)

FIGURE 9.13 Independent Practice from Lesson Plan for Lesson 4 of Community Unit

As they did during the learning set, effective teachers move around the classroom noting students' accurate performance and providing corrective feedback as needed. If teachers notice that students are making similar errors or if many are asking similar questions, they should move back to guided practice, reconfirm correct student responding, and sequentially move toward independent practice. During the sample community lesson plan, teachers move around the classroom, check student work, and praise group cooperation while they complete their problem-solution-effect visual displays.

EVALUATION

Lessons should be evaluated in terms of student performance, teachers' instructional interactions with students, and the structure of the lesson.

Student Performance

Student performance is assessed on learning objectives after they complete practice activities that may extend for several lessons. For example, they might describe the principle factors that influence the development of a community after they complete ten lessons in the curriculum sequence depicted in Figure 9.4.

Instructional Interactions with Students

In contrast, teachers should evaluate their instructional interaction with students for each instructional activity following each lesson. Teachers may evaluate their instructional interactions by addressing four fundamental questions: (1) Did I provide numerous opportunities to respond to relevant examples during the activity? (2) Was there a high ratio of correct to incorrect responding (approximately an 8:2 ratio)? (3) Were students on-task for more than 90 percent of the time during the activity? and (4) Was the allocated time for instructional phases (learning set, new material and guided practice, and independent practice) and activities within phases sufficient?

Structure of Lesson

By examining student performance and instructional interactions with students, teachers may identify changes that are needed in the structure of the lesson, the activities used within the lesson, and the interactions with students described in the activity formats that might improve their performance and instructional efficiency.

In general, large changes in instructional procedures and activity formats are warranted when more than 20 percent of the students fail to meet a criterion of 80 percent correct or the performance criteria described in the instructional format (Hofmeister & Lubke, 1990; Stevens & Rosenshine, 1981). These changes may include adding activities to teach new concepts, reorganizing the sequence of examples and the instructional formats for particular activities, providing additional practice examples, changing activity grouping structures, and changing time allocations for activities.

Smaller changes designed to improve instructional efficiency might be called for when students meet performance targets but problems are apparent in the interactions during the lessons. These problems include activities in which students have few opportunities to respond, make frequent errors, or are frequently off-task. Some changes that teachers might consider, depending on the evaluation data collected, include: increasing academic or behavioral praise, varying the way in which students respond, reducing the amount of content taught at one time, clarifying or condensing explanations or questions, and clearly structuring corrections to promote success with low-performing students.

SUPPORTING RESEARCH

This chapter describes how teachers might use Direct Instruction principles and an effective teaching structure to design and deliver small instructional units. Research that supports the analysis of knowledge forms and communication that characterizes curriculum planning was conducted in the field test and revision cycles conducted with commercially available Direct Instruction programs (see Chapter 2 for an extensive discussion of Direct Instruction research).

Two critical design features in Direct Instruction programs and highlighted in this chapter are big ideas and structuring the curriculum in cumulative information tracks. Instruction in big ideas permits an efficient use of classroom time, accommodates diverse students, and improves student achievement. In research evaluating big ideas applied to U.S. History, Carnine, Caros, Crawford, Hollenbeck, and Harniss (1997) found that students at-risk scored higher on measures related to content knowledge than students who used a traditional text and experiential approach to history instruction. In a follow-up study that addressed students' skills in writing applied content essays, lower-performing students scored lower than high performers in recalling and integrating historical facts. However, recall scores for low-performing students on the central concepts in the chapter were equivalent to recall scores for higher-performing students. In another investigation by Carnine et al. (1997), increases in vocabulary understanding were noted for students with diverse backgrounds instructed with a text organized around big ideas, while students who used the district adopted traditional curriculum showed little or no gain in vocabulary knowledge.

In a synthesis of research on videodisc core concepts math curricula organized around big ideas, Fischer and Tarver (1997) found consistently large effect sizes in studies that included students with disabilities, students at-risk, and students with average to high abilities. Taken together, these studies suggest that curricula organized around big ideas result in improved performance with a variety of students.

Several studies have shown the efficacy of organizing curricular information in cumulative tracks (Carnine, 1976; Gleason, Carnine, & Valla, 1991; Johnson, Gersten, & Carnine, 1987). For example, Gleason et al. (1991) taught ninety-five elementary and middle school students receiving remedial reading to identify the seven countries in Central America using a computer program. The students were divided into two treatment groups. For one group the countries were presented gradually with cumulative practice after each new country was introduced; for the other group, all the countries were presented at one time, then students practiced the entire set of countries. The results of this study highlight the efficiency of a cumulative curriculum design. While both groups of students eventually learned the material, the cumulative-introduction group required less than half the number of responses and less than half the time to meet criterion than students in the rapid introduction group. In addition, the students in the cumulative introduction group made almost five times fewer errors than students in the rapid introduction group. These results suggest that a cumulative programming strategy might be used effectively to teach and integrate more information in less time than a traditional curricular structure.

Using an effective lesson structure with validated instructional practices is also critical for successful teacher-designed instruction. The empirical basis for the effective lesson structure and practices suggested in this chapter are derived from over twenty-five years of research. Initially, researchers conducted large descriptive studies in elementary and high school classrooms (e.g., Brophy & Evertson, 1974; Capie & Tobin, 1981; Medley, 1977; Rosenshine, 1978) and with a broad range of populations including preschool children (Lane & Bergen, 1988), students with disabilities (Bickel & Bickel, 1986; Hudson, 1996, 1997), and in schooling in other countries throughout the world (Fuller, 1987). While the correlations between instructional variables and student performance were generally weak, the same set of instructional variables were identified consistently across studies: learning sets characterized by reviews, maintenance checks, and attention to prerequisite skills; new material and guided practice; and independent practice (see Hofmeister & Lubke, 1990; Hudson et al, 1993; and Hunter, 1984 for discussions of this research).

The early correlational research also led to studies that examined teaching practices that characterized effective teaching. These include the use of clear signals for student responding (Carnine & Fink, 1978), active student instructional engagement characterized by high rates of questioning and feedback (Anderson, 1980; Carnine, 1976; Delquadri et al., 1986; Greenwood et al., 1984; Sainato et. al., 1987), systematic error corrections that end with correct student responses (Barbetta, Heron, & Heward, 1993; Barbetta, Heward, & Bradley, 1993), and contingent praise for correct academic responding and behavior that supports active learning.

REFERENCES

Anderson, L. M. (1980). *An examination of classroom context: Effects of lesson format and teacher training on patterns of teacher–student contact during small group instruction.* Austin, TX: Austin Research and Development Center for Teachers. (Eric Document Reproduction Service No. ED189 075).

Barbetta, P., Heron, T. E., & Heward, W. L. (1993). Effects of active student response during error correction on the acquisition, maintenance, and generalization of sight words by students with developmental disabilities. *Journal of Applied Behavior Analysis, 26,* 111–119.

Barbetta, P., Heward, W. L., & Bradley, D. M. C. (1993). Relative effects of whole-word and phonetic prompt error correction on the acquisition and maintenance of sight words by students with developmental disabilities. *Journal of Applied Behavior Analysis, 26,* 99–110.

Becker, W. (1986*). Applied psychology for teachers: A behavioral cognitive approach.* Chicago, IL: Science Research Associates.

Bickel, W., & Bickel, D. (1986). Effective schools, classrooms, and instruction: Implications for special education. *Exceptional Children, 52,* 489–500.

Brophy, J. E., & Evertson, C. M. (1974). *Process–product correlations in the Texas Teacher effectiveness study: Final report.* Austin, TX: University of Texas (Eric Document Reproduction Service No. ED091 394).

Capie, W., & Tobin, K. G. (1981). Pupil engagement in learning tasks: A fertile area for research in science teaching. *Journal of Research in Science Teaching, 18,* 409–417.

Carnine, D. (1976). Effects of two teacher-presentation rates on off-task behavior, answering correctly, and participation. *Journal of Applied Behavior Analysis, 9,* 199–206.

Carnine, D. (1989). Designing practice activities. *Journal of Learning Disabilities, 10,* 603–607.

Carnine, D., Caros, J., Crawford, D., Hollenbeck, K., & Harniss, M. (1997). Five intervention studies evaluating *Understanding U.S. History. Effective School Practices, 16*(1), 36–55.

Carnine, D., & Fink, W. T. (1978). Increasing the rate of presentation and use of signals in elementary classroom teachers. *Journal of Applied Behavior Analysis, 11,* 35–46.

Carnine, D., Silbert, J., & Kameenui, E. (1997). *Direct instruction reading.* Columbus, OH: Merrill.

Christenson, S. L., Ysseldyke, J. E., & Thurlow, M. L. (1989). Critical instructional factors for students with mild handicaps: An integrative review. *Remedial and Special Education, 10*(5), 21–31.

Cibrowski, J. (1998). *Textbooks and the students who can't read them: A guide to teaching content.* Cambridge, MA: Brookline.

Delquadri, J., Greenwood, C. R., Whorton, D., Carta, J. J., & Hall, R. V. (1986). Classwide peer tutoring. *Exceptional Children, 52,* 535–542.

Engelmann. S., & Carnine, D. (1982). *Theory of instruction: Principles and applications.* New York: Irvington.

Engelmann, S., Davis, K., & Davis, G. (1981). *Your world of facts I: A memory development program.* Tigard, OR: C.C. Publications.

Englert, C. S. (1984). Effective direct instruction practices in special education settings. *Remedial and Special Education, 5*(2), 38–47.

Fischer, T. A., & Tarver, S. (1997). Meta-analysis of studies of mathematics curricula designed around big ideas. *Effective School Practices, 16*(1), 71–80.

Fuller, B. (1987). What school factors raise achievement in the third world? *Review of Educational Research, 57,* 255–292.

Gleason, M., Carnine, D., & Valla, N. (1991). Cumulative vs. rapid introduction of new information. *Exceptional Children, 57*(4), 353–358.

Greenwood, C. R., Delquadri, J., & Hall, R. V. (1984). Opportunity to respond and student academic performance. In W. L. Heward, T. E. Heron, & J. Trap-Porter (Eds.), *Focus on behavior analysis in education* (pp. 59–88). Columbus, OH: Merrill.

Gunter, P. L., Shores, R. E., Jack, S. L., Rasmussen, S. K., & Flowers, J. (1995). On the move. *Teaching Exceptional Children, 28*(1), 12–14.

Heward, W. L., Gardner, R., Cavanaugh, R. A., Courson, F. H., Grossi, T. A., & Barbetta, P. M. (1996). Everyone participates in this class. *Teaching Exceptional Children, 28*(2), 4–11.

Hofmeister, A., & Lubke, M. (1990). *Research into practice: Implementing effective teaching strategies.* Boston, MA: Allyn & Bacon.

Horner, R. H., & Rose, H. (1989). Generalized skills training with severely retarded students. *Direct Instruction News, 8*(2), 12–14.

Horton, S., Lovitt, T. C., & Slocum, T. (1989). Teaching geography to high school students with academic deficits: Effects of a computerized study guide. *Learning Disabilities Quarterly, 11,* 371–379.

Hudson, P. J. (1996). Using a learning set to increase learning disabled students' performance in social studies classes. *Learning Disabilities Research and Practice, 11,* 78–85.

Hudson, P. J. (1997). Using teacher-guided practice to help students with learning disabilities acquire and retain social studies content. *Learning Disability Quarterly, 20,* 23–32.

Hudson, P. J., Lignugaris/Kraft, B., & Miller, T. (1993). Using content enhancements to improve the performance of adolescents with learning disabilities in content classes. *Learning Disabilities Research and Practice, 8,* 106–126.

Hunter, M. (1984). Knowing, teaching, and supervising. In P. L. Hosford (Ed.), *Using what we know about teaching* (pp. 169–193). Alexandria, VA: Association for Supervision and Curriculum Design.

Johnson, G., Gersten, R., & Carnine, D. (1987). Effects of instructional design variables on vocabulary acquisition of LD students: A study of computer assisted-instruction. *Journal of Learning Disabilities, 20,* 206–213.

Kameenui, E., & Carnine, D. (1998). *Effective teaching strategies that accommodate diverse learners.* Columbus, OH: Merrill.

Kameenui, E., & Darch, C. (1995). *Instructional classroom management.* White Plains, NY: Longman.

Kameenui, E., & Simmons, D. (1999). *Toward successful inclusion of students with disabilities: The architecture of instruction.* Reston, VA: Council for Exceptional Children.

Kindsvater, R., Wilen, W., & Ishler, M. (1988). *Dynamic of effective teaching.* New York: Longman.

Lane, S., & Bergen, J. R., (1988). Effects of instructional variables on language ability of preschool children. *American Educational Research Journal, 25,* 271–283.

Medley, D. M. (1977). *Teacher competence and teacher effectiveness: A review of process–product research.* Washington, DC: American Association of Colleges of Teacher Education (Eric Document Reproduction Service No. ED143 629).

Palinscar, A. (1984). The quest for meaning from expository text: A teacher-guided journey. In G. Duffy, L. Rochler, & J. Mason (Eds.), *Comprehension instruction: Perspectives and suggestions* (pp. 251–265). New York: Longman.

Palinscar, A., & Brown, A. (1986). Interactive teaching to promote independent learning from text. *The Reading Teacher, 39,* 771–777.

Rosenshine, B. (1978). *Academic engaged time, content covered, and direct instruction* (Eric Document Reproduction Service No. ED152 776).

Rosenshine, B. (1986). Synthesis of research on explicit teaching. *Educational Leadership, 43*(7), 60–69.

Rosenshine, B., & Stevens, R. (1986). Teaching functions. In M. D. Wittrock (Ed.), *AERA handbook of research on teaching* (3rd ed., pp. 376–391). New York: MacMillan.

Sainato, D. M., Strain, P. S., & Lyon, S. R. (1987). Increasing academic responding of handicapped preschool children during group instruction. *Journal of the Division of Early Childhood, 12,* 23–30.

Sikorski, M. F., Niemiec, R. P., & Walberg, H. J. (1996). A classroom checkup: Best teaching practices in special education. *Teaching Exceptional Children, 29*(1), 27–29.

Skinner, C. (in press). An empirical analysis of interspersal research: Evidence, implications, and applications of the discrete task completion hypothesis. *Journal of School Psychology.*

Stein, M., Silbert, J., & Carnine, D. (1997). *Designing effective mathematics instruction: A direct instruction approach* (3rd ed.). Columbus, OH: Merrill.

Stevens, R., & Rosenshine, B. (1981). Advances in research on teaching. *Exceptional Education Quarterly, 2,* 1–9.

Test, D., Browder, D. M., Karvonen, M., Wood, W., & Algozzine, B. (2002). Writing lesson plans for promoting self-determination. *Teaching Exceptional Children, 35*(1), 8–16.

Woodward, J., Carnine, D., & Gersten, R. (1988). Teaching problem solving through computer simulations. *American Educational Research Journal, 25,* 72–86.

CHAPTER TEN

ASPECTS OF SCHOOLWIDE IMPLEMENTATIONS

NANCY MARCHAND-MARTELLA

Eastern Washington University

MOLLY BLAKELY AND ED SCHAEFER

Educational Resources, Inc.

OBJECTIVES

After studying this chapter you should be able to:

1. describe the elements and learning environments of effective schools;
2. define *opportunity to learn* in terms of time spent learning and time needed to learn;
3. explain how Direct Instruction fits into an effective school framework;
4. discuss critical issues and guidelines for implementing Direct Instruction programs;
5. describe coaching as a means of staff development;
6. explain the common types of coaching interventions;
7. discuss how we could provide effective coaching using the Direct Instruction coaching format;
8. characterize various tutoring models and procedures;
9. illustrate how to implement and evaluate a tutoring program;
10. summarize research conducted on tutoring using Direct Instruction programs;
11. note how we can structure the supervision of preservice teachers using an effective Direct Instruction supervision system;
12. discuss the research conducted on the Direct Instruction supervision system.

We have seen how urgent the need is to implement effective and efficient programs such as Direct Instruction. We have discussed the basic elements of DI programs. Additionally, we have discussed a myriad of DI programs in the academic areas of language, reading, writing, spelling, mathematics, and the content areas. We have also explored how to implement effective lesson plans following the effective teaching literature when no DI programs exist for what we want to teach. The chapters in Part III of this text (Chapters 9 and 10) take DI beyond the programs into areas of classroom implementation.

The implementation of DI programs requires coordinated efforts and quality training to ensure high levels of student achievement across the school. We cannot take implementation aspects lightly. We may hear that particular schools or teachers implement Direct Instruction programs with limited success. As educators driven by empirical evidence (i.e., those who make decisions based on the data), we must look to the environmental circumstances that may have produced these effects. What happened (or did not happen) when the program was implemented? What did the teacher do (or not do)? Amberge (2002) described reasons why an implementation of DI may not work. These include:

1. The students are not given placement tests to determine the appropriate program and level.
2. It is not used consistently in the order presented.
3. The teacher does not repeat a section until the students are firm.
4. The teacher alters the program, and chooses not to follow the script.
5. The students are not given specific praise to build their confidence in their own abilities (pp. 16–17).

In this chapter we describe various aspects of DI implementations. First, we describe the elements of effective schools. Opportunity to learn and those aspects that affect time spent learning and time needed to learn are discussed to enhance the development of an effective school. Second, we discuss how DI fits within an effective school framework. Third, we describe critical issues and guidelines for implementing DI programs to ensure proper implementation to ensure student success. Fourth, we highlight coaching as a means of staff development, with particular emphasis on the team-teach/side-by-side coaching model. Fifth, given that DI programs can be implemented by well-trained tutors within effective schools, we detail various aspects of effective tutoring programs. Finally, no chapter on DI implementations would be complete without a discussion of quality preservice teacher training and supervision at the university/college level. We describe a DI supervision system to help prepare "new" teachers.

ELEMENTS AND LEARNING ENVIRONMENTS OF EFFECTIVE SCHOOLS

We all want our schools to be effective learning environments for our children. What does it take to create an effective school? In a research synthesis of effective school practices, Cotton (1995) noted the following typical elements of effective schools:

1. Academic achievement is the school's top priority.
2. Strong leadership guides the instructional program.

3. Curriculum is based on clear goals and objectives.
4. Students are grouped for effective instruction.
5. School time reflects the academic priorities.
6. Learning progress is monitored closely.
7. Discipline is firm and consistent.
8. There are high expectations for quality instruction.
9. Incentives/rewards build strong motivation.
10. Parents are invited to become involved.
11. Staff strive to improve instructional effectiveness based on multiple sources of data related directly to student performance.

Effective schools are organized to enhance *student learning*; they recognize that creating an environment that promotes *staff learning* is one of the keys to promoting *student learning*. The student learning environment is of paramount importance. This environment includes the organization of curriculum, instruction, and classroom management that determines what students must do to achieve academic excellence in any subject area. Further, the staff learning environment includes the circumstances necessary for staff to create and sustain the desired student learning environment. Consequently, the staff learning environment "takes its cue" from the student learning environment. At a minimum, the staff learning environment addresses the academic mission of the school; systematic procedures for monitoring and responding to mission progress; the nature and scope of staff development; and the character, reach, and function of school leadership.

How do these two learning environments function to maximize academic achievement and to contribute to the growth of the school as an effective instructional organization? Forty years ago, Carroll (1963) gave us a useful analytic schema when he noted that academic achievement is determined by a student's opportunity to learn, defined as the ratio of time spent learning to the time needed to learn.

$$\text{Opportunity to Learn} = \frac{\text{Time Spent Learning}}{\text{Time Needed to Learn}}$$

Time spent learning is determined by the amount of criterion content covered and the amount of academic learning time invested in mastering the criterion content. Criterion content constitutes the academic agenda of a subject area: the scope and sequence of goals and objectives (knowledge and skills) that establish or enable a standard-meeting performance—for example, the fluent reading of sophisticated text. Effective schools recognize that there are no shortcuts to the successful attainment of higher-level learning objectives. They understand that higher-level skills are built on a strong foundation of basic skills. Effective schools recognize that many years of focused, sequential, and directed instruction are necessary if every student is to master the basic knowledge and skills that must be integrated and applied to higher-level performance (Brophy & Good, 1986).

Criterion Content Covered

Criterion content covered is the first variable that determines time spent learning. Effective schools recognize that they must establish a well-defined, systematically developed, multiyear curriculum of goals and objectives that, when mastered, enables any student to perform at high (criterion) levels. To accommodate any student, such a curriculum must include multiple entry points determined by objective, clearly defined placement procedures; frequent assessments of mastery or progress-to-date; and built-in systems to allow for adequate practice, correction, and remediation as well as methods of acceleration for students learning at a quicker pace. To educate all students well, effective schools acknowledge that, in each subject area, there can be only one curriculum sequence to which all students and staff adhere. Other programs or technologies are valued only to the extent that they build on or extend the core curriculum. This additional effort might occur, for example, to meet unique assessment or standards requirements in a given state.

Establishing the curriculum (including extensions) is the responsibility of school leadership, not individual teachers. Therefore, monitoring and supporting staff fidelity to, and student progress through, the core curriculum is a top priority of leadership. To accelerate all students through the curriculum, effective schools employ flexible, homogeneous grouping, based on present levels of student performance, in each priority subject area. Younger students and those functioning below grade level are given priority with respect to small group size. Procedures that place, group, and regroup students within a curriculum sequence are effective, efficient, and consistent. Managing this process is a high priority of leadership.

Academic Learning Time

Academic learning time (ALT) is a second variable that determines learning. Before we discuss academic learning time, we must first define the various levels of time in the school. There are four basic levels: available, allocated, engaged, and academic learning (Martella, Nelson, & Marchand-Martella, 2003). Available time is the amount of time available for all instruction. For example, if a school day is six hours, the total available time is six hours. However, the time in the school day must be allocated to many different activities; some of these are academic and some are nonacademic. Schools never have six hours available solely for instruction. Allocated time is the amount of time a teacher or school plans to devote to a given content/subject area. Engaged time involves the amount of time students are actively engaged in learning activities. Engaged time is also termed *on-task time*. Academic learning time is similar to engaged time in that students are actively involved in learning activities. However, academic learning time also involves the time when students are also *successful* (Olson & Platt, 2000). Academic learning time is the time when true learning takes place. Effective curricula such as Direct Instruction programs are designed to enhance academic learning time by their tight sequences, structured review, in-program assessments, and unison responding (to name a few important features).

Time allocations are the responsibility of the school as a whole and reflect the school's emphasis on academic achievement in priority subject areas. In each subject area, time sufficient to enable every student to excel is allocated and scheduled at the school level and protected at every level. Students functioning below grade level are allocated additional instructional time as needed to achieve grade-level status. Schedules that account for every minute of the instructional day are posted prominently in every classroom or instructional area. Instruction begins on time and proceeds unabated for the full instructional period—

every period, every day. Monitoring and supporting staff fidelity to the published schedules of allocated time is a critical leadership priority.

Additionally, student motivation to persevere and remain engaged in the learning process significantly enhances academic learning time and thus the opportunity to learn. Such commitments depend on how often students experience well-prepared and quickly paced lessons, short-term (daily) academic success, positive interactions with staff, and incentives or recognition for achievement. Monitoring and supporting the effectiveness of classroom instruction, rates of student engagement and success, and procedures to teach and reinforce responsible learning behavior are critical leadership functions.

The knowledge and skills required to maximize criterion content covered and academic learning time are at the core of the staff development agenda. Organizing, monitoring, and evaluating staff development are visible leadership priorities.

Minimizing Time Needed to Learn

The skills required to accelerate learning are at the core of the staff development agenda. Effective schools look first to employ curriculum (in any subject area) to prevent problems from arising. The curriculum provides frequent, objective, and short-term assessments of critical content and skills, especially those that most directly relate to upcoming instruction. Administering and responding to these assessments is a primary responsibility of the teacher. Monitoring student assessments, and the responses of staff to these assessments, is a primary responsibility of school leadership. Written lesson plans that embody the instructional routines are tightly aligned with the content, sequence, and assessments incorporated into the curriculum (see Chapter 9 for more details on lesson plans). They are sufficiently explicit to promote effective and efficient instruction for all students across teachers, grades, and years of instruction.

Effective schools recognize that both the content and the sequence of curriculum, instruction, and assessment are crucial. Within each subject area, these elements must be aligned and integrated into a seamless instructional program for all students, across teachers, grades, and years of instruction. Identifying, promoting, providing, and supporting such programs, therefore, is a hallmark of effective school leadership.

Pogrow (1996) noted that, in spite of the prodigious knowledge base on effective schools and teaching, the history of school improvement over the past thirty-five years has been "one of consistent failure of major reforms to survive and become institutionalized" (p. 657). Pogrow attributed this failure to the penchant of American educators to approach school improvement by disseminating generalized knowledge and then leaving it up to practitioners to figure out how to organize and apply that knowledge to local circumstances. Successful reforms or innovations are almost always highly structured solutions that are specifically focused, clearly defined (and therefore easily monitored), and systematic (include a complete system for implementation and dissemination). Pogrow called such a solution a *technology* or a systematic way of doing something effectively, efficiently, and consistently. Creating more effective schools to educate all our children well requires a *technology of implementation;* Direct Instruction is such a technology of implementation.

DIRECT INSTRUCTION IN AN EFFECTIVE SCHOOL FRAMEWORK

For over three decades, Direct Instruction programs have maximized the academic achievement of tens of thousands of students, regardless of their socioeconomic status, prior academic record, or initial levels of performance (Adams & Engelmann, 1996). A successful DI implementation will include every element of effective schools. Each DI program provides a completely integrated and aligned system of curriculum and instruction that spans multiple grade levels. Additionally, behavioral and classroom management routines crucial to the success of each program are also specified. Hence, the adoption of a specific DI program such as *Reading Mastery* provides a comprehensive technology of implementation needed to define and structure the student learning environment in that program area. With the adoption of any DI program, the staff learning environment (relative to that program area) becomes sharply focused and clearly defined; it becomes the substance of the academic mission and the monitoring of mission progress, the scope of the staff development agenda, and the compass of school leadership.

Figure 10.1 depicts student and staff learning environments and the place of DI in an effective school. The innermost circle, at the center of everything, represents the crux of the student learning environment in a subject area. It focuses on the students in relation to

FIGURE 10.1   Direct Instruction in an Effective School Framework

the staff. Direct Instruction programs provide the tightly coupled curriculum, also called the technology of implementation, that is necessary to maximize every student's opportunity to learn. The middle circle, closest to the students, surrounds and supports the student learning environment. The middle circle focuses on the staff in relation to the students and represents the staff learning environment. The outer circle notes those environmental elements shared by students and staff alike that enhance both sets of relationships, providing a bridge to the home and larger community.

CRITICAL ISSUES AND GUIDELINES FOR IMPLEMENTING DIRECT INSTRUCTION PROGRAMS

Next, we focus on critical issues and guidelines for implementing Direct Instruction programs. We highlight: the scope and sequence of implementation, organizing the student learning environment (placement, grouping, and scheduling), monitoring mission progress (student and staff performance), and professional development.

Scope and Sequence of Implementation

Whether initiating a new Direct Instruction implementation or expanding an existing one, the feasible scope of an implementation is determined by how many students and teachers will be involved with how many Direct Instruction programs, and at how many levels. The funding available for materials is an obvious constraint on the scope of any implementation or expansion. The start-up cost to outfit twenty-five students and their teacher with the materials required to implement the *Reading Mastery* program, for example, will be approximately $2000. Approximate materials costs for the second year and beyond will be about a third of the first year or start-up costs (sometimes considerably less, depending on the program and level).

Clearly, starting "small" has its advantages in terms of costs and manageability. A very feasible, small-scale start-up, noted by the National Alliance of Quality Schools (1995), is to begin with the oral language (*Language for Learning* and *Language for Thinking*) and reading programs (*Reading Mastery* or *Reading Mastery Plus*) for grades K and 1 only. Thereafter, one or possibly two grade levels would be added each year until the entire school was involved, or the complete DI oral language and reading sequence was implemented. Direct Instruction spelling (*Spelling Mastery*) could be introduced, beginning with the second grade, in Year 3. Another level of *Spelling Mastery* would be added each year thereafter. Beginning in Year 4, Direct Instruction math (*DISTAR Arithmetic* or *Connecting Math Concepts*) could be added at the K and 1 levels, with the next program level introduced each year thereafter. When starting small, it is best to begin with the lowest-grade students first and build up from there. The advantages to this scheme are cost, manageability, and students entering upper grades at significantly higher levels of achievement than previously. This scheme is certainly better for the children and will also reduce the emotional and fiscal costs of later remediation. The disadvantage here is that the greatest immediate need for intervention is probably at the higher grade levels. Although we can start with the higher grade levels and work down, we must be sure that the programs do in fact expand downward; otherwise the upper grades will forever be saddled with the burden of having to remediate academic and behavior problems that stem from weak programs in the lower grades.

An alternative, more complex and demanding, approach to establishing Direct Instruction involves the implementation of an entire program sequence (e.g., all six levels of *Reading Mastery* or *Connecting Math Concepts*) within one year. The advantage to this approach is obvious and significant: older students do not have to wait for effective instruction. The primary disadvantages are initial cost and the large amount of training and monitoring required by the multiple levels of the program. Because of the clear-cut advantage to the students, this is a very common implementation plan.

Spreading the implementation over two years ameliorates the disadvantages without sacrificing the full measure of advantages. Thus, a K–5 school could implement *Reading Mastery* in grades K–2 during Year 1, then finish the implementation for grades three to five in Year 2.

Other alternative patterns of implementation are simply matters of scaling up on the approaches we have already discussed. Likewise, the advantages and disadvantages are also matters of scale. The ultimate approach to a Direct Instruction implementation is to "bite the bullet" and fully implement all the programs within one to two years. Although the difficulties are indeed daunting, the potential rewards for students and staff are phenomenal.

Training and Monitoring Teachers.   The key factor in determining the feasible scope of a Direct Instruction implementation is the *school's ability to train and monitor its teachers*. Exceeding one's capacity to train and monitor staff performance will almost always result in failure (National Alliance of Quality Schools, 1995). Beyond preservice training at the university or college level, there are three categories of training used in DI implementations: initial (workshop), in-service, and coaching.

Initial Training.   Initial training occurs in a workshop setting, before staff begin teaching a program, preferably immediately before they begin teaching. Typically, this workshop includes concrete, hands-on practice (with feedback) in specific teaching techniques, rationales, and expected student outcomes for the designated level(s) of the program being trained. Participant groups of twenty-five to thirty teachers are common during initial Direct Instruction program training. Program level is also an important consideration for initial training: teaching *Reading Mastery I* or *II* is quite different and more difficult than teaching *Levels III-VI*. If a teacher has not previously taught a DI program, or is new to a significantly different level of a program, initial training is an absolute necessity. Typically, programs for grades K–2 require two full days of initial training, while one full day is usually adequate for the upper-level programs. Fortunately, certain levels of a single program can be combined for initial training; for example, *Reading Mastery I* and *II* may be combined into a single, two-day training or *Reading Mastery III-VI* can be combined into a single, one-day training. Consequently, an implementation or expansion that includes *Reading Mastery Levels I-IV* would require a total of three full days for training, although every teacher would not necessarily attend all three days (the *Reading Mastery III-VI* teachers would not need to attend the *Reading Mastery I-II* training). Financially, training means a stipend and possible travel expenses for one trainer for three days, or two separate trainers (one for two days and one for one day). Additional costs will be incurred if the participants must be compensated for their time.

In-Service Training.   In-service training occurs outside the classroom during the school year. It usually focuses on problem solving and teaching new instructional formats that will be introduced for the first time in the next ten to twenty lessons. Activities can include practicing/role playing formats, watching videos of expert implementation of programs, or discussing key procedures described in the teacher's guide that accompanies each level of every Direct Instruction program. During the first two or three months of initial implementation (or an expansion into new programs or levels of an existing program), the staff teaching a given level of a program would meet no more than thirty to sixty minutes per week. After the first few months, these meetings may occur every other week, then monthly. If the school employs an expert "coach" (either external or in-house), this person would be the ideal in-service leader. Fortunately, in-service training can be rather informal. If an expert trainer is not available or affordable, the training can be led by one or more in-house staff, including the principal. Staff availability and compensation must also be considered. In some schools, union contracts all but prohibit mandatory in-service training, or require compensation for the participants that make such training unaffordable. In-service training can be extremely beneficial; however, the inability to provide such training should *not* dissuade a school from implementing Direct Instruction.

Coaching.   The third type of training is "in-class coaching" involving an expert Direct Instruction teacher working in the classroom with another teacher demonstrating, observing, and providing immediate feedback to that teacher and the students. Coaching is a crucial element in any implementation, so much so that we will address this aspect of staff development at length later in this chapter. At this point, our concern is that the availability of coaching delimits the potential scope of an implementation or expansion. During the first semester of a new implementation (or an expansion into new programs or levels of an existing program), thirty to sixty minutes per month of in-class coaching should be provided to each teacher. Thereafter, the coaching schedule could become highly individualized, depending on the performance of students and staff within each group. The major limitation on coaching is the availability and cost of an expert coach. At thirty minutes per coaching visit, a coach can reasonably work with ten teachers per day. A staff of twenty, therefore, would require the availability of a coach for the equivalent of two days per month. Schools typically rely on external consultants or trainers to provide coaching during the first year of a new implementation. Hiring these individuals can be expensive (typical per diem costs for an expert trainer/coach/consultant range from $500 to well over $1000 per day plus expenses). Implementation plans should include provision for training a group of in-house staff who will become coaches and gradually reduce the need for external consultants. Although external coaches and trainers will eventually be replaced by in-house staff, this process (and the reliance on external consultants/trainers) usually requires three years.

Table 10.1 shows a list of Direct Instruction implementation companies and contact information as provided by the Association for Direct Instruction (ADI) (information on ADI is also noted in this table). This list is not exhaustive but represents companies who provide much of the DI training in the country. ADI is a nonprofit organization dedicated primarily

TABLE 10.1   Direct Instruction Association and Implementation Companies

Association for Direct Instruction
Bryan Wickman
Executive Director
P.O. Box 10252
Eugene, Oregon 97440
800-995-2464 (phone)
541-683-7543 (fax)
www.adihome.org

Molly Blakely
Educational Resources, Inc.
7105 Old Grant Creek Road
Missoula, Montana 59808
406-542-5010 (phone)
bgskycntry@aol.com

Ken Jackson
J/P Associates
284 East Chester Avenue
Valley Stream, New York 11580
516-561-7803 (phone)
jacksonkendeb@juno.com

Kurt Engelmann
National Institute for Direct Instruction (NIFDI)
P.O. Box 11248
Eugene, Oregon 97440
877-485-1973 (phone)
kurt@nifdi.org

to providing support for teachers and other educators who use DI programs. That support includes conferences on how to use the programs, publication of *Direct Instruction News* and the *Journal of Direct Instruction,* and the sale of various products of interest to its members.

Organizing the Student Learning Environment

Organizing the student learning environment is a matter of (1) placing each student correctly within a curriculum sequence, (2) forming homogeneous instructional groups (based on the placement results) and assigning each student to an appropriate group, (3) allocating and scheduling instructional time sufficient for each group to excel, and (4) providing a consistent yet flexible system to regroup students when necessary. The goal here is to establish a *system* that ensures that every student is instructed at a level in the Direct Instruction curriculum sequence that maximizes time spent learning while minimizing time needed to learn.

Every program includes very specific placement tests with precise directions and criteria for administration and scoring. Additionally, every program includes in-program mastery tests that occur every five or ten lessons. These in-program assessments can be used to further refine placement decisions. Students should not be placed in a program based on standardized test results as these instruments are insensitive to the sequence of instruction in the curricula. Even teacher recommendations should be verified via the placement tests and refined by the in-program mastery tests if necessary. Consistency in placement decisions is essential. Therefore, it is best to designate one person or a small group of staff to administer the entire placement testing process. These staff should be explicitly trained for this purpose.

Once every student's place in the curricular sequence has been established, students are then homogeneously grouped for instruction. This grouping is *not* the same as tracking because placement is flexible and a child may be with one group of students for reading and yet a different group of students (with possibly a different teacher) for language or math instruction. (For a thorough review of the research base on grouping and tracking, see Grossen, 1996.) It is very important to note that students in grades PK–2, and older students functioning below grade level, should be given priority with respect to small group size. Groups should be as small as possible given the number of staff available. For example, the placement results might indicate the need for fourteen groups; however, only twelve available staff are available. If the situation cannot be resolved via scheduling groups at different times, then the fourteen groups will need to be reconstituted as twelve groups. Therefore, a group placed to begin *Reading Mastery III* at lesson 40 might reasonably be combined with another group placed to begin *Reading Mastery III* at lesson 20. The new, combined group would then begin at lesson 20.

Patterns of Group Organization.   To maximize opportunity to learn in Direct Instruction, every program requires an allocation of sixty minutes per day per group. The only exception is *Spelling Mastery,* requiring only thirty minutes per day per group. There are three possible patterns of group organization: homeroom-based, team-based, and school-based.

Homeroom-Based.   The homeroom-based pattern is the most traditional organization of elementary and middle schools. Students are placed in a homeroom and then grouped by the teacher within the homeroom. The advantages to this scheme are that the teacher has total control over grouping and scheduling, and is not required to communicate or coordinate with other staff. Integrating the content or skills taught in Direct Instruction into other content areas, as well as communicating expansively to parents, is sometimes easier for the teacher in a homeroom-based pattern.

Nonetheless, the disadvantages of the homeroom-based system are severe. If the homeroom was created homogeneously with respect to the placement test results in a particular Direct Instruction program area, problems associated with tracking may arise. Especially vulnerable here are the lowest achieving homerooms that are frequently plagued by numerous behavior problems and other counterproductive issues (such as low expectations and motivation) caused by a history of failure. This environment is seldom conducive to learning. Furthermore, even though the students are grouped homogeneously relative to one subject area (e.g., reading), they may not be grouped homogeneously with respect to programs or subject areas. Finally, rates of learning differ among students and within the same student over time. Consequently, the homogeneity present in September may be different by December.

If the homeroom was created heterogeneously, the teacher could easily have five or more instructional groups (based on placement test results) in each subject area. Most teachers can teach no more than three groups in each subject area (e.g., three different levels of math) so students with radically different needs must be combined into groups. It is one thing to group students who are twenty lessons apart; however, it is a totally different thing to group students who are eighty lessons apart. Eighty lessons translates into an entire semester of a school year. Teaching these very heterogeneous groups compromises the learning of all the students.

The basic reality of grouping and scheduling is that students at the extremes of achievement (either high or low) will always challenge, and sometimes break, the system. The difference between challenging and breaking the system is determined by the size of the total student pool from which students are drawn and grouped.

Team-Based.   The team-based (and school-based, discussed below) patterns of organiza-tion are designed specifically to allow for more precise grouping of students with highly similar instructional needs. The key is scheduling a common instructional time during which all instruction in a subject area occurs.

In a team-based pattern, all teachers or homerooms at the same grade level or across two or three contiguous grade levels are formed into a team, and teach a designated subject area or Direct Instruction program at a common time. For example, all the students in grades K–2 could be scheduled to receive reading instruction (via the *Reading Mastery* program) from 8:30 A.M. to 9:45 A.M. each day. During this time, every student is placed in the reading group that best meets his or her needs no matter which team member is teaching it. This procedure greatly multiplies the number of groups available for each student. Cross-grade groups occur frequently, to the potential benefit of every student, by allowing appropriate placement for students at the extremes of achievement.

As a general rule at the primary level, students are not grouped with other students who are more than one grade level above or below them. For example, second graders may be grouped with first graders; however, second graders would probably not be grouped with kindergarten students. At the middle school level, the general rule for grade span increases to two grade levels (e.g., eighth graders with sixth graders is a feasible combination; eighth graders with fifth graders is probably not). Additionally, schools are advised not to group the lowest-performing students from one grade level with the highest performers from the grade below, even though all of them are scheduled to begin the school year at the same level and lesson of the same Direct Instruction program. The higher performers, though younger, will probably learn at a faster rate, soon surpassing the older students and destroying the homogeneity of the group. Rather, if necessary, group lower performers from one grade level with middle performers from the grade below; or higher performers with middle performers from the grade above.

Each staff member would be responsible for only one group during this common instructional time, allowing teachers to focus on the needs of a single group. Also, during this time, no pull-out (e.g., speech therapy) or special programs (e.g., art, music, PE) are scheduled or permitted for the K–2 students. So, in a K–5 school, we would have two teams (Grades K–2 and 3–5) and two common instructional periods, scheduled at different times, within the school day.

Sometimes, there are not enough staff to support reasonable group sizes during a single, common instructional period. Consequently, a variation of the team-based pattern involves doubling the time allocated to the common instructional period and then assigning two homogeneous groups to each teacher during that double period. Initially, the teacher directly instructs one group, while the other group works independently or under the supervision of a paraprofessional. At about the half-way point of the double period, the groups switch places and roles. Although this variation is more demanding for the teacher to manage, the clear benefit is that this doubles the number of available groups allowing for better placement while still giving each group the requisite amount of allocated time.

The primary disadvantage of the team-based pattern of organization is that it requires efficient procedures for communicating and coordinating among the team members. Especially relevant here are finding solutions to common instructional problems or issues and regrouping students needing to move ahead or back within the curriculum sequence. Regularly scheduled team meetings, chaired by an administrator or someone with administrative authority, are absolutely essential to the team-based pattern of organization. During the first month or two of school, these meetings should occur weekly. Thereafter, they may be scheduled less often, but seldom less than once a month.

Clearly, the advantage of the team-based pattern of organization is its ability to increase the probability that (1) the time officially allocated for instruction is actually allocated, and (2) students are placed and grouped into the most appropriate instructional level.

School-Based. A school-based model of organization addresses grouping problems by increasing the total student pool to its maximum size (i.e., the entire student body). Here, a single, common instructional period (either single period/single group or double period/double group) is designated for the entire school. As in the team-based pattern, no pull-out or special programs are scheduled or permitted during this common instructional time. Consequently, a school-based system provides an additional bonus not usually found in the team-based model: *every* staff member in the building (including special staff such as counselors, music teachers, and so on) is available to teach an instructional group. This influx of additional available staff reduces average group size or the size of the neediest groups.

The school-based pattern intensifies the advantages of the team-based pattern of organization. However, it does not necessarily worsen the disadvantages. Though communication and coordination must now occur on a schoolwide basis, students would still not be grouped with others more than one grade level (possibly two, in the case of the middle school) above or below them. Moreover, the instructional problems common to fourth-grade teachers would probably not be as relevant to those teaching first grade. Therefore, the school-based pattern could readily use a variation of the team-based pattern for organizing and scheduling meetings to solve common problems and regroup students as needed. In this scenario, team meetings need to be more flexible (e.g., sometimes involving the second and third grades, at other times involving the third and fourth grades). The critical role of school leadership in planning, coordinating, scheduling, and managing these meetings is accentuated within the school-based system of organization.

The school-based pattern may not be a possibility if, for instance, the union contract or state law absolutely forbids teachers from teaching outside their specific area of certification, or if a mandated number of minutes per week in a special area (e.g., music) cannot be guaranteed or scheduled because that special teacher is teaching reading for an hour or more every day. However, from the perspective of maximizing opportunity to learn for every child in the school, the school-based system is clearly the organizational model of choice.

Monitoring Mission Progress

Monitoring and responding to mission progress is a matter of quality control. The quality we seek in a Direct Instruction implementation is a high level of academic achievement on the part of every student in the school. The causes of academic achievement, which are controlled by the school, are the variables that determine time spent and time needed to learn. Therefore, monitoring needs to concentrate on those variables. The variables that determine *time needed to learn* are not readily quantified and, therefore, not easy to monitor directly or objectively. Fortunately, all the variables that determine *time spent learning* are readily quantified and, therefore, relatively easy to monitor in an objective manner. Moreover, if the various measures of *time spent learning* are at or above criterion levels, then there is every reason to believe that *time needed to learn* is indeed being minimized.

Quantitative Monitoring.   Quantitative monitoring of lessons that focus on *time needed to learn* include the following: (1) criterion content covered, (2) allocated time, (3) engagement and success rates, (4) correction ratios, and (5) praise ratios. Each of these is described below.

Criterion Content Covered.   In Direct Instruction programs, criterion content covered is measured in terms of the number of program lessons completed per unit of time (i.e., in a day, week, month, or year). *The goal in every Direct Instruction program is a lesson or more per day at mastery.* A monthly pacing guide can be used to monitor the lesson progress of groups of students.[1] A weekly pacing guide could be used for more intensive monitoring of criterion content covered.[2]

Allocated Time.   Given that criterion content covered or lesson gain at mastery is a concern (based on monitoring the monthly pacing guide), and in addition to the weekly pacing guide, leadership staff can monitor fidelity to the schedule of allocated time. Do teachers have the schedule posted prominently in the classroom? Do lessons consistently begin on time and continue for the entire period (i.e., the full allocation of time)? Monitoring such "bell-to-bell" teaching requires the supervisor to observe the beginning and the end of each scheduled instructional period. This sort of supervision is sometimes called "management by walking around" or MBWA. Though simple in nature, it is a crucial element in the monitoring of allocated time. In fact, it is the only way to monitor allocated time.

Engagement and Success Rates. Inadequate progress in the curriculum is frequently associated with low levels of student engagement and low levels of success. Monitoring engagement rates require the physical presence of an observer in the classroom. Monitoring student success rates can also be measured through classroom observation. Additionally, success rates may be monitored by analyzing student performance on daily independent work, as well as the mastery tests that accompany every level of every Direct Instruction program.

Students are academically engaged when they are participating in an activity directly related to the curriculum sequence. Their participation may involve speaking, writing, listening, or looking. If the students are not academically engaged, it is often helpful to know what other things they are doing.

The recording procedure entails a sequence of looking at an individual student, then immediately recording or categorizing that student's behavior; looking at the next student, then immediately recording the behavior; looking at the next student, then immediately recording the behavior; and so on until every student has been recorded once. The observer only records one student at a time, does not look ahead to other students or change a student's tally once it is recorded. In this manner, an observer can "sweep" a classroom of twenty to thirty students in about one minute. To get an accurate measure of engagement, the observer must be able to see each student's face before recording, and "sweeps" must be evenly spaced throughout the total observation period. The result of such recording is a series of "snapshots" that, when pieced together, provide a useful measure of student engagement. The criterion for engagement is 90 percent; that is, 90 percent of the students are engaged in the lesson.

In these observations, student responses, both group and individual, are analyzed. A correct group response includes three components: every student responds, all students answer on signal, and all students answer correctly. If even one of these components is missing, the response is recorded as an error. Individual responses are simpler; the only criterion for a correct individual response is accuracy. An appropriate ratio of group to individual responses is 10:1. Use of too many individual responses may offer a partial explanation for the slow pace of lesson gains. For example, many teachers use individual turns to redirect off-task student behavior. This procedure usually results in more, not less, off-task behavior, thus slowing the momentum of the lesson and the pace of lesson progress.

Success rates should also be analyzed. With few exceptions, every lesson of every level of every Direct Instruction program includes daily written independent work. The function of this activity is to review and apply knowledge or skills from previous lessons. Therefore, these assignments are a valid measure of student success on recent lessons. Additionally, mastery tests (sometimes called "checkouts") are built into every program after every five or ten lessons. There may also be out-of-program assessments (that must be purchased separately) that occur about every twenty lessons. All of these assessments must be consistently administered, checked, corrected, and recorded by the classroom teacher. It is essential that a common process for recording and reporting all this information be established and adhered to by every staff member. A quantitative monitoring guide could be used to assist staff in this endeavor.[3]

Another aspect of student success is their accuracy on the first opportunity with each task. These *first-time correct* data are gathered during a lesson and include the following. Every student response is counted as first-time correct if no mistake occurred in the group (or with an individual student) the first time it was presented. That is, all students responded accurately and on signal. For example, if there are fifty oral responses required by the students during a word attack exercise, the observer would track how many of those were answered correctly on signal the first time. If an error correction occurred on a response, the response would not be counted as first-time correct. The percentage of first-time corrects are an indication of how well teachers are ensuring mastery during their lessons over time. The criterion for this behavior is 85 percent or above.

Correction Ratios. Error correction is absolutely critical. Poor error corrections can result in inaccurate student performance and slow curriculum progress. The correction procedures used in Direct Instruction are included in the scripted lesson plans and are explained thoroughly in the teacher's guide that accompanies every level of every program. These procedures should be followed carefully. Observers should collect data on the adequacy of error corrections. The goal for appropriate error corrections should be 90 percent or above.

Praise Ratios. In Direct Instruction programs, the criterion praise ratio is about 9:1 (i.e., the teacher tells the students what they are doing right such as "nice reading that paragraph" or says generic words such as "good job" or "super" for appropriate student behavior nine times more often than redirecting or correcting inappropriate student behavior). Some Direct Instruction programs also provide a script with the inclusion of praise statements to help ensure that teachers tell students what they have done correctly (e.g., "yes, *mmm*").

Qualitative Monitoring. There are numerous occasions, however, when quantitative tools do not provide a sufficient description of what is happening in a Direct Instruction classroom. Consequently, a qualitative monitoring tool is also needed. A qualitative monitoring guide identifies teacher behaviors that are critical to the success of a Direct Instruction lesson, and places them into eight categories, arranged in a hierarchy.[4] They include:

1. Set up and preparation (e.g., group organization, use of materials).
2. Formats (e.g., follows script, provides clear phrasing, emphasizes key words).
3. Signals (e.g., clear signals, include "focus" cue).
4. Individual turns (e.g., name at end of directive, distributed across students).
5. Correction procedures (e.g., response and signal errors corrected).
6. Firm up (e.g., does a starting over to ensure mastery).
7. Pacing (e.g., quick lesson pace to ensure on-task behavior).
8. Behavior management (e.g., praise provided, point system utilized).

The qualitative monitoring hierarchy serves three important functions, in that it signals (1) the sequence in which teachers usually master strategic Direct Instruction behaviors, (2) the focus and priority for providing constructive feedback to teachers, and (3) the order in which one looks for solutions to problems of quality student performance.

Staff Development

The National Reading Panel (2000) suggests that several elements are required for staff/professional development to be most effective. First, the focus should be on changing both teacher and student behavior. This focus means that teachers must adopt new ways of teaching to produce corresponding changes in student behavior. Second, activities should be conducted regularly and should involve follow-up and support for further learning. These activities should involve teachers in the identification of what they need to learn and in the development of their learning experiences. Third, activities should be primarily school-based and built into day-to-day teaching schedules. Finally, these activities should be organized around collaborative problem solving, wherein teachers meet regularly to discuss strategies and methods that will maximize student academic achievement.

While in-service workshops and scheduled classroom observations conducted by school principals have been the traditional means of providing staff/professional development activities for teachers, Joyce and Showers (1995) propose that these approaches are not always the most effective in causing lasting change in their teaching practices. This finding is in large part due to teacher isolation and lack of regular supervision when they return to their classrooms to use the newly learned strategies and techniques. In fact, the absence of follow-up is the single most profound challenge in the professional development of teachers (Fullan, 1993). "Inadequate and insufficient professional support helps explain why so many attempts to improve student learning have failed" (Worrall & Carnine, 1995, p. 15). Coaching is one method to support teachers' implementation and maintenance of effective teaching practices (Carnine, Grossen, & Silbert, 1995).

COACHING AS A MEANS OF STAFF DEVELOPMENT

The term *coach* will be used in this chapter to refer to an individual who is responsible for the training and monitoring of teachers.

> Coaching has been defined as a confidential arrangement between peers that includes a focused classroom observation and feedback on that observation . . . it provides teachers a means of examining and reflecting on what they do in a psychologically safe environment where it is all right to examine, fail, revise, and try again (Raney & Robbins, 1989, p. 37).

The coach helps teachers provide effective instruction so that both they and the students can be more successful. Interestingly, Snippe (1992) reported that as few as two supervisory sessions, either with or without teachers having attended a previous workshop, can enhance their effectiveness in the classroom.

The ultimate focus of these supervisory sessions is on student learning. In order to improve student learning teachers must be provided feedback on their performance in the classroom. McLaughlin and Pfeifer (1988) defined feedback as the process of giving back information for the purpose of bringing about a change in the behavior of the person receiving it. The characteristics of effective feedback include: timeliness, specificity, clarity of purpose, and credibility of the source of feedback (McLaughlin & Pfeifer). Further, French (1997) noted that feedback should be descriptive rather than judgmental and should be directed toward performance, not toward the personal characteristics of the receiver. Coaches "must communicate the findings of their observations to classroom personnel in a way that establishes their credibility, focuses on quality ideas, provides depth of information, encourages changes in performance, and offers suggestions useful in improving instruction"

(Morgan, 1997, p. 8). Moreover, the methods of feedback should reflect and promote dialogue about classroom events, and should begin with the idea that information is the basis for all instructional decisions (Karant, 1989).

Along these lines, Gleason and Hall (1991) found the use of in-class feedback on the acquisition of teaching behaviors was more efficient and effective than after-class feedback. In-class feedback provides teachers an opportunity to practice the recommended changes immediately with their own students. In addition, when in-class feedback is provided, teachers are not required to wait until the next day to execute the changes, thus the amount of time that elapses between the feedback and the implementation of the changes is minimal. Coulter and Grossen (1997) reported that "in-class feedback resulted in faster acquisition of target behaviors than after-class feedback or no feedback" (p. 27). In addition, the in-class feedback method resulted in higher levels of performance for all participants. This in-class feedback involved comments and prompts provided to teachers *during* the lesson.

Common Types of Coaching Interventions

Five common types of coaching interventions used to train teachers include in-class demonstrations, meetings, workshops, in-class advice, and team-teaching procedures (Blakely, 2001). First, during in-class demonstrations, coaches may conduct model lessons with their students that teachers observe. Prior to demonstration lessons, it is critical that coaches and teachers have a conference to discuss particular strategies and techniques that will be demonstrated during the lessons. If this is not done, teachers may watch the style of the person teaching rather than the specific strategies and techniques. In Blakely's study, 22 percent of the 113 respondents stated that when they were acquiring new teaching behaviors demonstration lessons conducted by coaches was the preferred level of intervention, because "they felt at ease watching and observing a model provided by an expert: and that the visual example allowed them to better understand the strategy/technique" (p. 79).

A meeting is a second type of intervention. The coach and the teacher meet after school to discuss possible changes and/or adaptations following a demonstration. Approximately 10.6 percent of respondents in Blakely's (2001) study identified this kind of intervention as the preferred method of acquiring a new teaching behavior, because it "allowed time for discussion with the coach without any distractions" (p. 79). Johnson and Kardos (2002) reported that new teachers want an experienced coach to "watch them teach and provide feedback, help them develop instructional strategies, model skilled teaching, and share insights about students' work and lives" (p. 13).

Workshops are a third type of intervention. Teachers attend an after-school workshop or training session that focuses on various teaching strategies they can use in the classroom. During these workshops, coaches model specific teaching strategies and/or show video examples. Modeling is followed by teachers practicing the particular strategy or technique and discussing the impact they expect it to have on their students. However, Johnson and Kardos (2002) reported that new teachers who participated in workshops as their sole mode of professional development felt unprepared to meet the demands of teaching.

A fourth type of coaching intervention involves in-class advice: Coaches provide various verbal prompts, hints, or reminders while teachers instruct their students. For example, if a student read a word wrong during oral reading and the teacher provided no error correction, the coach might prompt the teacher by saying, "let's correct that error and have the student reread the sentence correctly."

Finally, during the team-teaching procedure (also called side-by-side coaching), coaches intervene during the lesson, provide a demonstration and a rationale for what they did, and then have the teachers repeat the instructional task. Blakely (2001) reported that over 60 percent of her respondents identified this model of coaching as the preferred level of intervention for learning new teaching behaviors. Further, the team-teaching procedure

> provided a 'hands-on' way to learn, therefore providing powerful shifts in the learning process; it was experiential rather than theoretical; and it limited the long-term effects of errors (pp. 79–80).

The team-teaching procedure is not commonly practiced because there are often concerns about the possibility of this type of method being overly intrusive and potentially undermining teacher authority. However, written responses from the participants in Blakely's (2001) study clearly indicated that the team-teaching procedure did not threaten or undermine teachers nor did it erode their credibility with students. An overwhelming number of teachers indicated that the procedure is powerful due to its experiential nature and that the immediate feedback allows for a positive "hands-on" approach to learning.

Direct Instruction Coaching Format

The coach should observe a typical thirty- to sixty-minute teaching session. During this observation the coach should ensure teacher skill acquisition and student success. Riley-Blakely and Schaefer (1999) outlined a sequence of training steps in a video entitled, *The Elements of Effective Coaching*:

1. Initiation
   A. The coach stops the teacher (e.g., "Let's pause here").
   B. The coach praises the students and the teacher for specific things they were doing well.
   C. The coach gives an assignment to the students to free up some time for the coach to interact with the teacher.
2. Intervention
   A. The coach describes what she observed (e.g., "Here's what is happening . . .").
      1. The coach describes student behavior and connects it to the teacher's behavior.
      2. The coach provides a teaching example and nonexample (if applicable).
   B. The coach describes the strategy to the teacher.
   C. The coach provides the teacher with a rationale for the strategy.
   D. The coach has the teacher watch as she models the strategy.
   E. The coach returns the teacher-presentation book to the teacher and asks her to reteach the format.
3. Intervention Summary
   A. The coach repeats the initiation above, being sure to praise students for their on-task behavior (including Parts A–C, with the coach providing feedback to the teacher as noted below).

B. The coach praises the teacher and connects teacher and student behavior for feedback purposes.

C. The coach summarizes the intervention.

   1. The coach has the teacher state or describe the strategy.

   2. The coach verifies the strategy.

The following example illustrates the use of this effective coaching format. For example, a coach was observing a new Direct Instruction teacher conduct a *Reading Mastery I* lesson. First, the coach entered the room unintrusively and sat next to the teacher so she could see both the teacher and the students. Next, the coach observed the teacher and intervened when the group made an error. For example, it is common for students not to provide a unison response when the teacher's signal lacks a clear, consistent focus. In *Reading Mastery I,* when a sound or a word is on a page, the teacher should point to the ball of the arrow, give the verbal prompt ("get ready"/"what word?"), and then provide a signal. Frequently, teachers will give the verbal prompt prior to securing a focus on the task, thus causing unnecessary errors, as students do not know what sound or word to focus on. When this error occurred in the lesson, the coach intervened by saying, "Let's pause here for a moment. Students, you did an excellent job coming to group quickly and quietly. Mrs. Jones, it is obvious you have taught them to transition from their learning centers to reading group. Also, in the first part of the format, the students did an excellent job holding the sounds for two to three seconds. That is an important prereading skill and you have done a great job teaching them to hold the continuous sounds. Students, we need you to practice the sounds on this page silently while we talk for just a moment. Mrs. Jones, here is what is happening . . . on Task 2, when students are required to identify sounds/words on the page, it is critical that they know where to focus their eyes prior to hearing the verbal prompt of "get ready/what word/what sound." In order to secure their attention, we focus on the ball of the arrow, give the verbal prompt, and then signal (example). What we don't want is to give the verbal prompt before providing a focus for the students (nonexample). So, the strategy is: focus on the task, give the verbal prompt, and then signal. By doing this, you will secure student attention and prevent unnecessary errors. I will demonstrate this with the group. Students, thank you for practicing these sounds silently and for waiting quietly for us to finish talking. You are really being respectful and we appreciate that. Now, I am going to do some of these sounds with you. When I touch the big ball of the arrow, I want you to look at where my finger is on the page."

The coach then models two to three examples or until students respond correctly. The coach then gives the teacher-presentation book back to the teacher and says, "Mrs. Jones, let's do that task again. Remember we will focus on the big ball of the arrow, thus securing student attention, then say 'get ready/what sound/what word,' and then signal."

At the end of the thirty-minute observation, the coach summarizes the session by stating the positive parts of the lesson and quickly summarizing the strategies modeled during the intervention(s).

"Mrs. Jones, you were very prepared to teach this lesson. You followed the script closely and the pace of your presentation was brisk and lively. You are positive with your students and they are motivated to work for you. In addition, when an error occurred, you did an immediate correction procedure and gave a delayed test on every item missed. You taught a very nice lesson. Let's remember that the first part of every signal is to focus on the task (e.g., word, sound). Next, you will give the verbal cue (e.g., "what sound, what word, get ready") and then signal. This procedure will ensure that students are focusing on the task and you will get a higher percentage of first-time correct responses that will minimize unnecessary errors. I know that you have a group in *Reading Mastery II* and the same strategy applies. So, when you teach your *Reading Mastery II* group, utilize the strategy of: focus on the task, give the verbal cue, and then signal. It was very nice to work with you and your students this morning. Keep up the good work. And students, give yourselves a pat on the back, you worked very hard today. Thank you."

Thus, it seems that the team-teaching procedure for coaching teachers is an effective and efficient way to improve the acquisition of Direct Instruction teaching behaviors. In turn, improvements in student performance as a result of better teaching in these programs will be evident.

TUTORING AS A MEANS OF INCREASING SUPPORT FOR STUDENTS

We have discussed how Direct Instruction implementations can be conducted to ensure teacher and student success. Another way of using Direct Instruction materials in a school is through tutoring. Tutoring can make the difference between success and failure for many students, particularly in times of diminishing school resources. Those who provide instruction to learners often note that "the problem is not what to teach or how to teach it, but finding enough (teaching) time and pairs of hands to do so" (Kamps, Locke, Delquadri, & Hall, 1989, p. 38).

Tutoring has been around for as long as we have provided instruction and mentoring to others (Enright & Axelrod, 1995); it has foundations dating back to ancient times (Martino, 1994). Tutoring refers to an alternative teaching arrangement whereby individuals serve as instructional agents for struggling learners. Tutoring may be used as a supplement to group instruction or may be used independently of other instruction as in adult basic literacy tutoring programs. Tutoring is an educational tool that many schools and organizations can utilize to improve the skills of those who struggle academically (or socially) (Martella, Marchand-Martella, Miller, Young, & Macfarlane, 1995; Meese, 2001).

What makes tutoring effective is that it is individually tailored to meet the unique needs of the learner. Learners are aided in skill development by a tutor who may be dealing, or have dealt with in the past, similar life and/or school issues. Bonds between the tutor and the learner are established. Trust ensues; success follows.

Direct Instruction programs work well in tutoring programs given their scripted nature and ease of implementation. For example, high school students who are at or above grade level in reading can successfully use *Corrective Reading* or *Spelling through Morphographs* to tutor peers who struggle in reading or spelling. Further, students who are reading above grade level (e.g., third graders in *Reading Mastery VI*) can be paired with struggling readers (e.g., third graders in *Fast Cycle II of Reading Mastery*) to listen to them read their storybooks and to ask comprehension questions; this approach could be used to provide additional opportunities to respond and obtain feedback to accelerate student performance. Finally, college students can be used to tutor lower performing first graders using *Teach Your Child to Read in 100 Easy Lessons.* Opportunities abound when tutoring is tied to Direct Instruction programs.

Advantages of Tutoring

When tutoring is used as an intervention, learners experience: a more favorable teacher-to-learner ratio (particularly with the use of one-on-one instruction); more on-task time via increased opportunities to respond with success and to receive feedback; immediacy of positive and corrective feedback so they stay on track and do not practice errors; and improved academic performance, motivation, and interpersonal skills and relationships (Utley, Mortweet, & Greenwood, 1997).

Tutors also realize benefits including: increased academic performance as a result of serving as a teacher; enhanced interpersonal skills and relationships; community service learning opportunities to expand tutor growth in human service related fields; opportunity to experience firsthand what it would be like to be a teacher; and important "life" skills such as patience, trustworthiness, and responsibility (Short, Marchand-Martella, Martella, Ebey, & Stookey, 1999; Wildman Longwill & Kleinert, 1998).

Tutoring Models

Several tutoring models and procedures have been used in schools and other organizations: (1) traditional tutoring, (2) cross-age tutoring, (3) classwide peer tutoring, and (4) tutoring using students with disabilities as tutors. Each of these models has been shown to be effective in increasing the academic performance of struggling students.

Traditional Tutoring.   In traditional tutoring, higher-achieving students are paired with learners who are lower-achieving (Maheady, 1990). For instance, Martino (1993) paired honors students with learners who were struggling in their high school classes. Additionally, with this model adult volunteers or college students may provide assistance to learners (e.g., Baker, Gersten, & Keating, 2000; Hock, Pulvers, Deshler, & Schumaker, 2001). Traditional tutoring has been shown to be effective across grades. It hinges on the fact that the tutors are already skilled in a particular subject (or social skill) area and, with training, can impart these skills to struggling learners. Researchers have studied the pairing of students without disabilities who served as tutors with learners who received special education services. For example, Martella, Marchand-Martella, Young, and Macfarlane (1995) noted improved academic and classroom behavior of a student with severe disabilities using trained high school peer tutors.

Cross-Age Tutoring.   In cross-age tutoring, tutors are students approximately two or more years older or younger than those receiving tutoring (Utley et al., 1997). Benefits abound for those receiving tutoring, particularly when older students work with younger students. For example, Van Zant and Bailey (2002) describe the Student-2-Student tutoring program in which eighth graders tutor sixth and seventh graders in math, science, social studies, and English. Positive effects of using cross-age tutoring have been noted across elementary to college/university settings including improved academic performance and enhanced social skills (Utley et al., 1997).

Classwide Tutoring. In the classwide peer tutoring (CWPT) approach, the entire class is organized into two teams and students tutor each other. Tutor and tutee roles are highly structured to ensure increased opportunities to respond and to obtain feedback (Arreaga-Mayer, 1998; Delquadri, Greenwood, Whorton, Carta, & Hall, 1986; King-Sears & Bradley, 1995). Tutoring occurs simultaneously for all tutor–tutee pairs while the teacher monitors the activities. Tutees earn points for their team for answering questions posed by their tutors. A winning team is determined daily and weekly. Several researchers have studied the efficacy of this approach. For example, Greenwood, Terry, Arreaga-Mayer, and Finney (1992) found that CWPT implemented by five elementary teachers and one student teacher increased spelling achievement.

Students with Disabilities as Tutors. In this approach students with disabilities tutor students with or without disabilities (Utley et al., 1997). Brown (1993) reported this arrangement as an alternative intervention for students with learning disabilities because improvements in academic achievement are evident. Maher (1984) described the successful implementation of a tutoring program involving adolescents with disabilities who tutored elementary-age students with disabilities across academic areas. Marchand-Martella et al. (1992) included elementary-age students with mild disabilities as first-aid instructors for their peers with moderate disabilities. Increased first-aid skill performance was noted for both the tutors and the tutees.

Implementing and Evaluating a Tutoring Program

In order to be effective tutoring sessions must be structured and contain several basic elements for success. First, an on-site supervisor should be selected to monitor the tutoring program. The on-site supervisor may also serve as the tutor trainer, teaching the skills necessary to be a successful tutor to those serving in this role. Clear expectations for tutors should be established. These expectations may include time commitments, professional behavior, and training they must complete. Volunteers should be recruited who are motivated to help others and who make a commitment to tutor on a consistent basis. They should be screened and matched with learners. Rapport-building activities such as "getting to know you" games may help break the ice and establish bonds between the tutors and tutees. Continuity enhances performance; that is, maintaining the same tutor/learner bond over time promotes increased rapport, comfort, motivation to learn, and reading success.

Tutoring sessions should occur daily with at least thirty minutes of instruction per session (if not daily at least two to three times per week). One-on-one tutoring is preferred, given the limited instructional background of the tutors, though an excellent tutor can work with two students at the same level. Tutors need a great deal of support and specific guidance. Direct Instruction programs are particularly well suited to tutoring programs. When reading is the focus, which is often the case in tutoring programs, phonemic awareness activities, sounds practice, word lists, and oral reading of text that incorporates previously taught sounds/words should be included (see Chapter 4 for further details). Further, oral reading, interspersed comprehension questions, and writing activities should be involved (again,

Chapter 4 provides details on these activities). Direct Instruction programs include these important reading elements. Other materials such as magnetic letter boards, dry erase boards/markers/erasers, and timers/stopwatches can be used during instruction. A record-keeping system should be developed to ensure tutors are conducting the program at a quality level and that learners are progressing. Learner performance data should be gathered on a daily basis. Charting learner performance data on graphs allows a visual display of improvements made in the program. (Marchand-Martella, Martella, and Waldron-Soler [2000] provide a manual published through the Association for Direct Instruction on how to establish a tutoring program involving the use of *Corrective Reading.* Forms to include in the program, such as data-collection sheets, observation forms, contracts, and tutor applications, are provided in this manual.)

During tutor training it is important to teach specific tutoring procedures. This training should include role-play and practice activities as well as problem-solving scenarios. Effective tutor-training programs include an *I do, we do, you do* approach (Martella, Marchand-Martella, & Cleanthous, 2002). In this approach, tutors watch a trainer demonstrate the tutoring skills, then they practice and receive feedback, typically using choral responding: the trainer acts as the student and the tutors conduct the lesson in unison. Finally, tutors break into pairs and conduct the lesson with supervised monitoring by the trainer. Following these experiences, tutors can begin working with learners.

Observations should be conducted on a regular basis during the tutoring program. Observations should include how tutors deliver instruction, provide praise and error corrections, and record learner progress. Feedback and coaching should also be provided. It is essential to conduct additional tutor training at scheduled intervals to maintain the tutors' skills. Tutor "drift" will occur without scheduled "tune-up" sessions. Regular meetings with tutors should be held to provide a forum for discussion and problem solving.

Tutors should be taught to follow the following seven guidelines:

1. Begin instruction immediately after the start of the tutoring session.
2. Provide clear instructions (e.g., "Read this list of words" rather than "Could you read this list of words?").
3. Use explicit teaching techniques (i.e., show learners what to do and provide opportunities for learners to practice with clear tutor supervision and feedback) rather than simply reading to the learners.
4. Include praise and encouraging words that are specific to the task at hand (e.g., "yes, the word is *brother*").
5. Use error corrections that include showing learners the correct response (e.g., "that word is *house*") and asking them to repeat it (e.g., "what word?").
6. Maintain a rapid pace of instructional delivery to keep learners focused and on-task.
7. Ignore inconsequential and unwanted learner behavior.

The following tips may prove helpful for those tutors who do not receive systematic training:

1. Be positive. Praise goes a long way with learners who struggle in reading. Provide positive feedback when correct responses are made (e.g., "yes, the word is *Sequoia*").

2. Stop learners immediately after an error. Model the correct response and provide them an opportunity to do it correctly (e.g., "That word is *trouble*. What word is this?"). Try not to use the word *no*.

3. Provide clear instructions (e.g., "Say this word" rather than "Would you say it?").

4. Record learner performance. Be mindful of mistakes made during the session. Review anything that learners miss or do not respond to confidently. Remember, learners "should say it like they know it."

5. Work from the beginning to the end of the period.

6. Keep tutoring sessions lively. Learner success and tutor support go a long way in keeping learners motivated to come back.

7. Try to ignore minor misbehavior. Focus on what learners are doing well rather than what they have missed.

8. Be patient. Show learners that you care about them by your commitment and encouragement.

Research on Tutoring Using Direct Instruction

Five published investigations have used Direct Instruction and tutoring (in the form of peer-delivered instruction). First, Marchand-Martella, Martella, Bettis, and Riley-Blakely (in press) assessed implementation aspects of *Corrective Reading* peer-delivered instruction in six high schools in the Pacific Northwest. Specifically, high schools provided details on supervising teachers, students receiving peer instruction, peer instructors, assessments, and funding. Across the six schools, 255 high school students received training from 167 peer instructors. Of the 255 students, seventy-eight (31 percent) were identified for special-education services. The majority (77 percent) of the peer instructors received college credit from a local university for their participation.

Second, Harris, Marchand-Martella, and Martella (2000) investigated the effects of a pilot program on the reading performance of at-risk high school students at one high school. Seventy-seven high school peer instructors and eighty-eight students in need of reading remediation were randomly assigned to dyads or triads. Peer instructors presented *Corrective Reading* and also conducted rate and accuracy measures. Results indicated that students' performance on a standardized reading assessment increased for both vocabulary and comprehension, as did their oral reading fluency and accuracy. These improvements were noted during an average of sixty-six days of instruction.

Third, Marchand-Martella, Martella, Orlob, and Ebey (2000) investigated the effects of a peer-delivered *Corrective Reading* program in another high school setting with students with disabilities. Twenty-two students with individualized education programs and twenty-two peer instructors participated in this investigation. The results of this study showed that students receiving the intervention during an academic year across levels of the *Corrective Reading* program showed stable grade-level performance in vocabulary and improvements in comprehension on a standardized reading assessment; stable performance on this reading assessment for both subtests was noted for the peer instructors. Additionally, improvements in reading fluency and accuracy were noted.

Fourth, Short et al. (1999) assessed the advantages of serving as peer instructors at one high school when *Corrective Reading* was delivered to peers who struggled in reading.

Eleven peer instructors participated in the study. Results showed that the peer instructors who scored below grade level on the vocabulary pretest of a standardized reading assessment increased to at or above grade level on the post-test; they exhibited stable performance on the comprehension subtest. Those peer instructors who scored at or above grade level on the reading assessment showed stable performance.

Finally, Parsons, Marchand-Martella, Waldron-Soler, Martella, and Lignugaris/Kraft (in press) assessed the effects of peer instruction using the *Corrective Mathematics* (CM) program. Ten learners and nine peer tutors participated in the study. Peer tutors instructed individuals or pairs of learners in the CM program for ten weeks. Results showed that students exhibited improved performance on two math subtests of a standardized academic assessment. The performance of the peer tutors also improved on both subtests of this assessment.

In addition, Marchand-Martella and Martella (2002) conducted an overview and research summary of peer-delivered *Corrective Reading* instruction, thereby summarizing the first four studies mentioned above.

EFFECTIVE SUPERVISION OF PRESERVICE TEACHERS

Note: The next section of this chapter will focus on a structured Direct Instruction supervision system; as such, it may be more relevant to university or college instructors, DI consultants/coaches, or school administrators wishing to establish effective guidelines for teachers or students completing practica or internships in the schools.

We have focused on the training and supervision of in-service teachers. However, Direct Instruction implementations would run more smoothly if teachers entered our schools already prepared to deliver programs effectively and efficiently. This training would include classes and structured field experiences in which these programs are utilized.

"Most teacher educators agree that field-based experiences are important in the preparation of teachers" (Hudson, Miller, Salzberg, & Morgan, 1994, p. 224). To ensure that these experiences are worthwhile, frequent and systematic observations coupled with feedback based on these observations are needed (Englert & Sugai, 1983). These observations can be conducted by university personnel, cooperating teachers (i.e., those persons already teaching in the classroom), or peer supervisors (i.e., those individuals in upper-level field experiences who supervise beginning students) (Gassman, Lignugaris/Kraft, & Marchand-Martella, 1991). Interestingly, more and more cooperating teachers are being asked to supervise students in field experiences (Kent, 2001). This occurrence may stem from decreased university resources to hire full-time personnel or the belief that those in the classroom daily are better prepared to supervise students compared to their university counterparts.

Direct Instruction programs provide a new challenge for those who supervise these field experiences. They offer a whole new set of teaching behaviors that require close observation and feedback. These programs should be carefully implemented following program-specific guidelines and procedures (Simon-Brynildson & Vreeland, 1991). Marchand-Martella, Lignugaris/Kraft and colleagues have conducted the most extensive research on the evaluation of preservice teachers using a Direct Instruction supervision system.[5] The following objectives are tracked in this supervision system on a Direct Instruction observation form.

1. *Teacher presentation.* A presentation involves three parts, including a correct cue (word, phrase, or question used to focus student attention on the task such as "What word?"), pause (at least a one-second waiting time), and signal (hand, touch, or auditory response presented by teacher to initiate a pupil response).

2. *Pupil responses.* Group responds simultaneously and correctly following the teacher signal (group response) or pupil responds correctly after cue and/or signal (individual response).

3. *Teacher corrections.* There are two types of errors requiring correction. A signal error occurs when students respond correctly but not on the teacher's signal. Signal-error corrections include two necessary components: (1) *address*—teacher tells pupils what they need to do such as, "Wait until I signal," and (2) *repeat*—teacher provides the original presentation to test the group's response such as, "What word?" A response error occurs when pupil(s) respond incorrectly. Response-error corrections include three required components and one optional component: (1) *model*—teacher tells pupils the correct answer within three seconds after the response error occurs such as "That word is *ranch*," (2) *lead*—this is an optional component and involves guiding the pupils through a response by saying it with them such as, "Say it with me. *Ranch*," (3) *test*—teacher requests group/individual to respond again by repeating the original cue such as, "What word?," and (4) *retest*—teacher tests pupils on what they missed, known as a "starting over" in Direct Instruction programs.

4. *Teacher praise.* There are two types of praise that can be delivered to pupils. Specific praise is a positive descriptive response following a desired behavior such as "Nice job saying *brother.*" General praise is a global or broad phrase that reflects a positive response to a desired behavior such as "Good job."

5. *Pacing.* One-word or number response or multiword or number responses (e.g., story reading).

After an observation, the supervisor conducts various calculations on the Direct Instruction observation form. These calculations are carried over for use on a Direct Instruction rating form. This form provides scales and mastery criteria. For example, the criteria for pacing are as follows: 9 responses or more per minute for one-word or number responses earns a rating of a 4.0, 7–8.9 responses per minute earns a rating of 3.0 and so on. Information gathered on the Direct Instruction observation form and translated Direct Instruction rating form are used to provide the basis for feedback on a general comments form. Finally, a Direct Instruction checklist can be used to provide feedback on more qualitative and subtle features of the lesson such as dressing appropriately and maintaining personal hygiene or using smooth phrasing and emphasizing key words during the lesson.

The Direct Instruction supervision system could be used as a self-evaluation system by new or preservice teachers. These individuals would need to videotape their own lessons and then take data on their performance using the Direct Instruction observation form. Again, the information would need to be translated to the Direct Instruction rating form to determine if mastery criteria were met. We are familiar with several universities that use this self-evaluation piece in their university practica/student teaching experiences. Using videotaped self-evaluation is similar to the procedures used by Simon-Brynildson and Vreeland (1991) when audiotaped self-monitoring was conducted.

Research on the Direct Instruction Supervision System

Four investigations have been conducted on the Direct Instruction supervision system developed by Marchand-Martella et al. (1995). First, Marchand-Martella and Lignugaris/Kraft (1992) described the performance of preservice teacher trainees in a highly structured Direct Instruction practicum in which one group of practicum students was supervised by university personnel and another by student teachers. Similar performance was found for students across both types of supervisors; however, the only teaching behavior on which these students contrasted sharply was lesson pacing. Practicum students supervised by university personnel fared better than those supervised by student teachers. Overall, most practicum students had difficulty with error corrections irrespective of type of supervisor.

Second, Lignugaris/Kraft and Marchand-Martella (1993) conducted an investigation with eight student teachers who served as supervisors for students enrolled in Direct Instruction practica. Students' presentation and error-correction skills improved throughout the practicum and students noted how much they enjoyed the experience. Lignugaris/Kraft and Marchand-Martella recommended the use of these advanced students as supervisors for beginning practicum students to increase the number of observations and opportunities to provide feedback.

Third, Marchand-Martella, Martella, and Lignugaris/Kraft (1997) used the Direct Instruction supervision system and summarized data across three-, six-, nine-, twelve-, fifteen-, eighteen-, twenty-one-, and twenty-four-minute observation sessions. Results indicated that, although there were minor variations in the percentages of teacher behaviors and scores received based on these percentages, the length of observation did not greatly affect the grade given to the teacher (as noted on the Direct Instruction rating form). The least amount of time required to obtain a representative sample of the teachers' instructional behaviors was twelve minutes.

Finally, Marchand-Martella and Lignugaris/Kraft (1997) described the use of the Direct Instruction supervision system using cooperating teachers as supervisors. Interobserver agreement was calculated comparing data and scores gathered by cooperating teachers to those data and scores gathered by a university coordinator. Results indicated high agreement percentages across teaching behaviors and overall ratings.

ENDNOTES

1. A monthly pacing guide may be obtained by writing to Dr. Molly Blakely, Educational Resources, Inc., 7105 Old Grant Creek Road, Missoula, MT 59808 (E-mail = bgskycntry@aol.com).

2. A weekly pacing guide may be obtained by writing to Dr. Molly Blakely, Educational Resources, Inc., 7105 Old Grant Creek Road, Missoula, MT 59808 (E-mail = bgskycntry@aol.com).

3. A quantitative monitoring guide may be obtained by writing to Dr. Molly Blakely, Educational Resources, Inc., 7105 Old Grant Creek Road, Missoula, MT 59808 (E-mail = bgskycntry@aol.com).

4. A qualitative monitoring guide may be obtained by writing to Dr. Molly Blakely, Educational Resources, Inc., 7105 Old Grant Creek Road, Missoula, MT 59808 (E-mail = bgskycntry@aol.com).

5. Direct Instruction supervision system forms developed by Marchand-Martella, Lignugaris/Kraft, Pettigrew, and Leishman (1995) can be obtained by writing to: Dr. Benjamin Lignugaris/Kraft, Department of Special Education and Rehabilitation Services, Utah State University, Logan, Utah 84322-2865 (E-mail = lig@cc.usu.edu).

REFERENCES

Adams, G., & Engelmann, S. (1996). *Research on Direct Instruction: 25 years beyond DISTAR.* Seattle, WA: Educational Achievement Systems.

Amberge, C. (2002). When Direct Instruction "doesn't work." *Direct Instruction News, 2*(2), 16–17.

Arreaga-Mayer, C. (1998). Increasing active student responding and improving academic performance through classwide peer tutoring. *Intervention in School and Clinic, 34,* 89–94.

Baker, S., Gersten, R., & Keating, T. (2000). When less may be more: A 2-year longitudinal evaluation of a volunteer tutoring program requiring minimal training. *Reading Research Quarterly, 35,* 494–519.

Blakely, M. R. (2001). A survey of levels of supervisory support and maintenance of effects reported by educators involved in Direct Instruction implementations. *Journal of Direct Instruction, 1*(2), 73–83.

Brophy, J., & Good, T. L. (1986). Teacher behavior and student achievement. In M. Wittrock (Ed.), *Third handbook of research on teaching* (pp. 328–375). New York: MacMillan.

Brown, J. (1993). Reverse-role tutoring: An alternative intervention for learning disabled students. *Canadian Journal of Special Education, 9,* 154–159.

Carnine, D. W., Grossen, B., & Silbert, J. (1995). Direct Instruction to accelerate cognitive growth. In J. Block, S. Everson, & T. Guskey (Eds.), *School improvement program* (pp. 129–152). New York: Scholastic Leadership Policy Research.

Carroll, J. B. (1963). A model of school learning. *Teachers College Record, 64,* 723–733.

Cotton, K. (1995). *Effective schooling practices: A research synthesis.* Portland, OR: Northwest Regional Educational Laboratory.

Coulter, G. A., & Grossen, B. (1997). The effectiveness of in-class instructive feedback versus after-class instructive feedback for teachers learning Direct Instruction teaching behaviors. *Effective School Practices, 16*(4), 21–35.

Delquadri, J., Greenwood, C. R., Whorton, D., Carta, J. J., & Hall, R. V. (1986). Classwide peer tutoring. *Exceptional Children, 52,* 535–542.

Englert, C. S., & Sugai, G. (1983). Teacher training: Improving trainee performance through peer observation and observation system technology. *Teacher Education and Special Education, 6,* 7–17.

Enright, S., & Axelrod, S. (1995). Peer tutoring: Applied behavior analysis working in the classroom. *School Psychology Quarterly, 10,* 29–40.

French, N. K. (1997). Management of paraeducators. In A. L. Pickett & K. Gerlach (Eds.), *Supervising paraeducators in school settings: A team approach* (pp. 91–169). Austin, TX: Pro-Ed.

Fullan, M. (1993). Why teachers must become change agents. *Educational Leadership, 24*(3), 12–17.

Gassman, G. W., Lignugaris/Kraft, B., & Marchand-Martella, N. E. (1991). Field-based supervision: A model for integrating university, cooperating teacher, and peer supervisors. *The Teacher Educator, 27*(2), 32–39.

Gleason, M. M., & Hall, T. E. (1991). Focusing on instructional design to implement a performance-based teacher training program. *Education & Treatment of Children, 14*(4), 316–332.

Greenwood, C. R., Terry, B., Arreaga-Mayer, C., & Finney, R. (1992). The classroom peer tutoring program: Implementation factors moderating students' achievement. *Journal of Applied Behavior Analysis, 25,* 101–116.

Grossen, B. (1996). *How shall we group to achieve excellence with equity?* Eugene, OR: University of Oregon.

Harris, R. E., Marchand-Martella, N. E., & Martella, R. C. (2000). Effects of a peer-delivered Corrective Reading program with repeated reading on the reading performance of at-risk high school students. *Journal of Behavioral Education, 10,* 21–36.

Hock, M., Pulvers, K., Deshler, D., & Schumaker, J. (2001). The effects of an after-school tutoring program on the academic performance of at-risk students and students with LD. *Remedial and Special Education, 22,* 172–186.

Hudson, P., Miller, S., Salzberg, C., & Morgan, R. (1994). The role of peer coaching in teacher education programs. *Teacher Education and Special Education, 17,* 224–235.

Johnson, S. M., & Kardos, S. M. (2002). Keeping new teachers in mind. *Educational Leadership, 59,* 12–16.

Joyce, B., & Showers, B. (1995). *Student achievement through staff development: Fundamentals of school renewal.* New York: Longman.

Kamps, D., Locke, P., Delquadri, J., & Hall, R. V. (1989). Increasing academic skills of students with autism using fifth-grade peers as tutors. *Education & Treatment of Children, 12,* 38–51.

Karant, V. (1989). Supervision in the age of teacher empowerment. *Educational Leadership, 35*(6), 27–29.

Kent, S. (2001). Supervision of student teachers: Practices of cooperating teachers prepared in a clinical supervision course. *Journal of Curriculum and Supervision, 16,* 228–244.

King-Sears, M., & Bradley, D. (1995). Classwide peer tutoring: Heterogeneous instruction in general education classrooms. *Preventing School Failure, 40,* 29–35.

Lignugaris/Kraft, B., & Marchand-Martella, N. E. (1993). Evaluation of preservice teachers' interactive teaching skills in a Direct Instruction practicum using student teachers as supervisors. *Teacher Education and Special Education, 16,* 309–319.

Maheady, L. (1990, June). *Peer-mediated instruction: An overview of methods.* Paper presented at the 14th Annual Intervention Procedures Conference for At-Risk Students, Logan, UT.

Maher, C. A. (1984). Handicapped adolescents as cross-age tutors: Program description and evaluation. *Exceptional Children, 51,* 56–63.

Marchand-Martella, N. E., & Lignugaris/Kraft, B. (1992, Spring). A descriptive analysis of preservice teacher performance in a Direct Instruction practicum using student teachers and university personnel as supervisors. *Direct Instruction News, 11,* 2–8.

Marchand-Martella, N. E., & Lignugaris/Kraft, B. (1997). Reliability of cooperating teacher supervisors in a Direct Instruction practicum. *Effective School Practices, 16*(4), 46–57.

Marchand-Martella, N., Lignugaris/Kraft, B., Pettigrew, T., & Leishman, R. (1995). *Direct Instruction supervision system.* Logan, UT: Utah State University.

Marchand-Martella, N. E., & Martella, R. C. (2002). An overview and research summary of peer-delivered Corrective Reading instruction. *Behavior Analysis Today, 3*(3), 214–221. Available from: www.behavior-analyst-online.org

Marchand-Martella, N. E., Martella, R. C., Agran, M., Salzberg, C. L., Young, K. R., & Morgan, D. (1992). Generalized effects of a peer-delivered first-aid program for students with moderate intellectual disabilities. *Journal of Applied Behavior Analysis, 25,* 841–851.

Marchand-Martella, N. E., Martella, R. C., Bettis, D. F., & Riley-Blakely, M. (in press). Project PALS: A description of a high school-based tutorial program using Corrective Reading and peer-delivered instruction. *Reading and Writing Quarterly.*

Marchand-Martella, N. E., Martella, N. E., & Lignugaris/Kraft, B. (1997). Observation of Direct Instruction teaching behaviors: Determining a representative sample of time for supervision. *International Journal of Special Education, 12,* 30–41.

Marchand-Martella, N. E., Martella, R. C., Orlob, M., & Ebey, T. (2000). Using peers as Corrective Reading instructors for students with disabilities in a rural high school setting. *Rural Special Education Quarterly, 19,* 20–30.

Marchand-Martella, N. E., Martella, R. C., & Waldron-Soler, K. (2000). *Implementation manual for Project PALS (Peer Assisted Learning System): Delivering Corrective Reading through peer-delivered instruction.* Eugene, OR: Association for Direct Instruction.

Martella, R. C., Marchand-Martella, N. E., & Cleanthous, C. (2002). *ADHD: A comprehensive approach.* Dubuque, IA: Kendall/Hunt.

Martella, R. C., Marchand-Martella, N. E., Miller, T., Young, K. R., & Macfarlane, C. (1995, Winter). Teaching instructional aides and peer tutors to decrease problem behaviors in the classroom. *Teaching Exceptional Children, 53–56.*

Martella, R. C., Marchand-Martella, N. E., Young, K. R., & Macfarlane, C. (1995). Determining the collateral effects of peer tutor training on a student with severe disabilities. *Behavior Modification, 19,* 170–191.

Martella, R. C., Nelson, J. R., & Marchand-Martella, N. E. (2003). *Managing behaviors in the schools: A school-wide, classroom, and individualized social learning approach.* Boston, MA: Allyn & Bacon.

Martino, L. R. (1993, January). When students help students. Worried about at-risk kids? Try peer tutoring. *The Executive Educator,* 31–32.

Martino, L. R. (1994). Peer tutoring classes for young adolescents: A cost-effective strategy. *Middle School Journal, 25,* 55–58.

McLaughlin, M. W., & Pfeifer, R. S. (1988). *Teacher evaluation: Improvement, accountability, and effective learning.* New York: Teachers College Press.

Meese, R. L. (2001). *Teaching learners with mild disabilities: Integrating research and practice* (2nd ed.). Belmont, CA: Wadsworth/Thomson Learning.

Morgan, R. L. (1997). Delivering feedback on teaching performance to improve student instruction: Looking for methods in hopes of avoiding madness. *Effective School Practices, 16*(4), 6–11.

National Alliance of Quality Schools. (1995). Planning for a Direct Instruction implementation. *Effective School Practices, 14*(3), 2–28.

National Reading Panel. (2000). *Report of the National Reading Panel: Teaching children to read: An evidence-based assessment of the scientific research literature on reading and its implications for reading instruction. Reports of subgroups.* Rockville, MD: NICHD Clearinghouse.

Olson, J. L., & Platt, J. M. (2000). *Teaching children and adolescents with special needs* (3rd ed.). Upper Saddle River, NJ: Merrill.

Parsons, J. L., Marchand-Martella, N. E., Waldron-Soler, K., Martella, R. C., & Lignugaris/Kraft, B. (in press). Effects of a high school-based peer-delivered corrective mathematics program. *Journal of Direct Instruction.*

Pogrow, S. (1996). Reforming the wannabe reformers: Why education reforms almost always end up making things worse. *Phi Delta Kappan, 77*(10), 656–663.

Raney, P., & Robbins, P. (1989). Professional growth and support through peer coaching. *Educational Leadership, 35*(6), 35–38.

Riley-Blakely, M., & Schafer, E. (1999). *The elements of effective coaching.* [video]. Eugene, OR: Association for Direct Instruction.

Short, C., Marchand-Martella, N. E., Martella, R. C., Ebey, T., & Stookey, S. (1999). The benefits of being high school Corrective Reading peer instructors. *Effective School Practices, 18*(2), 23–29.

Simon-Brynildson, K., & Vreeland, M. (1991). Effects of audiotape self-monitoring on DI teacher presentation techniques. *Direct Instruction News, 10,* 3–10.

Snippe, J. (1992). *Effects of instructional supervision on pupils' achievement.* Paper presented at the annual meeting of the American Educational Research Association, San Francisco, CA.

Utley, C., Mortweet, S., & Greenwood, C. (1997). Peer-mediated instruction and interventions. *Focus on Exceptional Children, 29,* 1–23.

Van Zant, S., & Bailey, E. (2002). Unlocking peer potential for tutoring. *Education Digest, 67,* 44–45.

Wildman Longwill, A., & Kleinert, H. L. (1998, May/April). The unexpected benefits of high school peer tutoring. *Teaching Exceptional Children,* 60–65.

Worrall, R. S., & Carnine, D. (1995). Lack of professional support and control undermines education: A contrasting perspective from health and engineering. *Effective School Practices, 14*(1), 3–16.

APPENDIX
Direct Instruction Programs

CONTENT AREA PROGRAMS

History/Social Studies

Understanding U.S. History Volume I

Carnine, D., Crawford, D., Harniss, M., & Hollenbeck, K. (1995). *Understanding U.S. history: Volume I through the Civil War.* Eugene, OR: Considerate Publishing.

Materials: Textbook

Understanding U.S. History Volume II

Carnine, D., Steely, D., & Silbert, J. (1996). *Understanding U.S. history: Volume II Reconstruction through to world leadership.* Eugene, OR: Considerate Publishing.

Materials: Textbook

Chemistry

Understanding Chemistry and Energy

Hofmeister, A., Engelmann, S., & Carnine, D. (1989). *Understanding chemistry and energy* [Videodisc]. Core Concepts in Science (available through MathMastery.com).

Hofmeister, A., Engelmann, S., & Carnine, D. (1989). *Understanding chemistry and energy* [Videotape]. Core Concepts in Science (available through MathMastery.com).

Earth Science

Hofmeister, A., Engelmann, S., & Carnine, D. (1989). *Earth science* [Videodisc]. Core Concepts in Science (available through MathMastery.com).

Hofmeister, A., Engelmann, S., & Carnine, D. (1989). *Earth science* [Videotape]. Core Concepts in Science (available through MathMastery.com).

Hofmeister, A., Engelmann, S., & Carnine, D. (1989). *Earth science* [DVD]. Core Concepts in Science (available through MathMastery.com).

Life Sciences

Carnine, D., Carnine, L., Vachon, V., Shindledecker, K. L., & Steely, D. (in preparation). *Understanding life sciences.* Eugene, OR: University of Oregon.

Your World of Facts

Your World of Facts I

Engelmann, S., Davis, K., & Davis, G. (1981). *Your world of facts: A memory development program,* Vol. 1. Columbus, OH: SRA/McGraw-Hill.

Teacher Materials: Teacher Presentation Book.

Student Materials: Workbook.

Your World of Facts II

Engelmann, S., Davis, K, & Davis, G. (1983). *Your world of facts: A memory development program,* Vol. 2. Columbus, OH: SRA/McGraw-Hill.

Teacher Materials: Teacher Presentation Book.

Student Materials: Workbook.

LANGUAGE PROGRAMS

Language for Learning

Engelmann, S., & Osborn, J. (1999). *Language for learning.* Columbus, OH: SRA/McGraw-Hill.

Teacher Materials: Presentation Books (4), Teacher Guide, Mastery Test Package, Behavioral Objectives Book, Skills Folder.

Student Materials: Workbooks (4).

Additional Resources: Picture Cards, Language Activity Blackline Masters.

Español to English

Engelmann, S., & Osborn, J. (1999). *Español to English.* Columbus, OH: SRA/McGraw-Hill.

Teacher Materials: Presentation Book, Teacher's Guide.

Language for Thinking

Engelmann, S., & Osborn, J. (2002). *Language for thinking.* Columbus, OH: SRA/McGraw-Hill.

Teacher Materials: Presentation Books (3), Teacher Guide, Mastery Test Package, Answer Key, Behavioral Objectives Book, Skills Folder.

Student Materials: Student Picture Book, Workbook.

Language for Writing

Engelmann, S., & Osborn, J. (2003). *Language for writing.* Columbus, OH: SRA/McGraw-Hill.

Teacher Materials: Presentation Book, Teacher Guide, Progress Monitoring System, Answer Key.

Student Materials: Textbook, Workbook.

Language III

Engelmann, S., & Osborn, J. (1987). *DISTAR language III.* Columbus, OH: SRA/McGraw-Hill.

Teacher Materials: Presentation Book, Teacher Guide, Annotated Edition Workbooks (3), Answer Key.

Student Materials: Workbooks (3), textbook.

MATHEMATICS PROGRAMS

Connecting Math Concepts

Lesson Sampler

Connecting math concepts lesson sampler. (2003). Columbus, OH: SRA/McGraw-Hill.

Connecting Math Concepts: Level A

Engelmann, S., & Carnine, D. (2003). *Connecting math concepts: Level A.* Columbus, OH: SRA/McGraw-Hill.

Teacher Materials: Presentation Books (2), Teacher Guide, Answer Key.

Student Materials: Student Workbooks (2).

Additional Resources: Math Fact Worksheets, Independent Worksheets.

Connecting Math Concepts. Level B

Engelmann, S., & Carnine, D. (2003). *Connecting math concepts: Level B.* Columbus, OH: SRA/McGraw-Hill.

Teacher Materials: Presentation Books (2), Teacher Guide, Answer Key.

Student Materials: Student Workbook (2).

Additional Resources: Math Fact Worksheets, Independent Worksheets.

Connecting Math Concepts: Level C

Engelmann, S., & Carnine, D. (2003). *Connecting math concepts: Level C.* Columbus, OH: SRA/McGraw-Hill.

Teacher Materials: Presentation Books (2), Teacher Guide, Answer Key.

Student Materials: Textbook, Student Workbook.

Additional Resources: Math Fact Worksheets, Independent Worksheets.

Connecting Math Concepts: Level D

Engelmann, S., Engelmann, O., & Carnine, D. (2003). *Connecting math concepts: Level D.* Columbus, OH: SRA/McGraw-Hill.

Teacher Materials: Presentation Books (2), Teacher Guide, Answer Key.

Student Materials: Textbook, Student Workbook.

Additional Resources: Math Fact Worksheets, Independent Worksheets.

Connecting Math Concepts: Level E

Engelmann, S., Carnine, D., Engelmann, O., & Kelly, B. (2003). *Connecting math concepts: Level E.* Columbus, OH: SRA/McGraw-Hill.

Teacher Materials: Presentation Books (2), Teacher Guide, Answer Key.

Student Materials: Textbook, Student Workbook.

Additional Resources: Independent Worksheets.

Connecting Math Concepts: Bridge to Connecting Math Concepts

Engelmann, S., Kelly, B., Engelmann, O., & Carnine, D. (2003). *Connecting math concepts: Bridge to connecting math concepts.* Columbus, OH: SRA/McGraw-Hill.

Teacher Materials: Presentation Books (2), Teacher Guide, Answer Key.

Student Materials: Textbook.

Additional Resources: Independent Worksheets.

Connecting Math Concepts: Level F

Engelmann, S., Kelly, B., & Carnine, D. (2003). *Connecting math concepts: Level F.* Columbus, OH: SRA/McGraw-Hill.

Teacher Materials: Presentation Books (2), Teacher Guide, Answer Key.

Student Materials: Textbook.

Additional Resources: Independent Worksheets.

Corrective Mathematics

Series Guide

Corrective mathematics series guide. (1981). Columbus, OH: SRA/McGraw-Hill.

Corrective Mathematics: Addition

Engelmann, S., & Carnine, D. (1981). *Corrective mathematics: Addition.* Columbus, OH: SRA/McGraw-Hill.

Teacher Materials: Presentation Book, Answer Key.

Student Materials: Workbook.

Corrective Mathematics: Subtraction

Engelmann, S., & Carnine, D. (1981). *Corrective mathematics: Subtraction.* Columbus, OH: SRA/McGraw-Hill.

Teacher Materials: Presentation Book, Answer Key.

Student Materials: Workbook.

Corrective Mathematics: Multiplication

Engelmann, S., & Carnine, D. (1981). *Corrective mathematics: Multiplication.* Columbus, OH: SRA/McGraw-Hill.

Teacher Materials: Presentation Book, Answer Key.

Student Materials: Workbook.

Corrective Mathematics: Division

Engelmann, S., & Carnine, D. (1981). *Corrective mathematics: Division.* Columbus, OH: SRA/McGraw-Hill.

Teacher Materials: Presentation Book, Answer Key.

Student Materials: Workbook.

Mathematics Module: Basic Fractions

Engelmann, S., & Steely, D. (1978). *Mathematics module: Basic fractions.* Columbus, OH: SRA/McGraw-Hill.

Teacher Materials: Presentation Book, Answer Key.

Student Materials: Workbook.

Mathematics Module: Fractions, Decimals, and Percents

Engelmann, S., & Steely, D. (1978). *Mathematics module: Fractions, decimals, and percents.* Columbus, OH: SRA/McGraw-Hill.

Teacher Materials: Presentation Book, Answer Key.

Student Materials: Workbook.

Mathematics Module: Ratios and Equations

Engelmann, S., & Steely, D. (1978). *Mathematics module: Ratios and equations.* Columbus, OH: SRA/McGraw-Hill.

Teacher Materials: Presentation Book, Answer Key.

Student Materials: Workbook.

DISTAR Arithmetic

DISTAR Arithmetic Level I

Engelmann, S., & Carnine, D. (1975). *DISTAR Arithmetic: Level I.* Columbus, OH: SRA/McGraw-Hill.

Teacher Materials: Presentation Books (3), Annotated Takehome Workbooks (3), Teacher Guide, Geometric Figure Cards, Form Boards, Acetate Page Protector, Group Progress Indicators.

Student Materials: Takehome Workbooks (3).

Additional Resources: Behavioral Objectives, Skills Profile Folders.

DISTAR Arithmetic Level II

Engelmann, S., & Carnine, D. (1975). *DISTAR Arithmetic: Level II.* Columbus, OH: SRA/McGraw-Hill.

Teacher Materials: Presentation Books (4), Annotated Takehome Workbooks (3), Teacher Guide, Group Progress Indicators.

Student Materials: Takehome Workbooks (3).

Videodisc and Videotape Programs

Problem Solving with Addition and Subtraction

Hofmeister, A., Engelmann, S., & Carnine, D. (1989). *Problem solving with addition and subtraction* [Videodisc]. Core Concepts in Science (available through MathMastery.com).

Hofmeister, A., Engelmann, S., & Carnine, D. (1989). *Problem solving with addition and subtraction* [Videotape]. Core Concepts in Science (available through MathMastery.com).

Mastering Fractions

Hofmeister, A., Engelmann, S., & Carnine, D. (1989). *Mastering fractions* [Videodisc]. Core Concepts in Science (available through MathMastery.com).

Hofmeister, A., Engelmann, S., & Carnine, D. (1989). *Mastering fractions* [Videotape]. Core Concepts in Science (available through MathMastery.com).

Mastering Informal Geometry

Hofmeister, A., Engelmann, S., & Carnine, D. (1989). *Mastering informal geometry* [Videodisc]. Core Concepts in Science (available through MathMastery.com).

Hofmeister, A., Engelmann, S., & Carnine, D. (1989). *Mastering informal geometry* [Videotape]. Core Concepts in Science (available through MathMastery.com).

Mastering Decimals and Percents

Hofmeister, A., Engelmann, S., & Carnine, D. (1989). *Mastering decimals and percents* [Videodisc]. Core Concepts in Science (available through MathMastery.com).

Hofmeister, A., Engelmann, S., & Carnine, D. (1989). *Mastering decimals and percents* [Videotape]. Core Concepts in Science (available through Math-Mastery.com).

Mastering Ratios and Word Problem Strategies

Hofmeister, A., Engelmann, S., & Carnine, D. (1989). *Mastering ratios and word problem strategies* [Videodisc]. Core Concepts in Science (available through MathMastery.com).

Hofmeister, A., Engelmann S., & Carnine, D. (1989). *Mastering ratios and word problem strategies* [Videotape]. Core Concepts in Science (available through MathMastery-com).

Mastering Equations, Roots, and Exponents

Hofmeister, A., Engelmann, S., & Carnine, D. (1989). *Mastering equations, roots, and exponents* [Videodisc]. Core Concepts in Science (available through MathMastery.com).

Hofmeister, A., Engelmann , S., & Carnine, D. (1989). *Mastering equations, roots, and exponents* [Videotape]. Core Concepts in Science (available through MathMastery.com).

Problem Solving with Addition and Subtraction

Hofmeister, A., Engelmann, S., & Carnine, D. (1989). *Problem solving with addition and subtraction* [Videodisc]. Core Concepts in Science (available through MathMastery.com).

Hofmeister, A., Engelmann, S., & Carnine, D. (1989). *Problem solving with addition and subtraction* [Videotape]. Core Concepts in Science (available through MathMastery.com).

Problem Solving with Multiplication and Division

Hofmeister, A., Engelmann, S., & Carnine, D. (1989). *Problem solving with multiplication and division* [Videodisc] Core Concepts in Science (available through MathMastery.com).

Hofmeister, A., Engelmann, S., & Carnine, D. (1989). *Problem solving with multiplication and division* [Videotape]. Core Concepts in Science (available through MathMastery.com).

Problem Solving with Tables, Graphs, and Statistics

Hofmeister, A., Engelmann, S., & Carnine, D. (1989). *Problem solving with tables, graphs, and statistics* [Videodisc]. Core Concepts in Science (available through MathMastery.com).

Hofmeister, A, Engelmann, S., & Carnine, D. (1989). *Problem solving with tables, graphs, and statistics* [Videotape]. Core Concepts in Science (available through MathMastery.com).

READING PROGRAMS

Corrective Reading

Series Guide

Corrective reading series guide. (1999). Columbus, OH: SRA/McGraw-Hill.

Corrective Reading Thinking Basics: Comprehension A

Engelmann, S., Hanner, S., Osborn, J., & Haddox, P. (1999). *Corrective reading thinking basics. Comprehension A.* Columbus, OH: SRA/McGraw-Hill.

Teacher Materials: Presentation Book, Teacher Guide.

Student Materials: Workbook.

Additional Materials: Mastery Test Package, Practice Standardized Test Format Blackline Master.

Corrective Reading Comprehension Skills: Comprehension B1

Engelmann, S., Osborn, S., & Hanner, S. (1999). *Corrective reading comprehension skills: Comprehension B1.* Columbus, OH: SRA/McGraw-Hill.

Teacher Materials: Presentation Book, Teacher Guide.

Student Materials: Workbook.

Additional Materials: Mastery Test Package, Practice Standardized Test Format Blackline Master.

Corrective Reading Comprehension Skills: Comprehension B2

Engelmann, S., Osborn, S., & Hanner, S. (1999). *Corrective reading comprehension skills: Comprehension B2.* Columbus, OH: SRA/McGraw-Hill.

Teacher Materials: Presentation Book, Teacher Guide.

Student Materials: Workbook.

Additional Materials: Mastery Test Package, Practice Standardized Test Format Blackline Master.

Corrective Reading Concept Applications: Comprehension C

Engelmann, S., Hanner, S., & Haddox, P. (1999). *Corrective reading concept applications. Comprehension C.* Columbus, OH: SRA/McGraw-Hill.

Teacher Materials: Presentation Book, Teacher Guide.

Student Materials: Workbook.

Additional Materials: Mastery Test Package, Practice Standardized Test Format Blackline Master.

Corrective Reading Word-Attack Basics: Decoding A

Engelmann, S., Carnine, L., & Johnson, G. (1999). *Corrective reading word-attack basics: Decoding A.* Columbus, OH: SRA/McGraw-Hill.

Teacher Materials: Presentation Book, Teacher Guide.

Student Materials: Workbook.

Additional Materials: Mastery Test Package, Practice Standardized Test Format Blackline Master.

Corrective Reading Decoding Strategies: Decoding B1

Engelmann, S., Johnson, G., Meyer, L., Carnine, L., Becker, W., & Eisele, J. (1999). *Corrective reading decoding strategies: Decoding B1.* Columbus, OH: SRA/McGraw-Hill.

Teacher Materials: Presentation Book, Teacher Guide.

Student Materials: Workbook.

Additional Materials: Mastery Test Package, Blackline Masters, High Interest Readers, Practice Standardized Test Format Blackline Master.

Corrective Reading Decoding Strategies: Decoding B2

Engelmann, S., Johnson, G., Meyer, L., Carnine, L., Becker, W., & Eisele, J. (1999). *Corrective reading decoding strategies: Decoding B2.* Columbus, OH: SRA/McGraw-Hill.

Teacher Materials: Presentation Book, Teacher Guide.

Student Materials: Workbook.

Additional Materials: Mastery Test Package, Blackline Masters, Tom and Ricky Series, Practice Standardized Test Format Blackline Master.

Corrective Reading Skill Applications: Decoding C

Engelmann, S., Meyer, L., Johnson, G., & Carnine, L. (1999). *Corrective reading skill applications: Decoding C.* Columbus, OH: SRA/McGraw-Hill.

Teacher Materials: Presentation Book, Teacher Guide.

Student Materials: Workbook.

Additional Materials: Mastery Test Package, Blackline Masters, Trail Blazer Series, High Adventure Series, Practice Standardized Test Format Blackline Master.

Funnix

Funnix Beginning Reading

Engelmann, S., Engelmann, O., & Davis, K. (2001). *Funnix beginning reading.* [Computer software]. Eugene, OR: Royal Limited Partnership. (Available at Funnix.com).

Materials: Computer program, Beginning Reading Workbook.

Funnix 2

Engelmann, S., & Engelmann, O. (2002). *Funnix 2.* [Computer software]. Eugene, OR: Royal Limited Partnership. (Available at Funnix.com).

Materials: Computer program, Funnix 2 Reader.

Horizons

Series Guide

Horizons series guide. (1998). Columbus, OH: SRA/McGraw-Hill.

Horizons Level A

Engelmann, S., Engelmann, O., & Davis, K. L. S. (1998). *Horizons—Learning to read: Level A.* Columbus, OH: SRA/McGraw-Hill.

Teacher Materials: Presentation Books (3), Teacher Guide, Answer Key, Letter Chart, Audiocassette, Literature Guide.

Student Materials: Textbooks (3), Workbooks (3).

Additional Resources: Literature Collection.

Horizons Level B

Engelmann, S., Engelmann, O., & Davis, K. L. S. (2000). *Horizons—Learning to read: Level B.* Columbus, OH: SRA/McGraw-Hill.

Teacher Materials: Presentation Books (3), Teacher Guide, Answer Key, Letter Chart, Audiocassette, Literature Guide.

Student Materials: Textbooks (3), Workbooks (3).

Additional Resources: Literature Collection of Trade Books.

Horizons Fast Track A/B

Engelmann, S., Engelmann, O., & Davis, K. L. S. (1997). *Horizons—Learning to read: Fast track A/B.* Columbus, OH: SRA/McGraw-Hill.

Teacher Materials: Presentation Books (3), Teacher Guide, Answer Key, Letter Chart, Audiocassette, Literature Guide.

Student Materials: Textbooks (3), Workbooks (3).

Additional Resources: Literature Collection of Trade Books.

Horizons Fast Track C/D

Engelmann, S., & Hanner, S. (1998). *Horizons—Reading to learn: Fast track C/D.* Columbus, OH: SRA/McGraw-Hill.

Teacher Materials: Presentation Books (3), Teacher Guide, Writing/Spelling Guide, Literature Anthology Guide.

Student Materials: Textbooks (3), Workbooks (3), Student Literature Anthology, Read-To Trade Books (2).

Journeys

Series Guide

Journeys series guide. (2000). Columbus, OH: SRA/McGraw-Hill.

Journeys: Level K

Engelmann, S., Engelmann, O., & Hanner, S. (2000). *Journeys: Level K.* Columbus, OH: SRA/McGraw-Hill.

Teacher Materials: Presentation Books (3 Language, 1 Reading), Teacher Guide, Answer Key, and Audiocassette.

Student Materials: Textbook, Workbooks (3).

Journeys: Level 1

Engelmann, S., Engelmann, O., & Hanner, S. (2000). *Journeys: Level 1.* Columbus, OH: SRA/McGraw-Hill.

Teacher Materials: Presentation Books (3 Reading, 1 Language), Teacher Guide, Answer Key, Literature Guide, Quick Start Presentation Book, Quick Start Blackline Masters, Audiocassette.

Student Materials: Textbook for Quick Start Lessons, Textbooks (3), Language Workbook, Reading Workbooks (3).

Additional Resources: Literature Collection (15).

Journeys: Level 2

Engelmann, S., Engelmann, O., Davis, K. K. S., & Arborgast, A. (2000). *Journeys: Level 2.* Columbus, OH: SRA/McGraw-Hill.

Teacher Materials: Presentation Books (3), Teacher Guide, Answer Key, Literature Guide, Audiocassette, Student Worksheet Blackline Masters (3 books).

Student Materials: Textbooks (3).

Additional Resources: Literature Collection (14 books).

Journeys: Level 3

Engelmann, S., & Hanner, S. (2002). *Journeys: Level 3.* Columbus, OH: SRA/McGraw-Hill.

Teacher Materials: Presentation Books (3), Teacher Guide, Answer Key, Literature Guide, Writing/Spelling Guide, Student Worksheet Blackline Masters (3 books).

Student Materials: Textbooks (3), Student Anthology.

Additional Resources: Read-to Books (4).

Language through Literature

Dodds, T. (2002). *Language through literature: Level 1 resource guide.* Columbus, OH: SRA/McGraw-Hill.

Dodds, T. (2002). *Language through literature: Level 2 resource guide.* Columbus, OH: SRA/McGraw-Hill.

Dodds, T. (2002). *Language through literature: Level 3 resource guide.* Columbus, OH: SRA/McGraw-Hill.

Dodds, T. (2002). *Language through literature: Level 4 resource guide.* Columbus, OH: SRA/McGraw-Hill.

Dodds, T. (2002). *Language through literature: Level 5 resource guide.* Columbus, OH: SRA/McGraw-Hill.

Dodds, T. (2002). *Language through literature: Level 6 resource guide.* Columbus, OH: SRA/McGraw-Hill.

Learning through Literature

Story Studies

Dodds, T., & Goodfellow, F. (1993). *Story studies package 1: People/friends.* Columbus, OH: SRA/McGraw-Hill.

Dodds, T., & Goodfellow, F. (1993). *Story studies package 2: Animals/Mice.* Columbus, OH: SRA/McGraw-Hill.

Dodds, T., & Goodfellow, F. (1993). *Story studies package 3: Caldecott winners/poetry.* Columbus, OH: SRA/McGraw-Hill.

Dodds, T., & Goodfellow, F. (1993). *Story studies package 4: Fairy tales/folk tales.* Columbus, OH: SRA/McGraw-Hill.

Novel Studies

Dodds, T., & Goodfellow, F. (1993). *Novel studies package 5: Ramona Quimbly, age 8 (Beverly Cleary).* Columbus, OH: SRA/McGraw-Hill.

Dodds, T., & Goodfellow, F. (1993). *Novel studies package 6: Philip Hall likes me, I reckon maybe (Bette Green).* Columbus, OH: SRA/McGraw-Hill.

Dodds, T., & Goodfellow, F. (1993). *Novel studies package 7. Little house in the big woods (Laura Ingalls Wilder).* Columbus, OH: SRA/McGraw-Hill.

Dodds, T., & Goodfellow, F. (1993). *Novel studies package 8: Stuart Little (E. B. White).* Columbus, OH: SRA/McGraw-Hill.

Dodds, T., & Goodfellow, F. (1993). *Novel studies package 9: The enormous egg (Oliver Butterworth).* Columbus, OH: SRA/McGraw-Hill.

Dodds, T., & Goodfellow, F. (1993). *Novel studies package 10: Ben and me (Robert Lawson).* Columbus, OH: SRA/McGraw-Hill.

Dodds, T., & Goodfellow, F. (1993). *Novel studies package 11: King of the wind (Marguerite Henry).* Columbus, OH: SRA/McGraw-Hill.

Dodds, T., & Goodfellow, F. (1993). *Novel studies package 12: Sign of the beaver (Elizabeth George Speare).* Columbus, OH: SRA/McGraw-Hill.

Reading Mastery Classic Edition

Series Guide

Reading mastery classic series guide. (2003). Columbus, OH: SRA/McGraw-Hill.

Reading Mastery Level I

Engelmann, S., & Bruner, E. C. (2003). *Reading mastery classic: Level I.* Columbus, OH: SRA/McGraw-Hill.

Teacher Materials: Presentation Books (3), Teacher Guide, Literature Guide, Spelling Book, Annotated Edition of Student Takehome Workbooks, Audiocassette, Page Protector, Group Progress Indicators, Behavioral Objectives Book Skills Profile.

Student Materials: Storybooks (3), Takehome Workbooks (3).

Additional Resources: Literature Collection (10 books), Independent Readers (2 sets), Seatwork, Benchmark Test Package, Assessment Manual.

Reading Mastery Level II

Engelmann, S., & Bruner, E. C. (2003). *Reading mastery classic: Level II.* Columbus, OH: SRA/McGraw-Hill.

Teacher Materials: Presentation Books (3), Teacher Guide, Literature Guide, Spelling Book, Annotated Edition of Student Takehome Workbooks, Audiocassette, Page Protector, Group Progress Indicators, Behavioral Objectives Book, Skills Profile.

Student Materials: Storybooks (2), Takehome Workbooks (3).

Additional Resources: Literature Collection (9 books), Independent Readers (2 sets), Seatwork, Benchmark Test Package, Assessment Manual.

Reading Mastery Fast Cycle

Engelmann, S., & Bruner, E. C. (2003). *Reading mastery classic: Fast cycle.* Columbus, OH: SRA/McGraw-Hill.

Teacher Materials: Presentation Books (4), Teacher Guide, Literature Guide, Spelling Book, Annotated Edition of Student Takehome Workbooks, Audiocassette, Page Protector, Group Progress Indicators, Behavioral Objectives Book, Skills Profile.

Student Materials: Storybooks (2), Takehome Workbooks (4).

Additional Resources: Benchmark Test Package, Assessment Manual.

Reading Mastery Plus

Series Guide

Reading mastery plus series guide. (2002). Columbus, OH: SRA/McGraw-Hill.

Reading Mastery Plus: Level K

Engelmann, S., Osborn, J., Bruner, E. C., Engelmann, O., & Davis, K. L. S. (2002). *Reading mastery plus: Level K.* Columbus, OH: SRA/McGraw-Hill.

Teacher Materials: Presentation Books (3 Language, 1 Pre-Reading, 1 Reading), Teacher Guide, Literature Guide, Behavioral Objectives Book, Skills Profile, Answer Key, Letter Chart, Page Protector, Group Progress Indicators, Audiocassette with Alphabet Song.

Student Materials: Story-Picture Book, Workbooks (3).

Additional Resources: Behavioral Objectives Book, Skills Folder, Literature Collection (7 books), Answer Key, Letter Chart Audiocassette.

Reading Mastery Plus: Level 1

Engelmann, S., Bruner, E. C., Engelmann, O., & Davis, K. L. S. (2002). *Reading mastery plus: Level 1*. Columbus, OH: SRA/McGraw-Hill.

Teacher Materials: Presentation Books (3 Reading, 1 Language), Teacher Guide, Literature Guide, Language Arts Guide, Guide to Independent Readers, Behavioral Objectives Book, Skills Profile, Spelling Book, Answer Key, Fast Start Presentation Book, Fast Start Blackline Masters, Page Protector, Group Progress Indicators, Audiocassette.

Student Materials: Storybook, Textbook, Language Workbook, Workbooks (3).

Additional Resources: Seatwork, Behavioral Objectives Book, Skills Folder, Literature Collection (15 books), Independent Readers (8 books), Language Arts Guide, Guide to Independent Readers, Spelling Book, Answer Key, Audiocassette.

Reading Mastery Plus: Level 2

Engelmann, S., Bruner, E. C., Engelmann, O., Davis, K. L. S., & Arborgast, A. (2002). *Reading mastery plus: Level 2*. Columbus, OH: SRA/McGraw-Hill.

Teacher Materials: Presentation Books (3 Reading, 1 Language), Teacher Guide, Literature Guide, Language Arts Guide, Guide to Independent Readers, Behavioral Objectives Book, Skills Profile, Spelling Book, Answer Key, Page Protector, Group Progress Indicators.

Student Materials: Storybook, Textbook, Workbooks (3).

Additional Resources: Seatwork, Behavioral Objectives Book, Skills Folder, Literature Collection (14 books), Independent Readers (9 books), Language Arts Guide, Guide to Independent Readers, Spelling Book, Answer Key.

Reading Mastery Plus: Level 3

Engelmann, S., & Hanner, S. (2002). *Reading mastery plus: Level 3*. Columbus, OH: SRA/McGraw-Hill.

Teacher Materials: Presentation Books (3), Teacher Guide, Literature Guide, Language Arts Guide, Writing/Spelling Guide, Answer Key, Activities Across the Curriculum.

Student Materials: Textbooks (3), Literature Anthology, Workbooks (3).

Additional Resources: Research Assistant CD-ROM.

Reading Mastery Plus: Level 4

Engelmann, S., & Hanner, S. (2002). *Reading mastery plus: Level 4*. Columbus, OH: SRA/McGraw-Hill.

Teacher Materials: Presentation Books (2), Teacher Guide, Literature Guide, Language Arts Guide, Writing/Spelling Guide, Answer Key, Activities Across the Curriculum.

Student Materials: Textbooks (2), Literature Anthology, Workbooks (2).

Additional Resources: Research Assistant CD-ROM.

Reading Mastery Plus: Level 5

Engelmann, S., Osborn, J., Osborn, S., & Zoref, L. (2002). *Reading mastery plus: Level 5.* Columbus, OH: SRA/McGraw-Hill.

Teacher Materials: Presentation Books (2), Teacher Guide, Literature Guide, Language Arts Guide, Test Book, Answer Key, Activities Across the Curriculum.

Student Materials: Textbooks (2), Literature Anthology, Workbook.

Additional Resources: Research Assistant CD-ROM.

Reading Mastery Plus: Level 6

Engelmann, S., Osborn, J., Osborn, S., & Zoref, L. (2002). *Reading mastery plus: Level 6.* Columbus, OH: SRA/McGraw-Hill.

Teacher Materials: Presentation Books (2), Teacher Guide, Literature Guide, Language Arts Guide, Test Book, Answer Key, Activities Across the Curriculum.

Student Materials: Textbooks (2), Literature Anthology, Workbook.

Additional Resources: Research Assistant CD-ROM.

Rewards

Archer, A., Gleason, M. M., & Vachon, V. (2001). *Reading excellence: Word attack and rate development strategies.* Longmont, CO: Sopris West.

Teacher Materials: Teacher Guide.

Student Materials: Student Book.

Teach Your Child to Read In 100 Easy Lessons

Engelmann, S., Haddox, P., & Bruner, E. (1983). *Teach your child to read in 100 easy lessons.* New York: Simon & Shuster.

SPELLING PROGRAMS

Spelling Mastery

Series Guide

Spelling mastery series guide. (1999). Columbus, OH: SRA/McGraw-Hill.

Spelling Mastery: Level A

Dixon, R., Engelmann, S., & Bauer, M. M. (1999). *Spelling mastery: Level A.* Columbus, OH: SRA/McGraw-Hill.

Teacher Materials: Presentation Book.

Student Materials: Workbook.

Spelling Mastery: Level B

Dixon, R., Engelmann, S., & Bauer, M. M. (1999). *Spelling mastery: Level B.* Columbus, OH: SRA/McGraw-Hill.

Teacher Materials: Presentation Book.

Student Materials: Workbook.

Spelling Mastery: Level C

Dixon, R., & Engelmann, S. (1999). *Spelling mastery: Level C.* Columbus, OH: SRA/McGraw-Hill.

Teacher Materials: Presentation Book.

Student Materials: Workbook.

Spelling Mastery: Level D

Dixon, R., & Engelmann, S. (1999). *Spelling mastery: Level D.* Columbus, OH: SRA/McGraw-Hill.

Teacher Materials: Presentation Book.

Student Materials: Workbook.

Spelling Mastery: Level E

Dixon, R., & Engelmann, S. (1999). *Spelling mastery: Level E.* Columbus, OH: SRA/McGraw-Hill.

Teacher Materials: Presentation Book.

Student Materials: Workbook.

Spelling Mastery: Level F

Dixon, R., Engelmann, S., Steely, D., & Wells, T. (1999). *Spelling mastery: Level F.* Columbus, OH: SRA/McGraw-Hill.

Teacher Materials: Presentation Book.

Student Materials: Workbook.

Spelling through Morphographs

Dixon, R., & Engelmann, S. (2001). *Spelling through morphographs.* Columbus, OH: SRA/McGraw-Hill.

Teacher Materials: Presentation Books (2), Teacher Guide, Blackline Masters.

Student Materials: Student Workbook, Reproducible Student Workbook.

WRITING PROGRAMS

Basic Writing Skills

Basic Writing Skills: Capitalization and Punctuation

Gleason, M., & Stults, C. (1983). *Basic writing skills: Capitalization and punctuation.* Columbus, OH: SRA/McGraw-Hill.

Teacher Materials: Teacher presentation book.

Student Materials: Workbook.

Basic Writing Skills: Sentence Development

Gleason, M., & Stults, C. (1983). *Basic writing skills: Sentence development.* Columbus, OH: SRA/McGraw-Hill.

Teacher Materials: Teacher Presentation Book.

Student Materials: Workbook.

Cursive Writing Program

Miller, S., & Engelmann, S. (1980). *Cursive writing program.* Columbus, OH: SRA/McGraw-Hill.

Teacher Materials: Presentation Book.

Student Materials: Workbook.

Expressive Writing

Expressive Writing 1

Engelmann, S., & Silbert J. (1985). *Expressive Writing 1.* Columbus, OH: SRA/McGraw-Hill.

Teacher Materials: Teacher Presentation Book.

Student Materials: Workbook.

Expressive Writing 2

Engelmann, S., & Silbert, J. (1985). *Expressive Writing 2*. Columbus, OH: SRA/McGraw-Hill.

Teacher Materials: Teacher Presentation Book.

Student Materials: Workbook.

Readers and Writers

Dodds, T., & Goodfellow, F. (1993). *Readers and writers: Becoming authors through genre studies*. Columbus, OH: SRA/McGraw-Hill.

Teacher Materials: Teacher Guide.

Student Materials: Biographies, Mysteries, Realistic Animal Stories, Science Fiction, Sports Stories, Writer's Portfolio.

Reasoning and Writing

Reasoning and Writing Lesson Sampler

Reasoning and writing lesson sampler. (2001). Columbus, OH: SRA/McGraw-Hill.

Reasoning and Writing: Level A

Engelmann, S., Davis, K. L. S. (2001). *Reasoning and writing: Level A.* Columbus, OH: SRA/McGraw-Hill.

Teacher Materials: Presentation Book, Writing Extensions Blackline Masters.

Student Materials: Workbooks (2).

Reasoning and Writing: Level B

Engelmann, S., Arbogast A. B., & Davis, K. L. S. (2001). *Reasoning and writing: Level B.* Columbus, OH: SRA/McGraw-Hill.

Teacher Materials: Presentation Book, Answer Key, Writing Extensions Blackline Masters.

Student Materials: Workbooks (2).

Reasoning and Writing: Level C

Engelmann, S., & Silbert J. (2001). *Reasoning and writing: Level C.* Columbus, OH: SRA/McGraw-Hill.

Teacher Materials: Presentation Book, Answer Key, Writing Extensions Blackline Masters.

Student Materials: Workbook, Textbook.

Reasoning and Writing: Level D

Engelmann, S., & Silbert, J. (2001). *Reasoning and writing: Level D.* Columbus, OH: SRA/McGraw-Hill.

Teacher Materials: Teacher Presentation Book, Answer Key, Writing Extensions Blackline Masters.

Student Materials: Textbook.

Reasoning and Writing: Level E

Engelmann, S., & Grossen, B. (2001). *Reasoning and writing: Level E.* Columbus, OH: SRA/McGraw-Hill.

Teacher Materials: Teacher Presentation Book, Answer Key, Writing Extensions Blackline Masters.

Student Materials: Textbook.

Reasoning and Writing: Level F

Engelmann, S., & Grossen, B. (2001). *Reasoning and writing: Level F.* Columbus, OH: SRA/McGraw-Hill.

Teacher Materials: Teacher Presentation Book, Answer Key, Writing Extensions Blackline Masters.

Student Materials: Textbook.

NAME INDEX

Acland, H., 11
Adams, G. L., 57, 135, 215, 241, 242, 309
Adams, M. J., 10, 68, 101, 142, 180
Agnew, E., 142–143
Agran, M., 326
Ahlgren, A., 249
Aladjem, D., 62
Algozzine, B., 288
Alley, G. R., 264
Allington, R. L., 8, 61
Amberge, C., 305
Anderson, D. M., 174, 175
Anderson, G., 249
Anderson, L. M., 145, 301
Anderson, R. B., 9, 58, 60, 61, 135
Anderson, R. C., 8–9, 101
Andre, T., 261, 262
Anthony, H. M., 145
Applebee, A. N., 270, 273
Aram, D. M., 67, 69
Archer, A. L., 134
Armbruster, B. B., 102
Arreaga-Mayer, C., 326
Arvold, B., 250
Ault, M. J., 21
Axelrod, S., 324
Azim, D., 242

Bailet, L. L., 141, 143, 144
Bailey, E., 325
Bain, A. M., 141, 143, 144
Baker, J., 242
Baker, L., 69
Baker, S. K., 13, 68, 325
Ball, E. W., 10
Bane, M. J., 11
Barbetta, P., 293, 301
Barenbaum, E. M., 273
Barnard, S., 143, 146
Bateman, B., 20, 21
Bawden, H., 102
Bean, R., 251
Beck, I. L., 68, 247, 252, 264

Becker, W. C., 8, 20, 21, 30, 31, 36, 47, 51,
    53–55, 57, 60, 72, 135–136, 286
Beers, C., 184
Beers, J., 184
Bender, R., 179
Benner, G. J., 69, 96
Bereiter, C., 19–20, 57
Bergen, J. R., 301
Berkeley, M., 136
Berliner, D. C., 16, 41, 261
Bernard, J., 96
Beron, K., 8
Bessellieu, F. B., 56
Bettis, D. F., 203, 328
Beveridge, M., 95
Bickel, D., 301
Bickel, W., 301
Binder, C., 7
Birdsell, R., 96
Bisbicos, E. E., 261
Blachman, B. A., 10, 68
Blake, G., 247, 250
Blakely, M. R., 304–334, 321–322
Blum, I. M., 53–54, 242
Borko, H., 249–250
Borman, G. D., 62
Bradley, D. M. C., 301, 326
Bradley, L., 10, 243
Brent, G., 243
Brett, A., 68
Brinton, B., 68, 69
Britton, B. K., 252
Brophy, J. E., 262, 301, 306
Brophy J. E., 47
Browder, D. M., 288
Brown, A., 291
Brown, J., 326
Brown, S., 62
Bruck, M., 180, 181
Bryant, D. P., 250
Bryant, P., 10
Buetow, C., 243
Burnett, R., 252

Burnette, A., 203
Burns, M. S., 68, 101, 143
Byrne, B., 10

Cahen L., 261
Campanile, C., 5
Campbell, M. L., 57
Cantwell, D., 69
Capie, W., 301
Carlson, C. D., 136
Carnine, D. W., 11–13, 20–22, 31, 36, 54,
     56–57, 144–146, 174, 210–211, 214,
     216, 230, 231, 236–241, 250–253, 267,
     269, 273, 275, 276, 283, 286, 291, 294,
     296, 298, 300, 301, 320
Caros, J., 251, 275, 276, 300
Carroll, J. B., 306
Carson, C., 18
Carta, J. J., 282, 301, 326
Casazza, M. E., 22
Cassar, M., 181
Catts, H. W., 10, 67
Cavanaugh, R. A., 293
Ceci, S., 8, 9
Cerva, T. R., 58, 60, 61, 135
Chall, J., 101
Chambless, D. L., 14
Chan, L., 21
Chapman, J. W., 8
Chard, D. J., 13, 18, 21, 57
Chislett, M., 134, 135, 171
Christenson, S. L., 282, 288, 291
Church, E. B., 56
Cibrowski, J., 290
Cipriano, K., 243
Cleanthous, C., 327
Cochran, C., 252
Cogan, L. S., 6–7, 209, 213
Cohen, D., 11
Cole, K. N., 62, 71, 95, 96
Cole, P., 21
Collier, C., 273
Collier, J. L., 273
Collins, M., 174, 181
Colvin, R. C., 6
Conrad, L., 135
Cooke, B., 203
Cooley, E., 22, 242
Cooney, T. J., 250

Cornwall, A., 102
Cotton, K., 305–306
Coulter, G. A., 321
Courson, F. H., 293
Craig, H. K., 68
Cramer, B. B., 68
Crawford, D. B., 206–245, 240, 242, 251,
     253, 267, 269, 275, 300
Cross, R. W., 174
Cullinan, D., 95–96
Cunningham, A. E., 10, 68
Curtis, M. E., 68
Curtiss, S., 69
Cusick, G. M., 69

Dale, P. S., 62, 71, 95, 96
Darch, C. B., 22, 95–96, 135–136, 181, 203,
     294
Davis, G., 291, 296
Davis, K., 291, 296
De Courcey Hinds, M., 11
Delquadri, J., 282, 301, 324, 326
DeLuca, K., 135
Dempster, F. N., 214
Deno, S. L., 197
Deshler, D., 325
Dickson, S., 57, 246–279
DiObilda, N., 243
DiPerna, P., 207
Dixon, R. C., 21, 135, 143–146, 178–205,
     179, 181–183, 184, 190, 194–196, 214,
     230
Dodds, E., 135
Dodds, M., 135
Dodds, T., 134, 135, 171, 172
Dolan, L. J., 101
Dole, J. A., 270
Donlevy, J., 249
Doyle, P. M., 21
Drabman, R. S., 201
Duchastel, P. C., 261
Duffett, A., 7
Duffy, G. G., 270
Duffy, T. M., 252
Duran, E., 56

Earl, L. M., 203
Earle, J., 252
Ebey, T. L., 203, 325, 328–329

Ekelman, B., 67, 69
Elashoff, J., 261
Ellis, A., 10
Ellis, E. S., 17–18
Engelmann, O., 231, 241
Engelmann, S., xix–xxvi, 2, 10, 18–21, 31, 47, 48, 54, 56–57, 135, 144, 154, 174, 179, 184, 190, 194–196, 215, 216, 231, 236–239, 241, 242, 276, 291, 296, 309
Englert, C. S., 145, 288, 329
Enright, S., 324
Epstein, A., 96
Epstein, M. H., 69, 95–96
Erickson, H. L., 250
Evans, C., 96
Evertson, C. M., 301

Farkas, G., 8
Faw, H. W., 261
Felton, R. H., 10
Fessenden, R., 208
Fielding, L., 9
Fielding-Barnsley, R., 10
Fink, W. T., 301
Finn, C., 247
Finney, R., 326
Fischer, T. A., 241, 300
Fister, S., 12
Fitzgerald, M., 203, 204
Flesch, R., 3
Fletcher, J. M., 9, 11
Flick, D., 198
Flowers, J., 295
Foorman, B., 10
Forness, S. R., 53–54, 242
Fox, R. W., 249
Francis, D. J., 9, 10, 136
Fredrick, L. D., 140–177, 147, 174, 175
French, N. K., 320
Friedman, K., 70–71
Friedman, P., 70–71
Fujiki, M., 68, 69
Fullan, M., 320
Fuller, B., 301

Gable, R. A., 12, 21
Gall, M. D., 261
Gardner, R., 293
Garner, R., 250

Garza, M., 95–96
Gassman, G. W., 329
Gates, S. L., 261
Gazdag, G., 70–71
Gersten, R. M., 13, 18, 53–56, 95–96, 135–136, 241, 298, 300, 325
Gertner, B. L., 68–69, 95–96
Gettinger, M., 203
Gillingham, M. G., 250
Ginits, H., 11
Ginn, P. V., 147, 174, 175
Giuliotti, N., 102
Glang, A., 22, 242
Gleason, M. M., 134–136, 141, 144, 300, 321
Glynn, S. M., 252
Gomez, O., 250
Good, T. L., 47, 211, 262, 306
Goodfellow, F., 171, 172
Gouws, D. A., 211
Graham, S., 141–144, 147, 181
Grant, K., 184
Graves, M. F., 252
Gray, B., 70–71
Greaves, R. C., 21
Green, C., 243
Greenwood, C. R., 282, 301, 325–326
Griffin, P., 68, 101, 143
Griffith, P. L., 69
Grimes, A. E., 144
Gromoll, E. W., 252
Grossen, B., 22, 55, 135, 137, 174, 175, 241, 314, 320, 321
Grossi, T. A., 293
Gulgoz, S., 252
Gunter, L., 182, 185, 189, 203
Gunter, P. L., 295
Guskey, T. R., 13, 261
Guthrie, J., 3
Gutlohn, L., 104

Haas, M. E., 247
Hadley, P. A., 68–69
Haladyna, T. M., 250
Hall, J. K., 144
Hall, P. K., 67, 69
Hall, R. V., 282, 301, 324, 326
Hall, T. E., 198, 321
Hamff, A., 250
Hangen, D., 252

Hanner, S., 21
Haring, N. G., 198
Harniss, M. K., 246–279, 251, 253, 267, 269, 275–276, 300
Harris, K. R., 142, 144, 147
Harris, R. E., 328
Hart, B., 7, 10, 70
Hartocollis, A., 5
Hatcher, P., 10
Hawke, H., 203, 204
Haycock, K., 5
Hedge, M., 70–71
Heiry, T., 53–55
Helfand, D., 6
Hempenstall, K., 1–27, 11
Henshaw, P., 243
Henson, K. T., 261
Herman, R., 62
Heron, T. E., 301
Herr, C., 57
Hesse, K. D., 55, 203, 204
Hester, P. P., 69
Heward, W. L., 293, 301
Hewes, G. M., 62
Heyns, B., 11
Hiebert, E. H., 101
Higgins, L., 252
Hill, C., 252
Hillocks, G., Jr., 146
Hinshaw, S. P., 69
Hock, M., 325
Hodges, J., 102
Hoffman, C. M., 4
Hofmeister, A. M., 241, 276, 288, 294–296, 298, 299, 301
Holden, C., 247–248
Hollenbeck, K. L., 246–279, 251, 253, 267, 269, 275, 300
Horner, R. H., 289, 294
Hornor, S., 203
Horton, S., 298
Hoskyn, M., 9, 18
Houang, R., 6–7, 209, 213
Hovermill, J., 249–250
HsingChi, W., 209
Hudson, P. J., 282, 286–288, 290, 291, 293, 296, 301, 329
Hulme, C., 10
Hunter, M., 288, 301

Hurley, M., 68
Huth, E., 243

Isaacson, S. L., 141–147, 212
Ishler, M., 293
Iskold, L., 250

Jack, S. L., 295
Jencks, C. S., 11
Jenkins, J. R., 62, 71, 95, 96
Jerrams, A., 95
Jitendra, A. K., 250
Johnson, B., 104
Johnson, G., 21, 300
Johnson, J., 7
Johnson, K. R., 144
Johnson, S. M., 321
Jones, C., 67, 69
Jorm, A., 9
Joyce, B., 21, 320
Juel, C., 9, 10
Jung, J. S., 54–55, 242

Kaestle, C., 3
Kageyama, M., 22
Kaiser, A. P., 69
Kameeuni, E. J., 21, 31, 57, 68, 101–103, 144–146, 214, 250–252, 262, 273, 281, 283, 286, 291, 294, 296
Kamps, D., 324
Karant, V., 321
Kardos, S. M., 321
Karvonen, M., 288
Karweit, N. L., 101
Kavale, K. A., 53–54, 242
Kearney, C. A., 201
Keating, T., 135–136, 325
Keel, M. C., 147, 174, 175
Kelly, B. F., 22, 55, 238–239, 241
Kemp, K., 12
Kemper, E. A., 57, 136
Kent, S., 329
Kinder, D., 22, 100–139
Kindsvater, R., 293
King, R. R., 67, 69
King-Sears, M., 326
Kinoshita, S., 22
Kintsch, W., 105
Kirsch, I., 3

Kitz, W. R., 241
Klau, K., 135
Klein, D., 210
Kleinert, H. L., 325
Knobel, M., 96
Knuth, E., 249–250
Koser, L., 51
Kozloff, M. A., 56
Kuhn, M. R., 56

Lane, S., 301
Langer, J. S., 270, 273
Larkin, M. J., 17–18
Larner, M., 62
Larsen, D., 188
Lasky, E., 67, 69
Layng, T. V. J., 144
Leach, D. J., 12
Lehr, F., 102
Leishman, R., 331
Lenz, B. K., 264
Lenz, K., 174
Leslie, L., 68
Levin, B., 4
Levy, F., 208
Lewis, A. B., 211
Lewis, L., 7
Liberman, D., 10
Ligas, M. R., 137
Lignugaris/Kraft, B., 242, 280–303, 282,
    286–288, 290, 291, 293, 296, 301, 329,
    331
Llinares, S., 249
Lloyd, J. W., 21, 53–54, 95–96, 242
Locke, P., 324
Loveless, T., 207
Lovitt, T. C., 298
Loxterman, J. A., 252
Lubke, M., 288, 294, 295, 296, 298, 299, 301
Lum, T., 180
Lyon, G. R., 4, 6, 7, 9, 11
Lyon, S. R., 282, 301

MacArthur, C. A., 144
Macfarlane, C. A., 324, 325
MacIver, M. A., 57, 136
Madden, N. A., 101
Madsen, C. H., 51
Maggs, A., 11, 95–96, 203, 204

Maguire, K., 96
Maheady, L., 325
Maher, C. A., 326
Malus-Abramowitz, M., 181
Manzo, K. K., 247
Marchand-Martella N. E., 57, 96, 135, 136,
    203, 242, 243, 304–334, 307, 325, 326,
    327, 328–329, 331
Marshall, J., 11
Martella, R. C., 52, 57, 96, 135, 136, 203,
    242, 243, 307, 324–329, 331
Martin, M., 242
Martin, R., 210
Martino, L. R., 325
Masarik, K., 249–250
Masem, E., 62
Masini, B., 207, 209
Matthews, R., 9
Mayer, R. E., 211
McCaffrey, M., 252
McCormick, C. B., 203, 204, 261
McGee, R., 9, 67, 69
McGlocklin, L., 171, 203
McGuinley, W., 273
McKenzie, M. A., 243
McKeown, M. G., 68, 247, 252, 264
McKnight, C. C., 209
McLaughlin, M. W., 320
McLaughlin, P. J., 21
McLaughlin, T. F., 188
McLean, R., 9
McLuhan, T. C., 264
McMahon, P., 62
McMillan, K., 203, 204
Medley, D. M., 301
Medo, M. A., 68
Meese, R. L., 324
Mehlenbacher, B., 252
Meyer, L. A., 135–136
Michelson, S., 11
Miller, D. E., 57, 96
Miller, P. D., 135
Miller, S., 251, 329
Miller, T. L., 282, 286–288, 290, 291, 293,
    296, 301, 324
Miller, Z., 208
Mills, P. E., 62, 71, 95, 96
Mitchell, M., 95–96
Moats, L. C., 8, 141, 143, 144

Moore, L. J., 241
Morath, P., 95–96
Morgan, D., 326
Morgan, R. L., 320–321, 329
Morris, D., 178–179
Morton, L. L., 180
Mortweet, S., 325–326
Mulligan, I., 62
Murnane, F., 208

Nagy, W. E., 8–9
Nakano, Y., 22
Nation, J., 67, 69
Nelson, J. R., 52, 69, 96, 307
Newcomer, P. L., 273
Niedelman, M., 276
Niemiec, R. P., 282, 291
Nolet, V. W., 247, 250
Noll, M., 70–71
Nordness, P. D., 96
Novy, D., 10
Nungester, R. J., 261

O'Brien, D. M., 136
O'Flahavan, J. F., 273
Ollendick, T. H., 14
Olson, J. L., 307
O'Malley, A., 62
Omanson, S. F., 211
Orlob, M., 328
Osborn, J., 19, 66–99, 72, 102
Overman, L. T., 62

Paik, S., 7
Palinscar, A., 291
Palmaffy, T., 2
Panagos, J., 70–71
Parsons, J. L., 242, 329
Patching, B., 203, 204
Pearson, P. D., 270
Pecora, R., 70–71
Peressini, D., 249–250
Perfetti, C. A., 68
Pettigrew, T., 331
Pfeifer, R. S., 320
Phelps, R. P., 247, 248
Phillips, M., 11
Plager, E., 51
Platt, J. M., 307
Pogrow, S., 308

Porpotage, F. M., 102
Porter, A., 212–213
Pratt-Struthers, J., 188, 201
Prawat, R., 276
Prelock, P., 70–71
Prenn, M. C., 252
Prochnow, J. E., 8
Proper, E. C., 58, 60, 61, 135
Pruitt, P., 249
Pryor, F. L., 102
Przychodzin-Havis, A., 242
Pulvers, K., 325

Raney, P., 320
Rankin, R., 203, 204
Raphael, T. E., 145
Rappaport, D., 210
Rashotte, C. A., 10
Rasmussen, S. K., 295
Ravitch, D., 247
Rebarber, T., 174
Recht, D., 68
Renouf, K., 250
Rescorla, L., 67–68
Resnick, L. B., 211
Rice, M. L., 68–69
Richards, J. P., 261
Riley-Blakely, M., 322, 328
Risley, T. R., 7, 10, 70
Rivers, J., 10–11
Roach, R., 135
Robbins, P., 320
Robinson, J. W., 55, 203, 204
Robinson, L., 68
Rochester, J. M., 3
Roehler, L. R., 270
Rogers-Adkinson, D. L., 69
Roid, G. H., 250
Romagnano, L., 249–250
Romance, N., 55, 276
Rose, H., 289, 294
Rosenshine, B. V., 16, 17, 41, 52, 251, 261,
    282, 288, 291, 293, 299, 301
Rosoff, A., 135
Rothkopf, E. Z., 261
Rothlein, L., 68
Rourke, B. P., 9
Rutherford, F. J., 249
Ryan, B., 70–71
Ryder, R. J., 68

Sachse-Lee, C. M., 18
Sainato, D. M., 282, 301
St. Pierre, R. G., 58, 60, 61, 135
Salas, B., 144
Salzberg, C. L., 326, 329
Sanders, W., 10–11
Schaefer, E., 52–53, 55, 304–334, 322
Schaffer, D., 102
Schieffer, C., 135, 136
Schmidt, T., 144
Schmidt, W. H., 6–7, 208, 209, 213
Schumaker, J., 174, 325
Schwartz, S., 144
Schweinhart, L., 62
Scott, J. A., 101
Scruggs, T., 21
Sexton, C. W., 55
Shanahan, T., 142, 270–273
Shannon, P., 21
Share, D. L., 9
Shavelson, R. J., 16
Shaywitz, B. A., 9
Shaywitz, S. E., 9
Shealy, B., 250
Shepherd, M., 180
Shores, R. E., 295
Short, C., 325, 328–329
Showers, B., 21, 320
Sikorski, M. F., 282, 291
Silbert, J., 21, 136, 144, 146, 211, 214, 230,
    236, 237, 240, 250, 286, 291, 320
Siler, C. R., 247
Silva, P., 9, 67, 69
Simmons, D. C., 10, 21, 57, 68, 101–103,
    145, 146, 262, 281, 283
Simmons, K., 142
Simon-Brynildson, K., 329, 331
Simonsen, F. L., 135, 136, 178–205, 182,
    185, 189, 203
Simpson, R. G., 181, 203
Sinatra, G. M., 252, 264
Singer, G., 22, 242
Skinner, C., 294, 298
Slater, W. H., 252
Slavin, R. E., 15, 53, 101, 261
Sloane, S., 252
Slocum, T. A., 28–65, 298
Smith, F., 144
Smith, M., 11
Smith, S., 252

Smith, S. B., 103
Snider, V. E., 56, 206–245, 242
Snippe, J., 320
Snow, C. E., 68, 101, 143
Snyder, T., 95–96
Snyder, T. D., 4
Sommers, J., 204, 242
Soter, A., 273
Spencer, J., 68
Stahl, S. A., 56, 68, 135
Stanovich, K. E., 8–10, 68
Stanton, G., 261
Stebbins, L. B., 58, 60, 61, 135
Stedman, L., 3
Steele, D. F., 250
Steely, D., 253, 267, 269
Stein, M. L., 100–139, 104, 143–146, 211,
    236, 237, 240, 291
Stennett, R. G., 203
Stevens, C., 250
Stevens, D. D., 145
Stevens, R., 52, 288, 293, 299
Steventon, C., 140–177
Stone, J. E., 11
Stookey, S., 325, 328–329
Strain, P. S., 282, 301
Struthers, T. B., 188, 201
Stuart, M., 68
Sugai, G., 329
Swanson, H. L., 9, 18

Tallal, P., 69
Tarver, S. C., 54–55, 241, 242, 300
Taylor, J., 207, 209
Taylor, R., 56, 95–96
Templeton, S., 178–179
Terry, B., 326
Test, D., 288
Thiagarajan, S., 253
Thomas, D. R., 31, 51
Thompson, M., 252
Thompson, S., 250
Thompson, V., 252
Thorpe, H., 241
Thurlow, M. L., 282, 288, 291
Tierney, R. J., 142, 270–273
Tindal, G., 198, 247, 250
Tish, N., 22, 242
Tobias, S., 261
Tobin, K. G., 136–137, 301

Todd, C., 69
Tomblin, J. B., 67, 69
Torgesen, J. K., 10
Towne, L., 15–16
Townsend, J., 69
Trafton, P. R., 211
Treiman, R., 181
Trout, A., 96
Tso, M. E., 57, 96, 203, 243
Tuckman, B. W., 21
Tunmer, W. E., 8

Ugel, N., 250
Uhry, J., 180
Utley, C., 325–326

Vachon, V., 134
Vail, J., 243
Valla, N., 300
Valverde, G. A, 208
Van Dusen, L., 252
Van Zant, S., 325
Vaughn, S., 18
Viadero, D., 2, 12
Vitale, M., 55, 276
Vreeland, M., 203, 243, 329, 331
Vygotsky, L. S., 40–41

Wagner, R. J., 10
Walberg, H. J., 282, 291
Waldron-Soler, K. M., 57, 66–99, 96, 135,
        136, 242, 327, 329
Wallace, D., 252
Waller, T. G., 261
Wandry, D., 249
Ward, B., 261
Ware, A. M., 136
Warner, D. A., 57, 96
Warren, S. F., 12, 21, 70–71
Wasik, B. A., 101
Waters, G. S., 180, 181
Watkins, C. L., 28–65, 58
Wayne, A. J., 6, 249
Weaver, C. A., 105
Weikert, D., 62
Weil, M., 21

Weiner, P. S., 67, 69
Weisberg, P., 57
Wellington, J., 243
Wenglinsky, H., 11
Wenner, G., 250
White, C. S., 250
White, O. R., 198
White, R., 11
White, W. A. T., 53–56
Whorton, D., 282, 301, 326
Wilde, S., 200
Wildman Longwill, A., 325
Wilen, W., 293
Wiley, D. E., 209
Wilkinson, I. A. G., 101
Williams, R. L., 67, 69, 188, 201
Willingham, D. T., 214
Willis-Yorker, C., 249–250
Wilson, P., 9
Wilson, S. F., 174
Winne, P., 261
Wolery, M., 21
Wolfe, R. G., 209
Wong, B., 21
Wood, J., 203
Wood, W., 288
Woodward, J., 12, 56, 276, 298
Wooley, C., 249–250
Worrall, R. S., 320
Worthington, L. A., 17–18
Wu, H., 211
Wulfeck, P., 69

Xin, Y. P., 250

Young, K. R., 325, 326
Young, M., 242
Young, R., 324
Youngs, P., 249
Ysseldyke, J. E., 282, 288, 291

Zawojewski, J., 211
Zheng, T., 250
Zigmond, N., 251
Zukowski, A., 181

SUBJECT INDEX

Academic learning time (ALT), 41–42, 307–308
Academic problems, 7–10
  increase in, 9–10
  Matthew Effects, 8, 18
  preventing academic failure, 10
  and reading participation, 8
  in vocabulary development, 8–9
Accelerated Reader, 134
Active student participation, 44
Activity planning, 286–287, 289–290
Add-A-Word spelling, 201
Addison-Wesley Mathematics program, 243
Adventures in Language (Dodds and Chislett), 171
Affective outcomes, 17, 58, 60
Age of students, 56–57
American Educational Research Association (AERA), 12
American Federation of Teachers (AFT), 2, 31, 62, 137
American Institutes of Research (AIR), 62
American Management Association, 7
American Psychological Association (APA), 14–15, 20
America Reads, 8
America's Education Choice, 208
Armed Services Vocational Aptitude Battery, 207–208
Assessment
  continuous, 43, 169–170
  in history/social sciences programs, 268–269
  in language programs, 93
  mastery tests, 93, 168, 198, 238–239, 268, 270, 272
  in mathematics programs, 237–239
  placement tests, 93, 167–168, 197–198, 202, 237–238, 314
  in reading programs, 132–133
  in science programs, 269–270, 271, 272
  in spelling programs, 197–198
  in writing programs, 167–170

Association for Direct Instruction (ADI), 312–313
Auditory signals, 92, 130, 166, 236

Background knowledge. *See* Primed background knowledge
Basic mathematics skills, 210, 211–212
Basic reading skills, 30
Basic skills outcomes, 58
Basic Writing Skills
  assessment in, 167–170
  content analysis of, 165
  described, 147, 150
  instructional format of, 165
  overview of, 148
  research on, 174
  teaching techniques for, 165–167
Becoming a Nation of Readers, 101
Behavior management, 44
Big ideas, 29–30
  in curricular design, 251, 254–259, 273, 283–286
  defined, 283
  in history/social science programs, 254–258, 273, 283–286
  in mathematics programs, 214–215, 216–219, 222–235
  problem-solution-effect (PSE) approach to, 254–255, 264–265, 273, 287, 294
  in science programs, 258–259
  sequencing, 286, 287
  in writing programs, 144–145, 154–159, 273
Bush, George W., 15, 21

California, 104, 175
Center for Research on the Education of Students Placed at Risk, 62
Chemistry and Energy program, 253, 254
Choral responding, 44–45, 267
Classwide peer tutoring (CWPT), 326
Clear communication
  in curricular design, 281

Clear communication (*con't*)
  principles of, 31–34
  of research results, 13
Clinical psychology, 14–15
Coaching, 312–313, 320–324
  defined, 320
  for Direct Instruction, 322–324
  models for, 321–322
Coalition for Evidence-Based Policy, 13
Cognitive-conceptual skills outcomes, 58
Cognitive deficits, reading problems and, 9–10
Cognitively Guided Instruction (CGI),
  242–243
College Board, 142
Commission on Excellence in Special
  Education, 6
Commission on Reading, 101–102
Communication. *See* Clear communication;
  Reading programs; Writing programs
Concept-based instruction, 250
Condition of Education, 7, 10
Connecting Math Concepts (CMC), 37–40,
  207
  assessment in, 238, 239
  content analysis of, 219–235
  described, 216
  extensions and adaptations of, 239–241
  implementation of, 310–311
  instructional format of, 219–235
  research on, 54–55, 241–243
Conspicuous strategies
  in curricular design, 251–252, 259–261,
  274
  in history/social science programs,
  259–261, 274
  in mathematics programs, 214–215,
  216–219, 222–235
  in science programs, 261
  in writing programs, 145, 159–160, 274
Constructivism, 210
Content analysis, 29–31, 283–286. *See also*
  Curricular design
  of *Basic Writing Skills*, 165
  of *Connecting Math Concepts (CMC)*,
  219–235
  of *Corrective Mathematics*, 219
  of *Corrective Reading*, 124–129
  in curricular design, 281, 283–286
  of *Cursive Writing*, 160–161, 162

  of *DISTAR Arithmetic*, 216–219
  of *Expressive Writing*, 154–156
  of history/social sciences programs,
  254–258, 259–262, 264–265, 283–286
  of *Horizons*, 119–124
  of *Language for Learning*, 74–84
  of *Language for Thinking*, 84–90
  of *Reading Mastery*, 110–119
  of *Reasoning and Writing*, 154–165
  of science programs, 258–259, 261,
  262–264, 265, 266
  of *Spelling Mastery*, 184–193
  of *Spelling Through Morphographs*,
  183–194
Content areas, 246–279. *See also* Curricular
  design; History/social sciences
  programs; Science programs
  assessment and troubleshooting in, 268–270
  defined, 247
  extensions and adaptations of, 270–275
  history/social sciences. *See Understanding
  U.S. History* program
  importance of, 248–249
  importance of content area instruction,
  249–250
  principles of curricular design, 251–252
  research on, 275–276
  science. *See Chemistry and Energy*
  program; *Earth Science* program;
  Understanding Life Sciences
  teaching techniques in, 266–268
Continuous assessment, 43, 169–170
Core Concepts videodisc, 241
Correction procedures, 48–51
  component skill errors, 236–237
  fact errors, 237
  general corrections, 92
  in history/social science programs, 267
  in language programs, 92
  in mathematics programs, 236–237
  in reading programs, 130–132
  repeat-until-firm procedure, 166–167
  in science programs, 268
  specific corrections, 92
  in spelling programs, 196–197
  statement corrections, 92
  strategy errors, 237
  in writing programs, 166–167
Correction ratios, 319

Corrective Mathematics, 207
  assessment in, 238
  content analysis of, 219
  described, 215–216
  instructional format of, 219
  research on, 241–243, 329
Corrective Reading, 124–129
  assessment in, 132–133
  content analysis of, 124–129
  critical features and lesson events, 106
  described, 107, 109–110
  extensions of, 107, 134, 135
  instructional format of, 124–129
  research on, 135–137, 328–329
  teaching techniques for, 129–132
  tutoring applications of, 324, 327, 328–329
Corrective Reading series, 20
Corrective Spelling Through Morphographs.
  See Spelling Through Morphographs
Critical thinking, 153–154
Cross-age tutoring, 325–326
Curricular design, 29–40, 280–303. *See also*
  Content areas; Direct Instruction;
  Program design in Direct Instruction
  big ideas in, 251, 254–259, 273, 283–286
  content analysis in, 281, 283–286. *See also*
  Content analysis
  in content areas. *See* Content areas;
  History/social sciences programs;
  Science programs
  evaluation in, 299–300
  lesson plans in, 286–299
  overview of, 281–283
  principles of, 144–147, 212–215, 251–252, 270–275
  sequencing content in, 286, 287, 310–313
  state and local requirements for, 280–281, 284
  supporting research on, 300–301
  unit objectives in, 283
Curriculum-based assessment (CBA), 197–198
Cursive Writing
  assessment in, 167–170
  content analysis of, 160–161, 162
  described, 147–150
  extensions of, 170
  instructional format of, 160–161, 162
  overview of, 148

  research on, 174
  teaching techniques for, 165–167
  troubleshooting in, 169–170

Decoding, 104, 124–127
Delaware, 142
Demonstration-practice-feedback approach, 17
Design of curriculum. *See* Curricular design
Developmentally appropriate practice, 56–57
Difference principle, in communication, 32–33
Direct Instruction
  components of, 29–52
  continued research and program development, 21–22
  described, 2
  effective teaching versus, 16, 52–53
  in history content area. *See Understanding U.S. History* program
  history of, 19–22
  implementation of. *See* Implementation of Direct Instruction
  increased interest in, 21
  language programs. *See Language for Learning; Language for Thinking; Language for Writing*
  mathematics programs. *See Connecting Math Concepts (CMC); Corrective Mathematics; DISTAR Arithmetic*
  organization of instruction in, 29, 40–43
  program design in, 29–40, 52, 74–90. *See also* Curricular design
  purpose of, 28–29
  reading programs. *See Corrective Reading; Horizons; Reading Mastery*
  research on. *See* Research on Direct Instruction methods
  in science content area. *See Chemistry and Energy* program; *Earth Science* program; *Understanding Life Sciences* program
  spelling programs. *See Spelling Mastery; Spelling Through Morphographs*
  students appropriate for, 53–57
  teacher preparation for, 311–313, 319–324
  teacher-student interaction in, 29, 43–52
  writing programs. *See Basic Writing Skills; Cursive Writing; Expressive Writing; Reasoning and Writing*

Discriminant learning theory (DLT), 242
DISTAR (Direct Instruction System for
    Teaching Arithmetic and Reading), 20.
    See also Direct Instruction; *Reading
    Mastery*
DISTAR Arithmetic, 207
    assessment in, 238
    content analysis of, 216–219
    described, 215
    implementation of, 310
    instructional format of, 216–219
    research on, 241–243
    teaching techniques for, 235, 236–237
DISTAR Language I, 71, 95–96. *See also
    Language for Learning*
DISTAR Language II, 71, 72, 95–97. *See also
    Language for Thinking*
DISTAR Language III, 71, 73, 95–96. *See
    also Language for Writing*
DISTAR Reading. See Reading Mastery

Early intervention
    impact of, 7, 57
    importance of, 10
    research on impact of, 57–58, 62
Earth Science program, 253, 254
    assessment with, 269–270
    content analysis of, 258, 265, 266
    extensions and adaptations of, 270, 271
    instructional format of, 258, 265, 266
    research on, 276
Educational outcomes, concern over, 4–5
Effective schools, 305–310
    Direct Instruction in, 309–310
    elements of, 305–306
    student learning in, 306–308
Effective teaching, 1–27. *See also* Curricular
    design; Direct Instruction
    characteristics of, 16–17
    concerns for educational outcomes and, 4–5
    Direct Instruction versus, 16, 52–53
    importance of, 10–11
    lack of, and disadvantaged status, 3–4
    in mathematics, 212–215, 216–235
    need for quality education, 2–3, 10–11
    in preventing academic failure, 10
    principles of, 17–18
    research and, 11–13, 15–19
    serious academic problems and, 7–10

for students who perform poorly, 5–7
    support for power of, 18–19
    in writing, 141, 144–147, 154–165
Effective teaching cycle, 286–289
Elementary and Secondary Education Act
    (ESEA), 15
Elements of Effective Coaching, The (video),
    322–323
Emotional and behavioral disorders (EBD),
    69, 175, 275–276
Empirically supported treatments (ESTs),
    14–15
Employment, 3–4, 7, 101–102, 207–208
Employment Policies Institute, 102
Engaged time, 307–308, 317–319
Entry Test, 93. *See also* Placement tests.
Errors. *See also* Correction procedures
    group unison responses and, 45, 46–47
    signals and, 46–47, 50–51
Español to English, 95
Evaluation. *See also* Assessment
    in curricular design, 299–300
    of tutoring program, 326–328
Explicit instruction, 211
Expository writing, 153
Expressive Writing
    assessment in, 167–170
    content analysis of, 154–156
    described, 147, 150–151
    extensions of, 170, 171
    instructional format of, 154–156
    overview of, 148
    research on, 174
    teaching techniques for, 165–167

Florida, 137
Fluency, 104, 117–118, 123–124, 126–127,
    134, 239–240
Fluent Reader, 134
Fractions equal to one, 230–235
Functional literacy, 3
Funnix, 129

General case programming, 31
General correction, 92
Good-bye List, 201
Great Britain, 13
Grouping, instructional, 40–41, 314–317
Group unison responses, 44–45

problems with, 45, 46–47
signals and, 45–47, 130, 235, 267
Guided practice, 211, 288, 295–297

Hand-drop signals, 91–92, 166, 195, 235–236
Handwriting skills, 141, 144, 147–150
Head Start, 10, 57
Higher-order thinking skills, 31, 152
High school graduation, 7, 101–102, 207–208
High-stakes tests, writing component of,
    140–141, 142
History/social sciences programs. *See also*
    Understanding U.S. History program
  assessment in, 268–269
  big ideas in, 254–258, 273, 283–286
  extensions and adaptations of, 270–275
  importance of, 248
  national assessments of, 247
  overview of Direct Instruction in, 253
  research on, 275–276
  teaching techniques in, 266–268
  troubleshooting in, 269
Holt Math Series, 243
Homeroom-based grouping, 314–315
Horizons, 119–124
  assessment in, 132–133
  content analysis of, 119–124
  critical features and lesson events, 106
  described, 107, 108–109, 119–120
  extensions of, 107, 129
  instructional format of, 119–124
  research on, 136–137

Implementation of Direct Instruction,
    304–334
  effective schools and, 305–310
  monitoring mission progress in, 317–319
  problems of, 305
  research on, 328–329, 331
  scope and sequence in, 310–311
  staff development in, 311–313, 319–324,
    329–331
  student learning environment in, 40–43,
    306–308, 313–317, 324–329
Implicit instruction, 210–211
Independent practice, 288, 298–299
In-service training, 312
Institute of Child Health and Human
    Development, 68, 180, 182

Instructional format, 34–36. *See also*
    Curricular design
  of *Basic Writing Skills*, 165
  of *Connecting Math Concepts (CMC)*,
    219–235
  of *Corrective Mathematics*, 219
  of *Corrective Reading*, 124–129
  of *Cursive Writing*, 160–161, 162
  of *DISTAR Arithmetic*, 216–219
  example of, 34–36
  of *Expressive Writing*, 154–156
  of history/social sciences programs,
    254–258, 259–262, 264–265
  of *Horizons*, 119–124
  of *Language for Learning*, 74–84
  of *Language for Thinking*, 84–90
  of learning set activities, 290–292
  of *Reading Mastery*, 110–119
  of *Reasoning and Writing*, 154–165
  of science programs, 258–259, 261,
    262–264, 265, 266
  "shifts" within, 36
  of *Spelling Mastery*, 184–193
  of *Spelling Through Morphographs*,
    183–194
Instructional grouping, 40–41, 314–317
Instructional interactions, 299
Instructional time, 41–42, 306–308, 317–319
Invitation to Mathematics, 242
Iowa Test of Basic Skills, 2
IQ scores, 53–55, 135, 242
Irregular words, 115–116, 125–126

Journeys, 107
J/P POWER Series, 135
Judicious review
  in curricular design, 252, 265–266, 275
  in history/social science programs, 265, 275
  in science programs, 266
  in writing programs, 146–147, 165, 275
Just for the Kids, 11

Language Activity Masters, 94
Language for Learning
  adaptations of, 94–95
  assessment in, 93
  content analysis of, 74–84
  described, 71–72
  extensions of, 94

Language for Learning (*con't*)
  implementation of, 310
  instructional format of, 74–84
  Language for Thinking compared with,
    72–73
  research on, 95–97
  teaching techniques for, 90–92
  troubleshooting in, 93
Language for Thinking
  adaptations of, 94–95
  assessment in, 93
  content analysis of, 84–90
  described, 72
  implementation of, 310
  instructional format of, 84–90
  Language for Learning compared with,
    72–73
  research on, 95–97
  teaching techniques for, 90–92
  troubleshooting in, 93
Language for Writing
  described, 73–74
  research on, 95–97
Language programs, 66–99. *See also*
    Language for Learning; *Language for*
    Thinking; *Language for Writing*
  assessment and troubleshooting in, 92–93
  extensions and adaptations of, 94–95
  importance of oral language, 67–69
  importance of oral language instruction,
    70–71
  research on, 95–97
  teaching techniques for, 90–92
Learning environment, 306–308, 313–317,
    324–329
  academic learning time in, 41–42, 307–308
  criterion content covered in, 306–307
  instructional grouping in, 40–41, 306–308,
    314–317
  minimizing time needed to learn in, 308
  opportunity to learn in, 306
  organizing, 313–317
  time spent learning in, 41–42, 306–308,
    317–319
Learning set activities, 286–295
  activity planning, 286–287, 289–290
  designing and delivering, 293–295
  formats of, 290–293
  purpose of, 286–288

Learning styles, 56
Learning Through Literature; Novel Studies
    (Dodds and Goodfellow), 172
Learning Through Literature: Story Studies
    (Dodds and Goodfellow), 171–172
Lesson plans, 286–299
  effective teaching cycle and, 286–289
  guided practice activities in, 211, 288,
    295–297
  independent practice in, 288, 298–299
  learning set activities in, 286–295
  new material in, 288, 295–297
Letter-sound correspondence, 112–113, 122,
    124–125, 130, 181
Lott, Thaddeus, 2, 11

Massachusetts, 11
Mastering Math Facts (Crawford), 240
Mastery learning, 48
Mastery tests, 93, 168, 198, 238–239, 268,
    270, 272
Mathematics Equals Opportunity, 207–208
Mathematics Modules, 238
Mathematics programs, 206–245. *See also*
    Connecting Math Concepts (CMC);
    Corrective Mathematics; *DISTAR*
    Arithmetic
  assessment and troubleshooting in, 237–239
  big ideas in, 214–215, 216–219, 222–235
  design principles for effective instruction,
    212–215, 216–235
  extensions and adaptations of, 239–241
  importance of mathematics, 207–208
  importance of mathematics instruction,
    208–212
  international assessments of, 6–7, 207,
    208–209, 212–213, 247–248
  research on, 241–243, 329
  teaching techniques for, 235–237
Math facts, 240
Math Their Way, 242–243
Matthew Effects, 8, 18
Mediated Learning (ML), 96
Mediated scaffolding
  in curricular design, 252, 261–264, 274
  in history/social science programs,
    261–262, 274
  in mathematics programs, 211
  in science programs, 262–264

in spelling programs, 191
in writing programs, 145, 160–161, 274
Medical research, 13–14
Metropolitan Achievement Test, 55, 61
Minority students, 5–6
Monitoring progress, 317–319. *See also*
    Assessment
    qualitative, 319
    quantitative, 317–319
Morphemic approach to spelling, 182–183,
    188–193
Morphographs, 30–31
Motivation of students, 51–52

Narrative writing, 152–153
National Academy of Sciences, 180–181,
    248–249
National Alliance of Quality Schools, 310,
    311
National Assessment of Educational Progress
    (NAEP), 5, 102, 207, 209, 247
National Center for Educational Statistics, 247
National Center for History in the Schools,
    248
National Center to Improve the Tools of
    Education (NCITE), 20–21, 251, 273
National Commission on Excellence in
    Education, 4
National Council of Teachers of Mathematics
    (NCTM), 209–210, 212
National Institute for Literacy, 3, 4
National Institute of Child Health and Human
    Development, 6
National Institute of Mental Health (NIMH),
    15
National Reading Panel (NRP), 8–9, 10, 101,
    102–105, 108, 135, 181–182, 319–320
National Research Council, 15–16
National Science Education Standards,
    248–249
Nation at Risk, A, 4
*Nation's Report Card: Fourth-Grade
    Reading*, 5
New Jersey, 175
New math, 210
New Zealand, 9
No Child Left Behind Act (2001), 13, 15
North Carolina, 142
Number families, 222

Objectives, unit, 283
Office of Educational Research and
    Improvement, 5–6
On-task time, 307–308
Oral language
    and beginning reading achievement, 67–68
    in group unison responses, 44–45, 46–47,
        130, 235, 267
    importance of, 67–69
    importance of instruction in, 70–71
    long-term effects of poorly developed, 69
    and reading comprehension, 68
    social interaction and, 67, 68–69
Oregon, 249
Organization of instruction, 29, 40–43,
    306–308
    continuous assessment, 43, 169–170
    instructional grouping, 40–41, 314–317
    instructional time, 41–42, 306–308,
        317–319
    scripted presentation, 42–43

Pacing of instruction, 47
*PALS-Performance-Based Activities &
    Literature Skills* (DeLuca), 135
Parents Are Teachers (Becker), 20
Phonemic approach to spelling, 181–182,
    184–188
Phonemic awareness, 68, 103, 110–112, 120,
    124–129
    oral blending, 110, 111
    oral segmenting, 110, 111
    rhyming, 111, 112
Phonics, 103–104, 112–117, 120–123,
    124–129, 134
    irregular words, 115–116, 125–126
    letter-sound correspondence, 112–113,
        122, 124–125, 130, 181
    regular words, 113–115, 122–123,
        125–126
    text selection, 116–117, 123, 126
Phonological skills, Matthew Effects and, 8
Picture Cards, 94
Placement tests, 93, 167–168, 197–198, 202,
    237–238, 314
Planned variation, 58
Praise ratios, 319
Presentations, scripted, 42–43
Preservice teachers, supervision of, 329–331

Primed background knowledge
in curricular design, 252, 264–265,
274–275
in history/social science programs,
264–265, 274–275
in science programs, 265
in writing programs, 146, 163–165,
274–275
Problem-solution-effect (PSE) approach,
254–255, 264–265, 273, 287, 294
Program design in Direct Instruction, 29–40,
52
clear communication, 31–34
content analysis, 29–31, 74–90. *See also*
Content analysis
instructional format of, 34–36, 74–90. *See
also* Instructional format
sequencing of skills, 36–37
track organization, 37–40
Project Follow Through, 19, 20, 57–61,
135–136
models used in, 59
outcomes measured in, 58, 60
Pronunciation, 114
Public Agenda, 4
Put Reading First, 102

Quality education. *See also* Curricular design;
Effective teaching
importance of, 10–11
need for, 2–3, 10–11

Reach System, 107
Reader's Club, 134
Readers & Writers (Dodds and Goodfellow),
172
Reading Excellence Act (1998), 15
Reading Mastery, 110–119, 281
assessment in, 132–133, 314
coaching in, 323–324
content analysis of, 110–119
critical features and lesson events, 106
described, 107–108
extensions of, 37, 107, 108, 109, 129, 134,
324–325
implementation of, 309, 310–311, 315
instructional format of, 110–119
research on, 135, 136
teacher preparation for, 311

teaching techniques for, 129–132
troubleshooting in, 133
tutoring applications in, 324–325
Reading Mastery Fast Cycle, 107, 109, 324
Reading Mastery Plus, 37, 107, 108, 109,
292, 310
Reading participation, impact of problems
with, 8
Reading programs, 100–139. *See also
Corrective Reading*; *Horizons*; *Reading
Mastery*
assessment and troubleshooting in, 132–133
critical components of, 102–105
extensions and adaptations of, 133–135
importance of reading, 101–102
research on, 135–137, 142, 328–329
teaching techniques for, 129–132
Reading Success, 135
Read Naturally, 134
Reasoning and Writing, 107
adaptations of, 173–174, 281
assessment in, 167–170
content analysis of, 154–165
described, 147, 151–154
extensions of, 170–172
instructional format of, 154–165
overview of, 149
research on, 174–175
teaching techniques for, 165–167
troubleshooting in, 170
Regular words, 113–115, 122–123, 125–126
Repeat-until-firm procedure, 166–167
Report of the Education Trust, 11
Report of the National Reading Panel,
102–105
Reprimands, 51
Research (general)
in clinical psychology, 14–15
on effective teaching, 11–13, 16–19
lack of impact on educational practice,
11–13
linking professional practice and, 13–16
in medicine, 13–14
need for communication and, 13
obstacles to research-driven teaching, 12
Research on Direct Instruction methods,
21–22, 53–62
in content area programs, 275–276
in curricular design, 300–301

on implementation of Direct Instruction, 328–329, 331
language programs, 95–97
mathematics programs, 241–243, 329
Project Follow Through, 19, 20, 57–61, 135–136
reading programs, 135–137, 142, 328–329
science programs, 276
spelling programs, 203–204
supervision of preservice teachers, 331
tutoring, 328–329
writing programs, 142, 174–175
REWARDS, 134
REWARDS Plus, 134
Rhyming, 111, 112
Rote learning, 30–31, 180

Sameness principle, in communication, 33
SAT, writing component of, 140–141, 142
Scaffolding. *See* Mediated scaffolding
School-based grouping, 316–317
Science for All Americans, 249
Science programs. *See also Chemistry and Energy* program; *Earth Science* program; *Understanding Life Sciences*
assessment in, 269–270, 271, 272
big ideas in, 258–259
importance of, 248–249
international assessments of, 6–7, 207, 208–209, 212–213, 247–248
overview of Direct Instruction in, 253, 254
research on, 276
teaching techniques in, 266–268
troubleshooting in, 270
Science Research Associates (SRA), 2, 21, 94, 154
Scripted presentations, 42–43
Second International Mathematics and Science Study (SIMSS), 247
Self-esteem, 17, 58, 60
Sequencing
of content, 286, 287, 310–313
of skills, 36–37
Setup principle, in communication, 32
Signals, 45–47, 50–51
auditory, 92, 130, 166, 236
hand-drop, 91–92, 166, 195, 235–236
in language programs, 90–92
in mathematics programs, 235–236

in reading programs, 130
in spelling programs, 194–196
touch, 91, 166, 195, 235
with unison responding, 45, 130, 235, 267
visual prompts, 130
in writing programs, 166
Social interaction, oral language and, 67, 68–69
Socioeconomic status (SES)
mathematics and, 207–208, 209
oral language and, 70
Specific correction, 92
Spell-checkers, 179–180, 183
Spelling contests, 202–203
Spelling Mastery, 30–31, 179, 181
adaptations of, 201–203
assessment in, 197–198
content analysis of, 184–193
described, 183–184
extensions of, 200–201
implementation of, 310, 314
instructional format of, 184–193
research on, 203–204
teaching techniques for, 193–197
troubleshooting in, 199–200
Spelling programs, 30–31, 178–205. *See also Spelling Mastery*; *Spelling Through Morphographs*
assessment and troubleshooting in, 197–200
extensions and adaptations of, 200–203
importance of spelling, 179–180
importance of spelling instruction, 180–181
morphemic approach to spelling in, 182–183, 188–193
phonemic approach to spelling in, 181–182, 184–188
research on, 203–204
teaching techniques for, 193–197
whole-word approach to spelling in, 182, 188
Spelling Through Morphographs, 107, 134, 179, 181
adaptations of, 201–203
assessment in, 197–198
content analysis of, 183–194
described, 184
extensions of, 200–201
instructional format of, 183–194
research on, 203–204

Spelling Through Monographs (*con't*)
  teaching techniques for, 193–197
  troubleshooting in, 199–200
  tutoring applications in, 324
Spiral curriculum, 212–214
Staff development
  coaching in, 312–313, 320–324
  for content area instruction, 249–250
  for Direct Instruction, 311–313, 319–324,
    329–331
  elements of, 319–320
  supervision of preservice teachers,
    329–331
Statement corrections, 92
Stipulation, 187
Story grammar, 152
Strand curriculum, 213, 214, 216, 217,
    219–222
Strategic integration
  in curricular design, 251, 259, 273–274
  in history/social science programs, 259,
    273–274
  in science programs, 259
  in writing programs, 145–146, 161–163,
    273–274
Student-2-Student tutoring, 325–326
Students at risk, 11, 53–55, 250, 275–276
Students of different ages, 56–57
Students with disadvantages, 5–6, 55–56, 57
  in history of Direct Instruction, 19–22
  lack of effective teaching, 3–4
Students with diverse language backgrounds,
    55–56, 69, 95, 175
Students with diverse learning needs, 53–55,
    71, 95, 175
Students with learning disabilities, 6, 326
  concept of, 21
  history programs and, 275–276
  language programs and, 95
  writing programs and, 175
Students with various learning styles, 56

Tables, 226–230
TBI (traumatic brain injury), 22
Teachers. *See also* Curricular design;
    Effective teaching; Staff development
  error correction in classroom. *See*
    Correction procedures
  role in motivation of students, 51

signaling by. *See* Signals
  supervision of preservice, 329–331
Teacher-student interactions, 29, 43–52
  active student participation, 44
  correction procedures, 48–51
  group unison responses, 44–45
  motivation, 51–52
  pacing, 47
  signals, 45–47
  teaching to mastery, 48
*Teaching Disadvantaged Children in the
    Preschool* (Bereiter and Engelmann),
    19
*Teach Your Child to Read in 100 Easy
    Lessons*, 129, 324–325
Team-based grouping, 315–316
Tennessee, 11
Testing principle, in communication, 34
Test of Written Language (TOWL), 175
Texas, 2, 11, 56
Text comprehension
  oral language and, 68
  in reading programs, 105, 118–119, 124,
    127–129, 135
Text selection, 116–117, 123, 126
Think sheets, 145
Third International Mathematics and Science
    Study (TIMSS), 6–7, 207, 208–209,
    212–213, 247–248
Time needed to learn, 317–319
Time spent learning, 41–42, 306–308,
    317–319
Touch signals, 91, 166, 195, 235
Track organization, 37–40
Troubleshooting
  accuracy of responses, 93
  in history/social sciences programs, 269
  in language programs, 93
  loud and draggy responses, 93
  in mathematics programs, 237–239
  in reading programs, 133
  in science programs, 270
  in spelling programs, 199–200
  in writing programs, 169–170
Tutoring, 324–329
  advantages of, 325
  defined, 324
  guidelines for tutors, 327–328
  models for, 325–326

program evaluation, 326–328
program implementation, 326–328
research on, 328–329

Understanding Chemistry and Energy, 253, 254, 276
Understanding Life Sciences, 253, 259, 261, 262–264, 265, 266
Understanding U.S. History program, 253. *See also* History/social sciences programs
content analysis of, 254–258, 259–262, 264–265, 283–286
instructional format of, 254–258, 259–262, 264–265, 265
research on, 275–276
U.S. Department of Education, 4–7, 10, 13, 15, 57, 207, 208
U.S. Department of Labor, 3–4, 102
University of Illinois, 19–20

Visual prompts, 130
Vocabulary development
impact of problems with, 8–10
in oral language instruction, 70–71
in reading programs, 104–105, 118, 124, 127–129, 134–135
Volume of a solid, 230

Washington, 249
Wechsler Intelligence Scale for Children (WISC-R), 242

What Do Our 17-Year-Olds Know? (Ravitch and Finn), 247
Whole-word approach to spelling, 182, 188
Wide Range Achievement Test, 53–54
Wording principle, in communication, 31–32, 34
Word problems, in mathematics, 222–226, 240–241
Word Problems Made Easy (Crawford), 240–241
Write-Say spelling, 201
Writing programs, 140–177. *See also Basic Writing Skills*; *Cursive Writing*; *Expressive Writing*; *Reasoning and Writing*
assessment and troubleshooting in, 167–170
big ideas in, 144–145, 154–159, 173
design principles of effective instruction, 141, 144–147, 154–165, 270–275
in extension of spelling programs, 200–201
extensions and adaptations of, 170–174, 281
handwriting skills and, 141, 144, 147–150
importance of writing, 140–143
importance of writing instruction, 143–144
research on, 142, 174–175
teaching techniques for, 165–167

Your World of Facts, 266, 291

Zone of proximal development (Vygotsky), 40–41